# A Concise History
of the
# Middle East

### SEVENTH EDITION

# A CONCISE HISTORY

## of the

# MIDDLE EAST

## SEVENTH EDITION

Arthur Goldschmidt Jr.

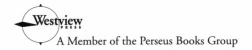

A Member of the Perseus Books Group

Copyright © 2002 by Westview Press, A Member of the Perseus Books Group

Westview Press books are available at special discounts for bulk purchases in the United States by corporations, institutions, and other organizations. For more information, please contact the Special Markets Department at The Perseus Books Group, 11 Cambridge Center, Cambridge MA 02142, or call (617) 252-5298.

Published in 2002 in the United States of America by Westview Press, 5500 Central Avenue, Boulder, Colorado 80301–2877, and in the United Kingdom by Westview Press, 12 Hid's Copse Road, Cumnor Hill, Oxford OX2 9JJ

Find us on the World Wide Web at www.westviewpress.com

Goldschmidt, Arthur, 1938-
  A concise history of the Middle East / Arthur Goldschmidt Jr.—7th ed.
     p. cm.
  Includes bibliographical references (p. ) and index.
  ISBN 0-8133-3885-9 (pbk.)
    1. Middle East—History. I . Title.

DS6,2 .G64 2001                                                                                          2001045326

The paper used in this publication meets the requirements of the American National Standard for Permanence of Paper for Printed Library Materials Z39.48–1984.

10      9      8      7      6      5      4      3      2

*To the Memory of*
*AGNES INGLIS O'NEILL,*
*teacher, counselor, friend*

*She taught every subject with a spirit of fun*
*and each pupil in a spirit of love.*

# CONTENTS

# ILLUSTRATIONS

## Maps

## Tables

## Figures

# PREFACE

When I started to teach Middle East history, I was sure that I would never write a textbook. Nothing in my graduate training or early research experience had led me to value writing for beginners in my field. Textbooks were a means by which second-rate minds made their reputations or feathered their financial nests. When I wrote the first edition of *A Concise History of the Middle East* after twelve years of teaching, I feared it might reveal a deflated self-image or a touch of avarice. Would it, I wondered, meet a general need?

Evidently, it has. I have met or heard from countless people who have either taught from the book or gotten their first exposure to Middle East history from having to read it for a class. I thought that teachers and students needed a book that reflected current scholarship, did not hide its ideas behind a pseudoscholarly style addressed to pedants, and did not reinforce political or ethnic biases. Students—and members of the wider English-speaking public—deserve clear explanations of the Arab-Israeli conflict, the Middle East's role in the energy crisis, and the Islamic resurgence. The book has gone through six editions and, despite the appearance of other general Middle East histories, has become ever more widely used in universities.

More and more scholars, both Middle Eastern and Western, are enlarging what we know about the history of the area. We can—and we must—share their findings with university students, both to arouse their interest in the Middle East and to make them more aware of themselves by exposure to other lifestyles, other areas, and other eras. Teachers and textbooks cannot free themselves from bias, but let us at least make sure that our students see more than one side of the burning issues of the present and the past. Let us also reveal what we know to the wider public. Many people—not only students—care about what is going on now in the Middle East and how things came to be that way.

Any work of art or scholarship follows conventions. When writing a book that introduces a recondite subject to students and general readers, the author must tell the audience what these conventions will be. The English system of weights and measures is giving way to the metric system; this book uses both. Prices expressed in non-American currencies, ancient or modern, are given in 2001 U.S. dollar equivalents. All dates are based on the Gregorian calendar. But let no one forget that Muslims follow a twelve-month lunar calendar dated from the year in which Muhammad and his associates moved from Mecca to Medina. Quite naturally, they use this calendar when they teach or learn Islamic history. Conversion between the two systems is cumbersome and prone to error. When dates appear in parentheses following a ruler's name, they refer to the span of his or her reign. Personal names in languages using the Arabic script are transliterated according to the Library of Congress system, minus the diacritics, except for a few persons and places mentioned often in the press. The same applies to technical terms that cannot be translated simply and accurately into English. I have kept these to a minimum.

This book has an immense number and variety of sources. Almost every book or article that I have read and most people with whom I have conversed have left an imprint on what I think and write. I chose not to use footnotes, which might distract student readers, but wrote a long bibliographic essay at the end. In some places I singled out scholars who have influenced my treatment of certain topics because I wanted Middle East history students to know about them. No doubt I omitted some leading authorities. I expect instructors to fill in the gaps for their students.

I set out to write the first edition in the style I might use to write a series of personal letters to young adults, taking into account their concerns and experiences. I was looking for a middle ground between telegraphic brevity and boring thoroughness. At times I shot from the hip. Not surprisingly, I often hit my foot. Professors James Jankowski (University of Colorado) and Glenn Perry (Indiana State University) read and critiqued the original version, which I used in mimeographed form for my classes from 1977 to 1979. My students helped me to improve the style and coverage of the book by their comments and criticisms and also by what they showed, in their written or oral tests and in classroom discussions, to be understandable or abstruse. Some sacrificed Sunday afternoons to meet in our living room to review the book in minute detail while I was revising it for publication. Patricia Kozlik (now Kabra) was notably generous with her time, effort, and advice. With each succeeding edition, I have sought help from Penn State students and alumni, including R. Mark Sirkin (who teaches at Wright State University), Lawrence Conrad (now at Hamburg University), Kenneth Mayers, Joshua Novak, Sabrina Ramet (now at the Henry Jackson Center), Yoram Egosi, Geoffrey Perry, Katherine Lovette, and Amber Cistaro. I have also taken advice from faculty at other institutions, including Jose Alvarez, Jere Bacharach, Herbert Bodman, John Bohnstedt, Neil Caplan, Nancy Gallagher, William Griswold, G. L. Penrose, Donald Reid, Mark Seifter, and Canfield Smith. Via electronic mail, I have heard from Nihaya Dugan, Ibrahim Hooper, Michel Lieberman, and Alexander B. Umacob. I also drew on suggestions offered to me by Samuel Koenigsberg, a friend of my father for seventy years. Special thanks go to my colleague, Timothy Gianotti, whose wise and perceptive corrections have graced the newer editions.

Don Kunze (then a graduate student, now an associate professor of architecture, at Penn State University), aided by Barbara Droms and later by Chuck Siegel, drew the original maps to my sometimes protean specifications. They have now been redone by Mark Wherley of Penn State's Deasy Cartographic Laboratory, using computer techniques unknown in the 1970s. Financial help for the first edition came from the Department of History, the College of the Liberal Arts, and the Central Fund for Research of the Pennsylvania State University, as well as from my parents, the late Arthur E. and Elizabeth Wickenden Goldschmidt. Westview Press helped fund my revisions to what has become a decreasingly concise history of the Middle East. Numerous editors, proofreaders, indexers, and production managers at the Press have improved one or more versions of this book. Finally, I must pay tribute to Frederick A. Praeger, one of the giants in American book publishing, who encouraged me in 1977 to complete my mimeographed typescript and to submit it to Westview Press.

My wife, Louise, deserves a special acknowledgment for her encouragement, patience, and constant love. Our sons, Stephen and Paul, now fully grown and launched on their own careers, lived through my early efforts to write this book, often at the cost of my being the father they wanted.

Although I am grateful to all persons named in this preface and to others I have neglected to cite, I remain accountable for all errors of fact or interpretation. I welcome, as always, readers' comments and advice. The word processor enables me to act on your suggestions for the book's revision. When we can reach one another through cyberspace, textbook writing at last resembles letter writing. I have come full circle. If you wish to reach me by computer, my Internet address is axg2@psu.edu.

The work of a great teacher never perishes; hence my original dedication of this book—to an elementary school teacher and principal whose knowledge, ideas, and enthusiasm live on in thousands of her former pupils—shall endure.

*Arthur Goldschmidt Jr.*

# ONE

# Introduction

In this book I will introduce the Middle East to students and other readers who have never been exposed to the area. *Middle East* is a rather imprecise term describing a geographical area that extends from Egypt to Afghanistan, or the cultural region in which Islam arose and developed. I plan to make the term clearer in this chapter. First, let me tell you why I think history is the discipline best suited for your introduction to the Middle East. After all, you might look at the Middle East through its systems for allocating power and values, using the discipline of political science. An economist would focus on the ways in which its inhabitants organize themselves to satisfy their material needs. A student of comparative religions would examine their various systems of belief and worship. A geographer would study the interaction between the people and their physical surroundings. Sociologists and cultural anthropologists would analyze the institutions and group behavior of the various peoples who constitute the Middle East. You could also view the various cultures of the region through its languages, literature, architecture, art, folklore, and even its cuisine.

## What Is History?

Why history? Some of you may have picked up a rather dismal picture of history from schools or books. History is supposed to be the study of events that took place in the past. These events have been carefully gathered together, checked for accuracy, and written down in chronological order by historians, a strange breed of antiquarians who shamble between dusty libraries and musty archives. History teachers pass these accounts along to young people by means of textbooks and lectures. They are organized according to the reigns of rulers or the life spans of nation-states, divided into manageable chunks of time. Students memorize this "history"—as little as they can get away with—in the form of facts, names, and dates. Only an occasional concept, casually communicated and dimly grasped, adds some seasoning to the stew. A kind teacher may tell a class just to learn the "trends." These are interpreted by the students to mean vague statements unsupported by evidence from the unheeded lectures or the unread textbook. History, in this all-too-common conception, is a dreary bore, a dead subject suited only to cranks, to antique-lovers, or perhaps to a few students looking for bits of small talk with which to impress their peers. It is not useful. It will not get them jobs. It cannot predict what will happen in the future. History does not repeat itself, even if historians repeat other historians.

But let me respond. I do have some better ideas of what history is, how it should be studied and taught, and why we bother to learn it. Some of my ideas may seem obvious if you have already taken several college or university courses in history. Or you may already be an avid reader of history books. My ideas may change in the years to come. In time, you may want to set me straight. But first let me say what I think about this subject and how it relates to your introduction to the Middle East.

History belongs to all of us. Whenever you talk about something that happened to yourself, your friends, your community, or your country, you are relating history through events that took place in the past. Everyone does this at least some of the time. History has no technical vocabulary, except what is needed to describe a particular time or place, society or culture. It can cover politics, economics, lifestyles, beliefs, works of literature or art, cities or rural areas, incidents you remember, stories older people told you, or subjects you can only read about. Broadly speaking, everything that has ever happened up to the moment you read these lines is history, or the study of the past.

As an academic discipline, though, history mainly examines those aspects of the past that have been written down or passed on by word of mouth. Historians cannot write or teach about an event that was never recorded. The unrecorded event might be trivial: What did Columbus have for breakfast on 12 October 1492? Or it might be a big question: When Muhammad was dying on 8 June 632, whom did he want as his successor? Historians do not treat all recorded events as being equally important, any more than you would if you were calling home just after you had arrived at a new place. They evaluate past events, stressing some while downgrading or even omitting others. What historians think is worth mentioning can also change over time or vary from place to place. We will look at this historiographical dimension later.

How do historians pick the events they mention or stress? Often, they base their choices on the degree to which those events affected what later happened. Just as chemistry goes beyond spotting the elements on the periodic table, history deals with more than just isolated happenings. Historians look at cause-and-effect relationships. The Pilgrims sailed to Plymouth in 1620 *because* they wanted to worship God in their own way. Russian intellectuals, workers, and peasants hated the autocratic (and inefficient) rule of Czar Nicholas II; *therefore*, they organized revolutionary movements until they overthrew him in 1917. We ask not only *what* events occurred but also *why*.

Did the institution of slavery cause the Civil War? Did Roosevelt's New Deal end the Great Depression? Was the creation of Israel in 1948 the result of Hitler's attempt to destroy the Jews of Europe during World War II? When we study cause-and-effect relationships, we are studying processes. What makes individuals or groups act, react, make decisions, or refrain from acting? The answers usually depend on the time and the place. We may have our own ideas about what forces motivate human actions. I will share some of mine as the story unfolds and in my concluding chapter. As we study more recent events, we may think we know more about the people's motives; but our own feelings may color our views. We may also have to do without some of the sources we need, such as memoirs and government documents, which are often closed for at least a generation to protect people's careers and reputations.

There is another dimension to history, one we tend to overlook even though it colors our thinking. What makes our society or civilization, country or culture, different from others existing at the same time? How does American life in the twenty-first century differ from what it was in the nineteenth? To word the question another way, do different cultures in our modern age have qualities in common, making the contemporary United States and Egypt similar to each other now and different from what both were like a century ago? Do the English have certain traits that span differences of time or region, such that an English person of 1800 and one of today are more like each other than either is like, say, Iranians of the corresponding dates? Historians often make such comparisons.

Now let me raise still another issue. What are the most meaningful units of historical study? The West has a strong tradition of studying national history—that of the United States, Britain, France, Russia, or, for that matter, China or Japan. In other parts of the world, including the

Middle East, political boundaries have changed so often that nation-states have not existed until recently, let alone served as meaningful units of historical study. In the Islamic and Middle Eastern tradition, historical studies tend to center on dynasties (ruling families), whose time spans and territories vary widely. The Ottoman Empire, for example, was a large state made up of Turks, Arabs, Greeks, and many other ethnic groups. Its rulers, called *sultans*, all belonged to a family descended from a Turkish warrior named Osman. It was not a nation but a dynastic state—one that lasted a long time and affected many other peoples. But Middle East historians are now devising a system of periodization that is less political and more closely related to changes in people's economic and social life. This book will straddle the issue. At some times I will use the old dynastic divisions of time and space; for the modern period, I may use a country-by-country approach, making major wars and crises the points of division. At other times I will examine the history topically, in terms of "Islamic civilization" or "westernizing reform." As professional historians learn more about the Middle East, our writing will become more systematic and sophisticated.

From what we now know about Middle East history, I believe that our most meaningful unit of study is not the dynasty or the nation-state but the civilization. Although the term *civilization* is easier to describe than to define, this book, especially in its earlier chapters, focuses on an interlocking complex of rulers and subjects, governments and laws, arts and letters, cultures and customs, cities and villages—in short, on a civilization that has prevailed in most of western Asia and northern Africa since the seventh century, all tied together by the religion of Islam. You will see how Islamic beliefs and practices produced institutions for all aspects of Middle Eastern life. Then you will learn how Muslim patterns of belief and action were jarred by the impact of the West. You will look at some of the ways in which the peoples of the Middle East have coped with Western domination, accepting the best but rejecting the rest of European and U.S. culture. You will also see how they have won back their political independence and started to regain their autonomy as a civilization. I believe this to be the best way to get started on studying the Middle East.

## THEN AND NOW, THERE AND HERE

But why, you may ask, should anyone want to study the Middle East, let alone the history of Islamic civilization? I argue that studying any subject, from philosophy to physics, is potentially an adventure of the mind. Islamic history is a subject worth learning for its own sake. Confronted by distances of time and space, and by differences of thought patterns and lifestyles, we learn more about ourselves—about our era, area, beliefs, and customs. Islam is somewhat like Christianity and Judaism, but not entirely so. The peoples of the Middle East (like those of the West) are partial heirs to the Greeks and the Romans. To a greater degree, however, they are direct successors of the still earlier civilizations of Egypt, Mesopotamia, Persia, and other lands of the ancient Middle East. As a result, they have evolved in ways quite different from ours. They are rather like our cousins, neither siblings nor strangers to us.

In another sense, our culture is their debtor. Our religious beliefs and observances are derived from those of the Hebrews, Mesopotamians, Egyptians, Persians, and Greeks who lived in the Middle East before Islam. Moreover, many Westerners do not know what they have learned from Islamic culture. Some of the technical aspects of cultural transmission, especially in philosophy, mathematics, and science, I will save for later. For now, a glance at the background of some everyday English words backs up my point.

Let us start with what is closest to ourselves, our clothes. The names of several things we are apt to wear have Middle Eastern backgrounds: cotton (from the Arabic *qutn*), pajamas and sandals (both words taken from Persian), and obviously caftans and turbans. Muslin cloth once came from Mosul (a city in Iraq) and damask from Damascus. The striped cat we call *tabby* got its name from a type of cloth called *Attabi*, once woven in a section of Baghdad having that name. Some Arabs claim that the game of tennis took its name from a medieval Egyptian town, Tinnis, where cotton cloth (used then to cover the balls) was woven. Am I stretching the point? Well, the name for the implement with which you play the game, your racquet, can be traced back to an Arabic word meaning "palm of the hand." Backgammon, chess, polo, and playing cards came to the West from the Middle East. The *rook* in chess comes from the Persian *rukh* (castle) and *checkmate* from *shah mat* (the king is dead). As for household furnishings, we have taken *divan, sofa, mattress,* and of course *afghan* and *ottoman* from the Middle East.

You may already know the Middle Eastern origin of such foods as shish kebab, yogurt, tabbouleh, hummus, and pita. Some of our other terms for eatables have been naturalized over longer periods: *apricot, artichoke, ginger, lemon, lime, orange, saffron, sugar,* and *tangerine. Hashish* is an Arabic word denoting, in addition to cannabis, weeds and grass, depending on the context. Both *sherbet* and *syrup* come from the Arabic word for drink.

Muslims may not use intoxicating liquor, but the very word *alcohol* comes from Arabic. So do words for other familiar beverages: *coffee, soda* (derived from the word for headache, which the Arabs treated with a plant containing soda), and *julep* (from the Persian word for rosewater).

Indeed, many words used in the sciences, such as *alembic, azimuth,* and *nadir,* are Arabic. In mathematics *algebra* can be traced to *al-jabr* (bonesetting) and *algorithm* to a ninth-century mathematician surnamed al-Khwarizmi. The word *guitar* goes back, via Spain, to the Arabs' *qitar.* Other Middle Eastern instruments include the lute, tambourine, and zither. *Mask* and *mascara* both derive from an Arabic word meaning "fool." Let some miscellaneous words round out the digression: *alcove* (from *al-qubba,* a domed area), *admiral, arsenal, magazine* (in the sense of a storehouse), *talc, tariff* (from *al-ta'rifah,* a list of prices), and *almanac* (from *al-manakh,* meaning "weather"). Middle East history gives us some background to what we have, what we do, and what we are.

Getting back to more practical matters, we must look to the recent history of the Middle East to explain what is happening there now. This area gets more than its share of the news: Arab-Israeli wars (or possibly peace), assassinations, oil diplomacy, the Greek-Turkish conflict in Cyprus, Iran's revolution, terrorism, and the Gulf War. Current events in the Middle East affect us as individuals, as members of religious or ethnic groups, and as citizens of our countries. Can history give us clues as to how we should respond? I think it can. This book will risk relating past events to current ones. As a historian, I care about what happened, how it happened, and why it happened. But all of us who live in this world, entering a new millennium, want to know what these happenings mean for ourselves, here and now.

As this caravan (originally a Persian word) of Middle East history starts off, let me wish you *rihlah sa'idah, nasi'ah tovah, safar be-khayr* (and may you have a fruitful intellectual journey).

## THE PHYSICAL SETTING

Before I can write anything about its history, we must settle on a definition of the Middle East. Even though historians and journalists throw the term around, not everyone agrees on what it means. It makes little sense geographically. No point on the globe is more "middle" than any other. What is "east" for France and Italy is "west" for India and China. Logically, we could say "Southwest Asia," but would that not leave out Egypt and European Turkey? Our conventional view of the "Old World" as having three continents—Europe, Asia, and Africa—breaks down once we think about their physical and cultural geography. Do Asia and Africa divide at the Suez Canal, or at the border between Egypt and Israel, or somewhere east of Sinai? What differences are there between peoples living east and west of the Ural Mountains or the Bosporus? For us humans, continents are not really logical either.

So let me write about a "Middle East" that the press, radio, and television have made familiar to us. Its geographical limits may be disputed, but for the purposes of this book the Middle East runs from the Nile Valley to the Muslim lands of Central Asia (roughly, the valley of the Amu Darya, or Oxus, River), from extreme southeast Europe to the Indian Ocean. I may stretch or shrink the area when discussing a given historical period in which political realities may have altered the conventional outline. After all, the lands south and east of the Mediterranean were *the* East to our cultural forebears, until they started going to India and China, whereupon the Muslim lands became the Near East. World War II made it the Middle East, and so it has remained, despite UN efforts to rename it "West Asia." For navigation and aviation, for peacetime commerce and wartime strategy, and for journalism and politics, the area is very much in the middle, flanked by centers of population and power.

## SOME DESCRIPTIVE GEOGRAPHY

History waits upon geography. Before you can have a play, there must be a stage. Perhaps we should spend a lot of time on topography and climate, flora and fauna, and other aspects of descriptive geography. Some textbooks do, but they may remind you of the bad old way of teaching geography by making schoolchildren memorize the names of mountains, rivers, capitals, and principal products of countries. Let us stick to the few essential points that you need to master before starting your study of Middle East history. We can add the details later.

### Climate

The Middle East tends to be hot and dry. Most parts get some rainfall, but usually in amounts too small or too irregular to support settled agriculture. Yet the world's oldest farming villages have been unearthed in the highlands of Anatolia (Asiatic Turkey), Persia, and Palestine. Others have been found in the western Sahara. What happened? It seems that as the polar ice caps (from the last, great Ice Age) retreated some 10,000 years ago, rainfall diminished in North Africa and Southwest Asia. Hunting and food-gathering peoples, living in lands that could once have been like the Garden of Eden, had to learn how to control their sources of sustenance. Rain-watered areas became farther and farther apart. Some peoples moved into the marshy valleys of the great rivers: the Nile, the Tigris, and the Euphrates. By 3500 B.C.E. ("before the common era," that is, the equivalent of B.C.) or so, they had learned how to tame the annual floods to water their fields. Other peoples became nomads; they learned how to move up and down mountains or among desert oases to find forage for their sheep, goats, asses, and eventually camels and horses.

The sedentary farmers who tamed the rivers needed governments to organize the building of dams, dikes, and canals for large-scale irrigation that would regulate the distribution of the floodwaters. They also needed protection from wandering animal herders. The latter group, the nomads, sometimes helped the settled peoples as soldiers, merchants, and purveyors of meat and other animal products. But at times they also became the bane of the farmers and their governors when they pillaged the farms and sacked the cities. Herders and farmers often fought, like Cain and Abel, and yet they also needed each other. In arid lands characterized by long hot summers and cold winter nights, both groups had to coexist in order to survive.

## Location

The Middle East is the natural crossroads of the Afro-Eurasian landmass. It is also the "land of the seven seas." It lies athwart the water route from southern Ukraine to the Mediterranean, via the Black Sea, the Bosporus, the Sea of Marmara, the Dardanelles, and the Aegean Sea. In various eras an area between the Nile Delta and the Sinai Peninsula has been adapted to facilitate shipping between the Mediterranean and the Red Sea. Ever since the taming of the one-humped camel around 3000 B.C.E., men and women have crossed the deserts with their merchandise, flocks, and household goods. Even the high mountains of Anatolia and Persia did not bar passage to people with horses, donkeys, or two-humped camels. Invaders and traders have entered the Middle East from Central Asia, Europe, and Africa since prehistoric times. Rarely in the past 4,000 years have Middle Eastern peoples known any respite from outside pressures or influences.

Consider what this accessibility means for the Middle East, compared with some other parts of the world. Chinese civilization developed in relative isolation; invading "barbarians" were first tamed and then absorbed into China's political system. The peoples of Britain lived for centuries in what they smugly called "splendid isolation" and viewed foreign affairs as "something, usually unpleasant, that happens to someone else." The United States long saw itself separate from the outside world. Writing as an American to my fellow citizens, who may at times question the political attitudes and actions of Middle Eastern peoples, I urge that we ask ourselves these questions: When did we last fight a war on U.S. soil? When did we last experience a foreign military occupation? When did we even fear hostile raids from across our borders? Middle Easterners have, by contrast, known conquest, outside domination, and a continuing exchange of people and animals (but also of goods and ideas) with both the East and the West throughout their history.

## Natural Resources

Nature did not endow the Middle East as lavishly as North America or Europe. There are no more grassy plains. More than nine-tenths of the forests have been cut down. Partly as a result of deforestation, drinkable water is scarce almost everywhere and has become so precious that wars have been fought over it. Some coal and lignite are mined in Anatolia. A few mountainous areas harbor deposits of copper, iron, and other metals; in many instances they have been worked since ancient times. These resources are meager. More plentiful are sand and limestone, other building materials, and sunlight (a blessing if solar energy becomes the main source of power).

But what about oil? It is true that some areas, especially those around the Persian Gulf, have immense petroleum deposits, more than half of the world's known reserves. Oil has lately magnified the Middle East's importance. Its blessings, though, are showered on but few countries, mainly Saudi Arabia, Iran, Kuwait, Iraq, and the United Arab Emirates. Exploitation of Middle Eastern oil did not start until the twentieth century; it assumed large-scale proportions only after 1945. For most of history, crude petroleum was a medicine, a pitch for caulking riverboats, or the cause of mysterious fires that were objects of religious veneration, but not the source of wealth and power that it has now become. And who knows how long it will last?

## Human Diversity

The Middle East's geography has contributed to the diversity of its inhabitants. On the one hand, varied landscapes—mountains and plains, river valleys and deserts—require differing lifestyles. Relatively inaccessible mountains, further isolated in winter and spring by fast-flowing streams, have shielded religious and ethnic minorities in such countries as Lebanon, Yemen, and Iran. On the other hand, frequent invasions have brought new races and folkways into the Middle East. The result is a vast mosaic of peoples, a living museum of physical types, belief systems, languages, and cultures.

This diversity may not always show up on statistical tables, such as the one at the end of this book. Even when it does, remember that the religion of nine-tenths of the people in the Middle East is Islam. Half the population of the area speaks Arabic; most of the other half speaks either Turkish or Persian. The mosaic of separate religious and ethnic groups has started to crumble. General primary schooling, Walkman personal stereos and CD players, television, VCRs, and mobile telephones are spreading a universal culture, especially among the young. Oil revenues, the proliferation of factories, and the growth of cities have also made the people seem more alike.

But cultural and religious differences persist and promote conflicts. Lebanon's civil wars were partly due to the feeling of many Muslims that they have not enjoyed equal power and prestige with the Christians, who claim to be the majority in the country. Syria's current elite comes disproportionately from a minority sect, the Alawis, who used the army officer corps to rise to power in a society otherwise dominated by Sunni Muslims. Christian Arabs, especially the Greek Orthodox who make up less than 5 percent of Syria's population and 10 percent of Lebanon's, outstripped the Muslims in promoting the early spread of Arab nationalism in those countries. Iraq's politics are bedeviled by differences between Sunni and Shi'i Muslim Arabs, both of whom have resisted attempts by the Kurds (about a fifth of the country's population) to form a separate state. Israel, though mainly Jewish, has a million Arabs living within its pre-1967 borders and has been ruling more than 2 million additional Arab Muslims and Christians in lands it has controlled since the June 1967 war. Israel's Jews are divided between those of European origin, called *Ashkenazim*, and those who came from Asian or African countries, called *Sephardim* or Orientals. You may now be confused by these sectarian and ethnic differences, but I will cover them in more detail later. If you cannot wait to have these terms defined, look for them in the Glossary.

## CONCLUSION

The interaction between human beings and their physical surroundings is a fascinating subject, more so than most students realize. As you read through the historical narrative, do not be put off by the names of deserts and mountains, rivers and seas (most of which can be found in the Glossary). Think of the challenges they have posed to humanity and the stratagems by which Middle Eastern peoples have overcome them. Once we get into their history, you will have little trouble absorbing the geographic data, as nomadic tribes confront farming villages, as urban centers absorb invading soldiers, or as oil discoveries shower sudden benefits on desert areas. History is not limited to shaykhs and shahs or to presidents and politicians; it is also the story of traders and teachers, artisans and farmers, herders of goats and warriors on horseback. In the chapters that follow, you will see how they used the mountains, plains, and valleys that appear on Map 1 and how they filled the Middle East with cities, dynastic kingdoms, and contending nation-states.

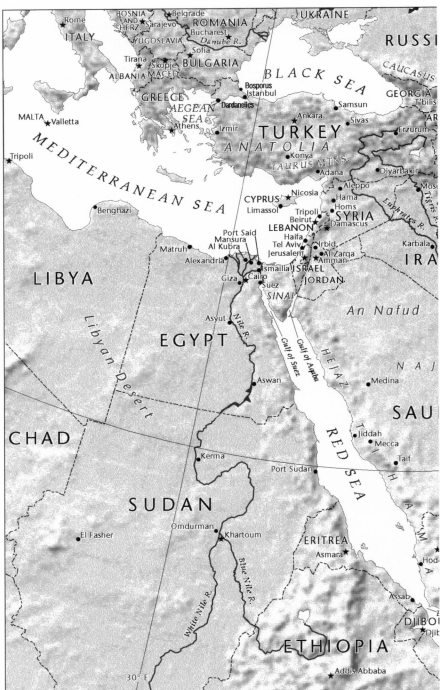

MAP 1 Physical features of the Middle East

# TWO

# The Middle East
# Before Muhammad

When does the history of the Middle East start? At what point should this supposedly concise history begin? Every profession has its unique hazards. For historians, it is the urge to trace causal relationships as far back as possible. We are trained to see that every event or trend must have come from something, which in turn must have been caused by something else. Does this quest take us back to Adam, Eve, and the serpent in the Garden of Eden? If history can be defined as humanity's recorded past, then the Middle East has had more history than any other part of the world. Although the human species probably originated in Africa, the main breakthroughs to civilization occurred in the Middle East. It is here that most staple food crops were initially cultivated, most farm animals first domesticated, and the earliest agricultural villages founded. Here, too, arose the world's oldest cities, the first governments, and the earliest religious and legal systems. Writing and the preservation of records were Middle Eastern inventions. Without them history would be inconceivable.

Also inconceivable would be a complete coverage of all aspects of Middle East history in a concise narrative. It is easy to cut out trivia, but I hate to omit the whole span of recorded history from the earliest river valley civilizations up to the decline and fall of the Roman Empire. This subject is by no means trivial, but its omission reduces the time we must cover from sixty centuries to fifteen. History courses on Western civilization or the ancient world usually drop the Middle East after Rome's fall. The conventional date of this event is 476 C.E. ("of the common era," the equivalent of A.D.), but perhaps you know that the center of Roman power and culture had already shifted to the eastern Mediterranean, where it would last for almost another millennium. It is just where traditional Western civilization courses leave the Middle East that this concise history should start.

## A MINIMUM OF ANTIQUITY

How admirable are the ways in which human beings adapt to seemingly adverse conditions: the heat of Libya or the cold of Siberia, the crowds of Calcutta or the vast emptiness of the Great Plains, the bureaucratized anonymity of a big university or the insularity of a small college. Note how people turn adversity into advantage: The Yankee farmer scrabbles a living out of his rocky hillside, the camel nomad finds seasonal water and vegetation in a barren desert, and the architect designs a handsome structure to fit an oddly shaped city block. I see much adaptability in the history of the Middle East.

During the last 10,000 years before the birth of Christ, the peoples of the Middle East developed various skills to cope with their challenging environment. They tamed asses and cattle to bear their burdens and share their labors. They built ovens hot enough to fire clay pottery. As the uplands grew dry and parched, they learned to harness the great rivers in order to grow more crops. They fashioned tools and weapons of bronze and, later, of forged iron. They devised alphabets suitable for sending messages and keeping records on tablets of clay or rolls of papyrus. They developed cults and rituals, expressing the beliefs that gave meaning to their lives. They absorbed Medes and Persians coming from the north and various Semitic peoples from Arabia. They submitted to Alexander's Macedonians in the fourth century B.C.E. but soon absorbed them into their own cultures. Finally, in the last century before Christ, the lands east and south of the Mediterranean were themselves absorbed into the Roman Empire.

## PERSIA AND ROME

The two great empires existing at the dawn of the common era, Persia and Rome, took many pages from the books of their imperial precursors. During the period of the Achaemenid dynasty (550–330 B.C.E.), Persia, the land that we now call Iran, ruled over various ethnic and religious groups in an area stretching from the Indus to the Nile. The kings and nobles followed the religion of Zoroaster, who had lived in the sixth century

B.C.E. He had taught the existence of a supreme deity, Ahura Mazda ("Wise Lord"), creator of the material and spiritual worlds, source of both light and darkness, founder of the moral order, lawgiver, and judge of all being. An opposing force, Ahriman, was represented by darkness and disorder. Although Zoroaster predicted that Ahura Mazda would ultimately win the cosmic struggle, all people were free to choose between Good and Evil, Light and Darkness, the Truth and the Lie. The Zoroastrians venerated light, using a network of fire temples tended by a large priestly class. Zoroastrianism appealed mainly to the high-born Persians, not to commoners or to the other peoples under their rule. The Achaemenid kings tolerated the diverse beliefs and practices of their subjects as long as they obeyed the laws, paid their taxes, and sent their sons to the Persian army. Their empire set the pattern followed by most—but not all—of the multicultural dynastic states that have arisen since ancient times. When Alexander the Great humbled the Achaemenids and absorbed their empire into his own, he hoped to fuse Hellenic (Greek) ways with the culture of the Middle East. Many of the ideas, institutions, and administrators of the Egyptians, Syrians, Mesopotamians, and Persians were co-opted into his far-flung but short-lived realm.

Cultural fusion likewise occurred later, when Rome ruled the Middle East. By uniting under its rule all the peoples of the Mediterranean world, the Roman Empire stimulated trade and the interchange of peoples and folkways. Several Middle Eastern religions and mystery cults spread among the Romans. Two of these were Mithraism, a cult that had begun in Persia and won the backing of many Roman soldiers, and Christianity, originally a Jewish sect whose base of support was broadened by Paul and the early apostles. Most of the early church fathers lived in Anatolia, Syria, Egypt, and North Africa. These areas—later Islam's heartland—saw the earliest development of most Christian doctrines and institutions. By the late third century, Christianity (still officially banned by the Roman Empire) actually prevailed in the eastern Mediterranean. Its appeal, relative to rival religions, may have been due to its success in borrowing the attractive aspects of earlier faiths. For instance, the Egyptian people could identify the risen Christ with Osiris, one of their ancient gods.

When Rome's emperor Constantine (r. 313–337) became a Christian, he redirected the course of history, both Middle Eastern and Western. Rome now became a Christian empire. The emperor ordered the construction of a new capital, strategically situated on the straits linking the Black Sea to the Aegean. He called it Constantinople after himself. Its older name, Byzantium, survives in the parlance of historians who call his "new" state the Byzantine Empire. Actually, you may get away with calling it Rome, just as people did in the fourth century and long afterward. Even now, when Arabs, Persians, and Turks speak of "Rum," they mean what we term the Byzantine Empire, its lands (especially Anatolia), or the believers in its religion, Greek Orthodox Christianity. Rum was far from the Italian city on the banks of the Tiber, but the old Roman idea of the universal and multicultural empire lived on in this Christian and Byzantine form. Later, Arabs and other Muslims would adopt this idea and adapt it to their own empires.

Roman rule benefited some people in the Middle East. Their trading and manufacturing cities flourished, just as before. Greek, Syrian, and Egyptian merchants grew rich from the trade among Europe, Asia, and East Africa. Arab camel nomads, or bedouin, carried cloth and spices (in addition to the proverbial gold, frankincense, and myrrh) across the deserts. Other Middle Easterners sailed through the Red Sea, the Gulf, and the Indian Ocean, to lands farther east. Surviving remains of buildings at Leptis Magna (Libya), Jerash (Jordan), and Ba'albek (Lebanon) give us a hint of the grandeur of Rome in the Middle East.

But Roman dominion had its darker side. Syria and Egypt, the granaries of the ancient world, were taxed heavily to support large occupying armies and a top-heavy bureaucracy in Rome and Constantinople. Peasants, fleeing to the big cities to escape taxes, could find no work there. Instead, they became part of rootless mobs that often rioted over social or religious issues. In principle, an urbane tolerance of other people's beliefs and customs was the hallmark of a Roman aristocrat. But we know that long before Rome adopted Christianity, its soldiers tried to put down a Jewish rebellion by destroying the Second Temple in Jerusalem. Many of Jesus' early followers were tortured or killed for refusing to worship the Roman emperor.

Christian Rome proved even less tolerant. The spread and triumph of Christianity brought it into the mainstream of Hellenistic (Greek-influenced) philosophy. Major doctrinal crises ensued, as Christians disputed the precise nature of Christ. The debated points are nowadays hard to grasp and may puzzle even Christians, as well as everyone else. Let me simplify the issues. The essence of Christianity—what distinguishes it from Judaism and Islam, the other monotheistic (one God) religions—is its teaching that God, acting out of love for an often sinful humanity, sent His son, Jesus, to live on earth among men and women and to redeem them from their sins by suffering and dying on the cross. If you hope, after your death, to be reunited with God in the next world, you must accept Jesus as Christ (Greek for "anointed one," or "messiah") and as your personal savior. Christ's central role as mediator between God and humanity led the early Christians into many disputes over his nature.

### Dissident Christian Sects

One Christian group, the Arians, which arose in the early fourth century, taught that Christ, though divinely inspired and sired, was still a man not equivalent to God. The Arians' foes argued that if Christ were merely a man, his crucifixion, death, and resurrection could not redeem humankind. They won the church's acceptance of Christ's divinity at a council held in Nicaea in 325. Arianism became a heresy (a belief contrary to church doctrine), and its followers were persecuted as if they had been traitors to the Roman Empire. Most Christians, though, accepted the divine trinity: God as Father, Son, and Holy Spirit. Was Christ thus the same as God? If so, do Christians accept the Gospel stories of his mother's pregnancy, his birth, baptism, mission, and suffering—all essentially human attributes? The early church fathers, heirs to a rich tradition of Hellenistic thought, debated these matters. Even for the poor, humble, and unlettered masses, the nature of Christ was a burning issue, especially in the Middle East's main Christian centers: Alexandria, Antioch, and Constantinople. While learned scholars disputed, Christian mobs brawled, rioted, and pillaged over the true nature of the Prince of Peace!

In Antioch grew up a school of theologians called the Nestorians. They saw Christ as two distinct persons, divine and human, closely and inseparably joined. A church council at Ephesus condemned this view in 430, after which the emperor and the Orthodox church tried to suppress Nestorianism throughout the Byzantine Empire. Many Nestorians found refuge in Persia and sent out missionaries to Central Asia, India, China, and even southern France. Some of their opponents, called Monophysites, went to the opposite extreme, claiming that Christ contained within his person a single, wholly divine nature. Though centered in Alexandria, this Monophysite idea won followers throughout Egypt, Syria, and Armenia (an independent kingdom in eastern Anatolia). The Egyptian Monophysites called themselves Copts, the Syrian ones Jacobites; their churches (plus the Armenian one) have survived to the present day. The majority of Orthodox bishops, meeting at Chalcedon in 451, declared that the Monophysites were heretics, like the Arians and the Nestorians. The Orthodox church found a compromise formula: Christ the savior was both perfect God and perfect man. His two natures, though separate, were combined within the single person of Jesus Christ. Whenever the Byzantine emperor upheld the Chalcedon formula, the Orthodox bishops would use their political power to persecute Egyptians and Syrians who would not recant their Monophysite (or Nestorian) heresy. This policy turned dissenters against Constantinople and would later lead to the Arab conquests and the subjection of Middle Eastern Christianity to Islam.

Do you find this issue petty? Some modern historians think that material motives caused the disputes among Middle Eastern Christians. No doubt the Egyptians and Syrians resented the high Byzantine taxes. Others hated having their bishops subordinate to the Constantinople patriarch. Ancient Middle Eastern mysticism inevitably clashed with Hellenistic rationalism. Personality conflicts and power struggles did arise: Christian bishops were all too human. Keep in mind, though, that Christological issues were vital to these Middle Eastern peoples, whose lives in this world were guided by religion to prepare for the Judgment Day and the life to come. Someday, perhaps, our descendants will wonder why we fought over abortion, affirmative action, and gun control.

### Rome's Persian Rival

The Roman Empire never monopolized the Middle East. There was always a rival state in Persia that covered not just today's Iran but also what we now call Iraq (Mesopotamia), in addition to lands farther east, such as present-day Afghanistan, Pakistan, and Central Asia. Mountain ranges, such as the Zagros in lands north of the Gulf, the Elburz just south of the Caspian, and the Khurasan highlands, accumulated enough rain and snow to support the hundreds of hillside agricultural villages. Some Persian farmers shrewdly channeled groundwater through underground *qanats*, a sophisticated irrigation system that sustained farms and homes in otherwise parched lowlands. The Persians were better than the Romans at bronze casting and iron working. Both East and West drew on Persian architectural motifs, such as domes mounted on squinches, shaded courtyards, and huge bas-relief murals.

From 250 B.C.E. to 226 C.E., Persia was ruled by the Parthians, a poorly understood dynasty. Their written histories have come from the Romans, who could never subdue them, and the Sasanids, the Persian dynasty that supplanted them. We can hardly expect these sources to be sympathetic. But archaeological excavations have proved that the Parthians, who were enthusiastic horseback riders and hunters, patronized architects and artisans. They preserved Persian culture and the Zoroastrian religion, yet they welcomed Buddhists and Jews into their country to live.

Their successors, the Sasanid dynasty, usually get credit for Persia's revival. Between the third and seventh centuries, they amassed an extensive empire (shown on Map 2), established Zoroastrianism as the state religion, and set up a strong and centralized administration. The early Sasanids sent out scholars to many other countries to collect books, which were translated into the Pahlavi (Middle Persian) language, to trade, and to collect scientific and technical lore. Many foreign scholars were attracted to Persia, a tolerant kingdom in which Nestorian Christians, Jews, and Buddhists could worship and proselytize freely. Driven from a bigoted Byzantine Empire in the fifth century, Nestorian savants found refuge at the legendary Persian academy of Jundishapur, a center for the preservation of Hellenistic culture—indeed, the humanistic heritage of the whole ancient world. Scholars and students came from all parts of Europe and Asia to teach and study there, unhindered by racial prejudice, religious dogma, or political restrictions.

Persia's influence spread far. Although Zoroastrianism's appeal was limited mainly to Persians, it gave birth to a more popular dualistic faith called Manichaeism, which spread throughout Europe and Asia during the Sasanid era. Meanwhile, Persian art influenced architecture, sculpture, painting, and even jewelry and textile design, from Western Europe to China. Ctesiphon, the Sasanid capital just south of what is now Baghdad, featured vaulted buildings higher and wider than any to be found in the Roman Empire. Small wonder that this highly cultured kingdom defied the Romans and their Byzantine successors. With the help of their bedouin allies in Arabia, Persian soldiers managed to overrun Syria, Palestine, and Egypt early in the seventh century. This climax would, however, be brief.

## THE ARABS

It was not the Persians who ended the Hellenistic age in the Middle East but their Arab allies. How did the Arabs come into being? The domestication of the camel, a slow process that took place between roughly 3000 and 1000 B.C.E., enabled bands of people to cross the vast deserts of Arabia, eastern Persia, and eventually North Africa. The Arabian dromedary, or one-humped camel, is famous for its ability to go for days across great distances without needing water, owing to its drinking capacity of 100

22

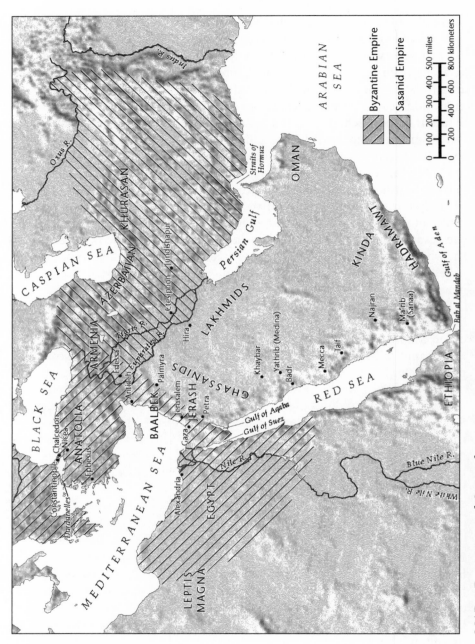

Byzantine Empire

Sasanid Empire

| | | | | | | |
|---|---|---|---|---|---|---|
| 0 | 100 | 200 | 300 | 400 | 500 miles | |
| 0 | 200 | 400 | 600 | 800 kilometers | | |

MAP 2 Byzantine and Sasanid empires circa 600

quarts (95 liters) in ten minutes, its retention of liquids once consumed, and its memory for desert water holes. Relative to other animals, the camel loses little water through perspiration, skin evaporation, and urination. Padded feet, short hair, and a high ratio of skin surface to body mass all help it withstand the heat. Camels can subsist on thorny plants and dry grasses that other animals cannot digest. They store fat—not water—in their humps as a reserve against scarcity. It is hard for Westerners to learn how to ride and guide camels, but the reputation of these animals for stubbornness and spitefulness is ill deserved. Our jokes and songs about camels reveal our ignorance, not their character.

The people who tamed the camel, probably first for food and only later for transportation, were Arabs. No one is sure where the Arabs came from. Popular legends identify them as descendants of Ishmael, Abraham's son by his Egyptian maid, Hagar. Scholars think that the Arabs are kin to the ancestors of other peoples who speak Semitic languages, such as the Hebrews, the Assyrians, and the Arameans. The difference is that these peoples settled in the Fertile Crescent (Syria and Mesopotamia). In ancient times, as some groups of people became sedentarized, others would leave the settled areas. When population outstripped the means of subsistence in such well-endowed areas as the Fertile Crescent, some groups would take to herding sheep and goats in lands where no crops could grow. A few ventured farther away and migrated from one desert oasis to another (just as others moved up and down mountains) to find seasonal water and vegetation for their flocks. Those who had mastered the camel could move even farther away from the lands of the peasant, the shepherd, and the tax collector.

## Conditions in Arabia

The Arabian Peninsula was just such a place: desolate, bereft of rivers and lakes, cut off by land and sea from all but the bravest invader. (The sole exception is the mountainous southern region, the Yemen, which I will discuss later.) The prevailing west winds from the Mediterranean, which carry winter rain to Syria and Anatolia, rarely bring moisture as far south as Arabia. What rain does come is usually blocked by the hills of the Hijaz, the western part, leaving central and eastern Arabia bone dry. Now and then a freak storm can send floods coursing down the dry valleys, but most of the water runs off because the ground is too hard to absorb it. Fortunately, underground water does reach the surface in springs, water holes, and oases, where date palms flourish. The Arabs learned to move around constantly, following the seasonal availability of groundwater and forage for their animals. Milk and dates—occasionally meat and bread—made up their staple diet.

It would have been hard for an individual or even a small band of people to survive in such a harsh environment. Great military empires or mercantile city-states would not have arisen there. The Arabs were organized into clans and tribes, extended families that migrated together and held their property in common. Significantly, the tribes protected their members against other nomads and the settled peoples. The Arabs were belligerent and zealous in defending their honor, on which their freedom depended. Tests of strength, such as raids and skirmishes, were common. Each tribe was governed by a council of adult men who represented the various clans or smaller family groupings. The council chose a *shaykh* (elder), usually the member of the tribe most respected for his bravery and generosity, except in a few tribes where the leadership was hereditary. The council decided on questions of waging war or making peace, inasmuch as the tribe increased its meager income by raiding other tribes and "protecting" the commercial caravans that plied between Syria and the Indian Ocean. Some members of tribes served as auxiliaries in the Persian or Roman armies; one of the third-century Roman emperors was named Philip the Arab. Others built trading cities on the fringes of the settled areas, such as Palmyra in Syria, Petra in Jordan, and Najran in the Yemen. Still others took up farming land, as in the region around Yathrib (now called Medina). But camel breeding and raiding remained the Arabs' favorite and most respected activities.

## Arabian Culture

The bedouin Arabs, owing to their adaptation to desert life, may have lacked the refinement of the Romans or the Persians, but they were not barbarians. They were warlike; hunger or habit led them to prey on one another or on outsiders. Their constant movement gave them no chance to develop architecture, sculpture, or painting. But they did possess a highly portable form of artistic expression—poetry. Pre-Islamic poetry embodied the Arab code of virtue, the *muruwwah*: bravery in battle, patience in misfortune, persistence in revenge (the only justice possible at a time when no governments existed), protection of the weak, defiance toward the strong, hospitality to the visitor (even a total stranger), generosity to the poor, loyalty to the tribe, and fidelity in keeping promises. These were the moral principles that people needed in order to survive in the desert, and the verses helped to fix the *muruwwah* in their minds. Recited from memory by the tribal Arabs and their descendants, these poems expressed the joys and tribulations of nomadic life, extolled the bravery of their own tribes, and lampooned the faults of their rivals. Some Arabs loved poetry so much that they used to stop wars and raids yearly for a month in which poets might recite their new verses and match wits with one another. Pre-Islamic poetry helped to shape the Arabic language, the literature and culture of the Arabs, and hence the thoughts and actions of Arabic-speaking peoples even now.

## Southern Arabia

During the time when Rome and Persia seemed to dominate the Middle East, there was actually a third power, far off and almost ignored. Southern Arabia, with its monsoonal rain and lush vegetation, seemed a world apart, but it fostered the growth of several city-states. Saba (whence came that mythic queen of Sheba to call on Solomon) is the best known. Even before the time of Christ, its people, the Sabaeans, had developed a thriving trade between their base in Yemen and the far shores of the Indian Ocean. They were the first people to make India and its products known to the Roman world and to colonize East Africa. The Sabaeans dammed up mountain streams and terraced the Yemen hillsides to support an elaborate agriculture. Their main export crop was frankincense, used by the pagan Romans to mask the offensive odor when they cremated their dead. The spread of Christianity, which replaced cremation with burial, hurt the frankincense trade. When Ethiopia turned Christian and teamed up with the Byzantines, the Yemeni Arabs, whose kings had by then converted to Judaism, got caught in the middle. Several dam breaks, an Ethiopian invasion, and a commercial depression combined during the sixth century to weaken southern Arabia.

## Sixth-Century Conditions

The political situation in Arabia then ranged from complex to chaotic. The last of the great south Arabian kingdoms was reduced in 525 to an Ethiopian dependency. Three outside powers contended for control: the Byzantine Empire, champion of Orthodox Christianity; Sasanid Persia, ruled by Zoroastrians but harboring Nestorian Christians, Jews, Buddhists, dissident Manichaeans, and other sects; and Ethiopia, which espoused the same Monophysite Christianity as the Byzantines' rebellious

Egyptian subjects, the Copts. Each empire had a client Arab tribe that it paid handsomely and furnished with the trappings of monarchy in return for military service. The peninsula was often ravaged by wars among these three tribes: the pro-Byzantine Ghassanids of the northwest; the pro-Sasanid Lakhmids, with their capital at Hira, near the Euphrates; and the Christian tribe of Kinda, situated in central Arabia and friendly to Ethiopia. Other Arab tribes, some still animist (believing that natural objects embodied spiritual powers), others partly Zoroastrian, Jewish, or Christian (though usually not Orthodox), would mix in their quarrels. Southern Arabia underwent two consecutive foreign occupations: Ethiopian (ca. 525–575) and Persian (ca. 575–625).

## Mecca

Most of central and northern Arabia kept a precarious independence. In times of peace the area was crossed by the camel caravans plying the overland trade route from Syria to Yemen. Despite the falling demand for frankincense, overland trade was gaining in importance as the shoals and pirates of the Red Sea made sailing comparatively risky. The Byzantine-Sasanid wars also tended to divert trade toward western Arabia. One of its Arabian towns, formerly tied to the Sabaean kingdom as a religious shrine, emerged in the sixth century as a major caravan station. This was Mecca, set inland from the Red Sea among the mountains of the Hijaz. Hot and dry, Mecca was useless for farming. It gained some of its wealth and power from trade. But its primacy among Arab towns stemmed from three additional assets: a yearly poets' fair at nearby Ukaz; Mount Arafat, already a pilgrimage site; and its Ka'bah, a cube-shaped structure of unknown antiquity that housed idols (reportedly 360 of them) standing for the various deities venerated by the tribal Arabs. Also nearby were lesser shrines honoring individual goddesses, notably al-Lat, al-Uzza, and al-Manat, who were worshiped by the pagan Meccans themselves.

Later, some Muslims would portray pre-Islamic Mecca as a sinkhole of wanton vice and corruption. Although they believed that Abraham and Ishmael had earlier built the Ka'bah for the worship of the one true God, the shrine had been corrupted in the intervening centuries. In reality, Mecca must have been an amalgam of goodness and iniquity, a merchant's haven. Its rulers belonged to a sedentarized Arab tribe called the Quraysh, later to become both famous and infamous in the annals of Islamic history. Every Muslim caliph for more than six centuries could trace his ancestry back to this family of traders, shrinekeepers, and politicians.

Under their leadership, the centers of Middle Eastern power would shift from the Mediterranean Sea and the Persian plateau to the Arabian desert and the Fertile Crescent. In the conventional usage of historians, this change marked the transition from the ancient to the medieval era. The prime cause of this transition will soon become clear: Muhammad, the last and the greatest of Islam's prophets, was a Meccan of the Quraysh.

## CONCLUSION

It is customary for historians of Southwest Asia to divide themselves according to their specialization into those of the ancient world, those of medieval Islam, and those of the modern Middle East. Although this practice reflects our training (especially the languages that we learn), you, as a student first learning about the Middle East, should avoid falling into the trap of dismissing as irrelevant the history of the area before Islam. The achievements of the Egyptians and Mesopotamians in hydraulic engineering have lasted (with periodic renovations, to be sure) up to now. The world's first law code was proclaimed in Mesopotamia by Hammurabi. The development of monotheism by the Egyptians and especially by the Jews was a necessary precursor to both Christianity and Islam. Greek ideas and Roman laws are part of the heritage of the Middle East as well as the West. The doctrinal disputes in early Christianity eventually set the direction of Catholic and, hence, of Protestant theology, although they also weakened Christendom's ability to withstand the impact of Islam. Sasanid Persia's imperial kingship, bureaucratic traditions, and tolerance of dissident faiths set a pattern for later Muslim-ruled, multicultural, dynastic states. The experience of the Arabs before Islam formed the matrix for the rise of Muhammad and his mission as a prophet. None of these themes is irrelevant to this book, for ancient institutions and customs lived on in medieval Europe and in the early Muslim world.

# THREE

# The Prophet of Mecca

Around the year 570 (by our reckoning) an Ethiopian army marched northward from Yemen with a baggage train of elephants and tried to take Mecca. It failed. Legend has it that some birds flew over the Ethiopians and pelted them with stones. Smallpox broke out among the troops, and they withdrew to Yemen. Soon afterward they were driven out of Arabia entirely. From then on, the "Year of the Elephant" was remembered by the Arabs—Meccans most of all—as a lucky one. Most people think that Muhammad was born in that year, a few months after his father's death. Before Muhammad was six, his mother also died. His grandfather, taking responsibility for the boy, sent him out to live with bedouin Arabs. Meccans often farmed out their children so that they might learn to speak more grammatical Arabic and get a healthier start in life than they could in the city. When his grandfather died, Muhammad's upbringing was taken over by his uncle, a caravan merchant named Abu-Talib, from whom he learned the business of buying, selling, and transporting goods. Muhammad's family was called the clan of Hashim, or Hashimites. They were a reputable, if relatively poor, branch of the ruling Quraysh tribe. But if you leave out the legends, nothing in this orphan's background could have told you that he would become a prophet of God, a popular leader in war and peace, and a shaper of world history.

## MUHAMMAD'S EARLY LIFE

Now that so many historians look to psychology as a key to understanding great men and women of the past, it is frustrating to know so little about Muhammad's childhood. To be sure, the Quran (the book of God's revelations to Muhammad) tells us a little about his formative years. Early

Muslims, amassing all they could learn about the man they called "the seal of the Prophets," added more data. We know far more about Muhammad than about Jesus. Yet I wonder how heredity and environment combined to form this deeply religious man who was also a brilliant political leader. What truths lurk behind the legends, recorded by early biographers, that angels opened five-year-old Muhammad's chest to cleanse his heart, or that a Christian hermit later pointed out a mark of prophethood between the lad's shoulders?

We do know that Muhammad, despite the handicaps of being orphaned and without property in a materialistic society, grew up to be a capable and honest merchant. When he was a young man, a merchant widow named Khadijah entrusted him with the care of her caravan. When he acquitted himself well, she broke with Arab custom and proposed marriage to him. Although she was said to be forty, fifteen years older than Muhammad, the marriage proved to be happy. She bore six children, and Muhammad took no other wives during her lifetime. The business (hence his reputation) did well. In the normal course of events, Muhammad should have become one of Mecca's leading citizens, even though the Umayyads, the strongest clan in the Quraysh tribe, looked down on the Hashimite family to which he belonged.

*Confrontation with Pagan Arab Values*

Muhammad was not wholly content. The *muruwwah* code of ideal Arab behavior, which parents still taught to their children, was no longer being upheld by Mecca's leaders, whose moneymaking activities as merchants or shrinekeepers had made them acquisitive and self-centered. Bravery in battle and generosity to the poor were noble ideals for nomads (what, asked the Meccans, did they have to give away?), but these sedentarized Arabs admired the ability to bargain in the marketplace.

What, then, did the Meccans believe? The Arabs' polytheistic animism and ancestor worship were no longer a living faith, even though pilgrimages to the Ka'bah and other shrines continued and were indeed a major source of Meccan income. The nomads believed in their gods only so long as they did what the nomads wanted. They were more apt to fear the jinns (or genies), invisible creatures who could do both nice and nasty things to people. There were some Christians in Mecca, and whole tribes and cities elsewhere in Arabia had converted to Judaism or to some sect of Christianity. There were other pious folk, neither Christian nor Jewish but leaning toward monotheism, known as *Hanifs*. But Mecca's merchants, profoundly practical, scoffed at such notions as the bodily resurrection or the Day of Judgment and at holy laws that might interfere with their pursuit of money and more money. To Muhammad, though, the Jews, Christians, and Hanifs just might have answers to the problems that were gnawing at the core of Meccan society. On many evenings he went to a nearby cave to meditate.

## First Revelation

One night in 610, during the Arabic month of Ramadan, Muhammad was visited by an angel, who exhorted him to read aloud. In awe and terror, he cried out, "I cannot read" (for Muhammad, Muslims believe, was illiterate). Hugging him so hard that he almost choked, the angel again ordered:

> Read: in the name of thy Lord who created,
> created mankind from a blood-clot.
> Read: for thy Lord the most generous;
> He has taught by the pen
> taught man what he knew not. (Quran, 96:1—5)

Everywhere he looked, he saw the same angel looking back at him and saying: "O Muhammad, thou art the messenger of God, and I am Gabriel." Fearing that he had gone mad, Muhammad hurried home and asked Khadijah to cover him with a warm coat. His quaking subsided, but then he saw Gabriel again, and the angel said:

> O thou who art shrouded in thy mantle,
> rise and warn!
> Thy Lord magnify,
> Thy robes purify,
> And from iniquity flee! (Quran, 74:1—5)

Khadijah, as it happened, had a cousin who was a Hanif (or, some say, a Christian). She went to see him, and he assured her that Muhammad, far from being mad, was God's long-awaited messenger to the Arabs. She returned to her husband and gave him the backing that he needed. Hesitantly, Muhammad realized that what he had heard was God's exhortation to make the divine presence known to the Arabs. Also, he had to warn them (just as God had sent earlier prophets to warn the Jews and the Christians) of a Judgment Day when all would be called to account:

*When the earth shall quake with a predestined quaking,*
*When the earth shall bring forth her burdens,*
*and men shall ask, "What ails her?"*
*Upon that day shall she tell her news*
*with which thy Lord has inspired her,*
*Upon that day shall men come out in scattered groups*
*to be shown what they have done.*
*Then he who has done one atom's weight of good shall see it*
*And he who has done one atom's weight of evil shall see it. (Quran, 109:1—8)*

Being God's messenger to the Arabs was an awesome task for an unlettered, middle-aged merchant, an orphan who had gained a precarious hold on a little wealth and status. Muhammad was tempted to shirk the responsibility; and yet, when he received no messages for a while, he feared that God had abandoned him. During this time, he kept asking himself whether he really was a prophet, but his wife never doubted him. A few of his friends and relatives believed in him, too. Once new revelations reached Muhammad, he came to know that his mission was real.

## The Early Muslims

The first believers, although they came from every class and many of Mecca's clans, were mainly young men from the upper-middle stratum—that of the "nearly haves" from which so many revolutions elsewhere have sprung—rather like Muhammad himself. Some converts were sons or younger brothers of the leading merchants; others were notables who had somehow lost (or failed to attain) the status they wanted within pagan Mecca. A few were "weak," which meant that they came from outside the system, that they had no clan to protect them against harm from other Arabs, or that their families lacked the political clout of the Umayyads or the Hashimites. You may be surprised to learn that Muhammad's uncle, Abu-Talib, never embraced Islam, yet he went on protecting his nephew. Abu-Talib's son, Ali, raised in Muhammad's own home, was probably his first male convert, certainly the first who never had bowed to idols, who grew up as a Muslim. Later, he would marry the Prophet's daughter, Fatimah, and become a leader of early Islam. Other early converts were Abu-Bakr, Muhammad's best friend and a man of wealth and social standing; Arkam, a young member of a strong clan, who let the Muslims meet at his home; Umar, an imposing figure from a weak clan; Uthman, an elegant but quiet youth of the powerful Umayyad family; Bilal, an Ethiopian slave set free by Abu-Bakr; and Zayd ibn Harithah, a captured Christian Arab whom Muhammad adopted.

Even if the early Muslims had kept a low profile, they would have attracted the notice—and hostility—of Mecca's leaders. Often Muslims and pagans were related to one another. Muhammad's message disrupted families and threatened the established order. W. Montgomery Watt, whose books on the life of the Prophet have won wide acceptance, summarized his early message in five main points: (1) God is good and all-powerful; (2) God will call all men and women back to Himself on the Last Day and will judge and reward them on the basis of how they acted on earth; (3) people should thank God, through worship, for the blessings He has given the earth; (4) God expects people to share their worldly goods with others needier than themselves; and (5) Muhammad is God's designated messenger to his own people, the Arabs. Later Quranic revelations taught that Muhammad was a prophet for all humanity.

Let me put in a semantic point here. During Muhammad's mission, those who believed in him as God's messenger came to be known as Muslims. The Arabic word *muslim* means "one who submits"—to God's will. The act of submission is *islam*, which became the name of the religion. You may see *Mohammedanism* used in place of *Islam* in older books, but Muslims detest the term. *Moslem* is the same as *Muslim*. Please do not say "Ali became an Islam" when you mean "Ali became a Muslim." Do not say "Mecca is an Islam city" for "Mecca is a Muslim (or Islamic) city." Some usages are confusing. An "Islamic scholar" may be a learned Muslim, but the same term is used for a non-Muslim who has studied a lot about Islam. "Islamic history" may mean the story of Islam's evolution as a religion or of the community of Muslims as distinct from non-Muslim states or of any Muslim peoples wherever they have lived. You and I must make our terms as clear as we can.

## Meccan Opposition

The Meccans who rejected this message feared that Muhammad might try to take away their wealth and power. What right did he have to attack business practices that they deemed necessary for their success? If God had decided to reveal himself then and there, why had he not chosen one of Mecca's leaders? Why did the early Muslims pray facing Jerusalem? If the pagan tribes accepted Islam, would they stop making their annual *hajj* (pilgrimage) to the Ka'bah and other sacred shrines in Mecca? We now know that Muhammad respected the Ka'bah and never wanted to displace it as a center for pilgrims. Nor was he trying to undermine Mecca's economy. A few accounts depict Muhammad as having been so eager to win the Meccan leaders' acceptance that he even conceded that the three pagan goddesses, al-Lat, al-Uzza, and al-Manat, were "sacred swans" worthy of veneration. This accommodation horrified many Muslims. When Muhammad realized what he had done, he denounced what he had mistaken for a divine revelation, and the Quran addressed the Quraysh regarding those goddesses:

> What, would you have males and He females?
> That would indeed be an unjust division.
> They are nothing but names you and your fathers have named,
> God has sent down no authority touching them. (Quran, 53:21—23)

When Muhammad disowned the goddesses, the Meccan leaders became angry, for the keepers of their nearby shrines were Mecca's allies. Unable to attack Muhammad while he had Abu-Talib's protection, the Meccans tried a boycott of the whole Hashimite clan. It failed. Still, they could torment the most vulnerable Muslims, some of whom took refuge in Christian Ethiopia. Then Muhammad made what, to the pagan Meccans, was a still more incredible claim. Following a Quranic revelation, he said that he had journeyed in one night upon a winged horse, first to Jerusalem, then up through the seven levels of Heaven, where he saw the celestial Ka'bah and received from God the fundamentals of the Islamic creed, and that he had talked to Moses during his return to earth. Although the Quran confirmed Muhammad's claims, the pagans mocked them. They averred that he had spent that whole night sleeping in his bed.

In 619 Muhammad lost the two people who had most helped him in his early mission: Khadijah and Abu-Talib died. Muhammad would later marry many women, but none could match the loyalty and support of his first wife. Without his uncle, Muhammad had no protector within the Hashimite clan, and so the persecution grew worse. The Muslims realized that they would have to leave Mecca. An attempt to take refuge in nearby Taif failed, because of its close ties with the Meccan leaders. Muhammad had to abase himself to find a new Meccan protector so that he and his followers could safely return home. The Muslims' situation in Mecca had become untenable, but where else could they go?

## THE EMIGRATION (HIJRAH)

During the pagan pilgrimage month in 620, Muhammad was visited by six tribal Arabs from an agricultural oasis town called Yathrib (now Medina), located about 270 miles (430 kilometers) north of Mecca, just after they had completed their hajj rites at the Ka'bah. They told him that fighting between Yathrib's two pagan tribes had grown so bad that they could no longer protect themselves against the three Jewish tribes with which they shared the oasis. They wanted Muhammad to come and, because of his reputation as an honest man, arbitrate their quarrels. The next year more pilgrims came from Yathrib and some converted to Islam. In return for Muhammad's services as an arbiter, they agreed to give sanctuary to the Meccan Muslims.

This was a great opportunity for Muhammad. He quickly grasped that his mission as God's spokesman would be enhanced once he became the chief judge of a city (even if it was only a motley collection of settled tribes) rather than the spiritual leader of a persecuted band of rebels split between pagan Mecca and Christian Ethiopia. Besides, the Jewish presence in Yathrib made him hope that he might be accepted as a prophet by people who were already worshiping the one God—his God—revealed to the Jews by earlier scriptures. In the following months, he arranged a gradual transfer of his Muslim followers from Mecca to Yathrib. At last, he and Abu-Bakr departed in September 622.

This emigration, called the *hijrah* in Arabic, was a major event in Islamic history. Rather than a "flight," as some call it, the *hijrah* was a carefully planned maneuver by Muhammad in response to his invitation by the citizens of Yathrib. It enabled him to unite his followers as a community, as a nation, or (to use an Arabic word that is so hard to translate) as an *ummah*. From then on, Muhammad was both a prophet and a lawgiver, both a religious and a political leader. Islam was both a faith in one God as revealed to Muhammad (and the earlier prophets) and a sociopolitical system. Muhammad and his followers drew up the Constitution of Medina as a concrete expression of their *ummah*. No wonder the Muslims, when they later set up their own calendar, made the first year the one in which the *hijrah* had occurred.

## The Struggle for Survival

Once the *ummah* was set up in Yathrib, renamed Medina (or *madinat al-nabi*, the "city of the Prophet"), Muhammad faced new challenges. Medina's Arabs did not all become Muslims at once, their quarrels proved hard to settle, and it was harder still for him to win the allegiance of the city as a whole. If the Jews of Medina had ever harbored any belief in Muhammad as the Messiah or the messenger of God, they were soon disillusioned. His revelations did not agree with what they knew from the Bible, and they rejected his religious authority. Muhammad, for his part, saw Islam as the first and most natural monotheism, not as a pale imitation of Judaism or Christianity. His divine revelations, which now were becoming known as the Quran, repeatedly called Abraham a Muslim, a man who submitted to God's will. He wanted the Jews to acknowledge that Adam, Noah, Abraham, and other prophets had lived prior to the emergence of Judaism as a distinct religion. He had brought into Islam some Jewish practices (as he understood them), such as fasting on Yom Kippur (the Day of Atonement) and leading Muslim worship while he and his followers faced Jerusalem. The Jews were not convinced. Even the Medinans who converted to Islam, called *ansar* ("helpers"), grew tired of supporting the Meccan emigrants, who showed no aptitude for farming, the economic basis of their oasis. The emigrants were cut off from commerce, which they did know how to conduct, so long as pagan Mecca controlled the caravan routes and paid protection money to the nearby bedouin tribes.

If Muhammad was ever to lead Medina's Jews and *ansar*, the emigrants would have to find ways to support themselves. The Quran suggested that they might raid the Meccan caravans:

> To those against whom war is made
> Permission is given [to those who fight] because they are wronged;
> and surely God is able to help them. (Quran, 22:39)

Perhaps, in time, they would control enough of the trade route between Syria and Mecca to compete with the Meccans. But this was not as easy as you might think, for their caravans usually went armed and had many of the bedouin tribes on their side. Being a few generations removed from bedouin life, Muhammad and his men knew little about raiding techniques. But raid they did, and after a few fiascoes, they hit the Meccans hard enough to hurt. To do this, they attacked even during the month in which pagan Arabs were forbidden to raid because of their traditional pilgrimage to Mecca. This shocked many Arabs, but a Quranic revelation stated:

> They will question you about the holy month and fighting in it,
> Say "Fighting in it is wrong, but to bar from God's way,
> and disbelief in Him,
> and the sacred Ka'bah, and to expel its people from it—
> that is more wicked in God's sight;
> and persecution is more wicked than killing." (Quran, 2:213)

The pagan Meccans did not agree. In the second year after the *hijrah*—March 624, to be exact—the Muslims were zeroing in on a rich Umayyad caravan returning from Syria, just as Mecca was dispatching a retaliatory army of almost 1,000 men. They met Muhammad's forces (86 emigrants, 238 *ansar*) at an oasis called Badr, southwest of Medina. Clever tactics helped the Muslims win, but nothing succeeds like success. To Muhammad's people, victory was a tangible sign of God's favor, a chance to gain captives and booty. The latter was divided among the warriors, except for a fifth that the Prophet took to support poor members of the *ummah*.

In addition, the victory at Badr enhanced the prestige of Islam—and of Medina—in the eyes of the tribal Arabs. Even though the Meccans avenged themselves on the Muslims in 625 at Uhud, just north of Medina, they could not take the city itself. The *ummah* survived. Islam was taking root and could not be wiped out. In 627 Mecca sent a larger force to capture Medina, but the Muslims foiled the army by digging a trench around the city's vulnerable parts. The ditch was too broad for the Meccans' horses and camels to cross, so they turned back in disgust. Meanwhile, Muslim raids from Medina were endangering the Meccan caravan trade. The Arab tribes began to break with Mecca and make treaties with Muhammad to join in these lucrative attacks.

## Muslim Life in Medina

On the domestic front, Muhammad was becoming the head of both a large household and a small state. God's revelations now laid down laws about marriage and divorce, inheritance, theft and other crimes, and interpersonal relations, more than they told of God's power and the impending Judgment Day. Besides, regarding those practical matters on which the Quran was silent and to which old Arab customs were no longer applicable, Muhammad's own sayings and actions were becoming an authoritative guide for Muslim behavior. For the most part, a non-Muslim can readily admire the humane common sense that underlay Muhammad's conduct of his public and private life and thus respect his role as a model for Muslims. But non-Muslims often note two accusations that have been made against him: his lust for women and his mistreatment of the Jews. Any critic now raising these issues runs the risk of judging a seventh-century Arab by the standards of our own time and place, hardly a fair judgment. All I can do is present some facts and let you draw what conclusions you will.

*Muhammad's Marriages*

Before Islam, Arab men used to take as many wives as they could afford, unless they belonged to tribes in which women were dominant. Various forms of extramarital sexual relations were also accepted. Seeking to limit this license, the Quran allowed Muslim men to marry as many as four wives, provided that they treated them all equally, but this permission was granted in the context of a revelation concerning the welfare of widows and orphans—a natural concern, given Muhammad's own background and the heavy loss of young men in raids and battles. It is true that after Khadijah died, he gradually took other wives, possibly as many as ten. Several were widows of his slain followers, for whom he offered to provide support. Other marriages involved the daughters of tribal chieftains whom Muhammad wanted as allies. Aishah, who became his favorite wife, was the daughter of Abu-Bakr, his best friend, and she was nine at the time she came to live with him. Muhammad's critics pointed to his marriage to Zaynab, whom he came to know while she was married to his adopted son, Zayd. A new Quranic revelation allowed Zayd to divorce her, but even Aishah was quick to attack Muhammad for marrying her. Muhammad believed that his marriages were prescribed for him by God, and he always enjoyed the company of women. One can find other inconsistencies in his behavior: He forbade wailing at funerals until the death of his infant son, and he forgave many of the foes he faced in battle, but not the poets who made fun of his mission. Prophets were human beings, not plaster saints.

*Muhammad and the Jews*

Muhammad's relations with the Jews of Medina deteriorated as his own power grew. Some Westerners find this disturbing, for we have been slow to overcome anti-Muslim prejudices that go back to the Crusades; a few draw unwarranted parallels to the modern Middle East conflict. Muhammad viewed many biblical figures as prophets, or as men to whom God had spoken. He respected Jews and Christians as "People of the Book," since they worshiped God as revealed by sacred scriptures. Why could he not have been more magnanimous in Medina? Part of the answer is that he expected the Jews to recognize him as God's messenger, just as he had accepted their prophets; but they could not reconcile his Quran with their sacred scriptures. There were too many discrepancies. They opposed the Constitution of Medina, and they were turning some of the less sincere *ansar* against him, by trying to trick him with clever arguments and by mocking him and his followers in public. Perhaps the Jews saw the Muslims as potential competitors in the marketplace. The split widened. Following a Quranic revelation, Muhammad changed the direction of prayer—south toward Mecca instead of north toward Jerusalem. The one-day fast of Yom Kippur ceased to be obligatory, and Muslims started fasting instead during the daylight hours of Ramadan, the month in which Muhammad's first revelation had come. Sabbath observance was replaced by Friday congregational worship with a sermon. Dietary laws were eased. Islam was becoming not only more distinct but also more Arabian.

After winning at Badr, Muhammad expelled one of the Jewish tribes for conspiring with his Meccan foes but let its members keep their property. The Muslims expelled another Jewish tribe after their defeat at Uhud, seizing its groves of date palms. According to traditional accounts, the last of the three tribes suffered the worst fate: The men were killed, and the women and children were sold into slavery. Muhammad believed that this tribe, despite an outward show of loyalty, had backed the Meccans in 627 during their siege of Medina's trench. He sought the advice of an associate who seemed neutral but who in fact coveted the Jews' property. His advice led to a slaughter that enriched some Muslims and raised Muhammad's prestige among the Arab tribes, for it showed that he had no fear of blood reprisals. We should understand the situation as people then saw it. The Jews were not defenseless. The Muslims could have lost their grip on Medina and fallen prey to the Meccans and their tribal allies. Neutralizing their enemies was essential to their security, if not to their survival. Partly because of these confrontations, the Quran contains some harsh words about the Jews. These events did not poison later Muslim-Jewish relations, nor did Muhammad's policies cause what we now call the Arab-Israeli conflict.

## The Winning of Mecca

It is an historical irony that Mecca's pagans who persecuted Muhammad later gave in to him and then prospered under the new order, whereas the Jews of Arabia, whose beliefs were closer to his, rejected him as a prophet and then suffered severely. The story of Mecca's final capitulation seems almost anticlimactic. The emigrants in Medina missed their homes, their families (many were the sons and daughters of leading Meccan merchants), and the Ka'bah, so Muhammad, in 628, led a band of would-be pilgrims toward Mecca. They encountered Meccan troops at Hudaybiyah, slightly north of the city, and the two sides worked out a truce that ended their state of war. The Muslims had to return to Medina then but would be admitted into Mecca the next year as pilgrims. In effect, the Meccans accepted the Muslims as equals. Three months after the Hudaybiyah truce, two of the best Arab fighters, Khalid and Amr, embraced Islam. They eventually went on to greater glory as warriors for the *ummah*. Muhammad made some more key converts during that pilgrimage in 629. The next year, claiming that some clans had breached the terms of Hudaybiyah, he collected 10,000 troops and marched on Mecca. The Meccan leaders, overawed, quickly gave in, letting the Muslims occupy the city peacefully. Soon almost everyone in Mecca became Muslim.

Bolstered by Meccan troops, the Muslims defeated a large coalition of Arab tribes from around Taif. The Hijaz was now united under Islam. From then on, other tribes and clans, recognizing Muhammad's power, began sending delegations to Medina, which remained the capital of the new state. As a condition for his support, Muhammad required the tribes to accept Islam and even to pay taxes, a condition that the Quraysh tribe had never been able to impose. Traditional accounts maintain that by 632 nearly all the Arab tribes were Muslim. It is more likely, though, that only certain clans, factions, or individuals within each tribe embraced Islam. More on this later.

## Muhammad's Death

The Prophet's last years were clouded by worries about would-be rivals in Arabia, heavy political responsibilities, marital problems, the death of his infant son and several daughters, and failing health. He did manage to lead a final pilgrimage to Mecca in March 632. Thus he finished incorporating into Islam the rituals of the hajj, which he had cleansed of its pagan features. In his final sermon he exhorted his followers: "O ye men, listen to my words and take them to heart: Every Muslim is a brother to every other Muslim and you are now one brotherhood."

Soon after his return to Medina, Muhammad retired to Aishah's room. He appointed her father, Abu-Bakr, to lead public worship in his place. Then, on 8 June 632, he died.

## ASSESSMENT

How can we evaluate Muhammad and what he did? For Muslims he has always been the exemplar of Muslim virtues, such as piety, patience, humor, kindness, generosity, and sobriety. Non-Muslim Westerners, recalling Christian battles and disputations with Islam, have often judged him harshly. He has been called a renegade bishop thwarted in his ambition to become pope, a businessman turned brigand, an impostor who summoned mountains to come to him, an epileptic, and even a madman. Such attacks are unfounded. Yet these different assessments may remind us that observant Jews and sincere Christians do not believe, as Muslims must, that Muhammad was obeying God's commands as revealed to him by the Angel Gabriel.

The life of any famous person becomes a lens or mirror by which other people, individually or in groups, view themselves and the world. The biographer or the historian stresses some facts and omits or downplays others. The reader seizes upon a few points and expands them to fit a preconceived image. How, then, to judge Muhammad? I see him as a kind and sincere man, more urban than urbane (he could not tolerate poets' mockery, for instance), who came to have an overwhelming faith in God and in himself as God's final messenger. As such, he had to warn the Arabs and other people about the impending Judgment Day and to form the *ummah*, a religious community, within which Muslim believers could best prepare themselves for that dread occasion. Yet he had a sense of humor, saying: "Let a man answer to me for what waggeth between his jaws, and what between his legs, and I'll answer to him for Paradise." He let his grandsons climb on his back even while prostrating himself in worship. He must have been a skilled political and military tactician, for who else has ever managed to unite the Arabs? He took terrible chances when he accepted his prophetic mission and forsook his home city for an unknown future. The power that he gained came later, and the fame that he earned would not be evident until after his death. But what you can conclude about Muhammad's life will depend on how well you know Islam, the religion for which he did so much. I will give you the basic points in Chapter 4.

# FOUR

# What Is Islam?

When we think about Islam—or any religion that has lasted for a long time—we should remember that it has evolved through history and will continue to do so. It has varied from time to time, from place to place, and maybe even from one person to another. As personal belief systems, religions are hard to describe: How do you speak or write about someone else's deepest thoughts? Let me try to answer the question anyway.

## BASIC BELIEFS

Islam is the act of submission to the will of God (*Allah* in Arabic). In the broadest sense, every object in the universe has its own "islam." It must conform to God's rules, or to what atheists might call nature's laws. Rocks and trees, birds and beasts all submit to God's will because they were created to do so. Human beings, creatures capable of reason, have been made free to choose whether and how to submit to God's will. Many refuse out of ignorance or because they have forgotten the divine commandments they once knew. Some Christians and Jews may have been misled by their scriptures or, rather, by the way they have interpreted them. But anyone who submits to God's will, worships him, and expects his reward or punishment in the world to come is, broadly speaking, a "muslim."

### God

In common usage, though, a Muslim is anyone who believes that God's will for all humanity was last revealed through the Quran to Muhammad. What is God? It is hard to describe the Infinite. To Muslims, God is all-powerful and all-knowing, the creator of all that was and is and will be, the righteous

43

judge of good and evil, and the generous guide to men and women through inspired messengers and divine scriptures. God has no peer, no partner, no offspring, no human attributes, no beginning, and no end.

*La ilaha ill Allah, Muhammad rasul Allah* (There is no god *whatever* but the one God, and Muhammad is the messenger of God). This is the first of the famous five pillars of Islam; it can be found in the muezzin's call to worship; it is emblazoned in white letters on the green flag of Saudi Arabia. Anyone professing Judaism or Christianity agrees that there is only one God, but monotheism entails more than rejecting a pantheon of gods and goddesses. There can be no other Absolute Good; all else is relative. All material blessings—our houses, furniture, cars, clothing, and food—must be valued less highly than the one true God. The pleasures we pursue are (if lawful) fine, but finer yet is the satisfaction of God's commands. Spouses and consorts, parents and children, friends and teammates may be ever so dear, but they must remain second to God in our hearts. God is the giver of life and death. Some Muslims think that God has predestined all human actions. Others argue that God has given us free will, making us strictly accountable for what we choose to do. God wants willing worshipers, not human robots.

## Angels

Muslims believe that God works in a universe in which dwell various creatures, not all of whom can be seen, heard, or felt by human beings. Jinns, for instance, do much good and evil here on earth and are addressed in some Quranic revelations. But more powerful in God's scheme of things are angels, the Heavenly servants who obey the divine will. God did not reveal the Quran directly to Muhammad but sent the Angel Gabriel to do so. Angels taught him how to pray. An angel will blow a horn to herald the Judgment Day. When each of us dies, we will be questioned by a pair of angels. Satan, called Iblis or al-Shaytan in Arabic, was a jinn who flouted God's command to bow down to Adam. Having fallen from grace, he now tries to corrupt men and women. He seems to be doing well.

## Books

How was God's existence made known to humanity? How does the Infinite reveal itself to finite minds? Christians say that the Word became flesh and dwelt among us: God became a man. But Muslims argue that God is revealed by the words placed in the mouths of righteous people called prophets. These words have been turned into books: the Torah of the Jews (consisting of the first five books of the Bible), the Gospels of the

Christians, and the Quran of the Muslims. They also believe that God's earlier revelations, in the form we know them, were corrupted and had to be corrected by the Quran. Modern scholarship has shown that the books of the Bible were written down only after some time had passed since they were revealed. Muslims ask, therefore, whether Jews changed some passages of the Torah to depict themselves as God's chosen people (a concept rejected by Islam) or whether Christians rewrote the Gospels to prove the divinity of Jesus of Nazareth (for Muslims maintain that no human can be God). The Quran, however, is God's perfect revelation. It has existed in Heaven since time began. It will never be superseded. After Muhammad's death it was carefully compiled ("from scraps of parchment, from thin white stones, from palm leaves, and from the breasts of men," wrote an early Muslim) by his followers. Some parts had actually been written down while Muhammad was still alive. If any passage had been misread, a Muslim who had heard Muhammad give the passage would surely have put it right. Seventh-century Meccans had prodigious memories.

The Quran is not easy reading. It is the record of God's revelations, via the Angel Gabriel, to Muhammad. It contains laws, stories from the past, and devotional pieces intended for guidance and recitation, not for literary entertainment. Most of its 114 chapters bring together passages revealed at different times. The chapters, except for the first, are arranged in order of length. Those revealed in Medina, filled with injunctions and prohibitions, tend to precede the Meccan chapters, which stress God's power and warn of the coming Judgment Day. Because the Quran was revealed in Arabic, most Muslims do not think it can or should be translated into any other language. As its usage reflects that of seventh-century Meccans, even Arab Muslims may now need help to understand parts of what they read. The Quran's language is rhymed prose (not metrical like poetry), but it can sound lyrical when chanted by a trained reciter. Try to hear one. Muslims venerate the Quran for many reasons: Its language and style are inimitable, the book sets Islam apart from all other religions, and its teachings have stood the test of time. The speech and writing of pious Muslims are studded with Quranic expressions. No other book has affected so many minds so powerfully for so long.


*Messengers*

God's books were revealed to mortal people called prophets or messengers. Although Islam stresses that Muhammad was the last of the prophets, Muslims recognize and venerate many others, including Adam, Noah, Abraham, Moses, Jonah, and Job. Biblical personages (such as King Solomon) reappear in the Quran as prophets. Christians may be astonished that Muslims count Jesus as one of God's messengers. The Quran affirms that he was born of the Virgin Mary, that he is a "word" of God, and that he will some day return, but it doubts that he was crucified and denies that he was the son of God. All prophets must be revered; no one prophet, not even Muhammad, may be exalted above the others. No more prophets will come before the Judgment Day. Many people nowadays do not know what prophets can do. They do not predict what will happen or perform miracles unless God enables them to do so; they are just good people chosen to bring God's message to other men and women.

## Judgment Day

Among Islam's basic tenets, none was preached more fervently by Muhammad than belief in a final Judgment Day, from which no one can escape. On this day of doom all living people will die, joining those who have gone before them. All will be summoned before the heavenly throne to be judged for the good and the bad things they have done. Later Muslims built up the imagery: A tightrope will stretch across the fires of Hell, and only the righteous will cross over safely into Heaven. The Quran depicts Paradise as a shaded garden with cooling fountains, abundant food and drink, and beautiful maidens for the eternal bliss of righteous men. Righteous women, too, will enter Heaven, but the Quran is less specific on what they will find. Popular Islam teaches that they will go back to the age at which they were most beautiful. Both men and women will know peace, live in harmony, and see God. Hell is everything that is horrible in the Arab mind: fearsome beasts, fiery tortures, noxious vapors, foul-tasting food to eat, and boiling water to drink. There will be no peace and no harmony, God will not be present, and (for the worst sinners) the torments will never end.

## THE FIVE PILLARS OF ISLAM

How can the believer obey God? What are the divine commands? The Quran and Muhammad's teachings are full of dos and don'ts, for Islam (like Judaism) is a religion of right actions, rules, and laws. I cannot cover all of the Islamic rules, but they are symbolized by five obligatory acts: the five pillars of Islam.

## Witness (Shahadah)

I have already mentioned the first duty: witness or testimony that there is no god but God and that Muhammad is God's messenger. Anyone who says these words—and really means them—is a Muslim. Any Muslim who associates other beings with God, or denies believing in Muhammad or any of the other prophets, is no longer a Muslim but an apostate. Apostasy may be punished by death.

## Worship (Salat)

The second pillar of Islam is worship, or ritual prayer—a set sequence of motions and prostrations, performed facing in the direction of the Ka'bah in Mecca and accompanied by brief Quranic recitations. Worship reminds men and women of their relationship to God and takes their minds off worldly matters. It occurs five times each day, at fixed hours announced by the muezzin's call from the minaret (tower) of a mosque, a building constructed for congregational worship. Muslims may worship anywhere, but men are encouraged to do so publicly as a group; women usually worship at home. All adult men should go to a mosque on Friday noon, as congregational worship at that time is followed by a sermon and sometimes by major announcements. Before any act of worship, Muslims wash their hands, arms, feet, and faces. Worship may include individual prayers (that is, Muslims may call on God to bring good to or avert evil from them and their loved ones); but such invocations, called du'a in Arabic, are distinct from salat.

## Fasting (Sawm)

Muslims must fast during the month of Ramadan. From daybreak until sunset they refrain from eating, drinking, smoking, and sexual intercourse. Devout Muslims spend extra time during Ramadan praying, reciting from the Quran, and thinking about religion; lax ones are apt to sleep in the daytime, for the nights are filled with festivities, bright lights, and merrymaking. The discipline of abstinence teaches the rich what it is like to be poor, trains all observant Muslims to master their appetites, and through the shared experience of daytime fasting and nighttime feasting creates common bonds among Muslims. The Muslim calendar has exactly twelve lunar months in each year. With no month occasionally put in, as in the Jewish calendar, the Muslim year consists of only 354 days. Thus Ramadan advances eleven or twelve days each year in relation to our calendar and to the seasons. In the northern hemisphere the fast is relatively easy to keep when Ramadan falls in December, but great self-discipline is needed when it falls in June (as it did in the early 1980s). A Muslim who gets sick or makes a long trip during Ramadan may put off all or part of the fast until a more suitable time. Growing children, pregnant women and nursing mothers, soldiers on duty, and chronically ill Muslims are exempt. Yet nearly all Muslims who can fast do so, even those who have given up other outward observances of the faith.

## Tithing (Zakat)

All Muslims must pay a specified share of their income or property to help provide for the needy. This payment is called *zakat*, often translated as "alms," even though it began as a tax levied on all adult members of the *ummah*. In recent years, many Muslim countries have stopped collecting the *zakat* as a tax, but their citizens are still obliged to make equivalent charitable donations. Lately, though, some Muslim governments have gone back to exacting the tithe. In either case, wealthy and pious Muslims make additional gifts or bequests to feed the hungry, cure the sick, educate the young, or shelter the traveler. Many fountains, mosques, schools, and hospitals have been founded and maintained by a type of endowment called a *waqf* (plural: *awqaf*), about which you will read later. In essence, the fourth pillar of Islam is sharing.

## Pilgrimage (Hajj)

The fifth duty is the hajj, or pilgrimage to Mecca during the twelfth month of the Muslim year. All adult Muslims should perform the hajj at least once in their lives, if they are well enough and can afford to make the journey. Each year, from all parts of the world, observant Muslims, their bodies clad in identical unsewn strips of cloth, converge on Mecca to perform rites hallowed by the Prophet Muhammad, although some are taken from earlier Arab practices. These rites include circling the Ka'bah, kissing the Black Stone set in one of its walls, running between the nearby hills of Safa and Marwa, stoning a pillar near Mina representing the Devil, sacrificing sheep there, and assembling on the plain of Arafat. Some of the rites may have begun as pagan practices, but Muhammad reinterpreted them in monotheistic terms. Thus Muslims believe that Abraham and Ishmael found the Black Stone and erected the Ka'bah around it.

Running seven times between Safa and Marwa commemorates Hagar's frantic quest for water after Abraham had expelled her and Ishmael from his tent. The sacrifice of a sheep recalls Abraham's binding of Ishmael (Muslims do not believe it was Isaac) at God's command and the last-minute sacrifice of a lamb provided by an angel. The day of sacrifice is a high point of the hajj and the occasion for a major feast throughout the

Muslim world. The pilgrimage rites have served throughout history to bring Muslims together and to break down racial, linguistic, and political barriers among them.

## Other Duties and Prohibitions

The five pillars do not cover all Muslim duties. There is another, which some call the "sixth pillar of Islam," called *jihad,* or "struggle in the way of God." Non-Muslims think of the jihad as Islam's holy war against all other religions. This is not entirely true. To be sure, the Quran (9:29) commands Muslims to "fight against those who do not believe in God or the Judgment Day, who permit what God and His messenger have forbidden, and who refuse allegiance to the true faith from those who have received scriptures, until they humbly pay tribute." This would mean fighting Christians and Jews in some situations, and pagans in any case (for the passage was revealed when the Muslims were at war with Mecca before its conversion). But Islam also decreed tolerance toward the earlier monotheistic faiths.

Just how militant should Muslims be? I can give part of the answer now and the rest later on. Muslims strove to expand the territory controlled by their *ummah,* not to convert conquered Christians or Jews. Those who agreed to live in peace and to pay tribute were entitled to Islam's protection; those who resisted or rebelled against Muslim rule were crushed. Some modern Muslims interpret jihad to mean defending Islam against attacks, whether military or verbal, from non-Muslims. In order to protect the *ummah,* Muslims must first cleanse their souls of error, pride, and forgetfulness. Islam is a religion of community: Every Muslim is a brother or a sister to every other Muslim. If some err, or forget their duties to God or to other Muslims, the others, like good brothers or sisters, must correct them.

Prohibited to Muslims are all intoxicating liquors, all mind-affecting drugs, gambling, and usury. They may not eat the flesh of pigs or of any animal not slaughtered in the name of God. Men may not wear silk clothes or gold jewelry. The Quran lays down harsh penalties for murder, theft, and certain other crimes. There are also punishments for Muslims who make or worship idols, but this does not mean a total prohibition against artistic depictions of living creatures, as some people suppose. But Muslims have not, until modern times, sculpted statues, and pictures of living creatures rarely appear in mosques. I will write more about Islamic art in Chapter 8.

Muslims believe that sexual relations are meant to beget children and thus should not occur outside marriage. Most marriages are arranged by the parents of the bride and groom; in bygone days the young couple often met for the first time on their wedding day. Strict rules used to separate the sexes in order to ward off inappropriate love relationships. These rules led in practice to the seclusion of women from the mainstream of political and social life and subjected them to the command of their fathers, brothers, and husbands. Wearing the veil has been customary for urban women in many ancient Middle Eastern societies. A late Quranic revelation required Muhammad's wives to do so when they went outside, and eventually most Muslim women veiled their faces, at least in the cities. Nowadays they are less apt to do so, but many continue to cover their hair. Adults of both sexes dress modestly and shun situations requiring nudity. Homosexual acts and masturbation are included in the prohibition against sex outside of marriage. Even if some Muslims privately flout some of these rules, public acceptance of the prohibitions remains the norm.

Cleanliness is close to godliness. In addition to ritual ablutions before worship, Muslims must wash themselves after performing an act of nature, before eating, upon awakening, and after handling certain objects considered unclean. Total immersion in running water is required after sexual intercourse and, for women, after menstruation and childbirth as well. Traditionally, Muslim men shaved or cropped their heads and body hair but let their beards grow. Women remove their body hair.

## CONCLUSION

This chapter has barely scratched the surface of its topic. Hundreds of books have been written and thousands of speeches made attempting to answer the question, "What is Islam?" Every life lived by a Muslim is a statement about Islam, which now has more than a billion adherents living in every part of the world (though they are most heavily concentrated in the southern third of Asia and the northern two-thirds of Africa). The religion prescribes a complete lifestyle. In later chapters you will learn about the Shari'ah, or sacred law of Islam, which was developed and assembled during the first three centuries after Muhammad's death. Let me say for now that the Quran, combined with the teachings and practices of Muhammad, provides a comprehensive and coherent pattern for Muslim actions and thoughts. Islam has no bishops or priests. Even the *ulama,* the learned men well versed in Islamic doctrines and practices, are not set apart from other Muslims. All Muslims are equal except in their obedience to God's will. Men and women, young and old, friends and neighbors—all have mutual rights and duties within Islam. All can find freedom, without giving up security, in this world and the next. It is more than a faith; it is a way of life.

# FIVE

# The Early Arab Conquests

Muhammad's death left a great void within the community of his followers, the Islamic *ummah*. As long as he was alive, he had been prophet, arbiter, lawgiver, and military commander. In fact, just about any issue that arose among Muslims had been referred to him. How could they make decisions without his guidance? This posed a crisis for the *ummah*, but Muhammad's survivors found new leaders. They overcame the challenge of an Arab tribal rebellion and went on to expand the area under their control. The mightiest empires of the Middle East—Byzantium and Persia—were humbled by the Arab warriors for Islam. Success bred dissension and later caused sectarian rifts that have never completely healed, but the momentum of expansion was only briefly broken. The early Muslims' ability to surmount these crises ensured that Islam would survive, that its civilization would flourish, and that its legacy would endure.

## THE SUCCESSION ISSUE

During his lifetime Muhammad never chose a successor. Some say this was a mistake, but Arab leaders did not usually name their replacements. Besides, how would he have sorted out the functions he could pass on to someone else? He probably did not expect to die as soon as he did. He would not have thought of designating another divine messenger, for he viewed himself as the seal of the prophets. No one after his death could receive revelations. Perhaps no more were needed, for the Judgment Day was supposed to come at any time. Yet, even if the *ummah* sought no successor-as-prophet, it still needed some sort of leader, comparable to a tribal *shaykh*, who could direct its affairs until the hour of doom.

Indeed, a leader was needed at once. Before Muhammad's body was cold, the *ansar* were choosing their own commander. Given the smoldering rivalry between their tribes, they probably could not have agreed on anyone from Medina. And how could a Medinan rule the nomadic tribes only lately converted to Islam? Some of them might have put forth their own *shaykhs*. The best hope would be to elect a leader from the prestigious Quraysh tribe—not one of the ex-pagans who had harassed the Prophet but one of the early converts who had emigrated with him to Medina. Umar, the most decisive of Muhammad's companions, carried the day by naming Abu-Bakr, who belonged (as did Umar) to a clan of the Quraysh that was neither Umayyad nor Hashimite. Abu-Bakr was a modest man, but he knew the Arab tribes and their relationships thoroughly. He had been Muhammad's closest friend, the first person the Prophet had converted outside his own family, the father of his beloved wife Aishah, and the designated worship leader during his final illness.

Later, some Muslims would claim that a member of Muhammad's family should have been chosen. As Muhammad had no surviving sons, they argued that his successor should have been his cousin and son-in-law, Ali, the son of Abu-Talib. But in 632 his name did not come up. If Muhammad had favored Ali, it surely would have. Later, you will learn about some Muslims, called Shi'is, who argue that Muhammad had indeed named Ali to be his successor and that his associates concealed this designation.

Abu-Bakr (r. 632–634) called himself *khalifat rasul Allah* (successor of the messenger of God), soon shortened to *khalifah*, or *caliph* in English. In common usage, the caliph was called *amir al-muminin* (commander of the believers). Abu-Bakr surely earned the title. As soon as the Arab tribes heard of Muhammad's death, most of them broke with the *ummah*. Later Muslims would call this event *riddah* (apostasy), seeing the break as a renunciation of Islam. To the tribes, however, the leader's death had ended all treaties that would have required them to pay *zakat*—which they viewed as a form of tribute—to Medina. Abu-Bakr realized that if they could evade paying the required tithe, the unity of the Arabs would be sundered and the *ummah* would lose revenue. Islam might vanish entirely. To avert these dangers, he sent his best generals, Khalid ibn al-Walid and Amr ibn al-As, to force the tribes to rejoin the *ummah*. Although the *riddah* wars were costly, the tribes capitulated, one by one, and were eventually forgiven. But what, beyond a superficial adherence to Islam or a fear of the caliph's army, could hold the Arab tribes together?

## THE INITIAL CONQUESTS

The caliphs' brilliant answer was to turn the bedouin's combative energies away from one another and toward conquering the settled lands to the north, the territories of the Byzantine (Roman) and Sasanid (Persian) empires. Abu-Bakr's successor, Umar (r. 634–644), forgave the tribal rebels and enlisted them in the service of the caliphate, in a jihad to expand the *ummah*'s lands. This momentous decision would lead to the capture of Rome's Middle Eastern possessions (Palestine, Syria, Egypt, and Cyrenaica) in little more than a decade. It took a generation to absorb the whole Sasanid Empire. Within a century Muslim soldiers would be stationed from Spain in the west, across North Africa and the Middle East, to the borders of China in the east. Western historians once viewed the Arab victories as the main events separating the ancient world from the Middle Ages. Europeans were almost cut off from the rest of the world. Christianity was set back, notably in the lands of its origin. But I would add that those conquests brought together the diverse cultures of North Africa, Egypt, Syria, Iraq, and Persia. Out of this combination would grow a new civilization matching those of Greece and Rome.

If you had asked someone in the streets of Damascus (or any place else) around 625 to predict who would be ruling the Middle East a generation later, he or she might have named the Byzantine emperor, the Sasanid shah, or perhaps some new Roman or Persian dynasty. No one would have expected the rulers to be Meccan Arabs. The speed of the Arab conquests amazed everyone, then and now. People still ask why they succeeded. As you try to come up with an answer, here are some points to keep in mind.

1. The Arab armies were small, usually under a thousand men, thus fewer in number and less well equipped—but more cohesive—than their Roman or Persian foes. They fought few engagements and chose them with care. Their victories were decisive ones that enabled them to gain vast expanses of territory. Their horses were the essential ingredient in their speed, but their camels gave them endurance and mobility in the desert. Arab victories took place in the desert or sufficiently close to enable the troops to get away from Roman or Persian legions if they had to. A common Arab tactic was to draw enemy forces into a *wadi* (valley) and then use the terrain to trap them. One of the Arabs' triumphs, the Battle of the Yarmuk River in 636, resulted from a dust storm that enabled Khalid to conceal his men from the Romans. This victory gave the Arabs

control over Syria. Another dust storm helped the Arabs to defeat the Persians in 637 at Qadisiyah and hence to overrun Iraq.

2. Contrary to their image in popular histories, not all Arab warriors were fired up with Muslim zeal. A few were, but others belonged to Christian tribes estranged from the Byzantine Empire. Being Christian did not bar an Arab from fighting for the caliphate. Some Muslim leaders and tribes may have believed in predestination and martyrdom as their passport to paradise. Most tribal Arabs believed in looting. Economic hardship in Arabia had brought many of them to the verge of starvation. In fact, the Arab conquests facilitated a Semitic emigration from Arabia comparable to those of the earlier Akkadians and the Arameans, for the Arabian Peninsula often became overpopulated.

3. Years of warfare between the Sasanid and Byzantine empires had depleted the resources and manpower of both. Up to about 620, the Sasanid Persians had seemed to be taking over the whole Middle East. Then the Byzantine emperor Heraclius managed to reorganize his forces to push the Sasanids back to Iraq and Persia. Remember that each side hired many mercenaries, mainly Arabs; but as the Byzantines could no longer afford to pay the Ghassanid tribe (see Map 2 in Chapter 2), southern Palestine was opened to Muslim penetration even in Muhammad's last years. The Persians, however, thought they were rich enough to get along without supporting their Lakhmid vassals. As a result, the pro-Byzantine and pro-Sasanid Arabs had both become unreliable by 632, and some converted to Islam.

4. The subject peoples, especially those under Byzantine rule in Syria and Egypt, were discontented. Although they had cultural and economic grievances, the open issue was theological or, rather, Christological. The Byzantine Empire held the Orthodox (or Chalcedonian) view, explained in Chapter 2, that Jesus Christ combined in his person both a divine and a human nature. The Egyptian Copts and their Syrian counterparts, the Jacobites, believed in his single and wholly divine nature, according to the Monophysite doctrine. Emperor Heraclius, anxious to win their support, proposed a compromise: Christ contained two natures within one will. Almost no one (except the Maronites of Lebanon, whom I will discuss later) liked that solution. The disgruntled Syrian and Egyptian Christians viewed the Muslim Arabs as liberators from the Byzantine yoke and often welcomed them. The Copts, for example, turned Egypt over in 640 to Amr's Arab force, which, even with reinforcements, numbered fewer than 10,000. Likewise, the Jews, numerous in Palestine and Syria, chose Muslim indifference over Byzantine persecution.

5. The sudden collapse of Sasanid Persia, after having been master of Egypt, Syria, and much of Arabia as recently as 625, caused a vacuum that the Arabs were quick to fill. Persia was falling back because of political chaos in Ctesiphon, its capital. Power struggles sapped the central administration, which was needed to supervise the irrigation system on the Tigris and Euphrates rivers. Farm production fell and discontent rose. Besides, the Christian, Jewish, and Manichaean peasants of Iraq did not care for either the Zoroastrian priests or the Sasanid absentee landlords who lived in the Persian highlands. As soon as Iraq fell, following the Battle of Qadisiyah (637), the Sasanid state broke up. The Arabs picked up one Persian province after another, until the last Sasanid shah died, a fugitive, in 651.

To recapitulate, during Muhammad's lifetime the lands of the *ummah* were limited to western Arabia as far north as the Gulf of Aqaba, in addition to parts of the rest of the peninsula in which the Arab tribes supposedly embraced Islam. Under Abu-Bakr, the government at Medina overcame the challenge of a tribal revolt. The conquest of the adjacent lands in Syria and Iraq began under Abu-Bakr while he was suppressing the *riddah*. Upon Abu-Bakr's death in 634, Umar became the new caliph. Granting a blanket pardon to the rebellious tribes, Umar turned what had been a few forays into a systematic policy of territorial acquisition. During his caliphate and that of his successor, Uthman, all of Syria, Iraq, Persia, Egypt, and Cyrenaica were added to the lands of the *ummah*. You can readily imagine the strain this put on the primitive government in Medina, where Muhammad and Abu-Bakr used to buy their own food in the market, mend their own clothes, cobble their own shoes, and dispense justice and money in the courtyards of their own homes. A more sophisticated government was needed.

## THE BEGINNINGS OF ISLAMIC GOVERNMENT

Umar, strong willed and hot tempered, an early Meccan convert who came from a minor clan of the Quraysh tribe, was the man on the spot. He was shrewd enough to see that the Arab tribes, easily led into battle by the lure of booty far richer than they had ever known, might become unruly when they were not fighting. Military discipline sat lightly on the shoulders of these Arab warriors, especially if their commanders did not come from their own tribe. What would happen when civilization's centers fell under the sway of these bedouin? Would they wreck the palaces and libraries first, or would the wine shops and dancing girls sap their martial skills and religious zeal?

## Military Discipline

For centuries, nomads and foreign armies have overrun the settled parts of the Middle East, only to fall under the influence of their own captives. Umar did not want his Muslims to become corrupted in this way. It was no mere quirk of character that made him stride through the streets and bazaars of Medina, whip in hand, ready to scourge any Muslim who missed the prayers or violated the Ramadan fast. Umar may have admired the military leader Khalid's skill at beating the Romans and Persians in battle, but he resented his illegally contracted marriages. That and Khalid's hiring of poets (the publicity agents of the time) to sing his praises led Umar to dismiss him, the "sword of Islam," as an example to other Arabs.

When the troops were not fighting, they had to be kept under strict discipline. Umar's policy was to settle them on the fringe between the desert and the cultivated lands in special garrison towns, notably Basrah and Kufah, both in Iraq, and Fustat, just south of what is now Cairo, Egypt. His purpose was to keep the Arabs and the settled peoples apart. The Arab soldiers were forbidden to acquire lands outside Arabia. Their right to seize buildings and other immovable war booty was restricted. One-fifth of the movable prizes of war had to be sent back to Medina, where Umar set up a *diwan* (register) that carefully divided the spoils into shares for members of the *ummah*, ranging from Muhammad's widows and associates to the humblest Arab soldier.

## Civil Government

Although Arab generals and Meccan merchants usually took the top posts of the newly won provinces, their civil administration was left almost untouched. That hypothetical person in the streets of Damascus would not have found life in 650 much different from what it had been in 625. Local administrators went on running affairs just as before. For those towns and provinces that had not resisted the Arab conquests, land and house taxes were lighter than before, but they now went to Medina rather than to Ctesiphon or Constantinople. Governmental languages did not change: Greek and Coptic were used in Egypt, Greek and Aramaic in Syria, Persian and Syriac in Iraq and Persia. Conquered peoples went on speaking the languages they were used to. Few Jews or Christians rushed to convert to Islam, for they were protected as "People of the Book." Zoroastrians and Manichaeans in Iraq and Persia were less tolerated and more apt to become Muslim, but even they changed slowly. It was hard for early Muslims to get used to the conversion of non-Arabs to Islam. Having assumed that Muhammad was God's messenger to the Arabs, they conferred honorary Arab status on any non-Arab male convert. They did this by making him a client member (*mawla*; plural *mawali*) of an Arab tribe. Persians and Arameans who flocked to the garrison towns were especially apt to turn Muslim. Soon the *mawali* outnumbered the Arabs living in such towns as Basrah and Kufah. How ironic, considering that those cities had been set up to keep the Arabs from being corrupted by Persian civilization! They soon became melting pots and centers of cultural interchange.

## Dissension in the *Ummah*

The garrison towns also became hotbeds of dissension and intrigue, especially after the guiding hand of Umar was removed by assassination. Before he died, Umar appointed a *shura*, or electoral committee, to choose the third caliph. Some modern writers have used the *shura* to prove that early Islam was democratic. In fact, it consisted of six Meccan associates of Muhammad, all caravan traders who belonged to the Quraysh tribe. Owing perhaps to personal rivalries, they ended up choosing the only man in the *shura* who belonged to the prestigious Umayyads, the clan that had long opposed Muhammad.

Their choice to succeed Umar, Uthman (r. 644–656), has come down in history as a weak caliph, eager to please the rich Meccan merchants and to put his Umayyad kinsmen into positions of power. But such an interpretation is unfair to Uthman, who had defied his clan to become one of Muhammad's earliest converts. He also defied many of Muhammad's companions when, as caliph, he decided on a single authoritative version of the Quran and ordered the burning of all copies that contained variant readings. Many reciters were appalled when their cherished versions of the Quran went up in smoke, but would Islam have fared better with seven competing readings of its sacred scriptures?

As for the issue of Uthman's relatives, it is true that some lusted after power and that others lacked the ability to govern. But Uthman meant to use his family ties to assert greater control over the government. His cousin Mu'awiyah (already appointed by Umar) administered Syria well. He and his foster brother in Egypt built Islam's first navy to conquer Cyprus in 655. Uthman's mistake was to continue Umar's policies in a more complex time, without having Umar's forceful character. Perceiving this, the Muslims in Iraq's garrison towns began plotting against him.

## Uthman's Troubled Caliphate

Traditional accounts stress the contrast between the second and third caliphs. "The luck of Islam was shrouded in Umar's winding-sheet," remarked a survivor. Uthman complained from the pulpit of Muhammad's mosque to the men of Medina: "You took it from Umar, even when he whipped you. Why then do you not take it from one who is gentle and does not punish you?" Why, indeed? Whereas Umar, during his caliphate, slept on a bed of palm leaves and wore the same wool shirt until it was covered with patches, Uthman amassed estates worth over $20 million while he was caliph.

Modern scholars play down the personality contrast, however, and stress changing conditions within the *ummah*. The influx of money and treasure enriched Medina and Mecca far beyond anything Muhammad could have anticipated and eventually beyond what his associates could assimilate. Greed and vice proliferated, especially among the young—according to their elders. Once the early conquests had reached their limits (Cyrenaica in the west, Anatolia's Taurus Mountains in the north, Khurasan in the east, and the Indian Ocean and upper Nile in the south), the Arab tribesmen could not change from border warriors into military police. They sat idly in their garrison towns, bewailed the lost opportunities for booty, and plotted against the caliphate in far-off Medina.

From about 650, Uthman's rule was threatened by a mixture of people: pious old Muslims, mostly Medinans, who resented the way the Umayyads were taking over the same *ummah* they once had tried to destroy; Quran reciters who had lost power because of Uthman's authorization of a single version; and tribal Arabs who chafed at having no new lands to seize and plunder. Of all the garrison towns, Kufah was the most restive. An open revolt started there in 655, spread to Arabia, and reached Medina in 656. The insurgents besieged the house of Uthman, who got no protection from any of Muhammad's associates. A group of rebels from Egypt broke in and killed the aged caliph as he sat with his wife, reciting from the Quran. Five days later, Ali (r. 656–661) agreed, reluctantly, to become the fourth caliph.

## Ali's Caliphate

Thus began Islam's first time of troubles, which the Arabs call their *fitnah* (temptation). It seems unfair, for Ali appeared highly qualified for the caliphate. He was the son of Muhammad's uncle and protector, his first male convert, the husband of the Prophet's daughter Fatimah, and hence the father of his only grandsons, Hasan and Husayn. Ali had risked his life so that Muhammad could safely leave Mecca during the *hijrah*. He had fought valiantly against the pagan Meccans, accompanied the Prophet on most of his expeditions, and advised the earlier caliphs on questions of dogma and policy. He was pious and generous. Regrettably, he proved to be a weak caliph. Either Ali came too late to do the office any good, or the caliphate came too late to do him any good.

## Challenges to Ali

Soon after his accession, Ali left Medina, never to return; Kufah would serve as his capital. But when he reached Basrah, he was challenged by two of Muhammad's associates, Talhah and Zubayr; Aishah joined in, branding Ali unfit to rule because he had not tried to protect Uthman. This was a strange accusation, as none of the challengers had liked or defended the third caliph. Their real motives were political and personal. Ali had allegedly denied government posts to Talhah and Zubayr, and Aishah had never forgiven him for having once accused her of infidelity to Muhammad. Ali and his troops defeated the challengers in a bloody affray, the Battle of the Camel, so called because it raged around Aishah's camel-borne litter. Talhah and Zubayr died in battle (as did, reportedly, 13,000 others), and Aishah was sent back to Medina. The Battle of the Camel was the first instance in which two Muslim armies fought against each other. It set an unhappy precedent.

A more dangerous challenge came from Mu'awiyah, Uthman's cousin and governor of Syria, whom Ali tried to dismiss. The Umayyad clan was understandably outraged when Uthman was murdered and replaced by Ali, a Hashimite, who seemed reluctant to find and punish the assassins. In Damascus Mu'awiyah displayed Uthman's bloodstained shirt and the severed fingers of his widow, who had tried to protect her husband, thus horrifying many Muslims at what seemed to be a political murder. Arab custom called for seeking revenge, especially once it became clear that the assassins would not be brought to justice. Mu'awiyah had a loyal garrison of Arab troops, and they challenged Ali. The two sides met in a series of skirmishes at Siffin (in northern Syria) in the summer of 657. Finally, when Ali's side seemed to be winning, wily old General Amr ibn al-As advised Mu'awiyah's men to stick pages of the Quran on the tips of their spears and to appeal for a peaceful arbitration of the quarrel. Ali suspected a trick, but his troops persuaded him to accept the appeal.

Ali and Mu'awiyah each chose a representative and agreed to let them decide whether or not the Umayyads were justified in seeking revenge for Uthman's murder. Soon afterward, some of Ali's men turned against him for agreeing to the arbitration. Called Kharijites (seceders), these rebels harassed Ali for the rest of his caliphate, even after he defeated them in battle in 659. Before then, the appointed arbiters of Ali and Mu'awiyah had met. Emboldened perhaps by the Kharijite revolt against Ali, Mu'awiyah's representative, Amr, tricked Ali's arbiter into agreeing to his master's deposition from the caliphate. Ali did not resign, but the arbitration undermined his authority. His followers faded away. One province after another defected to Mu'awiyah, who had himself proclaimed caliph in Jerusalem in 660. Finally, in 661, Ali was murdered by a Kharijite seeking revenge for his sect's defeat.

## CHANGES IN THE GOVERNMENT OF ISLAM

Ali's death ended the period known to Muslims as the era of the Rashidun (meaning "rightly guided") caliphs. All four were men related to Muhammad by marriage and chosen by his companions. Later Muslims would look back on this period as a golden age to which many longed to return. They contrasted the simple governments in Medina and Kufah with the swollen bureaucracies of Damascus and Baghdad, headed by kingly caliphs who succeeded by heredity. I agree that most of the Rashidun caliphs were admirable and that all four were interesting, but theirs was an era of frequent strife, many crises of adjustment to changing conditions, and much improvisation. Even the caliphate itself had begun as a stopgap measure, shaped by Umar into a lasting institution. It became the linchpin for a state that was doubling and redoubling in area, population, and wealth. Now, upon Ali's death, it seemed to be in peril.

### Mu'awiyah

The man who saved the *ummah* and the caliphate from anarchy was the Umayyad governor of Syria, Mu'awiyah. He never faltered in his determination to discredit Ali for the murder of Uthman, and his Syrian Arab troops (many of them Christian) rewarded him with their unstinted backing. He possessed a virtue prized among Arabs—the ability to refrain from using force unless absolutely necessary. As he himself put it: "I never use my sword when my whip will do, nor my whip when my tongue will do. Let a single hair bind me to my people, and I will not let it snap; when they pull I loosen, and if they loosen I pull." After Ali died, some of his diehard Kufan supporters pushed his son Hasan into contesting the caliphate. Mu'awiyah got him to withdraw his claim by sending what amounted to a blank check. A rich man now, Hasan retired to Medina and played no further role in politics.

It is interesting that Mu'awiyah first claimed the caliphate in Jerusalem, the city sacred to Jews, Christians, and Muslims. What if he had made it his capital, something no Arab or Muslim ruler has ever done? But Mu'awiyah had started his career as a Meccan merchant, and he chose to stay in Damascus, his provincial capital, because it was on the main trade route between Syria and Yemen. He seems to have viewed Syria as a stepping stone toward taking over all the Byzantine Empire. How can we prove this? Once the *fitnah* had ended, the Arab conquests resumed, targeted mainly against Byzantium. Each summer the caliph's armies would push their way into Anatolia. Meanwhile, his navy drove the Byzantine fleet from the southeastern Mediterranean and twice during his reign besieged the very capital of the empire. But Byzantium withstood the onslaught. The Arabs found consolation by advancing westward across Tunisia and eastward through Khurasan.

## Administrative Changes

Mu'awiyah, once called the "Caesar of the Arabs" by none other than the Caliph Umar himself, was more worldly than his precursors; but the changes that took place after 661 could not be ascribed to personality differences. Patriarchal government—namely, what had grown up in Medina on the model of the Arab tribal system, modified somewhat by the Quran and the Prophet's practices—could not meet the needs of a sprawling empire encompassing many peoples and religions. Mu'awiyah adopted some of the Byzantine imperial customs and the bureaucratic practices familiar to Egypt and Syria. Many of his administrators and some of his warriors were Syrians or Christian Arabs, often survivors or sons of the old Byzantine bureaucracy and soldiery.

Mu'awiyah realized that he depended on the Arab tribes for most of his military manpower, and he wisely flattered their sense of racial superiority. But he had each tribe send a representative (really a hostage) to his court in Damascus. Such troublesome areas as Iraq, where Arab tribes had terrorized the countryside during Ali's caliphate, were cowed by ruthless local governors. Notorious among these was Ziyad, whom Mu'awiyah won over from Ali's backers by acknowledging him as his own half brother (Ziyad bore the unflattering nickname "son of his father" because his mother had been a courtesan in Medina). Upon taking charge in Basrah, Ziyad warned the people from the pulpit of its main mosque:

> You are putting family ties before religion. You are excusing and sheltering your criminals and tearing down the protecting laws sanctified by Islam. Beware of prowling by night; I will kill everyone who is found at night in the streets. Beware of the arbitrary call to obey family ties; I will cut out the tongue of everyone who raises the cry. Whoever pushes anyone into the water, whoever sets fire to another's home, whoever breaks into a house, whoever opens a grave, him will I punish. Hatred against myself I do not punish, but only crime. Many who are terrified of my coming will be glad of my presence, and many who are building their hopes upon it will be undeceived. I rule you with the authority of God and will maintain you from the wealth of God's *ummah*. From you I demand obedience, and you can demand from me justice. Though I may fall short, there are three things in which I shall not be lacking: I will be ready to listen to anyone at any time, I will pay you your pension when it is due, and I will not send you to war too far away or for too long a time. Do not let yourselves be carried away by your hatred and wrath against me; you will suffer if you do. Many heads do I see tottering; let each man see to it that his own remains on his shoulders!

When at last Mu'awiyah knew that his days were numbered, he obtained in advance his followers' consent to the succession of his son Yazid to the caliphate. It was this act that later earned Mu'awiyah the condemnation of Muslim historians (even though Ali's attempt to appoint Hasan must have set a precedent). From that time until the caliphate was abolished in 1924, the highest political office in Islam was hereditary *in fact*, even if it remained elective *in principle*.

I wonder, though, whether Islam would have fared better if Mu'awiyah had not founded the Umayyad dynasty. True, most tribal Arabs, if given a choice, would have gravitated to the Kharijite view—namely, that any adult male Muslim could become caliph, no matter what his race or lineage, and that any caliph who sinned should be overthrown in favor of another. The Kharijite idea would recur throughout Islamic history, especially among the nomads in Arabia and North Africa. In fact, some modern Muslims wish to revive the caliphate without restricting the office to descendants of the Quraysh tribe. But a popular election of the Muslim ruler, based on Kharijite principles, would have caused anarchy in the seventh century—or even now. Although there were diehard supporters of the sons of Ali and of other companions, such as Zubayr, their appeal was limited to particular cities. Mu'awiyah alone could command the support of Syria and Egypt, and his allies could control Arabia, Iraq, and Persia. I concede that the Umayyads were lax Muslims. Mu'awiyah had resisted Muhammad until all Mecca surrendered to Islam, but he then turned 180 degrees and became the Prophet's secretary. Some of his descendants' drinking and sexual exploits, though amusing to read about, shocked the pious Muslims of their day. Nevertheless, the Umayyads went on controlling the caravan trade between Syria and Yemen, and their business acumen helped them to choose policies, reconcile differences, and neutralize opposition. The Umayyad dynasty, though condemned by most Muslim historians on moral grounds, built up the great Arab empire.

## Mu'awiyah's Successors

What Mu'awiyah achieved was almost buried with him in 680. Yazid, his designated successor, was hated by Muhammad's old Meccan companions and by some of the Arab tribes, despite his victories in earlier battles against Byzantium. The animosity went back to Yazid's childhood. His mother, one of Mu'awiyah's favorite wives, had detested the settled life of the Umayyad court and pined for the bedouin camps of her youth. To this effect she wrote a poem, grossly insulting to Mu'awiyah, that convinced him that she and her son, still young at the time, belonged in the desert. Yazid grew up with his mother's tribe, Kalb, becoming a bold warrior but a heavy drinker. Upon his accession to the caliphate, he favored his tribe over its great rival, Qays. During the early conquests, the tribes had formed two large confederations involving most of the Arab soldiers: one "southern" and including Kalb, the other "northern" and including Qays. During Yazid's reign, their rivalries escalated into a full-scale civil war, part of Islam's second *fitnah*.

## Husayn's Rebellion: The Beginning of Shi'ism

Before I discuss the second *fitnah*, let me tell you about a small rebellion, not in itself a threat to Yazid's power but one that has since taken on immense significance in Islamic history. Remember that some Muslims still abhorred the very idea of an Umayyad caliphate and wanted the leadership of the *ummah* restored to the Hashimite clan, preferably in the person of a direct descendant of the Prophet. Muhammad, as you know, had no sons. His son-in-law, Ali, had been killed, as had Hasan, leaving the Prophet's other grandson, Husayn, as the only possible claimant. Husayn was a pious man who had lived most of his fifty-four years quietly in

Medina. But when Yazid succeeded Mu'awiyah in 680, Husayn refused to recognize the new caliph as legitimate. Some Kufan foes of the Umayyads, thus encouraged, talked Husayn into rebelling against them. Intimidated by their governor, though, most Kufans withheld their support in Husayn's hour of need. When the Prophet's grandson reached Karbala, Iraq, he found he had only seventy-two warriors pitted against 10,000 Umayyad soldiers. Husayn's tiny band fought as bravely as they could, but they all fell in battle on 10 Muharram 61 *Anno Hegirae* (10 October 680). Husayn's severed head was laid at the feet of Yazid in Damascus. The Umayyads had, seemingly, triumphed once more.

The significance of these events was that the partisans of the Prophet's "martyred" descendants, Ali and now Husayn, vowed never to recognize the Umayyads as legitimate caliphs. They came to be called Shi'at Ali (the Party of Ali), from which came the name Shi'ites or Shi'is. From Iraq they spread throughout the empire, wherever Muslims sought a pretext to defy Umayyad rule. Nowadays the Shi'is make up the second largest Muslim sect, as contrasted with the majority group, called Sunnis, who accepted (often reluctantly) the ruling caliphs. Religious differences do exist between Sunnis and Shi'is, due mainly to the latter's conviction that only Ali and his descendants (diagrammed in Figure 1) had any right to lead the *ummah*. To Shi'i Muslims, even Abu-Bakr, Umar, and Uthman, let alone Mu'awiyah and his heirs, were usurpers, whereas Ali was the first imam (leader) and he bequeathed special powers and esoteric knowledge to his sons, his sons' sons, and so on.

As time passed, disputes arose among various brothers claiming the imamate, causing splits among their Shi'i followers. As you will soon see, some Shi'is managed—later—to form states in opposition to the Sunni caliphate. Since about 1500, for reasons I will cover in Chapter 9, Persia's rulers have been Shi'i Muslims. But to identify Shi'ism with Persian nationalism better illuminates the mind of the twentieth century than that of the seventh. Shi'ism began as a political protest movement couched in religious terms, appealing to Arabs as well as Persians. It found expression in pilgrimages to Najaf and Kerbala (the burial sites of Ali and Husayn, respectively), in annual processions mourning the martyrdom of Husayn, and in the passion play reenacting his tragic end.

### Other Challengers

The other challenges to the Umayyads, although they seemed more threatening then, are now largely forgotten. Abdallah ibn al-Zubayr, son

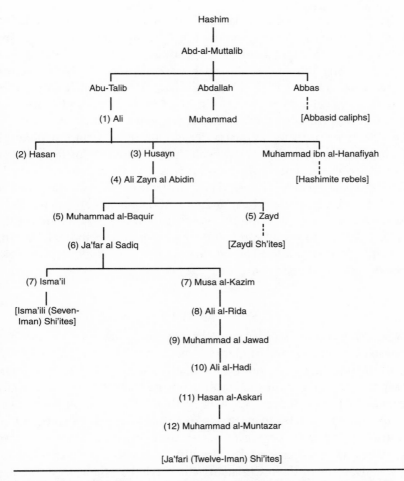

FIGURE 1 The Hashimite clan, showing Shi'i imams (numbered)

of the Zubayr killed in the Battle of the Camel, also refused allegiance to Yazid and escaped from Medina. But instead of courting the Kufans as Husayn had done, Abdallah ibn al-Zubayr stayed in Mecca and fomented rebellions elsewhere. When Yazid died in 683, leaving the caliphate to his sickly young son, Abdallah claimed the office for himself. Muslims in all the provinces, even some in Syria, promised to back him. The Arab tribes favoring Qays, the northern confederation, rose up against the Umayyads, who were linked to Kalb and hence to the southern Arabs. When the teenaged caliph died, leaving the Umayyads with no plausible candidate,

Abdallah had only to come to Damascus to claim the caliphate there. But he was allied with the pious descendants of Muhammad's associates living in Medina and Mecca. They hated Damascus and everything that smacked of Umayyad rule, so Abdallah stayed in Mecca. The oldest and most respected member of the Umayyad clan, Marwan, reluctantly agreed to oppose Abdallah's partisans, and in July 684 the Umayyad supporters defeated the opposing Arab tribes and drove them out of Syria.

Rebellions went on for almost a decade. In 685 a group of penitent Shi'is in Kufah started a two-year revolt that was notable for its appeal to non-Arab converts. There were several Kharijite uprisings—one could generally expect them whenever there was trouble. It took years for the Umayyads to crush the rival caliphate of Abdallah ibn al-Zubayr, but I must leave that story for Chapter 6. Never again would descendants of the emigrant companions and *ansar* put forth their own candidate for the leadership of the *ummah*. Never again would a large group try to make Mecca the capital city of Islam.

## Conclusion

Between Muhammad's death and the second *fitnah*, the *ummah* had grown so large that Arabia could no longer be its political center. The Arabian tribes that had carried out the conquests had formed a powerful aristocracy spread throughout the empire, but their effectiveness as a police force was fatally weakened by their rivalries. The government of the *ummah* had ceased to be an extension of either Arab tribal democracy or Muhammad's religious prestige; now it was firmly grasped by a Meccan mercantile clan based in Syria. Its administrative arm was a team of Arabs and Syrians, some of them Christian, who carried on the ruling practices of the Byzantines. Many of the Arabs, whether nomads, sedentarized Meccan traders, Medinan farmers, or tribal warriors living in garrison towns, felt alienated from this neo-Roman kingdom. Some of the non-Arab subjects had become Muslims, but these *mawali*, especially in Iraq, were second-class citizens who resented Arab claims to superiority. Shi'ite and Kharijite movements reflected these various tensions. Meanwhile, most of the caliphs' subjects remained Jews, Christians, or Zoroastrians, not Muslims who could be counted on to support the *ummah* whenever it was in danger. In sum, we should marvel that Islam survived Muhammad's death, that it gained new lands and adherents so quickly, and that it assimilated mighty empires and civilized societies. Yet, in spite of these achievements spanning half a century, Muslims were not yet secure.

# SIX

# The High Caliphate

For about a thousand years, history has been playing mean tricks on the Arabs. They have been wracked with internal factionalism and strife, external invasion, subordination to outside rulers, natural disasters, and exaggerated hopes and fears. But in the bleakest moments of their history, the Arabic-speaking peoples of the Middle East have comforted themselves with the memory of a time when their ancestors ruled most of the eastern hemisphere, when the Europeans and the Chinese feared and courted them, and when theirs was the language in which humanity's highest literary and scientific achievements were expressed. This was the time of the two great caliphal dynasties, the Umayyads and the Abbasids. This chapter uses a term coined by Marshall Hodgson to denote the years from 685 to 945: the High Caliphate.

During this period, the Islamic *ummah* was initially headed by the Marwanid branch of the Umayyad family, ruling in Damascus, and then by the Abbasids of Baghdad. Both dynasties belonged to the Quraysh tribe and were backed by those Muslims who came to be called Sunnis. The caliphal state was militarily strong, relative to Western Europe, the Byzantine Empire, India, and China. Territorial conquests continued until about 750, when the Abbasids took over from the Umayyads. After that time some land was lost, and the caliphal state began to break up. As long as any semblance of unity remained, though, the old Roman, Syrian, and Persian political practices and cultural traditions went on combining in new ways. Economic prosperity, based mainly on agriculture, was enhanced by commerce and manufacturing. These factors facilitated the movement of people and the spread of ideas, and hence the growth of an Islamic civilization.

The relative power of the various peoples shifted gradually during the High Caliphate. Under the Abbasids, if not earlier, Arab dominance waned, as many non-Arabs became Muslims and, in most instances, adopted the Arabic language as well. Beware of generalizations about Arab influence. The word *Arab* is ambiguous; it can mean bedouin, someone wholly or partly descended from tribal Arabs, someone who speaks Arabic, or a person living under Arab rule. When the term is used to pertain to a group, find out whether it bore arms for Islam and how it was paid. During this time, tribal soldiers from Arabia slowly gave way first to salaried troops, notably Persians from Khurasan, then to Turkish tribal horse soldiers paid with land grants.

As the caliphal state grew larger and more complex, it needed more people to run it. The early Umayyads had inherited Roman bureaucratic traditions, but now Persian administrators took over and introduced Sasanid practices. At the same time, there grew up a class of pious Muslims who could recite and interpret the Quran, relate and record *hadiths* (authenticated accounts of Muhammad's sayings and actions), systematize Arabic grammar, and develop the science of law (called *fiqh* in Arabic). Eventually they became known as *ulama,* which means "those who know," or experts on Muslim doctrines, laws, and history. Muslims also became interested in classical philosophy, science, and medicine, aided by the translation of many Greek works into Arabic. One result was the evolution of systematic Islamic theology. Muslims also developed some more esoteric ideas and rituals, leading to the rise of Sufism (organized Islamic mysticism), a topic you will read about later.

The caliphal state faced ongoing opposition from the Kharijites, who rejected any type of hereditary caliphate, and from Shi'i movements backing various descendants of Ali. Late in this period, many parts of the Muslim world came under the rule of Shi'i dynasties. Until about 1000, non-Muslims predominated in the lands of the *ummah,* but their relative power and influence were waning.

## RESTORATION OF THE UMAYYAD ORDER

Most scholars agree that Umar, Mu'awiyah, and Abd al-Malik should be listed among the caliphs regarded as the founding fathers of Islamic government. You have already learned about Umar, who presided over the early conquests, and about Mu'awiyah, who bequeathed the caliphate to his Umayyad heirs. But who was this Abd al-Malik? He took over the caliphate on the death of his aged father, Marwan, who had ruled briefly during what was (from an Umayyad viewpoint) the worst year of the second *fitnah.* When Abd al-Malik took charge, the northern Arab tribal confederation was rebelling against his family, in league with Abdallah ibn al-Zubayr, who was in Mecca claiming the caliphate. Every province except

Syria had turned against Umayyad rule. The martyrdom of the Prophet's grandson, Husayn, had further antagonized many Muslims, especially the Shi'is. One of Abd al-Malik's first challenges came from a revolt in Kufah of Shi'i penitents (so called because they regretted not having aided Husayn in 680). This revolt fizzled, but the Kufans rallied around an Arab adventurer named Mukhtar. His cause gained support from Persian and Aramean converts to Islam who, as *mawali*, resented being snubbed by the Arabs. Abd al-Malik could not stop this revolt, but, luckily for him, the army of Abdallah ibn al-Zubayr did. This was a time when Abdallah's partisans in Mecca were stronger than the Umayyads in Damascus.

## Abd al-Malik's Triumph

Although he took office in 685, Abd al-Malik waited until 691 to take Iraq from Abdallah's forces. The next year Hajjaj, an Umayyad general famed for his harsh government in Iraq and Iran, captured Arabia. His men had to bombard Mecca (even damaging the Ka'bah) before Abdallah's army surrendered. Hajjaj spent two years wiping out Kharijite rebels in Arabia before he went into Kufah. Wearing a disguise, he entered the main mosque, mounted the pulpit, tore the veil from his face, and addressed the rebellious Kufans: "I see heads ripe for the cutting. People of Iraq, I will not let myself be crushed like a soft fig. . . . The commander of the believers [Abd al-Malik] has drawn arrows from his quiver and tested the wood, and has found that I am the hardest. . . . And so, by God, I will strip you as men strip the bark from trees. . . . I will beat you as stray camels are beaten." The Kufans, thus intimidated, gave no more trouble, and Hajjaj restored prosperity to the Umayyads' eastern provinces.

Abd al-Malik laid the basis for an absolutist caliphate, one patterned after the traditions of the divine kings of the ancient Middle East instead of the patriarchal *shaykhs* of the Arab tribes. You can see the change not only in the policies of such authoritarian governors as Hajjaj but also in Abd al-Malik's decree making Arabic the administrative language. Before then, some parts of the empire had used Greek, others Persian, Aramaic, or Coptic, depending on what the local officials and people happened to speak. Many bureaucrats, especially the Persians, did not want to give up a language rich in administrative vocabulary for one used until recently only by camel nomads and merchants. But it is these Persians we can thank (or curse, if you study Arabic) for having systematized Arabic grammar, for they soon realized that no Persian could get or keep a government job without learning to read and write this complicated new language.

Following the old Roman imperial tradition of erecting fine buildings, Abd al-Malik had the magnificent Dome of the Rock built atop what had been Jerusalem's Temple Mount. It was a shrine erected around what local tradition said was the rock of Abraham's attempted sacrifice and what Muslims believe to be the site of Muhammad's departure on his miraculous night journey to Heaven. It was also a message to the Byzantine Empire and to Jerusalem's Christians that Islam was there to stay. With the Dome of the Rock set almost directly above the Western Wall, the sole remnant of the second Jewish Temple, you can see why Arabs and Jews now dispute over who should control Jerusalem's Old City, holy to all three monotheistic faiths. Another symbolic act by Abd al-Malik was the minting of Muslim coins, which ended the Muslims' dependence on Byzantine and Persian currency and made it easier for Arabs to distinguish among the various values of the coins. The use of Arabic-language inscriptions (often Quranic quotations) was a caliphal riposte to the Byzantine practice of stamping coins with the head of Christ. Eventually, Muslim rulers came to think that the right to issue coins in their own names symbolized their sovereignty. Erecting grand buildings served the same purpose.

## Resumption of the Conquests

The caliphal state was becoming an empire. It was no surprise that the Arab conquests resumed after the second *fitnah* ended. One army headed west across North Africa, while a Muslim navy drove the Byzantines from the western Mediterranean. The North African Berbers, once they had been bested by the Arabs, converted to Islam and joined their armies. Under Abd al-Malik's successor, a Muslim force crossed the Strait of Gibraltar and took most of what is now Spain and Portugal. It was not until 732— exactly a century after the Prophet's death—that a European Christian army stemmed the Muslim tide in central France. The greatest Arab thrust, though, was eastward from Persia. Muslim armies attacked the Turks, first in what is now Afghanistan, then in Transoxiana (the land beyond the Oxus River, or the Amu Darya), including Bukhara and Samarqand. They eventually reached China's northwest border, which became the eastern limit of the Arab conquests. Another force pushed north to the Aral Sea, adding Khwarizm to the lands of Islam. Yet another moved south, taking Baluchistan, Sind, and Punjab, roughly the area of modern Pakistan.

There was but one nut too tough to crack, the Byzantine Empire. From the time they conquered Syria, the Arabs seem to have felt that conquering all of Byzantium was their "manifest destiny," much as the United States viewed Canada and parts of Mexico in the nineteenth century. The Byzantines, though weakened by the loss of their Syrian and North African lands and shorn of their naval supremacy in the western Mediterranean, regarded the Arabs as a nuisance that, God willing, would soon pass away. They reorganized their army and the administration of Anatolia, making that highland area impregnable to Arab forces. Constantinople, guarded by thick walls, withstood three Umayyad sieges, the last of which involved an Arab fleet of a thousand ships and lasted from 716 to 718. Using "Greek fire," probably a naphtha derivative, that ignited upon hitting the water and (with favorable winds) set fire to enemy ships, the Byzantines wiped out almost the entire Arab fleet. After that, the caliphs seem to have concluded that Byzantium was too hard to take. Gradually they gave up their claim of being the new "Roman" empire and took on a neo-Persian aura instead.

## Fiscal Reforms

Whether the caliphs took on the trappings of Roman emperors or Persian shahs, their government favored the Arabs and depended on their backing. But most of their subjects were not Arabs, and they paid most of the taxes. Even those who became Muslims still had to pay the Umayyads the same rates as those who did not convert. The main levies were (1) the *zakat*, which Muslims paid on their animals, farm produce, or business earnings, as the Quran specified; (2) a property tax paid to the *ummah*, mainly by non-Muslims in conquered lands outside Arabia; and (3) a head tax or tribute paid by male Christians, Jews, and Zoroastrians in return for exemption from military service. The terminology and also the administration of these taxes were confused and rigged against the *mawali*, the converts to Islam who had become as numerous as the tribal Arabs themselves.

This problem was tackled by Umar II (r. 717–720), who alone among all the Umayyad caliphs is praised for his piety by later Muslim historians. Umar wanted to stop all fiscal practices that favored the Arabs and to treat all Muslims equally and fairly. When his advisers warned him that exempting the *mawali* from the taxes paid by non-Muslims would cause numerous conversions to Islam and deplete his treasury, Umar retorted that he had not become commander of the believers to collect taxes and imposed his reforms anyway. As he also cut military expenditures, his treasury did not suffer, and he did gain Muslim converts. He must have wanted conversions, because he also placed humiliating restrictions on non-Muslims: They could not ride horses or camels, only mules and donkeys; they had to wear special clothing that identified them as Jews or Christians; and they were forbidden to build new synagogues or churches without permission.

These rules, collectively called the *Covenant of Umar*, were enforced by some of his successors and ignored by many others. We cannot generalize about the conditions of Jews and Christians under Muslim rule—they varied so greatly—but conversion to Islam was usually socially or economically motivated, not forced. It was Hisham (r. 724–743) who finally set the taxes into a system that would be upheld for the next thousand years: Muslims paid the *zakat*, all property owners (with a few exceptions you need not worry about) paid on their land or buildings a tax called the *kharaj*, and Christian and Jewish men paid a per capita tax called the *jizyah*.

## THE DOWNFALL OF THE UMAYYADS

Despite the fiscal reforms of Umar II and Hisham, the Umayyad caliphate remained an Arab kingdom. Muslims could put up with this as long as the conquests continued. But as they slowed down in the 740s, the Arab tribes that supplied most of the warriors became worthless because of their constant quarrels. A few of the later caliphs also seemed useless, with their hunting palaces, dancing girls, and swimming pools filled with wine. Some of them sided with one or the other of the tribal confederations, raising the danger that the slighted tribes would stir up Shi'ite or Kharijite revolts that were hard to put down. Hisham faced these problems bravely; his less able successors did not.

Meanwhile, the *mawali* had become the intellectual leaders, the bureaucrats, and even the commercial elite of the *ummah*, but the political and social discrimination they had to endure dulled their support for the existing system. The best way for them to voice their discontent was to back dissident Muslim movements that might overthrow the Umayyads. Especially popular among the *mawali* was a Shi'i revolutionary movement called—ambiguously—the Hashimites. As you can see from Figure 1 (see Chapter 5), the name denotes Muhammad's family. The "Hashimites," as a conspiratorial group, concealed from outsiders just which branch of Shi'ism they were backing. In fact, their leaders descended from a son born to Ali by a woman other than Muhammad's daughter. In the early eighth century, some of the Hashimites conferred their support on one branch of their clan, the Abbasids, so called because they had descended from Muhammad's uncle Abbas. The Abbasids exploited these Shi'i revolutionaries and disgruntled *mawali* in order to gain power. Their power center was Khurasan, in eastern Persia.

The Umayyads' weakness was the Abbasids' opportunity. The Arab tribes were bitterly divided, the army was demoralized, river irrigation had raised Iraq's importance relative to Syria, popular opinion called for

Muslim equality in place of Arab supremacy, and Khurasan was a province in which thousands of Arab colonists mixed with the native Persian landowners. There, in 747, a Persian named Abu-Muslim unfurled the black banner of revolution on behalf of the Abbasids. Despite the heroic resistance of the last Umayyad caliph and his governor in Khurasan, the revolt spread. The Abbasids reached Kufah in 749 and laid claim to the caliphate for an Abbasid named Abu al-Abbas. Abu-Muslim's troops crushed the Umayyads' army in January 750, pursued their last caliph to Egypt, and killed him. Then they went on to wipe out all the living Umayyads and to scourge the corpses of the dead ones. The only member of the family who escaped was Abd al-Rahman I. After a harrowing journey across North Africa, he safely reached Spain, where he founded a rival caliphate that lasted almost three centuries.

## The Abbasid Caliphate

The Abbasid revolution is generally viewed as a major turning point in Islamic history. People used to think that it marked the overthrow of the Arabs by the Persians. This is, at best, a half-truth. The Abbasids were Arabs, proud of their descent from the Prophet's uncle. Their partisans included Arabs and Persians, Sunni and Shi'i Muslims, all united by a desire to replace an Arab tribal aristocracy with a more egalitarian form of government based on the principles of Islam. Like other historic revolutions, the overthrow of the Umayyads reinforced trends that had already begun: the shift of the power center from Syria to Iraq, the rise of Persian influence in place of the Byzantine-Arab synthesis of Mu'awiyah and Abd al-Malik, the waning drive to take over all the Christian lands of Europe, and the growing interest in cultivating the arts of civilization.

Even though most Westerners may not know who the Abbasids were, references to the caliph of Baghdad or Harun al-Rashid conjure up images of Disney's *Aladdin* and *The Arabian Nights*—a never-never land of flying carpets, genies released from magic lamps, and scattering gold and jewels. One could guess that the country was rich, that its rulers had the power of life and death over their subjects, and that the state religion was Islam. These guesses would prove true for the Abbasid Empire under its fifth caliph, Harun al-Rashid (r. 786–809).

### The Building of Baghdad

When Abu al-Abbas, Harun's great-uncle, was acclaimed as the first Abbasid caliph by the populace at Kufah in 749, Baghdad was just a tiny Persian village a few miles up the Tigris River from the ruined Sasanid capital, Ctesiphon. The early Abbasids wanted to move the government to Iraq, but they tried a few other cities before Abu al-Abbas's brother and successor, Abu Ja'far al-Mansur, chose that site in 762 for his capital. He officially named it the "city of peace," but it soon became better known by the name of the Persian village it replaced, Baghdad. It was located at exactly the point where the Tigris and Euphrates come closest together (see Map 3). A series of canals linking the rivers there made it easier to defend the site and also put Baghdad on the main trade route between the Mediterranean (hence Europe) and the Gulf (hence Asia). River irrigation in Iraq was raising agricultural output. It was also an area in which Persian and Aramean culture remained strong. Finally, it was closer to the political center of gravity for an empire still stretching east toward India and China.

Mansur wanted a planned capital, not a city that, like Kufah or Damascus, had long served other purposes. His architects gave him a round city. The caliphal palace and the main mosque fronted on a central square. Around them stood army barracks, government offices, and the homes of the chief administrators. A double wall with four gates girdled the city, and soon hundreds of houses and shops surrounded the wall. Across the Tigris rose the palace of the caliph's son, with a smaller entourage. The later caliphs built more palaces along the Tigris, which was spanned at one point by a bridge of boats. The building of Baghdad was part of a public works policy by which the Abbasids kept thousands of their subjects employed and their immense wealth circulating. It was a popular policy, for it led to the construction of mosques, schools, and hospitals throughout the empire, but its success depended on general prosperity, inasmuch as the people had also to pay the high taxes needed to support it.

*Public Piety*

The Abbasids made a public display of their piety, which had been their main justification for seizing power from the high-living Umayyads. Mahdi, the third Abbasid caliph, loved wine, music, and perfumed slave girls, but he also paid handsomely to expand the courtyard surrounding the Ka'bah and to set up guard posts and wells along the pilgrimage routes in Arabia. Harun al-Rashid went on the hajj every few years throughout his life, even walking once from Medina to Mecca in the hope of earning divine merit. Most of the Abbasids displayed their generosity during the great feasts of the Muslim calendar or at family celebrations, such as the

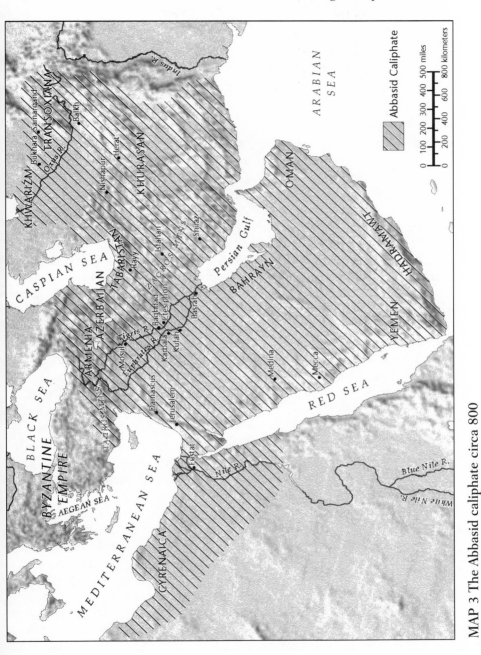

MAP 3 The Abbasid caliphate circa 800

birth or the circumcision of a prince. Harun personally led his army in a Muslim jihad across Anatolia that almost reached Constantinople before the Byzantines paid enough tribute to persuade the Abbasids to withdraw. Both merrymaking and holy wars were popular activities.

## Anti-Abbasid Revolts

With so much public piety, you might think that the Abbasids could have avoided religious uprisings like the ones that had troubled the Umayyads. Not so. The revolts became more frequent and varied than ever before, reflecting economic hardships and social discontent within the lands of Islam. Kharijite groups rebelled in Oman and North Africa, forming a few states of their own. The Shi'is were more dangerous, for they soon saw that the Abbasids had tricked them by using their help to oust the Umayyads. Two descendants of Hasan revolted in 762, one in Mecca and the other in Basrah. To crush their revolts, Mansur's troops killed thousands of Shi'i dissidents. In 788 another Shi'i led a Berber group in a rebellion that permanently severed Morocco from Abbasid rule. Shi'i revolts flared up in many different areas; I will not cover all of them, but you need to know that Shi'i Islam had now split into three branches, as shown in Figure 1 (see Chapter 5). You will learn more about these sects in Chapter 7.

Some of the revolts against Abbasid rule were anti-Islamic in spirit, especially those in which Persians took part. Why were they so restive? A dark curtain had shrouded Persia's history after the Arab conquests destroyed the Sasanid Empire, and for a century the Persians went into shock. Only a few became Muslims, but those who did so learned Arabic and adjusted to the new power relationships. The Umayyads' fall and Iraq's regeneration in the middle of the eighth century drew the Persians out of their shock. Many would back any hero who could restore their lost prestige.

Abu-Muslim was popular in Khurasan, where the Persians viewed him as their leader, not merely the standard-bearer of the Abbasid revolution. The first two Abbasid caliphs, Abu al-Abbas and Mansur, used him to defeat the Umayyads and crush the Shi'is. But Mansur feared that his own dynasty could be overthrown by the Persians. They charged that Mansur treacherously summoned Abu-Muslim to his court and had him put to death. Some Arabs called Abu-Muslim a *zindiq* ("heretic"), meaning that he may have carried on a few esoteric practices of a pre-Islamic Persian religion. He remains a controversial figure.

Abu-Muslim's execution brought the Abbasids no peace. Revolts promptly broke out in Khurasan. One of his friends, who may have been a

Zoroastrian, tried to destroy the Ka'bah. Then a "veiled prophet" claiming to be Abu-Muslim began a rebellion that lasted almost twenty years. Backed by thousands, he robbed caravans, wrecked mosques, and virtually ruled Khurasan. Years later, Azerbaijan saw another reincarnation of Abu-Muslim, a Persian named Babak whose rebellion also lasted twenty years. These uprisings were inspired by Persia's pre-Islamic religions, such as Zoroastrianism (the faith of the Sasanid establishment) and a peasant movement called Mazdakism. Moreover, the Manichaeans' philosophical dualism survived or revived in Persia among the Zindiqs. This group is hard to pin down, though, as pious Muslims branded most dissidents by that name.

*Persians in Power*

The resurrection of Persian influence did not always take dissident forms. Hundreds of Persians, especially from Iraq and Khurasan, rose to high positions within the army and the civil administration, replacing the Arabs and Syrians favored by the Umayyads. These men may have been more interested in the Sanskrit and old Persian classics than their Arab colleagues would have liked them to be, but they also learned Arabic and carefully toed the Abbasid line on religious matters. Some Persians became ulama and helped to shape Islamic ways. Loyal to their Abbasid masters, they helped them to suppress dissenting ideas and movements, but in fact they Persianized the state from within.

As the central administration grew more complex, Persian bureaucratic families rose to power. The greatest of these was the Barmakids, of whom three generations served the Abbasids from Mansur to Harun al-Rashid as bursars, tax collectors, provincial governors, military commanders, tutors, companions, and chief ministers. The title they bore, pronounced *wazir* in Arabic and *vezir* in Persian, came to be applied to any high-ranking official. Originally meaning "burden-bearer," it now is used to mean "cabinet minister" in most Middle Eastern languages. Harun unloaded many of his burdens onto his Barmakid *vezirs* (one of whom, Ja'far, you may recall from *Aladdin*), until he realized that he had let them take too much of his power and wealth. Then he dramatically killed the one to whom he was most attached and locked up his father and brother. So sudden was the move that many people ascribed it to a thwarted homosexual love affair that also involved a fictitious marriage between the murdered Barmakid and the caliph's sister, who later bore a child attributed to him. This account may humanize a rather pompous caliphate, but a truer explanation is that the Barmakids' power and prestige were eclipsing

Harun's own position. Either he or they had to go. How could Harun claim to be God's representative on earth and the fountainhead of justice if everyone looked to the Barmakids for patronage?

A less spectacular ladder for upwardly mobile Persians was a literary movement called the Shu'ubiyah. The Persians, especially in the bureaucratic class, used their knowledge of literature to prove their equality with (or superiority over) the Arabs. After all, they reasoned, Persians had built and managed mighty empires, prospered, and created a high culture for centuries while the Arabs were riding camels in the desert. The Arabs were quick to accuse the Shu'ubiyah of attacking Islam and the Prophet, but its scholars and bureaucrats were really working for equality within the system.

The greatest threat to the Abbasids came from those Persians who broke away to form separate dynastic states in Persia. These included a general who founded the Tahirids (r. 820–873) and a coppersmith who started the durable Saffarids (r. 861–1465). Indeed, the Abbasids themselves were being Persianized by their harems. So many caliphs had Persian wives or concubines that the genetic mix of the ninth-century Abbasids was more Persian than Arab. Harun's Persian mother pushed him into becoming caliph. The succession struggle between his two sons was intensified by the fact that the mother of Amin (r. 809–813) was Harun's Arab wife, whereas Mamun (the challenger and ultimate victor) was born of a Persian concubine.

## Mamun's Caliphate

Mamun (r. 813–833) deserves a high rank among the Abbasid caliphs, even though his rise to power resulted from a bloody civil war that almost wiped out Baghdad. A patron of scholarship, Mamun founded the Islamic equivalent of the legendary Sasanid academy in Jundishapur, a major intellectual center called Bayt al-Hikmah (House of Wisdom). It included several schools, astronomical observatories in Baghdad and Damascus, an immense library, and facilities for the translation of scientific and philosophical works from Greek, Aramaic, and Persian into Arabic.

Mamun's penchant for philosophical and theological debate led him to espouse a set of Muslim doctrines known collectively as the Mu'tazilah. This system of theology began as an attempt to refute Persian Zindiqs and the Shu'ubiyah but came to be seen as a rationalist formulation of Islam, stressing free will over divine predestination. Under Mamun and his two successors, each high-ranking Muslim official or judge was tested by being asked whether he believed that God had created all things, including the

Quran. A yes answer meant that he was a Mu'tazilite, one who opposed the popular idea that the Quran had eternally existed, even before it was revealed to Muhammad. (We will look at this issue carefully in Chapter 8.) The extreme rationalism of the Mu'tazilah antagonized the later Abbasids, who ended the test, and offended ordinary Muslims, who revered the Quran and believed that God had decreed all human acts. Mamun also tried to reconcile Sunni and Shi'i Muslims by naming the latter's imam as his successor. The plan backfired. Iraq's people resisted Mamun's concession to a descendant of Ali. The imam in question died, probably of poison.

## THE DECLINE OF THE ABBASIDS

Given so many dissident sects, revolts, secessions, and intellectual disputes going on between 750 and 945, you may wonder how the Abbasids ever managed to rule their empire. Well, as time passed, they no longer could. In addition to those aforementioned Shi'ite and Kharijite states in the remote areas of their empire, the Abbasids appointed some governors who managed to pass down their provinces to their heirs. An Abbasid governor, sent by Harun in 800 to Tunis, founded his own dynasty, collectively known as the Aghlabids. Their rule, over what now are Tunisia and eastern Algeria, was beneficent; they built or restored irrigation works, mosques, and public buildings. Intermittent Arab and Berber revolts did not stop the Aghlabids from raiding nearby Sicily, Italy, and southern France. These raids enhanced their prestige among Muslims at a time when Harun's successors were no longer taking Christian lands. Rather, Egypt's Christians overthrew their Abbasid governor in 832, and a Byzantine navy invaded the Nile Delta some twenty years later. Ahmad ibn Tulun, sent by the Abbasids in 868 to put Egypt in order, made the country virtually independent. As the Abbasids declined, the Byzantine Empire revived. Under its tenth-century Macedonian rulers, that Christian state would briefly retake southern Anatolia and even Syria.

Ahmad ibn Tulun was a Turk. In the ninth century some Turkish tribes from Central Asia came into the Middle East, seeking grazing lands for their horses and high-paying jobs for their warriors. In addition, individual Turks were incorporated into the Abbasid ruling system. Some captured in war became slaves for the caliphs. But under al-Mu'tasim (r. 833–842) the induction of Turks into the service of the caliphate became more systematic and large scale. Hundreds of boys were purchased from traders in Central Asia, taken to Baghdad, converted to Islam, and trained to be soldiers, administrators, or domestic servants for the Abbasids. Taught from a tender age to view the caliphs as the source of their material blessings, these Turkic slaves seemed more trustworthy than the Persian mercenaries. Soon they became the strongest element in the Abbasid army. Then they were able to manipulate the caliphs and murder anyone they disliked. Hardy and disciplined, the Turks took over the caliphal state—both the capital and some of its provinces—from within.

## CONCLUSION

The High Caliphate was the zenith of Arab political power. The Umayyads and Abbasids have come to be viewed collectively as great Arab leaders, yet only a few of these caliphs merit such a tribute. Some were brave, generous, and farsighted; most are now forgotten. Naturally, Arab chroniclers praised wise and magnanimous rulers, slighting what was really done by *vezirs* and ulama, traders and sailors, let alone artisans and peasants. Improved river irrigation and long-distance trade made Muslim lands prosper. The Arab conquests brought together people of diverse languages, religions, cultures, and ideas. The result was a flowering of artistic and intellectual creativity.

The political history, as you now know, was turbulent—a chronicle of palace coups, bureaucratic rivalries, and rural uprisings. Islam did not efface ethnic differences. Indeed, Muslim unity was more and more a facade, a polite fiction. No dramatic revolt toppled the Abbasids. Although their power ebbed away in the ninth and tenth centuries, their accumulated prestige and wealth enabled them to outlast most of the usurper dynasties. They went on producing caliphs in Baghdad until 1258, then in Cairo up to 1517. But dry rot had set in during the Augustan age of Harun al-Rashid and Mamun, if not before; for the political unity of the *ummah* had ended when the Umayyads had held on to Spain after 750. During the late ninth and tenth centuries, a welter of Muslim dynasties took control of the various parts of North Africa, Syria, and Persia. Finally Baghdad was captured in 945 by a Shi'i dynasty called the Buyids, and the Abbasids ceased to be masters even in their own house.

The decline of the Abbasids mattered less than you might think. As the caliphate declined, other types of political leadership emerged to maintain and even increase the collective power of the Muslim world. New institutions sustained the feeling of community among Muslim peoples, now that the caliphate could no longer fulfill that function. My next two chapters will treat these trends in greater depth.

## SEVEN

# Shi'is and Turks, Crusaders and Mongols

The period of Middle East history from the tenth through the thirteenth centuries challenges us. There is no one dynasty or country on which to focus our attention, so we must jump around. The Arabs were no longer dominant everywhere; they had given way to the Berbers in North Africa and to the Persians and Kurds in the lands east of the Euphrates River. Various Central Asian peoples, Iranian or Turkish in culture, came to dominate the successor states to the Abbasid caliphate, which lingered on in Baghdad but now had to obey other dynasties. Most of the Central Asians came in as slaves or hired troops for the Abbasids or their successors. Gradually they adopted Islam, learned Arabic and Persian, and became part of the culture of the Middle East. By the late tenth century, Turks on horseback entered the eastern lands in droves. Some, notably the Ghaznavids and the Seljuks, formed great empires.

Some of the greatest Muslim dynasties of this era were Shi'i, but not all from the same sect. Although we should note these sectarian splits and their effects on what people thought and did, we will find that geopolitical and economic interests mattered even more. The concept of being a Sunni or a Shi'i Muslim had just begun to form. Once people started to think in these terms, though, leaders often rose to power by exploiting the sectarian feelings of influential groups within a given area. As soon as they were securely entrenched, they tended to adopt policies that maintained a Muslim consensus.

During this time, the Byzantines briefly retook Syria, Spanish Christians began to win back the Iberian Peninsula, and (most notoriously) Christians from various European lands launched a series of crusades to recapture the "Holy Land" from the Muslims. Not all Muslim rulers aided their coreligionists, for some had ideological or economic reasons not to help rival Muslim states under Christian attack. The general effect of the Christian onslaught, though, was to make Islam more militant by the twelfth century than it had ever been before. Declining Byzantine power in the eleventh century enabled the Muslim Turks to enter Anatolia, which had until then been a land of Greek-speaking, Orthodox Christians. Thus Christians were gaining in some areas and Muslims in others. Two centuries later, however, Islam's heartland was hit by a dreadful disaster—the invasion of the Mongols, who had built up a great empire under Jenghiz Khan and his heirs. Nearly every Muslim state in Asia was conquered or forced to pay tribute to the Mongols. Only an unexpected victory by the Mamluks of Egypt saved Muslim Africa from the same fate.

You may be tempted (as I was) to call this chapter "One Damned Dynasty after Another," because so many ruling families came and went, but I hope you will see that Islamic civilization overcame sectarian disputes, throve despite Turkish infiltration and domination, drove out the Christian Crusaders, and subverted the Mongol vision of a universal empire. Muslim civilization survived because a growing majority of the people wanted to keep the coherent and comprehensive way of life made possible by Islam. It lived on because, in times of crisis, new leaders seized power and guided the governments and peoples of the various Middle Eastern lands. The dynasties founded by these leaders each underwent a cycle of growth, flowering, and decay, usually lasting about one century. Even if you cannot recall the names of all the dynasties mentioned here, I hope you will keep in mind the dynamics of this period in Middle East history.

## SHI'I ISLAM IN POWER

Periodization is a problem in any historical account, and certainly in the history of Islam. How do we decide when one period ends and another begins? The story of the past is a seamless web. The stars and planets move along their courses, the seasons follow their annual cycle, and people are born, grow up, carry on trades, marry, have children, and eventually die, almost oblivious to the periods designated by historians. Once scholars used the dates of caliphal and dynastic reigns; now we look to broader trends, social as well as political, to spot the turning points. I could start this chapter in 909, when the Fatimids seized Tunis and founded a Shi'i anticaliphate that later moved to Cairo. Or I could start it in 945, when Baghdad, seat of the Abbasid caliphate, was taken by a very different Shi'i dynasty called the Buyids. In either case, this chapter's first theme is the rise of Shi'ism as a political force.

*The Major Sects of Islam*

As you know, we tend to identify Muslims as being either Sunni, Shi'i, or Kharijite. Sunni Islam is often mistranslated as the "orthodox" version. I concede that some Muslims call anyone "Sunni" who follows the recorded practices (*sunnah*) of Muhammad. But when most people identify a Muslim as a Sunni, they mean that he or she acknowledged the Rashidun, Umayyad, and Abbasid caliphs as legitimate leaders of the entire *ummah* because most other Muslims accepted their rule. The person in question might have been a mystic, a rationalist freethinker, or a rebel against the laws of Islam; the "Sunni" designation is more political than theological. But it usually indicates that the Muslim in question adhered to one of the four standard "rites" of Islamic law, which I will explain in Chapter 8. As these rites were not clearly established until the ninth or tenth century, calling someone a "Sunni" used to be a novelty, a reaction against Shi'i dominance. It also meant accepting the religious norms of the *ummah*.

A Shi'i Muslim, in contrast, is a partisan of Ali as Muhammad's true successor, at least as imam (leader) or spiritual guide of the *ummah*, and of one of the several lines of Ali's descendants, shown in Figure 1 (see Chapter 5). Shi'is reject all other caliphs and all of Ali's successors not in the "correct" line, whose members are said to have inherited from him perfect knowledge of the inner meaning of the Quran and the whole message of Muhammad. Given these essentially genealogical differences, Shi'ism split into many sects. Some grew up and died out early, such as the Hashimites, who supported a son of Ali born of a wife other than Fatimah and then shifted their loyalty to the Abbasids just before they took power. Others stayed underground until the Abbasid caliphate grew weak, then surfaced in revolutionary movements.

The three Shi'i sects you are most apt to read about are the Twelve-Imam (or Ja'fari) Shi'is, the Isma'ilis (sometimes called Seveners), and the Zaydis, all shown in Figure 1. The first group believed in a line of infallible imams extending from Ali to Muhammad al-Muntazar, who is thought to have vanished in 878 but will someday return to restore peace and justice on earth. The Isma'ilis had by then broken with the Twelve-Imam Shi'is over the designation of the seventh imam, maintaining that Isma'il was wrongly passed over in favor of his brother. Soon after Isma'il died in 760, his followers founded a revolutionary movement that led to the emergence of the Qarmatians in Arabia and Bahrain, then the Fatimids in Tunisia, later the Assassins in Syria and Persia, and (in modern times) the Agha Khan in India. The Zaydis had broken off even earlier. Zayd, who rebelled against Umayyad Caliph Hisham (r. 724–743), was to his followers

the legitimate imam. By 900 Zayd's descendants were leading independent states in the Yemen and Tabaristan, both mountainous regions. Under the Zaydi system, each imam designated his own successor from
among the members of his family. The Zaydi imams of Yemen ruled up to
1962, when an army coup ousted them and set off a long civil war.

To round out this overview, let me remind you that the Kharijites were the
Muslims who had turned against Ali in 657. They believed that neither he
nor his descendants nor the Umayyads nor the Abbasids had any special
claim on the leadership of the *ummah*. They were prepared to obey any adult
male Muslim who would uphold the laws of Islam. But, if he failed to do so,
they would depose him. Even though their doctrines seemed anarchistic,
some Kharijites did form dynastic states, notably in Algeria and Oman.

As political unity broke down during the ninth and tenth centuries, various dynastic states emerged in the Middle East and North Africa in response
to local economic or social needs. Most have been forgotten, but two Shi'i
dynasties threatened the Sunni Abbasids in Baghdad: the Fatimids, who
challenged their legitimacy, and the Buyids, who ended their autonomy.

*The Fatimid Caliphate*

The Fatimids appeared first. You may note the resemblance between their
name and that of Fatimah, Muhammad's daughter who married Ali and
bore Hasan and Husayn. This choice of names was deliberate. The dynasty's
founder, called Ubaydallah (Little Abdallah) by the Sunnis and al-Mahdi
(Rightly Guided One) by his own followers, claimed descent from Fatimah
and Ali. He proposed to overthrow the Abbasid caliphate and restore the
leadership of Islam to the house of Ali, hoping for Shi'i—specifically Isma'ili—support. Perhaps because Isma'il's surviving teenaged son had
vanished at a time when other Shi'i sects either had living imams or had
worn themselves out in unsuccessful revolts, the Isma'ilis had become an
underground revolutionary movement, based in Syria. During the late
eighth and ninth centuries, Isma'ili Shi'ism slowly picked up support from
disgruntled classes or clans throughout the Muslim world. Toward this end,
it formed a network of propagandists and a set of esoteric beliefs, the gist of
which had allegedly been passed down from Muhammad, via Ali and his
successors, to Isma'il, who had enlightened a few followers before his death.

The Isma'ilis may remind you of the early communists, with their secret
cells, complex doctrines, and widespread propaganda against the established order. One branch of the Isma'ilis, the Qarmatians, formed a
bedouin republic in Bahrain, and its enemies accused it of being "communist" with regard to both property and marital relationships. The Qar-

matians picked up support in other parts of the Muslim world, but they deviated from the Isma'ili leadership in Syria. To continue my analogy, the Lenin of the Isma'ilis was Ubaydallah, who overthrew the Aghlabids and seized their North African empire in 909. His Red Army was the band of Berber nomads who had turned to Shi'ism to voice their opposition to their Aghlabid overlords, who were Sunni Muslim Arabs tied to the Abbasid caliphate. Berbers were spirited rebels.

To the Fatimids, Tunisia seemed too remote a base from which to build a new universal Muslim empire to replace the faltering Abbasids. Strengthening their corps of Isma'ili propagandists throughout the Muslim world, they set their sights on Baghdad. Instead, they found Egypt, a land that had played a surprisingly minor role in early Islamic history. It had been ruled by various dynasties since Ahmad ibn Tulun had broken away from Baghdad in 868. While fighting the Byzantine navy in the Mediterranean, the Fatimid general Jawhar saw that Egypt was in political chaos and gripped by famine. In 969 Jawhar entered Fustat, without any resistance, and declared Egypt a bastion of Isma'ili Shi'ism. Then the Fatimid caliph, Mu'izz, came with his family and government from Tunis to Egypt. It is said that a welcoming deputation of ulama challenged him to prove his descent from Ali. Mu'izz unsheathed his sword, exclaiming, "Here is my pedigree!" Then he scattered gold coins among the crowd and shouted, "Here is my proof." They were easily convinced.

The Fatimid caliphs chose a site north of Fustat for the capital of what they hoped would be the new Islamic empire. They called their city al-Qahirah (meaning "the conqueror," referring to the planet Mars); we know it as Cairo. It soon eclipsed Fustat in size and prosperity, becoming a rival to Baghdad as the Middle East's leading city. Its primacy as an intellectual center was ensured by the founding of a mosque-university called al-Azhar, where the Fatimids trained Isma'ili propagandists for two centuries. Cairo and al-Azhar outlasted the Fatimids and remained respectively the largest city and the most advanced university in the Muslim world up to the Ottoman conquest in 1517. Today Cairo, with its 15 million inhabitants, is again Islam's largest city, and al-Azhar remains a major university drawing Muslim scholars from many lands. The Fatimid government in Egypt was centralized and hierarchical. It promoted long-distance trade but not agriculture, for it neglected the Nile irrigation works. Like many Muslim states then and later, the Fatimids set up an army of slave-soldiers imported from various parts of Asia. Their strong navy helped them to take Palestine, Syria, and the Hijaz, but they lost interest in (and control over) their North African lands.

Surprisingly, the Fatimids did not try to convert their Sunni Muslim subjects to Isma'ili Shi'ism. They respected the religious freedom of the many

Christians and Jews over whom they ruled. The one exception was the Caliph al-Hakim (r. 996–1021), who has been depicted as a madman who persecuted Christians, destroyed their churches, killed stray dogs, outlawed certain foods, and eventually proclaimed himself divine. Modern scholars think that Hakim's hostility was aimed mainly against Orthodox Christians; he accused them of backing the Byzantines, who had just retaken part of Syria. His sumptuary decrees were meant to fight a famine caused by his predecessors' neglect of Nile irrigation. Far from claiming to be God, Hakim played down distinctions between Isma'ilis and other Muslims. One day he vanished in the hills east of Cairo; his body was never found.

Possibly Hakim's bad name among Muslims is due to the preaching done on his behalf by an Isma'ili propagandist, Shaykh Darazi, who convinced some Syrian mountain folk that Hakim was divine. These Syrians built up a religion around the propaganda of Darazi, from whom they got the collective name of Duruz, hence *Druze*. The Druze faith is a secret one that combines some of the esoteric aspects of Isma'ili Shi'ism with the beliefs and practices of other Middle Eastern religions. As mountaineers, the Druze people could not be controlled by Muslim governments in the low-lying areas. Thus, in the eyes of Muslim historians, they were troublemakers as well as heretics. They have survived to this day. The Druze take part in the tangled politics of modern Syria and Lebanon. Some own large estates and often become army officers. In northern Israel the Druze have backed the Jewish state and served in its armed forces. A proud and hardy people, the Druze share the language and culture of the Arabs, but their desire to retain their religious identity has kept them distinct politically.

The Fatimids ruled Egypt for two centuries, a long time for a Muslim dynasty, but they seem to have done better at building a strong navy and a rich trading center than at spreading their domains or their doctrines. Could they have won more converts? Sunni Islam seemed to be waning in the tenth and early eleventh centuries. The Abbasid caliphs were no longer credible claimants to universal sovereignty, for they had become captives of the Buyids, who were Persian and Shi'i. In fact, the strongest states resisting Fatimid expansion were already Shi'i and not impressed by these self-styled caliphs with their propagandists and their fake genealogies.

## The Buyid Dynasty

Best known for having captured Baghdad and the Abbasids in 945, the Buyids were one of several dynasties that aided the revival of Persian sovereignty and culture. By this time Persia was completing its recovery from the Arab conquest. This revival had already been manifest in Abu-Muslim's revolution, the later sects that rebelled in his name, the Shu'ubiyah literary movement, the Barmakid *vezirs*, Caliph Mamun's victory over his brother, and the ninth-century establishment of local Persian dynasties. During the tenth century, all Persia came to be ruled by such families: the Shi'i Buyids in the west and the Sunni Samanids in the east. Both consciously revived the symbols and practices of Persia's pre-Islamic rulers, the Sasanids. Persian language, literature, and culture made a major comeback at this time, but attempts to revive Zoroastrianism failed.

The Buyid family consisted of several branches concurrently ruling different parts of Iraq and western Persia; indeed, the dynasty was founded by three brothers, each with his own capital. The most important was Isfahan, in the prospering province of Fars, rather than Baghdad, whose politics were turbulent and whose agricultural lands were less productive than earlier. All Buyids were Twelve-Imam Shi'is, but they tolerated other Muslim sects. Although they allowed the Abbasids to retain the caliphate, they confined them to their Baghdad palace without independent means of support. One Abbasid caliph was blinded, another was reduced to begging in the street; but the institution of the caliphate was a useful fiction because it stood for the unity of the *ummah*. The Buyids' foreign policy was friendly to Christian Byzantium, to whoever was ruling Egypt, and to the Isma'ili Qarmatians. They were hostile to their Twelve-Imam Shi'i neighbors, the Hamdanids of Mosul, and to their fellow Persians, the Samanids of Khurasan. In short, when making alliances the Buyids heeded their economic interests more than any racial or religious affinities.

Domestically, the Buyids let their *vezirs* govern for them, promoted trade and manufacturing, and expanded a practice begun under the Abbasids of making land grants (*iqta's*) to their chief soldiers and bureaucrats instead of paying them salaries. The *iqta'* was supposed to be a short-term delegation of the right to use a piece of state-owned land or other property. Under the Buyids, though, it came to include the right to collect the land tax (*kharaj*) and to pass on the property to one's heirs. The *iqta'* system often caused landowners to gouge the peasants and neglect the irrigation works so necessary to Middle Eastern agriculture. Even more harmful to Buyid interests was a shift of the trade routes from Iraq toward Egypt and also toward lands farther east.

## THE TURKS

Before we can find out the fate of the Buyids, we must turn to Central Asia. Both the century of Shi'ism and the Persian revival were cut short by events taking place there, notably the rise of the Turks. The origin of the

Turkic peoples has been lost in the mists of legend; we will know little until archaeologists have excavated more of Central Asia and Mongolia, the probable birthplace of the Turks. We do know that they started as nomadic shepherds who rode horses and used two-humped camels to carry their burdens, although some became settled farmers and traders. Their original religion revolved around shamans, who were wizards viewed as capable of healing the sick and communicating with the world beyond. The shaman's spirit was thought to be able to leave his body at will. He also served as the guardian of tribal lore.

## Early Turkic Civilization

Around 550 the Turks set up a tribal confederation called Gokturk, better known to us (through Chinese sources) as the Tujueh. Its vast domains extended from Mongolia to the Ukraine. But soon the Tujueh Empire split into an eastern branch, which later fell under the sway of China's Tang dynasty, and a western one, which became allied with Byzantium against the Sasanids and later fell back before the Arab conquests. This early empire exposed the Turks to the main sixth-century civilizations: Byzantium, Persia, China, and India. It also led some Turks to espouse such religions as Nestorian Christianity, Manichaeism, and Buddhism. Some had even developed a writing system.

The transmission of cultures among the various Eurasian regions seems incredible until you stop to think that people and horses have crossed the steppes and deserts for ages, forming one of the world's oldest highways, the Great Silk Route. In the eighth century a group of eastern Turks, the Uighurs, formed an empire on China's northwestern border. Its official religion was Manichaeism and its records were kept in a script resembling Aramaic. These facts show you how far the Turks could take some of the ideas and customs they had picked up in the Middle East. Meanwhile, one of the western Turkic tribes, the Khazars, adopted Judaism, hoping to get along with its Christian and Muslim trading partners, while distancing itself from both sides.

## The Islamization of the Turks

Eventually, though, most Turkic peoples became Muslim. The Islamization process was gradual, and it varied from one tribe to another. Once the Arab armies crossed the Oxus River—if not long before then—they encountered Turks. Even in Umayyad times, some Turks became Muslims and served in the Arab armies in Transoxiana and Khurasan. Under the Abbasids, you may recall, the Turks became numerous and powerful in the government. The first Turkic soldiers for Islam were probably prisoners of war who were prized for their skill as mounted archers but viewed as slaves. Most historians think that the institution of slavery grew in Abbasid lands to the point where some tribes would sell their boys (or turn them over as tribute) to the caliphs, who would have them trained as disciplined soldiers or skilled bureaucrats. These slaves became so imbued with Islamic culture that they no longer identified with their original tribes. In addition, whole Turkic tribes, after they had embraced Islam, were hired by the Abbasids or their successors (notably the Samanids) as *ghazis* (Muslim border warriors) to guard their northeastern boundaries against the non-Muslim Turks. Much nonsense has been written about how the Turks "naturally" gravitated to Sunnism or Shi'ism. Actually, those who entered the service of a particular Muslim dynasty usually took on its political coloring. The *ghazis* cared nothing about such political or doctrinal disputes. Their Islam reflected what had been taught to them by Muslim merchants, mendicants, and mystics, combined with some of their own pre-Islamic beliefs and practices.

## The Ghaznavids

Two Turkish dynasties, both Sunni and both founded by *ghazi* warriors who had served the Samanid dynasty, stand out during this era. They are commonly called the Ghaznavids and the Seljuks. The Ghaznavids got their name from Ghazna, a town located 90 miles (145 kilometers) southwest of Kabul (the capital of modern Afghanistan), because their leader received that region as an *iqta'* from the Samanids in return for his services as a general and a local governor. The first Ghaznavid rulers, Sebuktegin (r. 977–997) and his son Mahmud (r. 998–1030), parlayed this *iqta'* into an immense empire, covering at its height (around 1035) what would now be eastern Iran, all of Afghanistan and Pakistan, and parts of northern India. It was the Ghaznavids who extended Muslim rule into the Indian subcontinent, although their efforts to force Hindus to adopt Islam have discredited them among some Indians.

## The Seljuk Empire

The other major dynasty, the Seljuks, takes its name from a pagan Turkic chieftain who converted to Islam about 956. Later he enrolled his clan as warriors for the Samanids. Seljuk's descendants proved to be one of the ablest ruling families in Islamic history (see Map 4). They made themselves indispensable first to the Samanids and then to the Ghaznavids as *ghazis* in Transoxiana against the pagan Turks. In return, they received *iqta's*, which they used to graze their horses and to attract other Islamized Turkic tribes, who would occupy the grazing lands with their sheep and goats, horses and camels. As more Turkic tribes joined the Seljuks, they increased their military strength as well as their land hunger. The trickle became a flood; in 1040 the Seljuks and their allies defeated the Ghaznavids and took over all of Khurasan. The Buyids had grown weak, leaving western Persia and Iraq open to these military adventurers who had the encouragement of the Abbasid caliph himself, eager to welcome Sunni Muslims.

When the Turks, thus encouraged, entered Baghdad in 1055, it was not to wipe out Arab sovereignty but to bring back caliphal authority, at least in name. The Turco-Abbasid alliance was cemented by the marriage of the Seljuk leader to the caliph's sister, and the caliph recognized him as regent of the empire and sultan (which might be translated as "authority") in both the East and the West. Soon the title was for real, as the Seljuks went on to take Azerbaijan, Armenia, and finally most of Anatolia following a major victory over the Byzantines at Manzikert in 1071. You would have to go back to the ninth century, when the Aghlabids took Sicily and raided the coasts of France and Italy, to find a time when a Muslim ruler had so successfully waged a war against Christendom. Not since the early Abbasids had so much land been held by one Muslim dynasty. Malikshah, the sultan at the height of Seljuk power, ruled over Palestine, Syria, part of Anatolia, the Caucasus Mountains, all of Iraq and Persia, plus parts of Central Asia up to the Aral Sea and beyond the Oxus River. "Praise be to God the Exalted," wrote a contemporary, "that the defenders of Islam are mighty and happy because the Turk carries the sword in his hand to the lands of the Arabs, Persians, Byzantines, and Russians, and fear . . . is firmly implanted in all hearts."

The Seljuk success story was too good to last. Soon after Malikshah's death in 1092, the empire began to crumble. By the end of the twelfth century nothing was left except a part of Anatolia ruled by a branch called the Rum Seljuks. *Rum* meant Anatolia, which historically was part of the Byzantine Empire. That empire, in turn, called itself *Rome*, which is why the Arabs, Persians, and Turks all called the area *Rum*. The Turkish "Rome," with its capital at Konya, lasted until about 1300. The Seljuk legacies helped transform the Middle East. Let me summarize them: (1) the influx of Turkic tribes from Central Asia; (2) the Turkification of eastern

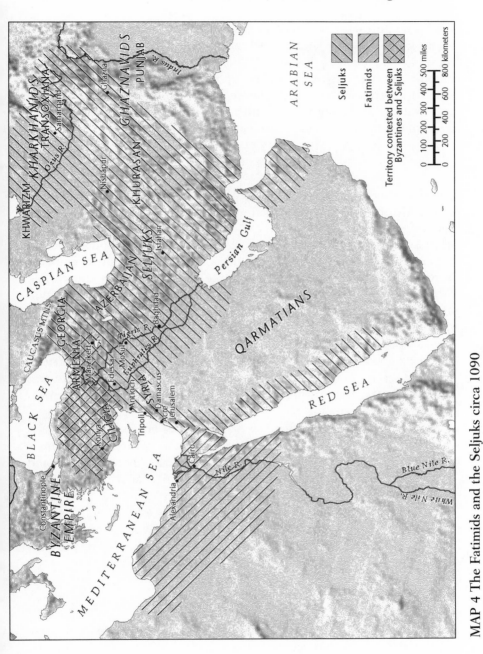

MAP 4 The Fatimids and the Seljuks circa 1090

Persia and northern Iraq, most of Azerbaijan, and later Anatolia (the land we now call Turkey); (3) the restoration of Sunni rule over southwest Asia; (4) the spread of Persian institutions and culture (both greatly admired by the Seljuks); (5) the development of the *madrasah* (mosque-school) for training ulama in Islamic law; (6) the regularization of the *iqta'* system for paying the tribal troops; and (7) the weakening of the Byzantine Empire in Anatolia, long its main power center.

## THE CRUSADES

The last of these enumerated results of Seljuk rule opened a new chapter in the history of Christian-Muslim relations. The Byzantines worried about the encroachment of Muslim Turkic nomads on the lands of Christian Greek peasants and were alarmed by the rise of Seljuk power during the eleventh century—so alarmed, in fact, that the Byzantine emperor begged the Roman pope, with whom the Greek Orthodox church had broken definitively forty years earlier, to save his realm from the Muslim menace. Pope Urban II, hardly a friend of the Byzantine Empire, responded to the call for help—but for his own reasons. Eager to prove the papacy's power in relation to the secular rulers of Christendom, Pope Urban in 1095 made a speech inviting all Christians to join in a war to regain the Holy Sepulcher in Jerusalem from "the wicked race." This call to arms inaugurated the first of what would be a series of Christian wars, known to history as the Crusades.

As the Crusades have inspired so many popular novels, films, and television programs, you may already know something about what seems a romantic episode in the history of medieval Europe. Many Catholics and Protestants have picked up a positive view of the Crusaders from their religious education. Many school and college sports teams are called the Crusaders; rarely is one called the Saracens (the word used for Arabs by the Crusaders themselves). You will soon see why this early confrontation between the Middle East and the West is less fondly recalled by Muslims in general and by Syrians and Palestinians in particular.

### Their Beginning

The emergence of the Turks in the Middle East was paralleled in Europe by the rise of the Norsemen (also called Northmen, Normans, or Vikings), who breathed new life into a poor and backward region. The resulting success of the Christian armies in pushing back the Muslims in

Spain and Sicily encouraged European kings and princes. During this time, travel overland or across the Mediterranean to the Middle East for trade or pilgrimage was becoming increasingly common. One of the telling points in Pope Urban's speech was his accusation that the Muslims (probably the Seljuks) were disrupting the Christian pilgrimage to Jerusalem.

Thousands of volunteers, mighty and lowly, rich and poor, northern and southern Europeans, left their homes and fields in response to the papal call. Younger sons from large noble families, unable to inherit their fathers' lands, were especially eager to carve out new estates for themselves. Led by the ablest European generals of the day (but not by rulers), the soldiers of the cross joined up with the Byzantines in 1097. They took Antioch after a nine-month siege, progressed southward along the Syrian coast, and reached the walls of Jerusalem in June 1099. Only 1,000 Fatimid troops guarded the city. After six weeks of fighting, the 15,000 Crusaders managed to breach the walls. Both Muslim and Christian accounts attest to the bloodbath that followed, as thousands of noncombatant Jews, Muslims, and even native Christians were beheaded, shot with arrows, thrown from towers, tortured, or burned at the stake. Human blood flowed knee-deep in the streets of Jerusalem. The Dome of the Rock was stripped of hundreds of silver candelabra and dozens of gold ones, then turned into a church.

Once the Holy Sepulcher was back in Christian hands, some of the European and Byzantine soldiers went home, but many stayed on to colonize the conquered lands. Four Crusader states were set up: the kingdom of Jerusalem, the principality of Antioch, and the counties of Tripoli and Edessa. The Crusaders also shored up a tiny state called Little Armenia, formed in southwest Anatolia by Armenian Christians who had fled from the conquering Seljuks. The Armenians would remain the Crusaders' staunchest allies.

### Muslim Reactions

You may ask how Islam, supposedly reinvigorated by the Turks' influx, stood by and let the Crusaders in. To some extent, the Crusaders were lucky. By the end of the eleventh century, Seljuk rule in Syria and Palestine had broken up, and the successor states were fighting one another. The Shi'i Fatimids farther south cared little about stopping an invasion that, until it reached Jerusalem, took lands from Sunni rulers. The Abbasid caliph in Baghdad was helpless; it is wrong to suppose that he was an Islamic pope who could command all Muslims to wage jihad against the Crusaders. Besides, the lands taken by the Crusaders were inhabited mainly by Christians of various sects, some of whom did not mind Catholic rule, or by Jews, Druze, or dissident Muslims. The Crusaders never took a city that really mattered to the political or economic life of Islam, such as Aleppo, Damascus, Mosul, Baghdad, or Cairo. Relative to the Muslim world in 1100 as a whole, the First Crusade was only a sideshow.

It is odd, though, that it took the Muslims so long to drive the Crusaders out. Part of the reason is that then, as now, they were divided into many small, quarrelsome states. Some Muslim rulers even formed alliances with the Crusaders against their own coreligionists. Fatimid Egypt usually had close ties with the Crusader states because of the lucrative trade going on between Alexandria and such Italian ports as Venice and Genoa.

The first turning point came in 1144, when Mosul's governor, Zengi, who had carved himself a kingdom from the decaying Seljuk Empire in eastern Syria, captured the county of Edessa from the Crusaders. The Second Crusade, led by the holy Roman emperor and the king of France, tried to take Damascus and thus the Syrian hinterland, including Edessa. The Crusaders botched the attack, however, and Islam resumed the offensive. Zengi had meanwhile been killed by one of his slaves, but his son, Nur al-Din, proved to be a worthy successor. Soon he controlled all of Syria, except for the narrow coastal strip still held by the Crusaders.

## The Rise of Salah al-Din

The scene then shifted to Egypt, still under the now-decadent Fatimid caliphs, who were by then declining. They had gradually given their powers over to their *vezirs*, who commanded the army and directed the bureaucracy. Both Nur al-Din in Damascus and the Crusader king of Jerusalem coveted the rich Nile Valley and Delta. But Nur al-Din got the upper hand through the political acumen of his best general, a Kurd named Shirkuh. Now Shirkuh had a nephew aiding him, Salah al-Din, known to the West as Saladin. Acting on behalf of their patron, Shirkuh and Salah al-Din fended off a Crusader invasion of Egypt and won for themselves the Fatimid vezirate. As the last Fatimid caliph lay dying, Salah al-Din quietly arranged to replace mention of his name in the Friday mosque prayers with that of the Abbasid caliph. In effect, Egypt rejected Shi'ism, a change hailed by the country's Sunni majority. In practical terms, it meant that Egypt was now led by a lieutenant of Nur al-Din, Syria's ruler, for Salah al-Din proclaimed himself sultan as soon as the Fatimid caliph died in 1171.

Salah al-Din seized power in Syria after Nur al-Din died three years later, but he needed at least a decade to overcome challenges by the Shi'is, particularly that colorful Isma'ili offshoot known as the Assassins. Then he managed to capture Jerusalem and most of Palestine from the Crusaders between 1187 and 1192. Salah al-Din was a master at perceiving his enemies' weaknesses and his own opportunities in time to capitalize on them. Both Muslim and Christian historians portray him as a paragon of bravery and magnanimity (what we call chivalry and the Arabs call *muruwwah*), unlike some of his Christian foes. For example, Reginald of Chatillon, one of the Crusader princes, raided caravans of Muslim pilgrims going to Mecca. When Salah al-Din sought revenge, he held off attacking Reginald's castle when he learned that a wedding feast was going on inside. Yet he could be vindictive toward Muslims who disagreed with him; he had many of the Fatimid courtiers and poets publicly crucified in Cairo, and the great Muslim mystic Suhrawardi was executed at his command.

Most Europeans thought that Salah al-Din had a master plan to drive the Crusaders out of the Middle East. If so, he was not wholly successful, for he failed to dislodge them from much of what we now call Lebanon. The Third Crusade, which lured France's King Philip and England's Richard the Lionheart to Palestine, took Acre from Salah al-Din in 1191. Some scholars think that he wanted to restore Muslim unity under the Abbasid caliphate, but his aims were less grandiose. Salah al-Din did manage to unite Egypt and Syria under his own family, which became the Ayyubid dynasty. The Ayyubids went on ruling these lands, though not always wisely or well, for almost two generations after Salah al-Din's death. Even though the Abbasid caliphate did revive at this time, the lands it recovered were in Iraq and Persia. Stranger still, in 1229 the Ayyubid sultan in Cairo chose to lease Jerusalem back to the Crusaders, who also held the coastal areas of Syria and Palestine. Twice they raided the Egyptian Delta. Egypt's Ayyubids resisted the Christian raiders by using their Turkic ex-slave soldiers, called Mamluks, who then took over the country for themselves.

In general, this era was one of greater Muslim militancy and intolerance in response to the Crusader challenge. Even the Ayyubid dynasty's founder, Salah al-Din, is revered as a symbol of Muslim resistance to the Christian West. Because he took Jerusalem back from the Crusaders, Muslims regained their self-confidence—just in time to face a far fiercer challenge from the East.

## THE MONGOL INVASION

The unwelcome interlopers from Asia were the Turks' cousins, so to speak—namely, the Mongols. For centuries these hardy nomads had lived on the windswept plateau north of the Gobi Desert, occasionally swooping down on China or on the caravans that plied the Great Silk Route linking China, India, and Persia. Most Mongols had kept aloof from the civilizations and religions surrounding them, worshiping their own deity, Tengri (Eternal Blue Sky). But in the late twelfth century, a warrior chieftain known as Jenghiz Khan united the eastern Mongol tribes into a great confederation. He started making forays into northern China but then turned abruptly toward Central Asia in response to a call for help from Turks who were being oppressed by a rival Mongol confederation called the Kara-Khitay. After having annexed their lands, Jenghiz faced the ambitious but foolhardy Prince Muhammad of the Khwarizm-Shah Turks. From 1218 to 1221 the Mongols chased Muhammad's army, laying waste to the great cities and some of the farmlands of Transoxiana, Khwarizm, and Khurasan. The atrocities perpetrated by the Mongol armies defy description: They slaughtered 700,000 inhabitants of Merv; their engineers broke the dams near Gurganj to flood the city *after* it had been taken; they poured molten gold down the throat of a Muslim governor; they carried off thousands of Muslim artisans to Mongolia as slaves, most of them dying on the way; they stacked the heads of Nishapur's men, women, and children in pyramids; and they even killed dogs and cats in the streets. The Mongol aim was to paralyze the Muslims with such fear that they would never dare to fight back.

Jenghiz Khan's death in 1227 gave Islam a respite, during which his successors ravaged China, Russia, and Eastern Europe. But one of his sons sent a large army into Azerbaijan, from which the Mongols could threaten both the Christian kingdoms of the Caucasus Mountains and the Muslims of Iraq and Anatolia. One result of this incursion was the defeat of the Rum Seljuks in 1243. The Mongols reduced them to vassal status and let the Turkish tribes carve up Anatolia into dozens of principalities. Another result was a lasting alliance between the Mongols and the kingdom of Little Armenia (which had earlier backed the Crusaders against Islam). This led many Europeans to think that a greater alliance between the Mongol East and the Christian West would crush the Muslim world forever.

## Destruction of the Caliphate

But the Mongols needed no help. In 1256 Hulegu, a grandson of Jenghiz, renewed the attack. He may have been spurred into action by the envoys whom the kings of Europe sent to the Mongol court, but he spurned their alliance offers. Although Hulegu was a pagan, his wife was a Nestorian Christian who might have inspired his hatred of Islam. The continued existence of the Abbasid caliph, with even a shadowy claim to the obedience of millions of Muslims, offended Hulegu, who could brook no rivals. After wiping out the Assassins, who had terrorized Sunni Muslims for two centuries, the Mongols crossed the Zagros Mountains into Iraq. The caliph's army resisted bravely until the Mongols flooded its camp, drowning thousands. Hulegu's forces proceeded to bombard Baghdad with heavy rocks flung from catapults until the caliph surrendered in February 1258. Then the Mongols pillaged the city, burned its schools and libraries, destroyed its mosques and palaces, murdered possibly a million Muslims (the Christians and Jews were spared), and finally executed all the Abbasids by wrapping them in carpets and having them trampled beneath their horses' hooves. Until the stench of the dead forced Hulegu and his men out of Baghdad, they loaded their horses, packed the scabbards of their discarded swords, and even stuffed some gutted corpses with gold, pearls, and precious stones, to be hauled back to the Mongol capital. It was a melancholy end to the independent Abbasid caliphate, to the prosperity and intellectual glory of Baghdad, and, some historians think, to Arabic civilization itself.

## Mamluk Resistance

The world of Islam did not vanish. Its salvation came from the Mamluks (their name literally means "owned men"), who in 1250 had seized control of Egypt from their Ayyubid masters, the descendants of Salah al-Din. In 1259–1260 Hulegu's forces pushed westward, supported by Georgian and Armenian Christians eager to help destroy their Muslim enemies. They besieged and took Aleppo, massacring its inhabitants. Damascus, abandoned by its Ayyubid ruler, gave up without a fight. Then Hulegu sent envoys to Cairo with this message:

You have heard how we have conquered a vast empire and have purified the earth of the disorders that tainted it. It is for you to fly and for us to pursue, but whither will you flee, and by what road will you escape us? Our horses are swift, our arrows sharp, our swords like thunderbolts, our hearts as hard as the mountains, our soldiers as numerous as the sand. Fortresses will not detain us. We mean well by our warning, for now you are the only enemy against whom we have to march.

But Hulegu suddenly learned that his brother, the Mongol emperor, had died. Grief-stricken (or perhaps power-hungry), he headed home from Syria, taking most of his men with him. In the meantime, the Mamluks murdered his envoys and entered Palestine, where they defeated the Mongols at Ayn Jalut (Goliath's Spring) in September 1260. The Battle of Ayn Jalut was doubtless a climactic moment in history, as it marked the high point of Mongol expansion against Islam. But it was hardly an Arab victory, for the Mamluks were mainly Turks at most one generation removed from the Central Asian steppes. Pro-Mongol chroniclers note that the Mamluks had twelve times as many men on the field. Hulegu could not avenge the defeat because he was fighting for power within the Mongol realm. Thus the Muslim world survived its Mongol ordeal.

## CONCLUSION

To end this gruesome tale, Hulegu and his descendants settled down in Iraq and Persia, calling themselves the Il-Khanid dynasty. Eventually they adopted Persian culture, including Islam, and repaired some of the damage they had done. The Mamluks survived for centuries, driving the last Crusaders out of Palestine in 1293. The kingdom they founded in Egypt and Syria became the major Muslim center of power, wealth, and learning for two centuries.

What can we learn from this mournful chronicle of invasions, conquest, and destruction, and from the bewildering succession of dynasties, few of which are known outside the Middle East? The rise and fall of Shi'i power and the Turkish influx benefited the area; however, the Crusaders and the Mongols did the Middle East more harm than good. But people cannot wish away the bad things that happen in their lives, nor can a country efface the sad events of its history. We learn from our misfortunes and overcome them. The religion and culture of Islam survived and grew stronger. You will find some of the sources of its resilience in Chapter 8.

# EIGHT

# Islamic Civilization

Now that we have covered almost seven centuries of political history, it is time to look at the civilization as a whole. But what should we call it? Scholars are divided between using *Islamic* and *Arabic*. Some say the civilization was Islamic because the religion of Islam brought together the various peoples—mainly Arabs, Persians, and Turks—who took part in it. The religion also affected its politics, commerce, lifestyle, ideas, and forms of artistic expression. But at least up to about 1000 C.E., Muslims were a minority within the lands of Islam. Inasmuch as they were relatively unlettered at first, many of the scholars and scientists active within the civilization were understandably Jews, Christians, Zoroastrians, or recent Muslim converts whose ideas still bore the stamp of their former religions. The civilization evolving in the Middle East drew on many religious and philosophical traditions.

The alternative term, *Arabic Civilization*, emphasizes the role of Arabic in the development of the culture. Not only because of its prestige as the language of the Quran and of the conquering elite, but also because of its capacity for absorbing new things and ideas, Arabic became the almost universal language of arts, sciences, and letters between 750 and 1250. But do not assume that all the artists, scientists, and writers were Arabs. The builders of the civilization came from every ethnic group within the *ummah*. Although many were Arabized Berbers, Egyptians, Syrians, and Iraqis whose present-day descendants would call themselves Arabs, only a few were wholly descended from tribal Arabs. Because *Islamic* is a more comprehensive term than *Arabic*, I have chosen "Islamic Civilization" for this chapter's title. It was not an easy choice.

## The Rules and Laws of Islam

Islam begins with a profession of faith but is manifested and elaborated by what Muslims do and what they condemn. Ever mindful of the impending Judgment Day, Muslims wish to know and obey the rules of behavior that will please God and maintain a harmonious society. These rules have been carefully compiled and organized into a law code called the Shari'ah (an Arabic word meaning "way"). It is somewhat like the Talmud for Orthodox Judaism; there is nothing comparable in Christianity. The Shari'ah tries to describe all possible human acts, classifying them as obligatory, recommended, neutral, objectionable, or forbidden by God, the supreme legislator. In addition to some commercial and criminal law, the Shari'ah includes rules about marriage, divorce, child rearing, other interpersonal relationships, property, food, clothing, hygiene, and the manifold aspects of worship. At least up to the Mongol era, there was nothing a Muslim might experience or observe on which the Shari'ah was silent.

## Development of Jurisprudence

The first Muslims based their ideas of right and wrong on the norms of the society they knew, that of western Arabia. Caravan traders had worked out elaborate rules about commercial transactions and property rights, but criminal law still held to the principles of retribution based on the tribal virtues (*muruwwah*). Muhammad's mission broadened and strengthened the realm of rights and responsibilities. The Quran spelled out many points. Muhammad's precepts and practices (what later Muslims would call his sunnah) set some of the laws for the nascent *ummah*. After the Prophet died, his successors tried to pattern their lives on what he had said or done and on what he had told them to do or not to do. Muhammad's companions, especially the first four caliphs, became role models for the Muslims who came later; indeed, their practices were the sunnah for succeeding caliphs and governors. Gradually, Arabia's traditional norms took on a Muslim pattern, as the companions inculcated the values of the Quran and the sunnah in their children and instructed the new converts to Islam. Even after the men and women who had known Muhammad died out, the dos and don'ts of Islam were passed down by word of mouth for another century.

Because of the Arab conquests, the early Muslims picked up many concepts and institutions from Roman and Persian law. Quran reciters and

Muhammad's companions gradually gave way to arbiters and judges who knew the laws and procedures of older, established empires. As the *ummah* grew and more disputes arose about people's rights and duties within this hybrid society, both the leaders and the public realized that the laws of Islam must be made clear, uniform, organized, acceptable to most Muslims, and enforceable. By the time the Abbasids took power in 750, Muslims were studying the meaning of the Quran, the life of Muhammad, and the words and deeds ascribed to him by those who had known him. Thus evolved a specifically Islamic science of right versus wrong, or jurisprudence. Its Arabic name, *fiqh*, originally meant "learning," and even now Muslims see a close connection between the *fuqaha* (experts on the Shari'ah) and the ulama (the Muslim religious scholars, or literally "those who know").

*Sources of the Law*

Historians of Islam see in the Shari'ah elements taken from many ancient legal systems, but Muslims customarily view their law as having four, or at most five, main sources: the Quran, the sunnah of Muhammad, interpretation by analogy, consensus of the *ummah*, and (for some) judicial opinion. Strictly speaking, only the first two are tangible sources. The Quran, as you know, is the record of God's revealed words to Muhammad. It contains many commandments and prohibitions, as well as value judgments on the actions of various people in history. Here are some examples. The Quran lays down explicit rules, obeyed by all Muslims up to modern times, for divorce (2:226–238), contracting debts (2:281–283), and inheriting property (4:11–17). When it describes the wickedness of the dwellers in Sodom (7:78–82), the message is implicit: Their acts are unlawful for Muslims. But the variety of human actions far exceeds what the Quran could cover. It might command people to pray, but only the example of Muhammad taught Muslims how to do so.

The Prophet's sunnah was broader than the Quran, but Muslims had to avoid certain pitfalls in order to use it as a source for the Shari'ah. How could they be sure that a certain act had been committed or enjoined by the Prophet? There had to be a *hadith* (oral report) that specified that he had done it or said it. The hadith would have to be validated by a chain of reporters *(isnad)*. The recorder of the hadith would have to say who had reported this new information, and who had told his informant, and who had told him, and so on back to the person who had witnessed the action or saying in question. The *isnad* served the function of a source footnote in a term paper; it authenticated the information by linking it to an established authority. As the hadiths were not written down until more than a century had gone by, the *isnads* served to eliminate those falsely ascribed to Muhammad. What if the *isnads*, too, were fabrications? To weed out hadiths with false *isnads*, the early ulama became quite expert on the lives of the Prophet, his family, his companions, and the first generations of Muslims. If it could be proved that one link in the chain of transmitters was weak because the person at issue was a liar or could not have known the previous transmitter, then the hadith itself was suspect. After a century of dedicated labor by many scholars, there emerged several authoritative collections of hadiths—six for Sunni Muslims and several others for the Shi'i sects. They are still being used by Muslims today.

Meanwhile, various scholars helped to formulate the Shari'ah itself. This they did by writing books that compiled the laws of Islam for reference and guidance. Because of the many changes that had occurred in the *ummah* since the Prophet's lifetime, the Quran and hadith compilations could not, most ulama thought, cover every conceivable problem. Thus they adopted reasoning by analogy, or comparing a new situation with one for which legislation already existed. Because the Quran forbids Muslims to drink wine, the ulama reasoned that all liquors having the same effect as wine should also be banned. Frequently, too, Muslim scholars relied on the consensus of the *ummah* to settle hard legal points. This is not to say that they polled every Muslim from Cordoba to Samarqand. Rather, consensus meant that which could be agreed upon by those who had studied the law. It was through this practice that many rules from older societies could be incorporated into the Shari'ah. Accordingly, the laws of Islam could cover the lives of people far removed from conditions known to Muhammad: a sailor in the Indian Ocean, a rice farmer in the marshes of lower Iraq, or a Turkish horse nomad in Transoxiana. In addition, the Shari'ah incorporated decisions that had been made by reputable judges in difficult or contested cases, much as legal precedents are used in administering Anglo-Saxon law. The resort to "judicial opinion," frequent during the Arab conquests, later became rare. Whenever they could, Muslim legists relied on the Quran and the sunnah.

## Sunni Legal Systems

The compilation of the Shari'ah into authoritative books was, at least for the Sunni majority, completed by the late ninth century. Several "rites" or systems of Sunni legal thought (*madhhabs*, a term hard to translate into

English) resulted, of which four have survived: Hanafi, Maliki, Shafi'i, and Hanbali. The Hanafi rite is the largest of the four. It grew up in Iraq under Abbasid patronage and drew heavily on consensus and judicial reasoning (in addition, of course, to the Quran and the sunnah) as sources. Today it predominates in Muslim India and Pakistan and in most of the lands formerly under the Ottoman Empire. The Maliki rite developed in Medina and made heavy use of the Prophetic hadiths that circulated there. It now prevails in Upper Egypt and in northern and western Africa. The Shafi'i rite grew up in ninth-century Egypt as a synthesis of the Hanafi and Maliki systems, but with greater stress on analogy. It was strong in Egypt and Syria at the time of Salah al-Din; it now prevails in the Muslim lands around the Indian Ocean and in Indonesia. The fourth canonical rite, that of the great jurist and theologian Ahmad ibn Hanbal (d. 855), rejected analogy, consensus, and judicial opinion as sources. Because of its strictness, the Hanbali rite has tended to have a smaller following, although its adherents have included the thinkers who inspired the modern reform movement within Islam. It is also the official legal system in present-day Saudi Arabia. Other Sunni rites that used to exist have died out. The substantive differences among the four rites are minor except in ritual matters. Each (except at times the Hanbali rite) has regarded the others as legitimate.

## Shi'i Legal Systems

Shi'i jurisprudence also relies on the Quran, the sunnah (except that any *isnad* authenticating a supporting hadith should include one of the legitimate imams), analogy, and consensus. Some differences do exist between Shi'i and Sunni Muslims regarding the authenticity of certain statements by the Prophet, notably one concerning whether he wanted Ali as his successor. In some matters Shi'i law is more permissive: It allows temporary marriage, the female line receives a slightly larger share of the inheritance, and some sects let Shi'i Muslims conceal their religious identity if their safety is at stake. The major difference is that whereas most Sunni rites no longer allow the Shari'ah to be reinterpreted, in Shi'ism the imams can interpret the law. They are regarded as being, in principle, alive. Among Twelve-Imam Shi'is, whose last imam is hidden, qualified legists called *mujtahid*s may interpret the Shari'ah until the twelfth imam returns. This "interpretation" (*ijtihad*) does not mean changing the law to suit one's temporary convenience; rather, it is the right to reexamine the Quran and the hadith compilations without being bound by consensus. In this sense,

Shi'ism has kept a flexibility long since lost by the Sunni majority, and the Shi'i ulama, especially the *mujtahids*, have remained influential up to now in such countries as Iran. Indeed, the main issue for Sunni Muslim ulama committed to Islamic reform has been to regain the right of *ijtihad*.

### Administration of the Law

At the dawn of Islamic history, the administration and enforcement of the law were handled by the caliphs or their provincial governors. As society grew more complex, they began to appoint Muslims who knew the Quran and the sunnah (as practiced by the early caliphs as well as by Muhammad) to serve as *qadis* (judges). As the judicial system evolved, an aspiring *qadi* at first got his legal training under an experienced jurist. Then schools were founded in the big city mosques for training within one (or more) of the various legal rites. The training schools for propagandists of Isma'ili Shi'ism and, later, the *madrasahs* founded by the Seljuks and other Sunni dynasties became centers for training judges and other legal experts. Students would read the law books and commentaries under the guidance of one or several masters. When they had mastered enough information to serve *qadis*, they would be certified to practice on their own.

Various other judicial offices also evolved: the *mufti* (jurisconsult), who gives authoritative answers to technical questions about the law for a court and sometimes for individuals; the *shahid* (witness), who certifies that a certain act took place, such as the signing of a contract; and the *muhtasib* (market inspector), who enforces Muslim commercial laws and maintains local order. The Muslim legal system has never had lawyers. Opposing parties are not represented by attorneys in court cases. Muslims maintain that an advocate or attorney might enrich himself at the expense of the litigant or the criminal defendant. There were also no prosecutors or district attorneys. In most cases the *qadi* had to decide from the evidence presented by the litigants and the witnesses, guided by relevant sections of the Shari'ah and sometimes by advice from a *mufti*.

The caliph had to ensure that justice prevailed in the *ummah*, not by interpreting the Shari'ah but by appointing the wisest and most honest *qadis* to administer it. True, some Umayyad caliphs might have flouted the Shari'ah in their personal lives, but its rules remained valid for the *ummah* as a whole. We must always distinguish between what people can get away with doing in their home (or palace or residence hall) and what they can do in public, in the possible presence of a police officer. No Umayyad or Abbasid caliph could abolish the Shari'ah or claim that it did not apply to him as to all other Muslims. When the caliph lost the power to appoint *qadis* and other legal officers, the various sultans and princes who took over his powers had to do so. When the caliphate ceased to symbolize Muslim unity, then everyone's acceptance of the Shari'ah bridged the barriers of contending sects and dynasties. Even when the Crusaders and Mongols entered the lands of Islam and tried to enforce other codes of conduct, Muslims continued to follow the Shari'ah in their daily lives. And to a degree that surprises some Westerners, they do so now. You can go into a bazaar (covered market) in Morocco and feel that it is, in ways you can sense even if you cannot express them, like the bazaars in Turkey, Pakistan, or forty other Muslim countries. A Sudanese student greets me with the same *salam alaykum* ("peace to you") that I have heard from Algerians and Iranians. The common performance of worship, observance of the Ramadan fast, and of course the pilgrimage to Mecca are all factors unifying Muslims from all parts of the world.

*Applicability of the Law*

But is the Shari'ah relevant today? Its laws are fixed forever, and critics claim that they cannot set the norms for human behavior in a rapidly changing world. Even in the times we have studied so far, strong rulers tried to bypass some aspects of the Shari'ah, perhaps using a clever dodge but more often by issuing secular laws, or *qanuns*. The ulama, as guardians of the Shari'ah, had no police force with which to punish such a ruler. But they could stir up public opinion, sometimes even to the point of rebellion. No ruler ever dared to change the five pillars of Islam. Until recently, none interfered with laws governing marriage, inheritance, and other aspects of personal status. Islam today must deal with the same issue facing Orthodox Judaism: How can a religion based on adherence to a divinely sanctioned code of conduct survive in a world in which many of its nation-states and leading minds no longer believe in God—or at any rate act as if they do not? Someday, perhaps, practicing Muslims, Christians, and Jews will settle their differences in order to wage war on their common enemies: secularism, hedonism, positivism, and the various ideologies that have arisen in modern times.

What parts of the Shari'ah are irrelevant? Are the marriages contracted by young people for themselves more stable than those that would have been arranged for them by their parents? Has the growing frequency of fornication and adultery in the West strengthened or weakened the family? If the family is not to be maintained, in what environment will boys

and girls be nurtured and taught how to act like men and women? Has
the blurring of sex roles in modern society made men and women hap-
pier and more secure? Should drinking intoxicating beverages be allowed,
let alone encouraged, when alcoholism has become a public health problem in most industrialized countries? Does lending money at interest
(without shared risk between the borrower and the lender) promote or
inhibit capital formation? Do gambling and other games of chance enrich
or impoverish the people who engage in them? If the appeal to jihad in
defense of Islam sounds aggressive, on behalf of what beliefs were the
most destructive wars of the twentieth century fought? Would Muslims
lead better lives if they ceased to pray, fast in Ramadan, pay *zakat*, and
make the hajj to Mecca? Let those who claim that Islam and its laws are
anachronistic try to answer these questions.

## ISLAMIC SOCIETY

In early Muslim times, social life was far more formalized than it is today.
Every class had certain rights and duties, as did each religion, sex, and age
group. The rulers were expected to preserve order and promote justice
among their subjects, to defend the *ummah* against non-Muslim powers,
and to ensure maximum production and exploitation of the wealth of
their realm. Over time, Sunni Muslims developed an elaborate political
theory. It stated that the legitimate head of state was the caliph, who must
be an adult male, sound in body and mind, and descended from the
Quraysh tribe. His appointment should be publicly approved by other
Muslims. In practice, though, the assent given to a man's becoming caliph
might be no more than his own. Some of the caliphs were young boys. A
few were insane. Eventually, the caliphal powers were taken over by *vezirs*,
provincial governors, or military adventurers. But the fiction was maintained, for the Sunni legists agreed that it was better to be governed by a
usurper or a despot than to have no ruler at all. The common saying was
that a thousand years of tyranny was preferable to one day of anarchy.

The abuse of political power was often checked by the moral authority
of the ulama. The rulers were expected to work with the classes commonly called the "men of the pen" and the "men of the sword." The men
of the pen were the administrators who collected and disbursed the state
revenues and carried out the rulers' orders, plus the ulama who provided
justice, education, and various welfare services to Muslims. The Christian
clergy and the Jewish rabbinate had functions in their religious communities similar to those of the ulama. The men of the sword expanded and

defended the lands of Islam and also, especially after the ninth century, managed land grants and maintained local order.

### Social Groupings

Strictly speaking, Muslims dislike class differentials, but the concept of ruler and subject was taken over from the Sasanid rulers of pre-Islamic Persia. The great majority of the people belonged to the subject class, which was expected to produce the wealth of the *ummah*. The most basic division of subjects was between nomads and settled peoples, with the former group further divided into countless tribes and clans and the latter broken down into many occupational groups. Urban merchants and artisans formed trade guilds, often tied to specific religious sects or Sufi orders (brotherhoods of Muslim mystics), which promoted their common interests. The largest group was made up of farmers, generally lower in status and usually not full owners of the lands that they farmed. There were also slaves. Some served in the army or the bureaucracy, others worked for merchants or manufacturers, and still others were household servants. Plantations using slave labor were rare. Islam did not proscribe slavery, which existed in seventh-century Arabia, but it called on masters to treat their slaves kindly and encouraged their liberation. Slaves could be prisoners of war, children who had been sold by their families, or captives taken from their homes by slave dealers. These concepts of class structure did not originate in Islam, which stressed the equality of all believers; they went back to ancient times. Analogous classes have existed in nearly all agrarian societies.

Crossing these horizontal social divisions were vertical ones based on ancestry, race, religion, and sex. Although some hadiths showed that Muhammad and his companions wanted to play down distinctions based on family origins, early Islam did accord higher status to descendants of the first Muslims, or of Arabs generally, than to later converts to the religion. As you have read in previous chapters, Persians and then Turks gradually rose to equal status with Arabs. Other ethnic groups, such as Berbers, Indians, and Africans, kept a distinct identity and often a lower status even after they converted to Islam. Racial discrimination, however, was less acute than it has been in Christian lands in modern times.

The divisions based on religion, though, were deep and fundamental. Religion was a corporate experience—a community of believers bound together by adherence to a common set of laws and beliefs, rather than a private and personal relationship between each person and his or her maker. Religion and politics were inextricably intertwined. Christians and Jews did not have the same rights and duties as Muslims; they were protected communities living within the realm of Islam, where the Shari'ah prevailed. Though exempt from military duty, they were forbidden to bear arms. They did not have to pay *zakat*, but they were assessed the head tax (*jizyah*) plus whatever levies were needed to maintain their own religious institutions. They were sometimes not allowed to testify in a Shari'ah court against a Muslim or to ring bells or to blow shofars (rams' horns used at certain Jewish holidays) or to hold noisy processions that might disrupt Muslim worship. At times they found the limitations even more humiliating, and in a few cases their lives and property were threatened. But for centuries they managed to keep their identity as Jews or Christians and to follow their own laws and beliefs. The treatment of religious minorities in Muslim countries that upheld the Shari'ah was better than in those that watered it down or abandoned it totally and much, much better than the treatment of Jews in medieval Christendom, czarist Russia, or Nazi Germany.

As for social divisions based on gender, Islam (like most religions that grew up in the agrarian age) is patriarchal and hence gives certain rights and responsibilities to men that it denies to women. Muslims believe that biology has dictated different roles for the two sexes. Men are supposed to govern states, wage war, and support their families; women to bear and rear children, manage their households, and obey their husbands. Traditional history has little to say about women; a few took part in wars and governments, wrote poems, or had profound mystical experiences, but most played second fiddle to their husbands, fathers, brothers, or sons. Often they were more influential than the traditional histories admit.

## IMPORTANCE OF FAMILY LIFE

As you may have guessed, the family played the main role in early Islamic society. Marriages were arranged by the parents or by the oldest living relatives of the potential couple, for it was understood that a marriage would tie two families together or tighten the bonds between two branches of the same house. Marriages between cousins were preferred because they helped keep the family's property intact. Muslims assumed that love between a man and a woman would develop once they were married and had to share the cares of maintaining a household and rearing children. Romantic love did arise between unmarried persons, but it rarely led to marriage. The freedom of Muslim men to take additional wives (up to a total of four) caused some domestic strife, but many an older wife rejoiced when her husband took a younger one who could better bear the strains of frequent pregnancy and heavy housework. The "harem" of the Western imagination was rare. Only the rich and powerful man could afford to support the four wives allowed him by the Quran (provided he treated them equally); many poor men could not afford any, as the groom had to pay a large dowry. Islamic law made divorce easy for husbands and almost impossible for wives, but in practice divorce was rare, because the wife was permitted to keep the dowry. A Muslim marriage contract might discourage divorce by specifying that the groom must present a part of the dowry to his bride at once and the rest only if he later divorced her.

Another point worth making about family life is that parents expected (and received) the unquestioning obedience of their sons and daughters, even after they had grown up. Once a woman married, she had also to defer to her husband's parents. Women naturally wanted to bear sons, who would eventually give them daughters-in-law to boss around. Parents disciplined their children harshly but loved them deeply and, if those children were among the few to survive the rigors of growing up, took great pride in their later achievements. Although a boy usually learned his father's trade, the gifted son of a peasant or merchant could get an education and move into the ranks of the ulama or the bureaucracy. Likewise, a *vezir*'s son might prove to be a bum. Girls had few opportunities to get an education, but certain occupations were limited to women, and wives often worked beside their husbands in the fields or in domestic industries, such as spinning. Ties among brothers, sisters, and cousins had an intensity (usually love, sometimes hate) that is rare in the Western experience, because Muslim youths spent so much of their free time within the family circle.

## Personal Relationships

Even social ties outside the household were probably more intense than in our culture. The individual in early Islamic society knew fewer people than in our more mobile world, but his or her friendships (and enmities) tended to be stronger and more lasting. Physical as well as verbal expressions of endearment between same-sex friends were commoner than in the West and did not have to mean homosexuality (although such relationships did exist). Men's friendships were usually based on childhood ties or common membership in a mystic brotherhood, trade guild, or athletic club. Women's associations were limited by custom to kinfolk and neighbors, but they had mystic sisterhoods, too.

Both men and women entertained their friends, segregated by sex, at home. Mutual visiting, at which food and drink were shared and news exchanged, was the most common pastime for every class in Islamic society. The customary time for these visits was late afternoon or early evening as the weather cooled off, or at night during the month of Ramadan. Large groups of men (or women) liked to gather at someone's house to listen to poetry recitations or, less often, musical performances. Both sexes liked picnics; Egypt and Persia retained pre-Islamic holidays that required making a spring trip into the countryside for an outdoor meal. The two great Muslim festivals, the Feast of (Abraham's) Sacrifice during the hajj month and the Feast of Fast-breaking that follows Ramadan, were major social occasions everywhere. People often gave lavish parties to celebrate births, circumcisions, and weddings. Funeral processions, burials, and postburial receptions also played a big part in the social life of Muslims. Although a death was naturally mourned, survivors consoled themselves with the conviction that the deceased would soon be with God. Men also used to meet in mosques, bazaars, public baths, and restaurants. Women often saw their friends at the women's baths, at the public well where they drew their water, or at the stream where they did their laundry. Compared with our society, early Muslims had less freedom and privacy but more security and less loneliness.

## Food, Clothing, and Shelter

The foods early Muslims ate, the clothes they wore, and the houses in which they lived varied according to their economic condition, locality, and the era in question, so it is hard to generalize about how they met their most basic needs. Wheat was the chief cereal grain. It was usually ground at a mill, kneaded at home, and baked in small flat loaves in large communal or commercial ovens. Bulgur or parched wheat was used in cooking, especially in Syria and Palestine. Bedouins ate wheat gruel or porridge. Rice was rarer than now; corn and potatoes were unknown. Many fruits and vegetables were eaten fresh; others were dried, pickled in vinegar, or preserved in sugar. Milk from sheep, goats, camels, water buffaloes, and cows was turned into cheese, butter (clarified for use in cooking), and yogurt. The meat Muslims ate most often was lamb or mutton, commonly roasted, baked, or stewed. Various animal organs not highly prized by Westerners, such as eyes, brains, hearts, and testicles, were considered delicacies. Pork was forbidden to Muslims, as were fermented beverages. Lax Muslims drank wine made from grapes and other fruits, beer, and *araq* (fermented liquor from date palm sap, molasses, or rice). The observant majority drank fruit juices in season, sherbet (originally snow mixed with rose water or fruit syrup), and diluted yogurt. Coffee and tea did not come into widespread use until the seventeenth century. Middle Eastern food was moderately spiced, usually with salt, pepper, olive oil, and lemon juice. Saffron was used for its yellow coloring more than for its flavor, because Muslim cooks liked to enhance the appearance of their dishes. Honey served as a sweetener, but sugar cultivation gradually spread through the Muslim world from India.

Clothing had to be both modest and durable. Linen or cotton clothes were worn in hot weather and woolen ones in the winter—or throughout the year by some mystics and nomads. Loose-fitting robes were preferred to trousers, except by horseback riders, who wore baggy pants. Both sexes shunned clothing that might reveal their bodily contours to strangers. Early Muslim men covered their heads in all formal situations, with either turbans or various types of brimless caps. Different colored turbans served to identify status; for instance, green singled out a man who had made the hajj to Mecca. Arab nomads wore flowing *kufiyah*s (headcloths) bound by headbands. Muslims never wore hats with brims and caps with visors, as they would have impeded prostration during worship. Women used some type of long cloth to cover their hair, if not also to veil their faces, whenever male strangers might be present. Jews, Christians, and other minorities wore distinctive articles of clothing and headgear. Because the ways in which people dressed showed their religion and status, strangers knew how to act toward one another.

Houses were constructed from those materials that were most plentiful locally: stone, mud brick, or sometimes wood. High ceilings and windows provided ventilation in hot weather. In the winter, only warm clothing, hot food, and an occasional charcoal brazier made indoor life bearable. Many houses were built around courtyards that had gardens, fountains, and small pools. Rooms were not filled with furniture; people were used to sitting cross-legged on carpets or low platforms. Mattresses and other bedding would be rolled out when people were ready to sleep and put away after they got up. In rich people's houses, cooking facilities were often in separate enclosures. Privies always were.

## INTELLECTUAL LIFE

Time and space limitations prevent me from giving to the intellectual life of early Islam all the attention it deserves. Regrettably, many Westerners still believe that the Arab conquest of the Middle East stifled its artistic, literary, and scientific creativity. On the contrary, it was the Arabs who saved many of the works of Plato, Aristotle, and other Greek thinkers for later transmission to the West. In fact, no field of intellectual endeavor was closed to Muslim scholars. Although the Quran is not a philosophical treatise, nor Muhammad a philosopher, the Arab conquests brought Muslims into contact with the philosophical ideas of the Hellenistic world. Having flourished earlier in the neoplatonist academy of Alexandria and its Sasanid counterpart in Jundishapur, Hellenistic philosophy found its way into Mamun's Bayt al-Hikmah in ninth-century Baghdad. The encyclopedic writings of Aristotle, translated by Syrian Christians into Arabic, inspired such Muslim thinkers as al-Kindi, al-Farabi, Ibn Sina (Avicenna), and Ibn Rushd (Averroës).

As "Philosopher of the Arabs," Kindi (d. 873) rated the search for truth above all human occupations except religion, exalted logic and mathematics, and wrote or edited many works on science, psychology, medicine, and music. He was adept at taking complex Greek concepts, paraphrasing them, and simplifying them for students, a skill any textbook writer can appreciate. Everything Kindi did was done even better by Abu-Nasr al-Farabi (d. 950), a Baghdad-educated Turk who won such renown that later philosophers called him the "second teacher," the first having been Aristotle. Farabi was the first to integrate neoplatonic philosophy with Islamic concepts of God, angels, prophecy, and community. A prolific writer on logic, he was also a skilled musician.

Ibn Sina (d. 1037) also combined philosophy with medicine. His theological writings are unusually lucid and logical, though his devout contemporaries shunned them because he separated the body from the soul and claimed that every person has free will. He stated that the highest form of human happiness is not physical but spiritual, aiming at communion with God. His scientific writings include what amounts to an encyclopedia of medical lore. Translated into Latin, this work remained a textbook in European medical schools up to the seventeenth century. Like Kindi, he wrote on logic, mathematics, and music. The greatest Muslim writer of commentaries lived in twelfth-century Spain. Ibn Rushd (d. 1198) is noted for his works on the philosophy of Aristotle and on Muslim theologians. Because of his unorthodox religious views, many of his writings were burned, and some of his original contributions to knowledge may have been forever lost.

## THEOLOGY

Like medieval Christianity, Islam had to settle some burning issues: Does divine revelation take precedence over human reason? Is God the creator of all the evil as well as all the good in the universe? If God is all-powerful, why are people allowed to deny God's existence and disobey divine laws? If God has predestined all human acts, what moral responsibility do people have for what they do? Philosophical questions led Muslims into theology, as did disputations with their Jewish and Christian subjects, who were often more sophisticated than they.

Islam developed several systems of scholastic theology, climaxing with the Mu'tazilah (mentioned in Chapter 6), the system of the self-styled "people of unity and justice." Their main tenets are: (1) God is one, so His attributes have no independent existence; (2) He is just, rewarding the righteous and punishing the wicked; (3) He is not the author of evil; (4) man, responsible for his own actions, is not a tool in God's hand; (5) only reason, which agrees with revelation, can guide man to a knowledge of God; (6) it is right to try to justify the ways of God to man; and (7) the Quran was created. If such tenets seem reasonable, you may wonder why some Muslims rejected them. For example, was the Quran really created? It must have been known to God before Gabriel revealed it to Muhammad. How could God exist without divine knowledge? If God has always existed, then His speech (the Quran) must also have been around since time began, not having been created like all other things. Muslims have always revered the Quran as the means by which to know God; it occupies a place in Islam somewhat like that of Jesus in Christianity. On the issue of free will, if all people will be rewarded or punished for what they do, what will happen to babies and small children who die before they have learned to obey or to flout God's will? If the innocents automatically go to Heaven, is this fair to those who strove all their lives to obey the laws of Islam? Despite these objections, the Mu'tazilah was for a while the Abbasids' official theology, but its advocates attacked dissident Muslims so fiercely that a reaction set in, new ideas took hold, and the movement died out.

The reaction against the Mu'tazilites was spearheaded by Ahmad ibn Hanbal, founder of the Sunni legal system that bears his name, for he opposed their application of rigid logic to the Quran and the laws of Islam. His writings influenced a major theo logian named al-Ash'ari (d. 935). Though trained as a Mu'tazilite, Ash'ari, deeply concerned with God's justice, concluded that divine revelation was a better guide than reason for human action. The Quran, he argued, was an attribute of God—eternally existent yet separate from God's existence. Faith was absolute. If the Quran mentioned God's hand (or other human features), this allusion must be accepted as is—"without specifying how" or even interpreting the words allegorically, as the Mu'tazilites and some later theologians tried to do. Finally, Ash'ari and his disciples accepted the complete omnipotence of God: Everything people do is predestined, for God created all persons and all their actions; yet God assigned these actions to them in such a way that individuals remain accountable for what they do. Later Muslim theologians proved that Muhammad must have been God's messenger because no human being could imitate the content and style of the Quran. The capstone of early Muslim theology was the work of Abu-Hamid al-Ghazali (d. 1111), one of the greatest law teachers in Baghdad. His main achievement as a theologian was his use of Aristotelian logic to prove the main tenets of Islam, but he also wrote a stinging attack on Muslim philosophers. Among Muslims he is best remembered for harmonizing law, theology, and Sufism.

## Mysticism

Sufism is an experience, a path into the real nature of things, and ultimately to God. Defining it (as I did) as "organized Muslim mysticism" is perhaps too prosaic. Some Muslims scorn Sufism as a nonrational perversion of Islam; others make it the essence of their faith. Some Sufis regard their beliefs and practices as universal, hence no more (or less) Islamic than they are Buddhist, Christian, or Zoroastrian. Each religion, they say, contains the germ of ultimate truth; but when controlled by an unsympathetic and worldly hierarchy, a religion can degenerate into a meaningless cult. Sufis seek to uncover meaning that is veiled from our senses and impenetrable to human reason. In monotheistic religions such as Islam, finding ultimate truth is called communion with God. This communion can be achieved through meditation or esoteric rites, such as prolonged fasting, night vigils, controlled breathing, repetition of words, or whirling for hours in one spot.

Islam always contained elements of mystical spirituality, but Sufism emerged as a distinct movement during the second century after the *hijrah*. At first it was a movement of ascetics, people who sought to exalt their souls by denying themselves the comforts of the flesh. Their driving force was a strong fear of God, but this fear later evolved into belief in God's love. Sufism could cut through the intellectualism of theology and soften the legalism of "formal" Sunni (or Shi'i) Islam. It did not—as some modern writers claim—negate the Shari'ah. Rather, it complemented the exoteric law with an esoteric path. Sufi leaders, such as Ghazali, spoke of the *fiqh* of the heart as the inner version of the *fiqh* of the world. Sufism also enabled Islam to absorb some of the customs of converts from other religions without damaging its own essential doctrines—a capacity that facilitated Islam's spread to Central Asia, Anatolia, southeastern Europe, India, Indonesia, and Africa south of the Sahara. From the eleventh century to the nineteenth, Sufism dominated the spiritual life of most Muslims. Brotherhoods (and sisterhoods) of mystics, also called Sufi orders, grew up throughout the *ummah*, providing a new basis for social cohesion. The Safavid dynasty, which ruled Iran from 1501 to 1736, began as a Sufi order. Sufism also held together the warrior *ghazi*s who founded the Safavid dynasty's better-known rival, the Ottoman Empire. The Safavids were Shi'is and the Ottomans Sunnis; indeed, both of the main branches of Islam could accommodate Sufism.

### Review of Muslim Divisions

Let me go over with you the various bases of division within Islam. The first is political: After Muhammad died, should the leaders have been chosen by the *ummah* or taken from the male members of his household? The second, overlapping somewhat with the first, is legal: Which rite or system of jurisprudence can best guide the conduct of individual and communal Muslim life? The third raises theological issues: To what extent can people apply reason to expressing or arguing about Islamic beliefs? Is God responsible for human actions, or is each person accountable for what he or she does? The fourth can be termed spiritual: To what degree, if any, should Islamic practice include mysticism, or the search for hidden meanings not contained in outwardly tangible aspects of religion? Do not treat the resulting sectarian divisions as watertight compartments. For instance, an eleventh-century Egyptian could be a Sunni Muslim adhering to the Maliki rite and to Ash'ari's theology, and practicing Sufism within a mystic brotherhood, even while being ruled by the Shi'i Fatimids.

### Mathematics and Science

I alluded to mathematics, science, and medicine while discussing Islamic philosophy, for early Muslims did not split up the areas of human knowledge as finely as we do now. We tend to appreciate Muslim thinkers, if at all, for preserving classical learning until the West could relearn it during the Renaissance. Our debt is really much greater. Muslim mathematicians made advances in algebra, plane and spherical trigonometry, and the geometry of planes, spheres, cones, and cylinders. Our "Arabic numerals" were a Hindu invention, but Arabs transmitted them to Europe. Muslims were using decimal fractions at least two centuries before Westerners knew about them. They applied mathematics to business accounting, land surveying, astronomical calculations, mechanical devices, and military engineering.

In medicine the Muslims built on the work of the ancient Greeks, but they were especially indebted to Nestorian Christians. One of these was Hunayn ibn Ishaq (d. 873), who translated many Greek and Aramaic texts into Arabic but did his greatest work in the science of optics. I mentioned already Europe's use of Ibn Sina's work as a medical textbook. As a further illustration of the influence of Middle Eastern medicine, I might refer to the drawings in Vesalius's pioneering work on anatomy, which show many parts of the body labeled with Arabic and Hebrew terms. Physicians in early Islamic society studied both botany and chemistry to discover curative drugs as well as antidotes to various poisons.

Scientific and pseudoscientific methods of observation were often closely tied together. Chemistry would be mixed with alchemy and astronomy with astrology. A knowledge of the movements of stars and planets aided navigation and overland travel by night. But early Muslims, like most other peoples, thought that heavenly bodies affected the lives of individuals, cities, and states, and thus many of the caliphs kept court astrologers as advisers. Muslims also used astrolabes (devices for measuring the height of stars in the sky) and built primitive versions of the telescope. One astronomer is said to have built a planetarium that reproduced not only the movements of stars but also peals of thunder and flashes of lightning. Long before Copernicus or Galileo expounded their theories, Muslim scientists, though not the public, knew that the earth was round and that it revolved around the sun.

To come closer to earth, descriptive geography was a favorite subject of the early Muslims. Thanks to the Arab conquests and the expansion of trade throughout the eastern hemisphere, they liked to read books describing far-off lands and their inhabitants, especially if they were potential trading partners or converts to Islam. Much of what we know about Africa south of the Sahara from the ninth to the fifteenth centuries comes from the writings of Arab travelers and geographers. History was a major discipline, too. Nearly all Muslim scientists wrote accounts of the earlier development of their specialties. Rulers demanded chronicles either to publicize what they had done or to learn from their predecessors' successes and failures. Many Muslims read accounts of the early caliphs and conquests for amusement as well as instruction. Muslim historians were the first to try to structure history by looking for patterns in the rise and fall of dynasties, peoples, and civilizations. These efforts culminated in the fourteenth century with Ibn Khaldun's monumental *Muqaddimah*, which linked the rise of states with a strong group feeling (*asabiyah*) between the leaders and their supporters.

## Literature

Every subject I have discussed so far in this survey is part of the prose literature of the Muslim peoples. Although Arabic remained the major language of both prose and poetry, Persian revived during the Abbasid era, and Turkish literature emerged a little later. Poetry was a major means of artistic expression, instruction, and popular entertainment. There were poems that praised a tribe, a religion, or a potential patron; some that poked fun at the poet's rivals; others that evoked God's power or the exaltation of a mystical experience; and still others that extolled love, wine, and God, or sometimes all three (you cannot always be sure which).

Prose works were written to guide Muslims in the performance of worship, instruct princes in the art of ruling, refute the claims of rival political or theological movements, or teach any of the thousand and one aspects of living, from cooking to lovemaking. Animal fables scored points against despotic rulers, ambitious courtiers, naive ulama, and greedy merchants. You may have read the popular stories that we call *The Arabian Nights*, set in Harun al-Rashid's Baghdad but actually composed by many ancient peoples, passed down by word of mouth to the Arabs, and gradually set to paper in the late Middle Ages. But you may not have heard of a literary figure beloved by many Middle Eastern peoples. The Egyptians call him Goha, the Persians say he is Mollah Nasroddin, and the Turks refer to him as Nasroddin Hoja. One brief story must suffice. A man once complained to Goha that there was no sunlight in his house. "Is there sunlight in your garden?" asked Goha. "Yes," the other replied. "Well," said Goha, "then move your house into your garden."

## Art

Muslims do not neglect the visual arts. Some of the best proportioned and most lavishly decorated buildings ever erected were the large congregational mosques in Islam's greatest cities. They had to be monumental to accommodate all their adult male worshipers on Fridays. Some have not survived the ravages of either time or the Mongols, but the congregational mosques of Qayrawan, Cairo, Damascus, and Isfahan are impressive enough. Muslim architects also devoted some of their time and talents to palaces, schools, hospitals, caravanserais, and other buildings, as well as to gardens, reflecting pools, and fountains. Artists worked in many different media. Although painting and sculpture were rare until modern times, early Muslim artists did illustrate manuscripts with abstract designs, beautiful pictures of plants and animals, and depictions of the everyday and ceremonial activities of men and women. Calligraphy (handwriting) was the most important art form, used for walls of public buildings as well as for manuscripts. Many artistic creations were in media we usually regard as crafts: glazed pottery and tile work; enameled glass; objects carved from wood, stone, and ivory; incised metal trays; elaborate jeweled rings, pendants, and daggers; embroidered silk cloths; and tooled-leather bookbindings. You have doubtless seen some "oriental" carpets. Most of the genuine ones were woven or knotted in Middle Eastern countries.

## CONCLUSION

The social, cultural, and intellectual life of early Islam was so rich and varied that it defies rapid description. The Muslim peoples of the Middle East drew on their own pre-Islamic traditions and those of the various civilizations that they encountered, many of which had been flourishing for centuries. They absorbed the customs and ideas that fit in with their basic belief in the unity of God and the mission of Muhammad. The others they rejected. Over many centuries and under many dynasties they went on developing and enriching this multifaceted civilization, through trade and manufacturing, the spoken and written word, the erection of imposing mosques and the design of refreshing gardens, and the formulation of lofty theological and philosophical ideas. Even the destruction of Baghdad and other great cities during the Mongol invasions did not stop these processes. Nor did centuries of Muslim-Christian warfare stop Europe from learning the arts and sciences of Islam at the dawn of the Renaissance. In fact, the apogee of Muslim power and artistic expression was not reached until the sixteenth century, the gunpowder era that will be the subject of Chapter 9.

# NINE

# Firearms, Slaves, and Empires

Because we tend to equate the history of the Middle East with that of the Arabs, we assume that Muslim military might, political power, and artistic elegance all peaked sometime before the Mongol conquests. This is wrong. To be sure, the Mongols abused Muslims in thirteenth-century Transoxiana and Khwarizm, Khurasan and Persia, Iraq and Syria. Their record for mass murder and destruction stood unbroken until the time of Hitler and Stalin. Their champion wrecker, Hulegu, hated Islam generally and its political claims specifically. Yet his descendants, the Il-Khanid dynasty, converted to Islam within half a century and adopted Persian culture. Indirectly, Hulegu and his heirs laid the groundwork for a succession of Muslim military states: the Mamluks in Egypt and Syria, the Safavids in Persia and Iraq, the Timurids in Central Asia and later in India (where they became known as the Mughals), and most notably the Ottoman Empire, which ruled the Balkans, Anatolia, and most of the Arab lands up to modern times.

What do firearms have to do with Muslim empires? None of the states I have just listed started out using them. I chose this title because all those that took power after the Il-Khanids either learned to use firearms or died out because their enemies had done so. The harnessing of gunpowder, used in fireworks since ancient times, transformed the nature of European and Middle Eastern politics and society. Once this change occurred, in the fourteenth century roughly, any army or navy that failed to adapt to the use of firearms in sieges and later in battles got crushed. Cannons and muskets required disciplined foot soldiers trained to load, fire, and maintain them. The need to recruit, train, and pay foot soldiers led to the rise of central governments and the fall of feudal lords who fought on horseback and protected themselves with plated armor and walled castles. The states that successfully made the transition to the gunpowder age were those that strengthened their administrative and commercial classes at the expense of the landowning aristocracy. No Middle Eastern country succeeded as well in this as England and Holland. The one that came closest was the Ottoman Empire.

Because the Middle East is so central within the Afro-Eurasian landmass, the area is apt to be measured during any given period by military yardsticks: Were its governments strong or weak? Did they win wars or lose them? Did they gain land or give it up? Did their soldiers go into foreign territories, or did other armies occupy their lands? Although this chapter has no defined beginning and ending dates, it could start with a Muslim victory, that of the Mamluks over the Mongols at Ayn Jalut in 1260, and terminate in 1699, the date of a widely recognized Muslim defeat, when the Ottoman Empire ceded Hungary to Habsburg Austria. Between these two dates, the Muslims recovered from the Mongol shock, formed new political institutions, expanded the lands of Islam by taking the Balkans and parts of India and by peacefully penetrating West Africa and Southeast Asia, reached new heights of prosperity, and built monumental works of art—such as the Taj Mahal—that still set a standard for created beauty.

## THE MAMLUKS

You may recall from Chapter 7 that the Mamluks who saved Egypt from the Mongol menace in 1260 were Turkish ex-slaves who had recently seized power from the Ayyubids, the descendants of Salah al-Din. This illustrious ruler had adopted the practice of many Muslim dynasties, going back to the Abbasids, of importing Turkish boys (*mamluks*, or "owned men") from Central Asia and training them to be soldiers. Under Salah al-Din's descendants, the Mamluks became the largest group within the Ayyubid armies. In the thirteenth century, Egypt, not Jerusalem, bore the brunt of the Crusader attacks. The Seventh Crusade, led by France's King Louis IX (later "Saint Louis"), occupied the coastal town of Damietta in 1249 and was about to take Mansurah when the Ayyubids sent the Mamluks to stop his forces. In the process, the Mamluks captured Louis and his army. Back in Cairo, meanwhile, the Ayyubid sultan died, with his son and heir presumptive far away. For six months his widow, Shajar al-Durr, concealed his death and ruled in his name. When the son returned to Cairo, the dominant Mamluk faction, seeing that he preferred a rival group, killed him before he could ascend the throne. The murderers proceeded to make Shajar al-Durr the new sultan—one of the few times in Islamic history that a woman has ruled in her own name—but in reality the

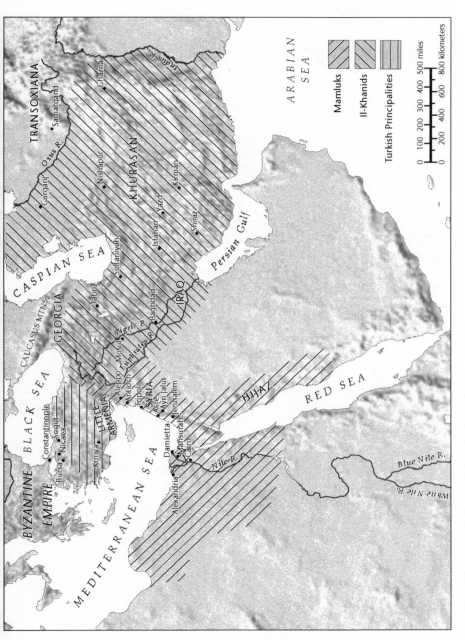

MAP 5 The Mamluks and the Il-Khanids circa 1300

Mamluks took over (see Map 5). Their commander made this clear when he married Shajar al-Durr a few months later.

## The Mamluk Ruling System

The Mamluks developed a succession pattern unique in Middle East history. Although a son would often succeed his father as sultan, he usually (especially after 1382) had only a brief reign during which the major factions would fight for power. As soon as one Mamluk party had defeated the others, its leader would seize the sultanate. It should have been the worst governmental system in history; oddly enough, it worked for more than 250 years.

One reason was that it enabled several gifted leaders to rise to the top and stay there. My favorite example is Baybars (r. 1260–1277), who had served his predecessor as one of his generals at Ayn Jalut. Soon after the victory, he killed his master and conned the other Mamluks into accepting him as their new sultan. Ever mindful of the Mongol threat to the east, Baybars tried to bring much of Syria under Mamluk control. This meant absorbing a few lands still under Ayyubid princes, reducing the Crusaders' territories to a coastal strip (they held Acre until 1291), and ravaging the kingdom of Little Armenia, the Mongols' most faithful ally. But Baybars did not let religion or nationality stop him from making useful alliances. He courted the Byzantines and the Christian rulers of Aragon, Sicily, and several Italian city-states, all of which became Egypt's trading partners. He sided with the Mongols in Russia—the Golden Horde (which had become Muslim)—against their Il-Khanid cousins in Persia. Baybars made Egypt the richest Muslim state. He also took in a fugitive Abbasid prince from Baghdad and proclaimed him caliph, thereby gaining some prestige. But Muslims cared more that Baybars earned the title of "Servant of the Two Holy Cities," when Mecca and Medina accepted Mamluk sovereignty. The implication of this title was that until those cities were taken by the Ottoman Empire in 1517, any Muslim making the hajj passed through Mamluk lands.

It has become so normal for army officers to seize power in the Middle East that modern readers may picture Baybars as a thirteenth-century prototype for Saddam Husayn. But there is a difference. Baybars set up a lasting political system. Only lately have Muslim and Western scholars begun to find the secrets of Mamluk power and endurance. A mamluk, as you know, is a slave. Slavery in early Islam was not as bad as we tend to think, for it often enabled gifted young men to rise to power through the army or the bureaucracy. In remote Middle Eastern areas—the steppes of

Central Asia (home of the Turks and the Mongols), the eastern shore of the Black Sea (inhabited by Circassians), the northern Zagros Mountains (Kurdistan), and even the Mediterranean islands—lived families that were willing to let their sons go, via slave traders, to serve Muslim rulers. In the thirteenth and fourteenth centuries, the greatest source of new mamluks was the Kipchak Turkic tribe. Then, after 1382, the Circassians took the lead, sending their sons to the barracks and their daughters to the harems of Muslim sultans and *amirs* (princes).

A boy usually became a mamluk when he was between ten and twelve, not yet adolescent but old enough to take care of himself and to learn to ride a horse, if indeed he had not been riding since he was old enough to walk. He would be sold into the service of the reigning sultan (if he was lucky), or to one of the amirs, and put into a barrack or dormitory with other mamluks his own age. All the boys would receive basic instruction in Islam and Arabic. They would be drilled in the care and riding of horses, taught to fight with lances and swords, and trained in archery. This rigorous education lasted eight to ten years, during which the youths were kept under the strictest discipline (a visit to the public baths was the high point of their week), but each cohort developed a feeling of unity that lasted the rest of their lives. Each mamluk, upon completing his military training, received his liberation paper, a horse, and his fighting equipment.

Even as a freed soldier of fortune, though, the mamluk stayed loyal to the sultan or amir who had trained and liberated him, to his teachers and proctors, and to the men who had gone through training with him. Each cohort of trainees tended to become a faction within the army, rather like a house in a boarding school or a pledge class in a fraternity. If the master died or lost his position, often his mamluks would suffer demotion or exile rather than attach themselves to someone else. Not surprisingly, the leaders of mamluk factions formed larger alliances, took power, and became amirs or, after 1250, sultans. In other words, men who had themselves been trained as mamluks often became the owners and trainers of new mamluk boys from Central Asia or the Caucasus mountains. The ties between master and mamluk were much like those within a family. In fact, few sons of mamluks entered the system. Those who did ranked below the sultan's mamluks and even those of the amir; they preferred to become ulama or administrators. Succession to the sultanate was seldom hereditary. The Mamluk sultans rose through the ranks of the sultan's mamluks. Their ability to reach the top depended on their military skills and political acumen. No Muslim dynasty that you have studied so far managed to rule Egypt and Syria for as long as the Mamluks did.

## The Decline of the Mamluks

In time, however, favoritism replaced advancement by ability, the rigor of the mamluks' training declined, and the quality of Mamluk rule (especially under the fifteenth-century Circassian sultans) deteriorated. The system caused the mamluks to crave wealth and power, and, in fact, they amassed huge estates. They also taxed free peasants and merchants so heavily that many ran away to become nomads. The Black Death and other epidemics reduced the population of Egypt and Syria by two-thirds. Mamluk attempts to monopolize commerce in luxury goods so antagonized both European Christians and Asian Muslims that the lucrative trade routes began shifting away from Egypt during the fifteenth century. By the way, the Mamluks' killing of the goose that laid their golden eggs led to Portugal's efforts to sail around Africa and also to Columbus's voyages to the Americas. At a time when other armies were adopting cannons and muskets, the Mamluks relegated the use of firearms to minor corps of mercenary foot soldiers and continued to fight on horseback, wielding their accustomed swords and spears, and shooting with bows and arrows. This failure to keep up with developments in military technology caused their dramatic defeat by the disciplined Ottoman army in 1516 and 1517.

## THE MONGOL IL-KHANIDS

The Mamluks' first rivals were the Il-Khanids, descendants of the Mongol conquerors of Iraq and Persia. Their founder, Hulegu (d. 1265), established his capital at Tabriz. He had good reasons for this choice: Tabriz was in the Azerbaijan highlands, it was close to the Great Silk Route leading to China and to southeast Europe, and it was also near large concentrations of Christians then remaining in Anatolia and northern Iraq. You will see that this proximity to other ethnic and religious groups raises an interesting issue.

## THE RELIGIOUS ISSUE

The 64,000-dinar question for Hulegu and his successors was which religion they would adopt, now that they were living among sedentarized peoples. They might well have become Christian. Indeed, Europeans believed that somewhere beyond the lands of Islam they might find a mighty Christian ruler, whom they called "Prester John." They hoped that this potentate—mythical, of course—would attack the Muslim menace from the rear and save Western Christendom. In the late thirteenth century Prester John was thought to be a Mongol; two centuries later Europeans would seek him in Ethiopia. Driven by this strange combination of hope and fear, the popes of this era sent missions to make contact with the Mongol empires, open trade with them, and, if possible, convert them. The Roman church had little at the time to offer the Mongols, but some did adopt a form of Christianity already common in Iraq, Persia, and Central Asia—namely, Nestorianism. The Mongols also allied themselves with Georgians, Armenians, and other Middle Eastern Christians during their assault on Islam. The late thirteenth century was the last golden age for such Christian sects as the Nestorians and the Jacobites (Syrian Monophysites). Later, their political power and level of learning declined, and most of the world forgot about them.

Most of the early Il-Khanids preferred Buddhism, with which the Mongols had long been familiar. Buddhist temples were erected in many Persian towns, and saffron-robed priests seemed as numerous as turbaned ulama. But the Il-Khanids tolerated all faiths and did not try to convert Muslims, clearly the majority of their subjects. In time, tribal Mongols intermarried with Turkish or Persian Muslims, adopted their language, and then took on their religion. The death in 1294 of Qubilai Khan (the "Kubla Khan" of Coleridge's poem) severed the remaining ties between the Il-Khanids and the great Mongol Empire, which was now becoming just one more "Chinese" dynasty. A year later, a new Il-Khanid ruler, Ghazan Khan (r. 1295–1304), formally embraced Islam. Persian Buddhism, an exotic growth, soon shriveled and died.

Ghazan and his successors converted temples into mosques and repaired much of the damage done to Persia by their ancestors. Ghazan's successors proved to be weaker, conflicts broke out between Sunni and Shi'i factions, and by 1360 Il-Khanid rule had fragmented and vanished.

### Effects of Il-Khanid Rule on Persia

The Mongol era was not so tragic a chapter in Persia's history as we might imagine from the massacres and destruction caused by Jenghiz Khan and Hulegu. Even before they became Muslims, the Il-Khanids encouraged and supported architects, artists, poets, and scholars. Some of the great mosques, such as those of Yazd and Kerman, date from the Il-Khanid period. Many of the monuments of Mongol architecture, however, have not survived the ravages of time, earthquakes, and later invaders. Several of the Il-Khanids commissioned great new complexes, with mosques, public baths, bazaars, hostels for travelers and Sufi mystics, schools, libraries, hospitals, and monumental tombs for themselves, in or near Tabriz. One remnant is the eight-sided tomb of Ghazan's successor, Oljeitu (r. 1304–1317), which supports a dome 250 feet (75 meters) high. This mausoleum stood in what was to have been the center of a new capital city called Sultaniyah, set in the mountains of Azerbaijan, but today all its other buildings have crumbled away.

The Mongol conquests made Persian artists and craftsmen more aware of the achievements of Chinese civilization, and so they produced some beautiful manuscript illustrations, glazed tile walls, and other ceramic creations. Hulegu, contrite at the damage he had wrought, patronized the great Persian scholar, Nasiruddin Tusi (d. 1274), who saved the lives of many other scientists and artists, accumulated a library of 400,000 volumes, and built an astronomical observatory that became the model for later observatories in both the Middle East and Europe. Some Persian Muslims became *vezirs* to the Il-Khanids and other Mongol dynasties. Two of these men, Ata Malik Juvaini (d. 1284) and Rashid al-Din (d. 1318), wrote universal histories—a rare achievement in any culture; these are chronicles from which we learn much about the Mongol empire and its accomplishments. Two of Persia's best-loved poets, Sa'di (d. 1291) and Hafiz (d. 1390), lived in Shiraz, a city the Mongols hardly harmed at all. In general, the late thirteenth and fourteenth centuries were a time of economic revival and intellectual brilliance for Persia. Islamic civilization east of the Tigris took on a distinct Persian character. Once again, as in the days of the Arabs and the Seljuk Turks, the Mongol era proved the old adage that captive Persia always subdues its conquerors.

## Tamerlane and the Timurids

Just as the Il-Khanid state was fading, a new military star rose in the east. A petty prince, Timur Leng, often called "Tamerlane," was born in 1336 in Transoxiana, a land suffering from constant bickering among Turkish and Mongol tribes. From his childhood, Timur associated with the most influential amirs and generals. He gathered an army of Muslim Turks (or Turkish-speaking descendants of the old Mongol tribes), with which he hoped to build a universal empire like that of Jenghiz Khan. Even before he could subdue his turbulent homeland, Timur crossed the Oxus in 1369 and proceeded to plunder and pacify Khurasan. When Russia's Mongols, the Golden Horde, tried to line up the principalities of eastern Anatolia and western Iran against him, Timur led his troops through Azerbaijan, Georgia, Armenia, northern Iraq, and parts of southern Russia. Everywhere they went, he had thousands of men, women, and children put to death. Cities were razed and farms destroyed. Posing as a devout Muslim, Timur inflicted special torments on Middle Eastern Christians.

After a brief rest, during which he embellished his capital at Samarqand, he invaded Persia a second time, crossed Iraq and Syria, and brought his empire to the eastern shore of the Mediterranean. Then, giving the Middle East a respite, he turned against India. He defeated its Muslim amirs, sacked Delhi, and filled his coffers with Indian booty, using its proceeds to march westward once more. Between 1400 and 1403 he took Aleppo and Damascus from the Mamluks and almost wiped out the rising Ottoman Empire at Ankara. But even when his Middle Eastern realm matched the Asian empire of Samarqand, Timur pined for a vaster domain to match that of Jenghiz Khan. Only his sudden death in 1405 stopped Timur's soldiers from setting out to conquer China itself.

Formerly, history buffs may have admired the ambition of an Alexander, a Napoleon, or a Jenghiz Khan to build by war a universal empire in which all peoples would live together in peace. There is something rather untidy about a world full of contending tribes and kingdoms, or one like ours with its 200 nation-states. Besides, the conquerors I have named were men of vision. They esteemed scholars, artists, and artisans, and left legacies in the fields of political or military organization. The Mongols may even have spread the use of gunpowder. Given our growing focus on social history, though, we cannot praise Timur, whose legacies were mainly pyramids of human heads and smoking ruins where great cities once had stood. To be fair, he did erect in Samarqand monumental *madrasah*s, mosques, and mausoleums. His descendants patronized scholars, manuscript illustrators, and jewelers. His great-great-grandson, Babur (r. 1483–1530), later founded a large Muslim state in India. Usually we call it the Mughal Empire, though it started out as a Timurid offshoot. It would last up to 1858, when Britain took full control of India.

Except for Central Asia, Timur's conquests broke away soon after he died. The Mamluks recovered Syria, the Turkish amirs of Anatolia won back their independence, and various dynasties took over in Persia. Most memorable of these dynastic states were those of the Shi'i Black Sheep and the Sunni White Sheep Turcomans, who fought each other for most of the fifteenth century. Out of this chaos would come a new dynasty, the Safavids (1501–1736), to spur yet another Persian cultural revival.

## GUNPOWDER TECHNOLOGY

In its earliest and most primitive phases, written history recounted the battles and the deeds of kings. War and diplomacy preoccupied most traditional ruling classes, so this is what they paid their clerks and scholars to record. It was basically a "drum-and-trumpet" history of Europe and the United States that our great-grandparents learned in school. Even now, what you get in Middle East history tends to stress politics and war, though literary and archaeological sources are now pointing us into economic and social history. One new field is the history of military technology. For example, Carlo M. Cipolla's *Guns, Sails, and Empires* shows how the development of gunpowder weapons and long-distance sailing ships enabled the Europeans to expand at the expense of the Muslim world in the sixteenth century. But the author also uses Turkish sources to show that some Muslim armies used siege cannons and field artillery as early as the Western Christians did, several centuries before the sixteenth.

The spread of gunpowder and firearms was as momentous a technological change at that time as the proliferation of nuclear weapons has been since 1945. Gunpowder had been used in China for fireworks since the tenth century, possibly earlier. It was being used as an incendiary device during the Mongol era, spreading from northern China to Europe. By 1330 both Christian and Muslim armies in Spain were loading gunpowder into cannons in order to fire huge projectiles against enemy fortifications. The big guns were too clumsy to do much harm to an enemy soldier, but, by injuring or frightening horses, they could block a cavalry charge. During the fourteenth and fifteenth centuries, Italian and German gunsmiths were refining these weapons. Bronze (easy to cast but very costly) gave way to iron, the diameters of the barrels were slowly standardized, and the weapons were made easier to load and to move around. Simultaneous improvements were being made in the related areas of mining, metallurgy, designing and assembling the component parts, harnessing draft animals, and building roads.

New methods of recruitment and training were devised to produce disciplined corps of foot soldiers and sailors who could maintain and fire these gunpowder weapons. Any European ruler who wanted to keep his territory—or even to survive—had to obtain these new implements. Those Muslim states that opposed Europe had also to get firearms. The amir of Granada had them by 1330 and the Mamluks (although they used them reluctantly) by 1365, but the greatest Muslim gunpowder state was the Ottoman Empire.

## THE OTTOMAN EMPIRE

Our tale begins with a humble Turkish principality located in the area of Sogut, a mountain village in northwest Anatolia. At the end of the thirteenth century it was one of several dozen such petty states, fragments of the once mighty Rum Seljuk sultanate. The growth of this principality into a sprawling empire, perhaps the greatest power of the sixteenth century, is an amazing success story that has been told time and again. According to ancient legend, the empire's origins went back to the Turkic Kayi tribe, whose members fled westward from their ancestral lands in Khurasan to escape from the Mongol invaders in the thirteenth century. The Rum Seljuk sultan was fighting the Byzantines when one of the Kayi chieftains, Ertogrul, happened to come along. Ertogrul's offer of his 444 horse soldiers turned the tide of battle in favor of the Seljuks, who rewarded him with an *iqta'* (land grant) at Sogut. Upon Ertogrul's death (sometime between 1280 and 1299), the leadership passed on to his son, Osman, who was girded by a Sufi leader with a special sword and commanded to wage ceaseless jihad against his Christian neighbors, the Byzantines. He took the title of *ghazi* (frontier warrior for Islam). From that time until the empire's end in 1923, Osman's descendants—the Ottomans—would upon accession be girded with his sword and commanded to fight for Islam against the Christian rulers of Europe.

Now, we do not know whether Ertogrul really lived. Recent studies suggest that Osman's ancestors had lived in Anatolia since 1071, when the Seljuks defeated the Byzantines. But in history we care as much about what people believe to have happened as we do about the literal truth. The legend stresses the Ottoman opposition to the Mongols and to the Byzantines (both of whom were, as you know, non-Turkish and non-Muslim) as well as Ottoman loyalty to the Seljuks and to the tradition of militant Islam. If you keep these attitudes in mind, you will understand the spirit of the Ottoman state. (The succession of Ottoman sultans, to which you may need to refer later, is diagrammed in Figure 2.)

### Beginnings

In the late thirteenth century the Byzantine Empire was recovering from a terrible blow it had sustained in 1204—not a Muslim raid as you might think, but the Fourth Crusade, a Venetian occupation of Constantinople itself. For almost sixty years the Venetians ruled this historic capital; only a rump of the Byzantine Empire survived in western Anatolia with its

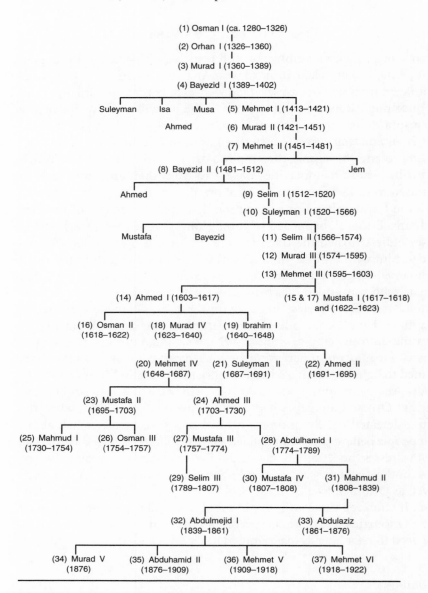

FIGURE 2 The Sultans of the Ottoman Empire (numbered). The dates in parentheses refer to the periods during which they reigned.

main city at Nicaea. Once the Byzantines had regained Constantinople in 1262, their grip on Asia began to weaken. By this time, the Rum Seljuk sultanate was an enfeebled kingdom that had been humiliated by the Mongols in 1243. No longer could it control the Turkish *ghazis* whose ancestors it had brought into Anatolia. Soon there were many principalities that were virtually independent of the Seljuks in Konya. The mountainous lands of western and northern Anatolia were what historians call marches, border regions contested by two or more groups. The local settled population was Greek-speaking and Orthodox Christian. The hillside nomads were Turkish-speaking and Muslim, either Sunni or Shi'i but almost always Sufi. Raiding the settled peoples was their favorite occupation, and the traditions of jihad reinforced their militancy.

Osman's *iqta'* at Sogut may have been tiny, but it was well situated on a hill overlooking Byzantine lands. Osman I (r. ca. 1280–1326) was a warrior chief who led a band of pastoral nomads and cavalry adventurers on raids into Byzantium to win new territories for Islam and for other Turkic tribes from the east, who constantly sought more grazing lands for their flocks. Although other Turkish rulers occasionally made peace with the Byzantine Empire, Osman never did. The chance for perpetual raiding attracted the land-hungry nomads to move west and fight for Osman. More sedentary Turks also came from the east, drawn by Osman's ties with the militant trade guilds, called *akhis* in Turkish, and they set up his rudimentary government. For nine years the Turks besieged the Byzantine stronghold at Bursa; as Osman lay dying, they finally took the city. It became the first real capital of the Ottomans (the name that Europeans would give to Osman's descendants).

## Expansion

Orhan (r. 1326–1360) was the first Ottoman to have coins minted in his name and to take on other attributes of Muslim sovereignty as he expanded his realm northwest to the Dardanelles and east to Ankara. Twice his armies were invited to cross the Straits into Europe by Byzantine emperors seeking Ottoman support against internal rivals and external foes. In 1354 Orhan's men crossed over a third time, took Gallipoli, and refused to go back to Anatolia. Orhan's son, Murad I (r. 1360–1389), conquered many parts of the Balkans, including Thrace, Macedonia, and Bulgaria. The Byzantine Empire became a mere enclave on the European side of the Bosporus, a shriveled husk that survived on Ottoman awe and protection. The great Christian power in southeastern Europe was Serbia. Its king,

Lazar, amassed a force of Serbs, Albanians, Bosnians, Bulgars, and Wallachians (totaling possibly 100,000 men) to defend his bastion against the Ottoman menace. Murad, leading perhaps 60,000 troops, defeated Lazar's coalition at Kosovo in 1389. Both rulers lost their lives, but Serbia also lost its independence. The new Ottoman ruler, Bayezid I (r. 1389–1402), started to besiege Constantinople in 1395. The Europeans perceived this new threat to Christendom, and Hungary's king led English, French, German, and Balkan knights in a great crusade against the Turks. They were defeated at Nicopolis, though, and the Ottoman Empire emerged as master of the Balkans. Symbolically, they moved their capital from Bursa (in Anatolia) to Edirne (in Thrace) and waited for nearby Constantinople to fall. It did not.

If Bayezid had stuck to his father's policy of expanding mainly against Christians in Europe, the Ottomans might have taken Constantinople and expanded farther into the Balkans, but he craved the same prestige accorded to other Muslim empires. The trouble came when Bayezid began conquering nearby Turkish principalities in Anatolia. His expansionist policies incurred the wrath of Timur, who was invited into Anatolia by the dispossessed Turkish amirs. The armies of Bayezid and Timur clashed near Ankara in 1402. The Ottoman sultan, deserted by his Turkish vassals, was defeated and taken prisoner. His newly won Anatolian lands were restored to their former rulers. Bayezid died in captivity, and four of his sons started quarreling over what was left of the Ottoman Empire.

After an eleven-year interregnum, Mehmet I (r. 1413–1421) overcame his brothers and started to rebuild the empire. Toward that end, he had to fight new wars against the Turkish amirs in Anatolia, the Venetian navy in the Aegean Sea, and a Christian ex-vassal in the Balkans. He also suppressed revolts by a popular Sufi leader and by a hostage of the Byzantines who claimed to be his lost brother and hence the true sultan. Murad II (r. 1421–1451) pressed farther into Europe but was stymied by the Hungarians. After several Ottoman setbacks between 1441 and 1444, the king of Hungary was encouraged to call a crusade, just when Murad had turned over his throne to his twelve-year-old son, Mehmet. The Christians reached the Black Sea port of Varna, whereupon Murad came out of retirement to take charge of the Ottoman army and defeat the latter-day Crusaders. Having resumed the sultanate, Murad led expeditions against John Hunyadi of Transylvania and Skanderbeg of Albania, two Christian warriors whose resistance to the Turks would make them legendary among their people.

## The Ottoman Zenith

When Mehmet II (r. 1451–1481) resumed his throne, he was influenced by a *vezir*, a Greek Christian by origin, who urged him to conquer Constantinople. They soon built a castle on the European side of the Bosporus, facilitating Ottoman movement between Anatolia and the Balkans while cutting the Byzantines off from any aid they might have gotten from their Christian allies at Trebizond, a Black Sea port city (see Map 6). In 1453 Mehmet did what so many Muslim rulers since Mu'awiyah had tried: He laid siege to the walled city of Constantinople. But this time the Ottoman ships and guns succeeded where earlier Arab and Turkish attacks had failed. Constantinople was taken, pillaged for three days, and converted into the new Ottoman capital. The city, which gradually came to be called Istanbul, was repopulated with Turks, Greeks, Armenians, and Jews. Soon it grew as rich as it had ever been under the Byzantines. The Greek patriarch was given civil and religious authority over all Orthodox Christians in the Ottoman Empire. Monophysite Christians and Jews later received similar confessional autonomy under what you will soon learn to call the *millet* system. This live-and-let-live policy was in striking contrast to the fanatical bigotry of Christian states at the time. Balkan peasants in Mehmet's time used to say, "Better the turban of the Turk than the tiara of the pope." By the end of his reign, they had gotten what they called for, as Mehmet's troops took the Morea (southern Greece), most of Albania, and the coast of what we now call Croatia. In 1480 the Ottomans landed on the heel of Italy and threatened to march on Rome, but Mehmet's death saved the Roman church from the fate of Greek Orthodoxy. What would our history have been like if Mehmet "the Conqueror" had lived longer?

Mehmet's son, Bayezid II (r. 1481–1512), was relatively passive, compared with the others of the first ten Ottoman sultans. His pacifist policies were due, however, to the captivity of his brother and rival, Jem, under several different European rulers. If Bayezid had ordered another attack on Rhodes, Italy, or Hungary, the Christians would have unleashed Jem to raise a Muslim revolt in Anatolia, where many resented the Ottomans' high taxes and reliance on converts from Christianity (I will explain why they did so later in this chapter). Anatolian peasants and nomads often adopted Shi'ism to voice their hatred of Ottoman repression. In fairness to Bayezid, though, he did manage to bring rival factions into balance, restore lands confiscated by his father to their rightful owners, and end debasement of the currency. He also sent his troops against the Mamluks to

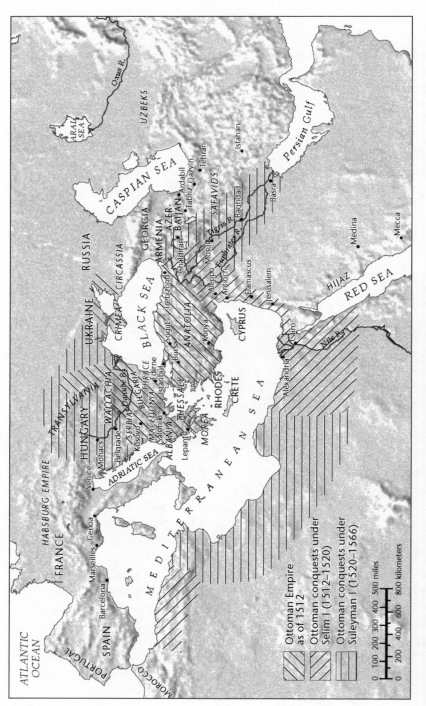

MAP 6 The Ottoman Empire in the sixteenth and seventeenth centuries

take Cilicia and against Venice for some of the Aegean islands. More threatening was the Shi'i challenge from the Turks of Anatolia, spurred by the rise of the Safavids in Azerbaijan. When their first shah, Isma'il, started a Turkish nomad rebellion that had spread as far west as Bursa by 1511, Bayezid's son, Selim, decided to seize control.

Selim I "the Inexorable" (r. 1512–1520) transformed the Ottoman Empire from a *ghazi* state on the western fringe of the Muslim world into the greatest empire since the early caliphate. Equipped with firearms and highly disciplined, Selim's forces routed the Safavids at Chaldiran in 1514 and even entered their capital, Tabriz, before withdrawing from Azerbaijan. Two years later they likewise defeated the Mamluks and took over their vast empire. As the new masters of Syria, Egypt, and the Hijaz, the Ottomans now ruled the heartland of Arab Islam. Even if we discount the story that the puppet Abbasid caliph in Cairo turned over his position to Sultan Selim, it is true that the Ottoman capture of Cairo made Selim the most prestigious ruler in the Muslim world. Islam's holy cities, Mecca, Medina, and Jerusalem, were also under Ottoman rule.

Suleyman "the Lawgiver" or "the Magnificent" (r. 1520–1566) had no living brothers to challenge his succession to Selim. Seen as the greatest of the Ottoman sultans by Turks and Westerners alike, Suleyman headed the forces that took Rhodes and Belgrade, defeated the Hungarians, besieged Vienna, captured most of the North African coast, drove Portugal's navy from the Red Sea, and twice defeated the Safavids. He revamped the government and laws of the Ottoman Empire. Regrettably, though, he delegated too many of his functions to his *vezirs*. Late in life he fell under the influence of his favorite wife, who caused him to have one of his sons (by another wife) killed and another exiled, thus leaving the throne to her son, Selim II "the Sot" (r. 1566–1574). Few of the remaining sultans would match the quality of the first ten.

## Causes of Ottoman Success

You may have inferred that the power and the glory of the Ottoman Empire stemmed from the personalities and policies of those first ten sultans. Rarely in history has one state enjoyed such a succession of just and brave rulers for almost three centuries. No doubt the Ottoman Empire owed some of its strength to these capable sultans, who learned the principles of government from their fathers and from their on-the-job training in the provinces. They gained power by competing against their brothers, and usually the best man won. To avoid costly power struggles, they established a rule that the man who succeeded to the sultanate should have all his brothers put to death. They let no religious prejudices stop them from using the administrative (and sometimes even the military and naval) skills of their Anatolian and Balkan Christian subjects to benefit the Ottoman Empire. When rival factions arose in the army and the bureaucracy, they kept them balanced and thus under control. "No distinction is attached to birth among the Turks," wrote a sixteenth-century envoy from the Habsburg Empire:

> The deference to be paid to a man is measured by the position he holds in the public service. There is no fighting for precedence; a man's place is marked out by the duties he discharges. In making his appointments the sultan pays no regard to any pretensions on the score of wealth or rank, nor does he take into consideration recommendations of popularity; he considers each case on its own merits, and looks carefully into the character, ability, and disposition of the man whose promotion is in question . . . Among the Turks, therefore, honors, high posts, and judgeships are the rewards of great ability and good services.

## Political Institutions

The strength and efficiency that awed the sixteenth-century Europeans were made possible by the ruling class, the so-called *Osmanlilar* ("Ottomans"). Following standard Islamic practice, the functions of the ruling class were to expand and defend the lands of the Ottoman Empire and to ensure the maximum exploitation of its sources of wealth. The main competing groups in the ruling class were the landowning aristocracy, made up of conquered Christian princes in the Balkans and Turkish amirs in Anatolia, and a group of slaves taken by force from their families as boys, converted to Islam, and trained for military or administrative service. The system of recruiting and training this group was called the *devshirme* ("boy levy"). The same word can mean the group of soldiers and bureaucrats produced by this system.

In theory, any male Ottoman subject could get into the ruling class by taking on the following attributes: (1) complete dedication of his life and worldly goods to the sultan's service; (2) acceptance and practice of Islam, although this rule seems not to have been enforced until the sixteenth century; and (3) learning and practicing the elaborate system of customs, behavior, and language known as the *Ottoman way*. As in the Mamluk system, special schools were set up in the capital and the main provincial centers to train youths for Ottoman government service. Nearly all of these boys were taken from Christian families under the *devshirme* system. Although some families resisted this apparent theft of their preadolescent sons (they could protect them by arranging early marriages for them), others actually brought them to the recruiters, for the *devshirme* afforded young men ways to climb as high in the government as their talents and aspirations might carry them.

The ruling class contained four branches: administrative, military, scribal, and cultural. The administrative branch was the palace; it included the sultan's wives, children, and household servants (sometimes called the inner service); and the cabinet (*divan*), which supervised all the other branches of the Ottoman government (and hence was called the outer service). The chief administrator of the outer service was the grand *vezir*, who was authorized to take the sultan's place on military campaigns or in the *divan*. By the time of Suleyman, the *vezir*s often did both. They were considered second in power and prestige to the sultan himself. The early *vezir*s were usually Turkish princes or administrators from older Muslim states; Christian converts to Islam began serving as chief ministers under Mehmet the Conqueror and almost monopolized the post from the reign of Suleyman on.

The military branch was important, too, for the Ottoman Empire often resembled an army camp. There were many subdivisions, both administrative and functional, but we need only concern ourselves here with the horse soldiers (*sipahi*s), who fought with lances or bows and arrows, and the foot soldiers (notably the janissaries), who were trained to use firearms. Although the *sipahi*s played the lead role in the early conquests, it was the well-armed, highly disciplined janissary corps that enabled the Ottomans to defeat the Safavids, the Mamluks, and the Habsburgs in the sixteenth century. The janissaries, whose origins are shrouded in legend, were by far the most numerous and important product of the *devshirme* system. Their training and discipline were extremely strict. Confined to barracks except during campaigns, the janissaries were forbidden to marry or to own land, so that their whole loyalty could be focused on the sultan and his state. The *sipahi*s, on the other hand, received estates, called *timar*s, which they were entitled to exploit only as long as they reported for duty and outfitted a specified number of horse soldiers whenever the sultan needed them. As armies made more use of siege cannons and field artillery during the sixteenth century, the *sipahi*s declined in power relative to the janissaries whose cohesion was reinforced by their belonging to a Sufi brotherhood called the Bektashis.

The janissaries and other foot soldiers had to get their food, clothing, and shelter from the government, and by the sixteenth century they also received salaries, plus accession money each time a new sultan came to the throne. The Ottoman Empire needed a well-run treasury to meet these demands. This function was performed by the scribal branch, which took in the revenues and paid salaries and other government obligations. Tax collection was not usually done by salaried officials, as in our system; rather, it was farmed out to Ottomans known as *multezims*. A *multezim* (tax farmer) was entitled to collect all the taxes that he could from a given area of land (or block of houses or shops in a bazaar) on the condition that a fixed amount or specified percentage of his take be remitted to the treasury. The *multezim* pocketed the rest. On the same principle, many officials were authorized to collect fees, called *bakhshish* (a word that has come to mean "bribe" or "handout" in the modern Middle East), for services rendered, not from the state treasury but, rather, from the public. As long as the Ottoman government was strong, this delegation of the right to collect taxes or fees ensured that officials would carry out their duties efficiently.

Later on, as the treasury needed more money than it could collect from the *multezims*, clerks had to buy their posts in the scribal branch and then recoup their investment by levying exorbitant taxes and fees on the public. Thus the system came to exploit and oppress Ottoman subjects.

The cultural branch of the ruling class was what you know as the ulama. These Muslim scholars took charge of the administration of justice, the management of *waqf*s (Islamic endowments) to support schools and hospitals, the education of most Muslim youth, and the various religious functions usually handled by ulama. Sometimes they also served as a buffer between the subject peoples and the other branches of the ruling class. What was new in the Ottoman system was that the higher ulama became a recognized branch of the government, headed by an official called the *shaykh al-Islam*, appointed by the sultan.

The subject class (*re'aya*) included everyone in the Ottoman Empire who did not belong to the ruling class. Its function was to produce the wealth of the empire. Herders and peasants, miners and builders, artisans and merchants, were all *re'aya*. Their cohesion was strengthened by trade guilds, Sufi orders, and athletic clubs. Their political and social organization was the *millet*, which may be translated as "religious community." The Greek Orthodox church was a *millet*, headed by a patriarch who served at the pleasure of the sultan. All ecclesiastical, judicial, educational, and other benevolent activities involving Orthodox Christians in the Ottoman Empire, from Bosnia to Basrah, were handled by their *millet*. The

Armenian *millet* performed similar functions for Armenians (and, in theory, other Monophysite Christians), wherever in the empire they lived. Later on, the Ottoman sultan appointed a chief rabbi to head the Jewish *millet*, with similar jurisdiction over Ottoman Jews. The Muslim *re'aya*, who made up less than half the population of the Ottoman Empire at its height, viewed themselves as part of the Islamic *ummah*. They, too, often called themselves a *millet*, but the cultural branch of the ruling class was their equivalent of an ecclesiastical organization.

Europeans living or doing business in the Ottoman Empire, being Catholic or (from the sixteenth century) perhaps Protestant, did not care to be a part of any of these *millets*. Nor did they have to be. The Ottoman government adopted a practice, dating back to the Ayyubids, of issuing "Capitulations" that gave autonomy to foreigners living in a Muslim territory. In effect, European nationals were freed from having to obey Ottoman laws or pay local taxes. Although older history books claim that the Capitulations started with a treaty between Suleyman the Magnificent and the king of France, in fact the system was taken over from the Mamluks. The deal was reciprocal: Muslim merchants received the same concessions when living in foreign states. It may seem odd that the Ottoman sultans would agree to a system that kept them from prosecuting criminals within their empire, if they had the protection of a foreign power. Indeed, when the European states grew stronger and the Ottomans weaker in the eighteenth and nineteenth centuries, many Westerners did abuse the privileges they enjoyed under the Capitulations. Muslims conceive of the law as binding on people who espouse the religion from which it stems, not on those who happen to be living in a particular place. The Capitulations also attracted European traders and technicians to live in the empire, while sparing the Ottomans the trouble of settling their quarrels.

## Ottoman Decline: Signs and Causes

The accession of Selim II in 1566 and the defeat of the Ottoman navy at Lepanto in 1571 are commonly identified as the first signs of decline. Some of its root causes go back earlier, though, and the outward signs were not visible for quite a long time. Well into the seventeenth century, Ottoman armies went on attacking European Christians and Persian Shi'is almost at will.

True, the Ottoman princes no longer got on-the-job training, nor were they put to death if they did not reach the throne. Rather, they were confined to the imperial harem and manipulated by factions of janissaries or bureaucrats until they reached the throne unfit to rule. And true, occasional border setbacks showed that the janissaries were no longer keeping up their high training standards of yore or using the latest weapons and techniques of war. In fact, they were living outside their barracks, getting married, enrolling their sons in the corps, rioting to obtain more privileges, and taking up trades more lucrative than soldiering. The Ottoman navy was still using oar-driven galleys when rival powers had converted to sailing ships and could blockade the Turks in the Mediterranean, the Black Sea, and even the Gulf.

Other aspects of Ottoman society were also declining, but most Europeans did not notice any problems until the late seventeenth century. The Ottoman army besieged Vienna in 1683. It had done so once before, only to be driven back by an unusually cold October; but during that second siege the superior arms and tactics of the Europeans saved the Habsburg capital and drove back the Turks, despite their greater numbers. By 1699, when the Ottomans signed the Treaty of Karlowitz, ceding control of Hungary to the Habsburg Empire, they were clearly on the defensive. The Ottoman Empire had ceased to be the scourge of Christendom; in another century it would be called the sick man of Europe.

Why did the Ottoman Empire start to decline in the sixteenth century? No state has yet found a political fountain of youth that would arrest its ultimate downfall. Will the United States hold up as long as the Ottoman Empire did? Perhaps we should admit that countries, like people, have life spans that, though variable in length, are never infinite. But historians have noted other causes of the Ottoman Empire's decline. One was its insistence on having only one army, for the experience of previous Muslim states had been that dividing their forces resulted in breaking up their realms. Besides, the army was, in principle, led by the chief *ghazi*—that is, either by the sultan himself or by his authorized representative, the grand *vezir*. Under these conditions, the army could fight only one campaign at a time, and never farther from Istanbul than it could march during the campaign season (April to October), because the *sipahis* went home in the autumn to supervise their *timars* and the janissaries wintered in Istanbul. If two states could coordinate an attack on the Ottoman Empire from two different sides, the army might well be defeated. By the end of the sixteenth century, the Ottomans lagged behind the West in weaponry and fighting techniques. Officers and troops liked the old ways; learning new ones would require more work and might threaten their power.

Economic conditions, too, were getting worse. Europe's discovery and exploitation of the New World and of sea routes around Africa to the riches of Asia weakened the role of the Muslim countries as intermediaries controlling the main trade routes. Cheap American silver flooded Europe and the Middle East, causing a general price inflation in the late sixteenth century. Some states, such as England and Holland, had ambitious merchants and manufacturers who were ready to expand their business activities; other countries, including Spain as well as the Ottoman Empire, suffered severe economic disruption because of the inflation. Indeed, many Ottoman merchants and artisans were ruined by foreign competitors sheltered by the Capitulations. Besides, extortionate tax collection by the *multezims* and rural overpopulation caused many peasants to leave their farms and flock to the cities. When they found no work, they became vagabonds and brigands, further impoverishing the economy.

Many Westerners believe that Islam engenders fatalism and discourages individual initiative. If this were universally true of Muslims, it would be hard to account for their successes under the High Caliphate, the early Mamluks, or the Ottomans up to 1566. But the Ottoman ulama became far too conservative. As guardians of the Muslim law, the Shari'ah, they had to be wary of blameworthy innovations. They carried this caution to absurd lengths when they forbade the introduction of Arabic and Turkish printing presses into the Ottoman Empire until the eighteenth century, lest a printed Quran violate the principle that God's work was written, and (in a more practical vein) lest Muslim scribes be thrown out of work. The ulama also amassed considerable power as interpreters of the laws, managers of the *waqfs*, and local administrators, and would resist any threat to their position.

The most basic reason for the Ottoman loss of power, though, was the disappearance of the balance among the various forces within the ruling class. English-speaking peoples often call for a balance of power within their government, whereby an equilibrium among its branches or special-interest groups helps protect the individual citizen from official tyranny. The Ottoman balance of power served a different purpose. The early sultans had encouraged competition between the traditional leaders (the landowners and ulama) and the men who had been recruited and trained under the *devshirme* system. When Suleyman the Magnificent appointed a succession of *vezirs* all taken from the *devshirme*, he tilted the balance in favor of that group. By the end of his reign, neither the old aristocracy nor anyone else could check the power of the *devshirme* administrators. Matters grew worse under his successors. A comparable imbalance occurred in the army, where the janissaries, who used firearms, overpowered the various corps of horse soldiers, who did not. The janissaries were emboldened, therefore, to demand the right to marry, to live outside the barracks, to enroll their sons in the corps, to practice trades other than fighting, and to neglect their training. By the end of the seventeenth century, they were no longer effective defenders of the empire. The Ottoman government took no more levies of Christian boys, and it phased out the rigorous training schools for janissaries and administrators. Appointment and promotion came to be based on family ties and favoritism, in place of merit. Once the ruling class had called its members "slaves of the [sultan's] gate"; now the Ottoman sultan was their servant, a captive within his own palace harem.

## PERSIA UNDER THE SAFAVIDS

Let us compare the Ottoman Empire with a contemporary Muslim state less known or feared in the West, Safavid Persia. The Safavid dynasty grew out of a militant Sufi order centered in Ardabil, a city in Azerbaijan. Although Sunni at first, the Safavids became ardently Shi'i some time after the Mongol conquest. The rapid breakup of Timur's empire after his death in 1405 led, in Persia, to a lot of small dynastic states, most of them ruled by quarrelsome nomadic tribes such as the Black Sheep and White Sheep Turcomans mentioned earlier. Under the leadership of Shaykh Junayd (d. 1460) and the protection of the Black Sheep Turcomans, the Safavids began converting large numbers of Turks in Azerbaijan and Anatolia to Shi'ism. These Shi'i Turks came to be called *kizilbash* (red heads) because of their distinctive headgear. When the Black Sheep Turcomans betrayed Junayd and drove him out of Ardabil, he made political and marital alliances with their White Sheep rivals, even though they were Sunni.

The Safavids kept on growing in strength and numbers, even after Junayd's death, until they threatened the power of their new patrons. The White Sheep Turcomans proceeded to kill or to lock up almost the whole Safavid family. By 1494 no leader of the *kizilbash* revolutionaries remained free except a seven-year-old grandson of Junayd, Isma'il, who eluded his pursuers during a house-to-house search of Ardabil and escaped to another part of Persia. During the summer of 1500 young Isma'il and his *kizilbash* followers stirred up a revolt in central Anatolia against their oppressors. Turkish Shi'i tribal warriors came in droves, and in early 1501 the White Sheep Turcomans were decisively defeated.

### Rise of Safavid Power

The Safavid state began in Azerbaijan when Isma'il, now thirteen, entered Tabriz, proclaimed himself shah, and declared that Twelve-Imam Shi'ism would henceforth be the sole religion of the state. This stance amounted to a declaration of war against the Ottoman Empire, which, as you know, was Sunni and not securely in control of the Anatolian Turks, who leaned toward Shi'ism. In fact, just about every Muslim dynasty in 1501 was Sunni, which made the Safavids quite distinctive. It was hard for them even to find books expounding the fundamentals of Shi'i Islam, and they had to import their ulama and their books from what is now southern Lebanon. Nevertheless, Isma'il aspired to conquer the whole Muslim world for Shi'ism, and he enjoyed the unswerving support of his *kizilbash* warriors. Even though most of the Turkish nomads and Persian peasants living in Safavid lands were Sunni, Isma'il was determined to unite the country both politically and religiously. Within a decade the Safavids, though Turkish by race, had taken control of all Persia. It took longer to win over the local inhabitants to Shi'ism, especially in the eastern provinces; but, once converted, the Persians came to view their sect as a badge of national identity. Likewise, they thought of the Safavids as a Persian dynasty, just as we view George III as English and Eisenhower as American in spite of their German ancestries. Indeed, the Safavid era was one of the most glorious for the history of Persian art and political power.

True, the Safavids could not match the might of the Ottoman Empire. You may remember that in the Battle of Chaldiran (1514), the janissaries with their firearms defeated the *kizilbash* fighting on horseback. The Ottomans entered Tabriz but left after a week, for the janissaries would spend the winter only in Istanbul. The Safavids lost some of their lands in Anatolia and Armenia, but Persia was saved from Ottoman rule. However, the fanatical loyalty of the *kizilbash* Turks to Isma'il Shah was shaken by the Chaldiran defeat, and the impetus to spread Safavid rule to other lands controlled by Sunni Islam was lost. So shaken was Isma'il that he became a recluse and spent the last decade of his life hunting and drinking. Why did the Safavids lag behind the Ottomans in adopting gunpowder weapons? Like the Mamluks, the *kizilbash* knew about them but viewed them as unmanly and awkward to carry on horseback. Besides, the Safavids' other foes, the Central Asian Uzbeks, did not use firearms either.

## The Safavid Zenith

Some of the effort the Safavids did not put into conquering the rest of the Muslim world must have gone into creating a good life for themselves. Tabriz, Qazvin, and finally Isfahan became the capitals of their empire. Each in turn became a center for artists, artisans, and (most conspicuously) architects. Isfahan was a dazzling and beautiful city. Even now, its mosques, bazaars, *madrasahs*, and palaces are eloquent testimony to the opulent lifestyle of the Safavid shahs. But Isfahan is better seen, even in slides, than read about in a textbook. As the Persians say, *Isfahan nisf-i-jehan,* or "Isfahan is half the world."

The reign of Shah Abbas I (1587–1629) was the zenith of Safavid wealth and power. Earlier shahs had been manipulated by the *kizilbash* tribal chiefs, but Abbas brought them to heel by executing anyone he suspected of plotting against him and by taking away much of their agricultural land. Like many earlier Muslim rulers, Abbas brought in slave boys (called *ghulams* in Persian) to be indoctrinated and trained as salaried warriors and administrators. In the Safavid case, they were mainly Armenian and Georgian Christians, not all of whom converted to Shi'ism. Abbas hoped to set up a balance between his aristocracy (the *kizilbash*) and this new corps of *ghulams*, each competing to serve the Safavid state. Like the Ottoman sultans, the Safavids divided their government into branches: the royal household, the state administration, the military corps, and the religious-judicial system. Each branch contained two or more dignitaries competing for the shah's favor, giving him more leverage. This governmental system was not unique to this era; Persia's hierarchy can be traced back to the early caliphs, the Sasanids, and even the Achaemenids.

The Europeans courted Abbas. He brought in English advisers to train his *ghulams* to use cannons and handguns, strengthening the Safavid army against the Ottomans. Because of the hostility between the Christian West and the Ottoman Empire, every European country that hoped to be a naval and commercial power sent envoys and merchants to Isfahan, seeking Abbas's help against Istanbul. Spain, Portugal, France, England, and Holland had representatives at his court. Even Catholic missionaries entered Safavid Persia. Was Shah Abbas a new Prester John?

Certainly not. Abbas was a great Muslim ruler like Harun al-Rashid or Suleyman the Magnificent. His reign marked a turning point in the history of his dynasty (as had theirs). Significant changes were taking place within the Shi'i religious establishment as the Sufis who had formerly led the rulers and people lost their power and influence to the ulama. Among the ulama, too, the earlier school, which had based its doctrinal and legal decisions heavily on the Quran and the prophetic sunnah, gave way to one that accorded far-reaching authorization to the *mujtahids* (legists) to interpret the Shari'ah. Thus the basis was laid for an ever more powerful establishment within Persia's Shi'i ulama, with momentous consequences for the 1979 Iranian Revolution. Shah Abbas, troubled early in his reign by the *kizilbash*, suspected anyone else who had power. This category included his own sons, all of whom he had blinded or put to death, and thus his ultimate successor was a grandson of little account. The later Safavids continued Abbas's policy of putting more and more land under state control at the expense of the *kizilbash* chieftains. They may have needed money to pay the *ghulams*, but the Safavids took too much land and impoverished the countryside, for crown land administration never matched the quality of *kizilbash* management. Like the *devshirme* groups in the Ottoman Empire, the *ghulams* kept increasing their numbers and internal power—though not their strength as a fighting force—until they could manipulate and strangle the Safavid government.

## The Aftermath of the Safavids

By the eighteenth century, Safavid Persia was ripe for the plucking, but most of its imperial neighbors were equally decadent. In 1722, however, a group of tribal Afghans seized control of Isfahan, and the Safavids took to the hills of Azerbaijan, their first home. The Ottoman Empire, breaking a ninety-year truce, invaded the region. No match for the janissaries on the field, the Afghans skillfully sapped the loyalty of the Ottoman auxiliaries and negotiated a peace, ceding large areas of western Persia. This was more than the Persian people could stand. Under the inspiring leadership of a warrior named Nader Afshar, Persian and Turkish tribes joined forces to drive out the Afghan usurpers and then, more gradually, the dissolute Safavids. The victorious leader had himself crowned Nader Shah in 1736. His reign was the last hurrah for traditional Persia. Within a decade he had driven back the Ottomans and taken most of India. He might have become a world conqueror, had he not tried to convert the Persians from Shi'i to Sunni Islam, thus weakening his support back home. Upon his assassination in 1747, Nader Shah's empire collapsed. A succession of minor dynasties led Persia into a long night of political breakdown and social decay from which it would be slow to recover.

## CONCLUSION

In this chapter, or perhaps earlier, you may have seen a pattern emerging that will help you to chart the rise and fall of dynastic states. An area is divided among many states or nomadic tribes. In its midst a ruler emerges with a mission, probably related in some way to Islam, that inspires his followers to do great deeds and to mobilize others like themselves to overcome rival states. The conquerors lower taxes or improve public order, thus gaining peasant favor, increasing food production, and promoting economic well-being. As the empire expands, it builds up a large army and bureaucracy that it must then support, increasing the burden on its subjects. The ruling class and the ulama become rich, powerful, and conservative. The rulers' descendants prove to be less and less capable of ruling, and their subjects become more and more prone to rebel, until the empire falls and the cycle repeats itself.

All of the empires that you have studied here—the Mamluks and the Il-Khanids, the Timurids and their Mughal descendants (slighted here, because India is not in the Middle East), the Ottomans and the Safavids—were Muslim military states in an era when possession and mastery of gunpowder weapons became prevalent, then essential for survival. But some of these states lasted a long time because they also set up institutions that ensured the best use of their subjects' talents as soldiers and bureaucrats while keeping a power balance between their competing factions. When even this was lost, the Ottoman Empire and other Muslim states found another type of equilibrium that saved their independence: the European balance of power.

# TEN

# European Interests
# and Imperialism

In the eighteenth century, the West achieved and then maintained military, political, and economic superiority over the Middle East. This had not been the usual power relationship before. It may not be so in the future. Neither the rulers nor the subjects of the Ottoman Empire—or any other Muslim country—wanted this subordination to the European Christians, whom they had formerly looked down upon. But what could they do? Whereas once the Muslims had controlled the commercial routes between Europe and Asia and had dictated the terms of trade to both, now Europeans were selling their manufactures to the Middle East in exchange for raw materials and agricultural products. In addition, Europeans living or trading in Muslim lands dwelt in special quarters of the big cities and did not have to pay local taxes or obey local laws and regulations. Whereas once the Mediterranean Sea and the Indian Ocean had been dominated by Muslim navies (or pirates), now European sailing ships—military and merchant—controlled the high seas. Earlier, the Ottoman sultan could choose the time and place for any attack on Christian Europe and then dictate peace terms; now his armies were at the mercy of the stronger forces of Austria's Habsburgs and Russia's czars. To the Muslims, accustomed to victory on the battlefield, these changes seemed a cosmic error. There is no power and no strength save in God, the ulama would say; yet all could see that the West's temporal might menaced the *ummah*. Was this divine punishment for Muslims who had lost their purity of intention and strayed from God's plan for their community?

## OTTOMAN WEAKNESS

We can trace the changing relationship between the Middle East and the West by a series of dated events: In 1683 the Ottomans failed to take Vienna, the capital of the Habsburg Empire; in 1699 they signed a treaty at Karlowitz, ceding Hungary to the Habsburgs and the Aegean coast to the Venetians; in 1718 they signed away more of their European lands; in 1774 they lost the Crimea and allowed Russia to speak on behalf of *their* Orthodox Christian subjects; and in 1798 Napoleon Bonaparte occupied Egypt and invaded Palestine. Meanwhile, other Muslim dynasties, such as the Timurids (Mughals) of India, the Safavids and their successors in Persia, the Central Asian Uzbeks, and the Sharifian rulers of Morocco, were also weakening before the mounting might of eighteenth-century Europe. But the Ottomans were closest to the new powers, had traditionally fought as *ghazis* for Islam, and stood to lose the most if the Europeans partitioned their lands. My focus will, therefore, be on the Ottoman Empire.

### Some Symptoms and Causes

Some popular histories may make you believe that the Ottoman rulers cared nothing for their empire's fate. Enchanted by the charms of the harem, dulled by wine or hashish, hamstrung by janissary revolts or quarreling court factions, the sultans (so the story goes) lost interest in maintaining their regime or defending their lands. By the same token, the venal *vezirs* tried to keep the sultans out of their way, in order to profit from the corruption of the system. Bureaucrats bought their offices and sold subordinate posts to others, while everyone in power gouged the poor peasants and workers on taxes and fees (which were really assessed bribes). The janissaries, who should have been the backbone of the Ottoman army, became a hereditary caste of merchants and artisans who failed to keep in training or to learn how to use such modern weapons as muskets and bayonets. Worse, they overturned their soup pots and went on a rampage if anyone dared to call for reforms. As long as the state fed and paid them, they saw no need to reform, or to let other troops take their place. The ulama turned into *juhala* (ignoramuses), steeped in superstition and untouched by the expansion of knowledge taking place in Europe. Landowners and merchants were robbed by brigands, against whom they had no protection. Peasants suffered from rapacious landlords and tax-farmers; many ran away to become brigands themselves. So the mournful cycle turned. The easy answer is to blame incompetent or impotent sultans. As the Turks used to say: *Balik baş dan kokar* (The fish stinks from the head).

## The Reforming Sultans and Vezirs

There is, as usual in such popular accounts, a germ of truth in all this. The sultans were getting worse. No one denies the insanity of Sultan Ibrahim (r. 1640–1648), who had his 280 concubines tied up in sacks and drowned in the Bosporus. Mustafa II (r. 1695–1703) insisted wrongly on leading his troops into battle. His catastrophic defeat at the hands of Prince Eugen of Savoy, the military genius of the age, cost the Ottomans an army, the province of Hungary, and their military prestige. Alcohol abuse and harem intrigues afflicted the later sultans far more than they had the first ten. In addition, there were members of the ruling class who milked the Ottoman system to enrich themselves while failing to perform their duties. But one of the secrets of Ottoman longevity was that the system went on producing capable sultans and *vezirs* who saw the corruption and introduced reforms. Among the reforming sultans were Osman II (r. 1618–1622), whose attempt to form a new Turkish militia led to his being killed by the janissaries; Murad IV (r. 1623–1640), a powerful wrestler and champion archer who executed 25,000 rebellious subjects within a single year; Mahmud I (r. 1730–1754), the first to bring in Europeans to teach new fighting techniques; and Selim III (r. 1789–1807), who introduced a comprehensive reform scheme, the *nizam-i-jedid*, which I will describe in the next chapter.

What about the reforming *vezirs*? The Koprulu family produced six grand *vezirs* who enhanced Ottoman security abroad and imposed political, social, and aesthetic changes at home. The first, Mehmet (d. 1661), was taken from his Albanian Christian parents by the *devshirme* and started his career working in the imperial kitchen. As grand *vezir* to Sultan Mehmet IV (r. 1648–1687), he defeated the Venetians and quashed revolts in Transylvania and Anatolia, executing thousands in the process. His son, Ahmet, strengthened the *vezirate*, checked the Habsburgs, and took Crete as well as parts of Poland. His brother led the Ottoman troops to the gates of Vienna in 1683, but failed to capture the city. A nephew of Mehmet Koprulu, serving Mustafa II, reduced taxes on consumer goods, set up factories, and hoped to restore farm production to its earlier level.

Another major *vezir* was Damad Ibrahim, best known for diverting Sultan Ahmed III (r. 1703–1730) into building pleasure palaces and tulip gardens; but he also brought in European artists, commissioned Turkish translations of Western scientific works, and introduced the first Ottoman printing press. Mehmet Ragib, another *vezir*, tried in the mid-eighteenth century to better his subjects' lot through fiscal and legal reforms, while keeping the empire at peace. My point is that, even in this dark age of Ottoman history, some sultans and *vezirs* tried to bring in some light. More westernizing reformers would arise in the nineteenth century; you will read about them later. What I must make clear now is that reforms alone could not save the Ottoman Empire.

## THE EUROPEAN POWERS AND THE EASTERN QUESTION

Most historians think that the key to the Ottomans' predicament—but also, paradoxically, their salvation—lay in Christian Europe. Without the Renaissance, the Reformation, the age of exploration and discovery, the expansion of trade, the Enlightenment, and the Industrial Revolution, Europe would not have surpassed the Muslim world in the eighteenth century. The Ottoman Empire had not undergone all the changes these movements brought to Western culture. But neither had such traditional Ottoman foes as Venice, Poland, and Spain; by 1750 they no longer menaced Ottoman security. Habsburg Austria still played its customary role as Christendom's chief defender against Islam. But Austria's leadership was paling before a new star rising in the north, czarist Russia. Many English-speaking people have believed that Russia would have taken over all Ottoman lands, but for the determined opposition of the other European states. To test this belief, let us now look at the Middle East policies of the most important European countries of the nineteenth century—the Great Powers: Russia, Habsburg Austria, Britain, and France.

### Czarist Russia

Unlike all the other Great Powers involved in the Ottoman Empire, Russia had experienced Muslim rule under the Mongol Golden Horde. It had emerged in the fifteenth century as a small but independent state, centered on Moscow and close to the sources of the main rivers and portage routes of central Eurasia. Some historians argue that the expansionist policy of Muscovite rulers was made possible by their control of these rivers and dictated by their ceaseless quest for outlets to the high seas. Rivers flowing into the Baltic Sea or the Arctic Ocean are apt to be icebound for half the year; therefore, Russia needed the Black Sea as a warm water outlet for trade. In the seventeenth century this body of water was almost completely surrounded by Ottoman lands. As a result, Peter the Great and his successors fought several wars against the empire in the eighteenth century in order to ensure Russian access to the Black Sea. By the middle of the nineteenth century, the Russians could regard the Black Sea as mainly theirs, but their ships still had to pass through the Ottoman-ruled Bosporus and Dardanelles (the Straits) in order to reach the Aegean and hence the Mediterranean. So Russia sought control of the Straits, or at least assurances that the Ottomans would not bar passage to its warships and merchant vessels. Russia also wanted to rule the Straits in order to better defend its Black Sea ports from naval attacks from invaders.

Some Russians had an additional motive to seize the Straits: They wanted to rule that great city on the Bosporus—Istanbul. You may recall that, up to the Ottoman conquest, it had been Constantinople, capital of the Byzantine Empire, hence the "Second Rome," and chief jewel of the Greek Orthodox church. When Constantinople fell, Russia became the greatest Greek Orthodox country and declared Moscow as the "Third Rome." A Muscovite prince married the niece of the last Byzantine emperor. Their descendants, Russia's czars, sometimes sought to gain control of Constantinople (which they called Czargrad) and restore the power and prestige of Greek Orthodoxy to the level of Roman Catholicism. Besides, many Orthodox Christians lived under Ottoman rule, mainly in the Balkans. Austria captured some of them in the early eighteenth century, but the Habsburgs, being Catholic, were unsympathetic. Mother Russia would be a better protector for the Serbs, Bulgars, Albanians, Romanians, and Greeks seeking freedom from Muslim rule, for they were nearly all Orthodox. So, when Catherine the Great defeated the Ottomans in 1769–1774 and thus could set the terms of the peace treaty, she secured Ottoman recognition of Russia's right to intervene diplomatically on behalf of Orthodox Christians living *within* the Ottoman Empire. The wording of this Treaty of Kuchuk-Kainarji is ambiguous, but Russians claimed later that it set a precedent for relations between Russia and Turkey (as the Ottoman Empire came to be called by the Europeans).

Later on, the Russians maintained that they had something else in common with many of the sultan's Balkan subjects—namely, that they were Slavs. Although Slavs were once considered a race, the term *Slav* really denotes membership in a language group. Russian and Ukrainian are Slavic languages; so, too, are Bulgarian, Serbian, and Croatian. During the nineteenth century, some Balkan peoples espoused a kind of nationalism called pan-Slavism that aimed to unite within a single state all peoples speaking Slavic languages. Russia, the largest Slavic country, claimed to be its leader. The Ottoman Empire feared the divisive effect of pan-Slavism as much as it had Russia's earlier sponsorship of the Orthodox Christians. But keep in mind that pan-Slavism was opposed by other European states such as Prussia and Austria with their many Polish subjects; thus Russia had to mute its pan-Slavism when it wanted to placate those powers. Indeed, many Russian officials preferred a policy of defending Ottoman integrity and maintaining good relations with the other European powers over any risky unity with either the Orthodox Christians or their Slavic cousins.

In the nineteenth century, Russia's drive toward the sea, leadership of the Orthodox Christians, and encouragement of pan-Slavism combined at times to produce an aggressive Middle East policy. Russian troops entered the Balkans during the 1806–1812 conflict, the Greek war for independence in the 1820s, the 1848 Romanian uprising, the Crimean War of 1853–1856, and the Russo-Turkish War of 1877–1878. In the last of these struggles, Russian troops came to within 10 miles (15 kilometers) of Istanbul and dictated the peace terms at San Stefano in February 1878. Because all the other Great Powers opposed Russia's military and political gains from that war, the sultan regained some of the Balkan lands in the comprehensive Treaty of Berlin, signed later in that same year. Russian encouragement of pan-Slavism even helped cause the Balkan Wars of 1912–1913 and the outbreak of World War I in 1914. Although you (like me) may feel overwhelmed by all the twists and turns of the "Eastern Question" from 1774 to 1917, you may safely assume that the Ottomans viewed Russia as their main enemy for nearly all of that time. (I will mention one exception later.)

The Eastern Question centered on whether Russia would gobble up Turkey's European possessions, especially the Straits, or be stopped from doing so by the other Great Powers. Although other countries at times accepted or even welcomed Russia's growing might (for example, when Russian forces helped defeat Napoleon in 1812–1814—or Hitler in 1942–1945, if I may jump ahead a bit), they usually tried to prevent a Russian capture of the Balkans and the Straits, lest it endanger the European balance of power.

Now, here is a concept that you may want me to explain. There was no way to decree that each state would have as much power as all the others. After all, Britain had industrialized first, built up the strongest navy, and acquired a large overseas empire. France derived more of its wealth from farming than manufacturing, but it, too, had a big empire and a very strategic location. Austria and Russia each controlled vast areas with large and diverse populations, necessitating big standing armies. Prussia (which did not become Germany until 1871) had an unusually well-armed and disciplined army. The balance of power did not, therefore, ensure that each state had equal power; it *did* mean that no state or coalition could become so strong that it could dominate all the other European countries. Failure to maintain that equilibrium had enabled Louis XIV and later Napoleon to impose French power over the rest of the continent, hardly an experience that the British or the Germans (or the Dutch, Belgians, Swiss, Italians, et al.) cared to relive. It was for the same reason that the British would later fight against Germany in the two world wars. On the same logic, many people in the nineteenth century feared that if Russia ruled the Balkans and controlled the Straits, all Europe would be at the mercy of the czars. The West felt a similar dread of Soviet influence over Turkey (and also over Central Asia and Afghanistan) during the cold war of 1945–1991; possibly, then, this need to keep a power balance will not seem strange to you.

Remember also that Russia was, like the United States, a continental power and an expanding one, except that the direction of its growth tended to be eastward (as well as southward). Not only the Ottomans, but also the Islamized descendants of the Mongols, Tatars, and Turks who had occupied Central Asia, fell under Russian control, especially during the nineteenth century. At times when the West feared that Russian influence in the Balkans would upset the European balance of power, the czars were also building an empire in cities like Bukhara and Samarqand, menacing Persia, Afghanistan, and Mughal (or British) India.

## Habsburg Austria

Russia's rivals had some positive reasons to get involved in the Ottoman Empire. The Habsburg Empire, for instance, bordered directly on Ottoman lands in southeastern Europe from the fifteenth to the nineteenth centuries. Having whetted its appetite by taking Hungary in 1699, Austria hoped to move down the Danube River toward the Black Sea. It also wanted to control lands south of the Danube, especially Croatia, Bosnia, and Serbia. The Habsburg emperors may have pursued commercial interests, but they also saw themselves as carrying on the old crusading traditions against the Muslim Turks. During the nineteenth century, as each of the Balkan states wrested its independence from the Ottoman Empire,

Austria would step forward as its patron, protector, and trading partner. Some seemingly traded one master for another. Bosnia and Herzegovina, two regions that were culturally and geographically close to Serbia (but with large Muslim populations), were placed under Habsburg military occupation as part of the 1878 Berlin Treaty. Thirty years later, with no prior consent from the Ottoman Empire (and to Russia's dismay), Austria annexed Bosnia and Herzegovina. But their acceptance of Habsburg rule was undermined by propaganda from nearby Serbia, leading to the 1914 assassination at Sarajevo of the heir to the Austrian throne. You may know that this was the spark that set off World War I. This takes us beyond where we should be, but some historians see Austria's Balkan policy as a cause of that great conflict once facetiously named "the War of the Turkish Succession."

## Britain and the Middle East

Britain was a naval, imperial, and Indian power. Safe sea transport to India became a primary British concern once it had consolidated its Asian empire by defeating France in the Seven Years' War (which U.S. history calls the French and Indian War) of 1756–1763. As long as most maritime transport between Europe and Asia went around South Africa, Britain hardly worried about the Ottoman Empire and at times even backed Russian expansionism in the Balkans. It did not, however, favor French expansionism in Egypt and Syria, as we shall soon see. From about 1820, the growth of steamship travel and the improvement of overland communications made it faster and safer to transship people and goods across Egypt or the Fertile Crescent, both nominally Ottoman lands, instead of taking the long route around Africa. Britain decided in the 1830s that the Ottoman Empire would be the best guardian of its routes to India and soon committed itself firmly to the empire's defense. It also had a commercial motive, for, as you will learn in the next chapter, Britain and the Ottoman Empire signed a treaty lowering their import duties on each other's goods. By 1850 the empire had become a leading customer of British manufactures and a major supplier of foodstuffs and raw materials to Britain. The British also came to share Austria's suspicions of Russia's Balkan aims.

The largest European conflict between Napoleon's defeat and the outbreak of World War I was the Crimean War of 1853–1856. Although popular legend has it that the war was sparked by a fight between Catholic and Orthodox priests in Jerusalem, the real cause was the fear of most European countries that Russia's growing strength in the Balkans would threaten the balance of power in Europe. By leading the anti-Russian coalition, Britain proved that it would go to great trouble and expense to defend Turkey against Russian expansionism and thus to preserve the balance of power. On the same logic, Britain sent part of its fleet into the Dardanelles in 1878 as a warning, after Russia had occupied most of the Balkan lands. In the next chapter you will see how Britain's commitment extended to pressing westernizing reforms on the Ottoman government at these critical times. In a further attempt to secure its routes to India, Britain also took Aden in 1839 and Cyprus in 1878, occupied Egypt in 1882, and made treaties with most of the Arab rulers along the Gulf from Oman to Kuwait. Several times Britain sent troops into Afghanistan or Persia to deter the advancing Russians, whose hope of reaching the Gulf nearly equaled their drive to the Straits. Britain feared that the Russian czars' hunger for new lands might also extend to the Himalayas, India, and even China. These nineteenth-century events foreshadowed Britain's attempt to dominate the Middle East in the early twentieth century.

## France: Protector and Civilizer

The best friend of the Ottoman Turks was usually France. Its strategic location, with ports on both the Atlantic and the Mediterranean, made France a frequent contender for mastery in Europe. Up to the nineteenth century its greatest Mediterranean rival was the Habsburg Empire, driving France into alliance with the Ottomans. France claimed to have the oldest Capitulatory treaty, and French merchants and investors almost always led the Europeans doing business in the Ottoman Empire. When it needed military or naval experts, engineers, or teachers, the Ottoman government usually sought French ones. Young Ottomans were more apt to choose France than any other foreign country for higher education or advanced vocational training.

Religion, too, strengthened the French connection. When Russia tried to protect Orthodox Christians under Ottoman rule, France advanced similar claims on behalf of the Catholics. Because they were relatively few in number, the Turks minded them less. One fateful result was the special bond between France and Syria. And one key to this tie was a Christian sect, the Maronites, who predominated in what is now northern Lebanon. In the seventh century, the Maronites had taken a compromise position between Orthodox and Monophysite Christianity, giving them a unique identity. They later entered into communion with Rome during the Crusades. They were allowed to keep their traditional practices (such as having prayers in Syriac and married priests). From the seventeenth century on, they had access to Western learning through a papal seminary for Maronites in Rome. When France emerged as the leading Catholic power, the Maronites welcomed French missionaries and merchants to Syria, where they built up a network of schools, churches, factories, and trading posts. France's primacy in Syria rested on ties with other Christians as well. Various Christian groups were breaking away from their native churches, usually Orthodox but also Jacobite (Monophysite) and Nestorian, and entering into communion with Rome as Uniates. These converts to Catholicism, like the Maronites, studied in the French schools and traded with French merchants. Some adopted other aspects of French culture, too, and viewed France as their patron and protector. When fighting broke out between Muslims and Christians in Syria in 1860, Paris would become the main interventionist power on behalf of the latter.

Strategically speaking, Egypt mattered more to France than Syria did. This concern was not widely felt in the eighteenth century, when Egypt's economy and society reached a low point, owing to Ottoman neglect and Mamluk misrule (about which you will read in the next chapter). But Napoleon Bonaparte, who called Egypt the world's most important country, occupied it in 1798. For three years Britain and Turkey engaged in a complicated series of military and diplomatic maneuvers to get the French troops out of Egypt. Following France's departure, a military adventurer named Mehmet Ali (the Arabs call him Muhammad Ali) rose to power in Cairo. Using French advisers, he started an ambitious reform program, built up a strong army and navy, and took Syria from the Ottomans in 1831. France abetted and applauded Mehmet Ali's gains. Not so the other Great Powers who saw these gains as a threat to the European balance of power and regarded Mehmet Ali as a French agent. It took British naval intervention to get his troops out of Syria in 1840, but Mehmet Ali retained his power in Egypt and founded a dynasty that would reign there until 1952.

France played the lead role in yet another Egyptian drama. Mehmet Ali's son, Sa'id, granted a concession in 1854 to a French entrepreneur to build a ship canal across the Isthmus of Suez. The British tried to block the project, fearing that it would put the French in control of a major route to India. But once the Suez Canal was opened in 1869, Britain became its main user. Soon it bought the Egyptian government's shares in the controlling company; then it sent troops into Egypt (France was supposed to send troops, too, but failed to act at the critical moment) to quell a nationalist uprising in 1882. France's economic and cultural ties with Egypt remained strong, but by the end of the nineteenth century, in spite of French opposition, Britain dominated the Nile Valley. France did, however, take control of most of the rest of North Africa. After World War I it would seek further compensation in Syria and Lebanon.

## CONCLUSION

This brings to a close my rapid survey of the Middle Eastern interests and policies of the major European powers. I went beyond the eighteenth century, hoping to give you a context for events occurring later on. You may ask why I focused on Russia, Austria, England, and France, to the exclusion of all other countries. Admittedly, I have oversimplified the scenario somewhat. The complete cast of characters in the Eastern Question would include Swiss archaeologists, Belgian bankers, German military advisers, American Protestant and Italian Catholic missionaries, Greek grocers, and Armenian photographers. By 1900 the German, Italian, and U.S. governments had also acquired bit parts in the political drama. Persia was becoming more important as well, especially as an object of Anglo-Russian commercial and military rivalry.

This chapter also treated the Middle East not as an area acting but as one acted upon. This, too, is a distortion. Even if it did lose lands in the Balkans and North Africa, the Ottoman Empire remained independent throughout this time. Even if Western ambassadors and advisers might have overdirected sultans and *vezirs*, the scope of their actions was limited by Muslim conservatism and their need to prevent another country's intervention. Likewise, Persia staved off the Russians and the British until both agreed to split the country into zones of influence in 1907. Most Middle Eastern peoples went on living their lives as if Europe were on another planet. The changes affecting them were the westernizing reform policies of their own rulers. It is to these reforms that we must now turn.

# ELEVEN

# Westernizing Reform in the Nineteenth Century

Europe's power rose so dramatically between the sixteenth and nineteenth centuries that every other part of the world had to adapt or go under. Some human groups, such as the Fuegian Indians at the southern tip of South America and the natives of Tasmania, were totally wiped out by white people's diseases, alcohol, or deportation. Others, such as the North American Indians and the Australian aborigines, lost nearly all their lands and liberties to the English colonists. Some peoples mixed with the European settlers, creating a hybrid culture, as in Brazil. Many west Africans were uprooted, enslaved, and shipped to strange and distant lands. Such ancient countries as India, Java, and Vietnam were absorbed into European empires. Japan kept its independence but copied Western ways on a large scale. Several other Asian states tried to stay independent by grafting onto their traditional societies those Western customs and institutions that they believed to be sources of power. China, Thailand, Persia, and the Ottoman Empire followed this path, which seemed moderate, logical, and appropriate for countries with deeply ingrained norms and values. Islam, for instance, was both a faith and a way of life. Muslim countries wanted to strengthen their armies and navies, their governments and economies, but not to cast off a lifestyle they had built up and followed for centuries. Reformers had to choose with care the institutions and practices they borrowed from Europe, but they soon learned that a westernizing program in, say, defense could not be blocked off from the rest of society. Military, political, and economic reforms sparked reactions in seemingly remote areas, often catching the reformers off guard.

You may have a problem defining *reform*. In a Western country, the reformer often comes from outside the power elite, challenges the system, and, if successful, changes it. He or she may resort to violent revolution, but most successful reforms are achieved through the ballot box, the legislature, or the forum of public opinion. They may well reflect social and economic changes that have already taken place. When we speak of the Reform Bills in English history, we mean the acts of Parliament that extended voting rights to more classes of people during the nineteenth century. A *reform party* in U.S. politics usually refers to an out-group fighting against corrupt or unjust practices within a city, state, or national government.

We commonly assume that reformers come from below. In a few cases they have, even in the Middle East. You learned earlier about the Kharijite and Hashimite rebels under the Umayyad caliphate. In the seventeenth and eighteenth centuries there were peasant revolts in Anatolia and the Balkans, but they aimed at breaking away from, not reforming, the Ottoman government. A better example would be the Wahhabis. They were a puritanical Muslim group, growing out of the Hanbali rite of Sunni Islam, that seized power in central Arabia during the eighteenth century. Led by a family named Sa'ud (hence the modern state named Saudi Arabia), these Wahhabis wanted to conquer the Arabian Peninsula (if not more) and to purify Islam from practices they deemed corrupt. They built up a fairly strong state in the late eighteenth century; then they were checked by the Ottomans and Mehmet Ali in the nineteenth but made a strong comeback early in the twentieth century. Many of their ideas have won acceptance from Muslim thinkers outside Saudi Arabia. Call them reformers if you wish. There have been many other movements within Islam in the past two centuries that aimed to restore Islamic civilization's grandeur or to bring Muslim institutions into harmony with modernity. They have come not from below but from the intellectual elite. At times they have been started by the rulers themselves.

In Middle East history, you may assume that significant and effective reforms have usually come from above. They have been instituted by the rulers, or by their *vezir*s, generals, or local governors. They have seldom been demanded by the poor, or done this class much good once put into effect. In particular, we will look at those governmentally imposed reforms that imitated the ways of the West, often at the expense of Islam as the people understood it. Westernization was—and still is—often confused with modernization. This chapter will focus on westernizing reform in Egypt, the rest of the Ottoman Empire, and Persia.

## EGYPT

If Rip Van Winkle had nodded off in Cairo around 1795 and roused seventy-five years later, he would have been amazed—if not bewildered—by the changes that occurred during his nap. Egypt made the fastest and most dramatic transformation of any Middle Eastern country in the nineteenth century. Since 1517 the country had been ruled by the Ottoman Empire, but an early rebellion had taught Istanbul to leave most local control to the Mamluks, the aristocracy of ex-slave soldiers who had ruled Egypt since 1250. During Ottoman times, the Mamluks continued to bring in Circassian boy slaves and to train them as soldiers and administrators. It might have been a good system once upon a time, but no longer; by the eighteenth century the Mamluks had turned into rapacious tax-farmers and cruel governors. Caught up in factional struggles, they failed to provide the irrigation works and security needed by the peasants, whose well-being and population plummeted to new lows. Starved for revenue, the *madrasahs*, including the ancient university of al-Azhar, declined in intellectual caliber. Most ulama became incompetent, lazy, and corrupt. Their Christian and Jewish counterparts were no better. The Ottoman governors could do nothing. Soldiers and peasants revolted, sometimes successfully, but they too could not reform the system. Egypt was running down. It took two extraordinary foreigners to get the country moving again: Napoleon Bonaparte and Mehmet Ali.

### Napoleon's Occupation

Napoleon was sent by France's revolutionary government in 1798 to conquer Egypt and, if possible, Syria and Iraq. That government probably wanted to get the ambitious young general out of Paris and may have hoped to retake India, where France had lost its colonies to the British in 1763. Napoleon aspired to emulate the conquests of Alexander the Great. To do this, he would have had to lead his army from Egypt via the Fertile Crescent to Persia, Afghanistan, and what is now Pakistan. It was a fantasy never realized, but Napoleon did defeat the Mamluks easily and occupied Cairo. Seeking to win over the Egyptians, he posted manifestos, like this excerpt:

> Peoples of Egypt, you will be told that I have come to destroy your religion. This is an obvious lie; do not believe it! Tell the slanderers that I have come to you to restore your rights from the hands of the oppressors and that I, more than the Mamluks, serve God . . . and revere His Prophet Muham-

mad and the glorious Quran. . . . Formerly in the land of Egypt there were great cities, wide canals, and a prosperous trade. What has ruined all this, if not the greed and tyranny of the Mamluks? . . . Tell your nation that the French are also faithful Muslims. The truth is that they invaded Rome and have destroyed the throne of the Pope, who always incited the Christians to make war on the Muslims . . . Furthermore, the French have at all times declared themselves to be the most sincere friends of the Ottoman sultan and the enemy of his enemies. The Mamluks, on the contrary, have always refused to obey him . . . Blessing upon blessing to the Egyptians who side with us. They shall prosper in fortune and rank. Happy, too, are those who stay in their dwellings, not siding with either of the parties now at war; when they know us better, they will hasten to join us. . . . But woe upon woe to those who side with the Mamluks and help them to make war on us. They will find no escape, and their memory shall be wiped out.

The Egyptians loved the Mamluks little, but they soon loved the French even less. Napoleon and his men were not Muslims, nor did they restore Ottoman sovereignty. France's occupation of Egypt was harsh, heavy-handed, and hated. Taxes and government fees, high but sporadic under the Mamluks, were now collected regularly from everyone, making them seem more oppressive. Ignorant of local mores and customs, the French troops shocked pious Muslims by their lewd conduct, public drinking, and blasphemous behavior, which included firing on al-Azhar to quell a local uprising. When the British navy sank most of Napoleon's ships in the Battle of Abu-Kir, then when the French army marched into Palestine but failed to take Acre from the Turks, and when Napoleon himself slipped through the British blockade to return to France, the Egyptians became even more hostile. Yet the French occupation lasted until 1801. The Egyptian people were sullen but unarmed. Their Mamluk ex-rulers were divided and weakened. It took a joint Anglo-Ottoman landing at Alexandria, followed by a general European treaty, to get the French forces out of Egypt. The British navy left soon afterward.

Popular histories tend to play up the French occupation because Napoleon was so colorful and because France would later form strong cultural ties with Egypt. More important, the French expeditionary force included about 100 scholars, scientists, and artists, who went around Cairo and the countryside studying almost every aspect of Egypt. The published results of their studies, consisting of nine volumes of text and fourteen of illustrations, give us a surprisingly thorough and fairly accurate description of the country's condition and the life of its people. The French brought in a printing press and set up a research institute, which attracted the notice of a few inquisitive ulama. Few historians now think, as we once did, that these events caused the intellectual awakening of Egypt. It had not been asleep, but Napoleon's invasion did (1) lead to on-going competition for Egypt between Britain and France; (2) destroy whatever notions Ottoman Muslims still cherished about their superiority over Europe; and (3) weaken the Mamluks, creating a leadership vacuum once the last British troops pulled out in 1802.

## Mehmet Ali and His Reforms

The man who eventually filled that vacuum was a soldier of fortune named Mehmet Ali. He had come to Egypt as second in command of the Albanian regiment in the Ottoman expeditionary force that tried, unsuccessfully in 1799 but victoriously two years later, to dislodge the French. Mehmet Ali used to underscore his personal ambitions by remarking, "I was born in the same year as Napoleon in the land of Alexander." He patterned his career after both men: By 1805 he had emerged from the pack of contenders for power and secured recognition from a group of ulama and local notables. Later that year he incited a revolt against the Ottoman governor and secured the sultan's consent to take his place. Like many of the Ottoman reformers, Mehmet Ali realized that losses on the field of battle showed the glaring weakness of the existing army and the government behind it. Unlike the others, though, he realized that adopting European uniforms, weapons, and tactics, or even importing foreign instructors and technicians, could not solve their military problems. Wholehearted and far-reaching reforms were a must. If the Western ways displeased Muslims, Mehmet Ali would be ruthless and dictatorial.

Fortunately for him, the Nile Valley made Egypt a proverbially easy land to govern, once all rival power centers were wiped out. The Mamluks posed the major obstacle; in 1811 Mehmet Ali had them all massacred. Because the ulama enjoyed great power and prestige, he exploited their internecine rivalries, then weakened them by taking away most of the land they had managed as *awqaf*. He also put most privately owned land under state control, thereby wiping out the tax-farmers and the rural aristocracy. His government thus gained a monopoly over Egypt's most valuable resource, its agricultural land. The state now decided which crops the peasants might grow; supplied them with seeds, tools, and fertilizer; purchased all their crops; and sold them at a profit. To make it easier to move goods from one part of the country to another, Mehmet Ali drafted peasants to build roads and dig barge canals. New irrigation works made it possible to raise three crops a year in fields that used to produce just one.

Egypt became the first Middle Eastern country to make the shift from subsistence agriculture (in which peasants raised essentially the crops they consumed, plus what they had to pay in rent and taxes) to cash crop farming (in which peasants raised crops to sell on the market). Tobacco, sugar, indigo, and long-staple cotton became major Egyptian crops. Using the revenues they produced, Mehmet Ali financed his ambitious schemes for industrial and military development.

Mehmet Ali was the first non-Western ruler to grasp the significance of the Industrial Revolution. He realized that a modernized army would need textile factories to make its tents and uniforms, dockyards to build its ships, and munitions plants to turn out guns and bayonets. French advisers helped the Egyptian government build and equip them. Hundreds of Turkish- and Arabic-speaking Egyptians were sent to Europe for technical and military training. Western instructors were imported to estab- • lish schools in Egypt for medicine, engineering, and military training. Finally, a new Arabic printing press was set up to publish translated textbooks and a government newspaper.

### Mehmet Ali's Military Empire

Mehmet Ali was also the first ruler since the Ptolemies to use Egyptian peasants as soldiers. The peasants hated military service. They regarded it as tantamount to death, for few of the conscripts ever saw their homes again. Despite their ingenious attempts at draft-dodging, they got dragged into the army all the same. Turkish, Circassian, and European officers whipped this new Egyptian army into a potent fighting force. It served Mehmet Ali (at the Ottoman sultan's request) against the Wahhabis, who had taken over Mecca and Medina. He also put together an Egyptian navy, with which he helped the Ottomans against the Greeks, who were fighting for their independence. After the Great Powers stepped in to help the Greeks defeat the Turks, however, Mehmet Ali turned against the sultan himself. He sent his son, Ibrahim, in charge of a large expeditionary force that marched into Palestine and Syria. By the end of 1832 he held most of the Fertile Crescent and the Hijaz. Ibrahim proceeded to impose his father's westernizing reforms in Syria, but the Syrians proved less docile than the Egyptians. Revolts broke out in the mountains as Syrian peasants resisted agricultural controls and the confiscation of their firearms. Taking advantage of Ibrahim's troubles, the Ottoman government tried to win back some of his land. Mehmet Ali and Ibrahim struck back, moving deep into Anatolia. By 1839 it looked as if Cairo would take over the whole Ottoman Empire as the imperial fleet deserted en masse to Alexandria and a sixteen-year-old prince was girded with the sword of Osman. Only intervention by the Great Powers (mainly Britain) forced Mehmet Ali to pull his troops out of Syria and settle for autonomy within Egypt.

Mehmet Ali's stature shrinks somewhat when you realize that he cared little for the Egyptian people. After his diplomatic defeat he lost interest in his economic and military reforms. Most of the schools and nearly all the state-run factories were closed. The state monopolies and other controls on agriculture lapsed. Most of the lands were parceled out to his friends and relatives. Nevertheless, upon his death Mehmet Ali could bequeath to his children and grandchildren a nearly independent Egypt with recent memories of military might. Also, his empire had been based on agricultural and industrial development, using no money borrowed from Western governments, banks, or investors. Few of his heirs ever matched this final boast.

## WESTERNIZATION OF THE OTTOMAN EMPIRE

Less impressive results came from efforts by Mehmet Ali's contemporaries to reform the Ottoman Empire. The first was Sultan Selim III (r. 1789–1807), whom a leading historian of Ottoman Turkey, Stanford Shaw, has depicted as a transitional figure among the westernizing reformers. Shaw divides the Ottoman government's attempt at internal reform into three phases. In the first, such reformers as the Koprulu *vezirs* of the late seventeenth century tried to restore the administrative and military system to what it had been when the empire was at its height in the sixteenth. When this effort failed, some of the eighteenth-century sultans and *vezirs* adopted a selective westernizing policy, chiefly in the army; but this second phase did not check Russia's advance into the Balkans or Napoleon's occupation of Egypt. In the third phase of Ottoman reform, mainly in the nineteenth century, the state tried to westernize many imperial institutions in an effort (only partly successful) to halt the secession or annexation of its territories.

### The Nizam-i-Jedid

Selim III was alarmed at the European designs on his country; he was also aware of its internal problems, with some provinces in open revolt, a war with Austria and Russia in progress, and a serious shortfall in tax revenues. In response, he planned a full-scale housecleaning, a *nizam-i-jedid* ("new order") that would reform the whole Ottoman government. But with the military threat so imminent, Selim concentrated on creating the westernized elite army to which that name is usually applied. The training of the *nizam* soldiers, many of them recruited from Istanbul street gangs, had to be done secretly. Selim knew that the janissaries—and their friends—would react violently once they found out. He was right. The janissaries feared that an effective fighting force, trained by European instructors and using modern weapons, would show them up as useless parasites of the state. They also were not about to let their privileges be jeopardized by military reform, however necessary. They revolted, killed the new troops, locked up Selim, and started a bloody civil war. The tragedy is that Selim could have built up his new army and stopped the Russians if he had carried out the comprehensive reform scheme he had originally proposed. But his plan was bolder than he was. Selim therefore seems to stand between the phase of selective westernization and the nineteenth-century effort to reshape the entire Ottoman Empire along European lines.

## Mahmud II

An ill-fated attempt by Selim's successor to revive the *nizam* sent the janissaries on such a rampage that they killed all the male members of the Ottoman dynasty but one, a cousin of Selim named Mahmud II (r. 1808–1839). Understandably, Mahmud mounted his throne in fear and trembling. Not only could the janissaries stir up the city mobs, trade guilds, and *madrasah* students to defend their privileges, but the whole empire was in danger. Some of the Balkan provinces had become independent in all but name under local warlords. A Serbian nationalist uprising threatened to influence other subject peoples. Local landowners in parts of Anatolia were taking the government into their own hands. Garrisons in such Arab cities as Aleppo and Mosul were held by dissident mamluk or janissary factions. Worse yet, Russia had again gone to war against the empire and had invaded its Danubian principalities (now called Romania), while Napoleon's forces were battling the British navy for control of the eastern Mediterranean. The Ottoman outlook was bleak, but Mahmud surprised everyone. Like his late cousin, he wanted to reform and strengthen the Ottoman state. But Mahmud also saw that (1) westernizing reforms must include every aspect of Ottoman government and society, not just the military; (2) reformed institutions would work only if the ones they replaced were wiped out; and (3) any reform program must be planned in advance and accepted by the country's leaders.

At first Mahmud kept a low profile, quietly cultivated groups that favored centralization of Ottoman power, and slowly built up a loyal and well-trained palace guard, to be used against the janissaries and their supporters when they were strong enough. Only in 1826 did Mahmud feel ready to strike. In a move reminiscent of Mehmet Ali's fifteen years earlier, he ordered a general attack on the janissaries. This time the sultan had a strong army, the ulama, the students, and most of the people on his side. The janissaries were massacred, their supporting groups (including the Bektashi Sufi order) abolished, and their properties seized for redistribution among Mahmud's backers. So glad were the people to be rid of the janissaries that the massacre has come down in Turkish history as the "Auspicious Event." It cleared the way for a large-scale reform program that took up the last thirteen years of Mahmud's reign.

Highest priority went, predictably, to forming a new military organization to replace the janissaries and other outmoded units, for the Greeks, backed by the Great Powers, were rebelling against Ottoman rule. Mahmud gathered into his new army soldiers from all units of the old system, to be issued European uniforms and weapons and subjected to Western drillmasters and instructors. Ottoman youths had also to be trained in technical fields that served the military. Existing schools of military and naval engineering were expanded, a new medical college was founded, and other schools were set up to teach European marching music and military sciences. In addition, a system of secondary schools was started to help boys bridge the transition from the mosques that provided most primary education to these new technical colleges and military academies.

It was hard to create schools in Istanbul based on French, German, or Italian models. The first teachers were all European. So, too, were the books they assigned. As a result, the boys had to master French or German before they could study medicine, engineering, or science. Even now this condition remains a problem in the Middle East, owing to the rapid growth of human knowledge. University students in Turkey, Iran, Israel, and (to a lesser extent) the Arab countries still use European or U.S. textbooks for specialized courses in engineering, medicine, business, and even the humanities. But the problem was more acute 150 years ago in the Ottoman Empire. Printed books in any language were rare, and Turkish books on the European sciences still had to be written. Some French and German textbooks were translated, but never enough of them. Special courses were set up to train Turkish Muslims to become translators and interpreters for the Ottoman government, replacing the Greeks who could no longer be trusted, now that there was an independent Greece. Like Mehmet Ali, Mahmud started a newspaper to print government announcements. He also sent some of his subjects to study in European universities, military academies, and technical institutes.

The general aim of the Ottoman reforms was to transfer power from the traditional ruling class to the sultan and his cabinet. Government ministries were reorganized to get rid of overlapping jurisdictions and superfluous posts. Mahmud abolished the system of military land grants (*timars*) that had sustained the *sipahis* since the dawn of Ottoman history. He could not imitate Mehmet Ali by putting all farmland under state control—the Ottoman Empire was larger and more diverse than Egypt—but he could at least tax the rural landlords. Building better roads aided the centralization of power. Mahmud had to overcome opposition from local and provincial officials, feudal *sipahis*, old-fashioned government clerks, and ulama. There were too few who shared Mahmud's dream of an empire reformed and reinvigorated, like Russia under Peter the Great. It would not benefit them enough.

*Military Defeat and European Protection*

Westernizing reform in the Ottoman Empire had another grave fault: It did not stop the army from losing wars. By 1829 the Greeks had won their independence, although their tiny kingdom in the Morea held only a minority of all Greek-speaking people. Their success was due mainly to intervention by Russia, which fought the Ottomans again between 1827 and 1829 and won a lot of land east of the Black Sea. Ibrahim's advances into Syria were another blow to the Ottoman Empire, especially when Mahmud's new army failed to dislodge them. Outside help would be needed if the empire were to survive. The first choice should have been France, but it was backing Mehmet Ali and Ibrahim, so Mahmud turned instead to his mighty northern neighbor. In a treaty bearing the euphonious (if forgettable) name of Hunkar-Iskelesi, Russia agreed in 1833 to defend the territorial integrity of the Ottoman Empire. In other words, the fox would guard the henhouse!

This pact between two states that had fought four wars in sixty years hit the West like a bombshell. Britain believed that the Hunkar-Iskelesi Treaty gave Russian warships the right to pass through the Straits, from which Western naval vessels were barred, and it railed vehemently against the threat of Russian domination of Istanbul. How could the British outbid the Russians? Luckily, the Ottomans wanted more trade with Britain. In a commercial treaty signed in 1838, the Ottoman government increased Britain's Capitulatory privileges and limited to 9 percent its import tariffs on British manufactures. This low rate stimulated British exports to the empire, thus wiping out many Ottoman merchants and artisans who could not compete against the West's more mechanized factories. One unexpected result of the 1838 treaty was to increase Britain's economic interest in the Ottoman Empire and hence its desire to keep it alive. That outcome soon benefited the Turks.

## The Tanzimat Era

Mahmud II died while Ibrahim's army was invading Anatolia, whereupon his navy, laboriously rebuilt with British and U.S. help after the Greek war for independence, defected to Alexandria. Mahmud was succeeded by his young son, Abdulmejid (r. 1839–1861). Although he seemed ill prepared for the duties of government, Abdulmejid reigned during the greatest Ottoman reform period, the era of the Tanzimat ("reorganizations"). The guiding genius of the early Tanzimat was Mahmud's foreign minister, Mustafa Reshid, who happened to be in London seeking British aid against Mehmet Ali at the time Abdulmejid took over. Advised by both the British and Reshid, the new sultan issued a proclamation called the "Noble Rescript (*Hatt-i-Sherif*) of the Rose Chamber," authorizing the creation of new institutions to safeguard the basic rights of his subjects, to assess and levy taxes fairly, and to conscript and train soldiers. Tax-farming, bribery, and favoritism would end. But how would these promises, revolutionary for the Ottoman Empire, be fulfilled? Well, Mustafa Reshid was surrounded by young and able officials who believed that liberal reforms would save the Ottoman Empire. Almost all aspects of Ottoman public life were restructured: A system of state schools was set up to produce government clerks; the provinces were reorganized so that each governor would have specified duties and an advisory council; the network of roads, canals, and now also rail lines was extended; and a modern financial system was set up with a central bank, treasury bonds, and a decimal currency.

The Tanzimat was not a total success. Some Ottoman leaders lost the power and prestige they had customarily enjoyed. The subject nationalities expected more from the 1839 rescript than the actual reforms could deliver. Balkan Christians did not want centralization of power; they wanted autonomy. Some now sought independence. The Romanians were among the many European peoples who rebelled in 1848; it took a Russian invasion to quell their revolt. Without firm British backing, the Ottoman reform movement would have collapsed. Unfortunately, Britain's insistence on upholding Ottoman territorial integrity was on a collision course with Russia's attempt to spread its influence in the Balkans. The crash was the Crimean War of 1853–1856. The Ottoman Empire, aided by British and French troops, defeated Russia and regained some lands in the Balkans and the Caucasus. But the price for Western support was a second official proclamation, Sultan Abdulmejid's 1856 Imperial Rescript (*Hatt-i-Humayun*). Its gist was that all Ottoman subjects, whether Muslim or not, would now enjoy equal rights under the law. This was a revolutionary statement. Most Ottoman Muslims opposed giving Christians and Jews the same rights and status as themselves, an act contrary to the basic principles of the Shari'ah. Some of the *millet* leaders feared they would lose their religious autonomy. Discontented Christian subjects still rebelled, but now there were also uprisings by Muslim conservatives who objected to the new Ottoman policy. The Tanzimat reforms continued, though, in such areas as landownership, codification of the laws, and reorganization of the *millet*s (or at least those of the Armenians and the Jews, who were not yet seeking separate states). Following the Crimean War, the Ottoman Empire was admitted to full membership in the European Concert of Powers, and no one dared—until later—to speak of its imminent collapse or partition.

## PERSIA UNDER THE QAJARS

Persia was the only Middle Eastern country outside the Arabian Peninsula that was never fully absorbed by the Ottoman Empire. Even if the Safavid shahs had often fallen back before the might of the janissaries in the sixteenth and seventeenth centuries, they had always retained control at home. After the Safavids' fall in the early eighteenth century, a succession of dynasties (most of them Turkic in origin but Persian in culture) ruled over that sprawling and heterogeneous country, in either uneasy alliance or open contention with the nomadic tribes, rural landlords, urban merchants, and Shi'i ulama. Following the meteoric career of Nader Shah (d. 1747), the country went into a long decline. The Qajar dynasty (1794–1925) ineffectually resisted dissolution from within and encroachments from without. Russia was pushing into the Caucasus region and into such Central Asian lands as Transoxiana, Khwarizm, and Khurasan. The czars' ultimate goal was to conquer the Gulf region. Britain, concerned with the defense of India, vacillated between a policy of backing

Persia's government and one of seizing parts of its southern territory. The Qajars designated Tehran, hitherto an obscure mountain town, their capital. Their rule rarely reached the countryside, which was controlled by absentee landlords and nomadic tribes. For the most part, the shahs seemed intent on enriching themselves and enlarging their families. My favorite example is Fath Ali Shah (r. 1797–1834), who was survived by 158 wives, 57 sons, 46 daughters, and almost 600 grandchildren. This helps you understand an old Persian saying that "camels, lice, and princes can be found everywhere."

Persia had no Mehmet Ali, no Mahmud II, and precious little Tanzimat. We could make a grudging exception for Nasiruddin Shah (r. 1848–1896). He had gotten some on-the-job experience as crown prince ruling in Tabriz, but because his father, the ruling shah, disliked him (and his mother), young Nasiruddin received no funds with which to feed and clothe his soldiers and officials or even to heat his palace. When he succeeded his father at the age of eighteen, his progress from Tabriz to Tehran was impeded by tribal and village leaders who importuned him for accession gifts he could not provide. Nasiruddin never forgot his humiliation. He began his reign with a program of military, economic, and educational reforms. A variety of factories was opened, and Tehran got its first bank and its first technical school. But the credit for these reforms goes to his energetic prime minister, who antagonized Nasiruddin's mother, a powerful figure in the Qajar court. He was suddenly executed in 1851. After that, Persia got embroiled in a war with Britain over control of port cities in the Persian Gulf and mired in tribal and religious uprisings, many of which were fueled by social and economic discontent against the government. Even women took part in urban riots when bread and other foodstuffs became scarce and expensive.

One religious movement that would have fateful consequences was the revolt of a Shi'i Muslim who proclaimed himself the Bab, or precursor to the hidden Twelfth Imam. Although the Bab was put to death in 1850, he had a successor named Baha'ullah who was exiled to Baghdad, which was then a part of the Ottoman Empire. Later, he proclaimed himself a prophet and founded the Baha'i faith, a universal religion of peace and unity that has won growing support in the West but is now regarded as a heresy in Iran, where since 1979 its adherents have been persecuted by the Islamic republic.

Persia's state treasury never had enough money to pay for the things Nasiruddin wanted to do, like building palaces and traveling to Europe. To supplement revenues from taxes, which were hard to collect, the government set up monopolies over such economic activities as mining and manufacturing. The shah began selling these monopolies as concessions to British and other European investors. He also hired Russian cossack officers to train his army. Instead of using reform to protect Persia from foreigners, the shah encouraged them to take over his country.

## SOME AFTERTHOUGHTS

Westernizing reforms seemed to be a cure-all for the ills of the nineteenth-century Middle East. Yet they seldom worked as well in practice as they had looked on paper. What went wrong? First, the reforms posed a threat to Muslim culture and values. Moreover, they were costly. Modern armies and westernized bureaucracies could not subsist on the traditional Islamic taxes: the *kharaj* paid on land and other fixed property, the *jizyah* paid by Jewish and Christian subjects, and the canonical *zakat*. Each of the countries we have studied would, in later years, stub its toes on finance, having run up a foreign debt so high (by nineteenth-century standards) that it had to accept European control over its governmental receipts and expenditures.

A related problem for all reformers was a shortage of trained personnel to run the westernized institutions they had set up. True, Europeans were often there to do the work. Some were talented, dedicated to their jobs, and cooperative with native officials. Others were incompetents who could not have held a job back home, fugitives from an unhappy past, alcoholics, or snobs who hated the local leaders. Turks, Arabs, and Persians could also be trained to administer the reforms. If they were sent abroad for their training, though, they often picked up some of the less admirable aspects of Western civilization: drinking, gambling, dueling, and even worse habits. Some resisted such temptations and came home well trained, only to be stymied by the old-style bureaucrats. If the native reformers got their education at the newly formed local schools, remaining subject to steadying influences from home and mosque, they could turn into half-baked Europeans unable to grasp either the values of the West or the real needs of their own societies. Such "Levantines" should have been a bridge between Europe and the Middle East. Most were not.

The best members of the generation that got its education from the reforms of Mehmet Ali, the Tanzimat, or Nasiruddin's *vezir* became imbued with ideas that were in a sense opposed to those of the early reformers themselves. Instead of hoping to centralize power in the hands of the ruler, they called for constitutions that would protect the individual's rights against a powerful government. Some rulers even encouraged this idea. Mehmet Ali's grandson, Isma'il, the khedive ("viceroy") of Egypt from 1863 to 1879, was as ambitious a reformer as his illustrious ancestor. During his reign, parts of Alexandria and Cairo were turned into copies of Paris, railroads crisscrossed the valley and delta of the Nile, and Egypt took on such attributes of modernity as law codes, schools, factories, and even an African empire. But Isma'il also set up a representative assembly and a newspaper press, both of which started out tamely enough, yet turned later into noisy critics of his government. He may even have fostered a nationalist party in his army, but let me save that story for Chapter 12.

The Ottoman reaction to the reforms was more complex. Some officials and ulama resisted them. They were encouraged to do so by Sultan Abdulaziz (r. 1861–1876), who patronized pan-Islam—an ideology that called on all Muslims, no matter where they lived, to unite behind Ottoman leadership and to uphold their traditional institutions and culture against Western influences. There were also bureaucrats, army officers, and intellectuals who reacted against the Tanzimat in the opposite direction, demanding more individual freedom, local autonomy, and decentralization of power. They called themselves New Ottomans, whom we must try not to confuse with the Young Turks of the next generation.

Great Power policies, briefly discussed in Chapter 10, often hindered reforms more than they helped. Britain and France stepped up their competition for control of Egypt after the Suez Canal became a major waterway. When Khedive Isma'il ran up a debt of nearly 100 million pounds, Britain and France first set up a financial commission in 1876, then made him appoint foreigners to key posts in his cabinet, then ordered the sultan to depose him, and finally threatened to suppress the Egyptian nationalist movement, all in order to guard their financial and strategic interests. Russia's zeal for protecting Orthodox Christians, gaining control of the Straits, and promoting pan-Slavism led in 1875 to revolts against Ottoman rule in several parts of the Balkans. In that same year, the Ottoman government admitted that it could no longer repay its debts, and the Europeans set up a financial commission to make sure their creditors got whatever the Ottoman government owed them. The next year the New Ottomans seized control of the government, drew up a liberal constitution for the empire, and tried to persuade the powers to let them settle their internal affairs in peace. Some countries agreed, but Russia distrusted the Ottoman promises, invaded the Balkans, and set off the Russo-Turkish War. Turkey's humiliating defeat put an end to the Tanzimat, the New Ottomans, and their constitution.

Persia also suffered from foreign imperialism. Its northern part, especially the key province of Azerbaijan, was occupied by Russian troops much of the time. European entrepreneurs (usually backed by their governments) went about gaining concessions—for which they paid Nasiruddin Shah handsomely—to run Persia's mines, banks, railroads, and public utilities. The sale of its assets reached the point where a concession to process and market all the tobacco raised in the country was sold to a British firm. This event touched off a nationwide tobacco boycott in 1892. It worked so well that the shah himself could not smoke his water pipe in his palace! The boycott was led by Shi'i ulama, who from then on would remain politically active. Its success was a warning to the West, little heeded at the time, that the patience of Middle Eastern peoples had limits. Someday they would strike back. But this brings us to the rise of nationalism, a subject that deserves a chapter of its own.

# TWELVE

# The Rise of Nationalism

Of all the ideas that the Middle East has imported from the West, none has been more popular and durable than nationalism. Often called the religion of the modern world, this ideology or belief system is hard to pin down. Drawing on the Western historical experience, I define nationalism as the desire of a large group of people to create or maintain a common statehood, to have their own rulers, laws, and other governmental institutions. This desired political community, or nation, is the object of that group's supreme loyalty. Shared characteristics among the peoples of Egypt and also among those of Persia stimulated the growth of nationalism in those two countries in the late nineteenth century. Other nationalist movements have grown up around shared feelings of opposition to governments, institutions, and even individuals regarded as foreign.

Nationalism was itself foreign to the world of Islam. In traditional Islamic thought, the *ummah*, or community of believers, was the sole object of political loyalty for Muslims. Loyalty meant defending the land of Islam against rulers or peoples of other faiths. All true Muslims were supposed to be brothers and sisters, regardless of race, language, and culture. Although distinctions existed between Arabs and Persians, or between them and the Turks, common adherence to Islam was supposed to transcend all divergences. Nationalism should not exist in Islam.

Yet it does, and religion has deeply influenced nationalism in the Middle East. Arab nationalism at its start included Christians and even Jews, but its most conspicuous expressions since World War II have been resistance to Christian control in Lebanon and to Jewish colonization in Palestine (Israel since 1948). The rhetoric of nationalism often confuses the Arab nation with the Islamic *ummah*, as when an Arab nationalist cause is termed a jihad.

Other Middle Eastern nationalist movements were based even more firmly on religion and called on their people to resist oppression by others having a different faith. These include Greeks and Armenians among the Christians of the Middle East, as well as Turks and Persians among the Muslims. Political Zionism, which called for Israel's creation as the Jewish state, drew its inspiration from Judaism, even if many of its advocates were not themselves observant. In all three monotheistic faiths, the rise of nationalism has meant substituting collective self-love for the love of God, enhancing life on this earth instead of preparing for what is to come after death, and promoting the community's welfare instead of obeying God's revealed laws.

During roughly the last forty years before World War I, the peoples of the Arab world, Turkey, and Persia began to develop feelings of nationalism. As this era was the heyday of European imperialism, we can see rising nationalism as a natural reaction to Western power. But it was also the end result of a century of westernizing reform, with its enlarged armies and bureaucracies, modern schools, printing presses, roads and rail lines, and centralized state power. One could not learn the techniques of Europe, most often taught in French, without absorbing some of the ideas of Europe. Middle Eastern students at French or German universities had plenty of chances to get exposed to Western ideas, even if they never attended lectures in political theory. There were newspapers and magazines being hawked in the streets, lively discussions in cafes, demonstrations (or riots), and occasional encounters with Western orientalists (the nineteenth-century counterpart of our Middle East historians and linguists) who could explain what was happening in Europe to a Turkish, Egyptian, or Persian newcomer. Even the students who learned their technical skills in Istanbul, Cairo, or Tehran were apt to get exposed to Western ideas through their European instructors. Besides, their schools usually had reading rooms. A Middle Easterner studying engineering could read works by Rousseau or other Western writers.

In short, as Middle Easterners learned how to work like Europeans, some also started to think like them. They learned that bad governments did not have to be endured (and of course many Muslims had in earlier centuries defied tyrannical rulers), that individuals had rights and freedoms that should be protected against arbitrary official coercion, and that people could belong to political communities based on race, language, culture, and shared historical experience—in short, they form nations. In the 1870s these liberal and nationalist ideas became current among many educated young Muslims of the Middle East, especially in the capital cities. While they faced the frustrations of these years and those that followed, their ideas crystallized into nationalist movements.

Many religious and ethnic groups formed nationalist movements in the Middle East before World War I. I will limit this chapter, however, to three that grew up within existing states that had governments and some experience with westernizing reform: those of the Egyptians, the Turks in the Ottoman Empire, and the Persians under the Qajar shahs. Arab nationalism and Zionism will be covered in later chapters. And nationalism among such Christian peoples of the Ottoman Empire as the Greeks and the Armenians will be discussed only as they affected the rise of Turkish nationalism.

## EGYPTIAN NATIONALISM

Western writers used to call Egypt "the land of paradox." Almost all its inhabitants were crowded into the valley and delta of the great River Nile, without which Egypt would have been only a desert supporting a few bedouin nomads. To European tourists of a century ago, Egypt was filled with relics of antiquity—temples, obelisks, pyramids, sphinxes, and buried treasures—and haunted by pharaohs whose tombs had been violated by bedouin robbers or Western archaeologists. To most Muslims, however, Egypt was the very heart and soul of Islam, with its mosque-university of al-Azhar, its festive observance of Muslim holy days and saints' birthdays, and its annual procession bearing a new cloth that would be sent to cover the Ka'bah in Mecca. Egypt meant Cairo, with its hundreds of mosques and *madrasahs*, ornate villas and bazaars—survivals of a time when the Mamluks really ruled and the city stood out as an economic and intellectual center. To a student who has just been exposed to Mehmet Ali's reforms and the building of the Suez Canal, Egypt was the most westernized country in the nineteenth-century Middle East.

Picture then, if you will, one of the newer quarters of Cairo or Alexandria in 1875, or the new towns of Port Said and Ismailia, their wide, straight avenues lined with European-style houses, hotels, banks, shops, schools, and churches. Horse-drawn carriages whiz past the donkeys and camels of a more leisurely age. Restaurants serve coq au vin or veal scallopini instead of *kuftah* (ground meat) or kebab; their customers smoke cigars in place of water pipes. The signs are in French, not Arabic. The passersby converse in Italian, Greek, Armenian, Turkish, Yiddish, Ladino (a language derived from Spanish and spoken by Sephardic Jews), or several dialects of Arabic. Top hats have replaced turbans, and frock coats have supplanted the caftans of yore. Each of these images fits a part of Egypt a century ago—but not all of it.

## Khedive Isma'il

The man who ruled over this land of paradox was Mehmet Ali's grandson, Isma'il (r. 1863–1879), a complex and controversial figure. Was he a man of vision, as his admirers claimed, or a spendthrift who would ultimately bring Egypt into British bondage? His admirers could tick off the railroads, bridges, docks, canals, factories, and sugar refineries built during his reign. It was also the time when the Egyptian government paid explorers and military expeditions to penetrate the Sudan and East Africa and worked to abolish slavery and slave trading within its empire. The Egyptian Mixed Courts were set up to hear civil cases involving Europeans protected by the Capitulations. Public and missionary schools—for girls as well as boys—proliferated in the cities. The Egyptian Museum, National Library, Geographical Society, and many of the professional schools first saw life under Isma'il.

But Isma'il's detractors point out that he spent money wildly in an effort to impress Europe with his munificence and power. Building the Suez Canal was costly for the Egyptian government, for the state treasury had to reimburse the Suez Canal Company when it was forced to pay wages to the peasant construction workers (the company had expected to get their labor for free). This was the fault of Isma'il's predecessor, Sa'id. But it was Isma'il who turned the canal's inauguration into an extravaganza, inviting the crowned heads and leaders of Europe to come—at Egypt's expense. Costing at least 2 million Egyptian pounds (worth $300 million in today's prices), it must have been the bash of the century, with enormous receptions, all-night parties, balls, parades, fireworks displays, horseraces, excursions to ancient monuments, and cities festooned with flags and illuminated by lanterns. New villas and palaces sprouted up, streets were widened and straightened, old neighborhoods were demolished, and even an opera house was erected in Cairo. Giuseppe Verdi, the Italian composer, was commissioned to write *Aida* for the inauguration of that opera house. Isma'il also paid huge bribes in Istanbul to increase his independence from the Ottoman government, changing his title from *pasha* ("governor") to *khedive* ("viceroy") of Egypt and obtaining the right to pass down his position to his son in Cairo rather than to a brother living in Istanbul. He also won a fateful privilege: that of taking out foreign loans without Ottoman permission.

## Financial Problems

But where could the money have come from? Egyptian taxpayers could not cover Isma'il's extravagance. The start of his reign had coincided with the American Civil War, which caused a cotton boom in Egypt. The British, cut off by the Northern blockade from their usual cotton supply, were willing to pay any price for other countries' crops to supply the textile mills of Lancashire. The high demand for Egypt's cotton stimulated output and greatly enriched both the Egyptian growers and the government. During this cotton boom, European investment bankers offered Isma'il loans on very attractive terms. When the boom ended after the Civil War, Egypt's need for money was greater than ever, but now he could get credit only at high interest rates. In 1866 Isma'il convoked an assembly representing the landowners to seek their consent to raise taxes. Soon they were taxing date palms, flour mills, oil presses, boats, shops, houses, and even burials.

Isma'il adopted still other stratagems to put off the day of reckoning. He promised substantial tax abatements to landowners who could pay three years' taxes in advance. He sold Egypt's shares in the Suez Canal Company—44 percent of the stock—to the British government in 1875. When a British delegation came to check up on rumors of Egypt's impending bankruptcy, the khedive agreed to set up a European commission to manage the public debt. But a low Nile in 1877, high military expenses incurred in the Russo-Turkish War, and an invasion of Ethiopia put the Egyptian government deeper in debt. In August 1878 Isma'il, pressed by his European creditors, agreed to admit an Englishman and a Frenchman to his cabinet, starting the so-called Dual Financial Control; he also promised to turn his powers over to his ministers. At the same time, he secretly stirred up antiforeign elements in his army. This was easy, for the Dual Control had cut the Egyptian officers' pay in half. A military riot in February 1879 enabled Isma'il to dismiss the foreign ministers and later to appoint a cabinet of liberals who began drafting a constitution, much as the Ottoman Empire had done in 1876. Britain and France, guarding their investors' interests, asked the Ottoman sultan to dismiss Isma'il. He did. When Isma'il turned over the khedivate to his son, Tawfiq, and left Egypt in July 1879, the state debt stood at 93 million Egyptian pounds. It had been 3 million when he came to power in 1863.

*The Beginnings of Nationalism*

Isma'il's successes and failures made him the father of Egypt's first nationalist movement. His new schools, law courts, railroads, and telegraph lines drew Egyptians closer together and helped to foster nationalist feeling. So did the newspapers he patronized in the hope of building up favorable public opinion. The Suez Canal and related projects drew thousands of

Europeans into Egypt; they became models for modernization and at the same time targets of native resentment.

Muslim feeling, always strong but usually quiescent, was aroused at this time under the influence of a fiery pan-Islamic agitator, Jamal al-Din, called al-Afghani (despite his claim of being an Afghan, he was really from Persia), who came to teach at al-Azhar. Afghani pops up in almost every political movement that stirred in the Middle East in the late nineteenth century. He soon clashed with the conservative ulama and quit al-Azhar to form a sort of independent academy that attracted many young Egyptians who would later become political leaders or Islamic reformers. Two of them were Muhammad Abduh, the greatest Muslim thinker of the late nineteenth century, and Sa'd Zaghlul, leader of Egypt's independence struggle after World War I. Afghani, like Isma'il, encouraged journalists; but his protégés were bolder ones, often Jews or Christians who turned more readily to secular nationalism than did most Muslims of the late 1870s.

Isma'il's financial troubles, which tied Egypt to Western creditors and to their governments, shamed Egyptians, especially members of his representative assembly. Once a subservient group of frightened rural landlords, it had now turned into a vociferous body of antigovernment critics. But the key breeding ground for nationalism was the army. Sa'id had started admitting Egyptian peasants' sons into the officer corps and had promoted some of them rapidly, whereas Isma'il held back their promotions and pay raises in favor of the traditional elite, the Turks and Circassians. Frustrated, the Egyptian officers formed a secret society to plot against their oppressors. It later would become the nucleus of the first National party.

Isma'il's deposition set back the nascent nationalists. During his last months in power, the Egyptian officers had joined with government workers, assembly representatives, journalists, and ulama to back the drafters of a constitution that would give to Egyptians some of the rights and freedoms enjoyed by Europeans in their own countries. But Tawfiq, the new khedive, thought it safer to back the European creditors than the Egyptian nationalists. He dismissed the liberal cabinet, restored the Dual Control, banned some of the newspapers, and exiled Afghani and other agitators.

## Ahmad Urabi

The nationalists seemed to be in eclipse, but I suspect that Khedive Tawfiq secretly encouraged them. Sa'd Zaghlul and Muhammad Abduh could still demand constitutional rule in the official paper that they edited. The disgruntled Egyptian officers continued to meet. In February 1881 these men, led by one Colonel Ahmad Urabi, mutinied and "forced" Tawfiq to replace his Circassian war minister with a nationalist, Mahmud Sami al-Barudi. Seven months later, 2,500 Egyptian officers and soldiers surrounded the khedive's palace and "made" him appoint a liberal cabinet. Moreover, they demanded a constitution, parliamentary government, and an enlarged army. The same demands were sought by the civilian nationalists; they were also feared by the European creditors, who wondered how Tawfiq or Urabi would ever find money to pay for these reforms.

During the next year Egypt came as close as it ever would to either democratic government (if you take the Egyptian nationalist view of history) or political chaos (if you buy the European—especially British—interpretation of what happened). A liberal cabinet drew up a constitution and held elections as Egypt's debts rose further. In January 1882 Britain and France sent a joint note, threatening to intervene to support Tawfiq (they really meant to restore the Dual Control). The nationalists called their bluff, declaring that Egypt's new Assembly, not the British and French debt commissioners, would control the state budget. Barudi took over the premiership and Urabi became war minister—bad news for the Turkish and Circassian officers in Egypt's army. The nationalists even thought of ousting Tawfiq and declaring Egypt a republic. More likely, though, they would have replaced him with one of his exiled relatives, a strange way to treat their secret patron.

As nationalism was so new in Egypt, we wonder if an outsider inspired these moves. A few English liberals helped Urabi, and the French consul in Cairo may have encouraged Urabi; however, the outside supporters seem to have been the Ottoman sultan and a dispossessed uncle of Tawfiq living in Istanbul. This fact may make the movement seem less than wholly nationalist. A book by a German scholar argues that what we usually call the National party was really a constellation of several groups with various political, economic, and religious interests. Still, the movement had become popular in Egypt by June 1882. What destroyed it was Britain's determination to send in troops, if need be, to protect European lives and investments in Egypt and also to defend the Suez Canal, which had become vital to British shipping.

Riots in Alexandria caused a general exodus of Europeans, and both British and French gunboats dropped anchor just outside the harbor. Then the British fired on Alexandria's fortifications, somehow much of the city caught on fire, and British marines landed to restore order (as the

French ships sailed away). Urabi declared war on Britain, but Tawfiq declared him a traitor and threw in his lot with the British in Alexandria. Other British Empire troops entered the canal and landed at Ismailia. Defeating Urabi's army was easy, and the British occupied Cairo in September 1882. Barudi's cabinet was dismissed, the nationalists were tried for rebellion, Urabi was exiled, the constitution was suspended, the nationalist newspapers were banned, and even the army was broken up by Tawfiq and his British advisers. The early nationalists had proved a weak force. Their party had been divided among Egyptian officers resenting Turkish and Circassian privileges in the army, civilians seeking parliamentary government, and reformers such as Afghani and Abduh who dreamt of an Islamic revival.

## Lord Cromer and the British Occupation

The British government that sent troops into Egypt in 1882 expected its military occupation to be brief. As soon as order was restored, Britain's troops were supposed to leave, and Egypt was to resume being an autonomous Ottoman province. But the longer the British stayed in Egypt, the more disorder they found to clean up and the less they wanted to get out. The financial situation in particular needed drastic economic and administrative reforms. The British agent and consul general in Cairo from 1883 to 1907, Lord Cromer, was a brilliant financial administrator. With a small (but growing) staff of British advisers to Egypt's various government ministries, Cromer was able to expand the Nile irrigation system to raise agricultural output, increase state revenues, lower taxes, and reduce the public debt burden. The British officials around him were highly competent, dedicated to the Egyptians' welfare, and scrupulously honest. His epitaph in Westminster Abbey would refer to him as the "regenerator of Egypt."

He may have been so, but Cromer is not well remembered in Egypt today. Many Egyptians living in his era felt that their own advancement in government posts or the professions was blocked by the numerous foreigners holding high positions in Cairo. Besides, they objected to Cromer's policy of limiting the growth of higher education. Some resented the fact that the Egyptian army, despite its British officers, lost the Sudan in 1885 to a rebellion led by the self-styled Mahdi (Rightly Guided One). After British and Egyptian troops won back the Sudan in 1898, it was placed under a condominium, with Britain effectively in control. Opposition to the continuing British occupation of Egypt came from a few British anti-imperialists; the French, who (despite their large economic stake in Egypt) had failed to intervene in 1882; and the Ottoman Turks, who resented losing another province of their empire. As long as there was no internal opposition, though, these groups could do little to thwart the British presence.

## The Revival of Egyptian Nationalism

Major resistance began when Abbas, Khedive Tawfiq's seventeen-year-old son, succeeded him in 1892. High-spirited and proudly guarding what he felt were his khedivial prerogatives, Abbas fought with Cromer over the right to appoint and dismiss his ministers and over control of the Egyptian army. Although the British consul won the battles by bullying the ministers and asking his own government to send more troops to Egypt, he lost the trust of the youthful khedive. Seeking to undermine Cromer, Abbas built up a clique of European and native supporters. Among the latter was an articulate law student named Mustafa Kamil, who emerged in 1895 as a potent palace propagandist in both Europe and Egypt. In the ensuing years, he gradually turned what had been Abbas's secret society into a large-scale movement, the (revived) National party. He founded a boys' school and a daily newspaper, the better to spread nationalist ideas. As his popularity grew, Mustafa became more interested in obtaining a democratic constitution and less concerned about the khedive's prerogatives. Of course, he and his followers always viewed the evacuation of British troops from Egypt as their main goal.

In 1906 an incident occurred that helped to spread Mustafa Kamil's fame. A group of British officers went to shoot pigeons in a village called Dinshaway. Due to some misunderstandings between the villagers and the officers, a fracas broke out. A gun went off, setting a threshing floor on fire. Another bullet wounded a peasant woman. The villagers began to beat the officers with clubs. One of the latter escaped, fainted after running several miles, and died of sunstroke. The British authorities, suspecting a premeditated assault, tried fifty-seven peasants before a special military court, which found many of them guilty of murder. Four were hanged and several others flogged in the presence of their families as an object lesson to the Dinshaway villagers. These barbarous sentences appalled Mustafa Kamil, most Egyptians, and even many Europeans, for at that time people were shocked by atrocities that now, after Hitler and Stalin, seem tame. Mustafa exploited those sentiments to win new followers and hasten Cromer's retirement. He publicly established the National party in December 1907 but tragically died two months later.

Mustafa's successors became divided over their tactics and aims. Was the National party for Muslims against Christian rulers or for all Egyptian people opposed to the British occupation? If the latter, could Egypt expect support from its nominal overlord, the Ottoman Empire? Should the party seek national independence by peaceful or revolutionary means? If the latter, would it oppose Khedive Abbas and other large landowners? Should it seek economic and social reform, or concentrate first on getting the British out of Egypt? How could a party made up mainly of lawyers and students, with little or no support in the Egyptian army, persuade Britain to leave? More moderate leaders, such as Ahmad Lutfi al-Sayyid, argued that constitutional government should precede independence. The British consul who replaced Cromer in 1907 neutralized the Nationalist threat by wooing Khedive Abbas and the more conservative landowners to Britain's side. The next consul won peasant support through his agrarian policies. By 1914 the Nationalist leaders were in exile. Only after World War I would the Egyptians build up enough resentment against British rule to form a truly national and revolutionary movement.

## OTTOMANISM, PAN-ISLAM, AND TURKISM

The rise of Turkish nationalism has been complicated by the fact that up to the twentieth century, no educated Ottoman, even if Turkish was his native tongue, cared to be called a Turk. The Ottoman Empire, though Europeans called it Turkey, was definitely not a Turkish nation-state. It contained many ethnic and religious groups: Turks, Greeks, Serbs, Croats, Albanians, Bulgarians, Arabs, Syrians, Armenians, and Kurds, to name but a few. Its rulers were Sunni Muslims, but it included Greek Orthodox, Armenian, and Jewish subjects organized into *millets* (which functioned almost like nations within the state), as well as many smaller religious groups. In Ottoman political tradition, its inhabitants were either *Osmanlilar*, who belonged to the ruling class, or *re'aya*, who did not, with nothing in between.

### Early Nationalism in the Ottoman Empire

Nationalism in the modern sense first appeared among the Greeks and the Serbs (who were most exposed to Western or Russian influences), then spread to other subject Christians. As independence movements proliferated in the Balkans, the Ottoman rulers worried more and more over how to hold their empire together and counter the Russians, who openly encouraged Balkan revolts. Westernizing reforms were their first solution, but these raised more hopes than could be met and did not create a new basis of loyalty. The reformers espoused the idea of Ottomanism (loyalty to the Ottoman state) as a framework within which racial, linguistic, and religious groups could develop autonomously but harmoniously. To this the New Ottomans of the 1870s had added the idea of a constitution that would set up an assembly representing all peoples of the empire. The constitution was drafted in 1876—the worst possible time, with several nationalist rebellions going on in the Balkans, war raging against Serbia and Montenegro (two Balkan states that had already won their independence), the Ottoman treasury nearly bankrupt, Russia threatening to send in troops, and Britain preparing to fight against the Turks to protect the Balkan Christians and against the Russians to defend the Ottoman Empire (a policy as weird to people then as it sounds now). Moreover, the New Ottomans had seized power in a coup, put on the throne a sultan who turned out to be crazy, and then replaced him with his brother, Abdulhamid II (r. 1876–1909), whose promises to uphold the new constitution were suspect.

Well, they should have been. The ensuing Russo-Turkish War put the empire in such peril that no one could have governed under the Ottoman constitution. Sultan Abdulhamid soon suspended it and dissolved parliament. For thirty years he ruled as a dictator, appointing and dismissing his own ministers, holding his creditors at bay, fomenting quarrels among the Great Powers to prevent them from partitioning the Ottoman Empire, and suppressing all dissident movements within his realm. People now looking back on him see him as a cruel sultan, reactionary in his attitudes toward westernizing reforms and devoted to the doctrine of pan-Islam. This movement alarmed Russia, Britain, and France, with their millions of Muslim subjects in Asia and Africa. It is interesting that Istanbul, seat of the sultan-caliph, became the final home of that wandering pan-Islamic agitator, Jamal al-Din al-Afghani. Many thought the sultan had him poisoned.

Abdulhamid is remembered for his censors and spies, his morbid fear of assassination, and his massacres of Armenians (some of whom were plotting against his regime). Although scholars trying to rehabilitate his image have shown how he furthered the centralizing policies of the earlier Tanzimat reformers, although the Ottoman Empire lost no European lands between 1878 and 1908, and although Muslims at home and abroad hailed him as their caliph, Sultan Abdulhamid was unquestionably incompetent, paranoid, and cruel. The empire's finances came under the control of a European debt commission, the freedoms of speech and assembly vanished, the army came to a standstill, and the navy deteriorated. The ablest reformers went into exile. Midhat, leader of the New Ottomans, was lured back with false promises, tried for attempted murder, locked up in the Arabian town of Taif, and secretly strangled there. It is said that Midhat's head was sent back to Istanbul in a box labeled "Japanese ivories, to be opened only by the sultan."

Many Ottomans, especially if they had attended Western schools, felt that the only way to save the Ottoman Empire was to restore the 1876 constitution, even if they had to overthrow Abdulhamid first. A number of opposition groups were formed. All of them tend to get lumped together as the "Young Turks," a term borrowed from Mazzini's "Young Italy," or perhaps from the "New Ottomans." Many were not Turks, and some were not even young, but the term has stuck. The key society was a secret one formed by four cadets—all Muslims but of several nationalities. It became known as the Committee of Union and Progress (CUP). Its history was long and tortuous, with moments of hope interspersed with years of gloom, centering at times on exiled Turkish writers living in Paris or Geneva, at others on cells of Ottoman army officers in Salonika and Damascus. Gradually, many Ottoman groups adopted the CUP's goals: that the empire must be strengthened militarily and morally, that all religious and ethnic groups must have equal rights, that the constitution must be restored, and that Sultan Abdulhamid must be shorn of power. Otherwise, Russia would move in and take what was left of the empire in Europe, including Istanbul and the Straits. Then the other Western powers would carve up Turkey in Asia, just as they had partitioned Africa and divided China into spheres of influence.

## The Young Turks in Power

The CUP was Ottomanist, not Turkish nationalist, as long as it was out of power. Responding in part to the reconciliation between the British and the Russians in 1907, the CUP inspired an army coup that forced Abdulhamid to restore the Ottoman constitution in 1908. Every religious and ethnic group in the empire rejoiced; the committee, even if most of its leaders were Turks, had the support of many loyal Balkan Christians, Armenians, Arabs, and Jews. Most wanted to go on being Ottoman citizens under the 1876 constitution. Western well-wishers believed that Turkey would now revive. Elections were held for the new Parliament, the tide of democracy seemed to be sweeping into Istanbul, and the CUP started so many changes that even now we call vigorous reformers "Young Turks." Indeed, their rise to power portended the many revolutions that have changed the face of Middle Eastern politics since 1908.

But if we examine what really happened to the Ottoman Empire under the Young Turks, we must give them lower marks for their achievements than for their stated intentions. They did not halt disintegration, as Austria annexed Bosnia, Bulgaria declared its independence, and Crete rebelled, all in late 1908. Their hopes for rapid economic development were dashed when France withdrew a loan offer in 1910. The next year Italy invaded the Ottoman province of Tripolitania. Then Russia incited Bulgaria and Serbia to join forces in 1912 and attack the empire in Macedonia. In four months the Turks lost almost all their European lands. Even Albania, a mainly Muslim part of the Balkans, rebelled in 1910 and declared its independence in 1913. And the Arabs, as you will see in the next chapter, were getting restless.

How could Istanbul's government, as set up under the restored 1876 constitution, weather all these problems? Soon after the CUP won the 1912 election by massive use of bribery and intimidation, the army forced its ministers to resign in favor of its rival, the Liberal Entente. It took another military coup and a timely assassination in 1913 to restore the CUP to power. By the outbreak of World War I, the Ottoman government was a virtual triumvirate: Enver as war minister, Talat as minister of the interior, and Jemal in charge of the navy. Democracy was dead in the Ottoman Empire.

## Turkish Nationalism

Amid these crises, the CUP leaders became more and more Turkish in their political orientation. Their early hope that the Great Powers and the empire's minorities would back their attempts at Ottomanism had been dashed. The powers grabbed territory and withheld aid. The minorities grumbled, plotted, or rebelled. What could the Young Turks do? Some stuck to their Ottomanist guns. Others argued for pan-Islam, which would have held the loyalty of most Arabs and also won needed support from Egypt, India, and other Muslim lands. But the new wave was pan-Turanism. This was the attempt to bring together all speakers of Turkic languages under Ottoman leadership, just as pan-Slavism meant uniting all speakers of Slavic languages behind Russia. Indeed, as most speakers of Turkic languages were then under czarist rule or military occupation, pan-Turanism seemed a good way to pay back the Russians for all the grief they had given the Ottoman Empire. Several of the leading pan-Turanian advocates were refugees from Russian Turkistan or Azerbaijan, but it was hard for the Ottoman Turks to forget their traditional ties to Islam or their own empire. Few believed that there really was a distinct Turanian culture. The CUP's efforts to impose Turkish in the schools and offices of their Arabic-speaking provinces stirred up Arab nationalism, which would further weaken their empire. The committee's influence on Central Asian Turks was almost nil. The Turks' ethnic and linguistic nationalism caused them more problems than it solved, until they limited their national idea to fellow Turks within the Ottoman Empire. The idea was not unknown. A Turkish sociologist named Ziya Gokalp was writing newspaper articles to promote what he called Turkism, but this idea would become popular only after World War I. By then it was too late to save the Ottoman Empire.

## NATIONALISM IN PERSIA

Persia, as you know, did not westernize as early as Egypt and the Ottoman Empire. However, it had a compensating advantage when it came to developing Persian nationalism. Let us look at what historians and political scientists usually cite as nationalism's components: (1) previously existing state, (2) religion, (3) language, (4) race, (5) lifestyle, (6) shared economic interests, (7) common enemies, and (8) shared historical consciousness. If you test Egyptian or Turkish nationalism against these criteria, you will find that they fall short on several counts. Not so Persian nationalism. The Qajar dynasty may have governed ineptly, but it was heir to a Persian political tradition traceable to the ancient Achaemenids, with slight interruptions owing to Greek, Arab, Turkish, and Mongol invasions. Persia was predominantly Muslim; but its uniqueness was ensured by its general adherence to Twelve-Imam Shi'ism, whereas its Muslim neighbors were mainly Sunni. Its chief written and spoken language was Persian (or Farsi), even though many of the country's inhabitants spoke Turkish while numerous Muslims in India and the Ottoman Empire read and wrote Persian well. *Race* is a treacherous term to use in a land so often invaded and settled by outsiders, but certainly the Persians regarded their personal appearance as distinctive. Their lifestyle, or culture, had withstood the tests of time, invasions, and political change. Both visitors and natives hailed the Persian way of life: its poetry, architecture, costumes, cuisine, social relationships—and even its jokes. The economic interests of nineteenth-century Persia seem to have been, if not homogeneous, at least complementary among city dwellers, farmers, and nomads. No other Middle Easterners could match the Persians' strong historical consciousness, expressed in their monumental architecture, painting, epic poetry, written history, and music, glorifying twenty-five centuries as a distinctive people.

### Early Resistance to Foreign Power

It should not surprise you, therefore, to learn that a Persian nationalist movement arose between 1870 and 1914. Basically, it was a reaction against the threat of a Russian military takeover, against growing dependence on the West, and against the divisive effects of tribalism in the rural areas. It was facilitated by the spread of roads, telegraphs, and both public and private schools. Nasiruddin Shah's policy of selling to foreign investors the rights to develop Persia's resources alienated his own subjects. In 1873 he offered a concession to one Baron de Reuter, a British subject, to form a monopoly that would build railways, operate mines, and establish Persia's national bank. Russian objections and domestic opposition forced the shah to cancel the concession, although the baron was later authorized to start the Imperial Bank of Persia. In 1890 Nasiruddin sold a concession to an English company to control the production, sale, and export of all tobacco in Persia. As I wrote in Chapter 11, a nationwide tobacco boycott, inspired by the same Afghani you saw earlier in Egypt, forced the cancellation of this concession. The boycott gave westernized Persians, Shi'i ulama, and bazaar merchants enough confidence in their political power to spur the growth of a constitutionalist movement in the ensuing years. Many observers noted the mounting problems of the Qajar shahs, their economic concessions to foreigners, the widening disparities between rich landowners and poor peasants (owing to the shift from subsistence to cash-crop agriculture), and Persia's growing dependence on Russian military advisers. Well might they wonder how long it would take for Russia to occupy Persia. Persians could see for themselves the British occupation of Egypt, the weakness of Abdulhamid's regime, and the foreign penetration of China. If the Russian troops did not come, some asked, would British investors take over Persia more subtly? As Russia was Persia's number one enemy, Britain was a close second. The shah, surrounded by fawning and corrupt courtiers, had sold most of his inherited treasures and was spending the proceeds of his foreign loans on palaces, European trips, and gifts to his family and friends.

## The Constitutionalist Movement

Patriotic Persians felt that the remedy to these ills was a constitution that would limit the arbitrary acts of their rulers. The idea spread among bazaar merchants, landlords, ulama, army officers, and even some government officials and tribal leaders. Secret societies sprang up in various cities, notably Tabriz (the main city in Azerbaijan) and Tehran (Persia's capital). The spark that set off the revolution was an arbitrary act by the shah's prime minister, Ayn al-Dowleh, who ordered the flogging of several merchants for allegedly plotting to drive up the price of sugar in the Tehran bazaar. The merchants took refuge in the royal mosque (which, by a time-honored Persian custom called *bast*, gave them sanctuary from arrest), but Ayn al-Dowleh had them expelled. This move enraged Tehran's ulama and swelled the number of protestors, who moved to another mosque. Desiring peace, the shah offered to dismiss his minister and to convene a "house of justice" to redress their grievances. But he failed to act on his promises. When the shah was incapacitated by a stroke, Ayn al-Dowleh attacked the protestors, who then got up a larger *bast* in Tehran. Meanwhile, the *mujtahids*, or Shi'i legal leaders, sought *bast* in nearby Qom and threatened to leave Persia en masse—an act that would have paralyzed the country's courts—unless their demands were met. Shops throughout Tehran closed. When Ayn al-Dowleh tried to force them to open, 15,000 Persians took refuge in the British legation, camping on its lawn for several weeks during July 1906. Finally the shah bowed to popular pressure. He fired Ayn al-Dowleh and accepted a Western-style constitution in which the government would be controlled by a Majlis, or representative assembly. So great was his aversion to the Persian nationalists, however, that only pressure from Britain and Russia (plus the fact that he was dying) kept him from blocking the constitution before it could take effect.

The Persian nationalists achieved too much too soon. In 1907 Britain and Russia reached an agreement recognizing each other's spheres of influence in Persia. Britain was to have primary influence over the southeast, the part of the country closest to its Indian empire. Russia acquired the right to send troops and advisers to the heavily populated north, including the key provinces of Azerbaijan and Khurasan, plus Tehran itself. Russia backed the new shah enough to enable him to close the Majlis in 1908. Though one of the main tribes helped the constitutionalists to regain military control of Tehran and then to reopen the Majlis in 1909, the Persian nationalist movement now lacked the fervent popular support it had enjoyed three years earlier. The revived Majlis got bogged down in debates and achieved nothing.

## Oil Discoveries

Persians might have welcomed news from the province of Khuzistan, located in the southwest, where a British company had begun oil exploration in 1901. In 1908 it made its first strike, and by 1914 thousands of barrels were being piped to a refinery on the Gulf island port of Abadan. When Britain's navy switched from coal to petroleum just before World War I, the future of Persian oil looked even brighter. But to the nationalists this growing industry was cold comfort. It was taking place far from Tehran, in lands traditionally controlled by tribal *shaykhs*. The revenues were going mainly to British stockholders—not to the Persian government, let alone its impoverished subjects. In the last years before World War I, Persia as a whole seemed to be drifting toward becoming a Russian protectorate.

## CONCLUSION

Nationalism in the West has gotten a bad name in the twentieth century, partly due to the destruction caused by two world wars, partly because of the excesses of such dictators as Mussolini and Hitler, and maybe also because our intellectual leaders have become more cosmopolitan. Even in the Middle East, it is now the fashion to attack secular nationalism and exalt Islamic unity, and nearly everyone recognizes the artificial character of most of the so-called nations that were set up by British or French imperialism.

Generally speaking, Middle Eastern nationalist movements fared badly before World War I. They surely did not increase the power, the lands, or the freedom of the Muslim states in which they arose. Except for a few successful moments, which now seem like lightning flashes within a general gloom, these movements did not win any wide popular support. There is no nationalism in Islam, said the critics, so these movements could appeal only to youths who had lost their religion because of Western education. Even when they reached a wider public, their success was due to popular misunderstandings. The uneducated majority often mistook the nationalist triumphs for Muslim victories. And these were few indeed. "Roll up the map of Islam," wrote a leading English sympathizer in his diary in 1911. Soon the European Christians would divide up what little was left of the independent Muslim world. Perhaps, the writer mused, only in Arabia, its birthplace, would Islam survive as an independent political force.

You may wonder why I told you so much about these unsuccessful nationalist movements. Why learn about them? History is not just the story of winners; sometimes we study losers whose grandchildren would be winners. History is more than a collection of mere facts, names, and dates; we must also look at the ways in which the peoples we care about view their own past. Ahmad Urabi and Mustafa Kamil are heroes to the Egyptian people today; Khedive Isma'il and Lord Cromer are not. In Istanbul, you can buy postcards that bear pictures of the leading New Ottomans. Every Turkish student sees the Young Turks as a link in the chain of national regenerators going from Selim III to Kemal Ataturk. The 1906 constitution remained the legal basis of Iran's government until 1979, and the Islamic Republic still remembers the Shi'i leaders and bazaar merchants who fought together against the shah to make the older constitution a reality. For the peoples of the Middle East, these early nationalist movements were the prologue for the revolutionary changes that were to come.

# THIRTEEN

# The Roots of Arab Bitterness

Few topics in Middle East history have generated as much heat—and as little light—as Arab nationalism. Few people are as poorly understood as today's Arabs. Even deciding who is an Arab or defining what is meant by Arab nationalism can easily get scholars and students into trouble, with both the Arabs and their detractors. Nevertheless, Arabs are becoming more politically active in the twenty-first century. In our analysis we may find that what is called Arab nationalism is now dissolving into many different movements, whose common feature is that they pertain to various Arabic-speaking peoples who seek to control their own political destinies. We must study these various manifestations of Arab feeling. And let us not fool ourselves: Arab feeling is strong and is likely to get stronger. It is also sometimes bitter, owing to some of the Arabs' unhappy experiences in the early twentieth century. Let us see what happened, and why.

## ARAB NATIONALISM

What is Arab nationalism? Simply put, it is the belief that the Arabs constitute a single political community (or nation) and ought to have a common government. Right away we can see problems. There is no general agreement on who is an Arab. The current definition is that an Arab is anyone who speaks Arabic as his or her native language. This is not enough. Many speakers of Arabic do not think of themselves as Arabs, nor do other Arabs so regard them: Take, for example, the Lebanese Maronites, the Egyptian Copts, and of course the Jews born in Arab countries who went to live in Israel. A more eloquent definition is one adopted by a conference of Arab leaders years ago: "Whoever lives in our country, speaks our language, is reared in our culture, and takes pride in our glory is one of us."

Up to the twentieth century, the term *Arab* was applied mainly to the camel-raising nomads of Arabia, the bedouin. To the settled peoples of Egypt and Syria, to be called an Arab was almost an insult. Turks used to call them *pis arablar* (dirty Arabs), which of course they resented. The ideas that Syrians and Egyptians might find glory in being Arabs, let alone in uniting their countries in the name of Arab nationalism (as happened in 1958 and almost recurred several other times), would have been taken as a joke. The question "What are you?" might have rated such answers as "I am a Syrian," "I am a Damascene," "I am a Sunni Muslim of the Shafi'i legal rite," or "I am a carpenter." Even a tribal affiliation might have been mentioned, but never "I am an Arab," at least not before the twentieth century. Even now, we note that there are some twenty countries that see themselves as part of the Arab world, each with its own government, flag, currency, stamps, identity card, and seat on the Council of the Arab League. None would deny the League's loyalty to the ideal of Arab unity, yet its member states go their separate ways. Even common opposition to the State of Israel did not bring the Arabs together; rather, it divided them even more.

## Historical Background

As we review the history of the Arabic-speaking peoples, we must remember that they have not been united since the era of the High Caliphate, if indeed then. Moreover, except for the bedouin, they did not rule themselves from the time the Turks came in until quite recently. The very idea of people ruling themselves would not have made sense to Middle Easterners before the rise of nationalism. For settled peoples, what mattered was that a Muslim government rule over them, defend them from nomads and other invaders, preserve order, and promote peace in accordance with the Shari'ah. It did not matter whether the head of that Muslim government was an Arab like the Umayyad caliphs, a Persian like the Buyid amirs, a Turk like the Seljuk and Ottoman sultans, or a Kurd like Salah al-Din and his Ayyubid heirs. Almost all rulers succeeded by either heredity or nomination; no one thought of letting the people elect them.

## The Arabs Under Ottoman Rule

From the sixteenth to the twentieth centuries most Arabs—all of them, really, except in parts of Arabia and Morocco—belonged to the Ottoman Empire. Even in periods of Ottoman weakness, the local officials and landlords were apt to be Turks, Circassians, or other non-Arabs. Since World War I the Arab nationalists and their sympathizers have denounced the horrors of Ottoman rule, blaming the Turks for the Arabs' backwardness, political ineptitude, disunity, or whatever else was amiss in their society. What went wrong? How did the state of the Arabs under Ottoman rule compare with what it had been earlier? In fact, the Arabs' decline cannot be blamed on Istanbul. You can even argue that early Ottoman rule had benefited the Arabs by promoting local security and trade between their merchants and those of Anatolia and the Balkans. If the eighteenth-century Ottoman decline and overly zealous nineteenth-century reforms hurt the Arabs, the Turks within the empire suffered too. If Ottoman rule was so oppressive, why did the Arabs not rebel?

Well, at times they did. I have already mentioned the Wahhabi revolt in eighteenth-century Arabia, but that group wanted to purify Islam, not to set up an Arab state. Peasant and military revolts sometimes broke out in Egypt, but for economic rather than national reasons. Some historians have found an anti-Ottoman angle in the policies of Mehmet Ali and Ibrahim. The latter, as governor of Syria, is supposed to have said: "I am not a Turk. I came to Egypt as a child, and since that time, the sun of Egypt has changed my blood and made it all Arab." But Mehmet Ali and his heirs spoke Turkish, viewed themselves as members of the Ottoman ruling class, and treated the Egyptians like servants. Urabi's name implied some Arab identity (many Egyptian peasants trace their lineage to Arab tribes), and he did rebel against Turkish and Circassian officers in the Egyptian army, but his revolution was an Egyptian one directed mainly against the Anglo-French Dual Control. Uprisings in Syria were frequent, but their cause was usually religious. Tribes in Iraq and the Hijaz often revolted against Ottoman governors, but over local—not national—grievances.

In weighing these facts, historians have come to feel that Arab identity played no great part in Middle East politics up to the twentieth century. Muslim Arabs felt that any attempt to weaken the Ottoman Empire was apt to harm Islam. Even under Sultan Abdulhamid, despite his faults, most Arabs went on upholding the status quo. Many served in the army or the civil administration. Some were among his leading advisers. They might have taken pride in being from the same "race" as Muhammad, but this did not inspire them to rebel against the Turks, who were Muslims too.

## Christian Arab Nationalists

Not all Arabs are Muslim. In the nineteenth century, perhaps as many as one-fourth of the Arabs under Ottoman rule belonged to protected minorities. Most of these were Christians, who were less likely than the Muslims to feel a strong loyalty to the empire. But we must pin down the time, the place, and the sect before we can discuss the politics of the Arabic-speaking Christians. The ones whose role mattered most in the birth of Arab nationalism lived in Syria, which then included most of what we now call Israel, Jordan, Lebanon, the Republic of Syria, and even parts of southern Turkey. Until they came under the rule of Ibrahim in 1831, or under that of the Tanzimat reformers, Arabic-speaking Christians cared little about who governed them. The *millet* system gave virtual autonomy to both Orthodox and Monophysite Christians. As for the others, they were usually so well protected by deserts, mountains, or river gorges that they hardly felt the Ottoman yoke. The Maronites (and other Catholics) enjoyed French protection by the nineteenth century. Russia took a growing interest in the welfare of the Greek Orthodox Syrians. From the 1820s on, U.S. and French missionaries founded schools in Syria, as did the British, Russians, and other Westerners, though to a lesser extent. Inasmuch as Syrian Christians naturally sent their children to mission schools closest to their own religious affiliation, Maronites and Uniate Catholics tended to go to French Catholic schools and to identify with France. How could the Orthodox Christians compete? Distressed by the low educational level of their own clergy, some were converting to Catholicism or Protestantism and sending their children to the relevant mission schools. But even those who stayed in their ancestral faith rarely chose either to enter the priesthood, because all higher clerical positions were held by Greeks, or to attend Russian mission schools, when few aspired to go to Russian universities.

The Americans provided an answer to their problem, but quite by accident they aided the rise of Arab nationalism. U.S. mission schools, especially their crowning institution, the Syrian Protestant College (now the American University of Beirut), tried to serve students of every religion. But most of them hoped also to convert young people to Protestant Christianity. Because Protestantism has traditionally stressed the reading and understanding of its sacred scriptures, the Bible was soon translated into Arabic for local converts. Many of the early American missionaries learned the language well enough to teach in it and even to translate English-language textbooks into Arabic. Until they realized that they could not recruit enough teachers and translate enough books under this system, the American mission schools and colleges used Arabic as their language of instruction. Reluctantly they switched to English in the late nineteenth century. Given this relative acceptance of their culture, many Arabs sent their children to American schools despite their Protestant orientation. The Orthodox Christians were especially apt to do so. The result was a higher standard of Arabic reading and writing among Syrian Orthodox youth, many of whom went into journalism, law, or teaching. Some became scholars and writers. Before long they were leading the Arabic literary revival, which (as so often happened in Europe) turned into a nationalist movement. The growth of nationalism was also fostered by such American ideas as using the schools to develop moral character, promoting benevolent activities, and teaching students to create new institutions to fit changing conditions.

Legend has it that the first Arab nationalist party was a Beirut secret society founded around 1875 by five early graduates of the American University. More recently, careful research by a professor at that institution, Zeine N. Zeine, has shown that these students, all Christians, were probably seeking the independence of what we now call Lebanon—not the whole Arab world—from the Ottoman Empire. Anyway, the secret society did not last long. But the commitment of students and alumni of the American University of Beirut, in both the nineteenth and the twentieth centuries, has nurtured the ideas of Arab nationalism and spread them among both Muslim and Christian speakers of Arabic. The American missionaries hoped to convert Arab youths to Protestantism through exposure to the Arabic Bible; the unintended outcome was to make them cherish more their heritage of Arabic literature and history. Their secular colleagues may also have taught them to respect Western ideals of liberalism and democracy, but the students applied them to building an Arab nationalist ideology. Teachers sow their seed in unknown soil; their pupils decide what they will cultivate and determine what posterity will reap.

*Muslim Arab Nationalists*

But Arab nationalism could never have won Muslim acceptance if all its advocates had been westernized Christians. The centralizing trend of Ottoman reforms, covered in Chapter 11, alienated some Arabs, high-ranking officials as well as local landlords, from what they were coming to view as a Turkish (rather than a Muslim) empire. The first example of a truly Muslim strain within Arab nationalism was a campaign during the 1890s, popularized by a writer named Abd al-Rahman al-Kawakibi, to revive the Arab caliphate, preferably in Mecca. Pan-Islam, strong among Muslims since the 1860s, had urged them to unite behind the Ottoman sultans. By juggling a few historical facts, their backers had claimed that the caliphate, maintained in Cairo by the Mamluks after the Mongol capture of Baghdad in 1258, had been transferred to the Ottoman sultans upon their conquest of Egypt in 1517. This claim may have angered some Muslims, for Sunni political theory states that the caliph must belong to Muhammad's tribe, the Quraysh of Mecca. The Ottomans were not Arabs, let alone members of the Quraysh tribe. Actually, they had seldom used the title of caliph before the late nineteenth century. Sultan Abdulaziz (r. 1861–1876) had done so, as part of his campaign to increase his support from Ottoman Muslims and to counter the harmful effects of Russian pan-Slavism. Sultan Abdulhamid exploited the caliphate even more, trying to win the backing of Egyptian and Indian Muslims ruled by Britain—one of the reasons for his bad reputation in Western history books. Britain's rising hostility to the Ottoman sultan may have stimulated Kawakibi's nationalism. Whatever the cause, his idea of an Arab caliphate did gain support from the non-Ottoman amirs in Arabia and even from Egypt's Khedive Abbas. Although the khedives were descendants of Mehmet Ali, originally an Albanian, they often tried to win Arab support away from the Ottoman sultans. In short, Kawakibi's campaign to free the Arabs from Turkish rule mattered more as a power ploy for diplomats, khedives, and amirs than for its popular following at the time.

## The Arabs and the Young Turks

The first breakthrough for Arab nationalism was the 1908 Young Turk revolution, which led to the restoration of the long-suspended Ottoman constitution. Suddenly, men living in Beirut and Damascus, Baghdad and Aleppo, Jaffa and Jerusalem, were choosing representatives to an assembly in Istanbul. Hopes were raised for an era of Arab-Turkish friendship and for progress toward liberal democracy in the Ottoman state. An Arab-Ottoman Friendship Society opened branches in many cities of the empire. Even some of the Syrian intellectuals who had fled from Abdulhamid's tyranny to Egypt or the New World packed their bags to return home.

Arab hopes soon faded, though. The Arab-Ottoman Friendship Society was closed down by the Committee of Union and Progress in 1909, although an Arabic literary society was allowed to meet in Istanbul as long as it steered clear of politics. Representation in Parliament tended to favor Turks against the many ethnic, linguistic, and religious minorities of the empire. Moreover, the elections were rigged to ensure that most of the deputies belonged to the CUP. The Young Turk government, imperiled by European imperialism and Balkan nationalism, resumed the centralizing policies of earlier Ottoman reformers. Consequently, the Arabs began to fear that their liberties, preserved by the weakness or indifference of earlier governments, would now be in danger. The imposition of Turkish as the language of administration and education (plus the apparent shift from pan-Islam to pan-Turanism) especially angered the Arabs.

But how could they react? Not since Muhammad's day had large numbers of Arabic-speaking peoples mobilized politically to gain unity and freedom. How could they oppose a government headed, at least in name, by a sultan-caliph? What good would it do Syria's Arabs to overthrow Turkish rule, only to become, like Egypt, a dependency of a Christian power? Few Syrians (other than some Maronites) sought French rule. Nor did Iraqi Arabs want Basrah to become (like Suez) a link in Britain's imperial communications.

The result of these deliberations was a low-profile movement of a few educated Arabs aimed not at separation but at greater local autonomy. It included three different groups: (1) the Ottoman Decentralization party, founded in 1912 by Syrians living in Cairo and seeking Arab support for more local autonomy instead of strong central control by the Ottoman government; (2) al-Fatat (Youth), a secret society of young Arabs, mainly Muslims, who were students in European universities and who convoked an Arab Congress, held in Paris in 1913, to demand equal rights and cultural autonomy for Arabs within the Ottoman Empire; and (3) al-Ahd (Covenant), a secret society of Arab officers in the Ottoman army, who proposed turning the Ottoman Empire into a Turco-Arab dual monarchy on the pattern of Austria-Hungary. Each of these groups found backers among educated Arabs living in Istanbul, other Ottoman cities (notably Damascus), and abroad.

But do not let the later strength of Arab nationalism fool you into rewriting its history before World War I. Most Arabs were not yet Arab nationalists; they remained loyal to the CUP, the Ottoman constitution that gave them parliamentary representation, and a government in which some Arabs served as ministers, ambassadors, officials, or army officers. If Arab nationalism had led to separation from the Ottoman Empire, the Egyptian khedive or the British might have gained more than the Arabs of Syria or Iraq. Even though Egypt was prospering, Arabs elsewhere did not crave British rule, let alone a French imperialism comparable to what already existed in Algeria. The Jewish settlers in Palestine, hardly numerous enough yet to threaten the Arab majority, might later aspire to separate statehood (see Chapter 16), and Arab nationalists opposed this potential threat even more strenuously than Turkish rule.

## WORLD WAR I

The next turning point in the rise of Arab nationalism occurred when the Ottoman Empire decided in August 1914 to enter World War I on the German side. The Young Turks, especially War Minister Enver, may have been influenced by their exposure to German military advisers, but their main motives were to win back Egypt from the British and the Caucasus Mountains from Russia. At the time, Muslim Arabs applauded these aims, even though later writers would castigate the Young Turks for committing the empire, already shaken by defeats in Libya and the Balkans, to war against the Western Allies. In 1914 Germany was respected for its economic and military might. The Germans were building a railway from Istanbul to Baghdad that would hold together what was left of the Ottoman Empire. A German military mission was in Istanbul, training officers and soldiers to use modern weapons. Two German warships, caught in the Mediterranean when the war started and pursued by the British navy, took refuge in the Straits, whereupon they were handed over by the German ambassador as gifts to the Ottoman government (complete with their German crews, who donned fezzes and claimed to be "instructors"). They replaced two ships then being built for the Ottoman navy in British shipyards, already paid for by public subscription, that had been commandeered by the British navy when the war broke out. So strongly did the Ottoman government and people support the German cause that after the new "Turkish" ships had drawn the empire into the war by bombarding the Russian port of Odessa, the sultan officially proclaimed a military jihad against Britain, France, and Russia. All three had millions of Muslim subjects who, if they had heeded the message, would have had to rebel on behalf of their Ottoman sultan-caliph.

### Britain and the Arabs

The British, especially those serving in Egypt and the Sudan, wondered how to counter this pan-Islamic proclamation serving the Turco-German war machine, which launched a well-publicized invasion of Sinai in late 1914, while Britain was declaring its official protectorate over Egypt. Some Ottoman army units reached the Suez Canal in February 1915, and one even crossed to the western side under cover of darkness. For three years, Britain had to station more than 100,000 imperial troops in Egypt—partly to intimidate the Egyptian nationalists, but mainly to stop any new Ottoman effort to take the canal, which the British now viewed as their imperial lifeline.

Britain's response was to make contact with an Arab leader in the Hijaz (western Arabia)—namely, Husayn, the sharif and amir of Mecca. Let me explain these grand titles. A sharif is a descendant of Muhammad, of which there were many in the Hijaz, especially in the Muslim holy cities. Being protectors of Mecca and Medina conferred prestige on the Ottoman sultans; they lavished honors on the sharifs but also exploited their rivalries to control them. The various clans of sharifs competed for the position of amir (prince), which carried some temporal authority.

During and after the Tanzimat era, however, the Ottoman government had tried to strengthen its direct rule over the Hijaz, using an appointed local governor. Sharif Husayn, the leader of one of the contending clans (which he called the Hashimites, the clan of the Prophet himself), had long struggled with the Ottoman sultan and his governors, enduring almost sixteen years of house arrest in Istanbul. Even though he still supported the Ottomanist ideal after he became amir in 1908, Husayn disliked the CUP's centralizing policies. One of his sons, Abdallah, had close ties with the Arab nationalist societies in Syria even before World War I. Abdallah went to Cairo to seek support from the British consul, Lord Kitchener, a few months before the war started. The British were not yet ready to plot against the Ottoman Empire, which they had long tried to preserve, but Kitchener did remember the meeting. When he went home to help plan Britain's war effort, London became interested in a possible anti-Ottoman alliance, involving these Arab Hashimite sharifs in Mecca. The British government instructed its Cairo representative to contact Husayn, hoping to dissuade him from endorsing the jihad or, better yet, to persuade him to lead an Arab rebellion against Ottoman rule.

## The Husayn-McMahon Correspondence

In Cairo, Britain's new high commissioner (the new title resulted from the declaration of the British protectorate over Egypt), Sir Henry McMahon, wrote to the sharif of Mecca. Britain wanted him to start a revolt against Ottoman rule in the Hijaz. Husayn in turn asked for a pledge that the British would support the rebellion financially and politically against his Arab rivals as well as against the Ottoman Empire. If he called for an Arab revolt, it was not for the sake of changing masters. The British in Egypt and the Sudan knew from talking with Arab nationalists living there that the Hashimites could not rally other Arabs to their cause—given the power and prestige of rival families living in other parts of Arabia—unless the Arabs were assured that they would gain their independence in the lands in which they predominated: Arabia, Iraq, and Syria, including Palestine and Lebanon. The Arab nationalists were not yet much interested in Egypt and the rest of North Africa.

Keeping these considerations in mind, the amir of Mecca and the British high commissioner for Egypt and the Sudan exchanged some letters in 1915–1916 that have since become famous and highly controversial. In the course of what we now call the Husayn-McMahon Correspondence, Britain pledged that, if Husayn proclaimed an Arab revolt against Ottoman rule, it would provide military and financial aid during the war and would then help to create independent Arab governments in the Arabian Peninsula and most parts of the Fertile Crescent.

Britain did, however, exclude some parts, such as the port areas of Mersin and Alexandretta (which today belong to southern Turkey), Basrah (now in Iraq), and "portions of Syria lying to the west of the areas [districts] of Damascus, Homs, Hama, and Aleppo." One of the toughest issues in modern Middle East history is to figure out whether McMahon meant to exclude only what is now Lebanon, a partly Christian region coveted by France, or also Palestine, in which some Jews hoped to rebuild their ancient homeland. Lebanon is clearly west of Damascus and those other Syrian cities more than is what we now call Israel. The Arabs argue, therefore, that Britain promised Palestine to them. But if the letter referred to the *province* of Syria (of which Damascus was the capital), what is now Israel and was then partly under a governor in Jerusalem may have been what McMahon meant to exclude from Arab rule. Not only the Zionists but also the British government after 1918, and even McMahon himself, believed that he had never promised Palestine to the Arabs. In my judgment, given that Britain cared more in 1915 about keeping its French connection than about reserving Palestine for the Jews, the area excluded from Arab rule in the Husayn-McMahon correspondence was Lebanon. Only later would Jewish claims to Palestine become the main issue.

The exclusion of these ambiguously described lands angered Husayn; he refused to accept the deal, and his correspondence with the British in Cairo ended inconclusively in early 1916. The Ottomans could have headed off any major Arab revolt, but for the stupidity of its governor in Syria, Jemal, who needlessly antagonized the Arabs there. As former naval minister and one of the three Young Turks who really ruled the Ottoman Empire when it entered World War I, Jemal had led the Turkish expedition to seize the Suez Canal and free Egypt from British rule. Although his first attempt failed, Jemal planned to try again. He settled down as governor of Syria while he rebuilt his forces, but he did little for the province.

Many areas were struck by famine, locusts, or labor shortages caused by the conscription of local peasant youths into the Ottoman army. Fuel shortages led to the cutting down of olive trees and also hindered the transport of food to the stricken areas. Meanwhile, the Arab nationalist societies met and pondered which side to take in the war. One of Amir Husayn's sons, Faysal, came to Syria to parley with both the Arab nationalists and Jemal in 1915, but he accomplished nothing. Then in April and May 1916, Jemal's police seized some leading Arabs, including some scholars who were not even nationalists, arrested them for treason, and had twenty-two of them publicly hanged in Beirut and Damascus. The executions aroused so much anger in Syria—and among Arabs in general—that Faysal hastened back to Mecca, a convert to the nationalist cause, and convinced his father that the time for revolt had come.

## The Arab Revolt

On 5 June 1916 Husayn declared the Arabs independent and unfurled the standard of their revolt against Turkish rule. The Ottoman Empire did not fall at once, but large numbers of Arabs in the Hijaz, plus some in Palestine and Syria, began to fight the Turks. But were the Arabs in these areas truly nationalists? Most probably did not care whether they were ruled from Istanbul or Mecca, so long as the outcome of the war was in doubt.

The Arab Revolt would have many ups and downs during the next two years, but let me keep the story short. Guided by European advisers, of whom T. E. Lawrence is the best known, the Arab supporters of Amir Husayn and his sons, among them Abdallah and Faysal, fought on the side of the Allies against the Ottoman Empire. Working in tandem with the Egyptian Expeditionary Force (the name used for the British Empire troops advancing from the Suez Canal), they moved north into Palestine. While the British Imperial troops took Jaffa and Jerusalem, the Arabs were blowing up railways and capturing Aqaba and Amman. When Britain's forces drew near Damascus in late September 1918, they held back to let Lawrence and the Arabs occupy the city, which then became the seat of a provisional Arab government headed by Faysal. Meanwhile, the Ottoman army, now led by Mustafa Kemal (later known as Ataturk), withdrew from Syria. The Turks were also giving way in Iraq before an Anglo-Indian army. Late in October the Ottoman Empire signed an armistice with the Allies on the island of Mudros. The Arabs, promised the right of self-determination by the British and the French, were jubilant. Surely their independence was at hand.

## The Sykes-Picot Agreement

But this was not to be. Fighting for its empire's survival, the British government during the war had promised Ottoman-ruled Arab lands to other interested parties. Russia had previously demanded Allied recognition of its right to control the Turkish Straits. In a secret treaty signed in London in 1915, Britain and France promised to back Russia's claim. For its entry into the war on the Allied side in 1915, Italy later demanded large portions of southwestern Anatolia. The Greeks, too, wanted a piece of Turkey, the land around Izmir, where many Greeks were living. France, tied down by the war against Germany on the Western Front (remember that the Germans held much of northeastern France from 1914 to 1918), could not give up its Middle Eastern claims. Given its historic ties with the Maronites, France wanted all of Syria, including Lebanon and Palestine. So Britain, France, and Russia drew up a secret treaty known as the Sykes-Picot Agreement (see Map 7). Signed in May 1916, it provided for direct French rule in much of northern and western Syria, plus a sphere of influence in the Syrian hinterland, including Damascus, Aleppo, and Mosul. Britain would rule lower Iraq directly. It would also advise an Arab government to be given lands between the Egyptian border and eastern Arabia, thus ensuring indirect British control from the Mediterranean to the Gulf. An enclave around Jaffa and Jerusalem would be under international government because Russia wanted a part in administering the Christian holy places. The only area left for the Arabs to govern without foreign rulers or advisers was the Arabian desert.

Arab apologists claim that Amir Husayn knew nothing about the Sykes-Picot Agreement until after World War I. T. E. Lawrence was wracked by guilt because he had worked with the Arabs on Britain's behalf, thinking that they would get their independence after the war, when in fact they were being manipulated by British diplomacy, if not duplicity. Now, I will not deny that Lawrence's *Seven Pillars of Wisdom* is a book worth reading, or that *Lawrence of Arabia* is a great film. But neither one is history. Amir Husayn did know about the Sykes-Picot Agreement. Not only had the Allied secret treaties been published by the communists after they had seized control of Russia in 1917, but Husayn learned about the agreement from Turkish agents trying to draw him out of the war and, indeed, from the British and French themselves. To Husayn, the advantages of directing an Arab revolt against the Turks, who had locked him up for so long, outweighed the perils of Sykes-Picot, which the British assured him would not involve the lands he wanted to rule. But to other Arab nationalists,

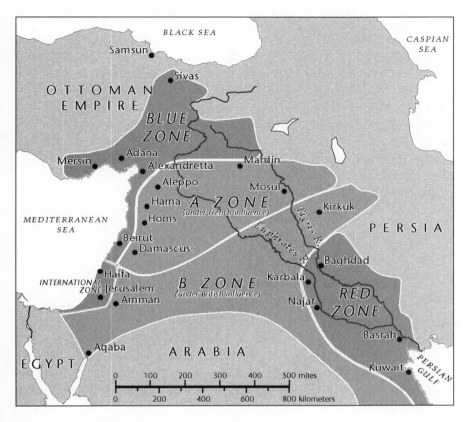

MAP 7 The Sykes-Picot Agreement, 1916

this Anglo-French agreement was a betrayal of their cause, worse because it was not made public until after the war.

## The Balfour Declaration

More public was a decision by the British cabinet to help establish a Jewish national home in Palestine, formally announced on 2 November 1917. This was the famous Balfour Declaration, so called because it came out as a letter from the foreign secretary, Lord Balfour, to Lord Rothschild, titular president of the Zionist Federation of Britain and Ireland. The letter will be analyzed in Chapter 16, but we can note now its salient points: (1) The British government would help set up a national home in Palestine for the Jews; (2) it would not undermine the rights or status of Jews choosing not to live there; and (3) it would not harm the civil and religious rights of Palestine's "existing non-Jewish communities." The Arabs' main objection to the Balfour Declaration was that they made up over nine-tenths of what would later become Palestine. How could anyone create a home for one group of people in a land inhabited by another? Worse still, the inhabitants had never been asked if they wanted their land to become the national home for a people who would be coming from far away. In addition, the Balfour Declaration never mentioned the *political* rights of non-Jewish Palestinians, a point that still stirs deep Arab resentment. If Britain tried to realize the Zionist dream of a Jewish state, what would be the political status of the Arabic-speaking Christians and Muslims of Palestine? Did this document not contradict the Husayn-McMahon correspondence and other statements meant to reassure Arabs who had thrown themselves into the revolt against the Turks?

## THE POSTWAR PEACE SETTLEMENT

How would these conflicting commitments be reconciled, once the war was over? In November 1918 the guns in Europe fell silent, and everyone hoped that the diplomats would make a lasting peace. During the war, President Woodrow Wilson, the greatest statesman of the day, had proposed a set of principles called the Fourteen Points, upon which he wanted the Allies to build the peace once the war was won. He denounced secret treaties, urged self-determination for all peoples (specifically including those who had been under Ottoman rule), and proposed the creation of a League of Nations to avert the threat of future wars. When he came to Europe to represent the United States at the Paris Peace Conference, Wilson was hailed everywhere as a hero and a savior.

But Britain and France, the Allies that had borne the brunt of the fighting and the casualties, were determined to dictate the peace. The defeated powers, Germany, Austria-Hungary, and the Ottoman Empire, could not attend the peace conference until it was time to sign the treaties. Russia (now a communist state that had signed a separate peace with Germany) was also left out. Georges Clemenceau, who headed France's delegation, expressed a popular mood when he insisted that Germany must be punished and that France must get control over all of geographical Syria. David Lloyd George, heading the British delegation, agreed that Germany should be punished, but he also sought a formula to bring peace to the Middle East without harming the British Empire. The Zionist (or Jewish nationalist) movement was ably represented by Chaim Weizmann. The Arabs had Faysal, assisted by Lawrence.

## The King-Crane Commission

No one could reconcile the Middle Eastern claims of the Arabs, the Zionists, the British, and the French, but the conferees did try. Wilson wanted to send a commission of inquiry to Syria and Palestine to find out what the people there really wanted. Lloyd-George accepted Wilson's idea, until the French said that unless the commission also went to Iraq (where Britain's military occupation was already unpopular), they would boycott it. The British then lost interest, and so the U.S. team, called the King-Crane Commission, went out alone. It found that the local people wanted complete independence under Faysal who had already set up a provisional Arab government in Damascus. If they had to accept foreign tutelage, let it come from the Americans, who had no history of imperialism in the Middle East, or at least from the British, whose army was already there, but never from the French.

The King-Crane Commission also looked into the Zionist claims, which its members had initially favored, and concluded that their realization would provoke serious Jewish-Arab conflict. The commission called for the reduction of the Zionist program, limits on Jewish immigration into Palestine, and an end to any plan to turn the country into a Jewish national home. Faysal and his backers hoped that the King-Crane Commission would persuade Wilson to favor the Arabs. Instead, Wilson was working to win U.S. support for his League of Nations. He suffered a paralytic stroke before he found time to read the commissioners' report, which was not even published for several years.

## Allied Arrangements: San Remo and Sèvres

What happened instead is that Britain and France agreed to settle their differences. France gave up its claims to Mosul and Palestine in exchange for a free hand in the rest of Syria. As a concession to Wilsonian idealism, the Allies set up a mandate system, under which Asian and African lands taken from Turkey and Germany were put under a tutelary relationship to a Great Power (called the mandatory), which would teach the people how to govern themselves. Each mandatory power had to report periodically to a body in the League of Nations called the Permanent Mandates Commission, to prevent any exploitation. Meeting in San Remo in 1920, representatives of Britain and France agreed to divide the Middle Eastern mandates: Syria (and Lebanon) to France, and Iraq and Palestine (including what is now Jordan) to Britain. The Hijaz would be independent. The Ottoman government had to accept these arrangements when it signed the

Treaty of Sèvres in August 1920. By then the French army had already marched eastward from Beirut, crushed the Arabs, and driven Faysal's provisional government out of Damascus. The Arab dream had been shattered.

## The Result: Four Mandates and an Emirate

What happened then to the Arabs of the Fertile Crescent? The French had absolutely no sympathy for Arab nationalism and ruled their Syrian mandate as if it were a colony. Hoping to weaken the nationalists, the French tried to split Syria into smaller units, including what would eventually become Lebanon, plus Alexandretta (which was handed over to Turkey in 1939), states for the Alawis in the north and the Druze in the south, and even Aleppo and Damascus as city-states. Lebanon's separation from Syria lasted because it had a Christian majority (as of 1921) that was determined to keep its dominant position. The other divisions of Syria soon ended, but the Syrian Arabs rebelled often against French rule, which in the 1920s and 1930s seemed unlikely ever to end (see Map 8).

The British were inconsistent backers of Arab nationalism, working with the Hashimite family. Husayn still had his government in the Hijaz, but the prestige he had gained from the Arab Revolt made him a troublesome ally for the British. He refused to sign the Versailles and Sèvres treaties, proclaimed himself "king of the Arabs," and later claimed to be the caliph of Islam. These actions so offended the British that, as the Saud family rose to power in eastern Arabia (see Chapter 14), they did nothing to stop the Saudis from marching into the Hijaz and toppling his regime in 1924. As for Iraq, British control was menaced by a general Arab insurrection in 1920. Needing a strong personality to pacify the country, the British brought in Faysal, who was approved in a rigged plebiscite as the new king of Iraq. Soon peace was restored. The British cooperated with Faysal's government and the local tribal *shaykhs* to speed Iraq toward independence. It is ironic that Iraq, once among the poorest areas of the Ottoman Empire, should in 1932 have been the first new state to gain its formal independence.

What would become of Abdallah, who had counted on ruling in Baghdad? After Faysal was ousted from Syria in 1920, Abdallah gathered about 500 tribal Arabs, occupied Amman, and threatened to raid the French in Syria. Although he could not have expelled them, the British wanted to keep him out of trouble. Winston Churchill, then the colonial secretary, met Abdallah in Jerusalem and persuaded him to accept—temporarily—

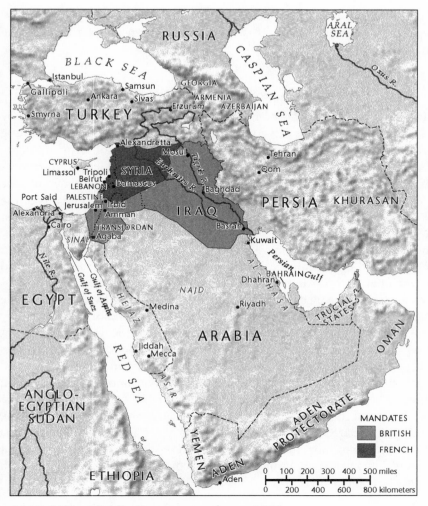

MAP 8 The Middle Eastern mandates, 1922

the part of Palestine that lay east of the Jordan River, until the French should leave Syria. This provisional deal was opposed by the Zionists, who wanted all of Palestine as defined by the 1920 peace treaties to be open to Jewish settlement and eventual statehood. France feared that Abdallah's new principality would become a staging area for Hashimite attacks on Syria. No one expected this Emirate of Transjordan to last long, but it did. While the rest of the Palestine mandate was seething with Jewish-Arab strife, Transjordan became an oasis of tranquil politics and economic development. The sad story of Britain's mandate in the rest of Palestine must be saved for Chapter 16.

## CONCLUSION AND SUMMARY

The Arabs had been roused from centuries of political lethargy, first by American teachers and missionaries, then by the revolution of the Young Turks, and finally by the blandishments of Britain and France during World War I. They recalled their ancient greatness and longed to recover it. From the West they learned about rights and freedoms, democratic governments, and national self-determination. Led by descendants of the Prophet Muhammad, a few Arabs had dared to rebel against the greatest Muslim state left in the world, the Ottoman Empire. In its place they hoped to set up one or more states that would have the same sovereign rights as all other independent countries. They helped the British and French defeat the Ottoman Turks in World War I, but later on the Allies failed to keep the pledges they had made to the Arabs. In the lands of the Fertile Crescent, where Arabs were clearly in the majority, where they hoped to form independent states, where some day the Arab nation might revive its former power and glory, the victorious Allies set up mandates that were mere colonies in disguise. Even if Britain and France governed their mandates well, promoting education and economic development, the Arabs wanted to rule themselves. Instead of coming together, the Arabs found themselves being pulled farther apart. One area, Palestine, was even declared to be the Jewish national home, leaving in doubt the future of its Arab inhabitants. These were the roots of Arab bitterness, put down eighty years ago. In the chapters to come, we shall see how this Arab anger bore bitter fruit.

# FOURTEEN

# Modernizing Rulers in the
# Independent States

In the last four chapters I have written about Middle Eastern peoples and countries that fell under European control. Actually, there was no area, except for the inaccessible deserts of Arabia and the highest mountains of Anatolia and Persia, that did not feel the impact of the West by 1914. As you have seen, Egypt and the Fertile Crescent came under Western rule, direct or indirect, before or during World War I. Even the regions that escaped—Anatolia, central Persia, and most of Arabia—were being eyed as potential colonies. The Allied secret agreements during the war would have awarded Istanbul and the Straits to czarist Russia and parts of western and southern Anatolia to Italy and France. Meanwhile, British agents were lining up the tribes of Arabia and Persia. Treaties were drafted that would have made their lands virtual British protectorates, as indeed Kuwait, Bahrain, the Trucial States (now called the United Arab Emirates), and Oman had become by 1914. Aden remained a settlement of the Indian government; it would not formally become a crown colony until 1937. In 1917 the Bolshevik Revolution pulled Russia out of the war and out of the contest for influence over its Middle Eastern neighbors, at least for a while. Once the Ottoman Empire and Germany surrendered in 1918, there seemed to be no one left to stem the spread of Western—especially British—power throughout the whole Middle East.

But the tide did turn. At least three areas of the Middle East did manage to salvage their independence after World War I. The Turks in Anatolia drove off the Western invaders, terminated the moribund Ottoman Empire, and set up the Republic of Turkey. A group of soldiers and civilian nationalists blocked British and Bolshevik attempts to take over Persia, reorganized the country, and then replaced the weak Qajar shah with a more dynamic ruler. In a remote part of east-central Arabia called Najd, a young man from an old ruling family combined a Muslim reform movement with a group of militant tribesmen to unite most of the peninsula in what we now call the Kingdom of Saudi Arabia.

Because most of the Middle East maps we see on television and in classrooms show political borders, we tend to think of "Turkey," "Iran," and "Saudi Arabia" as entities that have always been what they are today. In reality, Turkey and Saudi Arabia got their present names and boundaries only between the two world wars. Iran (as Persia came to be called in 1935), although its modern borders differ little from those of the 1890s, is a far cry from the Persia that was divided in 1907 into Russian and British spheres of influence. In each of these states, these changes resulted from the inspiration, the ingenuity, and the industry of a military commander who became a political leader: Mustafa Kemal Ataturk in Turkey, Reza Shah Pahlavi in Iran, and Abd al-Aziz ibn Abd al-Rahman (Ibn Sa'ud) in Saudi Arabia.

## TURKEY: PHOENIX FROM THE ASHES

When the Ottoman naval minister signed the Mudros Armistice in October 1918, ending his country's active role in World War I, the empire was nearly prostrate. Its armed forces had suffered some 325,000 deaths (more than the total number of U.S. casualties), 400,000 wounded, and 250,000 imprisoned or missing in action. High government spending had led to crushing taxes, deficit financing, and a severe price inflation that ruined many families.

Turkey's commerce, finance, and administration had already been disrupted by a fateful government policy: the deportation of the Armenians. Although they were Christians, most of these industrious people were loyal Ottoman subjects. Some had served in the army or the civil administration before the war. Others had made their mark in medicine, teaching, business, or skilled trades such as goldsmithing and photography. Only a few Armenians wanted a separate nation-state, for there was no Ottoman province in which they could have formed the majority of the population. But because some had earlier turned nationalist and rebelled against Sultan Abdulhamid, many Turks suspected them of treason. Once World War I broke out, the Ottoman government, abetted by its German advisers and fearing the Armenians as a potential fifth column, decided to clear them out of areas in eastern Anatolia near their coreligionists in enemy Russia. Many Armenians resisted deportation from their ancestral farms and pastures, villages and towns. The Ottoman army then turned local Turkish and Kurdish brigands loose on the Armenians, looting and killing them. Only the hardiest and luckiest escaped. Even Armenians living in southwestern Anatolia and Constantinople, far from Russia, were uprooted. About a million Armenians died. The survivors, having lost all that they had, were bitter and vengeful. Those living east of the lands under Turkish control formed an independent Republic of Armenia in 1918. Some hoped to enlarge this state and put it under a U.S. mandate. The American public was strongly pro-Armenian and anti-Turkish at the time, but eventually the U.S. government refused any direct responsibility for rehabilitating what we now call eastern Turkey. Part of Armenia was absorbed by Turkey in 1920; the rest became a Soviet republic. The Armenians, generally pro-Turkish up to World War I, now became Turkey's most implacable foes.

Turkey had other problems. Massive conscription and prolonged fighting had deprived many areas of the country of their young men. Farms and villages fell into neglect, and weeds choked once-fertile fields. Whole forests had been cut down to fuel the trains and run the factories when coal grew scarce. Demoralized by defeats, disease, arrears in pay, and poor food, many of the soldiers deserted their units and roamed the countryside as armed brigands. As you may know, the forces of the British Empire, aided by the Arab Revolt, had pushed the Ottomans out of the Fertile Crescent. Meanwhile, in the last year of the war, the Young Turk triumvirs, Enver, Talat, and Jemal, sent troops deep into the Caucasus. They hoped to build a new Turanian empire among the Muslims of what had been czarist Russia, now torn by civil war between the Whites (anticommunists) and the Reds (Bolsheviks). One of the ironies of World War I is that Germany and the Ottoman Empire surrendered while some of their troops still occupied foreign lands.

## Challenges to the Nationalists

The Mudros Armistice put an end to the Young Turk regime, Enver, Talat, and Jemal fled from Istanbul on a German warship just before the British and the French occupied the Straits. So anxious was the Ottoman sultan to keep his power that he aligned himself totally with the Western powers and was ready to do whatever they demanded. Soon his brother-in-law, Damad Ferid, took over the government, started dismantling the Ottoman army, and tried to pacify the country. French troops entered the area of southern Anatolia known as Cilicia (as specified by the Sykes-Picot Agreement), while the Italians laid claim to Antalya, in the southwest. Although the Bolsheviks renounced claims made on Istanbul and the Straits by previous Russian governments, Britain and France now occupied these areas on the pretext of aiding the White Russians against the communists. The winter of 1918–1919 was a nightmare for Istanbul's Turks. Influenza was rife, coal and wood were scarce, youth gangs roamed the darkened streets and robbed shopkeepers and passersby, food prices skyrocketed, and the Greek inhabitants flew their national flag openly. They even gave the French commander a white horse, on which he triumphantly entered the city, just as Mehmet the Conqueror had done in 1453.

By the time the Allies opened their postwar conference in Paris, they were prepared to divide Thrace and Anatolia—as well as the Arab lands discussed in Chapter 13—into spheres of influence. Some proposed a U.S. mandate over Anatolia as well as Armenia. The Turks, tired from wars that had taken their young men and drained their treasury since the Libyan War of 1911, might have accepted foreign tutelage and military occupation, but for an unforeseen challenge. Eleutherios Venizelos, the Greek prime minister, argued before the Paris Peace Conference that the west Anatolian city of Smyrna (now Izmir) should be awarded to Greece. Greek nationalists in Athens spoke of a reconstituted Byzantine Empire that would include Istanbul, Thrace, and western Anatolia, areas in which many Greek Christians still lived under Ottoman rule. Egged on by the Allies, especially Lloyd George, Venizelos acted to realize these ambitions. On 15 May 1919 some 25,000 Greek troops landed at Smyrna, welcomed by its mainly Greek and foreign inhabitants. No resistance came from the Ottoman government, which was trying to pacify a country that was close to anarchy. Yet this landing of the Greeks, long the most rebellious subjects of the Ottoman Empire, was the spark that lit the fires of Turkish nationalism in Anatolia. Four days later another landing, equally fateful for Turkish history, took place at the Black Sea port of Samsun.

### Mustafa Kemal Ataturk

Commanding the force that landed at Samsun was Mustafa Kemal, a general who had been sent by the sultan's government to disarm the people and restore order to the turbulent provinces of eastern Anatolia. Mustafa Kemal, later known to the world as Ataturk, had already won fame for his military triumphs in World War I. He had commanded the Turks' successful Dardanelles defense against the Western Allies in 1915. The following year his troops drove back the Russians in the east. He also directed the Turks' orderly retreat from Syria in 1918, gaining the respect of his British adversaries. His frank hostility toward the Young Turks had kept him from getting the positions or the power that he deserved. His ambitions thwarted by the CUP and the sultan's clique, Kemal had personal as well as patriotic reasons to resist the Ottoman government's subservience toward the Allies.

A myth has grown up that Kemal alone gave life to Turkish nationalism in May 1919. The truth is more complex. There were many groups in Thrace and Anatolia that were resisting the Greeks, the Armenians, their foreign backers, and the hapless Ottoman government. The driving spirit was Muslim as much as Turkish; ulama and Sufi leaders commanded great respect in the countryside. What Kemal did was to energize these "defense of rights associations" by publicly resigning from the Ottoman army and convoking a national congress in the central Anatolian town of Sivas. But leaders of the Eastern Provinces Society for the Defense of National Rights had already called a congress at Erzurum. Invited to the Erzurum conference, Kemal was elected its chairman. It was here that the Turks first drew up their National Pact, calling for the preservation of Turkey's existing borders (the Ottoman Empire minus the Arab lands lost in the war), opposition to any future changes in those borders, formation of an elected government, and denial of special privileges to non-Turkish minorities. Thus the stage was set for the September 1919 Sivas Congress, which rejected any foreign protectorate or mandate over Turkey and demanded the replacement of the weak Istanbul government by an elected one willing to uphold Turkish interests.

Such was the general mood that the grand *vezir* did resign—pushed by a nationwide telegraph operators' strike (Turkey's westernizing reforms had given the country an extensive communications network). A coalition cabinet including several of Kemal's men took over. New parliamentary elections gave the Turkish nationalists a whopping majority, but the popular government proved short-lived. In ratifying the National Pact, the Ottoman deputies antagonized the Allies, who formally occupied Istanbul and forced the coalition ministry to resign. Damad Ferid resumed power, and the *shaykh al-Islam* (as appointed head of the Muslim community) branded the nationalists as rebels against the sultan. Parliament was dissolved, and many of its deputies escaped (not without hardship) to Ankara, safely beyond the range of Allied gunboats and occupation forces. There, in central Anatolia, Mustafa Kemal convoked what he called the Grand National Assembly in April 1920.

The Kemalist movement now found itself at war with the Ottoman government in Istanbul, the (British-backed) Greek invaders around Smyrna, the Republic of Armenia in the east, the French in the south, and the British on the Straits. Poorly armed and half-starved Turkish irregulars had to fight against the well-supplied forces of the Allies and their Christian protégés. Underestimating the will of Kemal's nationalist following, the Allies in August 1920 forced the Ottoman government to sign the Treaty of Sèvres. The treaty would later turn out to be its death warrant.

Among its terms, the Sèvres Treaty provided that: (1) The Straits would be managed by a permanent Allied commission; (2) Istanbul could be taken away from Turkish administration if it infringed on minority rights; (3) eastern Anatolia would belong to an independent Armenia and possibly an autonomous Kurdistan; (4) Greece would have Smyrna and also Thrace; (5) Italy and France would each get parts of southwestern Anatolia; (6) the Arab lands would be divided into British and French mandates (as described in Chapter 13); and (7) the Capitulations, abolished by the Turks in September 1914, would be restored and extended. To the Turkish nationalists, the whole treaty was a slap in the face, but even this humiliation did not satisfy Venizelos. Encouraged by Lloyd George, the Greek forces pushed eastward, taking Turkish lands never awarded to the Greeks at Sèvres.

What saved Turkey was the aid it got from Soviet Russia. Both countries were embroiled in civil war and in fending off foreign attackers. Together, they wiped out the infant Republic of Armenia in late 1920. With no more challenge from the east, Kemal's forces managed to slow the Greek advance early in 1921. It gradually became clear that some Western countries would not back the Greeks either, once they claimed lands beyond what they had been offered by the Sèvres Treaty. France came to terms with the Kemalists after they had fought the Greeks to a standstill in a bitter battle close to Ankara in August and September 1921. Both France and Italy gave up their territorial claims in Anatolia. Only Britain continued to occupy the Straits, control the sultan, and cheer on the Greeks. In the summer of 1922 the Turks launched a fierce offensive that drove the Greek armies completely out of Anatolia. Then, at last, the British government decided to cut its losses by calling for another Allied conference to negotiate a new peace treaty with Turkey. The Ottoman sultan, shorn of his foreign support, fled from Istanbul, whereupon the Grand National

Assembly in Ankara abolished the sultanate altogether. On 29 October 1923 Turkey became the first republic in the modern Middle East.

The Turkish nationalists may have shown the world that they could wear down their opponents militarily, but the British still had to learn that they could also withstand political pressure. The British expected that the new peace conference, to be held in Lausanne, would be quick, letting them keep by diplomacy part of what their protégés had lost by war. General Ismet, chosen by Kemal to represent Turkey, stood firm and wore down his distinguished British counterpart, Lord Curzon, by feigning deafness and delaying the proceedings to get instructions from his government. When the Lausanne peacemakers finished replacing the Treaty of Sèvres, the Turks had freed their country of the hated Capitulations, all forms of foreign occupation, and any threat of an Armenian state or an autonomous Kurdistan. Most Greek Orthodox Christians living in Anatolia were deported to Greece as part of a population exchange that sent many Muslims from Bulgaria and Greek-ruled parts of Macedonia to a Turkey they had never known. The only setbacks for Turkey in the Lausanne Treaty were an international commission to supervise shipping through the Straits (which were demilitarized) and the failure to obtain Mosul (which the League of Nations later awarded to Iraq).

Thanks to the 1923 Lausanne Conference, Turkey became the only country defeated in World War I that was able to negotiate its own peace terms. Except for the 1936 Montreux Convention, which gave Turkey the right to fortify the Straits, and the annexation of Alexandretta in 1939, the Lausanne Treaty is still the basis of Turkey's place among the nations of the world. By contrast, the Versailles Treaty and all other postwar peace arrangements have long since been scrapped. Well might the Arabs, who had rebelled against the Turks to back the World War I victors, envy their erstwhile masters who had tied their fate to that of the vanquished!

## Kemal's Domestic Reforms

Mustafa Kemal devoted the last fifteen years of his life to changing Turkey from the bastion of Islam into a secular nation-state. Islam, the way of life and basis of government for the Turks since their conversion a thousand years earlier, was now to be replaced by Western ways of behavior, administration, and justice. If persuasion failed, then the changes would be imposed by force. Twice opposition parties arose within the Grand National Assembly, but in both cases Kemal suppressed them. A Kurdish uprising in 1925 was severely put down, and an attempt on Kemal's life led to the public hanging of most of his political opponents. As president of the republic, Kemal was authoritarian; yet he also detested fascism, opposed Marxist communism (although he utilized Soviet aid and was the first Middle Eastern leader to adopt state economic planning), and allowed free debate in the popularly elected assembly. Kemal admired democracy in theory, but he ruled as a stern father and teacher to his people, who he felt were not yet ready to govern themselves democratically.

Was Kemal a Muslim? He certainly flouted the rules of Islam in his card playing, drinking, and sexual escapades. Yet he also relied on Islamic symbols and joined with Muslim leaders to defend Turkey against the Greeks. Even if he kept some of the attitudes and practices of his Muslim forebears, though, he was determined to destroy Islam's power to block Turkey's modernization. He let a member of the Ottoman family retain the caliphate briefly, but abolished the position in 1924. Angry protests from Muslims in Egypt and India could not save the caliphate, and the Turks themselves were indifferent. After all, the caliphs had been powerless for a thousand years.

From 1924 on, the Grand National Assembly passed laws closing the Sufi orders and *madrasah*s, abolishing the *awqaf* and the position of *shaykh al-Islam*, and replacing the Shari'ah, even in the hitherto untouchable realm of family law, with a modified version of the Swiss Civil Code. Women, assured of equal rights with men in marriage, divorce, and property inheritance, also started to enter the higher schools and professions, as well as shops, offices, and factories. Given the vote for the first time in 1934, Turkish women elected seventeen of their sex to the Assembly the next year. The veil, which had begun to disappear in Istanbul and Smyrna before and during the war, was discarded (with Kemal's encouragement) during the 1920s.

Of great symbolic importance was a law forbidding Turkish men to wear the fez or any other brimless headgear. Muslim males had always worn turbans, skullcaps, *kufiyah*s, or other head coverings that would not hinder prostrations during formal worship. In common speech, "putting on a hat" meant apostasy from Islam. But Kemal, addressing a crowd in one of Anatolia's most conservative towns, wore a panama hat, mocked the traditional clothing of Turkish men and women, and announced that henceforth all males would have to wear the costume of "civilized" peoples, including the hat. It is ironic that Turkish men fought harder to go on wearing the fez, imposed by Sultan Mahmud a mere century earlier, than to save the caliphate, started by Abu-Bakr in 632! What people wear often reflects how they live, the way they think, and what they value most highly. At any rate, Turkish men and women soon dressed pretty much like Europeans.

Turkey faced west in other ways. The Ottoman financial calendar was replaced by the Gregorian one, and clocks were set to European time, a change from the Muslim system by which the date changed at sunset. Metric weights and measures replaced the customary Turkish ones, and the adoption of a formal day of rest (initially Friday, later Sunday) showed how Western the country had become. The call to worship and even Quran recitations were given in Turkish instead of Arabic. Even the Turkish constitution's reference to Islam as the state religion was expunged in 1928.

Turkish culture experienced an even more drastic change at about this time. Kemal announced that the Turkish language, hitherto written in an Arabic script ill suited to its sounds and syntax, would from then on use a modified Roman alphabet. Within three months all books, newspapers, street signs, school papers, and public documents had to be written using the new letters. Only a tenth of the people had been literate under the old system; now it was their national duty to learn the new one and teach it to their children, their neighbors, even to porters and boatmen (to use Kemal's own expression). The new alphabet, which was easier to learn and more phonetic, speeded up the education of the Turks. The number of school pupils doubled between 1923 and 1938. The literacy rate would climb to 85 percent in 2000. It was now easier for Turks to learn English, French, or other Western languages but much harder to study Arabic or Persian, or even to read classics of Ottoman Turkish prose and poetry. The new Turkish Language Academy began replacing Arabic and Persian loanwords with neologisms based on Turkish roots. As in other Middle Eastern countries, English and French words entered the language, producing such new terms as *dizel* (diesel), *frak* (frock coat), *gol* (goal, as in soccer), *gazöz* (soda, from the French *limonade gaseuse*), *kuvafür* (coiffeur), *kovboy* (cowboy), and *taksi* (taxi).

Another symbol of westernization, which has proved to be a convenience, was the law passed by the Grand National Assembly requiring all Turks to take family names. As society became more mobile and the need grew for accurate record keeping, the customary use of a person's given name—sometimes but not always combined with a patronymic ("Mehmet son of Ali"), military title, physical features, occupation, or place of origin—caused widespread confusion. Under the new law, Ismet, Kemal's representative at Lausanne, took the surname *Inonu*, the site of two of his victories over the Greeks. Mustafa Kemal became Ataturk (Father Turk). Old titles, such as *pasha, bey,* and *efendi,* were dropped. Kemal Ataturk even gave up the title of *ghazi* once used by Ottoman sultans and given to him by a grateful Assembly following his victory over the Greeks. Henceforth men had to prefix their names with *Bay,* comparable to Mr. Women were to use *Bayan* in place of the traditional *hanum.* But old practices die hard, and it was years before the Istanbul telephone directory came to be alphabetized by the new family names.

Because Ataturk launched a comprehensive westernization program, we would have expected him to push for economic growth. Actually, he seems to have been less interested in economics than, say, Mehmet Ali and some of his successors in Egypt. But Turkey did move toward industrialization, as factories sprang up in the large cities and around the coal-mining region near where the Black Sea meets the Bosporus. Kemal was among Asia's first noncommunist leaders to call for state ownership and control of the main means of production. Hoping to speed up modernization, he brought in Soviet economists to draft Turkey's first five-year plan. During the 1930s the Turkish government set up a textile spinning and weaving complex, a steel mill, and various factories for producing cement, glass, and paper. Agrarian reform limped in this land of 50,000 villages, some of them linked by a single donkey path to the rest of the world; but agricultural training institutes, extension agents, rural centers for health and adult education, and model farms did lead to some improvement.

Ataturk summed up his program in six principles, which were later incorporated into the Turkish constitution. Often called the "six arrows," from the symbol of Ataturk's Republican People's party (RPP), they are republicanism, nationalism, populism, statism, secularism, and reformism. Republicanism entails the selection of a leader from the citizenry, in contrast to the hereditary system of the Ottoman Empire and other dynastic states. Nationalism calls on the Turks to devote themselves to the needs of the Turkish nation, rejecting special ties to other Muslims or to foreign ideologies. Populism means that the government belongs to the Turkish people, working together for the common good, without distinction of rank, class, and sex. Statism, or state capitalism, requires the government to direct and take part in the country's economic development. Secularism amounts to the removal of religious controls over Turkey's politics, society, and culture. Reformism (originally called revolutionism) refers to the ongoing commitment of the Turkish people and government to rapid but peaceful modernization.

Kemal Ataturk was a westernizing reformer, but above all he was a Turkish nationalist. The linguistic reforms simplified Turkish, bringing the written language closer to what the Turkish people spoke. Moving the capital from Istanbul to Ankara stood for a rejection of the cosmopolitan Byzantine and Ottoman past in favor of an Anatolian Turkish future. The study of history now stressed the Turks, from their misty origins on the Asiatic steppes up to their triumph over the Greeks, instead of the Islamic caliphate rooted in the Arabic and Persian cultures. Even westernization was defended in terms of Turkish nationalism: Cultural borrowing was no cause for shame, considering how much Western civilization owed to the Turks. According to the "sun language theory," an idea popular in the 1930s but since discredited, all languages could be traced back to Turkish whose word for *sun* was said to have been the sound uttered in awe by the first articulate cave dweller. If the Turks had developed the first language, anything they now took from other cultures was only a fair exchange. In addition, the schools, armed forces, rail and motor roads, newspapers, and radio broadcasting all reinforced the Turkish sense of nationhood.

## The Legacy of Kemalism

The greatest tribute paid by the Turkish nation to Kemal Ataturk since his death in November 1938 is its continuation of the Kemalist program. To be sure, some of the extremes have been moderated. The Quran and the call to worship may now be chanted in Arabic, the Sufi orders have been allowed to resume their activities, and many Turks flock to the mosques on Fridays. But industrial and agricultural growth has moved ahead at a rate even faster than that during Kemal's lifetime. To many Turks, their country is European, not Middle Eastern. Turkey has joined the North Atlantic Treaty Organization, the Organization for Economic Cooperation and Development, and the Council of Europe. It wanted to become a full-fledged member of the European Union in 1997, once it revised its taxes and tariff duties, but was put off due to Greek objections and general doubts about the country's human rights policies, especially with regard to its Kurdish citizens. Many Turks worked in Europe, and those who have returned have exerted a strong westernizing influence. Although Turkey stayed out of World War II, it has since then built up its military might under U.S. tutelage and acquitted itself well in the war against the communists in Korea. Because of communal strife between the Greeks and Turks living in Cyprus, Turkey's armed forces intervened there in 1974; from that time on, the Turks have controlled the northern third of the island. Military experts rate Turkey's armed power second only to that of Israel among the countries of the Middle East.

Ataturk's methods and achievements were impressive, but let us put them into broader perspective. Keep in mind that his program was a link in the chain of westernizing reforms from Selim's *Nizam-i-jedid* to Mahmud II, the Tanzimat era, Abdulhamid, the Young Turks, and Ziya Gokalp. His ambivalent position between dictatorship and democracy may remind you of Turkey's brief attempts at constitutional government in 1877 and 1908, or of its ongoing search for a political system that is both popular and orderly. After Ataturk's death, Turkey evolved toward a two-party system, as the new Demokrat party rose to challenge the Kemalist Republican People's party. After a free election in 1950, the Demokrats took power peacefully, a rare occurrence in a Middle Eastern country. Basing its power on the support of entrepreneurs, peasants, and pious Muslims, the Demokrat party grew so strong that it alarmed the army officers, who overthrew the government in 1960. Under the army's watchful eye, civilian politicians in 1961 drew up a constitution for what would be called the Second Turkish Republic. They also outlawed the Demokrat party and hanged its leader. Yet the social forces that had made them popular soon created a new challenge for the Kemalists in the army and the Republican People's party. This challenge took the form of the Justice party, which won enough votes in the first election to enter into a coalition with the RPP and later was able to gain complete control of the government. The army intervened in 1971 to check what it deemed the excesses of the Justice party. The RPP made a comeback, but small Marxist and neo-Muslim parties also grew up during the 1970s. Soon every Turkish cabinet was a coalition of several diverse parties, making government impossible. In 1980, after recurrent clashes between left- and right-wing extremists killed hundreds of Turks, the army again took control of the government. General Kenan Evren banned all political parties, detained their leaders, and set up a caretaker cabinet.

For the next three years, it looked as if the Turks had traded their liberties for the sake of security. The caretaker cabinet convoked a consultative assembly that drew up a constitution giving vast powers to the president and curtailing the rights of academics, labor unions, journalists, and anyone who had been active in party politics before 1980. Nevertheless, a nationwide referendum approved the new document in 1982 and general elections were held in 1983. Turgut Ozal, who as deputy prime minister for economic affairs had taken heroic measures to stop inflation, led the new Motherland party to an electoral victory, becoming Turkey's first prime minister under its new constitution. Pressed by the Western European governments, Turkey hesitantly lifted its ban on political freedoms, and the Ozal administration helped the country achieve greater political stability and economic growth. Ozal himself moved from being prime minister to president in 1989, just as new economic problems beset the country, and died in 1993, to be replaced by Suleyman Demirel. Tansu Ciller became Turkey's first woman prime minister in the same year.

The resurgence of Islam (to be discussed in Chapter 19) has not spared Turkey, though, as an Islamist group, the Welfare Party, won a slight plurality in the 1995 election and briefly headed the government (until the army intervened to remove its prime minister and bring back the secularists). Turkey has been plagued with Kurdish nationalist uprisings, especially in the southeast, where they predominate. The country remains divided on religious issues. This problem is part of Ataturk's legacy. His westernizing reforms split the mind of Turkey between acceptance of secular values and a desire to go back to Muslim principles and institutions. Turkey is stronger now than it was before 1980. Beneath the surface, though, it is a troubled country.

## FROM PERSIA TO IRAN

Persia is unique among the countries or culture areas we have studied so far. Deserts and mountains give the land distinct boundaries, yet it has been invaded many times. Usually it has absorbed its invaders, but the absorption process has led to a mosaic of tribal nomads and sedentary peasants with distinctive folkways. Persian is the national language, but many of the people speak variants of Turkish, Kurdish, or Arabic. Its religion is Islam, but Persians (unlike their neighbors) have adhered to its Twelve-Imam Shi'i branch since the sixteenth century. More often than not in its history, Persia has been a distinct political entity, but we commonly describe it by the name of its ruling family during the time in question— and Persia's dynasties have been numerous indeed.

### Historical Recapitulation

You may recall that Persia's ruling family from the late eighteenth century was the Qajar dynasty. It was under the Qajars that the country shrank to what are now its recognized borders, losing to Russia the Caucasus Mountains and parts of Central Asia, and giving up all claims to Afghanistan and what is now Pakistan. Tehran, a village near the Elburz Mountains, became Persia's capital under the Qajars, and so it has remained ever since. Most Persians take no pride in the Qajar dynasty. Its westernization lagged behind that of the Ottoman Empire, and its resistance to Russian expansion was feeble. It invited commercial penetration and exploitation by British and other foreign merchants. Its subjects, led by their ulama (whom they call *mollahs*) and bazaar merchants, resisted political and economic subjection to these outsiders. This resistance was called Muslim fanaticism (by nineteenth-century imperialists) or Persian nationalism (by twentieth-century writers); no doubt political and religious feelings were mixed together. One result was the 1906 constitution, which set up a representative assembly, the Majlis, to limit the shah's power.

Constitutionalism alone could not build a great nation. Unable to weld the diverse military units into one army, hamstrung by strong and lawless tribes, lacking the power to collect the taxes to pay for its expenses, Qajar rule was weak. Besides, Britain and Russia agreed in 1907 to set up spheres of influence in Persia. Russian troops occupied the northern third of the country before and during World War I. Several armies vied to control the British-held parts of the south, protecting the new wells, pipelines, and refinery of the Anglo-Persian Oil Company. During the war, a German colonel formed a rebel army in lands just north of the Gulf. Elsewhere in central Persia, German agents incited acts of murder and sabotage against British or Russian consuls and merchants. The 1917 Bolshevik Revolution briefly reduced Russian pressure on Persia, as the new communist regime gave up all the czarist claims. Germany's defeat in 1918 left Britain as the sole foreign contender for control.

## The Apogee of British Power

In 1919 Britain seemed ready to absorb Persia as it had most of the Arab lands. British imperial troops occupied Iraq; guarded most of the Arab sultanates, emirates, and shaykhdoms along the Gulf; moved into the Caucasus republics that were formed as the Turks pulled out; and aided White Russian forces against the Bolsheviks. Britain offered the Qajars a treaty that would have turned Persia into a veiled protectorate, rather like Egypt under its last khedives. But popular opposition to the proposed treaty was so fierce that the Majlis never ratified it, and it eventually became a dead letter.

As I have tried to show in other chapters, 1919–1920 marked the high tide of British power in the Muslim world. The Kemalist revolt in Turkey, nationalist uprisings in Egypt and Iraq, Arab riots in Palestine, Britain's reluctance to defend the new Caucasian republics (Azerbaijan,

Armenia, and Georgia), its half-hearted attempt to oppose Soviet influence in Afghanistan, and the failure of Allied efforts to crush the Bolsheviks elsewhere, all taken together, marked a turning point in British policy. The public was clamoring for the troops to come home, and Parliament did not want to commit funds to a long-term occupation. The British government had, therefore, to cut back its presence in the Middle East.

But Persia's territorial integrity was still threatened. Separatist revolts broke out in 1920 in the northern provinces of Gilan and Azerbaijan, and the Bolsheviks landed troops to aid them. British officers remained in many areas as trainers for various Persian army units, but they were widely disliked. Trying to make both sides withdraw, the Persian government negotiated a friendship treaty with the USSR early in 1921. The Soviets pulled out their troops, renounced all extraterritorial privileges, canceled debts, and turned over all Russian properties in Persia. But the treaty had a fateful article allowing the USSR to send in troops whenever it felt menaced by the presence of another foreign army on Iranian soil. Although the Soviets would invoke this clause on later occasions, it helped Persia at the time to ease out the British.

## The Rise of Reza Shah

Five days before the Soviet-Persian pact was actually signed, an officer in the Persian Cossack Brigade (a local police force set up and led mainly by Russians) overthrew the government in Tehran. This officer, Reza Khan, born in 1878 in the mountainous province of Mazandaran, rose to prominence within the brigade during the tumultuous period after the war. Having helped to oust the brigade's pro-Bolshevik commander, Reza took charge of its infantry regiment and organized a secret society of Persian officers opposed to both British and Russian control. A general mutiny of the Persian cossacks resulted in the dismissal of all Russian officers left in the brigade. Reza, seeing how easily he had gained control of his country's strongest force, was encouraged to enter the political arena. Working with an idealistic young journalist, Sayyid Ziya ud-Din Tabatabai, Reza led his cossacks into Tehran and toppled the existing ministry on 21 February 1921. Sayyid Ziya became the new premier and Reza the commander-in-chief of the Persian army. A vigorous and comprehensive reform program began, but Ziya held power for only three months. Opposed by many of his own ministers and probably by Reza himself, he resigned and went into exile.

Persia's politics lapsed into their usual state of disorder. The Majlis opened a new session with demands from the deputies for financial and bureaucratic reform. The last of the Qajars, Ahmad Shah, kept trying to leave the country. The old politicians were divided and dispirited. Reza, who by now was war minister, became the real power behind the throne. He concentrated on uniting Persia by restoring public security, consolidating the various armies, and suppressing tribal rebels, communists, and other dissidents. Following an attempt on his life in 1923, Reza arrested the premier and forced Ahmad Shah to appoint him in his place. The shah then left for Europe, never to return.

Reza now intended to declare Persia a republic, following Kemal's example in Turkey, but the Shi'i ulama, fearing a secular regime, mobilized opposition throughout the country. After threatening to resign, Reza finally gave in. He evened the score by replacing the cabinet, putting in ministers who, though more competent, were also more compliant with his own wishes. He then went off on an expedition to quash a tribal revolt in Khuzistan, followed by a pilgrimage to the Shi'i shrines at Najaf and Karbala to mollify the *mollahs*. He returned to Tehran determined to strengthen his hold on the government. As the Majlis dithered, he acted alone to forge some major reforms. One of these now stands as his greatest achievement—the Trans-Iranian Railway, which connects the Caspian Sea to the Gulf. Aside from being an engineering marvel, this railway is notable because it was paid for without foreign loans. Construction costs were met by special taxes on sugar and tea, two staples of the Persian diet.

In a nationalistic spirit, the Majlis in 1925 adopted the old Persian solar calendar in place of the Muslim lunar one and required everyone to take a family name. Reza took the surname *Pahlavi*, the name of the pre-Islamic Persian language. The Majlis proceeded to depose Ahmad Shah, abolish the Qajar dynasty, and proclaim Reza Khan as Persia's new ruler. He officially became Reza Shah in December 1925 and then placed the Pahlavi crown on his own head in a formal ceremony.

## Reza's Reforms

Reza Shah was the regenerator of Persia just as Kemal, whom he admired, was the father of modern Turkey. The two leaders have often been compared, usually to Reza's disadvantage. But the conditions facing these nationalist reformers were not quite the same. Kemal had won fame as a successful general within a losing army, whereas Reza was known to just a few officers when he led the 1921 coup. Turkey was heir to more than a century of westernizing reforms; it had a cadre of trained officials and officers to carry out Kemal's programs. Persia had been cut off from the West, except for the dubious blessing of bordering on Russia. Kemal expressed the disillusionment toward Islam felt by many Turks and equated westernization with "civilization." Few Turks cared about their own pre-Islamic heritage in the far-off Asian steppes. Reza could make no such break with the Persian past. His people were still profoundly influenced by Shi'i *mujtahids* and *mollahs*. Even when he could fight this Muslim clerical influence, Reza recognized that Persia's pre-Islamic heritage was alive and meaningful to his subjects. This tie to the past could promote his reform program, too, as Sasanid monuments were spruced up, the Zoroastrian religion won official toleration, and the Persian language was purged of some of its Arabic words. But there was also a drastic break with the past, as Reza decreed in 1935 that his country's name should be changed from *Persia* to *Iran* (the land of the Aryans). The post office was even instructed to return any letters addressed to the old name of the country. These symbolic changes strengthened national pride and distanced Iran from Islam and the Arab world.

One of his ablest subordinates, General Hassan Arfa, summed up Reza's reforms under four convenient headings: (1) liberation from foreign political and economic domination, (2) establishment of internal security and centralized government, (3) administrative reforms and economic progress, and (4) social reforms and cultural progress. Let us examine each set of reforms in more depth.

Liberation from foreign domination entailed more than ousting British and Russian troops; it also meant replacing British with Iranian control along the Gulf coast, taking charge of banks, currency, telephones and telegraphs, and gaining the right to try foreigners accused of crimes and to fix and collect the customs duties on imports. Reza succeeded in implementing every reform until he tried to annul the Anglo-Persian (soon to be renamed Anglo-Iranian) Oil Company's concession. Britain took the issue to the League of Nations, and finally the company agreed to pay higher royalties to the Iranian government, which in turn extended its concession by thirty years. Many Iranians later accused Reza of granting this extension in exchange for British bribes, a charge that non-Iranians find hard to prove.

Strengthening Iran's national government could be achieved only by weakening the nomadic tribes. Many were forced to settle down, their chiefs in some cases being put under house arrest. Those allowed to remain nomadic often transported their flocks under police escort. The army was extensively reorganized, with vastly improved munitions, weapons, training, barracks, and health-care facilities. All security forces were placed under central control, and a rudimentary political police was set up.

Iran gradually acquired a civil service, European-style law codes and courts, a state budget, and a national system for registering births, land transfers, marriages, and deaths. Roads suitable for cars and trucks, almost nonexistent in 1921, crisscrossed the country by 1941. Often accused of taking away the peasants' lands to augment his own holdings, Reza claimed that he wanted his estates to serve as model farms to discover and teach new methods. Iran also built some modern factories and imposing public buildings during his reign, but their boost to morale probably outweighed their material benefit to the nation.

To Reza, social reform meant education. Schooling increased drastically at all levels, for girls as well as boys. Although Reza is well known for opening the University of Tehran in 1935, he cared most about the basic education of peasants and workers. Night schools proliferated, and the army became a vast training program. Officers were held responsible for teaching their troops to read, write, and do basic arithmetic. If any soldier did not gain these skills by the end of his two-year stint, then his unit commander would not get promoted. Sports and games had long been a part of Iran's culture, although many *mollah*s frowned on them, but Reza made a cult out of physical fitness and athletic contests. He did not attack organized Islam directly (as Ataturk had done), but he sometimes nettled the *mollah*s by drinking beer or wine in public, and he did insist that all men who wore the garb of ulama pass examinations proving their right to do so. He followed Ataturk's example by forcing an "international" costume on all Iranian men and surpassed him by forbidding women to veil their faces. This reform deeply offended conservative Muslims, who asked whether Westerners would be just as shocked if women of all ages were forced to go topless in public. Muslim opposition barred what I think would have been a sounder and more lasting reform: the romanization of the Persian alphabet.

## Reza's Downfall

Although Reza Shah tried in many ways to transform Iran, the results often disappointed him. An impatient man, he never could delegate tasks. Trying to reduce Iran's dependence on Britain, he brought in foreigners from other lands to advise him on reforms. When a U.S. mission improved Iran's fiscal administration in the 1920s but failed to attract American investors, Reza forced the director to resign and phased out his subordinates. The U.S. government did not step in, much to the Iranians' astonishment. Germany was more active. An able German director built up the National Bank of Iran in the early 1930s. After Hitler took power, German entrepreneurs and advisers flocked to Iran. Reza and many of his subjects were flattered by Nazi racial theories, because they viewed Iran as the original Aryan nation. After World War II began and Nazi forces overran most of Europe, the British had reason to fear Germany's presence in Iran. In 1941 a group of Arab nationalist army officers briefly seized control of neighboring Iraq. Suspecting them of pro-Nazi sympathies, Britain rushed in to install a pro-British regime. When Hitler suddenly invaded the USSR that June, both the British and the Soviets sent troops into Iran. Once again Iran's independence was violated. Unwilling to rule under a military occupation that threatened to undo twenty years' work, Reza abdicated in favor of his son, Mohammad. He went into exile and died three years later.

## Epilogue

When he succeeded his father, Mohammad Reza Shah Pahlavi seemed to be no more than a Western protégé. The tribes hastened to regain the power and lands they had lost. The Majlis asserted its constitutional right to govern. The World War II Allies treated Iran as a supply line, a source of oil, a convenient meeting place, and a subordinate ally. Once the war ended, the USSR tried to set up communist republics in northern Iran but withdrew its troops in 1946 under United Nations pressure. The communists then played on the rising discontent of the workers in the Anglo-Iranian Oil Company (AIOC). Iranian nationalists won control of the Majlis, electing Mohammad Mosaddiq as prime minister. Because it nationalized the AIOC, Mosaddiq's government became popular at home but was fiercely resented in Britain and the United States, so it was toppled in 1953 by a CIA-backed military coup. For the next quarter century, Mohammad Reza Shah ruled Iran as a dictator. Skyrocketing oil revenues enabled his government to build up its schools, industries, and armed forces. The shah's "White Revolution" promised changes in landownership, rural development, education, and women's rights beyond his father's wildest dreams. It also deprived the ulama of many of their lands and other sources of revenue.

The shah also inherited his father's authoritarian streak. When his reforms failed to meet his subjects' expectations, he fell back on propaganda, censorship, and his secret police (SAVAK) to stay in power. Although successive U.S. governments backed him as a bulwark against communism, many Americans questioned his commitment to human rights. Iranian students abroad and ulama at home stirred up opposition to the shah. They decried the erosion of Muslim values, the widening gap between rich and poor, the huge sums spent on arms, the failure of agrarian reform, and the shah's oppressive regime. A nationwide revolution, led by Shi'i ulama, sapped the shah's authority. He left Iran in January 1979, giving way to an "Islamic Republic." Iran's vaunted "modernization" was only superficial. Billions of dollars in oil revenues could not solve Iran's problems or keep a ruler in power after his people turned against him. This story will be resumed in Chapter 19.

## THE RISE OF SAUDI ARABIA

Nowadays most people think of Saudi Arabia as a rich, modern, and very influential country. This may be true today, but as late as 1945 it was poor and viewed as backward. The homeland of Islam and Arabism had been a backwater of history since the High Caliphate. If Istanbul was in the vanguard of westernizing reform movements up to this century, few parts of the Middle East could have opposed them more than central Arabia, especially the area known as Najd. Its location helped. Situated among barren hills, lacking an outlet to any sea, Najd offered no attractions to foreign traders or to Western imperialism. Most of its people were bedouin; a few small towns contained Arab merchants and ulama. So far I have hardly mentioned the area, except in connection with the rise of a puritanical Muslim sect called the Wahhabis, whose beliefs still prevail in today's Kingdom of Saudi Arabia.

### Historical Background

The story starts in the mid-eighteenth century, when a wandering young scholar, Muhammad ibn ("son of") Abd al-Wahhab, became a Hanbali—that is, an adherent to the strictest of the four canonical rites of Sunni Muslim law. The latter-day Hanbalis came to oppose certain practices associated with popular Islam (often taken from older Middle Eastern religions), such as venerating saints, their tombs, trees, and wells. When this Muhammad began preaching and writing in his hometown about cleansing Islam of these practices, his own relatives drove him out. Taking refuge in a nearby village, he converted his protector, Muhammad ibn

Sa'ud, to his strict doctrines. Thus leagued together, the two Muhammads set out to convert the nearby Arab tribes, with the son of Abd al-Wahhab as spiritual guide (hence our use of *Wahhabi* for the sect) and the son of Sa'ud as military and political leader (which is why we speak of the Saudi dynasty). In the late eighteenth and early nineteenth centuries, the Saudis managed to spread their rule and the Wahhabi doctrines to most of northern Arabia, using methods similar to those of the Kharijites centuries earlier. They even took Mecca and Medina, destroying or damaging many of the tombs and other shrines that are part of the Muslim hajj. You may remember that the Ottoman sultan sent Mehmet Ali's army to the Hijaz to drive away these Wahhabis, whose threat to the Ottomans in this sensitive area could undermine their legitimacy in other Muslim lands as well. After years of desert warfare, the Saudi-Wahhabi combine was defeated, and the Turks garrisoned the Hijaz. Although Wahhabi doctrines continued to spread to the Gulf region and even to India, the Saudi family was confined during the nineteenth century to central and eastern Arabia. Even there it contended for power with the Rashid dynasty, which enjoyed Ottoman backing and seemed by 1900 to have triumphed over the house of Sa'ud.

The man known to us as Ibn Sa'ud (the Saudis call him Abd al-Aziz ibn Abd al-Rahman) was born in Riyadh, the Saudis' home base, in 1880. When he was ten, the Rashids drove his family out. The Saudis took refuge near the Rub' al-Khali (the Empty Quarter, in the eastern part of the Arabian Peninsula) among the Bani Murrah, a tribe so poor and primitive that its people are called the bedouins' bedouin. Among these desert desperadoes Ibn Sa'ud learned to ride and shoot expertly and to deal with other tribal Arabs. Later the Saudis were given asylum by the *shaykh* of Kuwait, a fishing port near the head of the Gulf. There Ibn Sa'ud began learning about the outsiders who now coveted the Arabian Peninsula, one of the few lands not already carved up by the great European empires. Actually, Arabia in 1900 had a patchwork of local and foreign rulers, too many to be listed in a concise history. Let me just say that Sultan Abdulhamid was extending Ottoman control into formerly autonomous lands, such as the coastal region east of Najd called al-Hasa. Some of the Arab *shaykhs* along the Gulf had made treaties with the British that let them manage their defense and foreign relations. But young Ibn Sa'ud craved neither protection by foreign Christians nor dependency on the Ottomans, whom the Wahhabis saw as backsliders from Islam; he wanted to retake Riyadh from the Rashid tribe. Heading a small band of loyal Wahhabis on a nighttime raid, he successfully won back his ancestral capital in 1902. This was the first episode in an epic that has been told time and again by Saudi and foreign chroniclers.

## The Emergence of the Saudi Kingdom

This epic is the story of how, over the span of some thirty years, most of the tribes and emirates of the Arabian Peninsula became united under Ibn Sa'ud. The process involved many bedouin raids, battles, and wars between the Saudi-Wahhabi combine and other contenders for power. First they had to subdue the Ottoman-backed Rashid dynasty. After 1906 they began to win control over the tribes of central and eastern Arabia. Few outsiders noticed these struggles until Ibn Sa'ud's followers challenged the kingdom of the Hijaz, the state headed by Amir Husayn (see Chapter 13). When he conquered the Hijaz and took control of Islam's holy cities between 1924 and 1926, Ibn Sa'ud became the most respected leader in Arabia—indeed, in the whole Arab world. How different Arab history would have been if Britain had heeded its India Office during World War I and backed Ibn Sa'ud of Riyadh instead of the Hashimites of Mecca!

Why did he win? First, Ibn Sa'ud believed in Wahhabi Islam and enforced its rules strictly among his followers, using religious belief to temper the bedouins' love of battle and booty. His deep convictions, combined with his physical courage and personal magnetism, led thousands of Arabs to love and obey him. His skills were marital as well as martial; both his victories and his marriages were more than you could count. Most of Ibn Sa'ud's nuptials served to cement peace with the tribes he had subdued. In case you are wondering how he stayed within the Quranic limit of four, he divorced most of the wives he married and returned them, loaded with gifts, to their guardians. Yet people said that any woman who married Ibn Sa'ud, however briefly, loved him for the rest of her life. I wonder who could verify this—or how!

Another way Ibn Sa'ud controlled the tribes was to weld them into a religious organization called the *Ikhwan* (Brothers). These *Ikhwan*, though bedouin, were persuaded to give up camel nomadism for settled agriculture. Although many of them never learned how to push a plow, their settlement in farming villages made them easier to control, more willing to heed the teachings of Wahhabi ulama from Riyadh, and better disciplined when Ibn Sa'ud needed their military services. Without the *Ikhwan*, the Saudis could not have united most of Arabia within a generation.

But some parts of Arabia never fell under their control. Like Ataturk, Ibn Sa'ud knew his political limits. Once he had taken Asir, the tiny kingdom between the Hijaz and the Yemen, and had formally created the kingdom of Saudi Arabia in 1932, his conquests ceased. After a brief war two years later, Ibn Sa'ud gave up all claims to the imamate of Yemen. This magnanimity was wise, for the Yemeni highlanders were Zaydi Shi'is who would have bitterly resisted Wahhabi (that is, Hanbali Sunni) rule by the Saudis. He also disbanded the *Ikhwan* in 1930 after they took to raiding tribes in Iraq, then a British mandate. Rarely did the Saudis attack Arab rulers under British protection, such as Abdallah of Transjordan, the *shaykh* (later amir) of Kuwait, other *shaykhs* along the Gulf coast, the sultan of Muscat and Oman, or the rulers of southern Arabia east of Aden. By the 1940s Ibn Sa'ud had become the Arabs' elder statesman. Even his Hashimite rivals in Transjordan and Iraq, although they resented his expulsion of their father from the Hijaz, came to respect Ibn Sa'ud's leadership.

## Oil Discoveries and Their Effects on the Saudi Kingdom

Given the way the world is now, it is easy to forget that Ibn Sa'ud and his kingdom were extremely poor for most of his life. Najd was a sun-parched, mountainous land far from any sea, the Gulf provided only pearls and scanty trade to Hasa, Asir had some upland areas suitable for farming, and the Hijaz provided a meager income from the annual Muslim pilgrimage. Usually about 150,000 pilgrims came to Mecca each year; the figure of a quarter-million reported in 1926 (just after the Saudi conquest) was exceptional. The economy of Saudi Arabia as a whole depended on the date palm and the camel up to the late 1930s. Several British companies had tried with no success to prospect for oil in a few provinces of the kingdom. There were some abandoned gold mines, and it was widely thought that Arabia contained other valuable minerals; but its harsh climate, rapacious bedouin, and Wahhabi fanaticism all daunted outside prospectors. So desperately poor was Ibn Sa'ud that he was once heard to say, "If anyone were to offer a million pounds, he would be welcome to all the concessions he wanted in my country."

The man of the hour was an American whose surname you may recall from Chapter 13—Charles Crane, the plumbing manufacturer and philanthropist who took part in the 1919 King-Crane Commission. After a sojourn in the Yemen, where he financed a successful search for minerals, Crane visited Ibn Sa'ud in 1931. They discussed a similar quest in the Hijaz, hoping to find enough underground water to pipe it into Jiddah (the port town of Mecca). But Crane's mining engineer, Karl Twitchell, soon found that neither water nor oil existed in economic quantities beneath the largely barren Hijaz. Two years later, though, Twitchell came back, this time in the service of Standard Oil of California (now Chevron), which outbid a British representative of the Iraq Petroleum Company (now BP) for exploration rights in eastern Arabia. For a cash loan amounting to 50,000 gold sovereigns (about $300,000, now worth $2 million), plus an annual rent of 5,000 more, Ibn Sa'ud gave the Americans a sixty-year concession to search for oil in Hasa, with preferential exploration rights in other parts of his kingdom. They agreed that more loans would be made later if oil were found in marketable quantities, plus a royalty of one gold sovereign ($6) for every five long tons (a "long ton" is roughly equal to 2,240 pounds, or slightly more than one metric ton) of oil extracted from Saudi territory.

Five years of exploration and drilling ensued before the Americans struck oil in 1938 at Jabal Dhahran and began sending barrels to the British refinery on the nearby island of Bahrain, already an oil-exporting country. Soon they were building their own refinery, storage tanks, and a loading dock on the Gulf. Petroleum technicians, construction foremen, and equipment poured into Dhahran, which became a "Little America" complete with lawns, swimming pools, air-conditioned buildings, and a commissary at which the Americans could buy the canned goods, chewing gum, and cigarettes they had known back home. By this time, the Texas Oil Company had joined Standard Oil of California in setting up a subsidiary officially called the Arabian American Oil Company but almost always nicknamed Aramco. Tanker shortages during World War II halted its operations for a time, but eventually Aramco started selling oil to U.S. forces in the Pacific. After the war, new oil exploration and discoveries raised Saudi output by leaps and bounds to 1.3 million barrels per day in 1960, 3.8 million in 1970, and more than 10 million in 1981, when the kingdom's annual oil revenue reached $113 billion. Over a quarter of the world's proven petroleum reserves are thought to lie in Saudi territory.

The exploitation of Middle East oil was the most revolutionary change of that time. Karl Twitchell was surely no Karl Marx, but the result of his labors—amplified by Aramco's later geologists and explorers—drastically changed the economic, social, cultural, and moral life of the Saudi Arabs. No Middle Eastern people or country has been untouched by the shower of Saudi wealth. Its effects on the world economy will be discussed later, but let me say for now that oil wealth has made the Saudi government the most influential in the Arab world.

What is less well known is that Saudi Arabia had hardly any government in the modern sense during the reign of Ibn Sa'ud. For most of this period Saudi Arabia was "governed" insofar as Ibn Sa'ud had the personal charm and, if needed, the force to subdue (and collect tribute from) the bedouin tribes within his realm. Any money he got from the tribal *shaykhs*, the pilgrims, or Aramco went into his private treasury. It was used to maintain his palace, support his harem, increase his herds of Arabian horses and camels, or make sumptuous gifts to his foreign visitors or to his subjects, each of whom had the right to go directly to Ibn Sa'ud to vent his grievances and obtain justice. There was no formal cabinet; Ibn Sa'ud talked matters over with his relatives and a few foreign advisers, but he made his own decisions. There was no state bank; the gold sovereigns were stored in wooden chests. The laws were those of the Quran and the sunnah, administered by Hanbali ulama. Thieves had their hands chopped off. Murderers were beheaded. Disobedient tribes were fined or banished from their grazing lands. The Wahhabis forced all Saudi Muslims to pray five times a day, going from house to house to ensure compliance. Alcohol and tobacco were strictly forbidden to Muslims, as were Western clothes, movies, music, dancing, and even (for a while) radios and telephones.

Imagine, then, the effect of Little America in Dhahran, where the foreign Aramco employees lived in ranch houses with their wives (who did not veil their faces), built stills in their back rooms, threw parties, did not pray five times daily, and opened their clinic and hospital to Saudi Arabs, many of whom had never seen a doctor before. How could God bless these alien Christians more than the Muslims who feared and worshiped Him? Imagine, too, what must have happened when Ibn Sa'ud's sons and grandsons started to go abroad on diplomatic or educational missions. Palaces sprang up around Riyadh in crude imitation of what the Saudis had seen in Paris, London, and Hollywood. And camels gave way to Cadillacs, although it took time to train a cadre of local mechanics to maintain and repair them.

Ibn Sa'ud was totally unprepared for the sudden wealth that oil brought to his kingdom. Aging, lame, blind in one eye, he lived to see corruption and licentiousness spread among his courtiers and even some of his sons, deeply wounding his conscience and affronting his morals. He did not understand economics. When told that the price of food had outstripped his subjects' means, he ordered Aramco to double the wages it paid to Saudi employees, only to see the inflation get worse. Politics also bewildered him. He was troubled by the divisions among his fellow Arab rulers during and after World War II. He felt betrayed by the Palestine policies of the countries he had trusted, Britain and the United States. When he met President Franklin D. Roosevelt in 1945, Ibn Sa'ud asked him why the Allies could not take away the homes and lands of the Germans in order to house survivors of Hitler's atrocities, instead of punishing the Arabs of Palestine by calling for a Jewish state. Roosevelt promised not to act on the Palestine question (which you will read about in Chapter 16) without first consulting both Arabs and Jews. Six weeks later he died, and Truman ignored the promise. But Ibn Sa'ud could not really attack the Americans for helping to create Israel when their company was pumping his oil, filling his coffers, and building a railroad from Riyadh to the Gulf. Besides, the Saudis loathed Soviet communism even more.

*Ibn Sa'ud's Successors*

Ibn Sa'ud died quietly in his sleep in 1953. The ablest of his sons was Faysal, but the princes and the ulama agreed that the succession should go to the oldest surviving son, Sa'ud, a weaker figure. Within a few years Sa'ud had managed to run up a $300-million debt despite his government's rising income. The last straw was a sensational press story that Sa'ud had bribed a Syrian minister to kill Egyptian President Gamal Abd al-Nasir, then at the peak of his popularity in the Arab world. In 1958, a turbulent year in Arab politics, the Saudi princes agreed to turn over all executive powers to Faysal as premier. Six years later Sa'ud was deposed and Faysal became king. Under Faysal the Saudi government became much better organized, with regular ministries, an annual budget, development plans, new roads, schools, and hospitals. As Saudi Arabia plunged headlong into modernity, King Faysal became as influential among Arab rulers and Muslim conservatives as his father had ever been. His oil policies and eventual fate will be covered in Chapter 18.

## CONCLUSION

Three large Middle Eastern countries weathered the period between the two world wars—the high point of Western control over the area—without becoming colonies, protectorates, or mandates. Each country established the borders it has had ever since. Each government tightened its hold over groups that had checked the power of previous rulers. Personal income rose, more children (and adults) went to school, and public health improved.

These were not democratic regimes. In each case, the agent for change was a military leader whose successes in war won him the respect and obedience of his subjects. Other Middle Eastern countries were quick to learn from them. Army officers became the greatest force for modernization in the Middle East. As efficiency is essential in military operations, it is natural for commanders to apply the same standards and employ similar methods to modernize their countries. Nationalist leaders can persuade otherwise recalcitrant subjects to make sacrifices for the common good. But how much will they give up? And what if conditions change, as has happened (thanks to oil) in Iran and Saudi Arabia?

The men whose lives we have studied raise other issues. Can modernization be sustained without a set of shared values between those who order and those who obey? Kemal Ataturk saw Islam as a barrier to progress and tried to reduce its influence, but Turkish nationalism has not yet replaced Islam within the hearts and minds of many Turks. Divided almost evenly between westernizers and Muslim traditionalists, modern Turkey drifts without the rudder of ideological consensus. Reza Shah was ambivalent about Islam, but his reform program built up a westernized elite at the expense of Iran's Muslim leaders, who took their revenge after the 1979 revolution. Ibn Sa'ud's devotion to Islam united a disparate band of tribes under his rule, but his puritanical values could not cope with the innovations that flooded his country because of the oil revenues, and he died a bitterly disillusioned man. None of these leaders, however hard they worked to forge their people into nation-states, managed to establish a set of values to guide their successors. All equated westernization with modernization.

Some day, I hope, a synthesis will be achieved between Islam as a system of beliefs and behavioral norms on the one hand, and the values of a technical or industrialized society on the other. Until then, authoritarian leaders will probably be, as they have been up to now, the main agents for change in independent Middle Eastern countries.

# FIFTEEN

# Egypt's Struggle
# for Independence

For more than a century Egypt has loomed large in any discussion of Middle East politics, whether the country was acting or acted upon. One reason for this has been the Suez Canal, so strategically and economically important to any state that wanted to be a great power. Another is Egypt's position in the vanguard of westernizing reform, going back to the time of Napoleon and Mehmet Ali. In modern times Egypt has usually been the leader of the Arab countries, yet it underwent a long and complicated struggle for independence. For centuries, Egypt was valued by foreign powers, as an object to be seized and held, as a symbol of imperial might, as a means of influencing the rest of the Arab world, or as a stepping stone to Asia or the Mediterranean Sea—but never as Egypt.

What about the Egyptians themselves? Rather than actors, they had long been people who were acted upon. With centuries of experience as a doormat for outside invaders, oppressors, and explorers, many Egyptians, not surprisingly, distrusted the foreigners who lived or traveled within their country. After all, no Egyptian ruled Egypt from the time of the pharaohs to the fall of King Faruq in 1952. Even its aristocrats were mainly foreign—hence the popular proverb: *Fi bilad Misr khayruha lighayriha* (In the land of Egypt what is good belongs to others).

## BRITAIN'S ROLE IN EGYPT

Heroes come and go, and villains appear and disappear in most political dramas. But in Egypt's independence struggle, the main antagonist for seventy-five years was Britain. By rights, Egypt was an autonomous province of the Ottoman Empire from 1841 to 1914. In reality, as a land under military occupation from 1882 on, Egypt was a British colony in all but name. Important decisions about Egypt's administration were being made in London, not Istanbul, or (if locally) in the British Agency on the banks of the Nile, not in the khedive's palace, somewhat farther east in downtown Cairo. The ministers were puppets in the hands of their British advisers. Both the occupier and the occupied knew that theirs was a power relationship, with Britain dominant and Egypt either passive or protesting, although all sides observed the diplomatic niceties up to World War I.

Then, when the Ottoman Empire went to war against the Allies in November 1914, Britain had to bite the bullet. As it needed to hold Egypt to ensure the survival of the British Empire (at a time when hundreds of troop ships were carrying Australians, New Zealanders, and Indians through the Suez Canal to European war theaters), Egypt's Turkish tie had become an anomaly. Britain cut it decisively in December. No longer an Ottoman province, Egypt became a British protectorate. The change was no more legal than Germany's occupation of Belgium that August. It was certainly not approved by the Ottoman government, ratified by the Egyptian ministers, or accepted by the newly formed Legislative Assembly, which was adjourned indefinitely. Khedive Abbas, already barred from returning from Istanbul to Egypt by Britain's ambassador to the Ottoman Empire, was now accused of having taken the Turks' side in the war. Even though he had fled to neutral Switzerland to get away from the Turks, the British deposed him anyway. In Abbas's place they appointed a pliable uncle, Husayn Kamil (r. 1914–1917), who was given the title of "sultan" to underscore the break with the Ottoman Empire. The prime minister, Husayn Rushdi, stayed in office, believing that Egypt would get its independence once the war ended. Britain's chief representative became the high commissioner for Egypt and the Sudan, and his office came to be called the Residency. The Egyptian people accepted the changes passively, if a bit sullenly. Many hoped the Turks and Germans would win the war anyway.

## Anglo-Egyptian Relations: An Overview

As you know, they lost. The period from 1914 to 1956 has been termed by Elizabeth Monroe "Britain's moment in the Middle East." Since that period still looms large in the memories of most older Egyptians and Europeans, it seems a long time span, although it really was shorter than, say, Mongol rule in Persia. As long as the British were the top power in the area, the main drama was their relationship, rarely an easy one, with Egypt. "Egypt and England are like an old married couple," wrote a Frenchman in the 1930s. "They may quarrel from time to time, but they always make up in the end." Well, they eventually did get a divorce, but the comparison remains apt. A marriage can be built on many forces besides love. One common basis is power. One partner makes the decisions; the other goes along, out of either self-abnegation or stark necessity. Think of the domineering husband and the submissive wife in Ibsen's play *A Doll's House*. Britain, like Torvald, managed everything, whereas Egypt, in Nora's role, cajoled and intrigued to get its way. Eventually, Britain's power waned, and Egypt, never willingly obedient, found ways to sap its authority. The protectorate gave way in 1922 to a unilateral declaration of Egypt's independence, limited by four conditions called "reserved points." Then the two sides agreed in 1936 to formalize their relationship in a treaty, of which Egypt soon repented. Finally, after a bitter quarrel, they reached in 1954 a new agreement terminating Britain's occupation of Egypt in 1956. Even this conclusion had a sad sequel in the Anglo-French invasion of the Suez Canal late in that year. Each British concession was hedged with restrictions; each Egyptian demand went far beyond what any British government would grant. It must have been a very unhappy marriage.

Several explanations for this sad state of affairs come to mind. First, the British stayed in Egypt not out of love for the country or its people but because it was a stepping stone to India or to the oil wells of Arabia or Iran or a base in the contest against the Kaiser, the Nazis, or the communists. The Egyptians knew this and felt it deeply. The British did not even like them, to judge from the diplomatic reports, the social arrangements, and even the fiction of the age. The Egyptian, as viewed by the British, was a portly parody of a petty French official, a boastful coward, a turbaned Muslim fanatic, a noisy agitator blind to the benefits that British rule had given his country, or a "wog" (for "wily Oriental gentleman") selling dirty postcards in the bazaar. The Egyptians saw the British as coldhearted, exclusive (it was a sore point that, for many years, the only Egyptians who could enter Cairo's posh Gezira Sporting Club were servants), mercenary, and power-hungry. Egyptians tended to prefer the French or the Americans, but not (as their foes often alleged) the Germans or the Russians. Curiously, the British could relate well to almost any other people in the Arab world, especially the bedouin. France's influence on Egyptian schools and culture may have alienated the British, or perhaps it was the greater skill of desert Arabs at horseback riding, hunting, and other sports enjoyed by upper-class British males. But I suspect that the alienation stemmed from the way in which the British set themselves up as masters, whereas the Egyptians (unlike other Arabs) were used to being servants. Later, neither side adjusted easily to the way the other was changing.

## World War I

The quality of British administration in Egypt, top-notch up to 1914, declined during World War I. Many of the best Englishmen either left or were called home for military service, never to return. Hordes of new officials and officers poured into Egypt, making the country a vast army camp for the Allies. The new men, inexperienced and less sensitive than their precursors toward Muslims, often gave offense and overlooked the country's real needs. So much attention had to be paid to the war against Ottoman Turkey, especially the unsuccessful Dardanelles campaign of 1915 and the Egyptian Expeditionary Force that conquered Palestine and coastal Syria in 1917–1918, that vital problems were neglected in Egypt, which was placed under martial law for the duration of the war.

Cairo and Alexandria were becoming overpopulated. Food shortages drove up prices in the cities and other places in which troops were concentrated. Egypt's government, hoping to increase wheat harvests, limited the acreage for raising cotton, a more lucrative wartime crop for rural landlords and peasants. After having promised not to demand any wartime sacrifices from the Egyptian people, the British ended up requisitioning grain, draft animals, and even peasant labor for their Palestine campaign. "Woe on us, Wingate," sang the peasants in 1918, alluding to McMahon's replacement as British high commissioner,

> who has carried off corn
> carried off cattle,
> carried off camels,
> carried off children,
> leaving only our lives.
> For the love of God, now let us alone.

As the British grew in numbers, they lost touch with the Egyptians. The judicial adviser, an able and usually sympathetic Scotsman, drew up a note on constitutional reform that would have given Egypt a bicameral legislature, with a powerful upper house made up of Egyptian ministers, British advisers, and representatives of the foreign communities, which already dominated the country's economic life. Even though it would have ended the Capitulations, patriotic Egyptians could never have welcomed such a constitution, which would have tightened the foreign grip on their own country. When the plan became known in November 1918, it fueled the flames of fury among upper-class Egyptians. We would rather rule ourselves badly, the nationalists argued, than let ourselves be governed well by foreigners.

## The 1919 Revolution

No Englishman foresaw a revival of Egyptian nationalism after the war. The National party had declined. The followers of the moderate Ahmad Lutfi al-Sayyid, most of them landowners and intellectuals, were few—though powerful—in the 1914 Legislative Assembly. One of those followers was Sa'd Zaghlul, the elected vice president of that representative body, who then emerged as a prominent critic of the government and its British advisers. Sa'd had an interesting background. Son of a prosperous peasant, he was educated in the 1870s at al-Azhar University, where he fell under the influence of Jamal al-Din al-Afghani. He then edited the government journal and backed the 1882 Urabi revolution. Shortly after the British occupied Egypt, he was arrested for plotting to kill Khedive Tawfiq. After his release from jail, Sa'd studied law in France, returned to Egypt, became a judge, and married the prime minister's daughter. His wife's family introduced him to Lord Cromer, who urged his appointment as education minister during the nationalist reaction to the 1906 Dinshaway incident. In a public speech just before he left Egypt in 1907, Cromer described Sa'd Zaghlul in the following terms: "He possesses all the qualities necessary to serve his country. He is honest, he is capable, he has the courage of his convictions, he has been abused by many of the less worthy of his own countrymen. These are high qualifications. He should go far."

Sa'd did go far, but not in the way Cromer had hoped. His progress through the Egyptian cabinet was thwarted by his quarrels with both Khedive Abbas and Lord Kitchener, so he quit the cabinet in 1912. Many British officials would later wish they had continued to co-opt Sa'd to their side, instead of letting him join their opponents. During the war, with the legislature not meeting, Sa'd had ample time to plot against the government. He was secretly encouraged by Husayn Kamil's successor,

Sultan Fuad (r. 1917–1936), who hoped to increase his power, relative to that of the British in Egypt, as soon as the war ended.

Fuad's ambitions were matched by those of many Egyptian politicians, who wanted a parliamentary government, a liberal democracy, and Egyptian control over the Sudan, untrammeled by the British protectorate. Most of these men had also been disciples of Lutfi al-Sayyid before the war. High-minded and devoid of religious fanaticism, they looked to Sa'd as their spokesman, as he had been in the 1914 assembly.

On 13 November 1918, two days after the European armistice, Sa'd Zaghlul and two of his friends called on the British high commissioner, Sir Reginald Wingate, a man who had lived in the Nile Valley for twenty years, spoke Arabic, and knew the Egyptians well. In a cordial conversation, they announced their intention to form a delegation (Arabic: *wafd*) to go to London to argue for Egypt's independence. Wingate counseled patience but agreed to wire home for instructions. Britain's Foreign Office, preoccupied with the approaching Paris Peace Conference, refused to talk to this delegation of "disappointed and disgraced" politicians, or even to receive Husayn Rushdi, who had stayed on as premier through the war in the hope that Britain would end its protectorate as soon as peace returned.

During the winter Sa'd announced that he would head a six-man delegation to present Egypt's case for independence before the Paris Peace Conference. Though made up of landowning moderates, this delegation, the Wafd, enlisted the aid of the remaining supporters of the National party to circulate throughout Egypt copies of a petition whose signers authorized the Wafd to represent them in demanding complete independence, meaning an end to the British protectorate and evacuation of all foreign troops from Egypt and the Sudan. In March 1919 the Rushdi cabinet resigned and the British exiled Sa'd and his friends to Malta, whereupon the movement to support the Wafd turned into a popular revolution, the largest of all that have occurred in modern Egypt. Students and teachers, lawyers and judges, government employees and transport workers, went out on strike. Riots broke out in the villages, railroad stations were attacked, and telegraph lines were cut. Every social class demonstrated against the British protectorate; even women from wealthy families took to the streets. Muslim ulama preached in Christian churches, and Christian priests gave Friday mosque sermons, as Copts and Muslims walked hand in hand, demanding "Egypt for the Egyptians." A new national flag appeared, with the Christian cross where the star within the Muslim crescent had been. Only when the British government recalled

Wingate, appointed as the new high commissioner General Edmund Allenby (who had commanded the Egyptian Expeditionary Force that had taken Palestine), and freed Sa'd to go to Paris did the Egyptians go back to work.

When the Wafd went to Paris to present its case to the peace conference, nearly all Egyptians had high hopes. Would President Wilson, well known for upholding the political rights of subject nations, ignore those of the world's oldest one? Was Egypt not as entitled as the Arabs of the Hijaz to a hearing in Paris? Did it not have as much right to independence as, say, Yugoslavia or Albania? Apparently not. On the day the Wafd arrived in Paris, the U.S. government formally recognized what Egypt's nationalists were fighting to terminate—the British protectorate. The Wafd was never invited to address the peace conference. Sa'd Zaghlul and his companions could only make speeches that were unheeded and churn out letters that went unanswered by those with the power to redraw the political map of the Middle East.

## British Efforts at a Solution

Noting the ongoing unrest in Egypt, the British government decided to send a commission, headed by Lord Milner, to "inquire into the causes of the late disorders, and to report on the existing situation in the country, and on the form of constitution which, under the protectorate, will be best calculated to promote its peace and prosperity, the progressive development of self-governing institutions, and the protection of foreign interests." Egyptian supporters of the Wafd, now as well organized at home as in Paris, might desire peace, prosperity, and the progressive development of self-rule, but they did not want the protectorate. They organized a general boycott of the Milner mission, a boycott that (probably against the organizers' wishes) led to some attacks on British soldiers and Egyptian ministers. The Milner mission saw that Britain must somehow come to terms with Egyptian nationalism, but its leaders were in Paris, not Cairo. The Egyptian government managed to persuade Sa'd Zaghlul to talk informally with Milner, but neither could concede enough to reach a compromise. The British called Sa'd a demagogue trapped by his own propaganda. The Wafd thought that Britain, to protect its imperial communications, would never really let the Egyptians rule themselves. A Zaghlul-Milner memorandum, which would have replaced the protectorate by an Anglo-Egyptian treaty, failed to gain the support of the Egyptian government or its people when Sa'd himself declined to endorse it. But Britain had now clearly signaled its willingness to give up the protectorate. An official Egyptian delegation, headed by the new prime minister, Adli Yakan, went to London in 1921 to negotiate the terms, but Sa'd managed to use his popularity in Egypt to undermine support for Adli's negotiations with the Foreign Office.

Having thus failed to negotiate a new relationship with the Egyptians, either officially with Adli or unofficially with Sa'd, Britain seemed to be stymied on the Egyptian question. New waves of strikes and assassinations made action imperative. Continued control over the Suez Canal and the port of Alexandria, the radio and telegraph stations, the railroads and the airports—all communication links vital to the British Empire—could have been put at risk by a nationwide revolution backed by Sultan Fuad and his ministers and led by Sa'd Zaghlul and the Wafd. Britain's dilemma in 1921–1922 would become common in a later time of decolonization: How much should a strong country defer to the national pride of a weaker one and yet preserve its own essential interests? The British high commissioner, General Allenby, came up with a solution. He jawboned the British government into declaring unilaterally an end to its protectorate over Egypt on 28 February 1922. The declaration did, however, limit this independence by reserving to British control, pending future Anglo-Egyptian agreement, (1) protection of British imperial communications in Egypt, (2) Egypt's defense against foreign aggression, (3) protection of foreign interests and minorities in the country, and (4) administration of the Sudan.

## Egypt's Democratic Experiment

Despite these infringements on Egypt's sovereignty, which became known as the Four Reserved Points, the Egyptians took the half loaf and began to set up their new government. Fuad changed his title from sultan to king and watched nervously while a committee of Egyptian lawyers drew up a constitution modeled on that of Belgium. The British residency (Allenby kept his title as High Commissioner) encouraged this democratic experiment. It was a time when Britain, weary of war and especially of dickering over Middle East postwar arrangements, was willing to make concessions. Elsewhere, this policy meant accepting nationalist leaders in Turkey and Iran and trying to move toward self-rule in Iraq and Palestine. Late in 1923 Egypt finally held free elections. The Wafd, reorganized as a political party, won an overwhelming majority of the seats in the parliament. King

Fuad accordingly called on Sa'd Zaghlul to appoint a cabinet made up of Wafdist ministers.

## The Short Reign of the Wafd

The high hopes of Egypt's liberal nationalists lasted only a few months. The 1919 revolution had unleashed violent forces that its leaders could no longer contain. Even Sa'd himself was wounded by a would-be assassin in the summer of 1924. The attempt presaged the assassination that November of the British commander of the Egyptian army. Later investigations revealed that these and other terrorist acts were being perpetrated by a secret society backed by some of Egypt's leading politicians. Meanwhile, Allenby had handed Sa'd an angry ultimatum stating that the murder "holds up Egypt as at present governed to the contempt of civilized peoples." He also demanded an indemnity of 500,000 Egyptian pounds to the British government, the withdrawal of all Egyptian officers from the Sudan, and an undefined increase in the quantity of Nile River waters to be used—at Egypt's expense—in irrigating the Sudan. The Wafd could not submit to such an ultimatum, and Sa'd's cabinet resigned. King Fuad named a caretaker cabinet of palace politicians, who called for new parliamentary elections and tried to fix their outcome. When this measure failed to keep the Wafd out of power, the king dissolved Parliament and suspended the constitution. Allenby, whose ultimatum had been disowned by his home government, resigned and was replaced by an even sterner imperialist.

## The Power Triangle

As the battle lines were drawn, three sides, not two, emerged. For the sake of brevity, let me sum up the following decade of Anglo-Egyptian relations by describing the power triangle that was emerging. In one corner stood the British, anxious to protect their position in Egypt with respect to India and the rest of the Middle East but less and less interested in reforming Egypt's internal affairs. On several occasions the British government, especially in 1924 and 1929 when the Labour party was in power, tried to negotiate with Egypt for a treaty to replace the Four Reserved Points. These attempts always foundered on the intransigence of the second party to the struggle, the Wafd party. This was the popular Egyptian nationalist movement, led initially by Sa'd Zaghlul until his death in 1927, then less ably by Mustafa al-Nahhas until the 1952 revolution. The Wafd, in the words of Jean and Simone Lacouture, two French writers, was the expression of the entire people, of which in the fullest sense it was the delegate. Any attempt at defining it would involve a complete description of Egypt. It contained all the generosity, intellectual muddle, good nature, contradictions, and mythomania of its millions of supporters. It united the unlimited poverty of some and the insultingly bloated fortunes of others, the demand for change and the demand for conservatism, reaction, and movement. There was something spongy, lax, and warm about it which is typical of Egypt.

Its insistence on Egypt's complete independence made the Wafd the most popular political party by far, among Copts as well as Muslims. It could win any free election in which it chose to run candidates for Parliament. It might have held power longer had it not antagonized the third party in the power triangle, King Fuad, who wanted to augment his own power at the expense of parliamentary government. He could count on the cooperation of rival parties and politicians to form governments more amenable than the Wafd to his wishes. The king could also make appointments within the Egyptian army, civil administration, and ulama. In 1930, when the contest between the Wafd and the British grew too intense, Fuad and his prime minister declared a state of emergency, replaced the 1923 constitution with a more authoritarian one, and turned Egypt's government into a royal dictatorship for the following five years.

However chaotic the state of Egyptian politics during the 1920s and early 1930s, these years saw a remarkable renaissance of Arab culture in Egypt. The proliferation of political parties led to soaring numbers of newspapers, magazines, and publishing houses. Egyptian authors, often educated in France, began to publish novels, short stories, poems in meters never before used in Arabic, and essays about the country's problems. Taha Husayn, a remarkable writer trained at al-Azhar and the newly formed Egyptian National University, published many essays, one of which argued that most pre-Islamic Arabic poetry, long seen by Muslims as the formative influence on the Arabic language and hence on the Quran, had not in fact been composed until after the time of Muhammad. Another writer argued that Ataturk's controversial abolition of the caliphate in 1924 would do Islam no harm, for the religion did not require having a caliph. These essays caused widespread controversy when they were published, as educated Egyptians had to decide how much they wanted their country to break with hallowed Muslim traditions. Some Egyptians glorified the pharaonic past at the expense of their Arab-Muslim heritage. Later, when Taha Husayn wrote that Egypt's cultural heritage was as much Greek and Roman as it was Arab, many conservatives were scandalized. This was an era of intellectual ferment, one that also saw the beginning of Egypt's film and recording industries and the formation of Cairo University. Egypt clearly was emerging as the intellectual capital of the Arabic-speaking world. But let us return to Egypt's political problems.

## The Anglo-Egyptian Treaty

A series of fortuitous events in 1935–1936 seemed to resolve the Egyptian question. Mussolini's Italy, already ruling Libya, menaced both British and Egyptian interests by invading Ethiopia. This move helped bring the two sides together. Ever more frequent student riots in Cairo revealed the unpopularity of the existing royal dictatorship under the 1930 constitution. The British, hoping for a firmer relationship with Egypt, called for a return to the 1923 constitution and free elections. The death of King Fuad in 1936 and the succession of his sixteen-year-old son Faruq (under a regency) gave new hope to believers in Egyptian democracy. In accordance with the 1923 constitution, new elections were held in 1936, and the Wafd party predictably won. Mustafa al-Nahhas formed a Wafdist ministry, which successfully negotiated a treaty with Britain's foreign secretary, Sir Anthony Eden. Because it replaced the reserved points that had left Egypt's independence in doubt for fourteen years, this new Anglo-Egyptian Treaty was initially popular in both countries. In Britain's behalf it guaranteed for at least twenty years a large military base from which to defend the Suez Canal, plus bases in Cairo and Alexandria, as well as in other Egyptian cities in case a war broke out. The question of the Sudan, ruled in fact by Britain, was put on the back burner. For Egypt it meant a constitutional monarchy with ministers responsible to Parliament, ambassadors in other countries' capitals, membership in the League of Nations, and all the trappings of independence so long deferred. Young Faruq was hailed with wild ovations wherever he went, and Sir Anthony Eden became the first foreigner ever to have his picture on an Egyptian postage stamp.

## Disillusionment

Again the high hopes of Egypt's liberal nationalists were dashed. The Nahhas government lasted only eighteen months. King Faruq proved as adept as his father in locating anti-Wafd politicians willing to form cabinets he liked better than those led by Mustafa al-Nahhas. Even some of the Wafd party leaders found Nahhas so objectionable that they bolted in 1937 to form a rival party. Meanwhile, the government was doing little to solve Egypt's pressing economic and social problems. The extremes of wealth and poverty were grotesque, all the more so in a country where nearly all the people (about 16 million in 1937) lived on 3 percent of the land, in an area roughly equal to the entire state of New Jersey. Egypt was becoming much more urbanized and somewhat industrialized. Although foreigners continued to dominate the ranks of the owner and managerial classes, Egyptian industrial capitalists were gaining. In addition, there was a growing middle class of Egyptian professionals, shopkeepers, clerks, and civil servants. The Capitulations, long a drag on Egypt's independence, were abolished in 1937, and even the Mixed Courts, special tribunals for civil cases involving foreign nationals, phased out over the next twelve years. No longer would Egypt's large foreign (and minority) communities get special privileges and protection.

Still, most Egyptian people remained as poor after independence as they had been under the British, for the landowners and capitalists who dominated Parliament did not favor social reform. Poverty, illiteracy, and disease stalked the lives of most Egyptian workers and peasants to a degree unparalleled in Europe or elsewhere in the Middle East.

The failure of nationalism and liberal democracy to solve these problems led many Egyptians to turn to other ideologies. A few intellectuals embraced Marxist communism, even though the USSR seemed remote and—in that era of Stalin's purge trials and destruction of the free peasants—unappealing as a model for Egypt to follow. Besides, the communists' militant atheism made their doctrine abhorrent to the Muslim masses. Mussolini's Italy and Hitler's Germany provided alternative models more attractive to Egyptians disillusioned with liberal democracy, and a right-wing authoritarian party, Young Egypt, did arise. But the most popular Egyptian movement of the 1930s was one wholly indigenous to the country, the Society of the Muslim Brothers (*al-Ikhwan al-Muslimun*). The Muslim Brothers wanted Egypt to restore the customs and institutions of Islam established by Muhammad and his followers. Though best known for their attacks against Christians and Jews, as well as for their demonstrations against motion pictures, bars, modern female fashions, and other "Western innovations," the Muslim Brothers had a valid point. They were reacting against a century (or more) of westernizing reforms that had brought little benefit and much harm to the average Egyptian. For most Egyptians' values, the Brothers' slogan, "The Quran is our constitution," made better sense than the demands for independence and democratic government set forth by the Wafd and the other parties. The parliamentary system, helpless to solve Egypt's social problems or to meet the challenges of Young Egypt and the Muslim Brothers, stumbled from one cabinet to the next (most of them coalitions of independent or minor-party politicians) as the king kept the Wafd out of power.

## World War II

Britain and France declared war on Nazi Germany in 1939. As Hitler's troops overran most of Europe, many Egyptians expected Britain to fall and hoped to free their country from its army of occupation. In fact Egypt became a vast army camp for the Western Allies, although popular feeling was hostile. Even King Faruq and his ministers were trying to wriggle out of the 1936 Anglo-Egyptian Treaty, as General Rommel's crack Afrika Korps swept across Libya into Egypt's Western Desert in early 1942. With demonstrators filling Cairo's streets and calling for a German victory, the British ambassador, Sir Miles Lampson, sent tanks to surround the royal palace and handed an ultimatum to King Faruq: He must either appoint a Wafdist government that would uphold the Anglo-Egyptian Treaty or sign his own abdication. After some hesitation, Faruq caved in. Mustafa al-Nahhas, the Wafdist leader and hence the standard-bearer for Egypt's independence struggle, came to power at the point of British bayonets.

Neither Nahhas nor the king ever recovered from Britain's action, taken in the darkest hour of World War II to help save the Western democracies from the Nazi menace. Faruq, a handsome and beloved youth with high political ideals and moral courage, started to turn into the gargantuan monster and dissolute playboy older Egyptians and Westerners remember today. Probably, as Egyptians said after Faruq was deposed in 1952, he *had* been spoiled by the people who surrounded him, once he realized that the British would not let him rule Egypt. For the rest of the war, thousands of soldiers, sailors, and airmen from all parts of the British Commonwealth (and also the United States) poured into Egypt, which was also visited by such statesmen as Churchill and Roosevelt. Major economic activity throughout the Arab world (and Iran) was coordinated in Cairo by the British-run Middle East Supply Center. Industrial and agricultural employment and output boomed. So did price inflation, urban congestion, disruption, and crime. Everyone wondered if the end of World War II would lead to popular uprisings as massive as the great 1919 revolution.

## THE EGYPTIAN REVOLUTION

Between 1945 and 1951 Egypt experienced many uprisings, but no revolution. One reason was that Britain no longer seemed so potent as a foreign oppressor. Second, the prestige of the Western democracies rose following their decisive victory over Germany, Japan, and Italy. Many people hoped that the new United Nations Organization, of which Egypt was one of the founding members, would rid the world of war and colonialism. Third, the communists, who might have had the discipline to lead a revolution, were not nearly so strong in Egypt as were their counterparts in Europe. Besides, there were no Red Army soldiers in Cairo as there were in Warsaw and Budapest. Fourth, the Egyptian government managed to distract public opinion with a newfound enthusiasm for Arab nationalism.

Although few Egyptians had viewed themselves as Arabs before, both King Faruq and the Wafd began to identify Egypt more closely with the rest of the Arab world. They may have been reacting to the rising Arab-Jewish contest for Palestine. A more pressing challenge, in my opinion, was Iraqi Premier Nuri al-Sa'id's 1942 proposal for an organic union of all the Arabic-speaking countries of the Fertile Crescent: Iraq, Transjordan, Syria, Lebanon, and Palestine. Egypt, backed by Saudi Arabia and Yemen (which would also have been left out of Nuri's proposed union), countered by calling for a league of Arab states. This Arab League, formally set up in 1945, preserved the sovereignty of each Arab country while coordinating their policies on key Arab issues. Hoping to uphold its own influence at France's expense, Britain encouraged this trend toward Arab cooperation. The problem was that the Arab states could agree on only one issue: They did not want the Jews to form a state in Palestine.

### Frustration and Failure

Thus Egypt, with all its domestic problems, plus the unresolved issues of British rule in the Sudan (which almost all Egyptians wanted restored to their country) and British troops within its own borders, found its attention and energies being diverted to the Palestine issue. To be sure, the Egyptian government went on negotiating with Britain to reduce the number of its troops in the Nile Valley. Egypt's ablest palace politician, Isma'il Sidqi, did manage to negotiate a treaty with Britain that would have evacuated British troops from all parts of Egypt except the canal zone. But

Wafdist opponents proved that Britain and Egypt had not really settled the status of the Sudan, and so the treaty was never ratified. In 1947 the Egyptian government took the Sudan question to the UN Security Council, claiming that the 1936 treaty had been negotiated under duress and that it was contrary to the UN Charter. The Security Council, unimpressed by these arguments, called on the two parties to resume their long and fruitless negotiations.

Meanwhile, Egypt was being drawn into the web of Palestine. In the next chapter I will discuss conflicting Arab and Jewish claims to the Holy Land, but let me state here that Egypt set its policies less to block any Zionist threat to Arab interests than to counter what the other Arab governments might do. If Egypt ignored the Palestine issue, then Transjordan's Amir Abdallah would take the leading role among the Arab rulers. If he chose to resist any Jewish attempt to form a state in Palestine, he might succeed in taking control of much (or all) of the country, annexing it to his desert kingdom. If he chose to make peace with the Zionists, they might divide Palestine between them. Either outcome would strengthen Amir Abdallah at King Faruq's expense.

The UN General Assembly voted late in 1947 to partition Palestine into a Jewish state and an Arab one. Neither Egypt nor Transjordan considered letting the Palestine Arabs form a state in the areas allotted to them by the partition plan; instead, they resolved to fight the plan and to throttle the Jewish state as soon as it came into being. I do not mean that there were no valid objections to a partition plan that (as we shall soon see) assigned over half of Palestine to one-third of its 1947 population, but simply that the Egyptian government's policy was based more on Arab power politics. Many Egyptians, especially the Muslim Brothers, called for an Arab jihad to free Palestine from the threat of Zionist colonialism. King Faruq, sensing an easy victory in a popular war, made the fateful decision (without consulting his cabinet or the Egyptian General Staff) to commit his army to fight in Palestine in May 1948.

But, as you might have guessed, Egypt's army was unprepared for the Palestine War. Inept commanders, crooked politicians who bilked the government on arms purchases, an ill-timed UN cease-fire, and general demoralization of the Egyptian forces led to a crushing defeat. Some Egyptian units fought bravely in Palestine, but the victories heralded in the Egyptian newspapers and radio broadcasts were imaginary. Early in 1949 Egypt had to sign an armistice agreement with the new State of Israel. But even then there was no peace.

## The Fall of the Old Regime

Defeat in Palestine discredited Egypt's old regime: the king, the ministers, the high-ranking army officers, and the democratic experiment itself. The government clamped down on the Muslim Brothers after they assassinated the prime minister, but the unrest continued in 1949. Free elections in 1950 brought back the Wafd party, this time with an ambitious reform program plus a commitment to drive the remaining British troops from the Nile Valley. The latter aim eclipsed the former, as Premier Nahhas repudiated the 1936 Anglo-Egyptian Treaty he himself had signed and began sending Egyptian commandos to fight against British troops in the Suez Canal zone. Not surprisingly, the British struck back, killing fifty Egyptian policemen in January 1952. Now the rumble of popular anger turned into an explosion. On a Saturday morning hundreds of Egyptians, better organized than any mob of demonstrators had ever been before, fanned across central Cairo and set fire to such European landmarks as Shepheard's Hotel, Groppi's Restaurant, the Turf Club, the Ford Motor Company showroom, and many bars and nightclubs. Only after much of Cairo had burned to the ground did either Faruq or Nahhas try to stop the rioting, looting, and killing. "Black Saturday" proved that the old regime could no longer govern Egypt. Who would? Some people thought the Muslim Brothers had set the fire and were about to seize power. Others looked to the communists. Few suspected that the army, humiliated in Palestine and generally assumed to be under palace control, would take over Egypt and kick out the king.

## The 1952 Military Coup

However, on 23 July, the army did just that. An officers' secret society, using a popular general named Muhammad Nagib as its front man, seized control of the government in a bloodless coup d'état. Neither Britain nor the United States intervened to stop them. Three days later Faruq abdicated and went into exile. Sweeping reforms followed as the patriotic young officers, like their counterparts in Turkey a generation earlier, took the places and powers (though not the perquisites) of the rich leaders of the old regime. Political parties were abolished and the Parliament dissolved. The military junta would rule until a new political system, which the officers said would be more truly democratic, could replace the discredited 1923 constitution. A land reform decree limited the total acreage any Egyptian might own to about 200 acres (81 hectares). All excess lands were bought from their owners with government bonds and redistributed (along with the royal estates) to Egypt's landless peasants. Many schools and factories were opened. Foreign supporters began to claim that Egypt's new rulers, the first real Egyptians to govern the country in more than 2,000 years, were also the best Egypt had ever had. But early in 1954, the figurehead leader, General Nagib, widely viewed as a moderate, was eased from power by the real mastermind of the young officers, Colonel Gamal Abd al-Nasir (whose name was widely anglicized as "Gamal Abdel Nasser"). Nagib's removal and later house arrest dampened the enthusiasm of some foreigners—and Egyptians—for the revolution.

*Settlement of the Suez Canal Issue*

The early Nasir regime was determined to settle the Egyptian question once and for all. With heavy pressure put on Britain by the United States, which hoped to bring Egypt into a Middle Eastern anticommunist alliance comparable to NATO, Anglo-Egyptian talks resumed. Britain finally agreed in 1954 to leave its Suez Canal base, the largest military installation outside the communist bloc, but on terms that would let British troops reoccupy the canal in case of an attack on any Arab League country or on Turkey, presumably by the USSR. British civilian technicians might also stay in the canal zone. Some Egyptian nationalists balked at these conditions, as well as at Egypt's concession that the Sudanese people might decide by a plebiscite between union with Egypt and complete independence. They chose independence, despite the blandishments of the Egyptian officers. Nasir was widely accused of being a fascist or an imperialist lackey. The communists even called him Gamal Abd al-Dulles (referring to the U.S. secretary of state), but, on 18 June 1956, the last British soldier was out of the Suez Canal base. For the first time since 1882, there were no British troops in Egypt.

## A STRANGE ENDING

Egypt's independence struggle should have ended then, but it did not. In October 1956 British and French paratroopers landed at Port Said and reoccupied the Suez Canal, while Israel's army pushed westward across the Sinai Peninsula. You can read the full story of this sequel later, but a few points cannot wait. The British government that ordered the invasion was led by the man who had negotiated the 1936 Anglo-Egyptian Treaty and its 1954 replacement—Sir Anthony Eden. He attacked Egypt because

Nasir in July 1956 had nationalized the Suez Canal Company, the greatest symbol of Egypt's subjugation to foreign powers, but also the lifeline of the British Commonwealth and of European oil-consuming nations. The world's superpowers, the United States and the Soviet Union, joined forces to pressure the British, the French, and the Israelis to stop their attack and to pull out of Egypt's territory. Meanwhile, the Nasir government expelled thousands of British subjects and French citizens from Egypt and seized their property, thus ending much of what remained of Western economic power within the country. Nasir had finished the struggle for Egypt's independence, but at a cost of much Western anger against his regime and his country.

# SIXTEEN

# The Contest for Palestine

Palestine, the "twice-promised land" as British wags used to call it, has caused more ink to spill than any other Middle Eastern issue in the twentieth century—even more ink than blood. Many of you may have assumed when you began your study of Middle East history that the contest for Palestine, which in 1948 became the Arab-Israeli conflict, was the main cause of the troubles throughout the area. Actually, Palestine or Israel is only one of the trouble spots in the contemporary Middle East. Civil wars, hijackings, assassinations, kidnappings, revolutions, invasions, and refugee problems have occurred in many Middle Eastern countries. Yet it is hard to name any problem in today's Middle East that has not somehow been affected by the Arab-Israeli conflict. Certainly the attention the major powers, the United Nations, and legions of propagandists for both sides have paid to the conflict should show how large it looms in the world today.

## ORIGINS

How did the Arab-Israeli conflict begin? Does it go back to Abraham's two sons, Isaac (the ancestor of the Jews) and Ishmael (the Arabs' progenitor)? Did the wars between the Hebrews and the Canaanites, to whom Palestine had belonged earlier, start it? Did Muhammad's quarrel with the Jews of Medina intensify it? Is it a religious war between Judaism and Islam? The Arabs say that it is not and that the Jews were always welcome to settle and prosper in Muslim lands. The Zionists reply that the Jews under Muslim rule were usually second-class citizens (as were all other non-Muslims). Both sides agree that Christian anti-Semitism (a regrettable term for prejudice against Jews, inasmuch as Arabs are Semites, too) was worse, but that historic prejudice sets a poor standard for religious toleration.

Jews and Arabs have some common traits. Both use Semitic languages and they often resemble each other. Each looks back to a golden age early in its history, to an era of political power, economic prosperity, and cultural flowering. For each people, that era was followed by a long time span during which their political destinies were controlled by outsiders. Because of their long subjugation, the birth of nationalism (which began in the late nineteenth century for both Jews and Arabs) was slow, painful, and uncertain. Neither group felt good about leaving its revealed religion for a modern ideology of collective self-love. Both suspected others of exploiting them. Both feared that when the chips were down, the whole world would turn against them. On the strength of the Bible and 2,000 years of religious tradition, Zionist Jews believed that the land of Israel (basically parts of what are now Israel and Jordan) would be restored to them someday and that the Temple would be rebuilt in Jerusalem. Only in the land of Israel had the Jews flourished as a sovereign nation. Muslim Arabs believed that Palestine, for so long a part of the *ummah* and containing Jerusalem, a city holy to them as well as to Jews and Christians, could not be alienated from the lands ruled by Islam. How could Muslim and Christian Arabs, who had lived in Palestine for 1,300 years (indeed longer, for the seventh-century Arab conquest had not displaced the earlier inhabitants), give up their claim? Were the rights of the Palestinian Arabs any less than the national rights of the Turks, Iranians, Egyptians, or Arabs living elsewhere?

Such arguments as these have come up so often during our own times that we naturally think they always did. This really is not true. Although Jews and Arabs have claims to Palestine going back hundreds of years, the real contest was just starting when World War I broke out. At that time, few foresaw how strong it would be. The duration and intensity of what we now call the Arab-Israeli conflict were due to the rise of nationalism in modern times. We have already studied the Arab nationalist movement in Chapter 13, with additional glances in the intervening chapters; now it is time to look at the history of Zionism. This chapter carries the contest for Palestine (itself a debatable and ill-defined geographical term) up to the creation of Israel as the Jewish state. I hope you will see why I stress the struggle between Arab nationalism and political Zionism. In later chapters, as we go through the various phases of the Arab-Israeli conflict, you will also see why it is so intense, so hard to resolve, and so relevant to other Middle East conflicts.

## PREFATORY REMARKS

Let me first define *political Zionism*. Zionism is the belief that the Jews constitute a nation (or, to use a less loaded term, a *people*) and that they deserve the liberties of other such groups, including the right to return to what they consider their ancestral homeland, the land of Israel (or Palestine). Political Zionism is the belief that the Jews should establish and maintain a state for themselves there.

Not every Jew is a Zionist. Some Jews identify solely with the countries in which they are citizens or reject altogether the idea of nationalism or believe that the only meaningful affirmation of Jewishness is observance of their religion, its laws, and its traditions. Not every Zionist is a Jew. Some Christians believe that the restoration of the Jews to Palestine or the creation of Israel must precede the second coming of Christ. Many Gentiles (non-Jews) back Israel out of admiration for Jews or Israelis or out of guilt for past wrongs committed against Jews by czarist Russia and Nazi Germany. Even some Gentiles who dislike Jews support Israel, perhaps because Zionism stresses the uniqueness of Jews, as do anti-Semites (opponents of Jews), and because it opposes the assimilation of Jews into Gentile society. Likewise, anti-Zionists are not necessarily anti-Semites. Some may be pro-Arab out of sincere conviction. Some people who favor Jews and Judaism still think that Zionism and the creation of Israel have done them more harm than good. This is a point that Jews should keep in mind. For their part, non-Jews must realize that expressions of opposition—or even skepticism—toward Zionism and Israel do sound anti-Semitic to many Jews. We all must discuss Zionism with care if Jews and Gentiles, or Arabs and non-Arabs, are to understand each other and reach peace in the Middle East.

To return to my definition, Zionism is a nationalist movement similar to Arab nationalism and other Middle Eastern nationalisms we have already studied. It may seem odd to Americans that Jews should call themselves a "nation." We never speak of a Catholic or a Methodist nation in the United States. American Jews do not view themselves as Israelis, nor do Israelis so regard them. Nevertheless, a belief prevails among all Jews—Orthodox, Conservative, Reconstructionist, Reform, and nonobservant—that they do constitute one people and that their collective survival depends on mutual support and cooperation. Even persons of Jewish ancestry who do not practice Judaism—indeed, even those who have converted to another faith—are still apt to be regarded as Jews unless they make strenuous efforts to prove they are not. Most Gentiles realize these facts, at least dimly.

The idea that the Jews are a nation is deeply rooted in the Bible: A nomadic tribe, the Hebrews, came to think that their deity was in fact the one true God, YHWH (Jehovah in English). He had chosen them for his love and protection because they had chosen him; he had commanded them to keep his covenant and obey his laws from generation to generation; he had led them out of Egyptian bondage and brought them safely to Canaan, which they called the land of Israel, for he had promised it to the seed of Abraham. Because Arabs as well as Jews claim descent from Abraham, the term *land of Israel* restricts its possession to the descendants of Jacob (i.e., the Israelites). Even though the Israelites at times married outside their tribe and even though other peoples converted to their faith, they regarded all as being, at least in principle, children of Israel. Identification with the land of Israel was central to their religion. Their festivals were—and are—tied to its agricultural seasons. Many of their laws and customs can be understood only in relation to the land of Israel in which they were first practiced. Jerusalem is featured in prayers and common expressions and is a symbol of the Jewish people's hopes and fears. *Jew* originally meant "one from Judea," the region in which Jerusalem is the main city; only later did it take on a religious significance.

### The Jews in Dispersion

For at least two millennia, most Jews have not been Judeans, nor until recently could it be said that they possessed Jerusalem or even that they spoke Hebrew (although they did read the Bible in that language). Jews kept their identity as a people by their observance of the faith and laws of Judaism and by their wish to survive as one people, even without having land, a common tongue, a state, or most of the other attributes of nationhood. No matter how tenuous might seem the ties between the Jews and their ancestral land, they never forgot them. More in good times and fewer in bad, Jews went back to Jerusalem to devote portions of their lives to study and contemplation or to be buried near its walls. There were always some Jews living in Palestine, and many believed that only those who lived there could feel wholly Jewish. The common anti-Jewish attitude of European Christians enhanced Jewish solidarity and identification with the land. Jews in Muslim lands were better treated and knew that they were free to live in Palestine, but only a small minority actually did so.

The European Enlightenment and the rise of liberal democracy freed many Western Jews from discrimination and isolation. Some reacted against the idea of Jewish solidarity, which they associated with ghetto poverty, and against identifying with a land of Israel that most would never see. A Jewish enlightenment (Hebrew: *Haskalah*) grew up in the late eighteenth century, leading in Germany and the United States to what is called Reform Judaism and to greater Jewish assimilation into Western society. This assimilation caused some people to deny their Jewishness and convert to Christianity (e.g., Heinrich Heine and the parents of such famous men as Karl Marx, Felix Mendelssohn, and Benjamin Disraeli). If the *Haskalah* had been stronger and more pervasive, would all the Jews have assimilated? Then we might never have heard of Zionism. But most Jews did not live in the United States, England, or even Germany; the majority could be found in czarist Russia (especially Poland) and in various parts of the declining multinational empires of the Habsburgs and the Ottomans. When the peoples of Eastern Europe began to embrace nationalist ideas, they had to fight against desperate autocrats to gain their freedom. The local Jews got caught in the middle. Law-abiding and usually loyal to their rulers, they often were viewed by the nationalists as enemies in their midst. Some rulers also tried to deflect nationalist anger from themselves by using the Jews as scapegoats, stirring up pogroms (organized attacks) against Jewish ghettos and villages.

How did Jews react to this new persecution from governments they had long obeyed? Some withdrew into piety and mysticism. Some fled to Western Europe or North America. A few converted in order to blend into the majority culture. Others tried to revive Hebrew as a literary language (just as Arab nationalism had begun as a literary revival). A few Jews— and more than a few Christians—said that the only way to end persecution of Jews was for them to emigrate to Palestine to live and rebuild their state in the land of Israel. The idea that Jews constitute a nation (Zionism by my definition) is nothing new, but saying that the Jewish nation should revive its ancient state in Palestine (the idea I call political Zionism) was indeed revolutionary for the nineteenth century.

## THE BEGINNINGS OF POLITICAL ZIONISM

Like most revolutionary doctrines, political Zionism started with very few supporters. Most rabbis said that the Jews could not be restored to the land of Israel until after God had sent the Messiah. Jews must be careful. Many false messiahs had led people astray by their extravagant claims, causing much suffering. Some said that nationalism was a form of collective self-love that ran counter to Judaism's basic commandment: "You shall love the Lord your God with all your heart, and with all your soul, and with all your might" (Deut. 6:5). Nevertheless, some nineteenth-century rabbis began thinking along other lines. One wrote that the Jews should return to the land of Israel to await the Messiah. As early as 1843 another rabbi called on rich Jews to set up a corporation to colonize the country, train young Jews in self-defense, and teach farming and other practical subjects. Some *Haskalah* thinkers hoped that this rebuilding of the Jewish homeland would bring young people closer to nature and make them more like Gentiles. Moses Hess, one of the first German socialists, argued in *Rome and Jerusalem* (1862) that Jews could form a truly socialistic nation-state in the land of Israel.

Hess's book was little read (until much later), but another early Zionist work, Leon Pinsker's *Auto-Emancipation* (1882), had immense influence in Russia. Official persecution was reaching new heights at this time, as the czarist regime implemented a series of so-called May Laws that restricted Russian areas in which Jews might live and put artificially low quotas on the admission of Jews to the universities and the professions. Pinsker's book was the first systematic attempt to prove that Jews were vulnerable to anti-Semitism because they lacked a country of their own. It inspired Russian Jews to form Zionist clubs and study groups in Russia. Their federation, Chovevei Tzion (Lovers of Zion), spread from Russia to other countries where Jews lived. A more activist movement, BILU (Hebrew: *Beit Ya'cov lchu vnelcha*; To the House of Jacob go and we will follow), sent groups of young Russian Jews to Palestine. Immigrants in these two organizations made up what historians of Zionism call the "first aliyah." *Aliyah* really means "going up," the term Jews had long used for going to Jerusalem, set among the Judean hills, but it came to mean "going to the land of Israel." Jewish immigrants were called *olim* (ascenders).

## Early Jewish Settlers

The Zionist *olim* found other Jewish newcomers in Palestine. There were always mystics and scholars going to Jerusalem and the other main centers of Jewish culture: Tiberias, Safed, and Hebron. Moreover, there were already immigrants buying land and trying to farm it. They got help from a Jewish educational organization, the Alliance Israélite Universelle (Universal Jewish Alliance). The Alliance set up modern, French-speaking schools for Jews throughout North Africa and the Middle East, upgrading their standard of education in the late nineteenth century. It also founded an agricultural school near Jaffa in 1870, a great help to the settlers even though the Alliance did not favor a Jewish state. At this time the total number of Jewish settlers in Palestine could not have exceeded 20,000; the vast majority of the local inhabitants spoke Arabic. The government of the land was under the Ottoman Empire—inefficient, corrupt, and suspicious of the Zionists (owing, it seems, to the fact that so many had come from Russia, the Turks' enemy). Not a few Jewish settlers quit in disgust and went home—or to the United States.

*Theodor Herzl*

Zionism based solely on Russian resources—mainly youthful enthusiasm—probably would not have lasted. What gave the movement endurance and popular appeal was the works of an assimilated Jewish journalist living in Vienna, Theodor Herzl, who in 1896 wrote *Der Judenstaat* (The Jews' State), an eloquent plea for political Zionism. Because Herzl was a popular writer, his book carried the ideas of Pinsker and other early Zionists to thousands of German-speaking Jews. Their conversion to Zionism enabled Herzl to bring together the first International Zionist Congress in Basel, Switzerland, in 1897. At its conclusion, the conferees adopted the following resolution:

> The goal of Zionism is the establishment for the Jewish people of a home in Palestine guaranteed by public law. The Congress anticipates the following means to reach that goal:
>
> 1. The promotion, in suitable ways, of the colonization of Palestine by Jewish agricultural and industrial workers.
> 2. The organizing and uniting of all Jews by means of suitable institutions, local and international, in compliance with the laws of all countries.
> 3. The strengthening and encouraging of Jewish national sentiment and awareness.
> 4. Introducing moves towards receiving governmental approval where needed for the realization of Zionism's goal.

Herzl proceeded to work unremittingly toward the formation of the Jewish state by writing more books, making speeches, and courting support from rich Jews and various European governments as well as from the Jewish middle class. At one time he even got an offer from the British government (often misnamed the "Uganda Scheme") that would have let the Zionists settle in what later would be called the White Highlands of Kenya. But most of Herzl's followers, especially the Jews from Russia, emphatically refused to form a state anywhere outside the land of Israel, saying that "there can be no Zionism without Zion." The movement split on this issue and others. When Herzl died in 1904, it seemed likely that the high hopes of early Zionism would never be realized.

## The Second Aliyah

If Herzl's life and teachings constituted the first event that saved political Zionism, the second was the large-scale emigration of Jews from Russia following its abortive 1905 revolution. Even though most decided to seek freedom and opportunity in that *goldene medina* (a Yiddish expression meaning "land of gold") overseas, the United States, some of the most idealistic men and women chose Palestine instead. With intense fervor and dedication, these Jewish settlers of the "second aliyah" (1905–1914) built up the fledgling institutions of their community in Palestine: schools, newspapers, theaters, sports clubs, trade unions, worker-owned factories, and political parties. Because the Jews entering Palestine had spoken so many different languages in the countries from which they had come, the *olim* made a concerted effort to revive Hebrew as a spoken and written language. Soon Jewish children and young adults in Palestine were speaking Hebrew as their first language.

Their most famous achievement was a novel experiment in agricultural settlement called the *kibbutz* (collective farm), in which all houses, animals, and farming equipment belonged to the group as a whole, all decisions were made democratically, and all jobs (including cooking, cleaning, and child rearing) were shared by the members. Not all kibbutzim succeeded, but the best survived because their members were dedicated to rebuilding the Jewish national home and to redeeming the land by their own labor. Although most *olim* went to live in the cities, including what became the first all-Jewish city in modern history, Tel Aviv, those who chose the kibbutzim have come to typify Israel's pioneer spirit: idealistic, self-reliant, and rather contemptuous of outsiders. The kibbutzniks toiled extremely long hours for what at first were pitiful material benefits, but they were determined to develop their lands (bought for them by the Jewish National Fund at high prices from absentee Arab and Turkish landlords) without resorting to cheap Arab peasant labor.

Because the pioneers of the second aliyah were brave and resourceful people, the founders of what would become the State of Israel, we may forget that most of the *olim* soon lost their zeal for this risky and unrewarding adventure. Hot summers, windy and rainy winters, malarial swamps, rocky hills, sandy desert soil, and frequent crop failures dimmed the fervor of many young pioneers. Arab nomads and peasants raided the kibbutzim. Their cousins in Jaffa and Jerusalem eyed Zionism with suspicion. As their own nationalist feelings grew, the Arabs understandably opposed a colonization scheme that seemed likely to dispossess them, reduce them to second-class status, or break up Syria. Already they were protesting in their press and in the Ottoman parliament against these foreign settlers and their plans to build up a Jewish state in Palestine. The Ottoman government, both before and after the 1908 Young Turk revolution, obstructed Jewish colonization for fear of adding yet another nationality problem to those in the Balkans and the Arab lands that were even then tearing its empire apart. No European government would risk offending Istanbul by supporting Jewish settlement in Palestine.

## BRITAIN AND THE PALESTINE PROBLEM

World War I was the third event that saved political Zionism. Both sides needed Jewish backing. In 1914 Berlin was the main center of the Zionist movement. Most politically articulate Jews lived in (and backed) the countries that made up the Central Powers: Germany, Austria-Hungary, and the Ottoman Empire. Up to 1917, when the United States entered World War I on the side of the Allies, American Jews tended to favor the Central Powers because they hated the tyranny of czarist Russia, from which so many Jews had barely managed to escape. The overthrow of the regime slightly earlier in 1917 made Russia easier to support, but now the issue facing its new government (which most Russian Jews favored) was how to stay in the war at all. That year was crucial in World War I. Germany, too, needed Jewish support but could not espouse Zionism owing to its ties with the Ottoman Empire, which still held Palestine. This is when the British government stepped in.

## The Balfour Declaration

Britain, though it had relatively few Jewish subjects, could speak out most forcefully for Zionism. There the leading Zionist advocate was Chaim Weizmann, a chemist who won fame early in the war by synthesizing acetone, a chemical (hitherto imported from Germany) used in making explosives. Weizmann's discoveries made him known to leading journalists and thus to cabinet ministers. The prime minister, Lloyd George, had come to favor Zionism from reading the Bible. Weizmann also won the backing of the foreign secretary, Lord Balfour. It was he who informed British Zionists of the cabinet's decision to support their cause in a letter that became known as the Balfour Declaration. The letter stated:

> His Majesty's Government view with favor the establishment in Palestine of a national home for the Jewish people, and will use their best endeavors to facilitate the achievement of this object, it being clearly understood that nothing shall be done which may prejudice the civil and religious rights of the existing non-Jewish communities in Palestine, or the rights and political status enjoyed by Jews in any other country.

Since this declaration has come to be seen as the Magna Carta of political Zionism, it deserves our careful scrutiny. It does not say that Britain would turn Palestine into a Jewish state. In fact, it does not specify what would be the borders of Palestine, which the British were then in the process of taking from the Turks. The British government promised only to work for the creation of a Jewish national home *in* Palestine. Moreover, it pledged not to harm the civil and religious rights of Palestine's "existing non-Jewish communities"—namely, the 93 percent of its inhabitants, Muslim and Christian, who spoke Arabic and dreaded being cut off from other Arabs as second-class citizens within a Jewish national home. Both Britain and the Zionist movement would have to find a way to assuage these people's fears and to guarantee their rights. They never did. Here, in a nutshell, is what Arabs see as the nub of the contest for Palestine. Even now the hottest issue of the Arab-Israeli conflict is to define the legitimate rights of the Palestinian Arabs.

The Balfour Declaration also had to take into account the fears of Jews who chose to remain outside Palestine and who would not want to lose the rights and status they had won in such liberal democracies as England, France, and the United States. Up to the rise of Hitler, Zionism had the backing of only a minority of these Jews. What the Balfour Declaration seemed to ensure was that the British government would control Palestine after the war with a commitment to build the Jewish national home there. Let us see what really happened.

## The British Occupation

When World War I ended, Britain's Egyptian Expeditionary Force and Faysal's Arab army jointly occupied the area that would become Palestine. The British set up in Jerusalem a provisional military government that soon became embroiled in a struggle between Jewish settlers, who were entering Palestine in large numbers and hastening to form their state, and the Arab inhabitants, who were resisting their efforts. Zionist writers often accuse British officers and officials of having stirred up Arab resentment. This is unfair if they mean the period from 1918 to 1922, although later Britain did favor the Arabs in Palestine. True, some British troops came from Egypt or the Sudan and knew better how to treat Arabs, who were usually polite, than to deal with East European Jewish immigrants, who could be intransigent because of their past suffering under czars and sultans. Some British officials assumed that, because of the communist takeover in Russia, Jews from that country favored the Bolsheviks. In fact, only a few did. There were ample grounds for suspicion between British imperialists and Zionist settlers.

But Arabs could draw their own conclusions about Jewish immigration, the Balfour Declaration, the cover-up of the King-Crane Commission's anti-Zionist report, and Britain's suppression of revolutions in Egypt and Iraq. As early as April 1920, the Palestinian Arabs revolted, killing Jews and damaging property. It was the opening chapter in the Arab nationalist revolution in Palestine, a struggle still going on today. The Zionists complained, not unreasonably, that Britain encouraged it by punishing the rebels too lightly and protecting the Jewish settlers too little. This was also the time when the Allies agreed at San Remo on assigning the mandates in the Arab world, putting Palestine definitely under British control. Once the Colonial Office took over the administration of Palestine from the army, Britain should have devised a clearer and fairer policy toward both Jews and Arabs. But this was not to be.

## The Palestine Mandate

In the ensuing years, Britain's Palestine policy seemed to go in two opposite directions. In the international arena, on the one hand, it tended to back Zionist aims because of Jewish political pressure on London and, indeed, on the League of Nations, based in Geneva. In Palestine, on the other hand, British officials favored the Arabs, often influenced by concern for Muslim opinion in neighboring countries and in India. Remember that these were general tendencies, not hard-and-fast rules. When the League of Nations awarded the Palestine mandate in 1922, it specifically charged Britain with carrying out the Balfour Declaration. In other words, Britain had to encourage Jews to migrate to Palestine and to settle there, help create the Jewish "national home," and even set up a "Jewish agency" to assist the British authorities in developing that national home, which none dared to call a "state."

The Palestine mandate could not be the same as the League's mandates for Syria and Iraq, which were to help them develop into independent states (thus requiring that they be given constitutions within a three-year period). Syrians and Iraqis knew that the mandates were supposed to prepare them for self-rule. In Palestine, however, although most of the inhabitants at the time were Arabs, it was the Jewish national home that was to be created. The Palestine mandate called only for "self-governing institutions," with no definite deadline for their creation. The Arabs naturally suspected that the British mandate would hold them in colonial bondage until the Jews achieved a majority in Palestine and could set up their state.

*Beginnings of the Anglo-Zionist Rift*

In reality, though, the British started effacing the mandate's pro-Zionist features before the ink was even dry. In 1922 Colonial Secretary Winston Churchill issued a white paper denying that the British government meant to make Palestine as Jewish as England was English (Weizmann's expression) or to give preference to Jews over Arabs. Its fateful provision was to restrict Jewish immigration to conform with Palestine's "absorptive capacity." This restriction did not hurt Anglo-Zionist relations in the 1920s, when Jewish immigration rarely filled the quotas, but after the rise of Hitler the question of Palestine's ability to absorb Jews would become a major issue indeed.

Another British action that seemed to violate the mandate was the creation of the Emirate of Transjordan, effectively removing the two-thirds of Palestine that lay east of the Jordan River from the area in which the Jews could develop their national home. Actually, there could hardly have been many Jews wanting to settle in the lands once held by the heirs of Gad, Reuben, and Manasseh, but the Zionists viewed Britain's attempt to give Abdallah a kingdom as a needless concession to Arab nationalism. The British claimed that this first partition of Palestine was only temporary. But as the French did not leave Syria and as Abdallah built up a bureaucracy and an army (the British-officered Arab Legion) in Amman, the separation of Transjordan became more and more set in stone. Most Jewish leaders in Palestine still chose to go on working with the British, but some turned to direct and even violent resistance, especially a group known as the Revisionists. They were formed by Vladimir Jabotinsky, who had set up a Jewish legion during World War I and the Jews' first self-defense militia during the 1920 Arab riots. Jabotinsky represented the ultranationalist right wing of the Zionist spectrum, and his views would influence those of such recent Israeli leaders as Menachem Begin, Yitzhak Shamir, Benjamin Netanyahu, and Ariel Sharon.

### The Jewish Governor and the Nationalist Mufti

Britain's first civilian governor in Palestine was Sir Herbert Samuel. Although he was a prominent Zionist, he tried hard to be fair to all sides, so that Palestinian Arabs as well as Jews would accept him. He leaned so far over backward as to name an ardent young nationalist, Hajj Amin al-Husayni, to be the chief mufti (Muslim legal officer) of Jerusalem, even though other candidates for the post were backed by the Muslim notables. Samuel probably hoped to tame him with a small taste of power, but Hajj Amin used his control of the *awqaf* and appointments to key Muslim posts to make himself the leader of Palestinian Arab nationalism. Although his flamboyant personality won him enemies as well as friends among the Palestinian Arabs, he became so influential as a spokesman and revolutionary leader that the British finally deported him in 1937.

Samuel encouraged both Jews and Arabs to form their own institutions. The Jews in Palestine went on developing organizations covering nearly every aspect of their lives, including the Jewish Agency as a body representing world Jewry and the *Vaad Le'umi*, a consultative national council for the Jewish settlers. Political parties mushroomed, each having its own unique blend of socialism, nationalism, and religion. The general labor federation, called Histadrut, set up factories, food-processing plants, and even a construction company. It also organized the underground defense organization, Haganah, formed after the 1920 riots. The Arabs, divided by family and religious loyalties, failed to create comparable organizations or even a united nationalist party. Instead, they pursued an obstructionist policy that hindered their cause outside the country. Britain tried in 1923 to set up a legislative council that would have given the Arabs ten out of twenty-two seats, but the Arabs refused, saying that the two seats designated for the Jews and the ten for the British were disproportionately high for their numbers. The Palestinian Arabs are said to have sought out Sa'd Zaghlul, leader of the Wafd party, hoping for Egyptian support. After hearing their complaints, Sa'd bluntly told their delegation to go back and make peace with the Jewish settlers who were developing the country. Other Arab and Muslim leaders did more to encourage Palestinian Arab resistance, but as they were all outside Palestine and had problems of their own, they gave little or no material aid.

In the days of Samuel and his immediate successor, it looked as if Jewish-Arab differences could be resolved. The number of Jewish *olim* shrank; in 1926–1928 more Jews left Palestine than entered it. There was also a complementary relationship—ill concealed by the propaganda of the two sides—between settlers and natives, between Jewish technical expertise and Arab knowledge of local conditions, and between Jewish capital and Arab labor. Wise British administration could have moderated their differences. There were always Jews who advocated friendly relations with Arabs, as well as Arabs who, quietly, welcomed Jewish immigration and investment; maybe they would take the lead if both sides toned down their most extreme nationalist claims.

## A New Arab-Jewish Clash

These hopes were dashed by the 1929 Wailing Wall Incident. The issues were complex. The Wailing Wall (more properly called the Western Wall) is a remnant of the second Jewish Temple and an object of veneration to most Jews. To some it symbolizes the hope that some day the Temple will be rebuilt and the ancient Jewish rituals revived. However, the Western Wall also forms a part of the enclosure surrounding the historic Temple Mount or Sacred Enclosure (Arabic: *al-Haram al-Sharif*) on which stand the Dome of the Rock and al-Aqsa mosque, pilgrimage centers almost as important for Muslims as Mecca and Medina. Legally, it had been a *waqf* since the time of Salah al-Din. Muslims feared that Jewish actions before the Western Wall could lead to their pressing a claim to the Temple Mount.

In 1928 Jewish worshipers brought some benches to sit on and a screen to separate men from women. The police took them away several times, but the Jews kept putting them back. To Muslims this activity looked like an attempt by the Jews to strengthen their claims to the Wall, and they retaliated by running a thoroughfare past it to distract the worshipers. Several fights broke out between Arabs and Jews. During the following year, these escalated into a small civil war, causing hundreds of casualties on both sides. Arabs perpetrated massacres elsewhere in Palestine, notably Hebron, where they killed most of the Jewish inhabitants and forced the others to leave. British police could not protect innocent civilians. When the Jews complained, Britain sent a commission of inquiry, which later issued a report that seemed to justify the Arab position. Then the colonial secretary, Lord Passfield, issued a white paper blaming the Jewish Agency and Zionist land purchases from Arabs (which had rendered some peasants homeless) for the 1929 disturbances. The British also tightened restrictions on Jewish immigration. Weizmann was so incensed by this report that he resigned from the leadership of the Jewish Agency. Chagrined, the British government issued a letter explaining away the Passfield White Paper, an action that angered the Arabs. It taught them that Zionist influence was strong enough to sway the British government whenever it tried to favor Arab interests. The letter hardly mollified the Zionists either. This incident shows just how ineffective Britain's Palestine policy had become. I would even say that it doomed the mandate to failure.

## Jewish Immigration and Arab Resistance

During the 1930s, Jewish-Arab relations worsened. The rise to power of Hitler and his Nazi party in Germany put the Jews in that country—numbering almost a million—in dire peril. Many stayed in Germany despite discriminatory laws, official harassment, and hooliganism against Jews inspired by Hitler's inflammatory speeches, but other German Jews (not to mention Jews from nearby countries such as Poland) began trying to get out. Even the Nazis tried, for a while anyway, to help them leave. But which country would take them in? Most European countries were already crowded and had too few jobs during the worldwide depression, so they did not want to admit many German Jews. Neither did the United

States, which since 1924 had set strict limits on foreign immigration. This left Palestine. From 1933 on, the trickle of Jewish immigrants into that country turned into a flood, taxing the limits Britain had set out of concern for Palestine's absorptive capacity—or indeed for the extent of Arab tolerance. Naturally, the Arabs wondered how long it would be before they became the minority. They had not brought Hitler to power; why should their rights be sacrificed for the sins of the Germans? In contrast, the Zionists could see swarms of Arab workers coming into Palestine to take jobs as the British seemed to ignore that strain on the country's absorptive capacity!

## The Peel Commission and the White Paper

As Arab feelings of anger and impotence mounted, Hajj Amin al-Husayni took charge of a new Arab Higher Committee that represented nearly all Palestinian Muslim and Christian factions. The committee called a general Arab strike in 1936. The strike turned into a large-scale rebellion that practically paralyzed Palestine for several months. Again the British government sent out a commission of inquiry, this one headed by Lord Peel. The Arabs tried to impress the Peel Commission with their power by boycotting it until just before it departed in January 1937. As a result, the Zionists got a better hearing. The Peel Commission report, issued later that year, recommended partition, giving a small area of northern and central Palestine to the Jews to form their own state and leaving most of it to the Arabs. The Arab state was expected to join Abdallah's Transjordan. The small allotment for the Jews would hardly have given them much space, but perhaps this foothold would later have enabled the Zionists to rescue far more European Jews from persecution and death under the Nazis. The Palestine Arabs, backed by other Arab states, opposed partition, fearing that Britain's acceptance of the Peel Commission's plan would be a step toward their loss of Palestine. But as often happened in the contest for Palestine, Britain soon scaled down the offer and finally retracted it.

Seeking a peace formula that would satisfy all parties, Britain called a round-table conference of Jewish and Arab leaders (including Arabs from other countries) in London in early 1939. By then the differences between Palestinian Jews and Arabs had become so great that they would not even sit around the same table. No agreement was reached, and the conference ended inconclusively. A new war with Germany was by then imminent, and Britain needed Arab support. It issued a policy statement called the White Paper that announced that the mandate would end in ten years, whereupon Palestine would become fully independent. Until then, Jewish immigration would be limited to 15,000 each year up to 1944, after which it could continue only with Arab consent (which hardly seemed forthcoming!). The sale of Arab land to Jews was restricted in some areas and prohibited in others.

Like the Arabs earlier, the Jews now felt angry but helpless. The White Paper seemed to sell out Britain's commitment to help build the Jewish national home pledged in the Balfour Declaration and the mandate itself. Remember that this happened after Hitler's troops had marched into Austria, after the Western democracies had consented to the dismemberment of Czechoslovakia at the Munich conference, and during the time that Poland was being menaced by a German attack. Europe's Jews were in peril. They had nowhere to go but Palestine. Now Britain, bowing to Arab pressure, had shut its gates to the Jews. The Arabs, too, spurned the White Paper, because it postponed their independence and did not stop Jewish immigration and land purchases altogether.

During World War II, most of the Arab countries remained neutral. Some of their leaders (including the exiled mufti of Jerusalem) sought out the Nazis, hoping that they would free the Arab world from British imperialism and Zionism both. But the Jews in Palestine had no choice. The threat of annihilation by the Nazis outweighed the evils of British appeasement to the Arabs, so they committed themselves to the Allied cause. On the advice of the chairman of the Jewish Agency, David Ben-Gurion, the Zionists agreed that "we must assist the British in the war as if there were no White Paper and we must resist the White Paper as if there were no war." Thousands of Palestinian Jews volunteered for the British armed services, taking high-risk assignments in various theaters of war. Some also undertook dangerous missions to rescue Jews from the parts of Europe controlled by Hitler and his allies. As the Nazi threat receded, a few frustrated Zionists turned to terrorist acts, such as assassinating the British minister-resident in Cairo.

## The Growing Role of the United States

As it became clear that Britain would not lift its restrictions on Jewish immigration into Palestine or relent in its opposition to a Jewish state, the Zionists increasingly looked to the United States for support. Zionism had not attracted many American Jews earlier, but the rise of Hitler had alerted them to the dangers of anti-Semitism running rampant. Most American Jews still had friends or relatives in lands falling under Nazi control. Although they did not foresee that Hitler would try to kill them all, they did worry about their safety. If Germany, once among the safest countries for Jews, now persecuted them, was there any country in which Jews could always live as a minority? Maybe a Jewish state would not be such a bad idea after all, American Jews reasoned, even if few of them planned to settle there.

In 1942 American Zionists adopted what was called the Biltmore Program, calling on Britain to rescind the White Paper and to make Palestine a Jewish state. Soon the World Zionist Organization endorsed this resolution. U.S. politicians, aware of the feelings of their voters but not those of the Arab majority living in Palestine, began clamoring for a Jewish state. This was not just a knee-jerk response to the "Jewish vote," for many Christians hoped that the formation of a Jewish state would atone for Hitler's vile deeds (their full extent was not yet widely known) and for the past persecution committed by so many others. Why did they not admit more Jewish survivors into the United States? This might have alleviated the Palestine problem, but it also would have undermined what the Zionists wanted, a Jewish state. Besides, anti-Semitism still existed in the United States; most Christians and even some Jews did not want to raise the immigration quotas for these Jewish refugees from Europe.

## Civil War in Palestine

As World War II was winding down, violence in Palestine mounted. Zionist terrorist groups, such as the *Irgun Tzvei Le'umi* (National Military Organization) and the Stern Gang, blew up buildings and British installations in Palestine. The U.S. government began to pressure Britain to end restrictions on Jewish immigration and to accommodate demands for Jewish statehood. An Anglo-American Committee of Inquiry went to Palestine in 1946 and interviewed both mandate officials and nationalist leaders. It called for a continuation of the mandate, but its most publicized recommendation was to admit 100,000 European Jewish refugees at once and to end all restrictions on Jewish land purchases. The new Labour government in Britain rejected this advice and advocated instead a federated Arab-Jewish Palestine. This satisfied no one, and the fighting worsened. Finally, Britain went before the UN General Assembly in February 1947 and admitted that it could no longer keep the mandate. Its Palestine policy was bankrupt.

## The United Nations Partition Plan

It was up to the new world organization to settle the issue. The General Assembly responded to the challenge by creating yet another investigatory body, the UN Special Committee on Palestine. This group of ten member states toured Palestine during the summer of 1947 but could not come up with a policy on which they could all agree. Some favored a binational Palestinian state, shared by Arabs and Jews. The Arabs still made up two-thirds of the country's population, though, and they were expected to resist admitting any Jewish refugees from Europe. The majority of the UN Special Committee members recommended partitioning Palestine into seven sections, of which three would be controlled by Arabs and three by Jews. The seventh, including Jerusalem and Bethlehem, would be administered by the United Nations. If you look at Map 9, you can imagine how hard it would have been to carry out the plan, with borders crisscrossing in a crazy quilt pattern designed to ensure that nearly all Jewish settlements would be in lands allotted to the Jews (comprising 54 percent of Palestine). Even so, their area would contain almost as many Arabs as Jews. Perhaps the Arabs could be transferred, but understandably neither the Palestinian Arabs nor the governments of neighboring Arab countries welcomed a plan to set up an alien state in their midst, against the wishes of the Arab inhabitants of the land. But the communist countries, the United States, and nearly all the Latin American republics favored it. The partition plan passed in the General Assembly by a thirty-three to thirteen vote despite the opposition of all five Arab member states.

The Zionists did not like all aspects of this plan, but they accepted it as a step toward forming the Jewish state for which they had waited and worked so long. The Arabs threatened to go to war if need be to block its implementation. But words and deeds were not always the same. Jewish paramilitary groups in Palestine soon seized lands not allotted to their side, and Arab commandos often struck back at Jewish targets. Although Arab League members met to plot a common strategy, their public threats masked private quarrels and a general state of military unreadiness. Amir Abdallah of Transjordan contemplated annexing Arab Palestine; most other Arab countries opposed him, calling for volunteers to fight in Pales-

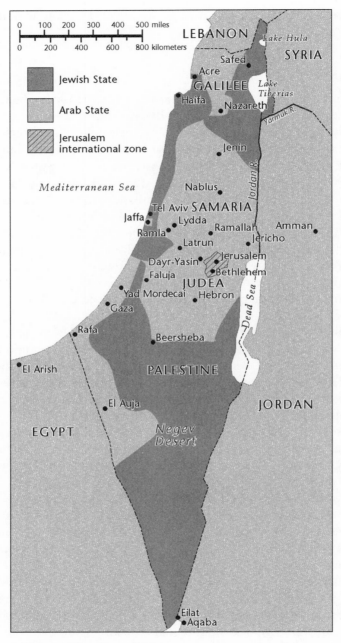

MAP 9   The United Nations partition plan for
Palestine, 1947

tine. At the end of 1947, it was not yet clear if they would commit their regular armies to action.

### The Creation of Israel

The 1947 partition plan was certainly not a peaceful resolution to the contest for Palestine. Both Jewish and Arab armies lined up volunteers and equipped themselves as well as they could. Both sides committed terrorist acts against innocent civilians. For example, the Irgun raided Dayr Yasin, an Arab village near Jerusalem, and massacred 254 men, women, and children. A few days later, an Arab group ambushed a bus going to the Hadassah Medical Center on Mount Scopus, killing 75 Jewish professors, doctors, and nurses. The British folded their arms and ignored the escalating violence, as they were preparing to withdraw totally from Palestine. Some hoped that they would be invited back by whichever side was losing the contest.

Mindful of the mounting violence in Palestine, the U.S. representative in the United Nations suggested in March 1948 that the partition plan be postponed for a ten-year cooling-off period under a UN trusteeship. This compromise might have satisfied the Arabs but certainly not the Zionists, with the Jewish state now almost in their grasp. Heavy pressure was brought to bear on President Truman, who finally reaffirmed his support for a Jewish state, over the objections of the State Department and his own secretary of defense. That spring, diplomats argued at the United Nations, Arab and Jewish terrorist groups in Palestine murdered civilians and sniped at each other, large numbers of Palestinian Arabs panicked and fled for safety to nearby countries, and finally the British troops pulled out of Jerusalem.

On 14 May 1948 the Jewish Agency Executive Committee, meeting in Tel Aviv, formally declared that those parts of Palestine under Jewish control were now the independent State of Israel. It also announced that the provisions of the 1939 White Paper limiting Jewish immigration and land purchases were null and void. The Zionists urged the Arab inhabitants of the new State of Israel "to preserve the ways of peace and play their part in the development of the state, on the basis of full and equal citizenship and due representation in all its bodies and institutions." They also called on the neighboring Arab states to cooperate with them for the common good of all. Even if these statements were sincere, they came too late. Many Palestinian Arabs, having fled from their homes during the early stages of the fighting, distrusted the Zionists and looked to their Arab neighbors for help. The next day five Arab governments sent their armies into Palestine to fight against the new State of Israel.

## CONCLUSION

The contest for Palestine entered a new phase. Arab nationalists and political Zionists had for years inflamed each other's worst fears under the bungling British mandate. Now they could fight each other openly. The Arab-Israeli conflict, as it must now be called, would become one of the most intractable problems of modern diplomacy. American journalist I. F. Stone quipped that if God is dead, he died trying to solve the Arab-Israeli conflict. Before 1948 a compromise might have been found between the extremes of Arab nationalism and political Zionism. But no attempt at accommodation worked, and the world continues to pay a high price for that failure.

# SEVENTEEN

# Israel's Rebirth and
# the Rise of Arab Nationalism

The 1948–1949 war between the new State of Israel and its Arab neighbors was a revolutionary event, setting in motion many drastic changes in the Middle East. To the Israelis and their admirers, the war was a struggle for Jewish independence, fought first against British imperialism and later against the armies of the Arab states. They saw Israel's victory as revolutionary because for the first time in the Middle East's modern history the citizens of a country managed to topple a colonial regime and set up a democratic government. From the Arabs' point of view, their defeat in Palestine was revolutionary because it humiliated their armies and discredited their regimes. In the ensuing years many Arab governments were ousted by military coups and many kings and prime ministers assassinated. The Palestine disaster uprooted more than a half-million Arabs who sought refuge in the Gaza Strip (a small part of Palestine occupied by Egypt in 1948), Jordan, Syria, or Lebanon. These Palestinian refugees emerged as a potent force. Some became ardent Arab nationalists. Others espoused any ideology or backed any leader who would give them back their dignity and their homes. The Palestinians' bitter opposition to Israel (and its Western backers) was matched only by their hostility to Arab governments that might want to make peace with the Jewish state. They became the revolutionaries of the Arab world. For both sides, the period from 1948 to 1967 was one of readjustment to the new conditions created by the war.

## ISRAEL'S WAR FOR INDEPENDENCE

How and why did Israel win the war? The Arab states were bigger and more populous. Some had large standing armies and ample military equipment. On 14 May 1948, when the Jewish Agency leaders declared Israel independent, the Arabs seemed likely to win. Armies of Egypt, Transjordan, and several other Arab countries went into Israel the next day. If for them the war was just starting, for the Israelis (as the Jews of Palestine now called themselves), it had been going on for years. As we saw in Chapter 16, it had been building up ever since World War II, chiefly against the British. Consequently, there were already many experienced Jewish fighters. But they had not all belonged to the same force. Aside from Haganah, which had become the military arm of the Jewish Agency, several of the political parties had their own militias. The best known was the Irgun Tzvei Le'umi, attached to the party that hoped to set up the Jewish state on both sides of the River Jordan. Under Menachem Begin, the Irgun conducted many terrorist attacks, of which the most notorious were the bombing of Jerusalem's King David Hotel in 1946 and the Dayr Yasin massacre of 1948. The Israelis were divided at first, for the Irgun and the even more extreme Stern Gang resisted absorption into Haganah, but the Arab invasion and what they viewed as the dire consequences of an Arab victory welded the people together. In a few weeks, the new Israel Defense Force (IDF) grew in numbers, equipment, and experience.

### The Contending Forces

The opposing Arab armies turned out to be smaller than expected. Countries such as Egypt held back most of their troops to preserve order at home. Saudi Arabia once promised to send 40,000 men, but as of October 1948 only 700 were on the field. Lebanon's 2,000 soldiers were little more than a glorified police force. The best-equipped and -trained army was Transjordan's Arab Legion, but its field strength of 10,000 could hardly match an Israeli army of more than 100,000 men and women. Even such pro-Israel accounts as Nadav Safran's *From War to War* state that the Jews had more troops committed to battle than all the Arab armies combined. This may not have been true by May 1948, when the reported success of several Arab guerrilla groups against the Jews in Palestine drew flocks of volunteers to join the regular armies of Egypt, Syria, Lebanon, Transjordan, and Iraq.

In the early days of the war, small bands of poorly armed Israelis had to ward off large Arab armies. In the northern Negev kibbutz of Yad Mordechai, for example, an Egyptian brigade headed for Tel Aviv was held up for six days—long enough for Israel to strengthen its defenses farther north—by a group of fewer than eighty men, women, and teenagers. In Galilee the beleaguered defenders of the Jewish quarter of Safed put together a makeshift "cannon," whose loud (but harmless) reports are said to have fooled the enemy into fleeing without a fight. It indeed mattered less that Jewish soldiers outnumbered Arab ones in Palestine than that the Arabs came to think they did. Ill informed about the character and abilities of the Jews in Palestine, Arab military leaders tended at first to underestimate them. When the Israelis gradually learned how to counter their early attacks, the Arabs overreacted and began to overestimate the Jews' strength. Poor morale was a major reason for the Arab defeat.

*The Outside Powers*

The attitudes and policies of the Great Powers confused both sides, but this confusion hurt the Arabs more than the Israelis. The United States and the USSR clearly favored Israel; both rushed to give it diplomatic recognition. Although most countries banned arms shipments to both sides, communist Czechoslovakia sold large quantities of weapons to Israel. In view of their later policies, why did the USSR and its allies back Israel in 1948? No doubt the Soviets acted partly on memories of their recent war against Nazi Germany and the destruction of European Jewry, but the main motives for their policy were (1) their desire to weaken British influence in the Middle East, (2) their hope that the new Jewish state would adopt socialism or even communism, and (3) their need to discredit "feudal" and "bourgeois" Arab regimes. The United States seemed to equivocate. Public opinion clearly favored Israel. With a presidential election approaching, Truman, an incumbent in deep trouble, vied with his Republican opponents in supporting the Jewish state. However, high officials in the State Department and the military feared that an anti-Arab stance would harm the growing U.S. oil interests in the Middle East. Entrepreneurs, educators, and missionaries who had spent years in the area argued cogently against policies that would antagonize the whole Arab world. But Israel's supporters, especially in Congress, had more clout.

The Arabs expected more support from Britain, which had been at odds with the Zionists since the 1939 White Paper. It had treaties with

Iraq and Egypt permitting British troops to guard airfields and strategic waterways. The commander of Transjordan's Arab Legion, Sir John Bagot Glubb, and many of his officers were British subjects. Britain also had major oil interests in Iraq and Kuwait. But although the Foreign Office and many senior diplomats did favor the Arabs, the British government depended too heavily on U.S. military and economic support to oppose publicly its Middle East policies. Continental Europe was recovering from the ravages of World War II, and most liberals sympathized with the Jewish state. Europeans who volunteered to aid the Arab armies often turned out to be unrepentant Nazis. Meanwhile, many Americans and Europeans rallied to Israel's cause as an act of atonement for the Holocaust.

## UN Mediation Attempts

The United Nations, overtaken by events in May 1948, tried to settle the Arab-Israeli conflict in ways that angered first one side, then the other, and sometimes both. It promptly sent a mediator, Sweden's Count Folke Bernadotte, who managed to get both sides to accept a monthlong cease-fire in early June. Both sides were exhausted from four weeks of intense fighting, but only the Israelis used this respite to obtain and distribute arms to its troops. Bernadotte published a plan that would have given the Negev Desert (assigned mainly to the Jews under the 1947 partition plan) and Jerusalem to Transjordan. In return, Israel was to get parts of western Galilee that had been allotted to the Arabs. Egypt, whose troops had occupied most of southern Israel, would get nothing. On 8 July fighting resumed on all fronts. During the next ten days, the Israelis took part of Galilee and the strategic towns of Lydda and Ramleh, expelling their inhabitants, as the Arab Legion drew back without a fight. But the UN secured another cease-fire before the Jewish forces could capture the Old City of Jerusalem (containing the revered Western Wall). On 18 July another uneasy truce descended on Palestine.

As both sides prepared for yet another round of fighting, the UN mediator made a new appeal to Arab support. Bernadotte added to his plan a stipulation that the Arab refugees be allowed to return to their homes in cities and villages now under Israeli control. How, with winter's cold and rain imminent, could these people wait in makeshift camps for a chance to return? Who could have known that Palestinian Arabs (and their descendants) would wait and wait and wait, as pawns or perpetuators of a conflict that the United Nations was supposed to settle in 1948? But the Israelis did not want to let these Arabs return, and Bernadotte was murdered in September by Stern Gang extremists.

Ralph Bunche, an American, became the new UN mediator. His first challenge lay in the northern Negev, mostly occupied by Egyptian troops. Because Israel needed to supply some isolated Jewish settlements, Bunche arranged for Egyptian and Israeli truck convoys to take turns using the roads. Egypt broke the agreement, giving Israel a needed pretext to resume fighting. Pushing back the Egyptians, the Israelis gained much of the northern Negev, including Beersheba. What they most wanted, though, was Judea, where Brigadier General Moshe Dayan attacked Arab Legion positions around Hebron and Bethlehem until the United Nations obtained a new cease-fire. Meanwhile, Israeli forces in Galilee drove the Syrian-backed Arab Liberation Army northward into Lebanon. While the UN members went on debating the Bernadotte plan in late 1948, Israel tried to push Egyptian and Arab Legion forces out of the Gaza area and the southern Negev. Another brigadier general, Yigal Allon, attacked the Egyptians at Auja, and by year's end the main fighting front had crossed the old Palestine border into Egyptian Sinai. When Egypt still would not sue for peace, Britain invoked the 1936 Anglo-Egyptian Treaty to thwart the Israelis. Cairo was embarrassed to turn to the British, but no Arab country was prepared to rescue Egypt.

The United Nations now began a bizarre exercise in diplomacy. No Arab state was willing to confer directly with Israel (and thus recognize de facto the Jewish state), but in January 1949 Ralph Bunche opened what were called "proximity talks" on the island of Rhodes. Egyptian and Israeli delegations, in separate suites of the same hotel, haggled over terms while Bunche carried proposals from one side to the other, finally securing an armistice agreement. Three months later, after the Arab Legion had lost the Negev areas it had occupied, Transjordan signed at Rhodes a separate agreement, one that in fact ratified a pact that King (formerly Amir) Abdallah had secretly made with Israel's army commanders. Israel now gained access to the Gulf of Aqaba, a fateful achievement that deprived Egypt and Transjordan of direct overland contact and enabled Israel to build a port at Eilat. Lebanon signed an armistice with Israel in March. Syria finally followed suit in July 1949. Iraq, which had also sent forces into Palestine, never signed an armistice (as it had no common border with Israel, this hardly mattered at the time) and fiercely opposed any Arab peace with Israel. It still does.

## THE WAR'S AFTERMATH

Would these armistice agreements lead to a comprehensive peace between Israel and the Arabs? The UN Conciliation Commission for Palestine set up a conference in Lausanne, where Israeli and Arab delegations were to settle their outstanding differences. But negotiations broke down before the two sides even met. Israel insisted on a comprehensive settlement, whereas the Arabs called on Israel to withdraw from the lands not allotted to the Jewish state by the 1947 Partition Plan. They also refused to negotiate with Israel until it let the Palestinian refugees return to their homes. The Arabs argued that these stipulations were contained in the General Assembly resolutions and that Israel had been admitted to the United Nations on condition that it comply with them. Israel replied that it was the Arabs who had first defied the General Assembly's Partition Plan. As such arguments went on and on, hopes for a settlement dissipated. Because most UN members recognized the Jewish state, Western observers thought that the Arab governments would soon admit that Israel was in the Middle East to stay. Later I will show why they did not.

### Arab Divisions

The main reason why the Arabs failed to defeat Israel in 1948, or in any of the later wars, is that they are politically divided. In principle, all the Arab states were opposed to the 1947 partition plan and to creating a Jewish state in Palestine. As members of the Arab League, they had vowed to fight against Israel, putting their armies under the nominal command of an Iraqi general. Some, however, had refused to appropriate funds or to commit troops as long as the British had stayed in Palestine. Transjordan's Abdallah still wanted to create a "Greater Syria." Even in 1948 he was willing to make a deal with the Jews in order to annex parts of Palestine to his own kingdom, a first step toward his annexing of Lebanon and Syria, some of whose citizens still backed the Greater Syria idea. You may recall from Chapter 13 how Mecca's Hashimite family had hoped to unite all the Arabs after World War I, but the French had taken over Syria and Lebanon. Abdallah was a Hashimite.

So was Iraq's ruling family, which supported his Greater Syria plan and Arab nationalism generally, provided of course that the Baghdad government became the senior partner. But both Egypt's Faruq and Saudi Arabia's Ibn Sa'ud opposed Hashimite claims to unify the Arab world. Egypt aspired to be the leading Arab country; it had the largest population, universities, newspapers, and broadcasting stations in the Arab world. The Arab League headquarters was in Cairo, and its energetic secretary-general was an Egyptian. And Egypt did not want to have a Hashimite king ruling in next-door Palestine and scheming to annex Syria and Lebanon. Ibn Sa'ud, having ousted the Hashimites from Arabia, agreed with Faruq.

In other words, while the Arabs claimed to be united and were threatening the Jews with defeat and even extermination if they dared to set up a state in Palestine, their leaders were really trying to outbluff one another. Up to May 1948, most Egyptian generals and cabinet ministers had hoped to avoid the expected war in Palestine. It was the zeal of the Muslim Brothers, the vanity of King Faruq, and the momentum of Egypt's own threats that sent the army in to fight a war for which it was unprepared. Amir Abdallah had assured Jewish emissaries that his Arab Legion would not fight, but he sent in his troops so that the other Arabs could not claim the glory if they won. Once the fighting started, the Egyptian army and the Arab Legion worked at cross-purposes. The Palestinians had an Arab Liberation Army, led by a Syrian, but it would not work with the British-officered Arab Legion. Abdallah also hated the best-known Palestinian Arab nationalist, Hajj Amin al-Husayni, Jerusalem's ex-mufti. Expelled from Palestine in 1937, the mufti had taken refuge in Lebanon and Iraq and then made his way to Berlin during World War II. Later he escaped to Cairo and was now working for Faruq. As long as the Arabs had a chance of defeating Israel in 1948, their leaders and armies competed to pick up the most land and glory in Palestine. Once Israel began driving the Arabs back, they began bickering over who was to blame.

## The Palestinian Arabs

Who looked out for the Palestinian Arabs? No Arab government heeded the needs or the interests of these people who, up to 1948, had formed the majority of Palestine's population. About 150,000 managed, by chance or by choice, to stay in their homes within lands controlled by Israel. They became Israeli citizens, an Arabic-speaking Muslim and Christian minority within a Jewish state, subject for years to harsh restrictions but also enjoying political rights, economic benefits, and educational opportunities unmatched by most of their Arab neighbors. The 400,000 Arabs who lived in those parts of Palestine not taken by Israel (including the Old City of Jerusalem) came under the military occupation of the Arab Legion. Abdallah soon annexed this region, now usually termed the "West Bank," to the state he renamed the "Hashimite Kingdom of Jordan." Most other Arab countries protested, but they could no more restrain Abdallah than they could defeat Israel. Although Israel opposed "Jordanian" rule over Jerusalem's Old City, its emissaries had secretly agreed to let Abdallah keep the West Bank, as they hoped to make a comprehensive peace settlement with Jordan later. Anyway, the Israelis held western Jerusalem, plus strategic chunks of Palestine not given to them by either the 1947 partition plan or the modifications later proposed by Bernadotte. There were also 200,000 Palestinians, many of them refugees, in the Gaza region, where Egypt set up an "all-Palestine government" under the former mufti. This political ploy against Abdallah foundered, leaving the Gaza Strip under Egypt's military administration, which did the local Palestinians no good at all.

The Palestinian refugees, whose numbers are widely disputed, suffered the most. The actual figure at the end of 1948 was somewhere between 550,000 and 800,000. Some had voluntarily left their homes even before the struggle started, whereas others fled (or were forced to flee) during the fighting. Who forced their flight? Israel's supporters claim that Arab governments broadcast orders to Palestinian civilians to get out so that their armies could more easily move in against the Israelis. The Arabs reply that Jewish extremists terrorized the Palestinians up to 14 May 1948 and that the Israel Defense Force drove out other Arabs during the later phases of the war. It is hard to determine who is right. No one has proved that the alleged Arab broadcasts were made. Both sides committed terrorist acts. Conditions varied from time to time and from place to place, but the outcome was that most Palestinians ended up in camps near Israel's borders in the Egyptian-held Gaza Strip, the Jordanian-ruled West Bank, Syria, and Lebanon. There was no state for the Palestinians.

The Arab countries would not absorb them, mainly for political reasons, but some would also have found it economically hard to do so. The Palestinians themselves rejected assimilation because they wanted to go back to their homes. Israel, busy absorbing European Jewish survivors and unwilling to take in a "fifth column" of implacable foes, would not readmit all the Palestinian refugees. The United Nations, realizing that something had to be done for these unfortunate people, set up the UN Relief and Works Agency (UNRWA) as a stopgap measure. But all it could do in 1949 was to house them in camps, give them enough food and clothing to survive, and educate or train their children, hoping that the problem would, someday and somehow, be solved. A few Arab refugees did manage to go back to Israel, and many younger Palestinians gradually became absorbed in the economies of the Arab countries; but many others stayed in the camps, growing more and more bitter against Israel, its Western backers, and, indeed, the Arab leaders who had betrayed them. I will have more to say about the Palestinians later.

## The Arab Countries

Let us look at the Arab world in the wake of what was soon termed the "Palestine disaster." In some cases, I will review the mandate era between the two world wars. If the details confuse you at times, keep in mind that no matter what claims to unity may have been made by Arab nationalists, there were several Arab states, many leaders, and various policies. Some Arab governments were stable, a few were popular, and many were neither.

### Jordan

The country most directly affected by the war was Jordan. What had been a desert emirate called Transjordan became the Hashimite Kingdom of Jordan. A half-million Transjordanians, most of bedouin origin, were joined by a million Palestinians, half of them local farmers or city dwellers in the newly annexed West Bank and the other half refugees in UNRWA camps. The Palestinians, all of whom were offered Jordanian nationality, tended to be more westernized and politically articulate than the Transjordanians over whom Abdallah had long ruled as a father figure. Most of the Palestinians were (or, in the case of the refugees, had been) subsistence farmers, but some were lawyers, teachers, merchants, or bureaucrats. Few were monarchists. For King Abdallah, having control of Jerusalem's Old City, with its Muslim shrines such as the Dome of the Rock, compensated for his father's loss of Mecca and Medina to Ibn Sa'ud a generation earlier. Content with his new lands and the tripled number of subjects, he negotiated secretly with Israel for rail access to Haifa in exchange for diplomatic recognition. Angry Palestinians, especially Arab supporters of the ex-mufti, denounced Abdallah as a traitor. In 1951 a young Palestinian murdered him in Jerusalem. His son was soon eased off the Jordanian throne due to alleged mental instability in favor of Abdallah's seventeen-year-old grandson, Husayn, who took charge officially in 1952.

During this time, Britain continued to subsidize Jordan's government, and Sir John Bagot Glubb commanded the Arab Legion. Although Jordan had become nominally independent in 1946, not until 1955 did the USSR agree to its admission to UN membership. There followed a brief period during which King Husayn flirted with Arab nationalism and the Palestinian Left. Westerners then argued that Jordan should have made peace with Israel and gained access to the Mediterranean. But the lesson of Abdallah's murder was clear. The Palestinians might have lost their homes and become second-class citizens in Jordan, but they could block any attempt to bury their claims by a peace settlement. Never would Husayn be the first to settle with Israel. As for Abdallah's Greater Syria ambitions, they faded like a desert mirage.

## Syria and Lebanon

What did happen to the rest of Greater Syria? The impact of the war on Lebanon and Syria was different but no less disruptive. What was now the Republic of Syria had grown embittered during a generation of unwanted French rule. After French troops had subdued Faysal's Arab army in 1920, they had taken control of all the areas mandated to France under the San Remo agreements. The French mandate administration, however benevolent, did its best to stifle Arab nationalism in the land of its birth. Syria was never prepared for independence as Wilson's mandate scheme had envisaged; it was not even offered a constitution until 1936, and then the French National Assembly rejected it. In the 1920s the French had fragmented Syria to keep its people from combining against the mandatory government. Most of the French divisions proved unworkable and had to be shelved, but two became permanent. One was the separation in 1938 of the region around Alexandretta and its formal annexation by Turkey in the following year. The other was the creation of Lebanon as a separate state, about which I must digress at length.

The mainly Christian area around Mount Lebanon enjoyed local autonomy from 1861 to 1914 within the Ottoman Empire, an arrangement that had been guaranteed by the European powers (but especially France) following a massacre of many Christians in 1860. Most of Mount Lebanon's Christians were Maronites, in communion with the Roman Catholic church. They traded with France and sent their children to French mission schools. Unlike most of Syria's inhabitants, they welcomed the French occupation after World War I. Hoping to buttress the Maronites' power over other religious groups, France created an enlarged Lebanon by adding the coastal towns of Tripoli, Beirut, and Sidon to the historic Mount Lebanon. The resulting entity, slightly more than half

Christian, proved stable (meaning pro-French) enough to be given a constitution and some local autonomy in 1926. French control of Lebanon lasted until 1943, while its large landowning families evolved into an elite of merchants and bankers. Their government was "democratic" in the sense that its legislators were popularly elected, but I would call it a constitutional oligarchy, for the wealth and power were concentrated within the leading families.

Lebanon's system also preserved religious divisions by allocating to each sect a fixed share of the parliamentary seats and administrative posts. The apportionment was based on a census taken by the French in 1932. But no census has been taken since then, as the Maronites and several other sects fear that any head count would show their relative decline. The influx in 1948 of some 150,000 Palestinian refugees complicated the arrangement. Lebanon quickly absorbed those who were Christian, but the Muslim majority was denied citizenship and settled in large refugee camps. Had any census been taken that included the Palestinians and left out those Christians who had moved to Europe or the Americas, it could have been proven that most Lebanese after 1948 were Muslim. Instead, the system of proportional representation by religious sects continued to reflect Lebanon's situation under the French mandate. By unwritten agreement, the president was always a Maronite Christian and the prime minister a Sunni Muslim; the other high posts went to the various smaller sects. The leaders also agreed to cooperate, in spite of their religious differences, to preserve Lebanon's independence and territorial integrity. This national pact meant that the Christians would not try to keep Lebanon tied to France or to recreate an autonomous Mount Lebanon under their own control, whereas the Muslims would not seek to reunite the country with Syria or any hypothetical pan-Arab state.

This understanding, to which all Christian and Muslim leaders subscribed in 1943, guided Lebanon through a coup d'état in 1952 and a civil war in 1958, up to the catastrophic breakdown that lasted from 1975 to 1990. Lebanon seemed to thrive under the system, but a few families retained most of its wealth and power, the government and army were too weak to protect the country or even to preserve order, and Beirut's free press became an arena for competing liberal, pan-Arab, and socialist ideologies. The influx of unassimilable Palestinians would undermine the system.

My digression on Lebanon may help show how Israel's creation affected Syria. The Syrians resented not only the amputation of Alexandretta and the creation of Lebanon during the French mandate era, but also the Western powers' decision to separate Palestine and Transjordan even earlier. Why not put back together what the West had divided? By the late 1940s the British and French had given up their mandates; surely, therefore, what had been Faysal's Arab kingdom in 1918 could now become a republic of Greater Syria. But there were two flies in the ointment. One was the creation of Israel, which the Syrians saw as an imperialist plot to keep the area divided and under Western control. The other was Abdallah and his family. Indeed, there was a group of Syrians, the People's party, who wanted Arab unity restored, under Hashimite rule, in the form of an organic union of all Fertile Crescent states, including Iraq. But the Syrians in power from 1945, i.e., the Nationalist party, wanted to keep the Hashimites from ruling Syria. They, too, desired Arab unity, but under the aegis of the Arab League, and they favored closer ties with Egypt and Saudi Arabia than with Iraq and Jordan. Accordingly, Syria fought against Israel in 1948 in alliance with Egypt and in competition with Jordan's Arab Legion. The poor showing of Syria's troops led to scandals in Damascus. The discredited civilian government was ousted by an army coup in 1949. Two more coups ensued that year. The leader who emerged from the pile was Colonel Adib Shishakli, whose populist dictatorship became the prototype for that of Egypt's Nasir and those of other Arab officers in the 1950s.

Deeply split by religious and local differences, Syria became notorious for instability and disunity; yet its leaders hoped to unite all Arabs against Zionism (meaning Israel and its backers) and imperialism. Shishakli's overthrow in 1954 led to another attempt at civilian government, but the system was unresponsive to the country's need for economic and social reforms. Syria became the birthplace of the first popular Arab socialist movement, the Ba'th (Renaissance) party, which appealed to young people, army officers, workers, and Palestinians, not just in Syria but also in many other Arab states. It demanded land reform, nationalization of basic industries, unification of the whole Arab world, and militant resistance to Israel and all vestiges of imperialism in the area. In such an atmosphere, no patriotic Syrian wanted peace with Israel or the absorption of the Palestinian refugees, even though land was being brought under cultivation in northeastern Syria. Indeed, Syria's own ethnic and religious minorities, such as the Armenians, other Christian sects, Shi'i Muslims, Alawis (an offshoot of Shi'i Islam), Druze (see Chapter 6), and of course the Jews, generally fared badly in this era of rising Arab nationalism.

## Iraq

Of all the Arab states in southwest Asia, the most populous is Iraq. With its two great rivers and its rising oil revenues, it might have become the strongest Arab country. There are several reasons why it has not. First, it was pasted together from parts of three different Ottoman provinces by the British, who had taken the area from the Turks during World War I. Although its rivers may seem to unite these parts, remember that the Euphrates and the Tigris both start in Turkey and that the former also flows through Syria. In addition, most of Iraq's arable land came under the control of the *shaykhs* of various quasi-independent bedouin tribes. The Muslim population was divided almost evenly between Sunnis and Shi'is, the latter having ties with neighboring Iran. Religious minorities included Jews and Assyrians (or Nestorians, covered in Chapter 2). Almost one-fifth of Iraq's population was Kurdish. A smaller share was Turkish. What these disparate groups had in common were four centuries of Ottoman rule, followed by a British military occupation in 1917. Shaken by a nationwide revolt in Iraq in 1920, the British sought a ruler who would serve their interests and unite its people. Faysal, driven by the French from Syria, fit the role admirably. The British made him king of Iraq and quickly handed local power over to his regime. In 1932 Iraq was the first Arab mandate to become independent and join the League of Nations.

Regrettably, Iraq's stability was upset by Faysal's early death in 1933, an Assyrian uprising that the Iraqi army put down violently, and a popular mood of strident Arab chauvinism in the late 1930S. Several coups brought military dictators into and out of power, culminating in 1941 with Rashid Ali al-Gaylani's ardently nationalist and pro-Nazi regime, which was crushed by the British. Meanwhile, Faysal's successor, Ghazi, died in a car crash in 1939, leaving the throne to his four-year-old son, Faysal II. A regency was set up under the boy's uncle, Prince Abd al-Ilah, who was allied with a shrewd politician named Nuri al-Sa'id, who managed to be both pro-British and Arab nationalist. Though trained as an Ottoman army officer, Nuri had joined the Arab revolt in 1916 and served the Hashimites from then on.

With British encouragement, Nuri proposed in 1942 a union of Fertile Crescent Arab states: Palestine, Transjordan, Syria, Lebanon, and Iraq. Such a combination would have been dominated by Iraq. This union was opposed by the Jewish settlers in Palestine. The French, still clinging to Syria and Lebanon, were hostile. But the fiercest objections to Nuri's plan came from Egypt and Saudi Arabia, which did not want Baghdad and the

Hashimites to lead the Arab world. As explained earlier, the Egyptian government, also with British backing, countered in 1944 by proposing the creation of what came to be called the Arab League. Iraq, unable to rally enough support for its Fertile Crescent scheme, joined the League and soon became the most vociferous Arab opponent of Zionism.

Iraq's army fought in the 1948 Palestine War, but the country suffered less from the defeat than did Israel's neighbors. Its rising oil revenues were being invested in river irrigation and other projects that promised future prosperity. Its cabinets changed with alarming frequency, the various minority problems festered (nearly all Jews were allowed to emigrate, minus their property, to Israel), the socioeconomic gap between the landowning *shaykhs* and the peasant masses widened, and the pro-Western monarchy lost popular support. But the West did not notice. Britain's remaining military presence was camouflaged politically in 1955 when Iraq joined with Turkey, Iran, Pakistan, and Britain to form an anticommunist alliance commonly called the Baghdad Pact. Iraq's government ignored its military ties with the other Arab League members. Relations between Baghdad and Cairo were usually bad. Both competed for the support of Syria and Lebanon. To Westerners, Iraq was the very model of a modernizing nation—that is, until its monarchy was felled by an army coup in 1958, one that they blamed on Egypt's press and radio attacks.

## Egypt's Nasir and His Policies

You may recall that in Chapter 15, I carried the history of Egypt up to the end of the British occupation in 1956. I did so because for most Egyptians at the time, their main political aim was to free the Nile Valley from British rule. Egypt's involvement in the contest for Palestine was really a struggle against the Hashimites for leadership of the Arab world. Gaining control of the Sudan came to seem less important, as Cairo's attention shifted to keeping either the Jews or Abdallah from taking over Palestine. The 1952 revolution that led to Nasir's rise to power can be viewed as the result of mounting frustration over either (1) Britain's prolonged occupation of the Nile Valley or (2) the Egyptian army's defeat by Israel. Most writers favor the latter interpretation because from 1948 to 1977 Egypt's energies were mobilized toward fighting against Israel and competing for the leadership of the Arab world. On the one hand, U.S. and Soviet pressure persuaded the British to give up their Suez Canal base in 1954. On the other, Egypt agreed to the Sudan's independence in 1956. Nile Valley unity was giving way to Arab nationalism.

It may help us to put Egypt's role as an Arab country into historical perspective. Even though the Arabs have not been politically united since the Abbasid revolution in 750—if indeed they were ever really united—the idea has grown up in the past century that the people who speak Arabic do constitute one nation. They should unite in a single state, as the Germans tried to do under Bismarck and Hitler or the Italians under Mazzini and Mussolini. Arab unity must include Egypt, the largest Arab country and the one linking North Africa's Arabs with those of Southwest Asia. The Egyptians believed that only a strong and united Arab world could withstand the domination of the Western powers. They viewed Israel's creation as a Western imposition on the Arabs, an attempt to maintain British and U.S. influence in the Middle East. They did not want to become communists, as some British and American observers thought in the 1950s, but because Russia had not ruled the Arab world in the past, the Arabs felt no hostility toward the USSR. Soviet diplomacy seized this chance to weaken the West's influence: It turned away from Israel and began to back the Arabs.

The rise of pan-Arabism in Egypt coincided with the overthrow of General Nagib, the titular leader of the 1952 revolution that ousted King Faruq, by Colonel Gamal Abd al-Nasir in 1954. For the next sixteen years, he would, as Egypt's president, loom larger than life in the words and imaginations of both those who loved him and those who hated him. He could be dictatorial or deferential, charismatic or suspicious, ingenuous or crafty. He reacted more than he acted. The son of an Alexandrian postal clerk and grandson of an Upper Egyptian peasant, Nasir had known poverty and humiliation in his youth. Moody and withdrawn, young Nasir read widely, especially history books and biographies of such leaders as Julius Caesar, Napoleon, and (closer to home) Mustafa Kamil. He embraced Egyptian nationalism, but not the parties of the 1930s. Unable to afford law school and yet eager to lead his country's fight for independence, he managed to enter the Egyptian military academy in 1937, the first year that young men without palace or aristocratic ties could be admitted into the officer corps.

After being commissioned, Nasir served in various army posts and slowly gathered a group of young officers from equally modest backgrounds. Intensely patriotic, these men chafed at Britain's power and their own army's weakness, shown by the British ultimatum to King Faruq in 1942 and Egypt's defeat by Israel in 1948. The bonding of these officers (reinforced by the social divisions within the army) led to a conspiratorial cabal, as they saw that only by ousting the rotten regime could Egypt be liberated and redeemed. Even after they had ousted Faruq in 1952, Nasir never lost this conspiratorial tendency. Once in power, he kept spies to observe and report on friends as well as foes.

Nasir started out leading from behind the scenes, but he engineered Nagib's overthrow in 1954 because the latter seemed to have become too popular. A ponderous speaker at first, Nasir did not win public support until he openly defied the West. An Israeli raid on the Gaza Strip early in 1955, allegedly in retaliation for Palestinian raids into Israel, made Nasir acutely aware of Egypt's need for more arms. His officers would have liked to get them from Britain or the United States, but neither country would sell any to Egypt unless it promised to join an anticommunist alliance and refrain from attacking Israel. Nasir rejected these strings on Western military aid. He attacked Iraq for joining the anti-Soviet Baghdad Pact in the spring of 1955. Egypt opposed any Arab alliance with the West.

Instead, as Nasir emerged as the leader of Arab nationalism, he adopted a policy that he called "positive neutralism" after his exposure to nationalist and communist leaders at the 1955 Bandung Conference of Asian and Middle Eastern states opposed to Western domination. Defying the West, he decided to purchase $200 million (then a huge sum) in arms from the communist countries. Arab nationalists outside Egypt, especially the Palestinians, hailed Nasir as their savior. He would lead the refugees back to their usurped homeland, just as Salah al-Din in 1187 had driven the Crusaders from Jerusalem. Egypt started arming bands of *fidaiyin* (Arabic for "those who sacrifice themselves for a cause"), made up mainly of Gaza Strip Palestinians, to provoke border incidents with Israel.

The U.S. government tried to deflect Nasir from his anti-Western drift by adopting a policy that now seems confused. On the one hand, Secretary of State John Foster Dulles wanted Nasir to leave the other Arab states and Israel alone, so he offered technical and economic assistance, notably a large loan to finance the construction of a new dam at Aswan. On the other hand, Dulles resented Nasir's "positive neutralism" between communism and the West, his threats against Israel and pro-Western Arab regimes, and his recognition of the People's Republic of China. In July 1956, just after Egypt had decided to accept the Aswan Dam loan offer, Dulles, hoping to humiliate Nasir, yanked it away. The Egyptian leader responded by nationalizing the Suez Canal Company, pledging to use its profits, most of which had gone to European investors since it opened in 1869, to finance the dam. "O Americans," he shouted before a vast crowd, "may you choke to death in your fury!"

It was not the Americans who choked. After all, the British and French were the canal's main users, mainly for oil imports from the Gulf. They began planning diplomatic (or if need be military) measures to get it back. That summer and fall saw several international conferences, trips to Cairo, and other Western stratagems aimed at prying the canal from Nasir's grip. Meanwhile, the Arabs hailed Nasir's defiance as just retribution for all the grief they had suffered from Western imperialism. When diplomatic attempts to subject the canal to international control failed, the British and French resolved to regain it by force—and to overthrow Nasir if they could. Significantly, they turned to Israel as an accomplice.

## ISRAEL'S EARLY YEARS

While the Arabs viewed Israel as an agent of Western imperialism, the Israelis saw themselves as an embattled nation seeking to ensure the survival of the Jewish people in the wake of the Nazi Holocaust. They regarded their war for independence as a struggle by an oppressed people for freedom from outside domination. Most of the Arab states against which Israel fought in 1948 were still influenced by British advisers and ruled by kings and landowners.

When revolutions later toppled the discredited regimes in Syria and Egypt, the Israelis were disappointed that the new leaders made no peace overtures to them. The republican Arab nationalists in uniform were no less bitter than the monarchical and feudal politicians in *kufiyah*s, fezzes, or turbans. However, the Israelis were busy rebuilding a war-torn country. In addition, they absorbed the thousands of Jewish refugees who had survived the war and the death camps of Europe. They also had to cope with the unexpected influx of even greater numbers of Jewish refugees from Arab countries, of whom many were transferred under complex secret agreements. Absorption of these new Israelis, so alien in language and culture from the earlier Jewish settlers, placed severe strains on the country.

### Problems of the Jewish State

Economic problems were daunting. The currency, cut loose from the British pound, plummeted in value. The new government could not borrow much money to pay its bills. But large amounts of U.S. government and private Jewish assistance, later augmented by German restitution payments to Jewish survivors of the Hitler era, eased the strain. In an extraordinary act of statesmanship, West German Chancellor Konrad Adenauer made an agreement with Israeli Premier Ben-Gurion to pay huge reparations to Israel for the Holocaust. All this financial aid provided capital for Israel's development and reduced (though it could never eliminate) its balance-of-payments deficit.

Equally crucial to the country's survival was the Israelis' conviction that the Jewish people must never again face the threat of extinction, whether by Christian fanatics, totalitarian dictators, or Arab nationalists. If any skeptics asked how the existence of tiny Israel, with a million Jews and as many problems, better guaranteed Jewish survival than the continued presence of 10 million Jews in the West (of whom few chose to move to Israel), the Zionists countered that Germany's Jews had prospered too, but who had rescued them from Hitler? If others accused the Israelis of creating an Arab refugee problem, they in turn blamed the Arab states. Israel was taking in Jewish refugees from Europe and the Arab countries as well. If it could not have peace without letting the Palestinian refugees return, as the United Nations insisted, then peace would have to wait.

Because the Israelis view their war against the Arabs as a struggle for independence, we forget that up to 1947 few Jews in Palestine or anywhere else really expected the Jewish state to be born in their lifetime. As a minority group within a mainly Arab land, the early Zionist pioneers had toiled to start farms in the wilderness; to build Tel Aviv amid the sand dunes north of Jaffa; to transplant the schools, theaters, and newspapers they had known in Europe; and to found new institutions, such as Histadrut, that combined labor and capital within a collectively governed organization. They had formed political parties espousing various combinations of socialism, nationalism, and Judaism. They had revived Hebrew as a spoken language and modernized it as a medium of written communication. But they had assumed that the Jewish national home would remain part of the British Commonwealth, that most of its inhabitants would be European, and that the Arabs would somehow get used to their presence and power. World War II, the Holocaust, and the 1948 war had belied these assumptions. Now Israel was an independent state, surrounded by Arab countries implacably opposed to its existence, with Jews pouring in from all parts of the world (mainly from the Middle East and North Africa), and with an unexpectedly small Arab minority. Despite their political inexperience and economic problems, though, the Israelis managed to build a nation-state with a democratic government and a remarkable freedom from repression—at least for Jews.

*Politics in Israel*

Israel's democracy is not an exact copy of Britain's. Political parties, some of them holdovers from Jewish movements in pre-1914 Eastern Europe, proliferated. No party could ever win the support of a majority of Israel's voters, which included doctrinaire socialists, observant Orthodox Jews, secular Zionists, and Arab nationalists. Furthermore, Israel did not adopt the system of geographical constituencies familiar to Anglo-Saxons; rather, it set up a representation system by which the percentage of votes cast in a general election for each party was exactly matched by the proportion of seats it held in the following session of Israel's legislature, the Knesset. In other words, if 1,000,000 Israelis voted in an election and 300,000 supported a particular party, then, out of the 120 Knesset seats, 36 would go to the top candidates on that party's list. To put it another way, the first 36 candidates listed by that party on the ballot would enter the Knesset, whereas those numbered 37 and beyond would not. Decisions on ranking the candidates were made beforehand in party caucuses, not by the voters. Following a pattern familiar to Europeans but not to Americans, executive power was vested in a council of ministers (or cabinet) responsible to the Knesset. The head of government, or prime minister, had to choose a cabinet acceptable to a majority of the Knesset members. As no party has ever won a majority of the votes (hence the Knesset seats) in any election, any leader wanting to form a government has had to combine his or her party with several others, compromising on ideological principles or policy preferences in the bargain.

In the early years of the state, Israel's leading politician was David Ben-Gurion, the leader of the moderate labor party known as *Mapai*. Even though Ben-Gurion came to personify Israel in the minds of most foreigners and even many Israelis, *Mapai* never won more than 40 percent of the vote in any general election. In order to form a cabinet, Ben-Gurion always had to form a coalition with other labor parties and usually with the National Religious party, whose leaders were determined to make Israel a more observant Jewish state. Even though Ben-Gurion and his followers were nonobservant in their private lives and secular in their public statements, they had to make compromises with the National Religious party. The result was a socialist republic with no formal constitution, no official religion, and no explicit reference to God in its declaration of independence. Yet the army and all government offices kept the kosher dietary laws, no buses ran on the Jewish sabbath (from sundown Friday until sundown Saturday) except in Haifa and mainly Arab areas, and all marriages and divorces were handled by the religious courts. State school systems were set up for Israelis who followed Jewish laws, for those who wanted their children to speak Hebrew but were nonobservant, and for Arabs who wanted their children to be educated in their own language and culture.

What made such a complex system work? Given Israel's huge economic problems, a population so diverse in culture, and no reliable outside power to protect the state against its numerous foes, many outsiders shook their heads in disbelief. Maybe Israel survived because the Arabs were so hostile. But it would be fairer to say that Israel's system worked because its leaders, haunted by the memory of what Hitler had tried to do, felt that no personal or ideological preference was more important than the security of the state, which they equated with the survival of the Jewish people. It was hard for a passionate Zionist like Ben-Gurion to admit that anyone could live a full Jewish life outside Israel, although experience soon proved that Israel needed the political and financial support of a strong and prosperous Jewish diaspora. It also became evident that the rebirth of a Jewish state strengthened the faith and practice of religion among Jews outside Israel, despite the corrosive influence of secularism and materialist ideologies on much of the modern world.

## Israel's Foreign Relations

It is true, though, that Arab hostility complicated Israeli life. All road and rail connections between Israel and its neighbors were cut. Planes going to and from Israel could not fly over Arab countries, let alone land in their airports. The Arab states refused to trade with Israel and boycotted the products of any foreign firm doing business there. Israeli citizens, Jews from abroad, and even foreign Gentiles whose passports showed that they had visited Israel were barred entry to many of the Arab countries. Ships carrying goods to Israel could not pass through the Suez Canal or even enter Arab ports. Egypt blockaded the Tiran Straits between the Red Sea and the Gulf of Aqaba, stifling the growth of an Israeli port at Eilat. Arab diplomats abroad shunned their Israeli counterparts. Arabic books, newspapers, and radio broadcasts virulently attacked Israel and its supporters.

Thus beleaguered, the Israelis might have been expected to develop symptoms of psychopathic hostility to outsiders. A few did. It was said (by Jews and Gentiles alike) that Israelis were rude and hard to deal with— like the native prickly pear (*sabra*) which has a tough skin and is covered with long thorns, yet is sweet once you get through its defenses. Almost every part of Israel was near an Arab country, and border raids occurred often. Frequent, too, were Israel's retaliatory strikes against Arab villages and refugee camps blamed for the raids. The winding armistice line between Israel and Jordan posed special security problems, especially when it cut off a village from its customary farming or grazing lands. Israel's retaliatory raid against Gaza in 1955 was what convinced Nasir that Egypt must buy communist bloc weapons to strengthen its armed forces. Israel bought some of the arms it needed from such friendly countries as France, but whenever possible it manufactured its own.

The growing frequency of Arab *fidaiyin* raids, plus the mounting fervor of hostile propaganda, led Israel's cabinet to take stronger military measures in 1956. When Britain and France prepared to attack Egypt, Israel quickly joined their conspiracy. All three hoped to punish the Arabs, mainly Nasir, for seizing the Suez canal and threatening Israel. The stated concern was for the safety of international waterways; the unstated one was Europe's growing need for Arab (and Iranian) oil.

## MIDDLE EASTERN OIL

Middle East history since 1948 risks becoming an account of the military and political struggle between the Arabs and Israel. But let us not ignore other developments that were taking place in the region. Not all Middle Easterners are Israelis or Arabs: Iranians and Turks have countries and concerns of their own; most Middle Eastern countries have minorities who do not share their governments' preoccupations; and there are times when Zionists and Arab nationalists think about matters unrelated to their conflict. Please keep these facts in mind.

At any rate, we cannot gloss over one development that took place after 1948 in Middle Eastern lands far from Israel: Oil exports were becoming the main source of income for the states bordering on the Gulf. The leading Middle Eastern oil producer for the first half of the twentieth century was Iran, which is not an Arab country. In 1951, amid a crescendo of nationalism, Iran's prime minister, Mohammad Mosaddiq, nationalized the Anglo-Iranian Oil Company. In retaliation, Britain and most of its Western allies refused to buy any oil from Iran, causing a spectacular rise in the demand for Arab oil, to the benefit of Iraq, Saudi Arabia, and Kuwait. Let me cite a few clarifying examples. Iraq's oil production rose from 3.4 million long tons (3.8 regular or 3.5 metric tons) in 1948 to 33.1 in 1955. For

Saudi Arabia, the increase was still more dramatic: from 1 million long tons in 1944 to 46 million in 1954. The champion, though, was Kuwait, whose oil output shot up from 800,000 in 1946 to 54 million in 1956.

Not only did the production and sale of Arab oil (and natural gas) sky-rocket, but the concessions were revised to favor the host countries. This meant that some Arab government revenues also rose dramatically. In 1950 the Arabian American Oil Company (Aramco) reached an agreement with the government of Saudi Arabia on a fifty-fifty sharing of all revenues. Soon other oil-exporting Arab countries won comparable increases in their royalty payments from the foreign oil companies. Oil revenues became the main source of income for most states surrounding the Gulf, enabling governments like Iraq to embark on ambitious development schemes, whereas patriarchal rulers expanded their palaces and replaced their camels with air-conditioned Cadillacs. The main example of the latter was Sa'ud, the king of Saudi Arabia from 1953 until his deposition in 1964. Later, these oil-rich desert kingdoms would gain the financial power to influence the policies of the other Arab states and even the West. Iran, for its part, agreed after Mosaddiq's overthrow in 1953 to place its nationalized oil company under the administration of a consortium of foreign companies, mainly U.S. firms—a fact noted by most Iranians and ignored by most foreigners at the time. The potential power of Iranian and Arab oil producers was not realized in the 1950s, or indeed the 1960s, so I will put off this topic. But keep in mind that by 1956 Europeans were using more oil than coal and they imported most of their petroleum and natural gas from the Middle East.

## THE GREAT POWERS AND THE ARAB WORLD

Nasir's notoriety resulted from his decision in July 1956 to nationalize the Suez Canal Company amid Arab applause—and to Western dismay. Britain, even though it had agreed in 1954 to give up its Suez Canal base, still viewed the canal as the imperial lifeline it had been in the two world wars. Prime Minister Eden likened Nasir to Hitler and Mussolini. Recalling his own opposition to Britain's appeasement policy in the late 1930s, Eden wanted Nasir stopped before he could undermine the West's position throughout the Arab world. France, too, wanted to stop Nasir, mainly because Egypt was backing, with words and weapons, the Algerian revolution. Both Britain and France got most of their oil from tankers that passed through the canal; the two countries were sure the Egyptians could not manage it. Though many Americans disliked Nasir for his hostility to

Israel and his ties with communist states, neither President Dwight Eisenhower nor Secretary of State Dulles sought a military showdown. Eisenhower was then seeking reelection on a slogan of "peace and prosperity." This was no time for a Suez war.

## The Suez Affair

Britain and France disagreed with the United States. They prepared openly to retake the canal by force, despite logistical problems that kept delaying the date of their attack. Israel, eager to clean out the *fidaiyin* bases in Gaza and to break Egypt's blockade of the Gulf of Aqaba, mobilized for a preventive strike against Egypt. Meanwhile, the UN Security Council debated measures to head off trouble. Egypt, which was running the canal more efficiently than anyone had expected, spurned proposals for international control and treated those military preparations as a big bluff.

They were not. On 28 October 1956, Israel called up its reserves, thereby doubling the number of its citizens under arms, and invaded Egypt the following day. As the attackers cut off Gaza and drove into Sinai, Britain and France issued a joint ultimatum to both countries, calling for an immediate cease-fire and for troop withdrawals to positions 10 miles (16 kilometers) from the Suez Canal. As Israel's forces were still in the eastern Sinai at the time, this ultimatum was really directed against Egypt. When Nasir rejected it, Britain and France bombarded Egypt's air bases, landed paratroops at Port Said, and occupied the northern half of the Suez Canal. Soviet arms did not enable Nasir's army to defend Egypt against what Egyptians called the "tripartite aggression." Soon Israel occupied all of Sinai, and only a heroic but futile civilian resistance delayed the British capture of Port Said.

But Nasir was not overthrown by either his army or his people. Instead, his military defeat turned into a political victory. The United States joined the USSR in condemning the attack in the United Nations. The General Assembly agreed to set up a United Nations Emergency Force (UNEF) to occupy Egyptian lands taken by the invaders. Britain and France did not get to keep the canal, Nasir was not discredited in the eyes of Egyptians or other Arabs, and Israel could not obtain recognition and peace from the Arabs, even after a four-month occupation of the Sinai Peninsula and the Gaza Strip. Israel finally withdrew under heavy U.S. pressure, and its main gain from the war was a vague guarantee that its ships could use the Gulf of Aqaba, hitherto blockaded by Egypt. A UNEF contingent was stationed at Sharm al-Shaykh, a fortified point controlling the Tiran Straits between the Gulf of Aqaba and the Red Sea. This arrangement, backed informally by the western maritime powers, lasted up to May 1967.

Nasir had survived the Suez Affair because the United Nations—and especially the United States—had saved him. Washington justified its opposition to the tripartite attack on Egypt as backing small nations of the Afro-Asian bloc against imperialist aggression. The abortive Hungarian revolution was going on at the same time. How could the United States condemn Soviet intervention to smother a popular uprising in Budapest while condoning a Western attack on Port Said? A more cogent reason, though, was that the crisis occurred only days before the presidential election, hardly the time for a confrontation with the USSR. Thus the U.S. government managed to alienate the British, the French, and the Israelis. It won little gratitude from Nasir and the Arabs.

The Eisenhower administration thought that its pro-Arab tilt in the Suez Affair would persuade the Arab governments to back the West against communism. The loss of the British and French hold in the Arab world seemed likely to create a power vacuum that the USSR and its allies would fill if the United States did not move in resolutely. Only Iraq had formally joined the anticommunist military alliance (the Baghdad Pact), and no other Arab state would commit itself so firmly to the West. Most cut diplomatic ties with France and Britain after the Suez invasion.

## The Eisenhower Doctrine

Yet some Americans thought that an aid offer might win over some Arab governments. Thus was born the Eisenhower Doctrine, a program in which the U.S. government offered military and economic aid to any Middle Eastern country trying to resist communist aggression, whether direct or indirect. When it was announced in January 1957, the Eisenhower Doctrine probably helped impress the American public with the importance of the Middle East. It may have deterred the USSR from a more assertive policy in the area, but its reception in Arab capitals was decidedly cool. Only Lebanon accepted it. Arab nationalists viewed it as a U.S. attempt to assume Britain's role as guardian of the Middle East. To them, the Suez Affair had proved that Zionism and imperialism endangered the Arab world more than did any hypothetical threat of communist aggression. Nasir in Egypt and the Ba'th party in Syria vehemently denounced the Eisenhower Doctrine, whereas Iraq's Nuri al-Sa'id endorsed it. He knew what was best for the Arabs. After all, as he remarked, he had helped lead the Arab Revolt before Nasir was born!

The struggle between the neutralist and pro-Western Arabs climaxed in Jordan. The annexation of the rump of Arab Palestine (the West Bank) by what had been Transjordan strained that country. The Palestinians were more urbanized, educated, and politicized than the Transjordanians. They hated Israel, the Western powers that they blamed for creating and sustaining it, and the Arab leaders who had failed to destroy it. Many Palestinians in Jordan loathed Hashimite rule; they saw King Husayn as a playboy propped up by his Arab Legion with its bedouin soldiers and British officers.

Trying to win Palestinian support, Husayn had given in to Arab demands in 1955 to keep Jordan out of the Baghdad Pact. Early in 1956 he dismissed General Glubb as head of the Arab Legion. Free elections in October resulted in a popular front cabinet that included Arab nationalists and even a communist minister. Britain began pulling its troops out of Jordan and stopped subsidizing its government, but Egypt, Saudi Arabia, and Syria agreed to take up the slack. Ba'thist and pro-Nasir officers within Jordan's army began replacing royalists; early in April 1957 they threatened to seize Husayn's palace. A few days later the Arab nationalists tried to capture a major Jordanian army base, but the king rallied loyal troops to his side and personally faced down the threat to his rule. He proceeded to dismiss the popular front cabinet, declare martial law, dissolve Parliament, and set up what amounted to a royal dictatorship. Dulles then announced that Jordan's territorial integrity was a vital U.S. interest and sent ships and troops to the eastern Mediterranean. In effect, the Eisenhower Doctrine was first used to thwart an Arab nationalist takeover in Jordan. Even backed by the Americans, Husayn's stance was precarious. Palestinians, especially the refugees, still opposed the monarchy, which was being assailed in Radio Cairo's widely heard broadcasts.

Meanwhile, the Lebanese government of President Kamil Sham'un accepted the Eisenhower Doctrine, despite Arab nationalist protests that to do so would violate Lebanon's neutrality. Pro-Western politicians, mainly Christians, held more power than the Arab nationalists, most of whom were Muslim. Some detractors accused Sham'un's government of increasing its power by rigging the 1957 parliamentary elections, in which many opposition leaders failed to get reelected. Arab nationalists, backed by Palestinian refugees in Lebanon and by Egypt and Syria, opposed the regime's pro-Western leanings and accused Sham'un of trying to keep himself in power. The stage was being set for Lebanon's 1958 civil war.

## The Contest for Control of Syria

A British journalist named Patrick Seale has written an analysis of Arab politics from 1945 to 1958 called *The Struggle for Syria*. As the title implies, he argued that any power, local or foreign, that seeks to dominate the Middle East must control centrally located Syria. Although geographic Syria includes Lebanon, Israel, and Jordan, even the truncated Republic of Syria has become a cockpit for international rivalries. Between the two world wars, France and Britain had competed for control over geographic Syria, and in the Cold War the United States and the USSR contended for its favor. Rivalries among the other Arab regimes have been even stronger. After World War II Amir Abdallah of Transjordan aspired to rule a "Greater Syria," so he sought allies within the country. So, too, did his main rivals, Kings Faruq and Ibn Sa'ud. Geography has almost dictated Iraq's interest in Syria, and Egypt has usually opposed this interest, no matter who ruled in Baghdad or Cairo.

Syrian politicians, sensitive to these rivalries, have tended to ally themselves with the outside contenders in their own power struggles in Damascus. After all, Syrians have usually been in the vanguard of Arab nationalism. It was Syrians who had formed the Ba'th party, which was committed to the unification of all Arabic-speaking peoples within a framework that would ensure individual freedom and build a socialist economy. The Ba'th constitution states: "The Arab nation has an immortal mission that has manifested itself in renewed and complete forms in the different stages of history and that aims at reviving human values, encouraging human development, and promoting harmony and cooperation among the nations of the world."

If the Arab nation were to fulfill this mission, the Ba'th would have to take over as many Arab governments as possible and weld them into an organic unity. Its first success was in Syria. In early 1957, after the Suez Affair had compromised the country's pro-Western politicians, a coalition of Ba'thists and other Arab nationalists won control of the government. Spurred by Radio Cairo broadcasts and generous Soviet loans, Syria's new rulers adopted what the West took to be a communist stance. Scarred by previous military coups backed by outsiders, Syria accused Washington of plotting its overthrow and expelled several U.S. embassy officials. As Turkey massed troops on its Syrian border, both the United States and the Soviet Union threatened to step in to help their client states. The crisis cooled off by November 1957, but it caused some Americans to view Syria as a communist satellite.

## The United Arab Republic

Not true! Syria's leaders were Arab nationalists, not communists. A communist takeover in Damascus would have stifled the Ba'th or perhaps set off a conservative countercoup like that of King Husayn in Jordan. The Ba'thists saw their salvation in a union with Nasir's Egypt. Nasir would have preferred a gradual federation of the two states, but Syria's leaders could not wait. In February 1958 Syria's president, meeting with Nasir in Cairo, agreed to combine their two countries. Henceforth, Syria and Egypt would be the "northern region" and the "southern region" of a new state, the United Arab Republic (UAR). Plebiscites held later that month in both regions ratified the agreement. The people voted almost unanimously for Nasir (the ballot offered no other choice) as their president. Outsiders accused Egypt of annexing Syria, but it was the Syrians who rejoiced loudest over the new union.

Union with Egypt settled Syria's internal unrest, at least briefly, but it put heavy pressure on other Arab governments to follow suit. The Hashimite kings, Jordan's Husayn and Iraq's Faysal II, reacted to the United Arab Republic by forming a rival union of their own, one more homogeneous but less popular. Saudi Arabia kept aloof but may have betrayed its concern when a leading Syrian politician accused King Sa'ud of offering him a bribe to murder Nasir and rupture the union with Egypt. As I mentioned in Chapter 14, this accusation led to the fall of Sa'ud (who had succeeded his father, Ibn Sa'ud, in 1953) from power. His brother and heir apparent, Faysal, took charge of Saudi finances and foreign affairs. Although he was widely regarded as pro-Nasir in 1958, Faysal stayed out of the UAR, preferring not to share his country's immense oil revenues with Egypt and Syria. Yemen's ultraconservative government did agree to federate with the UAR, but this action had no effect on its own internal politics. The Palestinians rejoiced at the union between Egypt and Syria, hoping that Nasir would soon restore them to their usurped homeland. But Israelis reacted calmly to this threatened Arab revival.

## Lebanon's First Civil War

However, the other non-Muslim state east of the Mediterranean—Lebanon—felt the winds of Arab nationalism. The lure of Arab unity was strong in Lebanon among several groups: Palestinians, especially those living in refugee camps; Muslim Lebanese, who felt that the status quo favored Christians; young people, mainly university students, who believed that Lebanon's aloofness from Arab nationalism benefited only Western imperialism; and those Lebanese politicians who were excluded from power by the Sham'un regime. Many groups made the short trip to Damascus to hail the union with Egypt. Demonstrations took place in many cities and villages. When Beirut's Muslim sections put up Nasir posters, Christians festooned their quarters with pictures of Sham'un. Tensions built up during the spring. The spark that lit the fire was the assassination of a pro-Nasir newspaper editor in May 1958. Arab nationalists were quick to blame the government and to accuse Sham'un of plotting to amend Lebanon's constitution to secure himself a second term as president. A heterogeneous opposition, led by city politicians and rural grandees, banded together as a "national front." Shooting incidents reignited ancient feuds in the countryside, the government declared a curfew, and the first Lebanese civil war began. In some ways, the war was like a comic opera: Bombs exploded at random, rebel leaders were allowed to use the government phone and postal facilities, and the army did nothing. The Sham'un regime accused Nasir of aiding the rebels by smuggling arms across the Syrian border. It appealed to the Arab League and then to the UN Security Council to stop this threat to Lebanon's independence. A UN observer group could not corroborate charges of massive infiltration from Syria, but observers confined their operations to daylight hours on major roads, so they could not see much.

Lebanon's civil war might just have wound down, once President Sham'un let the Parliament elect his successor. The rebel leaders did not really want Lebanon to join the United Arab Republic, even if they welcomed Nasir's support. What brought this war into the wider arena was a concurrent event in another Arab state, the Iraqi revolution of 14 July 1958. In a sudden coup, a group of officers seized control of the police camps, the radio station, and the royal palace in Baghdad. They murdered King Faysal II and his uncle, Abd al-Ilah, hunted down and shot Nuri al-Sa'id, and declared Iraq a republic. Most Arabs rejoiced at the monarchy's downfall, but the West was horrified. The new regime seemed the embodiment of Arab nationalism and communism combined, a triumph for Nasir, a harbinger of the fate awaiting Jordan and Lebanon, and a stalking horse for Soviet imperialism in the Middle East. Despite their refusal to stop Nasir in 1956, the Americans now wanted to invade Iraq.

## U.S. Military Intervention

The U.S. government immediately dispatched marines to Lebanon, responding to Shamun's plea for aid under the Eisenhower Doctrine, and

British troops were flown to Jordan, where Husayn's regime seemed to be in peril. The West would have intervened in Iraq if there had been any hope of restoring the monarchy, but Hashimite rule was finished in Baghdad, and few Iraqis wanted it restored. The new military junta ensured its own popularity by instituting land reform, proclaiming its support for Arab unity, and renouncing its military ties with the West. When the junta's fiery young nationalist who was second in command, Abd al-Salam Arif, flew to Damascus to meet Nasir, it seemed only a matter of time before Iraq would join the UAR. But the supreme revolutionary leader, Colonel Abd al-Karim Qasim, realized that Iraq's oil revenues would go a lot farther at home if they were not shared with 30 million Egyptians and 6 million Syrians. Arif was eased from power. Qasim started playing a risky game, balancing between Arab nationalists and communists. Iraq's new government bettered the lives of the masses, but many problems, notably the Kurdish rebellion in the oil-rich north, proved no easier for Qasim to resolve than they had been for the Hashimites.

## The Ideas of Nasirism

What did Nasir believe in? For many people in the Arab world, and some in other Asian and African lands, he stood for their wish to defy Western imperialism. Not only Egypt but most Arab countries—indeed, most "Third World" nations—felt humiliated by the way the West had treated them in the past. These feelings, and the conviction that the Arabs could build themselves a better future, led to an ideology often called "Nasirism." Its main ideas were pan-Arabism, positive neutralism, and Arab socialism.

Pan-Arabism is Arab nationalism with a stress on political unification. Nasir and his supporters saw how foreign imperialism and dynastic rivalries had split up the Arabic-speaking peoples of the Middle East into a dozen or more countries. Thus divided, the Arabs had lost Palestine in 1948 and were still subject to the machinations of outsiders. For instance, even in the 1950s, the benefits of Arab oil were going to a few hereditary monarchs and foreign companies when they should have been shared by all the Arabs. Political unification would increase the wealth and power of the Arab world as a whole. Nasir's opponents equated his pan-Arabism with Egyptian imperialism. They accused him of trying to seize control of the rest of the Arab world to enrich Egypt in general and his own regime in particular.

Positive neutralism, as I have mentioned, was Nasir's policy of not aligning Egypt with either the communist bloc or the anticommunist military alliances that the United States promoted. Rather, it invited other countries to join Egypt in a loose association of nonaligned states. Thus Egypt, together with such countries as India and Yugoslavia, could thwart U.S. and Soviet efforts to line up the other countries of the world on opposing sides. Neutralism could reduce world tensions and maybe even resolve the cold war. Critics called the policy one of working both sides of the street, a means by which Nasir could extract military and economic aid from the communist bloc and the West at the same time.

Arab socialism has never been easy to define. It is not a coherent set of beliefs that emerged, fully articulated, in Egypt or the other Arab countries at any given time. Rather, it has evolved in reaction to the economic system prevalent up to the 1950s in most parts of the Arab world, a system in which "capitalism" really meant foreign ownership of major business enterprises or a more primitive system (often misnamed "feudalism") in which land, buildings, and other sources of wealth belonged to a small native elite while masses of Arab workers and peasants lived in dire poverty. To bring about reform, Arab socialists called on their governments to run the major industries and public utilities so as to divide the economic pie more evenly among the people. They also believed that this pie could be enlarged by comprehensive state planning to expand manufacturing and modernize agriculture. Although they borrowed some of their ideas and rhetoric from the Marxists, most Arab socialists opposed communism for its atheism and tried to prove that their ideology was compatible with Islam. They argued that shopkeepers and small-scale merchants ("national capitalists") could play a constructive role in Arab socialism. They rejected the Marxian concept of class struggle; if it were stimulated, they feared, class war would divide the Arab world even more and would dissipate energies needed to develop a modern economy. Critics said that Arab socialism lacked theoretical rigor, inflated Egypt's already swollen bureaucracy, and discouraged foreign investment.

## The Ebb of the Pan-Arab Tide

In retrospect, the summer of 1958 was the zenith of pan-Arabism. Just as Qasim's Iraq soon went its own way, so too did Saudi Arabia under Crown Prince Faysal. The U.S. Marines in Lebanon confronted more Coke vendors than communists. Lebanon's parliament chose the neutralist Fuad Shihab, the general who had kept the army out of the civil war, to replace the pro-Western Sham'un. U.S. troops pulled out, all factions agreed to respect the independence and neutrality of Lebanon, and their leaders resumed their favorite activity: making money. Britain likewise withdrew its troops from Jordan, but Husayn's regime did not fall, to everyone's surprise. A military coup in the Sudan in November 1958, at first thought to be pro-Nasir, did not unify the Nile Valley. Some Syrians started to wonder why no other country followed theirs into the UAR. During 1959–1961 Egypt's heavy-handed bureaucracy made further inroads into Syria's hitherto capitalistic economy. Even the Ba'th chafed when Nasir insisted that it, like all other Syrian parties, must be absorbed by his new single party, the National Union.

For a while, Nasir mended his fences with the West, mainly because Iraq had repudiated his backers in favor of the communists. But the USSR was playing a growing role in the UAR economy, and Nasir came to believe that state planning and control of all major industries would be needed to fulfill his promise to double the national income during the 1960s. In his July (1961) Laws, he nationalized nearly all factories, financial institutions, and public utilities in Egypt and Syria; reduced to about 100 acres (42 hectares) the maximum landholding allowed an individual; and put a ceiling on the salary that a UAR citizen might earn. These laws angered bourgeois Syrians so much that two months later an army coup in Damascus ended their union with Egypt. Soon after that, the UAR (as Egypt continued to be called, in case Syria rejoined the union) ended its federation with Yemen, after its imam had allegedly written verses satirizing the July Laws. At the end of 1961, Nasir, the leader who still aspired to unite the Arab world, stood alone.

## Arab Socialism and Nasir's Comeback

The tide of Nasirism had receded. Egypt now looked inward and focused on building a new order under Arab socialism. Nasir convened a "National Congress of Popular Forces" to draw up what he called the "national charter," published amid great fanfare in 1962. A new single party, the Arab Socialist Union, replaced the flagging National Union, and half the seats in its national council were earmarked for workers and peasants. Workers were put on the managing boards of some nationalized companies. For the first time in Egypt's history, a worker and a woman took charge of cabinet ministries. If his socialist experiment promoted economic growth and social equality, Nasir reasoned, other Arab countries would imitate Egypt. Defying political isolation, he adopted a new slogan: "Unity of goals, not unity of ranks."

The first sign of a change was Algeria's independence in July 1962 after a bitter eight-year struggle against France. Algeria's leader, Ahmad Ben Bella, supported Nasir and all revolutionary Arab causes. The second sign was the revolution that broke out in Yemen that September, only a week after the old imam had died and Prince Badr had taken over. A group of military officers seized power in San'a and proclaimed Yemen a republic. Elated, Egypt's government hailed the new regime and assumed that Badr had been killed. In fact, he and his followers had fled to the hills, where monarchist tribesmen were ready to fight for their imam (who, as his title implies, was a religious as well as a political leader). They were backed by the Saudis, who feared a subversive Nasirite republic on their southern border. Nasir sent an Egyptian force to aid Yemen's new regime, but its leaders were inexperienced. The civil war that started as a contest between followers of Imam Badr (mainly Zaydi Shi'is in the hills) and republican officers (mainly Shafi'i Sunnis living near the Red Sea) became a five-year proxy struggle between conservative Saudi Arabia and revolutionary Egypt.

More heartening news for Nasir came in early 1963, when Ba'thist officers staged two successive coups: Qasim's ouster in Iraq by Abd al-Salam Arif, followed by the toppling of Syria's separatist regime. Soon Iraq and Syria adopted identical flags, swore eternal Arab brotherhood, and sent delegates to Cairo to negotiate with Nasir for a new United Arab Republic. Popular enthusiasm for Arab unity reached a new peak in April 1963, when Egypt, Syria, and Iraq published plans for organic unification. But again people's hopes were dashed, as Nasir and the Ba'th party failed to agree on how the new state should be led. For the rest of the year, disillusioned Arab governments, newspapers, and broadcasters hurled invectives at one another.

## The Jordan Waters Dispute

It was an Israeli move that brought the Arabs back together. Ever since Israel's rebirth, its scientists and engineers had tried to get more fresh water to irrigate its lands. Hydrologists argued that the Jordan River could be harnessed to irrigate both Israel and Jordan. An American emissary named Eric Johnston had secured an agreement from both countries on the technical aspects of a plan to share the Jordan waters, but Jordan's government rejected it on political grounds in 1955. For a few years, Israel hoped Jordan might relent, but then it decided to go ahead and build a national water carrier to meet its own needs, taking from the Sea of

Galilee the share of Jordan River waters that would have been allocated to Israel under the Johnston Plan.

Israel's tapping of the Jordan waters galvanized the Arab countries into action. If Jordan, Syria, and Lebanon could divert the main tributaries of the Jordan River, perhaps Israel would be deterred from completing its national water carrier. But Israel threatened preemptive air strikes against any Arab diversion projects. Nasir invited the Arab kings and presidents to Cairo to discuss the issue, and they all met at the Nile Hilton in January 1964. Though unable to act in concert against Israel, the Arabs decided to hold further summits in 1964 and 1965. The consensus was that the Arab armies could not yet confront Israel, but that they would build up their military strength so that Syria and Jordan could divert the tributaries of the Jordan River.

## The Palestine Liberation Organization

Another act of the 1964 summit meetings drew relatively little outside attention, but it would prove fateful for the Arab world. Arab leaders voted to form the Palestine Liberation Organization (PLO). This group was to act as an umbrella organization for all clubs, societies, and paramilitary groups serving the Palestinian Arabs. Encouraged by Nasir, Palestinian representatives met in Jerusalem's Old City in 1964, asked a veteran spokesman named Ahmad al-Shuqayri to appoint an executive board for the PLO, and adopted a national charter. Its main principles were that the Palestinian Arabs must fight to regain their homeland within what had been the British mandate borders and that they alone had the right of self-determination in Palestine, although Jews of Palestinian origin might still live in the liberated country. To replace the State of Israel, the Palestinians proposed a "secular democratic state" in which Jews, Christians, and Muslims would coexist in peace.

The PLO began assembling a conventional army, made up of refugees in Gaza, Jordan, and Syria. But a more dramatic and effective force was a guerrilla movement called al-Fatah (which can be translated as "Conquest" or Movement for the Liberation of Palestine). Fatah signaled its existence on 1 January 1965 by trying to sabotage part of Israel's national water-carrier system. Its leader was Yasir Arafat, who claimed to have come from Jerusalem, had fought against Israel in 1948, then became the leader of the Palestinian students in Egypt and lived for a few years in Kuwait. More than Shuqayri, Arafat spoke for militant younger Palestinians. Fatah's attacks, supported by Syria but generally launched from Jordan, caused serious casualties and property damage within Israel. The Israeli government, headed since 1963 by Levi Eshkol, decided to force the Arab armies to curb these commando operations. In late 1966 the Israeli army made a devastating retaliatory raid into the Jordanian West Bank, striking at commando bases in the village of al-Samu'. This move set off angry protests against Israel from Western as well as Arab governments. The UN Security Council unanimously condemned Israel's raid. Even some Israelis thought that they should have attacked Syria, which had backed the commandos materially and vocally, rather than Jordan.

## Background to the 1967 War

By the mid-1960s Syria had once again emerged as the most radical Arab nationalist state. Unable to form a union with Egypt or even with Iraq in 1963, its Ba'thist government pressed harder for Arab unity and military action against Israel. It spearheaded the attempts to divert the Jordan river sources, fired from the Golan Heights down on Israelis farming the no-man's-land at its border, and armed various Palestinian commando groups. An army coup in February 1966 brought to power an even more radical wing of the Ba'th party. Most of the new leaders belonged to a mysterious minority, the Alawi religious sect, many of whose members had joined the Syrian officer corps to advance themselves socially. Hoping to win over the Sunni majority in Syria, these young Alawi officers took pains to uphold the principles of Arabism and hence those of the struggle against Israel. By this time Nasir had realized that his army, still bogged down in Yemen's civil war, would not be ready to fight against Israel for a long time. Egypt's relations with Washington had sunk to a new low after its air force shot down a U.S. civilian plane and President Lyndon Johnson (whom Nasir detested) cut off surplus wheat sales. The USSR still backed Nasir but withheld the offensive weapons he needed to attack Israel. Nasir hoped to restrain Syria's new leaders from drawing Egypt into another war by making a military alliance with them.

This was a serious miscalculation. In April 1967 Syrian planes got into a dogfight with the Israelis and came out a poor second. Eshkol warned Syria that Israel would retaliate unless it stopped firing on Israeli settlements near its borders. In early May the Soviets told Nasir that Israel was massing troops in its north for a preemptive attack on Syria. Egypt called up its reserves, routed tanks through Egypt's cities and into the Sinai, and made threats against Israel. Nasir may have been bluffing to impress Syria, but no one thought so at the time. For months, his rivals, especially the

Saudis, had taunted him for hiding behind UNEF in Gaza and Sinai. On 16 May Nasir asked the United Nations to withdraw some of its peace-keeping units. Secretary-General U Thant promptly pulled out all UN forces (to Nasir's amazement), without even consulting the Security Council. Once UNEF had evacuated all the key points in Gaza and Sinai, Egyptian military units moved in. Among the strategic points they occupied was Sharm al-Shaykh, from which they renewed the Arab blockade against Israeli shipping through the Gulf of Aqaba. Nasir's prestige soared again throughout the Arab world.

This blockade, illegal according to Israel's supporters, has come to be seen as the main cause of the ensuing war of June 1967. Israel could not allow its trade from Eilat (important in asserting ties with South Asia and East Africa, though minor compared with its Mediterranean trade) to be throttled in this way. Besides, as Arab newspapers and radio stations were openly calling for a war to destroy the Jewish state, the Israelis could hardly assume that the Arab governments would stop at blockading the Gulf of Aqaba. But what should they do? Their passage through the Tiran Straits had been guaranteed by the Western powers. The U.S. government, mired in the Vietnam War, counseled caution. The European governments, realizing that they imported most of their oil from the Arab world, had cooled toward Israel since the Suez Affair. It seemed futile to wait for a Western flotilla to force open the Tiran Straits or to expect resolute action from the UN Security Council. Israel's leaders wanted peace, but they did not want to commit national suicide.

After King Husayn flew to Cairo on 30 May to conclude an agreement with Nasir on a joint Arab military command, Israel's cabinet assumed that war was inevitable. Most reserve units were called up, the whole economy was put on a war footing, and Israel's political leaders buried their quarrels to create a new cabinet that would represent nearly all parties and factions within the state. Especially significant was the appointment on 2 June of General Moshe Dayan as defense minister, despite his perennial personal and political differences with Prime Minister Eshkol. A hero in the 1948 independence war and the 1956 Sinai campaign, Dayan gave the Israelis new hope in what seemed to be their hour of peril. No one knew for sure what would happen next.

## CONCLUSION

The history of the Middle East after May 1967 was so dominated by the Arab-Israeli conflict that the preceding era seems serene by comparison.

But this chapter has shown that its political history was turbulent indeed. Outside powers deserve some of the blame for fishing in troubled waters, but how were those waters troubled in the first place? You may be confused by the clash of personalities and policies, especially in the Arab east. Are there no shortcuts, no generalizations, no keys to understanding all these details?

Rapid changes, especially in education and technology, were breaking down the customary modes of life and thought. Masses of people, most poor and young, flocked to the big cities. Alien ideas and customs, first embraced in these growing urban centers, spread everywhere by means of that underrated invention, the transistor radio, plus, of course, newspapers and magazines, schools and rural health centers, movies and (in some countries) television. Ideas of nationalism and progress seemed to make gains at the expense of religion and respect for tradition, just as the car and the truck replaced the camel and the donkey.

Was this good? Most people thought so at that time, but many nationalist slogans and ideologies have since proven false, and many Arabs did not understand these imported ideologies. As a blend of traditional and modern values, Nasirism now sounds like a personality cult. Positive neutralism was a natural reaction to the cold war, but why was Egypt's rejection of both the Western and the communist blocs deemed "positive"? Neutralism worked only so long as both sides were competing for Arab favor. Pan-Arabism overlooked the deep-seated differences within the Arab world, not just among leaders but also among their peoples, as well as between oil-rich and -poor countries. Arab nationalism tended to alienate religious and ethnic minorities, such as Lebanon's Maronites and Iraq's Kurds. Parliamentary democracy broke down when the masses were hungry and uneducated and when army officers and newly trained technicians were impatient to govern. Arab socialism failed to change Arab society from its traditional individualism, clannishness, and patriarchy into a collectivist economic system serving the common good.

Remember this book's early chapters, which told you how Islam as a doctrine and a way of life inspired the Arabs and their converts to submerge their cares and desires into one collective enterprise encompassing the conquests, the High Caliphate, and Islamic civilization. There have been many articulate Muslim thinkers, from Muhammad Abduh through Sayyid Qutb, but their voices were drowned out by those who spoke louder or tuned out by those who would not hear. Sayyid Qutb, a leading writer and Muslim Brother, was jailed and finally hanged in 1966 by Nasir's government despite pleas for clemency from other Arab countries.

How sad that no new Muslim leader came forth to recharge these batteries, to enlist the minds and muscles of men and women to rebuild the *ummah*, to harness the tools and techniques of modern industry to create an egalitarian society, and to make Islam a guide for right thoughts and actions in the modern world! What might the Arabs have achieved with stronger guidance and a more coherent set of beliefs?

Israel had problems, too. Political Zionism had achieved its goal of creating a Jewish state, but was it truly a light unto the Gentiles? Writing in 1963, Nadav Safran remarked that the most successful product that had come out of Israel since its creation was the Uzi submachine gun. Judaism as practiced during centuries of dispersion meant little to Israel's founders. Ben-Gurion and others wondered why so few Jews came to Israel from the West. With half of Israel's people having immigrated from elsewhere in the Middle East, were they becoming too much like their Arab neighbors? In reaction, Israelis developed cults of physical fitness and martial might, of archaeological quests to affirm their ties to the land, of redemption through the planting of trees. Divided on how Jewish they should be, they ranged from the ultra-observant (some refused to recognize the Jewish state until the Messiah came) to those who denied God's existence and the Bible's relevance to modern life. Jewish religious leadership was no better than its Muslim and Christian counterparts elsewhere. What part could the Arabs, a sixth of Israel's population, play in a state whose flag featured the Star of David and whose anthem expressed the Jews' longing for the land of Zion? What about the Arabs who had fled from Israel in 1948 and claimed the right to return? If Jews had remembered Zion for two thousand years, could Palestinians forget it in fewer than twenty? Amid the mists of ideological confusion and the dust of political combat brew the storms that have raged in the Middle East since 1967 and will dominate my final chapters.

# EIGHTEEN

# War and the Quest for Peace

On 5 June 1967 Israel launched a series of preemptive air strikes against its Arab neighbors who had threatened its very existence. Its consequent victory over Egypt, Syria, and Jordan took only six days. It refuted the notion, common after 1956, that the Jewish state could not defeat the Arabs without Western allies. It exploded the myth that "unity of goals" among the Arab states would enable them to defeat Israel and proved that the Israel Defense Force had attained high levels of skill, valor, and coordination in order to ensure the country's survival.

It also created a new myth, shared by supporters and enemies of the Jewish state, that Israel was invincible. This myth lasted until October 1973, when another war, begun by Egypt and Syria, exposed Israel's vulnerability. This October (or Yom Kippur) War was the most intensely fought, the costliest in lives and equipment, and the greatest threat to world peace of any war waged between the Arabs and Israel up to that time. It also set off a fourfold increase in the price of oil and nearly sparked a military showdown between the United States and the USSR. Its aftermath enlarged the U.S. role in trying to resolve the conflict. At first these attempts barely nudged Israel and the Arabs toward a settlement, but the peace process gained momentum through a series of interim agreements. Finally, Egypt's President Anwar al-Sadat broke the impasse in November 1977 with a dramatic flight to Jerusalem. A flurry of peace conferences and high-level meetings ensued. The end result was the Camp David Accords, followed by a treaty signed by Egypt and Israel in March 1979. But there was no comprehensive Arab-Israeli peace.

One of the overarching themes of Middle East history between 1967 and 1979 was the Arab-Israeli conflict. More than ever before, it held center stage in the Middle East drama. Many diaspora Jews turned into ardent Zionists. The Palestine question gained new significance in Arab states as remote as Morocco and Kuwait. Quarrels among the Arab countries and power struggles within them continued, but after 1967 they became secondary to the Arab-Israeli conflict. Hardly a month went by without some prediction that a new war was about to break out. Up to 1973 most people assumed that Israel—if adequately armed by the United States—would win any conventional war. Therefore, Palestinian *fidaiyin* came to dominate in Arab strategy against Israel.

After 1967 the USSR stepped up its role as arms supplier and adviser to many of the Arab states, as the United States did for Israel. This intensified superpower involvement in the conflict often threatened to escalate into World War III. As neither side wanted so drastic a confrontation, they frequently conferred together and with other powers over possible imposed solutions to the conflict. Many would suggest formulas. Neither the Arabs nor the Jews wanted the wars, the threats, and the tensions to go on forever. But at what price could each party accept peace with the other? The old Arab issue about the displaced Palestinians tended to give way to two others: return of Arab lands taken by Israel in June 1967 and recognition of the national rights of the Palestinian Arabs. The Israelis still demanded security and Arab recognition but argued among themselves over which of the captured lands—Jerusalem, the West Bank (which most Israelis call Judea and Samaria), the Gaza Strip, the Sinai, and the Golan Heights—they should give back in exchange for peace. Arms purchases claimed a growing share of every Middle Eastern government's budget, more young men in uniform risked dying before their time, and people's mental and physical energies had to shift from constructive to destructive endeavors. *Ma'lesh* (Never mind), said the Arabs; *Ma la'asot?* (What's to be done?), asked the Israelis. No matter, both sides felt: Survival and dignity were worth more than the highest price they (or their backers) could ever pay!

## THE JUNE 1967 WAR

The story of Israel's lightning victory over the Arabs in 1967 will be told and retold for years to come. It began when Israel's air force attacked the main air bases of Egypt—followed by those of Jordan and Syria—on the morning of 5 June and wiped out virtually all their war-making potential. Having gained air mastery in the first hour, Israel sent its army into Sinai and, in four days' fighting, took the whole peninsula. As he had done in 1956, Nasir ordered the Suez Canal blocked, but by taking Sharm al-Shaykh, Israel broke the blockade of the Gulf of Aqaba.

As King Husayn, hoping to share in any Arab gains, had made a pact with Nasir one week before the war that effectively put his army under Egyptian command, Jordan plunged into the war by firing into Israeli sections of Jerusalem. Israel's army then invaded the northern part of the West Bank (or Samaria) and also the north side of Arab Jerusalem to secure Mount Scopus (an Israeli enclave since the 1949 armistice) and to attack the Old City from its eastern side. On 7 June the Israelis took the city, after fierce fighting, and prayed at the Western Wall for the first time in nineteen years. Elsewhere on the West Bank Israeli forces drove back the Jordanians, under Husayn's direct command, in extremely tough combat. The Arabs accused Israel of dropping napalm on Jordanian troops and of using scare tactics to clear out some refugee camps and West Bank villages. Some 200,000 Arabs sought refuge across the Jordan, and new tent camps ringed the hills around Amman. Many Palestinians, after hearing promises from the Arab radio stations that Israel would be wiped out and that they would be allowed to return home, wondered why the Arab armies failed to work together for the desired victory.

Syria was the least helpful. Owing to recent border clashes with Jordan, the Syrians did nothing for Husayn until he was defeated. By then, Israel could storm Syria's well-fortified positions on the Golan Heights—no easy task—when no other Arab country would or could help the Damascus regime. If Israel and Syria had not agreed to a Security Council cease-fire on 10 June, nothing would have stopped the Israelis from marching into Damascus itself. Let me share with you the conclusion written by a Palestinian, Abdel Latif Tibawi, to his *Modern History of Syria* (1969): "Syria had often in history marched under the banner of Islam to victory and glory; it had yet to prove that it could do so under the banner of Arab nationalism."

*Reasons for the Outcome*

The 1967 war indeed discredited Arab nationalism. Beforehand the Arab forces had seemed superior on paper: Egypt alone had more men under arms than Israel, even if it mobilized all its reserve units; the Arabs had 2,700 tanks compared to 800 for Israel, 800 fighter planes to Israel's 190, and 217 ships to Israel's 37, and the population ratio was about 25 to 1. The Arabs enjoyed the wholehearted support of the communist bloc and most Asian and African nations, at a time when Washington's position (to quote a State Department spokesman) was "neutral in thought, word, and deed." Many Americans would have disputed this assertion, but with a half-million troops in Vietnam the United States could not have intervened, even if Israel had asked it to do so.

Why then did Israel win? One obvious reply is that Israel attacked first, destroyed most of the Arab fighter planes, and then kept complete control of the air. Another is that Egypt's best troops were still fighting in the Yemen civil war. The *New York Times* reported during the war that Israel probably had more troops on the field than its enemies, deployed better firepower, and used greater mobility in battle. Israel also had rapid internal transport and communication. The technical sophistication of Israel's soldiers—or even the fact that they all could read and write—helped. Israeli culture encouraged improvisatory thinking under pressure and egalitarian camaraderie between officers and fighting men. I do not claim that the Israeli soldiers were better than their Arab counterparts in strength, motor skills, or even bravery, but they did cooperate with their comrades-in-arms. Arab armies were riven by factionalism, and their governments did not trust one another. These factors contributed to the Arab defeat in 1948, as I wrote earlier. In 1967, even after most anachronistic monarchies and landowning elites had fallen from power, even after some fifteen years of pan-Arabism and social reform in Egypt and Syria, and even after billions of dollars worth of Soviet and Western arms had poured into the Arab world, the Arabs' divisiveness led to a swifter, more devastating defeat in 1967 than in 1948. Small wonder that Nasir, the Arab nationalist leader, tried to resign at the end of the war!

## The War's Aftermath

By the time the guns fell silent on 10 June, Israel had expanded its land area to three times what it had been six days earlier, having occupied the Gaza Strip, the Sinai Peninsula, the West Bank, and the Golan Heights (see Map 10). Almost a million Arabs, most of them Palestinians, had come under Israeli rule. Israel had not anticipated this. No one had drawn up contingency plans. Defense Minister Dayan and other Israeli officials had said during the war that they would defend, not expand, Israel's territory. Most Israelis were relieved just to find that they had not been annihilated and that the physical destruction and loss of Jewish lives, though certainly bad enough, were less than anyone had expected. Many hoped that the militant Arab leaders would be overthrown by the moderates or that the Arab governments would agree to talk about a peace settlement. In retrospect, it is too bad that both sides were not more accommodating. The Arabs would not negotiate from weakness (after all, some said, Hitler could not persuade Churchill to talk peace in 1940), whereas Israel decided to hold all the occupied lands as bargaining chips in the peace talks it hoped would ensue. Its new borders were shorter and more defensible

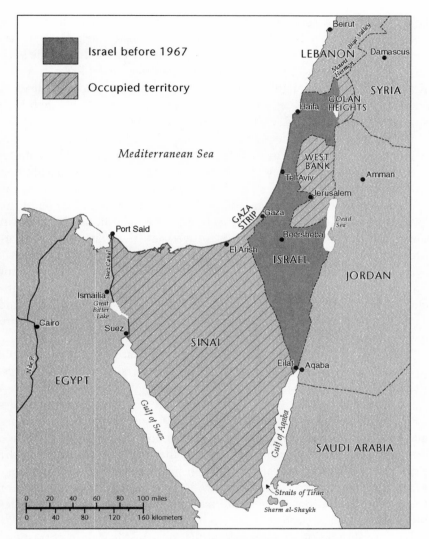

MAP 10 Israel and the occupied territories, 1967–1973

than the old ones had been. Soon some Israelis hoped to keep these lands, fueling Arab fears of Israeli expansionism.

## The United Nations

The Arabs believed that a just solution was more apt to come from the UN (as in 1956) than from direct negotiations. Responding to a Soviet call, the General Assembly held a special session that June, but none of the resolutions put forth by the various blocs could muster the necessary majority. After five futile weeks, the General Assembly handed the issue back to the Security Council. A summit meeting between Soviet Premier Alexei Kosygin and President Johnson also failed. In August the Arab leaders (none of whom had fallen from power because of the war) held their own summit in Khartum and resolved not to negotiate with Israel.

By the time the Security Council resumed its deliberations, both sides had hardened their positions. While the Arabs ruled out peace talks with Israel, the Israelis were making their occupation more visible in the captured territories. Arab houses were razed in Jerusalem's Old City to expand the space in front of the Western Wall. Suspected terrorists in Gaza and the West Bank were jailed or deported and sometimes their houses were blown up; whole villages and towns were destroyed. Jewish settlers, with government backing, began building settlements in the Golan Heights, the environs of Hebron, and East Jerusalem, notably on the hills connecting Mount Scopus with the western half of the city. Israel annexed East Jerusalem, including the Old City, defying a nearly unanimous General Assembly vote against the action. The USSR rearmed Syria and Egypt, sending them more technicians and advisers. The danger of a new war was rising.

It was left to the Security Council to devise a peace formula acceptable to Israel and the Arabs, as well as to the superpowers. During the debates, Britain's Lord Caradon devised a formula with the necessary ambiguity—the oft-quoted Resolution 242—to which all the permanent members could agree. It stressed "the inadmissibility of acquiring territory by war" and called for a just and lasting peace based on (1) withdrawal of Israeli armed forces from territories occupied in the recent conflict and (2) the right of every state in the area to "live in peace within secure and recognized boundaries free from threats and acts of force." It also called for freedom of navigation through international waterways and a "just settlement to the refugee problem."

Because Resolution 242 has joined the Husayn-McMahon correspondence and the Balfour Declaration in that gallery of ambiguous documents complicating the Arab-Israeli conflict, you should know what the parties to this conflict read into it. The Arabs saw the resolution as calling on Israel to return, as a precondition for peace, *all* the lands it had taken in the June war. Israel claimed that the resolution meant withdrawal from *some* of these lands, as each country was to live in peace within *secure* and recognized boundaries. Some Arabs interpreted the "just settlement to the refugee problem" to mean Israel's readmission of all displaced Palestinians wishing to return (the General Assembly had passed resolutions to that effect almost annually since 1948). Israel contended that the Palestinian refugees should be settled in the Arab countries. After all, the Arab states had expelled their Jewish citizens, most of whom had settled in Israel, and no one suggested letting them return to Iraq, Morocco, or Yemen.

Jordan, Israel, and Egypt agreed to abide by Resolution 242 (Syria, seeing it as a de facto recognition of Israel, rejected it until 1974), even though Arabs and Israelis disagreed on what it meant. Secretary-General U Thant asked a UN mediator, Gunnar Jarring, to bring the two sides closer together. But even as he began his ultimately fruitless mission in early 1968, the resolution's deficiencies were becoming apparent. One, clearly, was that each side expected the other to give in first. Another was that no limitation was put on the arms race, which was as feverish and financially debilitating as ever. Yet another was that the Arabs could still wage economic warfare against Israel and its backers—the boycott would go on. Finally, although this became clear only with the passage of time, Resolution 242 ignored the rights and interests of the Palestinian Arab people.

## THE PALESTINIANS

The emergence of the Palestinians as a separate factor in the Arab-Israeli conflict was one of the most dramatic developments in 1967. The idea that the Palestinians constitute a distinct people is novel. Never before in Middle East history had the Arabs living in Palestine sought or gained status as a separate and independent state. Quite the contrary, the Arabs of that region had usually chosen, if indeed they could exercise any choice at all, to claim a major identity: Muslim, Arab, or Greater Syrian. Before Israel's rebirth, Jews and foreigners often used the term *Palestinian* to denote the inhabitants of Palestine, but rarely had Arabs themselves used that label. Between 1948 and 1967, the Arabs from Palestine, especially the refugees in neighboring countries, had been the most ardent backers of pan-Arabism. They hoped to end all distinctions between them and the other Arabs whose aid they sought.

But Palestinians, because of their shared experiences and ideas, did come to see themselves as a people and then as a nation, just as surely as Eastern Europe's Jews had turned into Zionists in the early twentieth century. According to the Palestinians' view of their own past, the Jewish settlers in Palestine rejected the local Arabs before Israel attained statehood, expelled them during the 1948 war, and then refused to let them return to what had become Israel. The other Arab states would not, could not, and indeed should not have absorbed them. No country wanted them. But these refugees did not want to see themselves or to be seen by others as objects of pity, wards of the UN Relief and Works Agency, or causes of embarrassment to other Arabs. After the 1967 war revealed the inadequacy of the Arab states' armies, the Palestinians decided it was time to declare themselves a nation, get their own arms, train themselves to fight, and regain their lands, which the Arab armies had lost.

*Militant Palestinians*

As a result of the war, therefore, the Palestine Liberation Organization, set up in 1964 at the behest of the Arab governments, emerged as a more militant group. The older leaders, notably the loquacious Shuqayri, gave way to younger ones who, though no less determined to wipe out Israel by force of arms, knew better how to use the Western media to publicize their cause. It was easy to get support from the communist bloc, but the PLO wanted to win public opinion in Western Europe and North America over to the Palestinian cause. To do this, they could no longer call for Israel's destruction and the Jewish bloodbath or mass exodus that would most likely ensue. Rather, they claimed they would redeem what had been Palestine up to 1948 from the "false ideology" of Zionism, which debased the Jewish faith and oppressed the Christian and Muslim Arabs who had formerly constituted most of Palestine's population. Israel's leaders were likened to those of the white settlers of Rhodesia and South Africa. Palestinians viewed their *fidaiyin*, whom the Israelis called terrorists, as freedom fighters, like the Algerian Front de Liberation Nationale (National Liberation Front) under French rule or even like Partisans during the Nazi occupation of France. Some Americans, alienated by the Vietnam War, might be persuaded to identify Yasir Arafat, the leader of Fatah (the largest group of *fidaiyin*), with such contemporary New Left heroes as Che Guevara. Some did. But most could not equate Zionism with capitalism, racism, and fascism. The Palestine Liberation Organization also retained its covenant, calling for the destruction of Israel.

Early in 1968 the Israel Defense Force, stung into retaliatory action by Palestinian raids and bombings, attacked the Jordanian village of Karamah, some 25 miles (40 kilometers) west of Amman. Israel reportedly lost six jet fighters and twelve tanks in the battle before both sides accepted a new cease-fire. Many of Jordan's casualties were Palestinians from Fatah, whose role in resisting the IDF gave new luster to Arafat and his backers. Certainly Fatah outshone the regular armies of Egypt, Syria, and Jordan. Young men in the refugee camps and in many Arab cities and villages volunteered to join. Even King Husayn announced, after an IDF raid across the Jordan River, "We are all *fidaiyin* now." Foreign journalists flocked to interview Arafat and to visit his training camps. Some, impressed by his zealous nationalism, extolled his vision of a liberated Palestine that would be secular and democratic, a state where Jews, Christians, and Muslims might live together in peace, in contrast to the "unholy land" of Zionism they had seen. Skeptics asked whether any existing Arab state was secular, democratic, or capable of preserving concord among the various religious groups living within its borders. The Palestinians admitted that many Arab leaders were reactionary, bigoted perhaps, and tied to landholding or bourgeois class interests; but the *fidaiyin* were young, well educated, and free from these ties to the past. Would it be rude to ask whether those same reactionary and bourgeois Arab leaders were now bankrolling Fatah and the PLO, of which Arafat, a cousin of the ex-mufti, was elected chairman in 1969?

## ABORTIVE PEACE EFFORTS

Meanwhile, the U.S. government tried to resolve the Arab-Israeli conflict in quite a different way, through an accord among the major outside powers. President Johnson, Secretary of State Dean Rusk, and other American officials hoped somehow to reach agreements with the Soviet leaders, as well as with those of Britain and France. The United States hoped that the USSR might influence the leading Arab states, whereupon the Americans would use their leverage on Israel, probably by selling or withholding advanced weapons, to bring about a peace settlement based on Resolution 242. They hoped the Soviets wanted to stop pouring weapons into Egypt, Syria, and Iraq, arms that might never be paid for and that required large training missions. But Moscow liked having its arms and armies in Egypt and Syria, athwart what had been the main oil routes to the West. The naval and air facilities in these countries were aiding the Soviet buildup in the Mediterranean, where the U.S. Sixth Fleet had been dominant until the 1967 war.

During the war the USSR had ruptured diplomatic relations with Israel, and many of the Arab states had broken ties with the United States. The superpowers were now less capable of mediating in the Middle East. Israel argued that a peace settlement imposed by the superpowers would last only as long as the Arab states were too weak to defy it. Look at what had happened to the settlement imposed on Egypt after the 1956 war. Many Arabs, too, doubted that the U.S. and Soviet governments would resolve the root issues once they had served their own Middle East interests.

## "Evenhanded" Policies

Richard Nixon's victory in the 1968 presidential elections gave some hope to the Arabs; perhaps a new U.S. administration would take initiatives favoring their interests. Nixon sent a special envoy to the Middle East. He returned calling for a more "evenhanded" approach, implying that the Johnson administration had tilted against the Arabs. A major issue in the debates over U.S. Middle East policy has been the degree to which Washington should authorize arms sales to Israel or, indeed, to such pro-Western Arab states as Jordan. Johnson had arranged to sell Phantom jets to Israel, but the Nixon administration delayed the deal, hoping to make Israel accept territorial concessions to the Arabs.

## The War of Attrition

But the Egyptians, noting the attention paid to *fidaiyin* raids and Israeli retaliations, did not wait. In March 1969 Nasir announced that Egypt would step up the shooting that had been going on across the Suez Canal intermittently since 1967, starting the so-called War of Attrition. Nasir, a chess player, hoped to wear down the Israelis east of the canal by picking off men and planes every now and then. Instead, more Egyptians than Israelis were killed, the Egyptian cities west of the canal got shelled so badly that their civilian inhabitants had to be evacuated, Israeli commandos crossed over and raided Egyptian military targets, and Israeli jets flew sorties over Cairo and bombed various military bases and munitions factories in the Nile Delta. Many Egyptians feared a direct hit on the Aswan High Dam, which Soviet money and engineers had almost finished building. By 1970 Israeli troops had dug themselves in behind the Bar Lev line just east of the canal; in the meantime Egypt was becoming ever more vulnerable to Israel's planes, including new Phantom jet fighters supplied by the United States. Nasir had failed to predict how Israel would react to his decision to launch the War of Attrition; Israel equally misjudged Egypt's response to its deep-penetration bombing raids. Nasir flew to Moscow to get the USSR to send Egypt more guns, tanks, planes, missiles, and advisers. By the summer of 1970, Israeli fighter pilots engaging in dogfights high above the Suez Canal found that not only the MIGs but also some of their pilots came from the USSR. Israel did not want the Americans to get involved, but the danger of a superpower confrontation loomed.

## POLITICAL CHANGES: 1967–1970

Let us shelve the War of Attrition awhile to see some concurrent changes. I wrote earlier that no Arab government was overthrown as a result of the 1967 defeat. Nevertheless, leadership changes did occur. Alignments of Arab governments remained kaleidoscopic.

### The Two Yemens

During the 1967 Khartum summit, Egypt and Saudi Arabia agreed to wind down the five-year-old civil war in Yemen. Soon after Nasir pulled out his troops, the republican regime he had backed fell from power. Its successor edged toward accommodation with the imam, his tribal backers, and the Saudis. Yemen remained a republic, but in 1970 its government became a coalition that included royalists. Farther south, the British had tried for years to combine the urban and politicized citizens of Aden Colony with the tribal shaykhs and sultans of the southern Arabian Peninsula (the portion known as the Aden Protectorate). The combination was to be called the South Arabian Federation. The tribal leaders, most of them pro-British, were supposed to balance the urban radicals, but in the 1960s some nationalist groups arose among the unionized workers of the port of Aden. This outpost of empire was becoming too costly to Britain, so the Labour government decided in 1966 to let it go. Once it had announced its intention to pull all troops out of southern Arabia, the federation's Arab backers became disenchanted and the two leading nationalist groups began fighting each other for control of the entire area. In late 1967 Britain handed over southern Arabia to the victorious faction, the National (Liberation) Front. The new country was renamed the People's Republic of Southern Yemen. As its leaders hoped that it might someday be reunited with North Yemen, it later became the People's Democratic Republic of Yemen (PDRY), the sole Marxist state in the Arab world. Its politics continued to interact with those of North Yemen; in 1978 both countries' leaders were assassinated within two days, possibly by the same man. The two states' politics did gradually converge during the 1980s, and they united as the Republic of Yemen in 1990. The union has not been complete; a bitter civil war broke out between Aden (backed by Saudi Arabia) and the rest of the Republic of Yemen in 1994. Deep rifts endure in this supposedly unified country.

## Iraq

In Iraq, Abd al-Rahman Arif (who in 1966 had replaced his brother, Abd al-Salam, killed in a plane crash) was ousted by a rightist coup in July 1968. Two weeks later another Ba'th party splinter group seized power in Baghdad. The new regime soon quarreled with Syria over use of waters of the Euphrates River, even though both states were ruled by the Ba'th party. Relations with Iran were strained because both countries wanted to control the Shatt al-Arab, where the Tigris and the Euphrates meet before emptying into the Gulf. Iraq attacked Egypt and Jordan for having accepted Resolution 242, which tacitly recognized Israel. Kurds in northern Iraq went on fighting for their independence, and the government tried to distract popular opinion at home by publicly hanging fourteen convicted Israeli spies (nine of whom happened to be Jewish) in Baghdad. A tentative settlement with the Kurds in 1970 did not last; Iraq accused the shah of Iran of arming Kurdish rebels. As the Kurdish rebellion increasingly threatened Iraq's control over its oil-rich northern provinces, Baghdad moved toward a pro-Iranian policy. Meeting with the shah in 1975, Iraqi Vice President Saddam Husayn conceded to Iran sovereignty over the Shatt al-Arab on the Iranian side of its deepest channel, in return for Iran's cutting off all aid to the Kurdish rebels. The Kurdish rebellion subsided for a time but revived in the late 1980s.

## Libya

In 1969 military coups overthrew moderate governments in Somalia, Libya, and the Sudan. The most noteworthy was Libya's revolution, which brought to power an impetuous, articulate, and devout army colonel named Mu'ammar al-Qadhafi. This young officer emerged as the new champion of militant Arab nationalism. He persuaded the Americans and the British to evacuate their air bases in Libya, made all tourists carry travel documents written in Arabic, and volunteered his army for duty alongside Nasir's on the Suez Canal and the *fidaiyin* in Jordan and Lebanon. Nasir liked the Libyan revolutionary, who reminded him of himself as a young officer, before he had worn himself out combating Zionism and imperialism.

## Israel

Meanwhile, Ben-Gurion's successor as prime minister, Levi Eshkol, died suddenly in March 1969. His replacement was the former foreign minister and secretary-general of Mapai, Golda Meir. Although she was supposed to serve only as a caretaker until the November 1969 elections, disputes among other politicians and factions within Israel's ruling Labor Alignment made her the most acceptable standard-bearer for her party. And so, after the elections, she formed a broad coalition government. She proved to be a strong-willed, capable leader. Born in Russia and reared in Milwaukee, she managed to keep Israel's prima donnas, Yigal Allon and Moshe Dayan, from each other's throats. She could also make Americans view Middle Eastern events through Israeli glasses.

## The Rogers Peace Plan

As usual, the State Department was less influenced by Israel than any other branch of the U.S. government. In yet another attempt to break the Middle East impasse, Secretary of State William Rogers proposed in December 1969 the peace plan that has come to bear his name. Basically, the Rogers Plan called for a renewal of the Israeli-Egyptian cease-fire and a resumption of Jarring's mediation efforts between the two countries. Rogers envisaged a lasting peace "sustained by a sense of security on both sides," with borders that "should not reflect the weight of conquest"—meaning that Israel should give up almost all the lands it had taken in the war. He added that "there can be no lasting peace without a just settlement of the refugee problem," but he did not specify what that might be. As for Jerusalem, he opposed its annexation by Israel and proposed that it be united and accessible to all faiths and nationalities. Nasir turned down the Rogers Plan at first, but the Arab summit meeting held that month at Rabat offered him little additional military or economic aid to help Egypt fight the War of Attrition.

The escalation of the war during the first half of 1970 and the threat of superpower involvement may have made the Rogers Plan look better to Nasir; the Americans might give him by diplomacy what Egypt's armed forces had failed to gain by war. In a dramatic policy shift, Nasir announced Egypt's acceptance of the Rogers Plan on 23 July. Jordan, harassed by mounting *fidaiyin* activities on its soil, quickly followed suit. Israel questioned the wisdom of the new U.S. policy but reluctantly went along. A ninety-day cease-fire took effect, and Jarring resumed his rounds of Middle Eastern capitals (except Damascus, which still rejected Resolution 242). Israel's doubts seemed justified when Egypt moved some of its new surface-to-air missiles within range of the Suez Canal, an apparent violation of the agreement. Egypt replied that it had planned to move them before the cease-fire was arranged, because of Israel's earlier bombing raids. In October 1973 Egypt would use these missiles against Israel in the Sinai, but in 1970 Washington did not want to derail the negotiations by forcing a pullback. Israel then ended peace talks with Jarring, even though the United States had offered Jerusalem $500 million in credits, mainly to buy more Phantom jet fighters.

## Clashes in Lebanon and Jordan

The Rogers Peace Plan set off a crisis in Jordan. Its root cause was the Palestinian problem. The *fidaiyin* could not maintain bases within Israel or its occupied lands because of Israel's strict security arrangements and its harsh reprisals against terrorist suspects. Instead, they placed their guerrilla bases in refugee camps and peasant villages in southern Lebanon and east of the Jordan River. Since guerrilla activities led to Israeli retaliatory raids across the border, many Lebanese and Jordanians resented having the Palestinians in their countries. Several clashes took place in Lebanon in the fall of 1969. An accord reached in Cairo between the PLO and Lebanon's government limited the Palestinians' freedom to act there, causing them to step up their activities in Jordan in 1970. Quarrels broke out between the PLO and King Husayn's troops, many of whom were bedouin who had never liked the Palestinians.

The explosion was sparked by a Marxist splinter group, the Popular Front for the Liberation of Palestine (PFLP), led by George Habash. He believed that the Palestinians could reach their goals only by first attacking Western governments and civilians in order to dramatize their cause. Specifically, his group chose to hijack passenger airplanes, starting with an El Al jet that it diverted to Algiers in 1968. In September 1970 the PFLP climaxed its campaign by hijacking four Western planes, all filled with homeward-bound tourists, and forcing them to land in a desert airstrip near Amman. The harsh treatment of the passengers (especially those found to be Jewish) so embarrassed the Jordanian government that Husayn's army began attacking the Palestinians, civilians as well as *fidaiyin*, destroying whole sections of Amman and other cities and towns, an assault that has come to be called "Black September." Syria sent an armored column into Jordan to help the Palestinians but withdrew promptly when Israel (with U.S. support) threatened to intervene. Egypt's government again stepped in, as it had done in Lebanon, but it took literally all Nasir's remaining strength to mediate between Arafat and Husayn. On the next day Nasir died of a heart attack. Given his career as an Arab militant, it is ironic that Nasir's last act was to rescue Husayn from the Palestinians, thus saving a U.S. peace plan. His demise threw the whole Middle East situation into doubt.

## Egypt after Nasir

Nasir's death set off an extraordinary wave of public mourning in Egypt. *The Guinness Book of World Records* cited his funeral for having had more participants (4 million is a conservative estimate) than any other in history. Anwar al-Sadat, Nasir's vice president and one of the last of the original "free officers," was chosen to succeed him, but few expected him to last long in power. Other Nasirites competed against Sadat and with one another. Only on 15 May 1971 did Sadat assert full control of his government by a purge known as the "corrective revolution." While feigning loyalty to Nasir's principles, Sadat began making far-reaching changes. Nasir's elaborate internal security apparatus was dismantled. Sadat invited Egyptian and foreign capitalists to invest in local enterprises, even though such investment meant a retreat from socialism. The country's name, which remained the United Arab Republic even after Syria's secession, was changed to the Arab Republic of Egypt. Although Egypt's Soviet ties were seemingly tightened by a fifteen-year alliance treaty signed in May 1971, they were actually unraveling because Moscow would not sell offensive weapons to Sadat for use against Israel. The next year, Sadat's patience would become so frayed that he would expel from Egypt most of the Soviet advisers and technicians.

## The End of the Rogers Peace Plan

What happened to the U.S. government's efforts to bring peace to the Middle East? The temporary cease-fire was renewed several times during fall 1970 and winter 1971, as Jarring shuttled between Egypt and Israel. In February he sent notes to both sides, inviting them to accept certain points as a prerequisite to negotiations. Egypt would have to sign a peace agreement with Israel embodying the final settlement. And Israel would have to pull back to what had been the frontier between Egypt and Palestine (giving Egypt control of Sinai, but not the Gaza Strip). Sadat actually consented to sign a contractual agreement on the terms of a peace with Israel, something Nasir had never done. But Israel refused in principle to withdraw to the pre-June 1967 armistice line. Jarring terminated his mission and thus the Rogers Plan. Both Israel and Egypt did express interest in a partial settlement that would have included reopening the Suez Canal (closed since 1967), with Israel withdrawing slightly from the east bank. Washington tried to obtain agreement on this partial settlement, and Egypt and Israel might have saved many lives later by accepting it in 1971. Sadat took to calling 1971 "the year of decision," in which Egypt and Israel would either make peace or go to war. But in fact 1971 was not the year of decision, and neither was 1972.

The well-intentioned U.S. efforts to mediate an Israeli-Arab settlement by indirect negotiations failed to get at the roots of the problem: Israel's fear of attack (and hence extinction) by the Arabs and the Arabs' fear of expansion (and hence domination) by the Israelis. Israel could not risk its security by agreeing in advance to make concessions that might be matched only by some—or possibly none—of its Arab opponents. What if Israel gave up all or part of the Sinai, only to find that Sadat did not want peace after all or that he had been ousted by more militant Egyptian officers? What if Israel withdrew from the West Bank (presumably the sequel to abandoning the Sinai), and the land did not revert to Jordan but instead was given to a small, unviable, and discontented Palestinian state? Besides, Israel's right-wing parties had left the broad coalition government when it accepted the cease-fire for the Rogers Peace Plan. Any ill-conceived concession might bring down on Golda Meir's head the scathing condemnation of Menachem Begin, leader of the Herut (Freedom) party, and of other Israelis preoccupied with national security.

As for Egypt, Sadat felt he had bent as far as he dared. A separate peace would have probably isolated Egypt from the rest of the Arab world and dissuaded the oil-exporting countries from supporting the faltering Egyptian economy. Jordan would have made peace with Israel in return for its complete withdrawal from the West Bank, including Jerusalem's Old City. In 1972 King Husayn proposed a federation between these Palestinian areas and the rest of Jordan, to be called the "United Arab Kingdom." Neither Israel nor the Palestinians endorsed this idea. Syria maintained that Israel, as an expansionist state, would never give back peacefully what it had taken by force. The USSR, seeking détente with the West, did not block U.S. peacemaking efforts, but it did not push them either. Instead, it went on cultivating its own Middle

Eastern friends, including Syria and Iraq, as well as the chastened PLO and related guerrilla groups.

## DANGER SIGNS IN THE MIDDLE EAST

We now look back on the two years prior to October 1973 as the lull before the storm. Actually, there were danger signals. Qadhafi, having agreed to unite Libya with Sadat's Egypt, pressured him to go to war against Israel. Palestinian *fidaiyin* dramatized their cause in ways obnoxious to both Israel and the West. Their targets included Puerto Rican pilgrims in Israel's Lod Airport, Israeli athletes at the 1972 Olympic Games in Munich, the U.S. ambassador to the Sudan, and a trainload of Soviet Jewish emigrants entering Austria. Israeli planes struck back at Palestinian strongholds, also taking innocent lives. The UN condemned Israeli reprisals, but not the Palestinian actions that had inspired them.

Meanwhile, the Western press and people began to worry about the impending energy crisis and the risks of overdependence on oil imports. Europe and Japan felt especially vulnerable. Since World War II the industrialized countries had shifted from coal to oil as their main energy source. As Middle Eastern output skyrocketed, the oil companies had kept their prices low. They had even lowered them in 1959 and 1960 without consulting the host governments. As the two sides had agreed by then to split oil profits fifty-fifty, the companies' unilateral actions lowered the governments' incomes. These price cuts may have reflected low production costs and a glutted oil market, but petroleum and natural gas are irreplaceable resources as well as the main source of national income for some of the exporting countries. Five of them (Iran, Iraq, Kuwait, Saudi Arabia, and Venezuela) met in Baghdad in 1960 and set up the Organization of Petroleum Exporting Countries (OPEC). Later they were joined by Abu Dhabi (now the United Arab Emirates), Algeria, Ecuador, Indonesia, Libya, Nigeria, and Qatar.

During the 1960s, as long as the world's oil supply kept up with demand, OPEC had a low profile. But as its members came to know one another and learned more about oil economics, the organization became more assertive. In 1968 it recommended that its members explore for new resources on their own, buy shares in the oil companies, restrict their concession areas, and set posted (or tax reference) prices on their products (so that oil price drops would not reduce government revenues). Two years later the companies agreed to work toward uniform—and higher—posted prices and to pay higher taxes levied on their earnings. As world demand kept rising, the oil exporters started to flex their economic muscles.

What did this mean in terms of prices? As there are many kinds of oil and pricing arrangements, I can quote only some representative figures. One barrel (42 U.S. gallons or 159 liters) of Iraqi crude oil sold in 1950 for U.S. $2.41, dropping to $2.15 by 1960. The price rose back to $2.41 by 1970, reaching $3.21 in 1971 and $3.40 in 1972. Many would later object to the fourfold price hike in late 1973, so let me point out that oil had remained cheap for a generation. What other raw materials or manufactured goods kept the same prices between 1950 and 1970? The international accounting unit for oil is the U.S. dollar, whose value dropped considerably after Washington stopped selling gold at $35 per ounce in 1971. The price of an ounce of gold rose more than five times in terms of dollars between 1970 and 1978. Are the oil-exporting states any greedier than their customers?

## Prelude to War

In September 1973 the Middle East seemed calm and an Arab-Israeli war improbable. The Israelis, who had just feted their country's twenty-fifth birthday, were preparing for another Knesset election. The group that had ruled Israel since 1948 seemed likely to stay in power. The so-called Labor Alignment was a bloc of moderate and left-wing parties (but without the Arab and Jewish communists). Leading the alignment was *Mapai*, once headed by Ben-Gurion and now by Golda Meir. The ruling alignment was in coalition with the National Religious party, for which many Orthodox Jews would vote. Menachem Begin, head of the right-wing nationalists, took part in coalition cabinets under the Labor Alignment from 1967 to 1970, when he resigned to protest Israel's acceptance of the Rogers Plan. He then began welding Israel's conservative parties into a coalition called the *Likud*.

## U.S. Concerns

The United States, having pulled its forces out of Vietnam, was losing interest in foreign affairs. Most Americans had their minds on the scandals involving Nixon administration officials (mainly the Watergate affair). Those concerned with long-range issues watched the growing gap between U.S. consumption and production of petroleum and other fossil fuels, a deficit that was being met by rising oil and natural gas imports from the Middle East. Some oil companies argued that unless Washington took a more balanced approach to the Middle East conflict, the Arabs would stop selling oil and gas to the West.

Nixon, hoping to deflect Watergate brickbats, had just named his national security adviser, Henry Kissinger, as his secretary of state. A few Arabs feared that Kissinger, who was Jewish, might back Israel, but he publicly reassured the Arab countries of his fairness. Eager to promote détente, Kissinger hoped that the superpowers would stop the arms race and bring peace to the Middle East, where the danger of a confrontation remained high.

*Arab Frustrations*

Both Washington and Jerusalem underestimated the frustration of the Arab governments over Israel's prolonged and deepening occupation of the lands taken in 1967. Many pro-Israel observers knew this frustration existed; but, on the one hand, they assumed that the Arabs were harping on the territorial issue to distract outsiders from their real aim of destroying the Jewish state, and, on the other, they asserted that the Arabs lacked the will or the power to oust the Israelis. After all, the Arabs had never fought against Israel without having Egypt in their vanguard. Sadat seemingly weakened Egypt's ability to fight by ousting his Soviet advisers and technicians in 1972. However, he warned U.S. and European journalists that Egypt might soon attack Israeli troops somewhere in the Sinai to create a crisis that would force the superpowers to intervene. His warnings reminded his detractors of his fatuous threats about the "year of decision"; they branded him incapable of decision, either to wage war or to make peace with Israel.

Actually, Sadat wanted both. A war with Israel would be costly to Egypt, but if his army and air force, equipped with an impressive arsenal of Soviet tanks, planes, and missiles, could regain some of the lands Nasir had lost in 1967, Egypt would be in a better position (and a better frame of mind) to make peace with Israel. Even though Egypt's economic problems were acute, any peace overtures to Israel without such a war would cause the richer Arab states to cut off all aid to Egypt. Sadat had purged his government of any Nasirites who might have opposed his policies, but the military could have rebelled. Many officers and soldiers had been in a state of alert since 1967 and were thirsting for either a battle or a return to civilian life. Egypt's policy of "no war, no peace" had outlived its usefulness. The Egyptians watched Israel's election campaign, in which both the

Labor Alignment and the Likud made glowing promises about Jewish settlements and development towns in the Sinai, especially near the Gaza Strip. Sadat graphically expressed his reaction: "Every word spoken about Yamit [Israel's port near Rafah] is a knife pointed at me personally and at my self-respect."

*War Preparations*

Sadat began, therefore, to confer publicly and privately with other Arab heads of state about an attack on Israel. For personal and political reasons, he could no longer work with Qadhafi, who made frequent and often unannounced visits to Cairo to harangue the Egyptian people about the Arabs' duty to combat Zionism, the proper role of women in Islam, and the wickedness of Cairo's nightclubs. The projected union of Egypt with Libya, due to take effect on 1 September 1973, was put off and finally forgotten.

Instead Sadat looked to Saudi Arabia, Egypt's main financial backer, and to the other confrontation states, Syria and Jordan. These two countries had been rivals ever since King Abdallah's "Greater Syria" scheme. However, Hafiz al-Asad, who took over Syria late in 1970, was more interested than his precursors had been in building up his country's economy and less inclined to subvert Jordan's politics. Husayn wanted to end his kingdom's isolation in the Arab world. In early September, therefore, Sadat brought together the two leaders for a minisummit, at which they agreed to revive their united front against Israel. The next day Israel announced that it had shot down thirteen Syrian jets and lost one in a dogfight over the Mediterranean (Syria admitted to a score of eight to five). Israel may have tried to discredit the new solidarity vaunted by the Arab confrontation states. But high-level Egyptian and Syrian officers started quietly planning a coordinated surprise attack on the Israeli-occupied territories in the Golan Heights and the east bank of the Suez Canal.

Only after we have seen more published memoirs and documents will we know whether Syria and Egypt planned to invade and defeat Israel, presumably to liberate Palestine. This was not their stated goal. The Arab leaders planned to catch Israel off guard. They thought that the Americans, paralyzed by the Vietnam debacle and the Watergate scandals, would not intervene. They also agreed that Jordan, lacking missile defenses against Israeli aircraft, should stay out of the early phases of the war. Did Syria and Egypt deliberately choose Yom Kippur (the Jewish Day of Atonement) as the date of their attack? The experts disagree. The original plan was to launch it just after sundown, on a day when the moon was nearly full. The Soviets had just launched a spy satellite over the Middle East to guide the Arabs' maneuvers.

## THE OCTOBER (YOM KIPPUR) WAR

The war's outbreak was signaled by a massive Egyptian air and artillery (and water cannon) assault on Israel's Bar Lev line east of the Suez Canal, together with a large-scale Syrian tank invasion of the Golan Heights. With only 600 officers and soldiers on the Bar Lev line and seventy tanks guarding the Golan, Israel could not blunt this first Arab assault. Within a few hours, thousands of Egyptians had crossed the canal. Using their surface-to-air missiles to down Israeli planes, they effectively denied the enemy its accustomed control of the air; they also overran most of the Bar Lev line. The Syrians retook Mount Hermon and made inroads into the southern half of the Golan Heights; they might have invaded Israel itself.

### Israel's Unpreparedness

Mobilizing Israel's reserves was quick and easy; on Yom Kippur most reservists were either at home or praying in the synagogues. Soon hundreds of units were grouping and heading to the two fronts. Had the surprise attack occurred on any other day, it would have been harder for the IDF to call up its reserves. Nonetheless, Israel was taken by surprise. Both Israel and U.S. intelligence had noted the massing of Egyptian and Syrian troops in the preceding week but had assumed they were on routine maneuvers. Besides, they doubted that Muslim armies would attack during Ramadan, Islam's month of fasting. Israel did not want to call up its reserves, having done so at great expense a few months earlier. By the time it realized that war was inevitable, it had missed the chance to bring its front line up to the level of strength needed to stop the Arab armies. In an emergency meeting on the morning of 6 October, the cabinet discussed a preemptive air strike, but Meir ruled it out, lest Washington cut off all aid to Israel.

### The Course of the Fighting

The Arab assault worked at first but then stalled. The Egyptians could have pushed deep into Sinai, and the Syrians could have moved down the Golan Heights into northern Israel. Why did they hold back? They had not expected to start off so well and had no plan for what to do next. The Israeli troops, many of whom were hardened veterans of three or four previous wars, fought back. Seeing that Egyptian infantrymen carried lightweight surface-to-air missiles capable of hitting low-flying jets, Israeli pilots devised evasive maneuvers and diversionary tactics.

During the first week of fighting, the Israelis concentrated their forces in the north, fearing a revolt if Syrian forces broke through into mainly Arab areas, such as Galilee or the occupied West Bank. They soon drove the Syrians back beyond the 1967 armistice line. Israeli units reached a town halfway between Kunaitra (the main city of the Golan Heights) and Damascus; then they stopped, partly to avert any Soviet intervention or a massive onslaught by Jordan or Iraq, but also because Israel's main thrust had shifted to the Egyptian front. After crossing the canal, Egypt's armies took up positions about 6 miles (10 kilometers) deep into Sinai, but IDF intelligence found a weak spot in the middle, between the two armies. In the second week, amid tank battles as large as those in World War II, the Israelis pierced that middle zone, reached the canal, and crossed it. Egyptian fire and bombardment killed most of the Israeli advance units, but some managed to build a land bridge that enabled other troops to reach the west side of the canal. Egypt played down the crossing, but as the IDF headed for Suez, Sadat began to worry.

## Arms Supplies and the Oil Embargo

One major factor in turning the tide was the U.S. resupply of arms to Israel. Washington had put off sending ammunition and spare parts in the first week of the war, fearing it might antagonize the Arabs or perhaps hoping to make Israel more accommodating. Then it started a massive airlift. How could the Arabs discourage this resupply? The weapon that they had long neglected, an embargo on the sale of oil to the United States, now beckoned. Indeed, Arab oil-exporting countries had stopped sales to the West in the June 1967 war, but that embargo had fizzled after a few weeks. The difference was that oil had glutted the world market back then, whereas even before October 1973 most industrialized countries had feared oil shortages. Egypt had long urged the oil-rich Gulf states to deny oil to the United States as a means of making Israel give up the occupied territories. An *al-Ahram* editorial argued that American students, if forced to attend classes in unheated lecture rooms, would demonstrate for Israeli withdrawals as they had done for a U.S. troop pullout from Indochina.

Anyway, the day after the United States started flying arms to Israel, the Arab oil-producing states, meeting in Kuwait, announced that they would reduce their production by 5 percent that month and that these cutbacks would continue until Israel had withdrawn from all the occupied territories and had recognized the national rights of the Palestinians. Some OPEC members suddenly raised oil prices up to 50 percent. Then the Arab states (but not Iran) agreed to put an embargo on the United States and any European country deemed excessively pro-Israel. They singled out the Netherlands, not so much because of the Dutch government's policy but because most of the oil shipped to northern Europe came through the port of Rotterdam. The oil embargo failed to halt the airlift, but it did cause many European countries to deny landing rights to U.S. planes carrying arms to Israel. All these countries rushed to support the Arab interpretation of Resolution 242. Even so, oil supplies dwindled. With winter coming, European governments adopted austerity measures to reduce fuel consumption and avert a crisis.

### The Superpowers and the Cease-fire

By the third week of the longest war the Arabs and Israelis had fought since 1948, both Egypt and Syria faced military defeat. The USSR, anxious to avert their collapse, invited Kissinger to Moscow. The U.S. government might have exploited the Soviets' panic, but it was having its own problems. Aside from its fear of the Arabs' oil weapon and the threat that more Arab states might enter the war, Washington was in chaos. Vice President Agnew had just resigned. President Nixon had fired his special Watergate prosecutor and accepted his attorney general's resignation, thus damaging his own credibility. Kissinger flew to Moscow to work with Communist Party Chairman Leonid Brezhnev on writing a jointly-acceptable Security Council resolution. There was to be a cease-fire in place, a reaffirmation of Resolution 242, and immediate negotiations among the parties to the conflict. This resolution was adopted by the UN Security Council and accepted by Egypt and Israel—but not by Syria. Fighting continued on both fronts, however, with Egypt and Israel accusing each other of bad faith. By the time the Security Council passed a new resolution two days later, Israel's forces in Egypt had surrounded Suez City and in Syria had seized more land around Mount Hermon.

Many Israelis did not want this cease-fire; Egypt's Third Army was trapped in Sinai east of Suez, and they could have crushed it. But Kissinger reasoned that Egypt would be more apt to make peace if it could keep some of its initial gains. The cease-fire was shaky, the troop lines were intertwined, and most observers feared that fighting would resume shortly. U.S. forces were put on red alert the next day, allegedly because Soviet ships were unloading nuclear warheads at Alexandria. Nevertheless, the cease-fire held.

## THE WAR'S AFTERMATH

The June 1967 war had destroyed whatever influence the United States had in Egypt and Syria. One of the surprising results of the October 1973 war was that the United States actually regained that lost influence, thanks to the skill of Henry Kissinger. Even though he had never spent time in the Arab countries or shown much interest in them before he became secretary of state, he managed to deal shrewdly and yet compassionately with their leaders, to draw them away from their uncompromising stance toward Israel, and to strengthen their ties with Washington, which alone could put real pressure on Jerusalem. He tried various means to bring the Arabs and the Israelis together; if one failed, he suggested another. In early November Egyptian and Israeli army commanders met in a tent pitched near the Kilometer 101 marker on the Cairo-Suez road, to identify and unsnarl the lines separating the two sides and to arrange for sending food and medical supplies to Egypt's trapped Third Army. After these talks, Kissinger began organizing a general peace conference, to be held in Geneva in late December under the joint presidency of the superpowers. Syria stayed away because the PLO had not been invited, but Egypt and Israel both came. After a day of opening speeches, the conference adjourned as a technical committee began working on disentangling the Israelis and Egyptians around Suez. The Geneva Conference has been suspended ever since, but I will mention a 1977 attempt to revive it.

### Shuttle Diplomacy

In January 1974 Kissinger began flying between Jerusalem and Aswan (where Sadat spent the winter) and worked up a "separation of forces" agreement by which Israel's troops were to withdraw from all lands west of the canal and to establish its armistice line about 20 miles (35 kilometers) east of Suez (see Map 11). A new UN Emergency Force would patrol a buffer zone east of the canal, enabling Sadat to keep the lands his forces had taken and to regain those they had lost later in the war. The Israelis benefited because they could demobilize most of their reservists, who were needed in their factories, shops, classrooms, and offices back home.

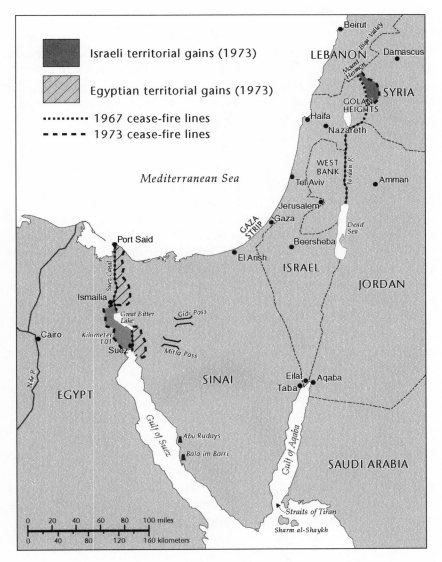

Israeli territorial gains (1973)

Egyptian territorial gains (1973)

·········· 1967 cease-fire lines

- - - - - 1973 cease-fire lines

*Mediterranean Sea*

Beirut

*Biqa' Valley*

LEBANON

Damascus

*Mount Hermon*

SYRIA

GOLAN
HEIGHTS

Haifa

Nazareth

WEST
BANK

*Jordan R.*

Amman

Tel Aviv

Jerusalem

Dead
Sea

Gaza

GAZA
STRIP

Beersheba

El Arish

ISRAEL

JORDAN

Port Said

*Suez Canal*

Ismailia

*Great Bitter Lake*

*Gidi Pass*

Cairo

*Kilometer 101*

Suez

*Mitla Pass*

*Nile R.*

EGYPT

SINAI

Eilat

Taba

Aqaba

*Gulf of Suez*

*Gulf of Aqaba*

Abu Rudays

Bala im Barri

SAUDI ARABIA

*Straits of Tiran*

*Sharm al-Shaykh*

| 0 | 20 | 40 | 60 | 80 | 100 miles |

| 0 | 40 | 80 | 120 | 160 kilometers |

MAP 11 The territorial situation at the end of the October 1973 war

So pleased was Egypt with this agreement that Sadat helped persuade King Faysal to lift the oil embargo. Syria, too, agreed to negotiate a disengagement of forces with Israel. This deal would prove much tougher to close. It kept Kissinger in the Middle East for most of May 1974, but finally the Israelis agreed to give back to Syria what they had taken in the

October War, plus the main city of the Golan Heights, Kunaitra. A UN Disengagement Observer Force was admitted into the Golan, but only for a six-month period that would have to be renewed by the consent of both sides. Despite some anxious moments at the end of each six-month period, Syria and Israel have renewed the deal ever since. Kissinger came home to a hero's welcome. Nixon, in peril due to Watergate, toured several Arab states and Israel in June, trying to reap some credit for what Kissinger had sown.

### Israel's Domestic Crisis

While Kissinger was conducting his virtuoso diplomacy, Israel's government underwent a severe political crisis. The general election, planned for October 1973, had been put off until late December because of the war. When it was held, the conservative Likud coalition scored significant gains at the expense of the Labor Alignment and its traditional coalition partners. The results were probably a voter reaction to the mistakes made by Meir's cabinet just before the war. In early 1974 she tried to form a new government, but her efforts were stymied by disputes between secularist and Orthodox parties over "Who is a Jew." A hoary Israeli issue that still has not been resolved, it centers on whether the government may confer citizenship rights on any Jewish immigrant desiring them (the secularist position) or whether it may do so only for an immigrant who can prove that he or she had a Jewish mother or has been converted according to Jewish law. Many North American Jews who belong to the Conservative or Reform movements oppose the latter definition, which implies that Israel does not accept their rabbis' authority to perform conversions to Judaism. Orthodox Jews argue that Israel must strive to be a truly Jewish state, not just one in which those people who call themselves Jews happen to form a majority. Meir, unable to reach a consensus on whether to include the National Religious party (the advocate of the Orthodox stance) in her coalition and stung by criticism about the war, offered her resignation. Once Israel's disengagement with Syria took effect in June 1974, Yitzhak Rabin became the new premier.

### Effects of the Oil Embargo

The 1973–1974 crisis posed major economic and political problems for the industrialized world. Crude oil prices fluctuated wildly for a while, as some countries took to bidding against one another to get what they needed to run their factories, drive their cars, and heat their houses. At one point the price per barrel reached $20, far above the average posted price of $3 charged in January 1973, but finally it settled at about $11.65. Oil shortages caused problems for industries and consumers in all parts of the world, and many buyers accused the oil companies of withholding supplies to raise prices charged to the consumer.

In the Middle East, though, the sudden spurt of oil income opened new vistas for economic development and political leverage to such countries as Saudi Arabia, Kuwait, and Iran. Libya, for example, gained ample funds to induce African governments to break diplomatic ties with Israel and also to back revolutionary causes in Ireland and Ethiopia. But even the oil exporters had problems, as Western entrepreneurs jammed their hotels and the waiting rooms of government officials, as ships loaded with machinery and consumer goods lined up around the Gulf states' inadequate ports, and as poorer countries such as Egypt (not to mention the PLO) importuned them for economic assistance.

Countries without oil, including such Arab states as Jordan, the Yemens, and the Sudan, could hardly pay the new prices. India, Pakistan, Bangladesh, and other Third World countries had to shelve needed development plans just to pay for oil. Europe, Japan, and the United States all suffered higher unemployment and price inflation in 1974. Such problems affected everyone who bought from these industrialized nations or tried to sell to them. Arabs and Iranians invested heavily in corporate stocks and bonds, real estate, treasury bills, and other forms of Western capital. At the rate they were acquiring petrodollars, the oil-exporting countries (said some alarmists) could soon own most of the world's assets. These fears proved unwarranted, but the economic power of Saudi Arabia, Kuwait, Iraq, Iran, Libya, and the United Arab Emirates continued to grow and to be translated into political—and military—power. U.S. arms sales to Middle Eastern rulers, to help pay for oil purchases, reached $9 billion in 1977. Egyptians, Yemenis, Palestinians, and Lebanese flocked to newly rich oil countries to find jobs and sent much of their earnings to their families, changing their lifestyles.

## PLO Power at Its Zenith

Foreign countries, hoping for better ties with the Arabs, backed the Palestinian cause more than they ever had before. Even though few had fought in the October 1973 war, the Palestinians were gaining leverage over the Arab governments. Many had already migrated to the oil-producing countries to make a living and now contributed heavily to the managerial elite and work force of such countries as Kuwait, where Palestinians made up one-fourth of the whole population. The Kuwaiti government also contributed heavily to the PLO. In October 1974 the Arab heads of state, meeting in Rabat, recognized the PLO as the "sole legitimate representative of the Palestinian people on any liberated Palestinian territory." Even King Husayn conceded to the PLO the right to negotiate for the West Bank. The UN General Assembly invited PLO Chairman Arafat to speak. It later recognized the Palestinians' right to independence and sovereignty and granted the PLO observer status at the UN. Meanwhile, the United Nations Educational, Social, and Cultural Organization (UNESCO) cut off financial aid to Israel because of its "persistence in altering the historical features of Jerusalem." In 1975 Israel became even more isolated when the UN General Assembly passed a resolution by a large majority, condemning Zionism as a form of racism, a resolution that it would repeal in 1991.

The PLO portrayed itself as a movement struggling for national liberation and rebutted Zionist efforts to discredit its actions as terrorist. It justified acts of sabotage and murder against civilian Israelis, especially virulent in 1974, as necessary steps toward Palestine's liberation. Skeptics wondered if their real purposes were to hamper Kissinger's peace efforts and to provoke Israeli air raids on the *fidaiyin* in southern Lebanon. Some people argued that if the Palestinians had a state on the West Bank and the Gaza Strip, they would become more responsible, out of fear that Israel would retaliate if they did not. But few Israelis at the time were willing to take a chance.

### A Return to Shuttle Diplomacy

In winter 1975 Kissinger launched a new series of talks with Egypt and Israel aimed at an interim Sinai agreement to keep up the momentum of the negotiations and to strengthen moderates such as Sadat against the Arab extremists. Again Kissinger tried his shuttle diplomacy, which had worked so well in 1974. But the talks foundered on Israel's refusal to hand back the Sinai oil fields or the strategic Gidi and Mitla passes and on Egypt's reluctance to pledge itself to nonbelligerency. When King Faysal of Saudi Arabia was killed in March by his nephew, the Arab world seemed to be entering a new era of political instability. The U.S. government began reassessing its Middle East policy, an apparent pro-Arab tilt. It delayed some arms deliveries to Israel and hinted that U.S. economic aid, totaling $2 billion since the 1973 war, might be pruned.

Later that year, though, both Egypt and Israel became more accommo-dating. In June Sadat reopened the Suez Canal and allowed passage to ships with Israeli cargos. After yet another round of shuttle diplomacy, Kissinger got a new Sinai accord. Israel gave up the passes and oil fields, as 100 U.S. civilian technicians joined the UN Emergency Force inside the buffer zone separating the Egyptian and Israeli armies. Egypt renounced war as a means of resolving the Middle East conflict, a statement widely interpreted in other Arab capitals as a sellout, but neither the Palestinians nor any Arab leader could stop Sadat's peace march.

## LEBANON: THE ARENA FOR A NEW ARAB STRUGGLE

In Lebanon a separate but related crisis was brewing: a civil war far more lasting, costly, and bitter than that of 1958. This long conflict makes sense only if we look at it from several angles.

### The Religious Angle

The conflict was initially seen as one between Christians and Muslims. Lebanon was a country deeply split along religious lines. The Maronites, the largest single Christian sect, had long wielded power disproportionate to their actual share of the population. Lebanon's Muslims, really a major-ity of the country's people, sought equal rights for themselves. Not all Christians lined up on the Maronites' side (many of the Greek Orthodox did not), and not all Muslims had the same interests. Shi'i Muslims were increasing, relative to the historically preponderant Sunnis, and as the war continued, they more stridently demanded recognition of their status. It is also hard to explain how the first spokesman of the "Muslim" side was Kamal Jumblat, a Druze landowner. In later years both Christians and Muslims would become split into factions at war with one another. Reli-gious issues mattered, but other problems also divided Lebanon.

### The Nationalist Angle

Some experts saw the war as one between Lebanese loyalists, who viewed their country as a link between the West and the Middle East, and Arab nationalists, who sought closer ties with Syria and other Arab states. This aspect of the conflict invited other Middle Eastern states to fish in troubled waters. Because no Arab state would openly favor Lebanese particularism over Arab nationalism, the policy adopted by any one government was apt to depend on how much it wished to please Syria. And Syria's policy, as you will soon see, changed several times. Supporters of Israel accused the Palestinians of attacking the Lebanese (meaning the Maronites). A half-million Palestinians lived in Lebanon, mainly in the south and in refugee camps around Beirut. Many felt cut off from Lebanon's political and economic life. Christian Arabs from Palestine had been assimilated after 1948, but not the Palestinian Muslims who helped to create a Muslim majority there. After 1970 the PLO, driven out of Jordan, made Lebanon its operational base. It did not want to enter the civil war, but it sided with any group that espoused Arab nationalism and wanted to liberate Palestine. It was a Maronite militia's attack on a Palestinian bus that sparked the fighting in April 1975, committing the PLO to the Arab nationalist side.

## The Economic Angle

The Lebanese conflict was also a struggle between a privileged class of landowners and merchants trying to preserve the status quo and a large mass of poor people (mainly Muslim) striving for more equality. The gap between rich and poor, especially in Beirut, was immense and scandalous. High-rise apartment buildings abutted on shacks built of cinder blocks and corrugated iron. Unable to tax the incomes of the rich, the government imposed high excise taxes on cigarettes and other goods consumed by the poor. Many employers did not pay the minimum wage, as they could hire Palestinian refugees or newcomers from rural areas, desperate for jobs, for less money.

## The Ideological Angle

Given such social conditions, some journalists and scholars saw the war as one between the Right (guardians of the status quo) and the Left (those wanting change). This was partly true. Those who were rich, well connected, and Christian *tended* to favor the Right; those who were not *generally* became Leftists. Some Marxist "progressives" did enter the fray. Besides, the Left's rifles and grenade launchers tended to be of Soviet manufacture, whereas U.S. and European arms were borne by the forces of the Right. Most Middle Eastern states had armed themselves to the teeth for years, and Lebanon had been a smugglers' haven even in peacetime. Naturally, some of its citizens possessed lots of bombs and guns.

## An Attempted Synthesis

All of these angles had some truth. None was wholly true. People fight for reasons other than religion, nationality, class interest, or ideology. Lebanese loyalties were also based on habit, family, patronage, or even region or neighborhood of habitation. Old grudges and dormant feuds were revived. Past favors or slights were paid back in kind—or worse. Lebanon had plenty of armed factions, ranging from street gangs to private militias. The two main Lebanese parties to the conflict were the Phalanges, a long-lived and largely Maronite force, and the Lebanese National Movement, which was led by members of the Jumblat family and tended to be mainly Muslim. President Sulayman Franjiyah openly backed the "Christian" side. The "Muslim" side won the support of PLO leader Arafat. Savage fighting alternated with shaky cease-fires for eighteen months, becoming most intense in and around Beirut, where the hotel district, the port, and residential areas became battle zones. Fighting with bazookas and grenades, both sides reduced buildings to rubble. It is estimated that 70,000 Lebanese (most civilians) were killed, over a half-million people were left homeless, and property damage exceeded $1 billion during 1975–1976.

## Syria's Role

One puzzling aspect of this war was Syria's 1976 policy shift. Syria had deeply resented France's severance of Lebanon during the mandate period, and since independence the Syrians had hoped that someday the two countries would be reunited. Mostly Muslim and generally the bellwether of Arab nationalism, Syria had tended to side with any faction that would weaken the pro-Western Maronites there. Naturally, then, President Hafiz al-Asad should have backed the rebels during the Lebanese civil war. At first he did, both morally and materially. But in January 1976 he managed to get Franjiyah and his opponents to accept a cease-fire and a political deal that would require a slight shift in Lebanon's power balance in the Muslims' favor. But the Muslim Lebanese, abetted by the PLO, rejected his proposed compromise. This rejection angered Asad and made him change sides. Syria sent tanks and troops to enforce its carefully crafted settlement, attacked Lebanese Muslims and the PLO, and battered them into submission by fall 1976.

An Arab summit meeting, held in Riyadh that October, devised a formula by which Lebanon would go on being occupied by an Arab League peacekeeping force, made up mainly of Syrians. Elias Sarkis was chosen to succeed Franjiyah as president. But why did Asad, a self-styled champion of Arab nationalism and socialism, protect Christian interests in Lebanon? He wanted to keep the PLO weak enough so that his government could control it; earlier he had quarreled with Yasir Arafat. Lebanon settled into an uneasy truce, but the fighting had in fact partitioned the country—and Beirut—between Christians and Muslims. Although some Christians still lived peacefully within "Muslim" zones such as west Beirut, the Maronites began building a new harbor and airport north of the city and treating their area as a Christian version of Israel. Indeed, the Israelis seemed to agree. As a foretaste of larger invasions to come, Israeli forces in 1976 entered southern Lebanon to destroy Palestinian bases and warned Syria to keep its troops away from Lebanon's southern border. Christian Lebanese in the south—cut off from their coreligionists in the rest of the country—began crossing into Israel to sell their produce, seek work, or get medical care. The Arabs accused Israel of using Lebanon to prove that multireligious states could not last in the Middle East, a traditional Zionist argument. Actually, most Middle Eastern governments cooperated in ruining a country that had once been reasonably free, democratic, and wealthy.

## THE ROAD TO CAMP DAVID

The U.S. government suspended its quest for Middle East peace during its 1976 presidential election. Both President Gerald Ford and his challenger, Jimmy Carter, pledged to back a strong and independent Israel and ignored the Palestinian Arabs. The United States was not unaffected by the Lebanese civil war, as its ambassador was assassinated in 1976 and the PLO helped the embassy evacuate U.S. civilians from Beirut. But Washington would not enter negotiations with the PLO; such parleys were ruled out by Kissinger during his 1975 peace talks and opposed by most American voters. After Carter was elected, though, he would try a new initiative to settle the Arab-Israeli conflict and perhaps the Lebanese civil war as well.

### Carter's Plans

The key to the new administration's thinking on the Middle East lay in a report prepared by the Brookings Institution and published in 1976. Called *Towards Peace in the Middle East*, it urged the Arab states to recognize Israel within its pre-June 1967 boundaries (with some minor border adjustments). Israel was to turn the Gaza Strip and the West Bank over to a government of Palestinian Arabs, but not necessarily the PLO. It also called for reconvening the Geneva Conference to reach the necessary agreements. One of the authors of the Brookings report was William Quandt, who would work with Carter's national security adviser, Zbigniew Brzezinski. Carter gave high priority to Middle East peace and began to talk with various heads of state, hoping to resuscitate the Geneva Conference before the end of 1977.

*Policy Problems*

New snags soon appeared. Israel was intensely suspicious of any conference that the USSR would cochair with the United States. Formerly, Kissinger's shuttle diplomacy had kept Moscow out of the peacemaking process. Now Washington seemed determined to invite the Soviets back in, embarrassing the Israelis and even Sadat. Besides, the Arab states insisted on having Palestinians at the proposed meeting. If they were left out, some Palestinian group or individual might kill someone or blow up something to block any peace settlement that might bypass their interests and aspirations. If they were included, would the PLO represent them, according to the 1974 Rabat summit resolutions? Negotiating with the PLO was totally unacceptable to Israel, which viewed Arafat as a murderer and his organization as the umbrella for a variety of terrorist groups. Israel argued that Jordan was a Palestinian state and that there was no need for another, especially one whose covenant called for Israel's destruction. For their part, the Palestinians wanted the PLO to represent them. As of 1976 all newly elected mayors of West Bank towns backed the PLO. Few expected the PLO to recognize Israel, but it wanted to speak for the Palestinians at the reconvened Geneva Conference.

Carter's advisers learned the hard way not to take Israel for granted. While the new administration was seeking peace, Israel was holding a general election. The Labor Alignment had been hurt by internal dissension between Prime Minister Rabin and Defense Minister Shim'on Peres, government scandals, galloping inflation, and mounting social problems. Israel's electorate turned against Labor. Some changed to a new party calling for peace and major reforms, but more voted for the right-wing Likud. Its head, Menachem Begin, managed to form a coalition with the National Religious party and thus to become prime minister. For the first time, the post was held by an Israeli not belonging to any of the labor parties. Begin's election seemed to be a giant step away from peace, as he was quick to assert that the West Bank (which he called Judea and Samaria) was an integral part of *Eretz Israel* (the Land of Israel) that had been liberated, not occupied, in 1967. He called on Jews to settle in strategic parts of that mainly Arab area. The Arabs called Begin a terrorist. As former head of the Irgun, he had carried out the 1948 Dayr Yasin massacre. It seemed unlikely that any Arab leader would talk to such a chauvinistic Israeli. Yet, amazingly, there was one—also a former terrorist.

## Sadat Leads the Quest for Peace

Speaking before Egypt's National Assembly, Anwar al-Sadat stated, rather theatrically, that he was willing to go before the Israeli Knesset to argue his country's case for peace. Questioned later by American television journalists, Begin said he would receive the Egyptian president at any time. Arrangements were made hastily, and on 19 November 1977 Sadat flew to Israel. The next day he delivered before the Knesset a speech that was carried to most of the world by radio and television. He offered the Israelis peace with Egypt if they withdrew from all lands they had occupied in the 1967 war and recognized a Palestinian state. Many people thought that Sadat's visit was so dramatic a step toward peace that Israel should have offered comparable concessions to Egypt. But no other Arab leader wanted the reconciliation with Israel that Sadat offered; Qadhafi and Arafat called him a traitor to the Arab cause. Israel was willing to make peace with Egypt, but Sadat was hoping for a comprehensive settlement including Syria, Jordan, and the Palestinians.

To follow up on his Jerusalem visit, Sadat called a general conference in December 1977; however, as only Israel and the United States agreed to come to Cairo, it ended inconclusively. Yet the Egyptian people, burdened by heavy state military expenditures, saw peace with Israel as a first step toward their economic recovery. Begin flew to Ismailia to meet with Sadat, and they agreed on concurrent negotiations: military talks in Cairo and political ones in Jerusalem. By the time they began in January, though, both sides cared less about peace and worried more about each other's motives. Begin's insistence that Jewish settlements on the West Bank and industrial towns in the Sinai must stay under Israeli army protection reminded Sadat of British efforts to keep their Suez base before 1956, so he pulled his negotiators out of Jerusalem.

Israel and Egypt also differed on how to resolve the Palestinian issue. Begin offered self-rule (with an indeterminate Israeli occupation) to the

Arabs in the occupied areas. Sadat wanted self-determination for the Palestinian people. How could Begin expect Sadat to accept indefinite Israeli control over the Palestinians, when the Arabs had struggled for most of the century to free themselves from foreign rule? How could Sadat expect Begin to jeopardize his country's security by committing his government, before any substantive talks, to return strategic areas to Arabs who had not recognized Israel's right to exist? Jewish Israelis did not care to admit that Palestinian Arabs wanted freedom as much as they did, whereas Egypt (and the other Arab countries) did not realize how Israel's concern for security resulted from Jewish fears of extinction after the Nazi Holocaust and years of tension due to the Arab-Israeli conflict.

Such tunnel vision was tragic, for both sides needed peace. The burden of military expenditures was becoming unbearable. Some Israelis were moving to other countries because they were tired of the confiscatory taxes, constant calls to military reserve duty, and ceaseless tension. Some Arabs, too, had gone abroad, especially educated young adults seeking intellectual freedom and professional opportunities. Egypt hoped to free funds earmarked for arms in order to rebuild its limping economy. Widespread food riots had broken out in Cairo and the Delta cities in January 1977, drawing world attention to Egypt's economic problems.

The U.S. government got more involved than ever before in the quest for peace. Americans feared that another Arab-Israeli war would be destructive and dangerous, that the USSR would gain if peace talks failed (during 1978 communism made gains in Libya, Ethiopia, South Yemen, and Afghanistan), and that Arab oil might be denied to Western buyers. Carter and his cabinet devoted a disproportionate share of their time and energy to the Arab-Israeli conflict, visits to Middle Eastern capitals, compromise formulas, balanced arms sales, and top-level meetings.

### The Egyptian-Israeli Treaty

A spectacular summit, consisting of Begin, Sadat, and Carter, along with cabinet ministers and advisers from the three corresponding countries, met at Camp David (the summer White House in Maryland) in September 1978. Twelve days of intense negotiations produced documents called "A Framework for the Conclusion of a Peace Treaty Between Egypt and Israel" and "A Framework for Peace in the Middle East." The latter was intended to bring other parties into the settlement. But Jordan, Saudi Arabia, and (not surprisingly) Syria and the PLO refused to join in these agreements, which offered the Palestinians little hope for self-determination. After long and bitter debate, Israel's Knesset agreed to pull its troops out of Sinai and hence its settlements and airfields from the lands it would give back to Egypt. Negotiations opened at Blair House, not far from the White House (clearly highlighting Carter's crucial role). But the Washington talks foundered on Egypt's attempt to link the establishment of diplomatic relations to Israel's loosening its control over the Gaza and West Bank Palestinians. The three-month deadline agreed upon at Camp David passed without a treaty.

Meanwhile, OPEC warned that during 1979 it would raise posted oil prices by 14.5 percent (later, after the Iranian revolution, it would boost them further and faster), increasing the West's balance-of-payments deficit. Fighting a war of nerves against each other, Egypt and Israel jockeyed for support from Carter, Congress, and the American people and avoided making compromises. The other Arab governments held a summit meeting in Baghdad in November 1978, offered Egypt inducements to quit the peace talks, and threatened reprisals if it signed a treaty. Hard-line Israelis warned that they would block any pullout from the lands Begin had offered to return to Egypt.

Concerned about the eroding U.S. position in the Middle East, Carter decided in early March 1979 to fly to Cairo and Jerusalem to complete negotiations for the peace accord. His risky venture paid off, as Carter and his aides managed to reconcile the differences between Sadat and Begin. A complex treaty, formally ending the state of war between Egypt and Israel, was signed on the White House lawn on 26 March 1979. It would prove costly for the United States, both economically and politically. Almost at once Begin and Sadat disputed the meaning of the document they had signed. Nearly all the other Arab governments condemned it. Most of all, the Palestinians accused Sadat of betraying their quest for justice and self-determination by agreeing to negotiate with Israel on the future of Gaza and the West Bank. Washington wanted peace, but most Middle Eastern peoples rejected the terms accepted by Cairo and Jerusalem.

## CONCLUSION

What do we mean by peace? Up to now I have assumed that you and I know what peace is. But do we? One simple answer is that peace is the absence of conflict. But in the Middle East many conflicts smolder for years, then flare up suddenly. The Arab-Israeli conflict was muted between 1956 and 1967, and yet there was no peace. We could define peace in another way: as a condition of harmony within and between every person, every group, and every nation in the world. Two people cannot be at peace with each other unless they feel at peace with themselves. If the members of a group disagree among themselves, they cannot agree with another group. A country riven with factional, sectional, or ethnic hostility cannot make peace with another state. Such an idyllic condition rarely occurs in human life, though. Most disputes in history merely have died down, enabling the parties to stop fighting each other, even if they have failed to reach an accord.

When addressing the question of peace with Israel, some Arabs say they will accept *salam* but not *sulh*. What is the difference? Both words mean "peace," but in modern usage *salam* connotes a temporary cessation of hostilities and *sulh* means "reconciliation." Arabs who make this distinction may envisage an armistice with Israel, a respite from hostilities, in which they can regain their political and economic strength, but not a true reconciliation with the Jewish state. Because this distinction naturally alarms Israel and its backers, harping on it will not lead to peace.

But then is Israel just a Jewish state? It is a country inhabited by Jews and Arabs who must find a basis of coexistence that does not involve domination or repression of one side by the other. Let us not kid ourselves. Arab Israelis—not to mention Palestinians under Israel's occupation—do not enjoy the same rights, power, and status as Jewish Israelis. Zionists who ignore the feelings of these 3 million Arabs also impede the quest for *sulh* and maybe even *salam*. There can be no peace without security. There can be no peace without justice. For both sides. Period.

# NINETEEN

# The Reassertion of
# Islamic Power

By 1979, a crucial year in Middle East history, the outlook for peace seemed about as stable as a roller coaster ride. Nearly everyone wanted a just and peaceful settlement to the Arab-Israeli conflict. Yet the roller coaster of war fears and peace hopes in the Middle East swooped and sank, lurched left and right, on and on. As the train veered past Camp David and the White House lawn, a new trouble spot sprang up—Iran. A country hailed by President Carter on a New Year's Day visit in 1978 as "an island of stability in one of the more troubled areas of the world" became, before the year ended, paralyzed by strikes and demonstrations. What about its ruler, the Shahanshah (King of Kings) Mohammad Reza Pahlavi *Aryamehr* (light of the Aryans)? Carter, in his New Year's toast, had said, "This is a great tribute to you, Your Majesty, and to the respect, admiration, and love which your people give to you." A year later the shah was gravely ill and cut off from his rebellious subjects, and Carter's officials were discussing ways to ease him out of Iran.

Meanwhile, the television cameras turned to an emaciated, dark-eyed, white-bearded octogenarian in a black turban, brown coat, and green tunic, living a spartan existence in a Paris suburb. Just who was this Ayatollah Ruhollah Khomeini? How could an aged Shi'i teacher win the hearts and minds of millions of Iranians, at home and abroad? For thirty-seven years, the shah had labored to modernize Iran—or so most Western governments thought—but now the forces of Muslim fundamentalism, reaction, and fanaticism were taking over. Suddenly, "Islam" was a force in the world, and

Middle East "experts" had to write books, give lectures, and teach courses about it. In early 1979 the shah left Iran "for an extended vacation," and the ayatollah came home to a tumultuous welcome. Soldiers gave up their arms and joined the mobs. Upper- and middle-class Iranians fled the country. The Iranians who stayed behind voted to set up an "Islamic republic." Islam, not Marxism, now seemed to be the wave of the future.

The U.S. and Iranian governments had long been diplomatic, military, and economic allies. The new regime, reacting against the old, vented its hatred against the United States. Militant students, abetted by their leaders, seized control of the U.S. Embassy in Tehran and took more than sixty Americans hostage, demanding the return of the shah, his relatives, and his property to Iran. As mobs filled the streets, shouting "Death to America," the American people and their leaders wondered what had gone wrong. Their country, the strongest nation on earth since World War II, seemed to have become a helpless giant among the newly assertive peoples of the Middle East. Its ambassadors could be killed and its embassies burned. The USSR could send 100,000 troops to occupy Afghanistan. The U.S. government could not effectively strike back. Its people could, however, elect the assertive Ronald Reagan in place of the more circumspect Jimmy Carter. On the day Reagan took office, the American hostages were released; but he soon had problems of his own in dealing with Iran and other parts of the Middle East.

Several regional conflicts intensified, as Middle Eastern leaders found that aggression pays—in the short run, at least. The Turks stayed in Cyprus and the Syrians in Lebanon, the Soviets tightened their hold on Afghanistan, Iraq invaded Iran in 1980, and the Israelis occupied the southern half of Lebanon in 1982. The cost of aggression proved high, but only slowly became clear, to the aggressors. By the decade's end, Afghan rebels backed by volunteers from throughout the Muslim world drove out the Soviets. Iran had expelled the Iraqi invaders but could not bring down the Iraqi regime. The Israelis had pulled back to a narrow "security zone," leaving Lebanon more chaotic than ever. Aggression did not pay after all.

Many officials labored to unravel these conflicts, only to entangle themselves and their governments more than ever. Sadat, who the West thought had done the most to promote Middle East peace, fell beneath a hail of machine-gun bullets in 1981. The United States sent a Marine contingent to join troops from three European powers in a multinational force to effect the withdrawal of Syrian and Israeli forces from Lebanon and to persuade the country's warring factions to reform their government. Instead, the Western powers had to leave, unable to defend even themselves against militant terrorists. No Westerner living in Lebanon was safe from kidnappers, mainly Iranian-trained Lebanese Shi'is. The Iran-Iraq War blazed fiercely until August 1988, costing close to $1 trillion and 1 million lives, and still its basic causes were not resolved. The Palestinian Arabs, always resistant to Israeli rule, launched a massive revolt, the *intifadah*, in December 1987 and declared the occupied territories "independent" a year later. Washington angered the Palestinians by continuing its aid to Israel and incensed the Israelis by talking to the PLO.

## Prefatory Remarks
## on Islam and Politics

Much has been written lately about the resurgence of Islam. A religious revival, or return to transcendental values, has taken place in many parts of the world, among Christians and Jews as well as Muslims. After thirty years of rising prosperity in the industrialized world, new problems set in. Some people who have never known poverty now question the goals and assumptions of materialism and quest after the life of the spirit. Old religious traditions are being revived. Secular-minded people are taking up various forms of meditation. Religion no longer retreats before the advance of science. My working assumption while I was writing this book was that people are motivated more by the need to prove their self-worth than by their material drives and desires. For many oppressed peoples, such as the Catholics of Northern Ireland and the Buddhists of Tibet, asserting religious beliefs and symbols has been a step toward attaining their freedom and dignity. Even though most Middle Easterners had known formal independence for a generation, old complexes about colonialism lingered. Indeed, because of the economic power of multinational corporations and the pervasive influence of U.S. pop culture, some forms of dependence have lately grown stronger. Many Muslims hail this revival as a response to the "Coca-Colanization" of their values and way of life. In the late twentieth century, the West's influence was cultural, economic, intellectual, and social; its threats were as virulent as those of the political and military imperialism of the late nineteenth century.

In the past, Muslims believed that their only legitimate state was the *ummah* founded by Muhammad and elaborated by his successors. As you read earlier, the *ummah* is the community of Muslim men and women who believe in God, angels, holy books, divine messengers, and the Day of Judgment. Its leaders should rule justly and in accordance with the Quran and Muhammad's example, or what you have learned to call the Shari'ah, to preserve internal safety and harmony. Non-Muslims may live, work, pray, and own property within *Dar al-Islam*, or the "house of Islam," but they may not take control. Lands not under Muslim rule are collectively called *Dar al-Harb*, or the "house of war." Most Muslims believe they should expand the *Dar al-Islam* against *Dar al-Harb*. For centuries they did so, but then the territorial losses inflicted on them by the Christians of Spain, and later those of Austria, Russia, France, and Britain, shocked Muslims. Their rulers began borrowing weapons, tactics, and military organization piecemeal from the West. When these stratagems failed, some adopted comprehensive westernizing reforms.

Although most of us would argue that westernization improved education, transport, and commerce, there was another side to the coin. Good customs got thrown out with the bad. The old moral and intellectual leaders, the ulama, were displaced but not really replaced, for the new westernized elites lacked the ulama's rapport with the people. Many artisans and traders lost their livelihoods. Government despotism and corruption, far from vanishing, grew more efficient with the telegram and the railroad. Bypassing Muslim political theory, native westernizers adopted secular nationalism, but this ideology did not halt the spread of Western rule. It did not stop the exploitation of poor people or local minorities. Instead, nationalism sapped popular institutions and exalted dictators such as Ataturk, Reza Shah, Nasir, and Qadhafi. Few Muslim states (Indonesia, Algeria, and South Yemen are exceptions) won their independence by revolutionary armed struggles. After independence, however, many failed to build national unity or even defeat their enemies. Muslim defeats—like those of the Arabs by Israel in 1948, 1956, and 1967—were traumatic. If nationalism failed to uphold the self-worth of modern Muslim states, other imported ideologies also proved unfit: Fascism degraded the individual to exalt the state, and communism denied the basic tenets of Islam altogether. People attain freedom and dignity not by aping others but by affirming what is true within themselves.

## THE IRANIAN REVOLUTION

Although the religious revival touched all parts of the Muslim world, its most dramatic impact has been in Iran. This country is unique in some ways: its language, its conscious cultivation of a pre-Islamic heritage, and its adherence to Twelve-Imam Shi'ism. In Iran the rise of nationalism was reinforced by the beliefs of the ulama and the people. The Shi'i ulama enjoyed great power and prestige. As you may recall from Chapter 8, they had more leeway than did their Sunni counterparts to interpret the Shari'ah. Their ideas had great revolutionary potential, especially their belief that no ruler's authority was legitimate, save that of the missing twelfth imam. Until this imam returns, the lawmakers for Shi'i Islam were the *mujtahids*, highly trained ulama. Their schools and mosques worked apart from (and often in opposition to) the secular rulers. The ulama, along with the bazaar merchant guilds and the athletic clubs, opposed the Qajar shahs during the 1892 tobacco boycott and the 1906 constitutionalist movement. They were inconsistent toward the Pahlavi dynasty, supporting it against the USSR and the procommunist *Tudeh* (Workers) party but resisting its secularizing reforms. Naturally, they opposed the shah's attempts to seize their endowed lands and to ally Iran with the Western powers, notably the United States. The Western press harped on the ulama's opposition to such features of the shah's White Revolution as women's suffrage. Inasmuch as neither women nor men could elect their representatives during most of the shah's reign, this press attack missed its mark. Muslim observance is so central in most Iranians' lives that you can be sure the ulama knew the people's feelings better than the shah and his ministers.

## The Monarchy

The Pahlavi dynasty ruled from 1925 to 1979. It consisted of two shahs: Reza Khan and his son, Mohammad Reza. They (along with their burgeoning family) took over a vast share of Iran's land, houses, shops, hotels, and factories (how vast no one knows, but the assets of the Pahlavi Foundation alone were estimated in 1977 at some $3 billion). Around them swarmed a cadre of bureaucrats, landlords, military officers, and professional people who tied their lives and fortunes to the Pahlavi kite. Some were patriotic Iranians who believed that the shah's policies would benefit their country; others were crafty opportunists who enriched themselves by exploiting the government. Reza Shah, covered in Chapter 14, was a dictator who admired and emulated Ataturk. His son, Mohammad, was more complex. He could be ruthless in his pursuit of power and in imposing his westernizing reforms against the wishes of powerful and entrenched groups in Iran, or he could court popularity. At times he shrank from wielding power. Early in his reign he left Iran's government to his ministers and let the tribal and local leaders regain powers they had lost under his father. Later he was eclipsed by a popular premier, Mohammad Mosaddiq, who nationalized the Anglo-Iranian Oil Company in 1951.

After the shah was restored to power by a CIA-backed army coup in 1953, he seemed overshadowed by his U.S. and military advisers. Because of its location between the USSR and the Gulf, Iran played a strategic role in U.S. efforts to contain Soviet expansionism. When the Baghdad Pact (later renamed the Central Treaty Organization, or CENTO) was formed in 1955, Iran joined. In the early 1960s Americans urged the shah to clamp down on groups they viewed as blocking Iran's modernization: landlords, ulama, and bazaar merchants. The White Revolution, proclaimed in 1963 after a popular referendum, called for land redistribution, nationalizing Iran's forests, the sale of state-owned enterprises to private interests, electoral law changes to enfranchise women, profit sharing in industry, and the formation of a literacy corps to aid village education. Riots instigated by the Shi'i ulama broke out in various parts of Iran. One of the fiercest critics of the White Revolution was a teacher in Qom, Ayatollah Ruhollah Khomeini. The shah's secret police, SAVAK, used various threats and inducements to silence him. When all else failed, Khomeini was exiled. The shah used money and patronage to reward those ulama who would endorse his policies. Some did. Others quietly disapproved and subtly conveyed this attitude to their younger disciples in the *madrasah*s of Qom and Mashhad. One of Khomeini's most telling points in mobilizing the ulama against the shah was his attack on an agreement exempting U.S. civilian and military personnel from Iranian jurisdiction. Even though such exemptions are common in foreign aid agreements, they reminded Iranians of the Capitulations. Khomeini's campaign was aimed at U.S. influence, not just against the White Revolution.

The shah's policies were revolutionary in their attempt to change the lifestyle of the Iranian people. Their results, in terms of dams, bridges, roads, schools, clinics, factories, and farmers' cooperatives, look impressive on paper. The upsurge of Iranian oil revenue, from $817 million in 1968 to $2.25 billion in 1972–1973 to more than $20 billion in 1975–1976, financed a boom in construction. Bottlenecks often belied the goals: long lines of ships waiting to unload, goods rotting on the piers for lack of transport, and more trucks imported than there were Iranians trained to drive and repair them. Iran's schools and universities proliferated and turned out thousands of graduates who, especially in liberal arts, law, and commerce, were too numerous for the economy to absorb. In these areas, but also in science, medicine, and engineering, Iranians went abroad to earn higher degrees, marry foreigners, and never come back. Those who did return, or who never left, chose to live in Tehran rather than in the provincial cities and villages where their services were most needed. The capital city swelled from about 1 million inhabitants in 1945 to 5 million in 1977. Its traffic congestion and smog became dreadful. Apartment rents in Tehran rose fifteenfold between 1960 and 1975.

Imagine the revolutionary potential of a growing army of unemployed (or underemployed) intellectuals concentrated in Tehran. SAVAK watched dissidents, censored their writings, and imprisoned thousands. Amnesty International reported that many jailed artists, writers, and ulama were tortured, mutilated, and even killed. As for the peasants, the White Revolution gave few of them any share of the great estates. Its rural cooperatives did not provide seeds, fertilizer, tools, or draft animals to the farmers who most needed them. Historically a grain exporter, Iran became a net importer as agribusiness firms turned farmlands into fields of fruits and vegetables to sell to Europe. Farmers flocked to the cities to seek lucrative factory jobs. Corruption spread among government employees and contractors, who "did not understand" (a euphemism for "opposed") the White Revolution's aims but tried to enrich themselves and their families. All envied the thousands of American advisers, imported by the shah's regime for what, by local or U.S. standards, were princely wages.

The shah's opponents, especially Iranian students in Western universities, often portrayed him as an evil dictator with an authoritarian personality or a puppet of U.S. imperialism. His ambitions were indeed presumptuous. He dreamt of raising Iran's industrial output to the level of Italy or France by 1990. He assembled a huge armory of guns, tanks, and planes, hardly enough to stop a hypothetical Soviet invasion of his country but adequate to placate his elite officers, to cow his civilian critics, and to make Iran the policeman of the Gulf after Britain withdrew in 1971. The shah revealed his megalomania in the elaborate ceremonies for the coronation of himself and his wife in 1967 and for the 2,500th anniversary of the Iranian monarchy in 1971 (at a reported cost of $200 million). But if you blame the shah personally for the failure of his White Revolution, you may ignore other causes. Here are some: (1) Iran's bureaucratic elite had less experience with westernizing reform than did those of Turkey and Egypt, but it faced greater resistance from traditional leaders such as the rural landlords, tribal chiefs, bazaar merchants, and ulama; (2) the burgeoning oil revenues created more wealth than the economy could absorb; (3) both the traditional elites and those individuals or groups that rode the oil boom to power became divided and corrupt; (4) Iranians were nationalistic in resisting foreign control but insufficiently patriotic, as they imported outside advisers to use against their rivals; and (5) materialist values challenged religious belief among all social classes.

Although Western observers knew about these problems, they tended to play down the domestic opposition to the shah. In fact, U.S. Embassy personnel were not allowed to meet with politicians from Mosaddiq's National Front, even though they were milder than the shah's truly strong opponents. The vociferous ones were the Iranian students abroad; they were discounted as inexperienced, infiltrated by SAVAK agents, and often too alienated to come home. Despite their protests against the shah, many students got financial aid for their studies from the Iranian government or the Pahlavi Foundation. If the shah's domestic foes had any ideological coloring, it was supposed to be red, but the old Tudeh party was weak. Paradoxically, Moscow backed the shah's government almost as long as Washington did. Why did the experts ignore the "black" opposition, the Shi'i ulama? When I was writing the first edition of this book in 1979, I could find neither a definition of *ayatollah* nor a description of Shi'ism's clerical structure. Scholars and teachers of Middle East history have blind spots; we may follow fashionable concerns (or the media) instead of leading and forming public opinion.

Carter's concern for human rights exposed a flaw in the shah's regime that should have troubled earlier administrations, which had given Iran free rein to defend the Gulf and to decide what arms it wanted to buy from U.S. and European companies. Most American Middle East specialists tended to disregard Iran because they cared most about a resolution of the Arab-Israeli conflict.

### The Fall of the Monarchy

When 1978 began, Iran seemed to be stable and the shah's position secure, as implied by Carter's toast. Trouble started a week later when the minister of information planted an article in Tehran's leading newspaper attacking Khomeini. This led to a sit-in by religious students in Qom. Police attacked them, and several were killed. From then on, riots would break out every forty days, it being the Muslim custom to hold a memorial service on the fortieth day after a death. All the shah did in response to the spreading protest was to replace his SAVAK chief and his prime minister. A fire in an Abadan theater, killing 477 people, was widely blamed on SAVAK agents. In early September troops opened fire on a mass demonstration in Tehran's Jaleh Square, causing between 300 and 1,000 deaths and many injuries. At this time, the leading ayatollah in Tabriz, Shariat-Madari, told the new premier that the riots would continue until he restored parliamentary government under the 1906 constitution and let

Khomeini come back from his fourteen-year exile in the Shi'i holy city of al-Najaf in Iraq. Instead of readmitting the ayatollah, the Iranian government asked Iraq to expel him.

This move hurt the shah, for Khomeini moved to a Paris suburb, where other exiled opposition leaders gathered around him. Soon the ayatollah, viewed in the West as a throwback to the Middle Ages, was spreading his fundamentalist message by means of long-distance phone calls, tape cassettes, and Western television news broadcasts. His call for a workers' strike almost shut down Iran's oil industry. Foreign companies and customers, remembering the Arab oil embargo of 1973, became jittery about new shortages. Oil prices shot up. As the gravity of the Iranian crisis became clear in Washington, Carter's advisers debated whether to offer the shah more military support or to ease him out, perhaps with a regency for his eighteen-year-old son under a liberal coalition government. The shah declared martial law in early November, named a general as his premier, and banned all demonstrations during the ten days usually devoted to mourning the martyrdom of Husayn (the Prophet's grandson). The oil workers' strike spread to other industries. Mobs sacked and burned Tehran shops, notably liquor stores, cinemas, and other symbols of Western influence. Almost all members of the royal family, most foreigners, and many rich and educated Iranians left the country. Rallies and riots continued. Carter's special envoy urged the shah to form a coalition cabinet that would include opponents of his regime. On 6 January 1979 he asked the National Front's vice president, Shapur Bakhtiar, to head a government; ten days later the shah left Iran for good.

Joyful demonstrations followed the shah's departure, but the crisis continued as Khomeini, still in Paris, called on Iranians to overthrow Bakhtiar's government. The ayatollah was gradually taking charge as he set up his Revolutionary Islamic Council and refused to compromise with Bakhtiar, who gave in to popular pressure to let him return. Within days after Khomeini's arrival, the Iranian army stopped protecting the government; many soldiers gave away their guns and joined the demonstrators. On 11 February the shah's imperial guard fell, and so did Bakhtiar's cabinet. At no time could the United States (or any other outside power) have intervened with force to save the shah's government.

## The Establishment of the Republic

The first revolutionary cabinet, headed by Mehdi Bazargan, an engineer who had managed Iran's nationalized oil industry under Mosaddiq, combined moderate reformers with extremist Muslims. It called on the strikers to go back to work (most did) and set up a national plebiscite on Iran's future government. Held in March, the referendum showed near unanimous support for an Islamic republic, as advocated by the ayatollah. An assembly of lawyers and ulama drew up a new constitution. Revolutionary committees effected drastic changes throughout the country. Royal symbols were destroyed in actions that ranged from blowing up monuments to cutting the shah's picture out of the paper money. Poor people seized and occupied the abandoned palaces. Streets were renamed, textbooks rewritten, political prisons emptied (soon they would be refilled), and agents of the old regime tried and executed. When Westerners deplored this reign of terror, Iranians asked why the shah's government had committed worse atrocities and yet had not been scolded by the Western media. Tehran's new regime was soon challenged by nationalist revolts—Turks in Azerbaijan, Kurds, Arabs, Baluchis, and Khurasani Turcomans—all seeking greater autonomy. It was the old story of regional and ethnic forces in Iran battling against the central government during a time of crisis. The revolutionary regime had to restore the army and the secret police—even some of the shah's personnel—to protect itself. Under the new constitution, legislative authority would be vested in a Majlis dominated by ulama. In contested cases, verdicts would be made by Khomeini, as the state's leading *faqih* (judicial expert). But in the summer and fall of 1979 the ulama did not yet have full control; Premier Bazargan and other moderates were trying to maintain some ties to the West, and both the left-wing revolutionary committees and the remaining right-wing generals posed potential threats to the regime.

## The Hostage Crisis

The revolution shook U.S.-Iranian relations. It exposed the weakness of Washington's Middle East policy, which was predicated on a stable, pro-Western regime in Tehran. Despite their cautious peace feelers, each side distrusted the other. Carter had just brought Egypt and Israel together to sign their peace treaty, arousing widespread Muslim (not just Arab) anger against Sadat. Iranians seized Israel's embassy in Tehran and gave it to the PLO, and the new regime invited Arafat to Iran. In February militants broke into the U.S. Embassy, but the government promptly drove them out. Iranians anxiously watched the deposed shah's movements, recalling how he had fled at the height of Mosaddiq's power in 1953, only to return following the CIA-backed army coup. Would history repeat itself? The shah moved from Egypt to Morocco to the Caribbean to Mexico as his health grew worse. Would he be admitted into the United States? The Carter administration, concerned about U.S. citizens still in Iran, hoped the shah would stay away. In October, though, his doctors advised him to go to New York for specialized treatment. Pressured by the shah's friends (among them Kissinger), the U.S. government let him in.

Iran's response to this provocation came from a group of women students, followed by armed men, who broke into the U.S. Embassy compound (whose marine guards had been ordered not to resist) and took sixty-three Americans hostage. They demanded that the United States send the shah back to Iran for trial and apologize for its role in his crimes against the Iranian people. The U.S. government and people were outraged at this gross violation of international law. Popular slogans such as "nuke Iran" articulated this anger. Most Americans urged Carter to punish Iran, but what could the United States have done without endangering the hostages? Attacking Iran would have enflamed anti-Western wrath throughout the Muslim world. The United States stopped buying oil from Iran, froze more than $11 billion in Iranian assets deposited in U.S. banks, required 50,000 Iranians holding U.S. student visas to register, and took various measures in other countries (and in NATO, the UN, and the World Court) to press Iran's government to make the militants set the hostages free from their captivity in the embassy. Nothing worked.

The United States' moderation could not stop angry mobs from storming its embassies in Pakistan and Libya. Sunni militants captured the main mosque in Mecca and held it for two weeks before the Saudi army and national guard took it back in a bloody affray. Shi'i militants demonstrated in eastern Saudi Arabia. In effect, the ayatollah and the militant students holding the U.S. Embassy came to symbolize Third World peoples' new assertiveness against Western power; in the eyes of the American public, they stood for their government's weakness against "militant Islam." People tended to forget that Iran and the United States, however much they hated each other in November 1979, would still need each other in the long run. The USSR reminded them the following month by sending 100,000 troops into neighboring Afghanistan.

The hostage crisis, during its 444-day duration, sparked major changes: Premier Bazargan's replacement by an avowed Khomeini supporter, the Soviet occupation of Afghanistan, the movement of U.S. forces into the Indian Ocean, the military takeover in Turkey to end fighting between its

Muslim and Marxist factions, Iraq's invasion of Iran in September 1980, and Reagan's decisive victory over Carter in the 1980 election. Iran could no longer sell oil to Western customers, causing domestic hardships such as unemployment and price inflation. The hostage crisis also strengthened the militant ulama against their rivals: secular nationalists, moderate reformers, Marxists, and separatists. When a secular nationalist won Iran's presidential election, causing Americans to hope that he would release the hostages, the ayatollah made sure that he was stymied by Muslim militants in the cabinet and in the new Majlis.

No Western-educated politician, no matter how strongly he had opposed the shah, could hold power in this new regime; but the army regained some of its luster (and power) when the U.S. attempt to rescue the hostages failed in April 1980 and when Iraq invaded Iran that September. Once Iran found itself at war with Iraq and needed more money and military spare parts, the American hostages were no longer worth keeping. By this time, the shah had died in Cairo. Following patient mediation by Algerian diplomats, Iran agreed to free its remaining fifty-two captives (it already had released a few) in return for releasing its frozen assets, from which would be deducted an escrow fund to cover claims made against the Iranian government (the amount returned was about $8 billion), and a pro forma U.S. promise not to meddle in its internal affairs. Iran's fears of dealing with President-elect Reagan may have forced this settlement. No U.S. administration would help Iran to recover the assets of the late shah's family outside the country.

Once the hostages were freed, Iran faded from Americans' minds. In 1981 political unrest intensified throughout the Middle East; bombs and bullets randomly killed ayatollahs, presidents, prime ministers, and party leaders. Iran's elected president won some popularity by visiting Iranian forces fighting against Iraq, but he was gradually shorn of his power. Finally forced to resign, he went into exile in France, where he joined the growing number of Iranians plotting to overthrow the ayatollah. The much-feared Soviet invasion never came, despite Iranian aid to the Afghan rebels. Rather, Moscow sent arms and advisers to the new regime, which consolidated its power but became as repressive as the late shah's government. By August 1979 the government had set up an auxiliary army, the Islamic Revolutionary Guard Corps, which trained Muslim (especially Shi'i) militants from many countries in the techniques of terrorist combat. The results of their labors would be seen in various terrorist incidents during the 1980s, notably in Lebanon and in some of the Gulf states.

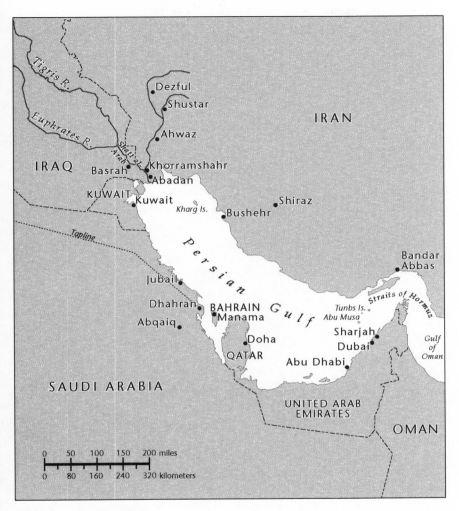

MAP 12 The Gulf area

## THE STRUGGLE FOR GULF SUPREMACY

During the 1970s most of the oil bought by noncommunist industrial countries came from states surrounding the Gulf: Oman, the United Arab Emirates, Qatar, Bahrain, Saudi Arabia, Kuwait, Iraq, and Iran (see Map 12). Huge tankers carried the oil through the Straits of Hormuz and the Gulf of Oman into the Arabian Sea and the Indian Ocean. Even when Iran, OPEC's second greatest oil producer up to 1978, cut its output during the revolution, the slack was soon taken up by Saudi Arabia and its neighbors. The revolution also ended Iran's role, taken over from Britain, as the policeman of the Gulf area. The other countries (except Iraq) had big oil resources and revenues, small native populations, and many immigrant workers. Usually young adult males, unmarried or without their families and often from countries far away, these workers might subvert conservative Gulf societies.

The U.S. government harped on a possible Soviet invasion across Iran, for the Russians had long been thought to harbor designs on the Gulf and its oil. The Soviet government, with good reason, noted various speeches and articles in which Americans threatened to seize the oil fields to protect them against revolutionaries. The local Arab rulers, hereditary monarchs except in Iraq, feared revolutions like the one that convulsed Iran but did not want to open their lands to U.S. military bases. When some Americans expressed the hope that Israel would defend their oil interests, the Arabs replied that they feared Israeli expansion more than the spread of Soviet power. This outlook was jolted a bit when the USSR, annoyed by the ineptitude of the Marxist regime it had helped set up in Afghanistan, invaded the country in late 1979. This sudden and massive influx of Soviet troops, into a mountainous land poor in oil resources but strategically close to both Pakistan and Iran, budged Arab perceptions slightly but galvanized Washington to act. Addressing Congress in January 1980, Carter warned that he would view any attempt by an outside force to gain control of the Gulf area as an attack on U.S. vital national interests and could lead to war. This Carter Doctrine, as it came to be called, was a risky declaration by the United States at a time when its embassy in Iran (the country most apt to be invaded) was occupied by militants backed by their government. It even seems foolhardy in retrospect, for the United States lacked the means to transport, deploy, and maintain a fighting force large enough to deter Soviet aggression, if any were contemplated. No Gulf state wanted to base U.S. naval or military personnel, most of whom would probably be (like their foreign workers) unattached young men who could stir up social problems. U.S. bases would make them more vulnerable if a war broke out between the superpowers. Did the Carter administration plan to use Egyptian troops, who had fought none too well against Libya in 1977, or Israelis, capable fighters but bound to provoke the hatred of local Arabs? Clearly, if the Gulf needed to be defended against an invader, the task should be performed by armies raised within that region. This perception led the Gulf states to buy more arms, train more troops, and coordinate their military planning, under their new Gulf Cooperation Council.

No superpower confrontation occurred in the Gulf region. Neither side would risk a war to occupy it. In 1979–1980 the United States was viewed as perilously weak, but the USSR soon turned out to be vulnerable, too, for about a fifth of its people—and a higher proportion of its youth—were Muslim. Most Soviet Muslims could be reached by Tehran radio, and they were open to Islamist and nationalist propaganda. The Soviets also found that their prolonged occupation of Afghanistan was costly in lives and equipment, insufficient to pacify the mountainous countryside, and bitterly resented in other Muslim countries, which took in about 4 million Afghan refugees. The United States and the USSR thus kept each other from becoming the dominant power in the Gulf, but both committed ships and troops to the region and escorted Kuwaiti oil tankers past would-be Iranian attackers under their own flags.

Broadly speaking, the Gulf states realized that their own security depends on never letting one country become strong enough to control all the others. As you may recall from Chapter 10, this is the balance-of-power concept that kept the peace in nineteenth-century Europe. During the 1970s the country that had dominated the Gulf was Iran, due to the shah's military buildup. When a rebellion, abetted by South Yemen (and indirectly by the USSR), had threatened Oman's sultan, Iranian troops came to his rescue in 1973. When the Kurdish revolt against Iraq heated up in 1973–1974, Iran stopped arming the rebels only after Iraq agreed in 1975 to share its control over the Shatt al-Arab waterway, an agreement that Iraq would denounce in 1980 and revive in 1990. The Islamic revolution eclipsed Iran's predominance, at least for a while. Saudi Arabia was too sparsely populated and inadequately armed to take Iran's place as the guardian of the Gulf.

But Iraq aspired to do so. The second largest of the eastern Arab states in both area and population, Iraq had used its abundant oil resources since the 1920s to build an economic infrastructure suited to both industrial and agricultural development. Political turbulence from 1958 to 1970 (plus the Kurdish revolt) slowed its growth, but after that it became more stable, under the forceful rule of Saddam Husayn, and developed rapidly. The country was armed by and aligned with the USSR.

Yet Iraq did not live up to its potential. With two rivers, abundant oil, deserts, mountains, and fertile valleys, it could have wielded greater power but for the divisions among its people. Iraq's Muslims are more than 55 percent Shi'i (with strong ties to Iran), and about 30 percent of its Sunni Muslims are either Kurdish or Turkish; yet the government has always been controlled by a Sunni Muslim and Arab elite. Still, Iraq aspired to unite the Arabs, as Prussia had led Germany's unification. It laid claim to Kuwait from the 1930s, trying to annex it in 1961 and occupying it in 1990. Iraq has never made an armistice agreement with Israel. It tried to block Sadat's peace efforts and gathered all the other Arab heads of state to condemn the Egyptian-Israeli peace treaty in 1979. When Egypt's Arab League membership was suspended, Iraq hoped to replace it as the leading Arab state. But how could Iraq prove itself?

Its answer was to attack revolutionary Iran, which threatened the security of its Arab neighbors, in September 1980. President Saddam Husayn accused Iran of violating the 1975 treaty (which he had negotiated on Iraq's behalf) by not giving up a piece of its mountainous territory closest to Baghdad. Iran had also kept three Gulf islands that the shah had annexed (from the United Arab Emirates) in 1971 because of their closeness to the Straits of Hormuz. Iraq expected the restive minorities in western Iran, especially the ethnic Arabs of oil-rich Khuzistan, to rebel against Tehran and help their Iraqi liberators. Iran, by the same logic, hoped to weaken Iraq by appealing to its Shi'i Muslim majority. Neither ploy worked. Each side tried using its air power to destroy the other's oil pipelines and refineries or to demoralize civilians. Iraq invaded the Iranian provinces of Kurdistan and Khuzistan, took Khorramshahr, and surrounded Abadan, whose oil refinery was nearly destroyed. Military and civilian casualties were high, higher than in any other modern Middle Eastern war, and the Iran-Iraq War lasted much longer than the Iraqis had planned. They had counted on Iran's internal instability, on its inability to buy spare parts for its inherited arsenal of U.S. weapons, and on possible Western support to help thwart Iran during the American hostage crisis.

Carter's administration backed neither side at first, fearing that an Iranian defeat would enhance Soviet power. The USSR sold its arms to both sides. Iraq got help from Jordan, Saudi Arabia, and even Egypt, whereas Iran had the support of Syria and Libya. In other words, the status quo states gravitated toward Baghdad and the revolutionary ones toward Tehran. Iran had lots of trained officers and soldiers, U.S. tanks and aircraft, and three times as many people as Iraq. The two sides settled into a stalemate for more than a year. Then in 1982 Iran made a comeback. Roused by the ayatollah's religious appeals, Iran's army (beefed up by teenaged volunteers) retook nearly all the lands Iraq had won earlier. Tehran demanded that Iraq admit to having started the war, pay an indemnity, and oust Saddam Husayn.

The Soviets veered toward Iran; Iraq, without renouncing its ties with Moscow, made overtures to the Reagan administration. Israel, too, entered the picture by bombing Iraq's French-built nuclear reactor in 1981 just before it was to go into operation and by selling arms and spare parts to Iran, despite Tehran's fierce anti-Zionist rhetoric, because it feared that an Iraqi victory would unleash Arab militants against the Jewish state. The United States publicly condemned this policy, but in 1986 it became known that the Reagan administration had covertly promoted the sale of missiles and spare parts to Iran in the hope of securing the release of Americans held hostage by Shi'i militants in Lebanon. The proceeds of the sales were funneled through secret Swiss bank accounts to aid Contra rebels who were trying to oust the Sandinista government in Nicaragua. Some reports revealed that Reagan's National Security Council had even urged Saudi Arabia and Egypt to help supply spare parts to Iran. To placate Iraq, Washington provided Baghdad with intelligence information, not wholly accurate, about Iran.

As the war continued, the United States and Israel hoped to prevent a decisive victory by either side. But the prolonged war threatened to impoverish both Iran and Iraq, to draw their backers into the fray, to endanger anyone shipping oil through the Gulf, and to weaken the economies of all oil-exporting states in the region. Both Iran and Iraq attacked oil tankers, not only each other's but those of neutral countries as well. The U.S. government reflagged some Kuwaiti vessels, and its navy escorted them past Iranian mines and speedboats. By 1988 Iran could no longer buy enough arms or spare parts. Iraq was using mustard gas and other chemical weapons against Iran and its Kurdish allies (who were Iraqi citizens). When a U.S. naval ship shot down an Iranian passenger plane and the chorus of protest was curiously muted, Tehran realized that it had few friends left in the world. Nearly bankrupt, Iran accepted a 1987 Security Council resolution calling for a cease-fire. The fighting ended in August 1988.

## THE RETREAT FROM CAMP DAVID

After having been enemies for thirty years and having fought five wars against each other, Egypt and Israel agreed in 1977–1978 to make peace because both needed a respite from fighting—or so they thought at that time. The protracted arms race and the destructiveness of their wars had impoverished Egypt and turned Israel into a fortress state. The prospect of an end to this cycle of war and rearmament encouraged both Egyptians and Israelis. The Americans, who perceived this hope, seemed wiser than the Soviets, who went on backing the rejectionist Arab states. The terms of the Egyptian-Israeli peace treaty, the Carter administration's greatest achievement, seemed to meet each side's basic needs: the phased restoration to Egypt of the Sinai Peninsula (taken by Israel in 1967); guarantees, backed by a multinational force that included Americans, that neither side would mass its troops to attack the other; mutual diplomatic recognition; and facilitation of trade, tourism, cultural exchanges, communications, and technical aid. The United States would assist ongoing talks between Israel and Egypt—plus, if possible, Jordan and the Palestinians—to arrange full autonomy for those Palestinians under Israeli administration.

Signing the peace treaty with Israel exposed Sadat to the wrath of the other Arab countries, but he contemptuously ignored their blandishments and parried their insults, even when the oil-rich countries cut off aid to Egypt. The Egyptian people did not like to abandon the Arab states to back Israel, but they also were tired of being the blood bank for every Arab war against the Jewish state. The Palestinians, so the saying went in Cairo, would go on fighting against Israel—to their last Egyptian soldier! If the Arabs had really wanted to humble Egypt, discredit Sadat, and derail the Camp David accords, they could have sent home the million Egyptian teachers, doctors, engineers, skilled workers, and peasants who had jobs in their countries and remitted their savings to Egypt. Their failure to do so suggests that they needed to use Egyptian brains and brawn more than they wanted to prove their ideological purity. Sadat expected the other Arab states to come around to support Egypt's peace policy. Many would do so late in the 1980s, but only Oman and the Sudan backed him in 1979.

If the other Arab states did not get on the peace bandwagon, part of the blame fell on Israel's government, which exploited its deal with Egypt to clamp down on the 1.4 million Arabs in Gaza, the West Bank, and the Golan Heights. "Full autonomy," Prime Minister Begin explained, was to be accorded to the *inhabitants* of these occupied areas, provided the Palestinians gained no control over defense, the police, or even the water supply on which their food and flocks depended. Jews were encouraged by subsidized mortgage loans to settle in these areas so that no outside power (let alone the UN) could ever turn the lands over to the Arab majority.

Of course, the Palestine National Council (the PLO's executive arm) thwarted the peace process, too, by its adherence to the 1964 charter calling for Arab control of all Palestine (meaning Israel's destruction) and by its murky involvement in terrorism. No one knew what the PLO could do to force or persuade the Israelis to hand their country over to the Palestinians. Could Israel somehow coerce or convince the Palestinians to renounce the PLO? The two sides disagreed on how to make peace.

*The Assassination of Sadat*

The peace treaty with Israel raised the Egyptian people's hopes that some money earmarked for defense could now be shifted into domestic programs. The regained Sinai would become a new frontier for settlement and development. Egypt at peace would draw Western investors and tourists, another boost to economic recovery. The Arab boycott of Egypt after it signed the 1979 treaty did not stop the country's economic revival. Although foreign investment was disappointing, revenues from the sale of Egypt's oil, Suez Canal tolls, tourism revenues, and emigrants' remittances did increase after Camp David, giving Egypt a balance-of-payments surplus in 1980 for the first time in years. This surplus did not recur, nor did growth benefit most of the Egyptian people. Sadat was not interested in economic or social issues. His open-door policy benefited only a small group of newly rich entrepreneurs.

The average Egyptian, squeezed by price inflation, housing costs, and deteriorating public services, longed to move to North Africa or the Gulf states. The villain is overpopulation. Egypt in 2001 has four times as many people as in 1952 but roughly the same amount of cultivable land. Its agriculture cannot feed its own population, increasing by 1.2 million per year. Birth control and family planning are on the rise, but so too are the housing and industry that compete with agriculture for Egypt's scarce land. Egypt produced in 1994 only 46 percent of the wheat that its citizens consumed (it has increased grain production since then in order to reduce the gap between imports and exports). Roughly one-fifth of the state budget subsidizes the purchase of basic necessities, to keep bread, sugar, butane gas, and kerosene affordable. These subsidies benefit all buyers, even rich Egyptians and foreign residents. Labor unemployment (or underemployment) holds down Egyptian salaries and wages.

Imagine how you would feel if you were an Egyptian man, aged twenty, studying law at Cairo University, where over 100,000 students use facilities intended for one-tenth of that number. Upon completing your arduous training, if you did not have to spend one to three years in the Egyptian army, you could expect to find a government job paying about 300 Egyptian pounds (U.S. $100) per month—more if you had good connections or worked in a private law firm that had rich clients. If you wanted to get married, you would have to wait until you had saved enough money from your earnings to buy an apartment or to be able to pay at least 3,000 pounds ($1000) in "key money" for a rental unit, in addition to the costs of furniture and appliances. This could prevent you from marrying until you were thirty or forty! It is not surprising that Egypt has many bachelors in their twenties and thirties who still live with parents or other relatives until they can save enough money to move out and get married. Women may marry younger, but often to men who are twice as old as they are. There are growing numbers of educated women who, if they find jobs, face sexual discrimination (including harassment) in a male-dominated work environment.

The frustration level in the early 1980s, therefore, was high. Many Egyptians felt that Sadat's policies could not or would not help them. Although some Egyptians (especially the most educated) became Marxists, scientific socialism had no general appeal in a highly religious society. Religion scored major gains, among Copts as well as Muslims, after Egypt's 1967 defeat. Islamic groups permeated nearly all aspects of Egyptian life. The Muslim Brothers survived Nasir's purges, and new secret societies arose. Some resorted to terrorist acts, inspired by the Iranian revolution. At first, Sadat promoted the formation of nonrevolutionary Muslim societies to counter the Marxist and Nasirite ones, especially at the universities. Muslims called for the application of the Shari'ah to all the laws of the country. The Copts, about one-tenth of Egypt's population, also became more politicized, and violent communal strife broke out in a workers' district of Cairo in July 1981. Even before then Sadat was clamping down on religious extremists, using popular referenda to pass laws to curb opposition to his policies, including peace with Israel. In September 1981 he banned the Muslim Brothers' popular magazine, *al-Da'wah;* imposed censorship on mosque sermons; and locked up 1,500 alleged opponents without trial. Because the U.S. government was spending $2 billion a year on economic, technical, and military assistance to Egypt, mainly as a result of the treaty with Israel, many Americans failed to see that Sadat had lost touch with his own people.

On 6 October, the eighth anniversary of Egypt's successful crossing of the Suez Canal to attack the Israelis occupying the Sinai, Sadat and most of his top officials were viewing a military parade in Victory City, a Cairo suburb. An army truck halted, apparently because of a mechanical failure, in front of the presidential reviewing stand. Four soldiers jumped out. Thinking they had stopped to salute him, Sadat rose to face them, whereupon they pointed their machine guns at him and opened fire, murdering the president and several of his aides. All but one of the assassins were killed. Police investigations unearthed a large conspiracy, both within the army and in Egypt generally, as well as a network of terrorist groups, of which the best known was called *al-Takfir wa al-Hijrah* (meaning, roughly, "Identifying Unbelief and Avoiding Evil"). Many of the terrorists, including the surviving assassin, were put on trial. Various Arab leaders, notably Libya's Qadhafi, rejoiced at Sadat's death; only a few Egyptians mourned him. The question remains: Was Sadat killed for having made peace with Israel, because economic and social conditions in Egypt were so bad, or due to the Islamic revival? Perhaps all three causes were relevant.

Vice President Husni Mubarak, who had commanded Egypt's air force during the 1973 war, was chosen by the National Assembly (followed by a popular referendum) to succeed Sadat. He declared a state of emergency, clamped tight controls on the universities and the press, and arrested more revolutionaries. But he also freed some of the political and religious leaders Sadat had jailed, busing them directly from prison to a reception at his office. He restored some public trust in the government by promising economic and social reforms and by linking himself with Nasir's legacy at the expense of Sadat's. Talks with Israel about Palestinian autonomy dragged on, and in April 1982 Egypt regained the rest of the Sinai. Israel's invasion of Lebanon in June 1982 caused Mubarak to recall Egypt's ambassador in Tel Aviv, and relations between the two states turned into a "cold peace." Israel suspected Egypt of backing away from the treaty to regain its leadership of the Arab world; the Egyptian government was embarrassed by Israel's occupation of southern Lebanon and its increasingly repressive policies in the West Bank and Gaza. Egypt did resume diplomatic ties with Jordan, aid Iraq in its war against Iran, and welcome Yasir Arafat to Cairo in 1983. But at the same time it took billions of U.S. aid dollars and continued its war of nerves with Qadhafi.

In 1984 Egypt had its freest parliamentary elections since 1952. Mubarak's National Democratic party won a majority of National Assembly seats, but opposition parties, notably the New Wafd, scored impressive gains. Egypt's economic problems grew worse as oil prices fell and 1986 security police riots frightened away foreign tourists. Relations with the United States and Israel became frayed at times, but peace prevailed, and Mubarak managed to stay in power. The other Arab governments restored diplomatic ties with Cairo, Egypt was readmitted to the Arab League, and Mubarak led in promoting the peace process.

## Israel's Rising Militancy

Peace with Egypt did not make Israel feel secure about its position as a Jewish island in an Arab sea. Increasingly, it felt that its only real ally was the United States. The Reagan administration came to power with the notion that it could develop a "strategic consensus" of governments opposed to Soviet expansion in the Middle East, including Egypt, Israel, Jordan, Saudi Arabia, and Pakistan. One means of building this consensus was to sell arms. Just after Sadat's assassination, the U.S. Senate—pressured by the White House in competition against the American Israel Public Affairs Committee (AIPAC), the powerful pro-Israel lobby—voted by a narrow margin to approve the sale of four airborne warning and control system (AWACS) planes to Saudi Arabia. Washington's efforts to court pro-Western Arab governments were both a result and a cause of Israel's ever more militant stance toward Arab governments and the PLO. Since its formation in 1977, Begin's government had followed a harsh policy against Palestinians living in the occupied areas. It also backed a group of Jewish militants, *Gush Emunim* (Bloc of the Faithful), in its plans to form new settlements or to raise the Jewish population of those already set up on the West Bank. The Jewish settlers had guns and might attack Palestinians at random; the Palestinians could be arrested for carrying knives or throwing rocks at Israeli military vehicles.

Although Palestinians in the occupied territories and other countries viewed the PLO as their representative, Israel regarded it as a terrorist group with which it would never negotiate for peace. If Israel wished to weaken the PLO, it had to attack Lebanon, its center of operations since Black September 1970. Reluctantly at first, the PLO was drawn into the Lebanese civil war in 1975, suffering a severe defeat when Syria intervened on the Christian side and captured the well-fortified Palestinian "refugee camp" (really a military base) of Tel Za'tar, near Beirut. Once the Syrians settled in as an occupying army, they gradually shifted to the side of the Lebanese Muslims and the PLO, which became dominant in various parts of Lebanon, including west Beirut. Palestinian *fidaiyin* often would launch dramatic raids against civilian targets inside Israel. The latter struck back by bombing the "refugee camps" in southern Lebanon. In March 1978 the Israel Defense Force occupied the area up to the Litani River. The UN Security Council condemned the invasion and set up a 4,000-man, multinational buffer force to replace the IDF and restore peace to southern Lebanon. Under U.S. pressure, Israel's cabinet agreed to withdraw the IDF, provided that the PLO be kept out of the buffer zone. The Israelis had no faith in any UN peacekeeping force; instead, they trusted the Christian militia of Sa'd Haddad, a renegade Lebanese colonel who in 1979 set up his "Republic of Free Lebanon" in the south. Israel absorbed the southern Lebanese Christians into its economy, thus gaining an added interest in Lebanon.

Israel went on making intermittent air raids against PLO strongholds in Lebanon, ignoring the UN presence there. These raids were usually intended as reprisals for Palestinian attacks, but Begin also asserted Israel's right to bombard "terrorists" in Lebanon even without prior provocation. The situation worsened in 1981 as Palestinians fired rockets into northern Israel and Israeli artillery pounded the coastal towns of Sidon and Tyre. Both sides stepped up their attacks. Twice in July, Israeli planes bombed Beirut, killing hundreds and injuring thousands of civilians, both Palestinian and Lebanese. Reagan's administration sent a special negotiator, Philip Habib, to arrange a cease-fire that Arafat, Begin, and all the Lebanese factions accepted, but Lebanon remained tense. Syria refused to remove the surface-to-air missiles it had installed in Lebanon's Biqa' Valley, despite Israel's threats to bomb them as it had Iraq's nuclear reactor.

Israel was showing greater hostility toward the Arabs in other ways. On the West Bank it periodically closed Arab schools and universities, expelled elected mayors who backed the PLO, and increased the size and number of Jewish settlements. Israel sought an alternative to the PLO as a negotiating partner, but few Palestinians came forward. Israel ascribed this attitude to PLO threats on the lives of would-be collaborators. But in spite of a long Israeli occupation that had materially benefited many Palestinians, few were willing to bargain directly with Jerusalem to gain more autonomy. Even replacing the military government with a civilian one did not soften Israel's occupation policies or make the Palestinians more compliant. Rather, they grew more sullen and militant during the 1980s.

As you know, in June 1981 Israel bombed and wiped out Iraq's nuclear reactor. Although Begin justified this belligerent act as protecting Israel's security, others wondered how secure the Arabs could feel living next door to Israel's functioning reactors and (unacknowledged) possession of nuclear arms. In December 1981 Begin's cabinet formally extended the application of Israeli law to the Golan Heights, which amounted to their annexation. The UN Security Council condemned both acts, but the world body's perceived anti-Israel bias blunted the moral force of these resolutions. Israel simply shrugged them off.

The Begin government did claim that it had carried out its treaty obligations to Egypt. Israel (with U.S. government aid) spent vast sums to move its military equipment from the Sinai to newly constructed bases in the Negev Desert. It offered Israeli settlers generous inducements to leave their homes, factories, and gardens in the Sinai, for Egypt did not want any Israelis to stay. When some in Yamit resisted, the IDF forcibly removed the recalcitrant settlers and bulldozed all buildings just before the area was returned to Egypt. When Egypt got back the rest of the Sinai in April 1982, the sole contested area was a 250-acre (105-hectare) plot along the Gulf of Aqaba containing an Israeli resort hotel in the village of Taba, just on the Egyptian side of the international frontier. Ironically, Taba had given its name to an earlier dispute between British-ruled Egypt and the Ottoman Empire, leading to the 1906 demarcation of that "international frontier" now separating Egypt and Israel. The new Taba Affair was finally submitted to arbitration and resolved in Egypt's favor in 1989.

## The Israeli Invasion of Lebanon

The strife in Lebanon—Christian against Muslim, rich fighting poor, Lebanese separatist versus Arab nationalist—went on and on. By the 1980s many of the fighters were teenaged boys who had never known peace. In May 1982 Israel bombed a Palestinian base near Beirut, killing twenty-five people. The Palestinians shelled northern Israel, and unidentified agents killed an Israeli diplomat in Paris and badly wounded Israel's ambassador in London. This last act provided the pretext for a massive IDF invasion of southern Lebanon on 6 June. Ignoring all outside diplomatic efforts to stop the fighting, Israel thrust northward, bypassing the UN troops and pushing back both PLO and Syrian forces. The Arabs suffered many casualties. Thousands of civilians, Lebanese and Palestinian alike, lost their homes. Taking advantage of surprise and complete control over the air, the Israelis bombed Beirut heavily and destroyed many Syrian missiles in the Biqa' Valley. Extensive press and television coverage showed the efficiency of the IDF invasion—and its cost in human suffering. Israel admitted using U.S.-made cluster bombs against "terrorists" (some of the victims were civilians). The Arab states, including Egypt, condemned the invasion as well as the U.S. vetoes that had blocked two Security Council resolutions against Israel. Noting that the U.S. kept on shipping arms to Israel, the Arabs suspected covert American support for the invasion. But no Arab state sent troops to help the Syrians and Palestinians in Lebanon. By mid-June the IDF had surrounded Beirut. For the first time, Israel was besieging an Arab capital, but the Arabs could not defend it. The USSR thundered and threatened—but did not act. It was at this time that Iranians set up their revolutionary training centers in the Biqa' Valley.

Washington was free to act, but the Reagan administration was split on what it wanted. Secretary of State Alexander Haig left office, probably because he would have backed Israel in destroying the PLO in Lebanon.

Other U.S. officials were angry at the Israeli invasion, anxious about possible Arab reprisals against American interests, and eager to bring peace to Lebanon. Some hoped for a general Middle East peace. The new secretary of state, George Shultz, drafted the Reagan Peace Plan, announced on 1 September 1982, calling for Israel's withdrawal from the West Bank and Gaza, free elections, and a five-year transition period to autonomy for the Palestinians and probable federation with Jordan. Israel and the PLO rejected the plan, Egypt accepted it, Jordan looked it over warily, and the Americans quietly shelved it. The Arab heads of state, meeting at Fez one week later, produced their own plan, proposing a Palestinian state and hinting at recognizing Israel.

But everyone was watching Lebanon, where Washington hoped to make peace. Earlier, Philip Habib had shuttled between Jerusalem, Beirut, and Damascus until he came up with an arrangement that provided for a partial Israeli pullback and a complete Palestinian withdrawal from the western half of Beirut, both of which were to be supervised by U.S. Marines and French and Italian soldiers. Negotiations would continue among the parties to set up a new government and to evacuate all foreign forces from Lebanon. In August the fighting in Beirut abated, allowing Israel's forces to pull back and permitting the PLO to get out. Meanwhile, Lebanon's parliament—unchanged for ten years—met to elect a new president. The sole candidate was Bashir Jumayyil, a leader of the Maronite paramilitary group called the Phalanges. Owing to his ties to the Christian side in the civil war, many opposition deputies boycotted the session at which Jumayyil was elected. Elated, Begin hoped Israel could reach a lasting peace with a Christian-dominated Lebanon.

The other side did not give up. On 14 September a bomb blew up the Phalanges' headquarters in east Beirut, killing the occupants, including Bashir Jumayyil. The IDF promptly occupied west Beirut and began rooting out PLO pockets of resistance that remained, in violation of Habib's peace plan. The IDF allowed the Phalanges to enter the Palestinian "camps" of Shatila and Sabra, where the Lebanese Christians massacred hundreds of Palestinian men, women, and children during a two-day rampage. Everyone was shocked, including the Israelis, who set up a commission to look into the cause of the massacres. The Israeli commission found that the IDF commander, Gen. Ariel Sharon, had facilitated the Sabra and Shatila massacres and recommended that he be excluded from future cabinets. The U.S.-French-Italian force was brought back into Beirut—for a longer stay this time—to restore peace. Lebanon's Parliament elected Amin Jumayyil, Bashir's older brother, to serve as president.

If Lebanon were to have peace, the domestic factions would have to revise their government's constitution and disarm their numerous militia groups. Foreign troops—the Syrians authorized by the Arab League to be in Lebanon; Palestinian *fidaiyin*; Israeli invaders; the UN buffer force; and the multinational force of France, Italy, and the United States (also joined by Britain)—would all have to leave the country. But in what order? The United States wanted a phased withdrawal, to be negotiated by all the involved parties. Syria wanted the other foreign troops to leave unconditionally. In late 1982 and early 1983, representatives of Lebanon, Israel, and the United States carried on lengthy deliberations leading to a treaty laboriously crafted by Shultz. It soon collapsed, as the IDF would not leave unless the Syrians and the PLO simultaneously withdrew their armies from the parts of Lebanon they were occupying. President Asad, opposed by Islamist Sunnis at home (he had massacred at least 20,000 of them and leveled half of Syria's conservative Muslim city, Hama, in 1982), refused to oblige the Americans by pulling out of Lebanon. Although Amin Jumayyil had signed it, the 1983 Lebanese-Israeli Treaty became a dead letter.

The emerging forces in Lebanon were ones that no one had ever bothered to notice. In the early years of the fighting, outside observers assumed that the main religious groups were Maronite Christians and Sunni Muslims. Westerners ignored the Shi'i Muslims, who predominated in the Biqa' Valley and parts of southern Lebanon. Gradually, though, they had become the country's largest sect, and many were flocking to Beirut's poorer districts in search of work. Many Shi'is at first welcomed Israel's invasion, hoping that it might weaken the Sunni Lebanese and the Palestinians. But when the Israelis stayed for months, the Shi'is turned against them. A growing number of Iranian agents found many Shi'i youths who were willing to become martyrs in an effort to drive out the Israelis and their perceived allies, the U.S. troops. A series of terrorist bombings ensued, hitting such targets as the U.S. embassies in Beirut and Kuwait, the U.S. Marine barracks at the Beirut airport, and even the French military headquarters (partly because France was arming Iraq against Iran). U.S. and Israeli reprisals against villages believed to be harboring the terrorists rendered many Lebanese homeless and further embittered the people against foreigners. The heavy loss of American lives in the Marine barracks blast, the threats against other U.S. citizens in Lebanon, and the murder of President Malcolm Kerr of the American University of Beirut sapped the will of the U.S. peacekeeping mission. Reagan decided to remove the contingent to the Sixth Fleet offshore. It was soon withdrawn "over the horizon." The French, British, and Italian contingents also pulled out in early 1984.

## The Terrorist Triumph

West Beirut fell under the control of Shi'i and Druze militia, and the fighting raged on in Lebanon. Amin Jumayyil's government could not restore order, even though it renounced its treaty with Israel. Internecine struggles split most of the sects and also the Palestinians, as Syria backed a faction opposed to Arafat. In the mid-1980s, U.S. and other foreign nationals still in Lebanon were being kidnapped by shadowy Shi'i gangs and held for ransom, which Western governments vowed never to pay (but sometimes did, secretly). The hijacking of passenger aircraft and even a cruise ship enhanced the Middle East's reputation for terrorism. The really striking development was that Lebanon's Shi'i Muslims achieved so much more than the PLO had at the expense of the Israelis, who withdrew from most of Lebanon—without a treaty—in June 1985. The Palestinian organization had the diplomatic and financial support of most of the Arab countries, but the Shi'i groups, the largely secular *Amal* (Hope) led by Nabih Berri, the breakaway Islamic Amal, and especially *Hizballah* (Party of God), earned the credit for driving Israeli and Western troops out of Lebanon. The major factor in the Shi'is' success, I believe, was their willingness to sacrifice their lives for their cause, inspired by the teachings of Khomeini, the success of the Iranian revolution, and especially the example set in 680 by Muhammad's grandson Husayn against his oppressors.

Terrorism is an old method of warfare practiced in most parts of the world whenever individuals and groups cannot attain dignity, freedom, or justice against powers that rely on armies, police, and other conventional forces to maintain their control. Its basic aim is to force other individuals or groups—and their countries—to take unwanted political actions that serve the terrorists' needs. In this book I have described the terrorism the Assassins used against the Sunnis, the Egyptians against the British in the Suez Canal, the Arabs and Jews against each other and against the British in Palestine, the Palestinians against the Israelis and their supporters, and Shi'i Muslims in Iran, Lebanon, and other countries against those people whom they have identified as their oppressors. Terrorists tend to be educated young men with lots of zeal and determination. They feel strongly that their religion or nationality has been oppressed and must be vindicated. Governments, too, sponsor terrorism, to demoralize their foes. Israel's bombardment of Palestinians in 1981 was a form of state-sponsored terrorism, as were Asad's massacre of his foes in Hama in 1982 and Saddam's attacks on Iraqi Kurds in 1988.

Middle Eastern governments and peoples have been victimized by terrorists to a greater extent than Americans and Europeans, but the terrorists prefer to strike at the West, to get not only vengeance but also the media publicity they crave. The Western countries profess an abhorrence of terrorism, but they do not agree on how to combat it. There are two basic schools of thought on the matter: (1) that terrorism can be deterred by striking back at its perpetrators and cowing them into submission and (2) that the only way to stop terrorism is to cure the conditions that cause it. But it is hard to deter terrorists when they are backed by so many of the people around them, when punitive action fails to strike at their source, and when the lives of innocent hostages are at stake. Reagan and his partisans attacked the Carter government for its weak handling of the American hostage crisis in Iran, but his own administration fared even worse in Lebanon and had to extricate itself from an embarrassing scandal involving the sale of U.S. weapons to Iran, the fountainhead of terrorism. It was nearly impossible to devise policies that would cure the conditions that cause terrorism, such as the ongoing Arab-Israeli conflict, the civil war in Lebanon, the Iran-Iraq War, urbanization, and poverty. The UN had tried with little success to address these issues for years.

## WESTERN POLICY FORMATION AND ISLAMIC POLITY

Formulating policies is hard for popularly elected governments, and especially for the United States, with its power divided between the White House and Congress. In the 1980s Washington lacked a Middle East policy, and its susceptibility to various lobbies made it even harder to formulate one. It was also a challenge for Israel, which from 1984 to 1988 was led by a shaky combination of the Labor party, led by Shim'on Peres, and the Likud coalition, headed after 1983 by Yitzhak Shamir. The two blocs won nearly equal numbers of seats in the 1984 Knesset elections, and they agreed to form a coalition cabinet in which Peres was prime minister until 1986, whereupon he was succeeded by Shamir for the following two years. The two men disagreed on their Arab policies: Peres favored and Shamir opposed an international peace conference that would probably lead to the return of most of the West Bank to Jordan. Shamir wanted indefinite Israeli control over the lands captured in the 1967 war. The Palestinians, too, were divided. Some called for an all-out struggle against the occupation, whereas others advocated that those who had been under Israel's administration for two decades should take an active part in Israeli politics, such as the Jerusalem elections. They also debated how far they could rely on the Arab governments to help them, but after December 1987 they chose to take their cause into their own hands. Policy debates on both sides did not bring peace.

What does it mean to have a policy? A government with a policy on a particular issue knows what goals it hopes to attain and chooses the means that it will adopt to reach them. As Iran in the early 1980s hoped to spread Islamic government throughout the Middle East, it formulated a policy of revolutionary subversion to undermine established governments in Muslim states by appealing to their *mostaz'afan* (literally "dispossessed," the people who felt alienated by the Middle East's westernization) and imbuing them with a zeal for self-sacrifice to combat their oppressors. This policy worked for a while in Lebanon, but it foundered on harsh economic realities in the war against Iraq, and eventually the Ayatollah Khomeini had to admit that Iran could no longer afford to fight Iraq and finance revolutionary Shi'i groups in Lebanon. Economic recovery became Iran's goal, and other means became more expedient. If Israel in the 1980s wanted to ensure its survival in a hostile Arab world, its obvious course was to defend itself so well and cow its enemies so thoroughly that no one would attack it. But these means could not ensure security, because the Lebanese Shi'is and Palestinians refused to be intimidated and stepped up their attacks on Israel. If the Reagan administration wanted a friendly Middle East, it initially thought that it could build a strategic consensus of governments opposed to the USSR, but this was a misguided policy, for most Middle Eastern governments feared one another (or internal revolutions) more than they feared a Soviet invasion. Later, he would seek peace between Israel and the Arabs and among contending factions in Lebanon based on compromises that ignored the true aims of both sides. Even later, he would try to soothe the American public, condemning hostage-taking in Lebanon and other acts of terrorism, yet at the same time sell arms to bargain, indirectly, with terrorist captors for the release of their hostages. Reagan used a feel-good approach; his was not a policy of ends and means.

To be blunt, policymaking was defective throughout the decade of the Ayatollah Khomeini. The Islamic Republic of Iran managed to survive all attempts—internal, Iraqi, and U.S.—to topple it, and it even repaid a $7 billion debt inherited from the shah; but it nearly ruined its economy and hastened the exodus of its richest, best educated, and most creative citizens. It persuaded no other country to become an Islamic republic. It claimed that it could reestablish the Shari'ah as the law of the land, but

Iranians still evaded its bans on women's cosmetics, drug addiction (opium abuse soared in Iran), and rock music. The Arab states continued to pursue policies that caused them to quarrel among themselves. Israeli policies demoralized the country and did not enhance its security. The U.S. government did not know how to deal with Middle Eastern fundamentalism, whether Muslim, Jewish, or Christian, and its attempts at repressing terrorism by bombarding Lebanese villages in 1983 and the Libyan capital in 1986 embittered peoples who might once have supported its interests. Khomeini's Islamic Republic, Menachem Begin's and Yitzhak Shamir's Greater Israel, Yasir Arafat's equivocation, and Ronald Reagan's patriotism all failed to illumine their policies.

The Islamic revolution in the Middle East, as inspired by the Ayatollah Khomeini, ended with his death in June 1989. Indeed, it had been declining for several years, as Iran's revolutionary zeal waned and Iraq regained the lands that it had earlier lost. Islam is a religion and a way of life; it is not a political ideology. Before 1979 Westerners underestimated the power of Islam over the hearts and minds of Muslims; during the 1980s we overestimated it. For most of the history that you have studied in this book, Islamic beliefs and institutions exerted a strong influence over the people of the Middle East, but no leader, not even Muhammad, was able to make Islam the sole determinant of what Muslims thought and did. The Shari'ah always coexisted with other systems of law, including the edicts of kings and governors. The imperial tradition of Achaemenid Iran coexisted through the ages with the Islamic vision of Muhammad. Civil officials and military officers exercised power in an ongoing symbiosis (or rivalry) with caliphs and ulama.

The Islamic revolution enabled the *mostaz'afan* to find their voice and to vent their anger on rulers and foreign advisers who exalted material wealth and power in the name of "modernization." Anger is a powerful tool for hopeful politicians everywhere, but it does not make policy, feed the hungry, shelter the homeless, win the war, or keep the peace. Islam gives meaning to the lives of individuals and groups; it teaches principles that make people more ethical and humane. But today's world is far more complex than the one in which the Shari'ah took form, and many skills are needed to meet its challenges, whether within the lands of Islam or between Muslims and non-Muslims. All countries touched by the "fundamentalist" revival must harness the wisdom of religion to solve economic and social problems, resolve conflicts, and create peace. It is time for Muslims and other religious people to work together on a basis of mutual understanding and respect; the need for violent confrontation is past.

# TWENTY

# The Gulf War and
# the Peace Process

Where is the Middle East headed? We live in a world of wrenching change and rising conflict between and within nations. People are frustrated with their governments, with the conditions of their daily lives, and with the lack of the respect from other people or governments that they feel they deserve. Frustration causes uprisings against entrenched regimes, religious and ethnic strife, demands for more popular participation in politics, and repressive governments. In the Middle East such problems were less visible in the 1990s than in other parts of Africa and Asia, but they lurked beneath the surface and have come back to haunt us in the new millennium. Following the collapse of the USSR, three Caucasian and five Central Asian states were born. Communism has lost its power and allure in the Middle East.

Meanwhile, Western news media and politicians have conjured up new threats in "terrorism" and "Islamic fundamentalism." By the same token, peoples in the Middle East have even more reasons to fear the power of the West. How did they see the military buildup in Saudi Arabia, answering Iraq's invasion of Kuwait in August 1990? And what about the 1991 Gulf War, in which the coalition of American, European, and Arab forces forced Iraq to pull out after aerial attacks that devastated much of the country but did not topple its leader? The Arab world felt divided, defenseless, and despondent about its inability to set its own course. Many Arabs who had once hoped to imitate Turkey's leap into westernization came to believe that imported ideologies and programs had divided them. Rather, Iran's Islamic revolution pointed a new direction to follow, but the model attracted mostly the people and not their governments. Arab leaders began open negotiations with Israel in Madrid and Washington, and secret ones in Oslo and other cities. Israel broke an ancient taboo when it talked to the PLO. A laborious peace process began between the two sides, but neither side was willing to offer what would most allay the other's fears. Threats of Arab violence and annihilation still haunt the Israelis, and the reality of Israel's domination and reprisals continues to hobble the Palestinians, who openly defy Israel's soldiers. Turkey wants to be a member of the European Union, but it cannot meet Western standards of respect for human rights when faced with a Kurdish rebellion in its southeastern provinces. Iran talks of exporting Islamic principles to the rest of the world, but its citizens have twice elected a president whose policies would shelve its revolution at home to rebuild its own society.

## THE PRESENT IN HISTORICAL PERSPECTIVE

Any historian who writes a textbook that includes the recent past walks on eggs. Events occur suddenly in the Middle East. Projections are hazardous. Who knows what a future reader will see as having been the major Middle Eastern events from 1990 to 2001? What happens in the coming years will highlight some events at the expense of others. Let me give you an example by looking backward. At the dawn of this century, a burning issue was the building of the Berlin-to-Baghdad railway by a German company. Our forebears believed that this railway would enhance German power in the Ottoman Empire and harm the interests of Britain, France, and Russia. In contrast, few noticed that a British subject obtained from the Persian government a concession that led to the first big oil discovery in the Middle East. Yet today we see Middle East oil as much more important than a railroad that was never completed. By the same token, will an incident that we now view as a major event seem trivial by 2010? Having given you this caveat, I would say that two issues dominate the Middle East as I am writing these lines in early 2001: The first is the Gulf War and its prolonged aftermath; the other is the faltering peace process between Israel on the one hand and the Arab states and the Palestinians on the other.

## THE GULF WAR

A geological fact created a historical anomaly. Petroleum and natural gas abound in the arid lands surrounding the Gulf where, until the 1960s, the population was sparse, mainly nomadic, and ignored by most of the world. Most of these lands remained under tribal *shaykhs* and amirs while army officers elsewhere in the Middle East were replacing monarchies with republics. During the middle third of the twentieth century, a motley assortment of states emerged. These ranged from Saudi Arabia, united by Ibn Saud and enriched by oil discoveries far beyond anything he or his subjects could ever have imagined, to such minuscule emirates as Fujaira, known best for its postage stamps, and Bahrain, a fading oil power with well-developed banking and touristic facilities. We call every country a "nation," but how could we claim that countries like Qatar and Dubai really owe their existence to the political loyalties of their citizens? The combination of two well-armed and populous countries possessing abundant oil reserves, Iran and Iraq, with many tiny states that also have oil but no means of self-defense was dangerous. The danger receded during the Iran-Iraq War in the 1980s, but the potential for local conflicts resurfaced once the war ended.

## Iraq's Complaints and Claims

Iraq suffers psychological complexes about being second in the Arab world. Egypt has more influential universities, publishing houses, newspapers, and radio and television stations. Syria pioneered the development of Arab nationalism, even though Iraq became independent sooner and championed Arab unity in the 1930s and 1940s. And Saudi Arabia's oil, although discovered later than Iraq's, has proved more extensive in terms of both output and reserves. Iraqis feel, therefore, that other Arabs (to say nothing of non-Arabs) do not respect them. Although many Arab states furnished huge loans and supplied arms to Saddam Husayn's regime during its 1980–1988 war against Iran, they failed to appreciate Iraq's expenditure of people and wealth to blunt the spread of Islamist militancy from Tehran to the Arab world.

A related complex is Iraq's belief that Western imperialism in general and Britain in particular tried to strangle its development by creating a separate emirate called "Kuwait." Iraq maintained that Kuwait had no right to independence. Its ruling Sabah family had recognized Ottoman suzerainty over Kuwaiti territory during the nineteenth century. In 1899, however, Shaykh Mubarak Al Sabah (r. 1896–1915) had signed a treaty with the British making them responsible for the defense and foreign relations of Kuwait, thus severing it from Ottoman control. The British, seeking to protect their routes to India, had already made similar treaties with other tribal leaders along the Gulf. During the twentieth century such pacts preserved an archaic political alignment in that area long after other Middle Eastern countries had cast off monarchical rule and colonial dependency. When the British fixed the borders of their Iraqi mandate in 1921, its leaders complained that the exclusion of Kuwait left Iraq with almost no access to the Gulf. Once Iraq gained its independence in 1932, it called for border adjustments. When Britain pulled its forces out of Kuwait in 1961, Abd al-Karim Qasim tried to replace them with Iraqis, but the other Arab states and Britain sent in troops to stop the Iraqi leader from annexing the emirate. Baghdad argued intermittently that Kuwait was legally Iraqi territory and that it had never formally ratified its recognition of Kuwaiti independence.

During its eight-year war with Iran, however, Iraq needed loans more than land, borrowing more than $15 billion from Kuwait—a sum it would not and could not repay after the war. Kuwait had islands, as yet undeveloped, that could have served as loading and shipping facilities for Iraq's petroleum trade with the rest of the world. Both Iraq and Iran needed more oil income after 1988 to rebuild their war-torn economies. Raising revenues would require either greater production or higher export prices, and Kuwait's aggressive oil sales (at cut-rate prices) helped neither Baghdad nor Tehran.

Kuwait's legendary wealth, derived wholly from selling oil discovered and developed by foreigners, served mainly to enrich the Sabah dynasty and a few Kuwaitis who could prove that their families had long lived in the emirate, not the flood of poor immigrants from other Arab states or from lands as far away as Bangladesh and the Philippines. These guest workers, however valued they might have been for their brawn, brains, and labor, did not enjoy the rights of Kuwaitis. Seldom could foreigners get Kuwaiti citizenship, even if they had worked in the country for forty years; nor could their children, even if they had lived there all their lives. By what special merit did a few Kuwaitis amass such fortunes, while most other Arabs remained poor?

Kuwaitis reply that in the eighteenth century their bedouin ancestors settled in a sheltered inlet near the northwestern end of the Gulf and set up a small fort (Arabic: *kuwayt*) there. In 1756 the settlers chose a member of the Sabah family to manage their affairs. Although many Kuwaitis remained nomadic and national borders were fixed only in the twentieth century, they were not just "tribes with a flag." Some Kuwaiti settlers took up trading, shipbuilding, pearl diving, and fishing. In the late 1930s, an Anglo-American firm found oil, but only after 1945 (when Kuwait's population totaled 150,000) did the tiny emirate become an exporter. Petroleum output, national wealth, and population skyrocketed after that.

Kuwaitis have been shrewd in using their oil revenues to build a modern infrastructure, educate their young people, invest money (estimated at $100 billion) abroad, set aside funds for a future when oil wells (or markets) may dry up, and support less opulent but more populated Arab states that might protect them against aggression. Because a quarter of Kuwait's inhabitants were Palestinians, the regime gave both economic and political support to the PLO and related Arab causes. Far from being a dependency of the West, Kuwait was the first small Gulf state to have close diplomatic ties with communist countries. And it was the only Gulf state that had a popularly elected parliament, although the amir dissolved it twice and suffrage was limited to males who could prove they descended from pre-1920 inhabitants. Did Kuwait deserve to be attacked for not raising its oil prices or for not curtailing production to assist Iraq's redevelopment after 1988? Was it wrong to expect Iraq to pay back its loans?

*Iraq's Annexation of Kuwait*

The Iraqi army invaded and occupied Kuwait shortly after midnight on 2 August 1990. The Kuwaiti amir, Shaykh Jabir Al Ahmad Al Sabah, some of his relatives and high officials, and many of his subjects fled to neighboring Saudi Arabia. From there they called on the international community, mainly the United States, to help them win back their country. Iraqi President Saddam Husayn had accused Kuwait of pumping his country's share of oil from their jointly owned Rumaylah oil field and of plotting to impoverish Iraq by overproducing oil in order to drive down its price on the world market. Efforts in late July by President Husni Mubarak of Egypt and King Fahd of Saudi Arabia to mediate between Iraq and Kuwait did not satisfy the Iraqi leader. Foreign intelligence sources knew that Iraqi forces were massing near Kuwait's border, but few expected Saddam to order an invasion. However much they quarrel, Arab states seldom invade one another.

Iraq's invasion and subsequent annexation of Kuwait ignited a dangerous diplomatic crisis. The other Arab states reacted slowly; an emergency Arab summit was called but then canceled. Did Arab leaders ignore the obvious danger? If Iraq could get away with invading a fellow Arab country, what was to stop other strong states from seizing their most vulnerable neighbors? By contrast, the U.S. government, emboldened by communism's retreat in Europe and by Soviet president Mikhail Gorbachev's tacit support, rushed in to fill the vacuum. It promptly condemned the invasion and froze all Iraqi and Kuwaiti assets in the United States. After winning the consent of the Saudi government, George Bush's administration began airlifting troops and supplies into the desert kingdom, which had formerly barred foreign troops from Saudi territory—or had kept their presence as inconspicuous as possible. By the end of October 1990, more than 200,000 American men and women in uniform were encamped at undisclosed locations around northeastern Saudi Arabia. In the following month, Bush would double the size of that force, adding offensive units to the mainly defensive ones he had already sent, a step that we now see as Washington's commitment to driving the Iraqi forces from Kuwait. Many other countries, including Egypt and Syria, sent troops to join the U.S. forces in what was officially termed Operation Desert Shield.

The UN Security Council passed a series of resolutions calling on Iraq to withdraw unconditionally from Kuwait and on other member states to impose economic sanctions against Iraq until it did so. Except for small amounts of food and medicine, Iraq could not import any goods from abroad, nor could it export any oil to earn the money needed to rebuild its war-torn economy. As the sanctions tightened and Saddam did not flinch, President Bush and British prime minister Margaret Thatcher threatened military action against Iraq. The United States and its allies rebuffed mediation attempts by King Husayn of Jordan and other leaders, calling on Iraq to obey the Security Council resolutions immediately and unconditionally. For Saddam and his supporters, these demands were a direct challenge; they refused to pull out.

Instead, Iraq heightened the tension by looting Kuwaiti homes and despoiling hospitals, schools, and businesses. Saddam's regime detained thousands of foreign nationals caught in Kuwait by the invasion, bused them to Baghdad, and housed some in Iraqi factories or military bases as "human shields" against foreign attacks. Baghdad ordered foreign embassies to leave Kuwait, proclaimed it Iraq's nineteenth province, destroyed written records, and tried to efface all evidence of Kuwait's existence as a separate state. Any resistance by the local inhabitants was suppressed. Thousands of Kuwaitis fled to other Arab countries, leaving whatever they owned to the Iraqi invaders.

Sadder yet was the plight of foreign workers in Kuwait and, to a lesser degree, in Iraq itself. Stripped of all the goods and money that they had acquired, Egyptians, Yemenis, Pakistanis, Indians, Sri Lankans, and Filipinos straggled across the desert to Jordan, where they filled up squalid, makeshift refugee camps until their countries could airlift them safely home. Most were young men and women who had come from poor households to Kuwait or Iraq to make money to send to their families. Now they had lost what they had earned, they and their dependents faced bleak employment prospects back home, and their countries would miss the hard-currency income formerly generated by their remittances.

A worldwide economic slowdown had been expected even before Iraq's invasion. Now, soaring oil prices, rising unemployment, and dislocations caused by the anti-Iraq sanctions worsened the recession in the Middle East and the West. How could countries wishing to send troops and supplies to assist Operation Desert Shield find the funds to pay for them? Germany and other European countries, as well as Japan, Saudi Arabia, and Kuwait's government-in-exile, pledged billions of dollars. With so many countries providing troops, tanks, planes, and money to the buildup, who would make the military decisions? How long would they remain united?

Although the near unanimity of the United Nations against Iraq's invasion of Kuwait raised hopes that other international disputes might soon be addressed and possibly resolved by the world body, diplomacy might not settle the first issue, let alone others that might be linked with it. Saddam cleverly offered to evacuate Kuwait only if all other foreign armies would withdraw from Middle East lands they were occupying, a stipulation meant to embarrass Israel and Syria. The specter of a prolonged war, marked by aerial bombardment of cities and public works, burning oil wells and refineries, missile attacks, poison gas, and even germ warfare, cast an ominous pall. During the fall of 1990, tensions rose in other conflicts, including the one between Israel and the Palestinians. Would Muslim peoples back the regimes that seemed united in condemning Iraq's actions?

### The Crisis of Arab Legitimacy

To many Arabs (and some non-Arab Muslims), Saddam was a folk hero who defied the West and made everyone reexamine the rules by which Middle East politics were conducted. He captured the hearts of the *mostaz'afan*. Most Palestinians, embittered by Western neglect, Israeli oppression, and abuse from other Arabs, admired him. Pro-Saddam demonstrations spread in Jordan and in Israel's occupied territories, as well as in more remote lands that favored Iraq, such as Tunisia, Libya, and Yemen. In countries that opposed Iraq for fear that it would become the leader of the Arab world, notably Syria and Egypt, some people vented pro-Saddam feelings in demonstrations that were promptly suppressed. There were also angry demonstrations against Saddam in countries whose people suffered indignities from the Iraqi army and had lost their livelihoods and remittances.

Iraq's political system, the way in which power is allocated and decisions are made, has been highly dictatorial. The state controls Iraq's major industries, all educational institutions, and the information media. Huge portraits of Saddam Husayn adorn street corners and public buildings. Any expression of opposition to his policies is punished. Summary executions, torture, and long jail terms without trial are common. Most of the military officers and civil officials who had belonged to his Ba'th party faction when it seized power in 1968 or who had helped him to become president in 1979 were later purged, exiled, or pensioned off. Saddam surrounded himself with a clique of relatives and friends from his hometown, Takrit. His army, including the Republican Guard, "popular forces," and reservists, constituted more than a million men and was the largest and best equipped in the Arab world. France, Germany, and the USSR had sold Iraq vast quantities of weapons during its war against Iran. Iraq's use of poison gas against Iranians and even Iraqi Kurds during that war enhanced the army's reputation for cruelty. One wonders how Iraqi soldiers, or the families of their fallen comrades, felt when Saddam announced in August 1990 (apparently trying to get Iran to defy the UN sanctions) that Iraq was ready to reinstate the 1975 agreement, thus allowing Iran to share with Iraq control over the Shatt al-Arab, and returning other lands Iraq had taken during eight years of war against Iran. And how could Saddam offer to give Iraqi oil to those Third World countries suffering from price hikes caused by the invasion, when he had just complained that Kuwait was depressing oil prices that Iraq wanted to raise? Clearly, Iraq's protean interests, which Saddam equated with his own, dictated these sudden and drastic policy lurches.

But what did the crisis tell us about Iraq's Arab rivals? Governments such as Syria and Egypt endorsed Operation Desert Shield in order to punish Iraq, ignoring their people's aversion to Saudi and U.S. policies. Other governments, such as Jordan and Yemen, backed Saddam because of their economic ties with Iraq, at the risk of offending their other neighbors. Almost every Arab regime feels insecure about its own legitimacy. In a crisis, most will resort to some form of coercion to ensure their citizens' obedience. Without a system of collective security, all of them are vulnerable to invasion. If wealthy Saudi Arabia needed Operation Desert Shield for defense against invasion (though Iraq never openly threatened to invade or to annex the Saudi kingdom), how would its government be viewed by its own subjects, who have no constitutional means of supporting or opposing its policies? What had the Saudis done with all the arms it had bought earlier at high prices from the United States and Britain? Until August 1990 the Saudi government could protect its own subjects and, more important for its legitimacy, guard the holy cities of Mecca and Medina. By January 1991 the whole country was guarded by a half-million foreign troops—most of them not even Muslim. Iraq had no foreign troops on its soil.

## OPERATION DESERT STORM

Saddam's rejection of the twelve Security Council resolutions demanding his unconditional withdrawal from Kuwait, combined with Bush's refusal to compromise with Iraq, led to the outbreak of hostilities on 17 January 1991. Operation Desert Storm, as the allied coalition renamed its campaign, began with massive aerial bombardments of Iraq's military facilities. After an initially weak response, Iraq launched Scud missile attacks on Israel (which was not part of the allied coalition), hoping to draw Jerusalem into the war. Baghdad hoped that if Israel began fighting against Iraq, the armies of Saudi Arabia, Egypt, and Syria would desert the alliance. Under heavy U.S. pressure not to retaliate, Israel complied but reserved the right to strike back at some future date, lest the Palestinians and other Arabs assume that Jerusalem was weak and had to hide behind a battery of U.S. Patriot missiles hastily set up by the Americans. Iraqi Scud attacks went on throughout the war, hitting Saudi Arabia as well as Israel, but they proved to have no strategic value.

Some of Iraq's other ripostes to the allied air strikes, which soon numbered in the thousands, were more damaging. Saddam ordered the Kuwaiti oil taps opened, spilling millions of gallons of crude petroleum into the Gulf, threatening beaches, wildlife, and even water desalination plants, as well as deterring an amphibious assault on Kuwait City. Allied pilots whom Iraq had shot down and captured were tortured and made to appear on state television to confess their "crimes" against the Iraqi people. Many Kuwaitis were kidnapped and taken to Iraq to serve as human shields (thus replacing the ones taken in August, whom Saddam had released in December as a futile goodwill gesture) against allied attacks. Then Iraqi troops began to set Kuwait's oil fields on fire. In the sixth week of Operation Desert Storm, Iraq tried a diplomatic ploy, sending its foreign minister, Tariq Aziz, to Moscow to enlist Soviet aid to stop the war.

Iraq and the USSR offered several compromise proposals for the evacuation of Kuwait, hoping to forestall an allied ground offensive. But Bush and the other coalition leaders ignored the deals and called on Iraq to obey all Security Council resolutions. When it rejected their demands, the allied coalition began a ground offensive that within 100 hours had driven Iraqi troops out of Kuwait. The guns fell silent on 27 February 1991.

*After the Storm*

The Bush administration and the United States seemed to have won a great victory in a surprisingly short time. Unlike the wars in Korea and Vietnam, the Gulf War was backed by most Americans. It opened new vistas for a *Pax Americana* in the region. I hoped at the time that the U.S. government would bring all the Middle Eastern countries together to settle their political differences. To a degree, it did. I feared at the time that fighting would continue in Iraq. It certainly did. With allied coalition forces occupying parts of southern Iraq, the local Shi'is rose up in rebellion against the Baghdad regime, as did the Kurds in northern Iraq. But the coalition offered no military help either to the Shi'is, who might have formed an Islamic republic in southern Iraq, or to the Kurds, whose formation of an autonomous Kurdistan might have inspired similar demands by Kurds in Turkey and elsewhere. It did not overthrow Saddam Husayn, who proved invulnerable to every attempt, military or civilian, to oust him.

Instead, the coalition tried to enforce the destruction of Iraq's nuclear, biological, and chemical weapons, maintaining for more than a decade the UN sanctions that impoverished the Iraqi people without ever harming their leaders. Saddam continues to believe that he won the war, for he stayed in power, whereas Bush was voted out of office in November 1992. Iraq was able to build up its army and the Republican Guard, menacing Kuwait again in 1993 and 1994 and defying UN weapons inspection teams in 1997 and 1998; in the meantime the Iraqi people suffered great privation. It is estimated that more than one million Iraqis have died due to the sanctions. After years of resistance, Saddam consented to a UN deal that allowed him to sell $2 (soon raised to $5 and now to an unlimited amount) billion worth of Iraqi oil every six months in exchange for imported food, medicine, and other necessities, starting in 1997. The UN inspectors, denied access to some of Iraq's military installations and presidential palaces, pulled out in 1998, just before an Anglo-American bombing campaign that hurt mainly civilian Iraqis. The embargo on Iraq was increasingly resented in the Middle East. By 2001, most Arab states,

Turkey, and Iran were trading with Iraq as though the sanctions had been lifted. And no outsider knew whether Iraq was stockpiling biological, chemical, or nuclear weapons, because the UN inspectors could no longer enter the country.

Kuwait promptly extinguished its burning oil fields and rebuilt its economy. It held parliamentary elections in 1992, although it still did not let women vote or extend citizenship rights to foreign workers. Most Palestinians who had built up its economy were exiled (without their property) and not readmitted. Their jobs were taken by Egyptians and other nationals.

## PALESTINIANS AND THE PEACE PROCESS

Lately, what we have been calling the "Arab-Israeli Conflict" has reverted to being the "Palestinian Question." Israel's backers used to attribute the problem to the refusal of the Arab states to recognize the Jewish state. Well, Egypt did so in 1979. Jordan did so in 1994. The Palestinians were victims of the conflict because the Arab governments refused to absorb them, unlike Israel, which had welcomed the Jews from the Arab countries after 1948. I used to argue that despite the propaganda put out by Arab nationalists and Zionists alike, the Palestinians were actually being absorbed or at least employed by both Israel and the Arab states. Recently, though, the Palestinians' plight has refuted my argument. Both Israel and the Arab countries have rejected the Palestinians, who now mainly comprise the descendants of the Arab refugees of 1948 from what became Israel. What has happened?

### The First Intifadah

The story starts in December 1987 with a small uprising of Gaza children and teenagers against Israel's occupying army. It soon spread throughout the occupied areas, adding an Arabic word to the world's stock of terms for "rebellion." The Palestinians under Israeli occupation became more coordinated in their opposition and more effective in refuting Israel's claim that most of them were happy and prosperous under its rule. The youthful stonings and tire burnings that launched their *intifadah* (which literally means "shaking off") made everyone see their distress, but their strongest ploy was to boycott Israeli manufactures, such as soap, cigarettes, and fabrics. Some Palestinians who used to go to Israel to work for higher wages than they could earn in the Gaza Strip or the West Bank stayed home. One village refused to pay taxes to Israel's authorities. The *intifadah* began spontaneously as a homegrown protest movement; it was not started by the Palestine Liberation Organization, located since 1983 in Tunis. Some of the local leaders, disillusioned with the secularist PLO, founded a Muslim resistance movement, patterned on Hizballah, called *Hamas* (meaning "Courage" or "Movement of Islamic Resistance").

Why did the uprising break out in December 1987? If the Palestinian Arabs had chafed under Israeli military occupation since 1967, why did it take twenty years for them to try to shake it off? Actually, there had always been resistance, both overt and covert, in the West Bank and Gaza Strip. Even though Palestinians (and of course Israelis) had benefited materially from their twenty-year symbiosis, there was much tension and little integration in their relationship. No one could be sure whether Israel's gradual absorption of the occupied territories would be reversed by an exchange of land for peace, probably with Jordan and under U.S. sponsorship, or brought to its logical conclusion by outright annexation and possibly, as some Israeli extremists proposed, by forced expatriation of all Palestinians. Many observers saw signs of rising Palestinian unrest due to the policies of the Israeli occupying authorities and the vigilante actions of the well-armed Jewish settlers. One key event shortly before the *intifadah* was the summit meeting held in Amman in November 1987, when the Arab heads of state paid lip service to the Palestinian cause but gave one another permission to resume diplomatic ties with Egypt, which had been isolated from most other Arab governments since 1979 for its separate peace with Israel. Soon Saudi, Kuwaiti, and even Iraqi ambassadors were back in Cairo. In 1989 Egypt would even be readmitted into the Arab League. The unspoken message to Palestinians was that the Arab states were not going to punish Egypt any longer and that the PLO should stop expecting their diplomatic and military support. The Palestinians took politics into their own hands and gained respect from other Arabs and people generally, even though hundreds of Palestinians were killed by the IDF or, indeed, at the hands of other Palestinians, whereas few Israelis died or even admitted to any hardship as a result of the *intifadah.*

The PLO viewed this uprising as a means to achieve foreign recognition and international legitimacy. King Husayn validated the rebellion by renouncing any Jordanian claims to the West Bank in July 1988, leaving the PLO responsible for ensuring that local officials got paid. In November of that year, the Palestine National Council voted to declare an independent "State of Palestine," which soon won diplomatic recognition from almost 100 other countries. Yasir Arafat publicly denounced terrorism and offered to recognize Israel, to the dismay of many Palestinian revolutionaries, in order to open negotiations with Washington. The Israelis vehemently rejected any idea that the PLO might be treated as a government-in-exile, let alone as a suitable negotiating partner, but many other people and countries argued that the only way to resolve the Arab-Israeli conflict was through a "two-state solution" with a Jewish Israel and an Arab Palestine. Many Palestinians likewise opposed efforts to make peace with Israel, which they viewed as their oppressor; their committing acts of terrorism soon derailed any rapprochement between the Bush administration and the PLO. The uprising continued, as Hamas coordinated acts of violence in Gaza and later on the West Bank. Some thought Israel had covertly aided its emergence as a rival to the PLO. As Hamas acquired firearms, violence intensified throughout the occupied territories.

## The End of Lebanon's Civil War

After the West had pulled out its troops in 1984, the government almost closed down in Beirut. No police remained to stop the abduction of U.S., European, and indeed Saudi and even Iranian hostages by the various militias. Partitioned, de facto, since 1976, Lebanon saw less fighting between Muslims and Christians than before 1984, but more *within* each religious or political grouping. As soon as one faction seemed ready to take charge and restore order, it would split into two or more competing splinter groups. The Shi'i Muslims fought the Palestinians in 1985; by 1988 they were fighting among themselves, with the somewhat secular and Syrian-backed *Amal* pitted against the militantly Islamic *Hizballah*, supported by Iran. Only diplomatic intervention by these two outside sponsors ended the intra-Shi'i quarrels. Meanwhile, the Maronites, who had clearly lost their plurality of Lebanon's population to the Shi'i Muslims by 1980, could not agree on a leader. When Amin Jumayyil's presidential term drew to a close in the summer of 1988, the parliament could not meet in Beirut to elect his successor because the militias prevented many members from attending. The presence of 40,000 Syrian troops gave Damascus a chance to say who Lebanon's next president should be, but the loudest voice among the Maronites was Iraqi-backed General Michel Awn, who demanded that all Syrians leave Lebanon and even moved into the presidential palace, opposing the rival pro-Syrian caretaker government under Sunni prime minister Salim al-Hoss.

In October 1989, after a year-long impasse, the Saudi government invited all surviving members of Lebanon's parliament (no popular election of deputies had taken place since 1972) to Taif to choose a new president. The man whom they elected, a moderate Christian acceptable to Syria, was assassinated in Beirut after only seventeen days in power, but the parliament bravely met again to elect a replacement, Ilyas Harawi. The Awn and Harawi Maronite factions fought each other as bitterly in 1990 as the Shi'i groups had among themselves in 1988. Only when Iraq became embroiled in occupying Kuwait did it withdraw its support from Awn. He was soon defeated by Harawi's forces, with the backing of Syria, whose troops did not leave Lebanon in 1990. They remain there as of 2001, as the people slowly rebuild their country. Lebanon and Syria signed a pact in May 1991, giving Damascus substantial control over Lebanon's foreign and military affairs. The 1989 Taif Accords proposed a division of power among Lebanon's sects, factions, and militias that came closer to their actual shares of the country's population. At last, Lebanon is at peace. Beirut and most parts of the countryside are returning to normal. Everyone is tired of fighting. Israel's troops, which had pulled back in 1985 to a "security zone" on the Lebanese side of its northern border, would withdraw completely in 2000.

## The Peace Process in Arab-Israeli Relations

The Gulf War changed Israel's relationship with its Arab neighbors and with the Palestinians. For one thing, the USSR altered its Middle East policy. Gorbachev's government did not oppose the U.S.-led coalition. It allowed its Jewish citizens to emigrate and resumed diplomatic relations with Israel, resulting in the influx of almost a million Russian Jews. It stopped arming Syria and other Arab confrontation states against Israel and Egypt. It aided U.S. efforts to convene a general peace conference. Then it dissolved as a union at the end of 1991, leaving the United States as the sole superpower that could act independently in the Middle East. If Israel's government could trust Washington to uphold its essential interests, it could be persuaded to engage in peace talks with Syria, Saudi Arabia, and Jordan (with an attached delegation of Palestinians, none of whom had public ties with the PLO). The oil-exporting Arab governments realized that their security depended on good relations with Washington and on averting any future threat to their security—a threat that seemed more apt to come from Iraq or Iran than from Israel. Syria was willing to enter peace talks if it stood a chance to regain the Golan Heights taken by Israel in the 1967 war. Besides, the loss of its Soviet sponsor left Syria with few real alternatives. For Jordan and the PLO, their public support of Iraq's policies had hurt their credibility among the oil-exporting regimes that had formerly supported them financially and diplomatically. Both had suffered losses from the Gulf War. Having few viable options, they agreed to negotiate with Israel.

After eight trips to the Middle East, U.S. Secretary of State James Baker managed to set up a general conference that opened in Madrid in October 1991. The mere fact that Arab delegates were meeting in the same room with Israeli representatives marked a step toward peace, even though the Madrid Conference produced no breakthroughs. Multilateral talks on various issues concerning the Middle East as a whole, such as water rights, refugees, economic development, and arms control, went on during the following years in various locations, making progress but getting little publicity. Bilateral parleys met, faltered, and resumed during 1992 and 1993, as first Israel and then the United States elected new and more liberal governments. But most of the news was bad. Terrorist acts carried out by Hizballah in Lebanon, Hamas in Israel's occupied areas, and the Islamic Group in Egypt asserted the growing power of radical Islamism at the expense of Israeli soldiers and civilians, Arabs suspected of collaborating with Israel, and foreign tourists. It even seemed that terrorism was spreading to the United States, as a group of expatriate Egyptians was accused of planting bombs that blew up part of New York's World Trade Center in February 1993. An exiled Saudi millionaire, Osama Bin Laden, set up terrorist cells in the Sudan and then in Afghanistan. He is widely suspected of having inspired the 1993 World Trade Center bombing and attacks on the U.S. embassies in Kenya and Tanzania in August 1998. U.S. punitive bombing raids on Bin Laden's suspected base in Afghanistan and on a pharmaceutical factory in Khartum did nothing to blunt his appeals to terrorism.

Let us take the story back to 1993. Israel continued to drop bombs on Lebanese villages (leaving a half-million villagers homeless) and also to wound or kill Palestinian demonstrators. It could also subject them to preventive detention, blow up houses, and impose curfews on parts of the Gaza Strip and the West Bank. Hopes for peace seemed to be receding again.

## The Oslo I Accord

Greater progress was made away from public notice, though, under the auspices of Norway's foreign minister and his wife, as secret talks were held between representatives of the PLO and of the new Israeli government, despite their protestations to the contrary. After the news leaked out in August 1993, Oslo agreed to turn over its mediating role to Washington. On 13 September 1993, the foreign ministers of Israel, the PLO, and the United States met for a public ceremony, held on the White

House lawn, to sign a formal Declaration of Principles, also called the Oslo I Accord. The ceremony included brief speeches by U.S. president Bill Clinton, Israeli Premier Yitzhak Rabin, and PLO Chairman Yasir Arafat and concluded with a handshake between the veteran Israeli and Palestinian leaders, symbolically ending their long enmity. Under the declaration, Israel was to withdraw its forces from the Gaza Strip and Jericho within three months, enabling the PLO to set up a "self-governing authority" as a first step toward full autonomy for the occupied territories other than east Jerusalem (whose status was to be discussed at a later time). The Palestinians would be permitted to hold free elections for a national assembly (whose size and powers were unspecified), once Israeli troops could be withdrawn from their main population centers. Jewish settlements in the West Bank and the Gaza Strip would remain under Israeli protection. Neither the Palestinians' demand for full autonomy nor the Israelis' security needs were fully met by the Declaration of Principles. But neither Arafat nor Rabin would benefit by abandoning the peace process.

The ensuing negotiations between Israel and the PLO have not validated Oslo I. The declaration left many issues unsettled, and both sides tend to play to their supporters. Israel did pull its troops out of those parts of Gaza and Jericho not settled by Jews, allowing Arafat to return and to start building political institutions. A Palestinian police force, recruited and trained mainly in Egypt, was charged with maintaining order but gradually became a militia fighting against Israelis. Foreign governments withheld much of the $2 billion they had pledged to support the PLO's "self-governing authority" (which gradually came to be seen as a state) and to rebuild the Palestinian economy because Arafat wanted full control of the money with no public accountability. His administration, hamstrung by rival authorities and security agencies, was also defied by the militant Islamist group Hamas. Palestinian police shot and killed a dozen Hamas demonstrators in the main mosque of Gaza, and one of its members was implicated in the murder of an Israeli civilian. Economic conditions in Gaza, far from improving, worsened. Conditions in the occupied lands not under the Palestine Authority also grew tense. For instance, an armed Jewish settler entered the mosque at the Tomb of the Patriarchs in Hebron and killed or maimed more than thirty Muslim worshipers before he was overpowered and killed. Distrust on all sides intensified.

*Gains and Losses in the Peace Process*

Even though the Declaration of Principles brought no peace or prosperity to the Palestinians, it did open the door to political deals with Israel by other Arab countries. Jordan's King Husayn had long talked secretly with Israel about peace, but now he and his government worked openly to end their state of war. In October 1994 Clinton, Husayn, and Rabin met at the border between southern Israel and Jordan to sign a formal Jordanian-Israeli peace treaty in a windswept desert. Then Israel offered King Husayn undefined supervisory powers over the Muslim holy sites in Jerusalem's Old City (a move perceived as a slight by the PLO, which claims eastern Jerusalem as its future capital). Tunisia and Morocco formed consular ties with Israel, and several of the small Gulf states hastened to make business deals with the Jewish state. Since 1994 most Middle Eastern countries have attended an annual economic development conference, though Arab governments critical of Israel's policies boycotted the 1997 meeting at Doha. The United States continued to hope that the Syrian government would sign a peace treaty with Israel in exchange for a phased withdrawal of Israeli troops from the Golan Heights, but even a personal visit from Clinton to Asad in 1994 did not bridge the chasm still separating Jerusalem from Damascus. The Arab states met in that year to coordinate their diplomatic strategies, for they had become as disunited in making peace as in waging war.

In September 1995 Israel and the Palestinians signed another agreement (often called Oslo II), containing an intricate plan for Israel's gradual withdrawal from the West Bank (but not any part of Jerusalem). Oslo II set up three West Bank zones. Zone A comprised eight West Bank cities, including Jericho, which was already Arab-controlled. Palestinian authorities would become responsible for its internal security and public order, except for parts of Hebron containing Jewish settlers. Zone B consisted of other West Bank towns and villages, where Palestinian police would eventually maintain order but Israel retained overriding authority for security. Zone C included Jewish settlements, unpopulated areas, and lands Israel viewed as strategic. Israel retained full security authority for Zone C, pending "final status" talks. The redeployment of Israeli troops was to occur at six-month intervals. Israel and the Palestinians were to form joint patrols, and Israel would build bypass roads for its settlers. The Palestinians were empowered to elect a president and an eighty-two-member council. The Arab inhabitants of Jerusalem could not run but could cast absentee ballots in the elections, which were indeed held in January 1996.

Events within Israel and actions by Palestinian extremists combined to derail the peace process. Prime Minister Rabin was killed by an Israeli assassin just after addressing a peace rally in November 1995. His successor, Shim'on Peres, did not enjoy as much popular support, as the May 1996 general elections showed. In part because of two suicide-bombing attacks, widely ascribed to Hamas, the Israeli electorate voted by a narrow margin to replace Peres and his Labor government with the leader of the Likud, Benjamin Netanyahu. The Likud had opposed peace talks with the PLO (and indeed the permanent-status talks were suspended) but promised to fulfill Israel's commitments under the Oslo Accords. Netanyahu even reached an agreement to withdraw Israeli troops from most of Hebron in January 1997. But Israel put off giving back the other West Bank areas because of new anti-Israel terrorist bombings that Netanyahu blamed on Arafat. Despite the opposition of many members of Netanyahu's cabinet, Clinton and his new secretary of state, Madeleine Albright, tried time and again to get him to give up occupied lands and Arafat to curb acts of terrorism. In the meantime, the Palestinians grew ever more frustrated at a peace process that gave them no hope for freedom or even employment. The Palestinians also resented Israel's policy of creating new Jewish settlements, symbolized by its construction of houses in Har Homa (which they call Jabal Abu Ghunaym), a part of Jerusalem which Israel had annexed in 1967.

Under the 1993 Declaration of Principles, a five-year transition period was to lead to final status talks, which were to occur in 1998, about such contentious issues as (1) the future of Jerusalem (which the Palestinians, like the Israelis, claim as their capital), (2) the right of dispersed Palestinians to return to their homes or to receive compensation from Israel, (3) the future of Jewish settlements in territories conceded to the Palestinians, (4) the configuration of final borders between Israel and the projected Palestinian state, and (5) the status of the Palestinian (Self-Governing) Authority. Netanyahu's intransigence and Palestinian terrorism combined to delay the final-status talks.

Israel held general elections in May 1999. Labor made gains at the expense of Likud and managed to set up a coalition cabinet that included several splinter parties and enjoyed the tacit support of Israeli Arabs. In the first separate election ever held for the position of prime minister, Ehud Barak handily defeated Netanyahu. Clinton and Barak hoped that they could make peace with both the Palestinian Authority and with Syria. Neither peace was concluded. Syria's Hafiz al-Asad (who died in 2000 and was replaced by his son, Bashar) would not parley with Israel unless he had a prior commitment to the complete return of the occupied Golan Heights to his country. Palestinian and Israeli representatives met at the Erez Crossing between Gaza and Israel, in Shepardstown (West Virginia), in an estate on the Wye River (Maryland), and finally with Bill Clinton in a three-way summit at Camp David. But there were no breakthroughs to peace. Israel would not allow the Palestinians to regain the entire West Bank and East Jerusalem, nor would it agree to readmit the

Palestinian refugees (and their descendants) from the 1948 war. Palestinians gave lip service to preventing terrorism, but in practice they allowed attacks on Israelis to continue. Barak's offers to Arafat seemed generous—perhaps overly so—to Israel and its backers. Arafat drew criticism from the Americans for not accepting offers never before dealt to the Palestinians. Meanwhile, though, Jewish settlers continued to build new settlements and increase the size of older ones on the West Bank (at the end of 2000 the Jewish settler population in the West Bank and Gaza exceeded 200,000). They seized water resources and sometimes land belonging to the Palestinians and crisscrossed the area with new highways.

### The Second Intifadah

On 28 September 2000 General Ariel Sharon made a highly public visit to the Muslim shrines atop the Temple Mount, or *al-Haram al-Sharif*, accompanied by more than a thousand soldiers and police. Partly because Sharon is viewed by most Arabs as a murderer, his act enraged the Palestinians, who began attacking Jewish settlements with rocks and sometimes firearms. The Israel Defense Forces struck back with massive retaliation raids, killing hundreds and maiming thousands of Palestinians, many of whom were innocent bystanders or even young children accidentally caught in the line of fire. What should have been a police action carried out jointly by Israel and the Palestinian Authority was instead a military operation that included blowing up houses, uprooting olive and orange trees, shooting demonstrators with live ammunition, and blanketing whole villages with teargas. The Israelis were especially upset when fighting broke out between Jewish soldiers and Israeli Arab civilians in Nazareth, because they had always assumed that Israeli Arabs would not attack them. The Palestinians suffered not only deaths and injuries, but also the loss of their livelihood as Israel closed border crossings to Palestinians who had been workers in Israel.

This Palestinian uprising was soon dubbed the Intifadah of al-Aqsa (referring to the large mosque on the Temple Mount), and it won the support of nearly all Arabs, who demanded that their governments cut all diplomatic and commercial ties with Israel. Only Egypt and Jordan (whose King Husayn had died of cancer and was replaced by his son, Abdallah II) maintained formal relations with Israel. The Israelis felt that their security was at risk, and angry debates took place in the Knesset because of what many politicians felt were the overly generous offers made by Barak at Camp David. The prime minister agreed to end his term early and seek reelection. His challenger proved not to be Netanyahu (who had given up his Knesset seat and hence was ineligible to run) but rather Ariel Sharon. Palestinians and other Arabs were disillusioned with Barak but viewed Sharon as a war criminal for his role in supporting the 1982 Sabra and Shatila massacres and in other military actions against Arabs during his long military career. During the campaign Sharon presented himself as the one leader who was tough enough to achieve peace between Israel and the Arabs. He defeated Barak by a margin of 20 percent. Since the election did not involve the Knesset, though, the Labor party still held its plurality of seats there, and Sharon decided to form a broad-based coalition, with politicians such as Shim'on Peres who became his foreign minister, that included Labor. It would be hard for this cabinet to devise a unified Israeli policy, or to reach a prompt settlement with the Palestinian Authority. The latter, still led by Yasir Arafat, was almost totally discredited among Palestinians for its corruption and ineptitude.

Hizballah and Hamas seized the initiative for the Palestinians by sending suicide bombers into Israel and shooting Israelis in West Bank and Gaza settlements. Israeli troops briefly reoccupied the Gaza Strip, bombarded Palestine Authority buildings from the air, and imprisoned many Palestinians without trial.

## WHITHER ISLAM?

The popular catchword of the 1990s was "Islam is the solution," even though this religious "fundamentalism" has failed to solve problems in Iran and other countries where it has been tried. Muslim groups often deliver welfare benefits to masses of newly urbanized Middle Easterners whose needs are not well served by governments or older charitable organizations. The revival of some Muslim customs, such as the growing of beards by men and the wearing of head-scarves by women, has spread throughout the whole Islamic world. Heightened religious observance may well be a positive development in a tense area and era. Clearly, though, the issue is the combination of Islam with politics.

### Islamist Gains and Losses

In such countries as Jordan, where public participation in politics is now encouraged, Islamist parties have won votes because of bad economic conditions, disillusionment with the peace process, and anger at the United States. In Egypt, where political parties have proliferated but those based on religion are banned, opposition to the policies of Husni Mubarak and his American backers has been expressed by acts of terrorism against government officials, Copts, foreign tourists, and secularist writers. Islamists won control of the professional unions of lawyers, physicians, and engineers in 1992 elections; since then, the Mubarak government has established new rules for their elections. But Mubarak cannot stamp out fundamentalism every time it pops up: A judge tried in 1995 to force a woman to divorce her husband, a Cairo University professor, after he published a scholarly article that the magistrate interpreted as anti-Islamic. The Sudan, impoverished by years of civil strife, has an avowedly Islamist government that exports propagandists to the rest of the Arab world. Possibly inspired by Osama Bin Laden, some Sudanese tried to assassinate Mubarak in 1995.

The Islamic revolutionaries who drove the Soviet army out of Afghanistan in 1987 now train other activists in many Muslim countries, including Egypt and the Sudan. In Afghanistan itself the *Taliban* (Muslim students) won control of most of the country against better-armed militias in 1996 and proceeded to impose severe restrictions on women and westernized intellectuals. In Iran, President Muhammad Khatami, elected in 1997, seeks to ease some Islamic restrictions and open better relations with the West, in contrast to the hard-line policies of the country's religious leader, the Ayatollah Khamanei, who retains most of the power under the 1979 constitution.

Turkey's pro-Islamist Welfare party won enough votes in the last general elections to lead a coalition government for a few months, but its diplomatic approaches to Iran and Libya, plus its threat to undo Ataturk's legacy, stirred up such opposition among the army officers that its leader voluntarily resigned in 1997 and let the secularists regain power. And yet Turkey's Islamist and the secularist governments alike have strengthened military ties with Israel. The country most threatened by this de facto alliance is Syria, where Islamist revolutionaries have failed to topple or to influence Hafiz al-Asad or the son who replaced him in 2000. Syria is the neighbor of Israel most resistant to making peace, especially if it cannot regain the Golan Heights by doing so. It also gets most of its irrigation water from Turkey, whose massive dams now control the Euphrates and the Tigris Rivers. Water is scarce everywhere and may cause the wars of the coming century.

The Islamists might somehow manage to oust a long-entrenched Arab regime. Jordan has been ruled by Hashimites since 1921, Syria by the Asad family since 1970, Yemen by Ali Abdallah Salih since 1978, Iraq by Saddam Husayn since 1979 (and informally long before that), Egypt by Mubarak since 1981, and Saudi Arabia by King Fahd since 1982. However, these countries' security forces make such a revolution seem improbable.

A more enticing prospect would be to take control of one of the emerging Caucasian or Central Asian republics, among which Azerbaijan, Kazakhstan, and Turkmenistan have oil reserves that are just beginning to be tapped. Turkey, Saudi Arabia, and Iran have all contended for influence in the lands when czars and commissars formerly held sway. So far, the Islamist appeal has not prevailed in any of these new countries.

Most of the Middle East's problems, such as overpopulation, scarcity of water and other resources, maldistribution of wealth, and inadequate infrastructure for industrialization, will not be solved by combining Islam with politics. Islamic leaders can do more by setting a higher moral tone for their societies, helping build democratic institutions, and denouncing leaders who fail to serve their people than they can by seizing power for themselves. No king or president now heading a Muslim Middle Eastern state possesses much popularity or vision; whether a populist army officer or intellectual can take over one of these governments is beyond my ability to predict. But the Middle Eastern states' lack of legitimacy will make their subjects seek solutions elsewhere, quite possibly in some form of religious fundamentalism. In the past, state control of radio and television broadcasting was able to restrict what the people learned, but as satellite TV stations and "dish" receivers spread, not to mention the Internet, many Middle Easterners now enjoy free access to facts and ideas that their governments might not have liked them to have.

## A PARTING MESSAGE

In reading the Middle East's history from the rise of Islam to the present, you may have noticed how much of your attention has been focused on confrontations, especially on wars. When you survey the history of any region or country, you do risk getting bogged down in its struggles and ignoring its cultural achievements or the everyday lives of its people. In this book the closer the past has moved toward current events, the more I have told you about Middle East conflicts: the United States versus the USSR, oil producer versus consumer, Islamist versus secularist, Christian versus Muslim, Shi'i versus Sunni, and Arab versus Israeli. Map 13 shows the Middle East's countries with their internationally recognized boundaries; it does not show which lands are really being governed by which states.

Textbook writers often make lists in order to condense their ideas. My last one sums up what I see as the main causes of Middle Eastern conflict: (1) the incomplete transition from communities based on religion and obedience to divine law to nation-states enforcing human-made laws to

MAP 13 The Middle East, showing internationally recognized borders, 2001

increase their security and well-being in this world; (2) the resulting belief on the part of many Middle Eastern peoples that their governments are illegitimate and not to be willingly obeyed; (3) the quest for dignity and freedom by highly articulate peoples (or nations) who have endured centuries of subjection and are determined never again to lose their independence; (4) the involvement of outside governments and individuals who, however good their intentions, cannot work with the hopes and fears of Middle Eastern peoples and, in the worst case, play on them to serve their own needs; (5) the growing concentration of highly destructive weapons in countries that are both volatile and vulnerable; (6) the rising need for food, water, and fossil fuels throughout the world as the amounts available for consumption decline; and (7) overpopulation of some countries and the widening gap between a few very rich people and the many poor.

The Middle East is the most troubled region of a turbulent world. Its people are not at peace with one another or with themselves. They suspect that outsiders do not understand them. I hope that this book has helped you to know them better. Is this all? Most of you will spend your adult lives in the twenty-first century. We have to share Spaceship Earth with the other world powers, with Israeli Jews, Arabs, Iranians, Turks, Kurds, and Armenians, as well as with a few billion other people. How will you get along with them? You can go on learning about their cultures and also about your own—not with a childish desire to prove that "We're right and you're wrong" but, rather, with a mature hope of promoting a genuine dialogue between Middle Eastern and Western ways of life. There is much that we can learn from them: hospitality, generosity, strong family ties, and true empathy for the needs and feelings of others. But I expect that clashes will continue. Do not expect to find easy solutions. Do heed the stated interests and concerns of the parties to the various disputes and conflicts of the area. Look for the unstated hopes and fears. Work for comprehensive conflict transformation from war to dialogue. Be subtle. Give generous credit to the parties involved for any quarrels they contain.

You have learned that the Middle East is an area that has always been vulnerable to invasion and exploitation, that could not escape from the ambitions of local and foreign rulers, and that has been prized for its natural resources or its strategic location. It has produced more than its share of scholars and poets, artists and architects, philosophers and prophets. We call it the cradle of human civilization. Let us hope it will not become its grave.

# CHRONOLOGY

| | |
|---|---|
| 570 | Muhammad born; Ethiopians invade western Arabia |
| 603–628 | War between Byzantine Empire and Sasanid Persia |
| 610 | First revelations of the Quran to Muhammad |
| 619 | Deaths of Khadijah and Abu-Talib |
| 620 | Abortive Muslim flight to Taif |
| 622 | *Hijrah* of Muhammad and his associates from Mecca to Medina, where first Muslim *ummah* is formed |
| 624 | Muslims defeat pagan Meccans at Battle of Badr |
| 625 | Meccan revenge at Battle of Uhud |
| 627 | Muslims foil Meccan attack at the Battle of the Trench |
| 628 | Hudaybiyah truce between Muhammad and Meccan pagans |
| 630 | Mecca's pagan leaders accept Islam |
| 630–632 | Arab tribal delegations accept Muhammad as their leader |
| 632 | Muhammad dies; associates choose Abu-Bakr as first caliph; rebellion (*riddah*) of the Arab tribes |
| 633 | Muslim armies crush *riddah* and finish conquering Arabian Peninsula |
| 634 | Muslims defeat Byzantine army and start conquests outside Arabia; Umar succeeds Abu-Bakr as caliph |
| 636 | Arab victory over Byzantines in Battle of the Yarmuk |
| 637 | Battle of Qadisiyah enables Arabs to take Ctesiphon and western Persia from the Sasanids |
| 639–642 | Arabs take Egypt from the Byzantine Empire |
| 640 | Arab garrison towns set up at Basrah and Kufah |
| 644 | Umar murdered; *shura* elects Uthman as caliph |
| 651 | Death of last Sasanid shah completes Arab conquest of Persia |
| 653 | Uthman establishes standard version of the Quran |

| | |
|---|---|
| 656 | Rebels murder Uthman; Ali declared caliph; Battle of the Camel opens first civil war (*fitnah*) |
| 657 | Mu'awiyah challenges Ali at Battle of Siffin; issues later submitted to arbitration |
| 659 | Arbitration goes against Ali, who is challenged by Kharijites |
| 661 | Kharijite kills Ali, whose son, Hasan, abdicates to Mu'awiyah |
| 661–750 | Umayyad caliphate in Damascus |
| 667 | Arabs cross Oxus River into partly Turkic Transoxiana |
| 669–678 | First Arab siege of Constantinople |
| 670 | Arab troops, crossing North Africa, found Qayrawan |
| 680 | Mu'awiyah designates son Yazid as his successor, then dies; Husayn challenges Umayyad rule and is killed at Karbala |
| 682–692 | Second *fitnah*, as Abdallah ibn al-Zubayr founds rival caliphate in Mecca; northern and southern Arab tribes quarrel |
| 684 | Pro-Umayyad southern Arabs defeat northern Arabs |
| 685–687 | Mukhtar leads *mawali* revolt in Kufah |
| 685–705 | Caliph Abd al-Malik restores order, resumes conquests, and later Arabizes his bureaucracy and coinage |
| 708–715 | Arabs conquer Sind, Transoxiana, and Spain |
| 717–720 | Caliph Umar II equalizes status of Arabs and *mawali* |
| 720–759 | Arabs conquer and occupy southern France |
| 724–743 | Caliph Hisham reorganizes the fiscal system |
| 732 | Europeans defeat Arabs in the Battle of Tours |
| 738 | Kharijite revolts in Iraq against Umayyad rule |
| 739–742 | Kharijite and Berber revolts in North Africa |
| 747 | Abu-Muslim, backed by Shi'i *mawali*, starts Abbasid revolt in Khurasan |
| 749 | Abbasids take Kufah and proclaim Abu al-Abbas as caliph |
| 750 | Abbasids defeat and murder Umayyads of Damascus |
| 750–1258 | Abbasid caliphate in Iraq |
| 751 | Arabs defeat Chinese; paper introduced into Middle East |
| 754 | Abbasids execute Abu-Muslim, alienating many Persians |
| 756–1030 | Umayyad dynasty in Cordoba |
| 762 | Baghdad founded as new Abbasid capital |
| 786–809 | Caliphate of Harun al-Rashid |
| 788 | Berber revolt brings Idrisids to power in Morocco |

| | |
|---|---|
| 800–909 | Aghlabid dynasty in Tunis |
| 803 | Harun al-Rashid dismisses Barmakid *vezirs* |
| 809–813 | Succession struggle between Amin and Mamun |
| 813–833 | Caliphate of al-Mamun, who courts Shi'i support, founds Bayt al-Hikmah, sponsors translation of ancient Greek writings, and espouses Mu'tazilite doctrines |
| 816–833 | Babak rebels in Azerbaijan |
| 820–873 | Tahirid dynasty in Khurasan |
| 825 | Arabs invade Sicily |
| 833–842 | Caliph Mu'tasim increases importation of Turkish slaves |
| 836–1465 | Saffarid dynasty in Persia |
| 874 | Disappearance of Muhammad, the twelfth Shi'i imam |
| 874–999 | Samanid dynasty in Transoxiana and Khurasan |
| 901–906 | Qarmatians ravage Syria and Iraq; later sack Mecca |
| 909 | Fatimids seize power in Tunis and found Shi'i caliphate |
| 929–1003 | Hamdanid dynasty in northern Syria and Iraq |
| 932–1062 | Buyid dynasty in western Persia and Iraq |
| 945 | Buyids occupy Baghdad |
| 956 | Turkic leader Seljuk converts to Islam |
| 960–1302 | Seljuk dynasty in Transoxiana, spreading to Persia, Iraq, and Anatolia |
| 962–1186 | Ghaznavid dynasty in Khurasan, spreading to India |
| 969–1171 | Fatimid dynasty in Egypt, sometimes also Syria and Hijaz |
| 970s | Seljuk Turks infiltrate Transoxiana |
| 971 | Al-Azhar University founded in Cairo |
| 996–1021 | Reign of Fatimid Caliph al-Hakim, venerated by the Druze |
| 998–1030 | Reign of Ghaznavid Amir Mahmud, conqueror of India |
| 1040 | Seljuks defeat Ghaznavids and take over Khurasan |
| 1055 | Seljuks take control of Baghdad |
| 1061–1091 | Normans take Sicily from the Arabs |
| 1063–1072 | Seljuks conquer Georgia and Armenia |
| 1071 | Seljuks defeat Byzantines at Manzikert and enter Anatolia |
| 1085 | Spanish Christians capture Toledo |
| 1090s | Rise of the Assassins in Persia and Syria |
| 1092 | Malikshah's death ends Seljuk unity |

| 1096 | First Crusade starts |
|------|---------------------|
| 1097–1098 | Crusaders take Antioch after long siege |
| 1099 | Crusaders found "Latin Kingdom of Jerusalem" |
| 1127 | Zengi, a former Seljuk officer, takes over Mosul |
| 1144 | Zengi leads Muslim capture of Crusader County of Edessa |
| 1146–1174 | Reign of Zengi's son Nur al-Din in Syria |
| 1147–1149 | Second Crusade fails to recapture Edessa |
| 1157 | Khwarizm Turks end Seljuk rule in Khurasan |
| 1171–1193 | Reign of Salah al-Din ("Saladin") in Cairo |
| 1171–1250 | Ayyubid dynasty in Egypt (1174–1260 in Syria) |
| 1180–1225 | Brief revival of Abbasid caliphate |
| 1187 | Salah al-Din defeats Crusaders at Hittin and takes Jerusalem |
| 1189–1193 | Third Crusade takes Acre, but not Jerusalem |
| 1202–1204 | Fourth Crusade takes Constantinople |
| 1206–1227 | Reign of Jenghiz Khan, Mongol conqueror |
| 1218–1221 | Fifth Crusade, directed against Egypt |
| 1220 | Jenghiz Khan defeats Khwarizm Turks, enters Khurasan |
| 1228–1229 | Sixth Crusade leads to treaty, letting Christians rule Jerusalem and other holy land cities for a ten-year period |
| 1236 | Spanish Christians capture Cordoba |
| 1243 | Mongols defeat Seljuks in Battle of Kose Dagh |
| 1248–1254 | Seventh Crusade, directed against Egypt, is repelled by the Mamluks |
| 1250–1517 | Mamluk sultanate in Egypt (1260–1516 in Syria and Hijaz) |
| 1256 | Mongols, led by Hulegu, capture Assassin stronghold in Persia |
| 1256–1349 | Il-Khanid dynasty in Persia |
| 1258 | Hulegu's forces sack Baghdad, ending Abbasid caliphate |
| 1260 | Mamluks defeat Mongols in Battle of Ayn Jalut |
| 1270 | Eighth Crusade, directed against Tunis |
| 1291 | Acre taken by the Mamluks |
| 1295–1304 | Reign of Ghazan Khan, Il-Khanid convert to Islam |
| 1299–1923 | Ottoman Empire |
| 1326 | After long siege, Ottomans take Bursa, which becomes their capital |
| 1354 | Ottomans cross Dardanelles, also take Ankara |

| | |
|---|---|
| 1361 | Ottomans capture Adrianople (Edirne) |
| 1369–1405 | Reign of Timur Leng (Tamerlane), who takes Central and Southwest Asia and founds the Timurid dynasty |
| 1371 | Ottomans conquer Bulgaria and Macedonia |
| 1378–1469 | Black Sheep Turcomans rule Azerbaijan and Armenia |
| 1387–1502 | White Sheep Turcomans rule Iraq and Anatolia |
| 1389 | Ottomans defeat Serbs at Kosovo |
| 1389–1402 | Reign of Ottoman Sultan Bayezid I |
| 1391–1398 | First Ottoman siege of Constantinople |
| 1396 | Ottomans defeat Crusaders at Nicopolis |
| 1397–1398 | Bayezid takes Konya and rest of Muslim Anatolia |
| 1400–1401 | Timur ravages Syria and invades Anatolia |
| 1402 | Timur defeats Ottomans at Ankara and captures Bayezid I |
| 1402–1413 | Interregnum and civil war in the Ottoman Empire |
| 1415 | Massive revolt against Mehmet I; Ottomans retake Izmir |
| 1421–1451 | Reign of Ottoman Sultan Murad II |
| 1441–1442 | John Hunyadi of Transylvania halts Ottoman armies |
| 1444 | Crusaders invade Balkans; repelled by Ottomans at Varna |
| 1451–1481 | Reign of Ottoman Sultan Mehmet II "the Conqueror" |
| 1453 | Ottoman capture of Constantinople ends Byzantine Empire |
| 1480–1481 | Ottomans occupy southern Italy |
| 1492 | Christians take Granada and expel Jews and Muslims from Spain |
| 1499–1503 | Ottomans take strategic Mediterranean islands |
| 1501–1736 | Safavid dynasty in Persia and parts of Iraq |
| 1507–1622 | Portuguese occupy Hormuz in the Gulf region |
| 1514 | Ottomans defeat Safavids at Chaldiran |
| 1516 | Ottomans defeat Mamluks and capture Syria |
| 1517 | Ottomans take Egypt, later also Medina and Mecca |
| 1520–1566 | Reign of Ottoman Sultan Suleyman "the Magnificent" |
| 1523–1536 | Ibrahim Pasha amasses great power as grand *vezir* |
| 1529 | First Ottoman siege of Vienna |
| 1535 | First Capitulations treaty between Ottoman Empire and France |
| 1571 | Christians defeat Ottoman navy at Lepanto; Turks take Cyprus |
| 1578–1639 | Long Ottoman-Safavid War over Iraq and Azerbaijan |
| 1587–1629 | Reign of Safavid Shah Abbas I |

| | |
|---|---|
| 1606 | Ottomans first recognize Habsburgs as equals in treaty |
| 1616 | British East India Company starts trading with Persia |
| 1638 | Ottoman Sultan Murad IV ends *devshirme* system |
| 1645–1670 | Ottoman-Venetian War in eastern Mediterranean |
| 1656–1678 | Koprulu *vezirs* begin Ottoman reforms |
| 1682–1699 | Ottoman Empire at war against Habsburg Austria |
| 1683 | Second Ottoman siege of Vienna |
| 1699 | Karlowitz treaty, Ottomans ceding Hungary to Habsburgs |
| 1703–1730 | Reign of Ottoman Sultan Ahmed III, the "Tulip Era" |
| 1718 | Passarowitz treaty, Ottomans ceding some Balkan lands |
| 1722 | Afghans invade Persia, weakening Safavid dynasty |
| 1729 | Turkish printing press introduced in the Ottoman Empire |
| 1736 | Nadir expels Afghans from Persia, becoming shah |
| 1739 | Nadir Shah takes Delhi from Mughals; Belgrade treaty restores some Balkan lands to Ottomans |
| 1747 | Assassination of Nadir Shah leads to anarchy in Persia |
| 1750–1794 | Zand dynasty in Persia |
| 1768–1774 | First Russo-Ottoman War |
| 1774 | Kuchuk-Kainarji treaty strengthens Russia on Black Sea and in Balkans and lays basis for Russian claim to protect Orthodox Christians |
| 1787–1792 | Russo-Ottoman War resumes, ending in Jassy treaty |
| 1789–1807 | Reign of Ottoman Sultan Selim III, who starts *nizam-i-jedid* |
| 1794–1925 | Qajar dynasty in Persia |
| 1798 | Napoleon occupies Egypt |
| 1799 | After failing to take Acre, Napoleon returns to France; Montenegro declares independence from Ottoman Empire |
| 1802 | Treaty of Amiens restores Ottoman control of Egypt |
| 1804 | First Serbian nationalist revolt |
| 1805–1849 | Reign of Mehmet Ali in Egypt |
| 1806–1812 | Ottoman Empire resumes war against Russia |
| 1807–1808 | Janissaries depose Selim, ending *nizam-i-jedid* |
| 1808–1813 | Russo-Persian War, ending in Treaty of Gulestan, in which Persia cedes part of Caucasus to Russia |
| 1808–1839 | Reign of Ottoman Sultan Mahmud II |
| 1811 | Mehmet Ali destroys Mamluks, attacks Arabian Wahhabis |

| | |
|---|---|
| 1812 | Bucharest treaty gives Bessarabia to Russia |
| 1814 | British treaty promises Persia protection from Russia |
| 1817 | Ottomans recognize Milosh Obrenovich as Serbian ruler |
| 1820 | Mehmet Ali starts conquest of Sudan; first British pacts with Arab shaykhs in the Gulf Region |
| 1821–1829 | Greek war for independence |
| 1826 | Mahmud II massacres janissaries |
| 1827 | Europeans destroy Ottoman-Egyptian fleet at Navarino |
| 1827–1828 | Russo-Persian War, ending in Turkmanchai treaty, ceding more of Caucasus mountain region to Russia |
| 1827–1829 | Fourth Russo-Ottoman War |
| 1829 | Adrianople treaty grants Serbian autonomy, Greek independence, and Balkan gains for Russia |
| 1831 | Ibrahim, son of Mehmet Ali, invades Syria |
| 1833 | Hunkar-Iskelesi treaty lets Russian warships pass through Straits in return for guarantee of Ottoman territorial integrity |
| 1838 | Anglo-Ottoman Commercial Convention lowers Ottoman import tariffs |
| 1839 | Ibrahim again defeats Ottomans, whose fleet deserts to Alexandria; Abdulmejid issues Noble Rescript of the Rose Chamber, promising administrative and fiscal reforms; British occupy Aden |
| 1840 | European powers confirm Mehmet Ali's autonomy in Egypt |
| 1841 | European powers sign Straits navigation convention |
| 1844 | Baha'i movement starts in Persia |
| 1848–1896 | Reign of Nasiruddin Shah in Persia |
| 1851–1857 | Cairo-Alexandria-Suez railway built |
| 1853–1856 | Russian occupation of Romania sparks Crimean War, in which France and Britain help the Ottomans defeat Russia |
| 1854 | Egyptian viceroy Said grants concession to French entrepreneur to build Suez Canal |
| 1856 | Paris treaty restores Bessarabia to Ottomans and demilitarizes Black Sea; Ottoman Imperial Rescript grants equality to Muslims, Christians, and Jews |
| 1856–1857 | Anglo-Persian War forces shah to evacuate Herat |
| 1860 | Druze-Maronite War in Lebanon leads to French intervention |
| 1861–1914 | Autonomous province of Mount Lebanon |

| | |
|---|---|
| 1863–1879 | Reign of Khedive Isma'il in Egypt |
| 1865 | Ottoman public debt administration established |
| 1866 | Syrian Protestant College (American University of Beirut) founded; first Egyptian representative assembly; rebellion in Crete |
| 1869 | Suez Canal opened |
| 1873 | Shah offers (but later revokes) concession to British company for railway and mining enterprises in Persia |
| 1875 | Isma'il sells Egypt's Suez Canal shares to Britain; rebellion in Bosnia and Herzegovina sparks Balkan crisis; Serbia and Montenegro declare war on the Ottoman Empire |
| 1876 | New Ottomans seize power; Bulgarian revolt crushed; Ottoman constitution issued; Egyptian debt commission established |
| 1876–1909 | Reign of Ottoman Sultan Abdulhamid II |
| 1877–1878 | Russo-Turkish War, in which Russians take Romania, Bulgaria, Thrace, and parts of eastern Anatolia |
| 1878 | San Stefano treaty sets up large Bulgaria; Ottoman constitution suspended; Berlin treaty reduces Bulgaria's size and curtails Russian power in Balkans; Anglo-French Dual Financial Control set up in Egypt |
| 1879 | Egyptian officers' uprising undermines Dual Control; Europeans press sultan to replace Isma'il with Tawfiq |
| 1881 | Europeans take control of Ottoman public debt; Egyptian Nationalist officers take over government; France occupies Tunis |
| 1881–1885 | Muhammad Ahmad, the Mahdi, leads revolt in Sudan |
| 1882 | British occupy Egypt and suppress nationalist movement |
| 1883–1907 | British consul in Cairo, Lord Cromer, reforms finances and irrigation, strengthening Britain's control over Egypt |
| 1885 | Mahdist rebels take complete control of the Sudan |
| 1885–1888 | Eastern Rumelia rebels, uniting with Bulgaria |
| 1888 | Constantinople Convention opens Suez Canal to all ships |
| 1890 | Persian shah sells tobacco concession to British company |
| 1892 | Nationwide tobacco boycott obliges shah to buy back concession |
| 1896 | Nasiruddin Shah assassinated; abortive Young Turk coup against Abdulhamid; Herzl publishes *Der Judenstaat* |
| 1897 | First Zionist congress in Basel; Ottomans defeat Greeks |
| 1898 | Anglo-Egyptian army recaptures the Sudan |
| 1899–1956 | Sudan condominium under Britain and Egypt |

| 1901 | British firm (later called the Anglo-Iranian Oil Company) given concession to explore southwest Persia for oil deposits |
| 1901–1953 | Reign of Ibn Sa'ud, initially in Najd, later in all Saudi Arabia |
| 1902 | Ottoman Empire engages German firm to build Baghdad railway |
| 1904 | Anglo-French *entente* ends rivalry over Egypt |
| 1906 | Persian revolution forces shah to grant constitution |
| 1907 | Anglo-Russian agreement creates spheres of influence in Persia; new shah tries to revoke constitution |
| 1908 | Committee of Union and Progress leads revolution to restore Ottoman constitution; Austria annexes Bosnia; Bulgaria declares its independence; first major oil strike in Persia |
| 1909 | Ottoman counterrevolt quashed; Abdulhamid is deposed; Russian troops occupy Tabriz and Tehran, but Persian constitution prevails |
| 1910 | Albanian revolt against Ottoman rule |
| 1911 | Russian pressure foils financial reforms in Persia; Italians invade Libya; Kitchener takes power in Egypt |
| 1912 | Ottomans give up Libya; Serbia and Bulgaria take most remaining European territories of the Ottoman Empire in first Balkan War |
| 1913 | CUP seizes Ottoman government; Ottomans defeat Bulgaria in second Balkan War; Albania independent; Germans send military mission to Istanbul |
| 1914 | Ottomans enter World War I on Germany's side; Britain annexes Cyprus, invades lower Iraq, and declares protectorate over Egypt |
| 1915 | Ottomans attack Suez Canal; McMahon promises British support for Arabs' independence if Hashimites rebel against Ottoman rule; Allied troops land at Gallipoli but fail to capture Dardanelles |
| 1916 | Sykes-Picot Agreement; Arab Revolt against Turks starts |
| 1917 | Britain takes Iraq and Palestine, issues Balfour Declaration |
| 1918 | Arabs occupy Damascus, set up provisional government under Faysal; Ottomans surrender; Allies occupy strategic Ottoman areas |
| 1919 | Proposed Anglo-Persian treaty stirs national opposition; Egyptians rebel against British; Paris Peace Conference sends King-Crane Commission; Kemal (Ataturk) resists Greek invasion of Turkey |
| 1920 | San Remo agreement gives mandates to Britain in Palestine and Iraq, and to France in Syria; Ottomans sign Sèvres treaty, which Kemal rejects; Faysal ousted; riots in Palestine; revolt in Iraq |

| | |
|---|---|
| 1921 | Reza Khan seizes power in Persia; British name Faysal king of Iraq and Abdallah amir of Transjordan (cut off from Palestine) |
| 1922 | Britain ends Egypt protectorate, subject to Four Reserved Points; Kemalist Turks expel Greek invaders |
| 1923 | Kemal abolishes Ottoman sultanate, declares Turkish Republic; Lausanne Treaty ends Capitulations and Allied occupation of Turkey; Egypt drafts constitution and holds elections |
| 1923–1938 | Presidency of Kemal Ataturk in Turkey |
| 1924 | Kemal ends caliphate; Ibn Sa'ud takes Hijaz from Hashimites |
| 1925–1941 | Reign of Reza Shah Pahlavi in Persia, renamed Iran |
| 1928–1929 | Wailing Wall Incident; Arab rebellion in Palestine |
| 1930 | Passfield White Paper blames Jewish immigration and land purchases in Palestine for the Arab rebellion |
| 1932 | Iraq given independence, but Britain keeps bases and oil interests; Kingdom of Saudi Arabia established |
| 1933 | Faysal dies; Assyrian uprising in Iraq suppressed; new Anglo-Iranian oil agreement signed |
| 1936 | Montreux Convention gives Turkey control of Straits; Arab rebellion in Palestine; Anglo-Egyptian treaty signed, limiting British control of Egypt |
| 1937 | Peel Commission calls for Palestine partition, opposed by Arabs |
| 1939 | British White Paper limits Jewish immigration into Palestine; most Middle East states declare neutrality as World War II breaks out |
| 1941 | British troops crush nationalist revolt in Iraq, occupy Syria and Lebanon; Britain and USSR invade Iran, and Reza Shah abdicates |
| 1941–1979 | Reign of Mohammad Reza Shah Pahlavi in Iran |
| 1942 | British make Egypt's Faruq appoint pro-Allied cabinet; Allies halt German advance at al-Alamain; Zionists issue Biltmore Program |
| 1943 | Lebanese Christians and Muslims adopt national pact |
| 1945 | Arab League formed; United Nations formed; Jewish resistance mounts against British in Palestine; French quit Syria and Lebanon |
| 1946 | UN pressures USSR to quit Azerbaijan; Anglo-American Committee of Inquiry visits Palestine; Transjordan becomes independent |
| 1947 | Truman Doctrine pledges aid to Greece and Turkey against USSR; Britain submits Palestine mandate to UN, which sets up Special |

| | Committee on Palestine; UN General Assembly accepts Palestine Partition Plan |
|---|---|
| 1948 | Israel declares independence as British troops quit Palestine; Arab armies attack but are defeated; most Palestinian Arabs flee |
| 1949 | Arab states and Israel sign armistice agreements; Abdallah annexes West Bank, creating Hashimite Kingdom of Jordan; three coups in Syria |
| 1950 | Turkey's Demokrat party defeats Republican People's party |
| 1951 | Mosaddiq nationalizes Anglo-Iranian Oil Company; Egypt renounces its 1936 treaty with Britain; Abdallah is murdered |
| 1952 | Egyptian mobs burn Cairo; military coup, led by Nasir, ousts Faruq and institutes land reform in Egypt |
| 1952–1999 | Reign of King Husayn in Jordan |
| 1953 | Shah's partisans, aided by United States, overthrow Mosaddiq |
| 1954 | Foreign consortium set up to manage Iran's oil; Anglo-Egyptian agreement calls for British evacuation of Suez Canal by 1956 |
| 1954–1970 | Presidency of Gamal Abd al-Nasir in Egypt |
| 1955 | Baghdad Pact formed; Israel raids Gaza; Egypt buys Soviet arms; United States offers Egypt loan to build Aswan High Dam |
| 1956 | United States retracts Aswan offer; Nasir nationalizes Suez Canal Company; British, French, and Israelis attack Egypt, but UN demands they quit Suez and Sinai; UN Emergency Force dispatched |
| 1957 | United States issues Eisenhower Doctrine; Husayn overthrows Arab nationalist government in Jordan |
| 1958 | Egypt and Syria form United Arab Republic; military coup ousts Iraq's monarchy; United States intervenes in Lebanese civil war |
| 1960 | Military coup in Turkey; Organization of Petroleum Exporting Countries formed in Baghdad to halt falling oil prices |
| 1961 | Kuwait made independent; new republican constitution enacted in Turkey; Syria withdraws from United Arab Republic |
| 1962 | Yemeni army coup deposes imam, leading to civil war and Egyptian military intervention |
| 1963 | Coups in Iraq and Syria lead to abortive unity talks with Egypt; shah proclaims White Revolution in Iran |
| 1964 | Jordan River waters dispute between Arabs and Israel; Palestine Liberation Organization formed in Cairo |
| 1964–1975 | Reign of King Faysal in Saudi Arabia |

| 1965–1966 | Syrian-backed Palestinians raid Israel, which attacks Jordan |
|---|---|
| 1967 | USSR falsely reports Israeli buildup near Syria; Nasir demands that UN withdraw its force from the Sinai and blockades Aqaba Gulf to Israeli ships; Israel attacks and defeats Arab states in lightning war, taking the Sinai, Jordan's West Bank, and Syria's Golan Heights; UN calls for peace settlement, mutual recognition, and Israel's withdrawal from occupied lands; British troops quit Aden and South Arabia; Egyptian troops quit Yemen |
| 1968 | Two military coups in Iraq |
| 1969 | Yasir Arafat elected PLO head; Nasir declares War of Attrition against Israel; Qadhafi leads coup in Libya |
| 1970 | Soviet arms buildup in Egypt; Rogers Plan for temporary cease-fire accepted by Egypt, Israel, and Jordan; indirect peace talks fail; Jordan crushes Palestinian rebellion; Nasir dies |
| 1970–2000 | Presidency of Hafiz al-Asad in Syria |
| 1970–1981 | Presidency of Anwar al-Sadat in Egypt |
| 1971 | Last British forces leave Gulf region |
| 1972 | Sadat orders most Soviet military advisers out of Egypt |
| 1973 | Egypt and Syria coordinate surprise attack against Israelis in the Sinai and Golan; after initial setback, Israelis penetrate Syria and cross Suez Canal; United States and USSR impose cease-fire; Arab oil boycott, price hikes, and production cutbacks pressure Israel and its backers; Geneva Peace Conference |
| 1974 | Kissinger arranges separation-of-forces agreements among Israel, Egypt, and Syria; Arab states affirm PLO as sole spokesman for Palestinians; UN General Assembly invites Arafat to speak |
| 1975 | Saudi King Faysal is assassinated and succeeded by Khalid; civil war starts in Lebanon; Egypt and Israel sign interim Sinai agreement; UN General Assembly calls Zionism a form of racism |
| 1976 | Syria intervenes in Lebanon; Arab summit at Riyadh tries to end Lebanese civil war, appointing Syrian troops as peacekeepers |
| 1977 | Begin is elected Israeli premier; Sadat flies to Jerusalem and addresses Knesset; Egypt and Israel start peace negotiations in Cairo |
| 1978 | Southern Lebanon invaded by Israelis, later replaced by UN force; Carter calls Begin and Sadat to summit at Camp David, where they draft tentative peace treaty; successive coups in the two Yemens; exiled Khomeini inspires mass demonstrations against shah, as workers' strike cuts Iran's oil output |
| 1979 | Shah names Bakhtiar premier and leaves Iran; Khomeini returns and proclaims Islamic Republic; oil shortages cause price hikes; |

Egypt and Israel sign peace treaty, causing other Arab states to break ties with Egypt; Saddam Husayn officially takes power in Iraq; Iranian militant students seize U.S. Embassy, holding Americans hostage; Muslim revolutionaries occupy Mecca mosque; USSR invades Afghanistan

1980    U.S. diplomatic pressure and military rescue attempt fail to release American hostages in Iran; shah dies in exile; military coup in Turkey; Iraq invades Iran, causing further oil price hikes

1981    Algeria mediates U.S.-Iranian agreement, releasing frozen Iranian assets in return for the hostages; Begin reelected; Israel bombs Iraqi nuclear reactor; Sadat assassinated during parade and is succeeded by Husni Mubarak; U.S. Senate authorizes AWACS aircraft sale to Saudi Arabia; Israel annexes Golan Heights

1982    Iran drives back Iraqi forces; Israel returns the Sinai to Egypt; Saudi King Khalid dies and is succeeded by Fahd; Israel invades Lebanon, drives back Syrian and PLO forces, and besieges Beirut; PLO troops withdraw under supervision of U.S., French, and Italian forces; President-elect Bashir Jumayyil killed in bomb blast; Israeli troops enter west Beirut as Lebanese Christians massacre Palestinians in camps; Amin Jumayyil is elected in his brother's place; Israel-Lebanon peace talks begin

1983    U.S. brokers peace treaty between Israel and Lebanon, calling for all foreign troops to leave Lebanon, but Syria refuses to pull out; Israeli forces withdraw to Awali River; truck bombers destroy U.S. Marine barracks and French headquarters in Beirut; Shamir replaces Begin as Israel's premier

1984    American University of Beirut president Malcolm Kerr assassinated; Western peacekeeping forces leave west Beirut as Shi'i extremists take control; inconclusive Knesset election in Israel produces broad coalition government, headed first by Shim'on Peres and then by Yitzhak Shamir; elections in Egypt and Turkey

1985    Israel quits Lebanon, except for self-defined security zone on southern border; militant Shi'is hijack TWA plane and demand Israel release its Lebanese prisoners; Israel bombs PLO headquarters in Tunis, following terrorist attack on Israelis in Cyprus; Palestinians step up terrorist acts

1986    Reagan orders bombing of Tripoli (Libya); U.S. and British hostages slain in Lebanon; U.S. Navy analyst admits to selling documents to Israel; Tehran reveals secret talks regarding U.S. arms sales to Iran, the proceeds to aid Contra rebels in Nicaragua

1987     Iranian troops besiege Basrah; presidential commission confirms U.S. arms sales to Iran via Israel and diversion of proceeds to Contras; United States agrees to protect Kuwaiti shipping in Gulf as Iran-Iraq War intensifies; UN passes Security Council Resolution 598, calling for end to Iran-Iraq War; more U.S. citizens kidnapped in Lebanon; Palestinian *Intifadah* breaks out in Gaza and West Bank, protesting Israeli occupation; elections held in Egypt and Turkey

1988     U.S. Navy involved in heavy Gulf fighting; Iraq and Iran accept Resolution 598, ending Iran-Iraq War; Lebanese parliament fails to agree on a new president, leaving Lebanon ruled by two separate governments; King Husayn disclaims Jordanian interest in regaining control of West Bank as *Intifadah* continues; inconclusive Israeli elections lead to broad cabinet with Likud and Labor ministers; Palestine National Council declares independent state of Palestine; Arafat formally renounces terrorism and recognizes Israel; U.S. begins direct talks with PLO representatives

1989     Shamir calls for West Bank and Gaza elections to choose Palestinian negotiators with Israel but rules out PLO role; Egypt's Mubarak and U.S. Secretary of State Baker propose peace plan; Ayatollah Khomeini dies and is succeeded by Khamanei as Iran's *faqih*; Majlis speaker Hashimi Rafsanjani becomes president; Saudi Arabia hosts meeting of Lebanon's parliament, which elects a moderate Christian president; when he is assassinated, parliament elects Ilyas Harawi; Awn refuses to give up power to elected president

1990     Arab leaders hold emergency summit as large numbers of Jewish emigrants from USSR enter Israel; two Yemens are united; Shamir's broad coalition government falls; Israel's religious parties enter right-wing coalition led by Shamir; Iraqi forces invade and occupy Kuwait; UN Security Council condemns Iraq and imposes economic sanctions; many countries, led by U.S., send forces and supplies to Saudi Arabia in Operation Desert Shield; Awn ousted from power in Lebanon

1991     U.S.-led coalition of forces in Saudi Arabia starts massive air attacks against Iraq; Iraq responds with SCUD missile attacks against Israel and Saudi Arabia; coalition's massive ground assault hastens Iraqi withdrawal from Kuwait; abortive rebellions by Kurds and Shi'is in Iraq; UN insists on removal of nuclear, biological, and chemical weapons from Iraq; Israel and Arab countries begin peace negotiations in Madrid

1992     General elections in Israel restore Labor to power; Yitzhak Rabin forms narrow coalition and authorizes secret contacts with PLO representatives in Oslo

1993     PLO and Israeli representatives sign Declaration of Principles on White House lawn, offering autonomy to Palestinians in Gaza and Jericho and eventually to rest of West Bank following Israeli troop withdrawals and elections for Palestinian council

1994     PLO-Israel talks over terms for troop withdrawals, elections, and Jewish settlements in occupied lands; Arafat returns to Gaza; Jordan and Israel sign peace treaty; U.S. seeks Syrian-Israeli treaty; other Arab states seek peace accords despite Islamist opposition

1995     PLO and Israel reach new agreement on phased Israeli troop withdrawals; Israeli extremist assassinates Rabin; Islamist party wins plurality in Turkish elections and forms government

1996     Elections held for Palestinian Authority in West Bank and Gaza; close Israeli elections restore Likud to power and Benjamin Netanyahu becomes prime minister; Israel-PLO peace talks stall over Jewish settlements, Jerusalem tunnel, and control over terrorism; Iraqi troops invade Kurdistan, setting off U.S. reprisals; Taliban take over most of Afghanistan

1997     Israel cedes control over most of Hebron; Turkish officers demand end to Islamist government; Iraq tries to bar UN arms inspectors from key sites, inviting confrontation with U.S.; Iranians elect Khatami president; terrorist attacks in Jerusalem and Luxor chill peace efforts

1998     Iraq's government continues to impede UN inspections for weapons of mass destruction, despite mediation of UN secretary-general Kofi Annan; inspectors quit Iraq as U.S. and Britain resume aerial bombardment

1999     Israelis vote Likud out of office, as Ehud Barak forms Labor coalition with small parties in Knesset; Husayn dies and is succeeded by Abdallah II as king of Jordan; severe earthquake in Turkey

2000     Hafiz al-Asad dies and is succeeded by his son, Bashar, as president of Syria; Israeli-Palestinian negotiations lead to Camp David summit, where Ehud Barak and Yasir Arafat fail to reach final peace settlement; Ariel Sharon's visit to Temple Mount sparks new Palestinian uprising, called the al-Aqsa Intifadah

2001     Ariel Sharon elected prime minister of Israel; Fighting intensifies between Israelis and Palestinians

# GLOSSARY

**Abadan** (ah-ba-DAHN): Iran's main oil refinery

**Abbas I, Shah** (awb-BOSS): Safavid ruler (1587–1629)

**Abbas II, Khedive** (ab-BASS): Egypt's viceroy (1892–1914)

**Abbasid dynasty** (ab-BAS-sid): Arab family descended from Abbas, Muhammad's uncle, that ruled from Baghdad over parts of the Muslim world (750–1258)

**Abd al-Ilah** (AB-dul-ee-LAH): Regent of Iraq (1939–1953)

**Abdallah** (ab-DULL-ah): Son of Amir Husayn of Mecca, participant in Arab Revolt, and amir of Transjordan (1921–1951)

**Abdallah II**: Jordan's king (1999– )

**Abdallah ibn al-Zubayr** (ab-DULL-ah ibn ez-zoo-BAYR): Mecca-based challenger to the Umayyads from 683 to 692, when he was killed

**Abd al-Malik** (AB-dul MA-lik): Umayyad caliph (685–705) who ended the second *fitnah*

**Abduh, Muhammad** (AB-doo, moo-HOM-mad): Egyptian Muslim reformer (d. 1905)

**Abdulaziz** (AB-dul-a-ZEEZ): Ottoman sultan (1861–1876)

**Abdulhamid II** (AB-dul-ha-MEED): Ottoman sultan (1876–1909) who advocated pan-Islam and opposed constitutional government

**Abdulmejid I** (AB-dul-me-JEED): Ottoman sultan (1839–1861)

**Abu al-Abbas** (AH-bull-ab-BASS): First Abbasid caliph (750–754)

**Abu-Bakr** (AH-boo-BEKR): First caliph (632–634), who put down tribal revolts and began conquests outside Arabian Peninsula

**Abu-Ja'far al-Mansur** (AH-boo JAH-far el-man-SOOR): Abbasid caliph (754–775) who began the construction of Baghdad

**Abu-Kir, Battle of** (ah-boo-KEER): British victory over Napoleon (1798)

**Abu-Muslim** (AH-boo-MOOS-lim): Persian leader of the Abbasid revolt (d. 754)

**Abu-Talib** (AH-boo-TAW-lib): Muhammad's uncle and protector (d. 619)

**Achaemenid** (AK-a-MEE-nid): Persian dynasty (550–330 B.C.E.)

**Aden** (AH-den): Port city between the Red and Arabian seas, ruled by Britain (1839–1967), now united with the Republic of Yemen

**Adli Yakan** (ODD-lee YEH-ghen): Egypt's prime minister in 1921

**Afghan** (AF-gan): Pertaining to Afghanistan, a mountainous country east of Iran

425

**al-Afghani, Jamal al-Din** (el-af-GHAW-nee, je-MAWL ed-DEEN): Influential pan-Islamic agitator and reformer (d. 1897)

**Agha Khan** (AH-gha KHAWN): Modern Isma'ili Shi'i leader

**Aghlabid dynasty** (AGH-la-bid): Arab family ruling Tunisia (800–909)

**al-Ahd** (el-AH-d): Nationalist secret society of Arab officers in the Ottoman army before and during World War I

**Ahmad ibn Hanbal** (AH-mad ibn-HAM-bal): Muslim jurist and theologian (d. 855)

**Ahmad ibn Tulun** (AH-mad ibn-to-LOON): Turkish founder of the Tulunid dynasty of Egypt (868–908)

**Ahmad Shah** (ah-MAWD SHAH): Persia's last Qajar ruler (1909–1925)

**Ahmed III** (ah-MET): Ottoman sultan (1703–1730) during Tulip Era

*al-Ahram* (el-ah-RAHM): Influential Cairo daily newspaper

**Aishah** (ah-EE-sha): Abu-Bakr's daughter, one of Muhammad's wives, and opponent of Ali at the Battle of the Camel (656)

*akhi* (AH-khee): Early Turkish trade guild

**Alawi** (AH-la-wee): Offshoot of Shi'i Islam prevalent in part of northern Syria

**Aleppo** (ah-LEP-po): City in northern Syria

**Alexander the Great:** Macedonian general and empire builder (d. 323 B.C.E.)

**Alexandretta:** Mediterranean seaport and its hinterland, now called Iskenderun, held by Turkey but claimed by Syria

**Alexandria:** Egyptian city on the Mediterranean coast

**Ali** (AH-lee): Fourth of the early caliphs (656–661), regarded by Shi'i Muslims as the first imam (leader) after Muhammad

**Alid:** Pertaining to Ali, his descendants, or partisans of their role as Muslim imams

**aliyah** (ah-lee-YAH): Jewish immigration to Israel

**Allenby, Edmund:** Commander of Egyptian Expeditionary Force in World War I, conqueror of Palestine, later high commissioner for Egypt and the Sudan (1919–1925)

**Allon, Yigal** (al-LAWN, yeeg-AHL): Israeli general and political leader (d. 1980)

**Amal** (ah-MAL): Lebanese Shi'i revolutionary movement, led by Nabih Berri and backed by Syria

**American Israel Public Affairs Committee (AIPAC):** Influential pro-Israel lobby

**Amin** (ah-MEEN): Abbasid caliph (809–813)

**amir** (ah-MEER): Muslim ruler or prince

*amir al-muminin* (ah-MEER el-muh-men-NEEN): Commander of the true believers, a title given to the caliph

**Amman** (am-MAN): Capital of Jordan

**Amr ibn al-As** (AHM ribn el-ASS): Early Arab general, conqueror of Egypt, and Mu'awiyah's representative in the arbitration (d. 663)

**Anatolia:** Peninsula between the Mediterranean, Black, and Aegean seas

**Anglo-American Committee of Inquiry:** Delegation that visited Palestine in 1946, urging continuation of mandate and admission of 100,000 Jews

**Anglo-Egyptian Treaty:** 1936 pact defining Britain's military position in Egypt, denounced by Egypt in 1951, and officially terminated in 1954

**Anglo-Ottoman Commercial Convention:** 1838 agreement limiting Ottoman import tariffs

**Anglo-Persian Oil Company:** Firm holding petroleum exploration, drilling, and refining rights in Iran; renamed Anglo-Iranian Oil Company; nationalized by Mosaddiq in 1951

**Ankara:** (1) Site of Timur's victory over Bayezid I in 1402; (2) capital of Turkey since 1923

*ansar* (an-SAWR): Medinan Muslim converts

**Antichrist:** Major antagonist of Jesus who Christians and Muslims believe will fill the world with evil before his return

**Antioch:** ancient city in southern Anatolia; important early Christian center

**anti-Semitism:** Popular term for prejudice against or persecution of Jews

**Aqaba** (AH-ka-ba): (1) Inlet from the Red Sea; (2) city in southern Jordan

**al-Aqsa** (el-AHK-sa): Important Jerusalem mosque

**Arab:** (1) Native speaker of Arabic; (2) person who identifies with Arabic cultural tradition; (3) inhabitant of Arabia; (4) citizen of a country in which the predominant language and culture are Arabic; (5) camel nomad

**Arab Higher Committee:** Palestinian nationalist organization of the 1930s

**Arab League:** Arab states' political association, founded in 1945

**Arab Legion:** Former name of the army of Transjordan (or Jordan)

**Arab Liberation Army:** Syrian-Palestinian group fighting against Israel in 1948

**Arab nationalism:** Movement seeking unification of all Arab countries and their independence from non-Arab control

**Arab Revolt:** British-backed rebellion of Arabs, mainly in the Hijaz, against Ottoman rule (1916–1918)

**Arab socialism:** Ideology advocating state control of Arab economies

**Arab Socialist Union:** Egyptian political party (1962–1978)

**Arabia:** Original Arab homeland, a peninsula bounded by the Red Sea, the Arabian Sea, the Gulf, and the Fertile Crescent

**Arabic:** (1) Semitic language spoken by Arabs; (2) pertaining to the culture of Arabs

**Arafat** (a-ra-FAT): Plain near Mecca

**Arafat, Yasir** (YAH-sir): Palestinian Arab nationalist, founder of al-Fatah, PLO chairman, and Palestinian Authority's president

**Aral Sea** (AR-al): Large lake in Central Asia

**Aramaic:** Ancient Semitic language

**Aramco:** Arabian American Oil Company, which developed the petroleum industry in Saudi Arabia

**Aramean** (a-ra-MEE-an): Native speaker of Aramaic

**Ardabil** (ar-da-BEEL): Northwest Iranian city, where the Safavids originated

**Arian:** Pertaining to the belief of some early Christians that Jesus was human, not of the same substance as God the Father

**Arif, Abd al-Salam** (AH-ref, AB-dus-sa-LAAM): Arab nationalist leader of Iraq (1958, 1963–1966)

**Arkam** (ar-KAM): An early Meccan convert to Islam

**Armenia:** (1) Mountainous region of eastern Anatolia; (2) kingdom of the Armenians, conquered by the Turks in the eleventh century

**Aryan:** Pertaining to the Indo-European language family (often used in juxtaposition with the term *Semitic*)

*asabiyah* (ah-sa-BEE-ya): Feeling of group solidarity

**al-Asad, Hafiz** (el-ASS-ed, HAW-fez): President of Syria (1970–2000); his son, Bashar (BAH-shar) al-Asad succeeded him

**al-Ash'ari** (el-ASH-ah-ree): Muslim theologian (d. 935)

**Ashkenazim** (ASH-ke-nah-ZEEM): Jews whose recent ancestors came from Eastern or Central Europe

**Assassin:** Member of a militant group of Isma'ili Shi'is who fought against Seljuks and other Sunni rulers (1092–1256)

**Assyrian:** Pertaining to Nestorian Christians in Syria, Iraq, and Iran

**Aswan** (ass-WAHN): (1) City in Upper Egypt; (2) site of the High Dam, built for Egypt by the USSR (1958–1970)

**Ataturk:** *See* Kemal, Mustafa

**Attrition, War of:** Artillery and air struggle between Egypt and Israel (1969–1970)

**Awn, Michel** (OW-un): Maronite general who claimed Lebanon's presidency (1988–1990)

**Ayatollah** (AYE-ya-TOL-lah): Title given by ulama to respected Shi'i legal experts

**Ayn Jalut** (AYN-ja-LOOT): Crucial Mamluk victory over Mongols in 1260

**Ayn al-Dowleh** (AYN-od-DOE-leh): Qajar minister opposed to 1906 Persian Constitutionalist Revolution

**Ayyubid dynasty** (eye-YOO-bid): Salah al-Din and his descendants, who ruled in Egypt (1171–1250) and Syria (1174–1260)

**Azerbaijan** (AH-zur-bye-JOHN): Mountainous region of northwestern Iran

**al-Azhar** (el-OZ-har): Muslim mosque-university in Cairo

**Babak** (BAH-bek): Ninth-century Persian revolutionary

**Babur** (BAH-ber): Founder of the Timurid (Mughal) dynasty in India (d. 1530)

**Badr:** Yemen's imam (1962), ousted by military coup

**Badr, Battle of:** Muhammad's first victory over the Meccans (624)

**Baghdad** (bagh-DAD): Iraq's capital; seat of Abbasids (762–1258)

**Baghdad Pact:** Anticommunist military alliance formed in 1955, renamed CENTO

**Bahrain** (bah-RAYN): (1) Island country in the Gulf; (2) eastern Arabia during the caliphal period

*bakhshish* (bakh-SHEESH): Gift, tip, bribe, or payment for services

**Bakhtiar, Shapur** (bakh-tee-YAR, shah-POOR): Iran's last shah-appointed prime minister (1979)

**Balfour Declaration:** Official statement in 1917 by British foreign secretary, supporting Jewish national home in Palestine

**Balkans:** Mountainous region of southeastern Europe

**Bandung Conference** (ban-DOONG): Meeting in Indonesia of Asian and Middle Eastern leaders in 1955

**Bar Lev Line:** Israel's defense line east of the Suez Canal breached by Egypt in October 1973

**Barak, Ehud** (ba-RAHK, ay-KHUD): Israel's prime minister (1999–2001)

**Barmakid** (BAR-ma-kid): Persian family of *vezirs* under the early Abbasids

**al-Barudi, Mahmud Sami** (el-ba-ROO-dee, mah-MOOD SA-mee): Egyptian nationalist prime minister (1882)

**Basel:** Site of first international Zionist congress (1897)

**Basrah** (BOSS-ra): Town in southern Iraq, founded by Umar to garrison troops

*bast* (BAWST): Individual or group act of taking refuge in a mosque or other public place to evade arrest, a Persian custom

**Ba'th** (BAHTH): Arab nationalist and socialist party ruling Syria and Iraq since the 1960s

**Baybars** (BYE-barce): Mamluk general and sultan (1260–1277)

**Bayezid I** (BYE-yeh-zeet): Ottoman sultan (1389–1402), who spread control in Balkans and Anatolia

**Bayezid II:** Ottoman sultan (1481–1512)

**Bayt al-Hikmah** (BAYT el-HIK-ma): Muslim center of learning under Abbasids

**bazaar** (ba-ZAWR): (1) Large trading and manufacturing center; (2) urban merchants as a corporate body, especially in Iranian cities

**Bazargan, Mehdi** (ba-zar-GAWN, meh-DEE): Iran's first prime minister after the Islamic revolution

**bedouin** (BED-a-win): Arab camel nomad(s)

**Begin, Menachem** (BAY-gin, me-NAH-khem): Leader of Israel's right-wing Likud coalition and prime minister (1977–1983)

**Beirut** (bay-ROOT): Port city, commercial center, and Lebanon's capital

**Bektashi** (bek-TAH-shee): Sufi order, popular among Ottoman janissaries

**Ben-Gurion, David:** Zionist pioneer, writer, politician, and Israel's defense and prime minister (1948–1953 and 1955–1963)

**Berber:** Native inhabitant of parts of North Africa

**Berlin, Treaty of:** Definitive peace settlement of the Russo-Turkish War, signed in August 1878 and replacing the San Stefano Treaty

**Berlin-to-Baghdad Railway:** Proposed rail line that, if completed, would have enhanced Germany's power in the Ottoman Empire before World War I

**Bernadotte, Folke:** Swedish UN mediator, murdered during the 1948 Palestine war

**Bethlehem:** Judean (or West Bank) city, south of Jerusalem

**Bilal** (bee-LAL): Muhammad's first muezzin, a Black Ethiopian

**Biltmore Program:** American Zionist resolution in 1942 openly demanding a Jewish state in Palestine

**BILU** (BEE-loo): Early Zionist movement in Russia

**Bin Laden, Osama** (bin LAH-den, oh-SAH-ma): Terrorist leader based in Afghanistan, originally from Saudi Arabia

**Biqa'** (be-KAH): Predominantly Shi'i valley in eastern Lebanon

**Black Sheep Turcomans:** Shi'i Turkish dynasty ruling in Persia (1378–1469)

**Bosporus:** Straits connecting the Black Sea and the Sea of Marmara

**British Agency:** Offices and residence of Britain's chief political and diplomatic officer in Cairo to 1914; later called the Residency and now the British Embassy

**Bukhara** (boo-KHA-ra): Central Asian city

**Bunche, Ralph:** U.S. diplomat and UN mediator in Palestine (1948–1949)

**Bursa:** City in northwestern Anatolia, early Ottoman capital

**Buyid dynasty** (BOO-yid): Family of Shi'i Persians who settled south of the Caspian, then conquered and ruled Persia and Iraq (932–1055); also called Buwayhid

**Byzantine Empire:** Eastern Roman Empire (330–1453), having its capital at Constantinople and professing Greek Orthodox Christianity

**Cairo** (KYE-ro): Egypt's capital, founded by the Fatimids (969)

**caliph** (KAY-lif): Successor to Muhammad as head of the *ummah*

**caliphate:** Political institution led by the caliph

**Camel, Battle of the:** First clash between Muslim armies (656), in which Ali defeated Talhah, Zubayr, and Aishah

**Camp David:** (1) U.S. president's vacation home in northern Maryland; (2) site of intensive peace talks by Begin, Carter, and Sadat in September 1978; (3) adjective applied to the Egyptian-Israeli accords or to the 1979 peace treaty; (4) site of abortive peace talks between Arafat, Barak, and Clinton in July 2000

**Canaanite:** Member of a Semitic group living in Palestine before the Hebrews

**Capitulations:** System by which Muslim states granted extraterritorial immunity from local laws and taxes to subjects of Western countries

**Caradon, Lord:** British diplomat who drafted Security Council Resolution 242

**Carter Doctrine:** U.S. policy statement declaring any foreign invasion of the Gulf to be an attack on vital U.S. interests

**Caucasus:** Mountain range between the Black and Caspian seas

**Central Treaty Organization (CENTO):** *See* Baghdad Pact

**Chalcedon:** Site of 451 Christian council at which the Orthodox bishops condemned the Monophysite view of Christ's nature

**Chaldiran, Battle of** (chal-dee-RAWN): Major Ottoman victory over Safavid Persia (1514)

**Chovevei Tzion** (kho-ve-VAY tsee-YAWN): Early Russian Zionist group

**Churchill White Paper:** Official statement in 1922 of British Palestine policy, limiting Jewish immigration to the country's absorptive capacity

**Cilicia** (si-LISH-ya): Southwest Anatolian region, also called *Little Armenia*

**Circassian:** Native (or descendant of a native) of the Caucasus region east of the Black Sea

**Committee of Union and Progress:** *See* Young Turks

**Constantine:** Roman emperor (306–337) who converted to Christianity

**Constantinople:** City on the Bosporus and Sea of Marmara, originally named Byzantium, which became capital of the Byzantine Empire (330–1204 and

1262–1453) and of the Ottoman Empire (1453–1922); called Istanbul since 1923

**constitutionalists:** Persons who believe that governments should uphold a set of basic laws limiting the rulers' powers; more specifically, Persian nationalists around 1906

**Copt:** Egyptian (or Ethiopian) Monophysite Christian

**Cordoba** (KOR-do-va): Spanish city, capital of the later Umayyads (756–1030)

**Cossack:** (1) Horse soldier of southern Russia; (2) member of a Persian brigade trained and chiefly officered by Russian Cossacks up to 1921

**Crane, Charles:** American manufacturer and philanthropist; member of the King-Crane Commission (1919) and adviser to Ibn Sa'ud (1931)

**Crimea:** Former Turkic region north of the Black Sea

**Crimean War:** Conflict among powers with imperial interests in the Middle East (1853–1856), in which Britain, France, and the Ottoman Empire defeated Russia

**Cromer, Lord:** British consul in Egypt (1883–1907), a financial reformer, who was resented by Egyptian nationalists

**Crusades:** European Christian military expeditions against Muslims (and sometimes Greek Orthodox Christians) between the eleventh and fifteenth centuries

**Ctesiphon** (TESS-a-fawn): Sasanid capital, south of modern Baghdad

**Curzon, Lord:** (KER-zen) Britain's main representative at the 1923 Lausanne Conference

**Cyprus:** Mediterranean island near Anatolia and Syria

**Cyrenaica** (sir-e-NAY-ka): Eastern Libya

**Damascus:** Syria's capital; seat of the early Umayyads (661–750)

**Darazi, Shaykh** (da-RAH-zee): Syrian founder of the Druze religion

**Dardanelles:** Straits connecting the Aegean to the Sea of Marmara

**Dayan, Moshe** (die-YAN, mo-SHEH): Israeli general and political leader (1915—1981)

**Dayr Yasin** (DARE ya-SEEN): Palestinian village near Jerusalem, where the Irgun massacred Arab civilians (1948)

**Declaration of Principles:** Formal name of the statement signed by Palestinian, Israeli, and U.S. representatives in 1993

**Demirel, Suleyman** (deh-mir-REL, suh-lay-MAHN): Turkish political leader and president (1993–2000)

**Demokrat party:** Turkish political party in the 1950s

**Desert Shield:** U.S. name for the multinational military buildup in Saudi Arabia opposing Iraq's occupation of Kuwait in 1990

**Desert Storm:** U.S. name for the multinational operation that attacked Iraq and drove its troops from Kuwait in 1991

*devshirme* (dev-shir-MEH): Ottoman system of taking Christian boys, converting them to Islam, and training them for military or administrative service

**Dhahran** (dhuh-RAHN): East Arabian city, site of first Saudi oil strike in 1938

diaspora (die-ASS-po-rah): Group of people, usually Jews but sometimes Armenians or Palestinians, who have been dispersed from their homeland to various parts of the world

Dinshaway Incident (den-sha-WYE): British atrocity against Egyptian peasants (1906)

*diwan* (dee-WAHN): (1) List of Arab troops entitled to share booty during early conquests; (2) council of ministers; (3) collection of poems. The Persian and Turkish word is *divan*

Dome of the Rock: Muslim shrine in Jerusalem, built in 692 on site of Jewish Temple; site of Abraham's sacrifice and of Muhammad's miraculous night journey

Druze: Pertaining to the secret religion practiced by some Arabs in Syria, Lebanon, and Israel, and founded by Shaykh Darazi, who preached that the Fatimid Caliph al-Hakim was the last of a series of emanations from God

*du'a* (doo-AH): Muslim prayer for divine intercession, as distinct from ritual worship

Dual Financial Control: Joint Anglo-French economic administration in Egypt (1876–1882)

Eden, Anthony: British prime minister during 1956 Suez Affair

Edessa: Northwest Mesopotamian town and Crusader state (1098–1144)

Egyptian Expeditionary Force: British group that captured Palestine and Syria during World War I

Eilat (ay-LAHT): Israel's port on the Gulf of Aqaba

Eisenhower Doctrine: Official U.S. policy statement opposing spread of communism in the Middle East (1957)

Elburz (el-BORZ): Mountain range in northern Iran

emirate: State ruled by an amir

Enver (EN-ver): Young Turk revolutionary leader (d. 1922)

Ephesus (EH-fuh-suss): West Anatolian town important in early Christian history; site of bishops' council that condemned Nestorianism in 430

Ertogrul (air-tuh-ROOL): Turkish *ghazi* leader (d. ca. 1280), father of Osman I

Erzurum (air-zuh-ROOM): East Anatolian city; site of 1919 Turkish nationalist congress

Eshkol, Levi (ESH-kol, LEH-vee): Israel's prime minister (1963–1969)

Ethiopia: East African country, mainly Christian since the fourth century, involved in Arabian politics up to Muhammad's time

Euphrates: The more western of Iraq's two rivers

Evren, Kenan (ev-REN, ke-NAHN): Leader of 1980 coup that restored order to Turkey

Fahd (FEHD): Saudi Arabia's king (1982–)

*faqih* (fa-KEEH or faw-GHEE), pl. *fuqaha* (foo-ka-HAH): (1) Muslim legal expert; (2) under Iran's 1979 constitution, the final lawmaking authority; (3) official title of the Ayatollahs Khomeini and Khamanei

al-Farabi (el-fa-RAW-bee): Muslim philosopher and theologian (d. 950)

**Faruq** (fa-ROOK): Egypt's last king (1936–1952)

**al-Fatah** (el-FET-ah): Palestinian guerrilla group founded by Yasir Arafat

**al-Fatat** (el-fa-TAT): Early Arab nationalist student group

**Fath Ali Shah** (FAT-haw-lee-SHAH): Qajar ruler (1797–1834)

**Fatimah** (FAW-tee-ma): Muhammad's daughter, who married Ali

**Fatimid dynasty:** Arab family of Isma'ili Shi'is claiming descent from Ali and Fatimah, ruling North Africa (909–972) and Egypt (969–1171), and claiming control of Syria, Hijaz, and Yemen

**Faysal** (FYE-sul): King of Saudi Arabia (1964–1975)

**Faysal I:** Son of Husayn of Mecca, Arab Revolt leader, who headed provisional Arab government in Damascus (1918–1920) ousted by the French, and who later became king of Iraq (1921–1933)

**Faysal II:** Iraq's last king (1939–1958)

**Feast of the Sacrifice:** *Id al-Adha* (Arabic) or *Kurban Bayram* (Turkish), annual Muslim holiday commemorating Abraham's obedience to God's command by offering to sacrifice his son, Ishmael (Isma'il); tenth day of the pilgrimage month

**Feast of the Fast-Breaking:** *Id al-Fitr* (Arabic) or *Ramazan Bayram* (Turkish), annual Muslim holiday following the Ramadan fast

**Ferid, Damad** (fe-REED, dah-MAWD): Ottoman prime minister backed by the sultan and the Western powers (1919–1920)

**Fertile Crescent:** Modern term for the lands extending from the eastern Mediterranean, via Syria and Mesopotamia, to the Gulf

**fez:** Crimson brimless head-covering worn by male officials in the later Ottoman Empire and in some successor states; outlawed in Turkey by Kemal Ataturk

*fidaiyin* (fe-DA-ee-yeen): Commandos, or people who sacrifice themselves for a cause, often applied to Palestinians fighting against Israel or to militant Shi'is

*fiqh* (FIK-h): The science of Islamic law (jurisprudence)

*fitnah* (FIT-na): Term applied to several civil wars in early Islamic history

**Four Reserved Points:** Britain's limitations on its unilateral declaration of Egypt's independence (1922)

**Fourteen Points:** President Wilson's plan to settle issues that had caused World War I, calling for self-determination of all peoples

**Franjiyah, Sulayman** (fran-JEE-ya, slay-MAN): Lebanon's president (1970–1976)

**free will:** Religious doctrine that God has created human beings who can choose their actions, as opposed to predestination

**Fuad I** (foo-ODD): Egypt's sultan and king (1917–1936)

**Fustat** (foos-TAWT): Egyptian garrison town in early Islamic times; later an administrative center, near modern Cairo

**Gabriel:** Angel who transmitted the Quran to Muhammad

**Galilee:** Mountainous area of northern Israel, containing many Arab villages

**garrison town:** City, such as Basrah, Kufah, or Fustat, set up by the early caliphs to house Arab soldiers

**al-Gaylani, Rashid Ali** (el-gay-LAH-nee, rah-SHEED AH-lee): Leader of the 1941 Arab nationalist government in Iraq, overthrown by the British

**Gaza Strip:** Small part of southwest Palestine held by Egyptian forces in 1948 and inhabited by Arabs, administered by Egypt (1948–1956 and 1957–1967), captured by Israel in 1956 and 1967, and governed by Israel (1967–1994) and by the PLO (since 1994)

**Geneva Conference:** December 1973 meeting of Israel, Egypt, and Jordan, cochaired by the United States and the USSR

**Gezira Sporting Club** (guh-ZEE-ra): Exclusive Cairo social club

**al-Ghazali, Abu-Hamid** (el-gha-ZA-lee, AH-boo-ha-MEED): Major Muslim theologian (d. 1111)

**Ghazan Khan** (gha-ZAWN KHAWN): First Muslim Il-Khanid ruler (1295–1304)

*ghazi* (GHAH-zee): Muslim border warrior

**Ghazi:** Iraq's king (1933–1939)

**Ghazna:** Afghan city, where the Ghaznavid Empire began

**Ghaznavid** (GHAZ-nah-vid): Turkish empire, comprising Afghanistan and parts of Iran and Central Asia, that conquered much of India (977–1186)

*ghulam* (ghoo-LAWM): Male slave, usually military or administrative, especially in Safavid Empire

**Gibraltar:** (1) Mountain in southern Spain; (2) straits between the Atlantic and the Mediterranean (originally *Jebel Tariq*, named after the Berber who commanded the Muslim conquest of Spain)

**Gidi Pass:** Strategic point in western Sinai, captured by Israel in 1956 and 1967 and relinquished to a UN force in 1975

**Gilan** (gee-LAWN): Region of northwestern Iran

**Glubb, John Bagot:** British commander of Jordan Arab Legion, dismissed in 1956

**Gokalp, Ziya** (geuk-ALP, zee-YAH): Theoretician of Turkish nationalism (d. 1924)

**Gokturk** (geuk-TEWRK): Sixth-century Turkic empire in Asia

**Golan Heights** (go-LAHN): Mountainous area of southwestern Syria, occupied by Israel since 1967 and scene of intense fighting in 1973

**Golden Horde:** Group of Islamized Mongols, having a Turkic majority, that ruled Russia from the thirteenth to the fifteenth centuries

**Granada:** Capital of the last Muslim state in Spain

**Grand National Assembly:** Representative legislature of the first Turkish republic

**Great Khan:** Title of Mongol emperor during the thirteenth century

**Great Silk Route:** Trade route connecting Iran with China, crossing the steppes and mountain passes of Central Asia

**Greek fire:** A liquid substance, probably a naphtha derivative, that ignited upon contact with water, used by Byzantine and later by Muslim sailors to destroy enemy ships

**Greek Orthodox:** Pertaining to the branch of Christianity that accepts the spiritual authority of the Constantinople patriarch and espouses the Christological doctrines adopted at the Nicaea (325) and Chalcedon (451) church councils

**Gulf, the:** Body of water separating Iran from the Arabian Peninsula and connecting the Shatt al-Arab to the Arabian Sea

**Gulf War:** (1) Iran-Iraq War (1980–1988); (2) campaign of U.S.-led coalition to make Iraq withdraw from Kuwait (1991)

**Gush Emunim** (GOOSH em-oo-NEEM): Group of religiously observant Israeli settlers on the West Bank

**Habash, George** (HOB-osh): Leader of the Popular Front for the Liberation of Palestine, a Marxist Palestinian Arab group

**Habib, Philip** (ha-BEEB): U.S. negotiator among Syria, Lebanon, and Israel (1981–1982)

**Habsburg** (HOPS-burg): German family that ruled over the Holy Roman Empire (1273–1806) and Austria (up to 1918)

**hadith** (ha-DEETH): A statement, documented by a chain of reliable witnesses, concerning a saying or action of Muhammad, or an action by one of his companions that he approved; hence an authoritative source of the Shari'ah

**Hafiz** (haw-FEZ): Popular Persian poet (d. 1390)

**Haganah** (ha-ga-NAH): Jewish Agency's army in Palestine (1920–1948)

**Hagar** (HAH-gar): Abraham's second wife, mother of Ishmael, ancestor of the Arabs

**Haifa:** Israel's main port city

**hajj** (HODGE): Muslim rite of pilgrimage to Mecca, or (with a lengthened vowel) a Muslim who has completed the pilgrimage rites

**al-Hajjaj** (el-haj-JAJ): Authoritarian governor of Iraq (d. 714)

**al-Hakim** (el-HACK-em): Fatimid caliph (996–1021), venerated by the Druze

**Hamas** (ha-MASS): Palestinian Islamist group

**Hamdanid dynasty** (ham-DAH-nid): Arab family with branches ruling in Aleppo and Mosul during the tenth century

**Hanafi** (HA-na-fee): Most widespread rite of Sunni Muslim jurisprudence, originating in Iraq, stressing communal consensus as a source of the Shari'ah

**Hanbali** (HAM-ba-lee): Rite of Sunni Muslim jurisprudence, very strict, requiring that all rules of conduct be based on the Quran and hadith

**Hanif** (ha-NEEF): Arab true believer before rise of Islam

**Harawi, Ilyas** (HRAH-wee, il-YASS): Lebanon's president (1989–1995)

**harem:** The portion of a Muslim house used by women and young children, not open to unrelated males

**Har Homa:** New Jewish settlement in Jerusalem's outskirts, on which construction was begun by Netanyahu's government in 1997, angering many Palestinians, who call the town Jabal Abu Ghunaym

**Harun al-Rashid** (ha-ROON er-ra-SHEED): Abbasid caliph (786–809)

**al-Hasa** (el-HAH-sa): Oil-rich Gulf coast region of Saudi Arabia

**Hasan** (HAH-san): Older son of Ali and Fatimah, named by Ali as his successor but pensioned off by Mu'awiyah; recognized as second Shi'i imam (d. 669)

**Hashimite** (HA-she-mite): (1) Member of the family descended from Hashim; (2) supporter of an extremist *mawali* Shi'i sect in late Umayyad times; (3) member of the dynasty ruling the Hijaz (1916–1925), Syria (1918–1920), Iraq (1921–1958), and Jordan (1921- )

**Haskalah** (hoss-ka-LAH): Era of Jewish enlightenment during the eighteenth and nineteenth centuries

**Hebrew:** Semitic language of ancient and modern Israel

**Hebron** (HEB-run): Town in Judea (the West Bank), revered by Jews and Muslims, site of a massacre of Palestinians in 1994

**Hellenistic:** Pertaining to the society and culture of the Mediterranean area that used Greek as its main literary and administrative language

**Heraclius** (he-RACK-lee-us): Byzantine emperor (610–641) who repulsed Sasanids but later lost Syria and Egypt to the Arabs

**Hermon** (hair-MOAN): Mountain in southwestern Syria, partly occupied by Israel since 1967; site of heavy fighting in 1973

**Herut** (khay-ROOT): Israel's right-wing party, led by Begin up to 1983; now part of the Likud coalition

**Herzl, Theodor** (HAIR-tsul, TAY-a-dor): Writer and founder of political Zionism (d. 1904)

**Hess, Moses:** Early German socialist and advocate of a Jewish state (d. 1875)

**Hijaz** (he-JAZZ): Mountainous area of western Arabia

**Hijrah** (HIJ-ra): Emigration of Muhammad and his followers from Mecca to Medina in 622 (year 1 of the Muslim calendar)

**Hira** (HEE-ra): Capital of pre-Islamic Lakhmid kingdom

**Hisham** (he-SHAM): Umayyad caliph (724–743)

**Histadrut** (hiss-tah-DROOT): Israel's major labor union, owner of many business enterprises, and manager of health insurance plan

**Hizballah** (hiz-BOL-lah): Shi'i commando group based in Lebanon

**Holy Sepulcher:** Jesus' reputed burial place and a major church in Jerusalem

**Hudaybiyah** (hoo-day-BEE-ya): Treaty made by Muhammad with the Meccans in 628, enabling Muslim emigrants to make the hajj

**Hulegu** (HEW-le-gew): Mongol ruler (d. 1265), Jenghiz Khan's grandson, who extended Mongol conquest of Persia and Iraq and founded the Il-Khanid dynasty

**Hunayn ibn Ishaq** (hu-NAYN ibn iss-HOCK): Scientist and translator (d. 873)

**Hunkar-Iskelesi** (HOON-kyar-iss-KELL-e-see): An 1833 treaty that made the Ottoman Empire virtually a Russian protectorate

**Hunyadi, John** (hoon-YAW-dee): Hungarian leader (d. 1456)

**Husayn** (hoo-SAYN): Younger son of Ali and Fatimah, killed in an anti-Umayyad revolt at Karbala (680), hence a martyr for Shi'i Muslims, also spelled *Hussein*

**Husayn:** Amir and sharif of Mecca (1908–1924), king of the Hijaz (1916–1924), and leader of the 1916–1918 Arab Revolt against the Ottomans

**Husayn:** Jordan's king (1952–1999)

**Husayn, Saddam:** *See* Saddam Husayn

**Husayn Kamil:** Egypt's sultan (1914–1917)

**Husayn-McMahon Correspondence:** Letters exchanged by Amir Husayn and Britain's high commissioner in Cairo (1915–1916), offering British aid for the Arabs' independence in exchange for Arab support against the Ottoman Empire

**al-Husayni, Hajj Amin** (el-hoo-SAY-nee, HODGE ah-MEEN): Mufti of Jerusalem and early Palestinian nationalist leader

**ibn:** Son of, often used in Arabic names, a cognate of the Hebrew word *ben* and pronounced *bin* in some dialects

**Ibn Khaldun** (ibn-khal-DOON): Noted historian and social thinker (d. 1406)

**Ibn Rushd** (ibn-ROOSHD): Muslim philosopher, known as *Averroës* in Latin (d. 1198)

**Ibn Sa'ud** (ibn-sa-OOD): Arab leader who conquered most of the Arabian Peninsula between 1902 and 1930 and ruler of Saudi Arabia (1932–1953), also called *Abd al-Aziz ibn Abd al-Rahman*

**Ibn Sina** (ibn-SEE-na): Muslim philosopher, theologian, and scientist (d. 1037); known as *Avicenna* in Latin

**Ibrahim** (ib-rah-HEEM): Mehmet Ali's son, conqueror and governor of Syria (1832–1840), also viceroy of Egypt (1848)

**Ibrahim I:** Ottoman sultan (1640–1648)

**Ibrahim, Damad** (dah-MAWD): Ottoman *vezir* under Ahmed III

*ijtihad* (ij-tee-HAD): Use of reasoning to determine a specific rule in Islamic law

**Ikhwan** (ikh-WAHN): (1) Sedentarized bedouin soldiers for Ibn Sa'ud; (2) members of the Society of the Muslim Brothers

**Il-Khanid** (il-KHAW-nid): Mongol successor dynasty in Persia (1256–1349)

**imam** (ee-MAWM): (1) Muslim religious or political leader; (2) one of the succession of leaders, beginning with Ali, viewed by Shi'is as legitimate; (3) leader of Muslim congregational worship

**Imperial Rescript:** Ottoman promise in 1856 of equal rights and status to all subjects, regardless of religion, sometimes called the *Hatt-i-Humayun*

**Inonu** (ee-nuh-NIEW): (1) Site of two Turkish victories over Greeks in western Anatolia (1921); (2) surname taken by Ismet, Turkish leader in those battles

*intifadah* (in-tee-FAW-duh): (1) Palestinian uprising against Israeli occupation (1987–1990); (2) Palestinian rebellion that followed Ariel Sharon's visit to al-Aqsa Mosque in 2000

*iqta'* (ik-TAH): Land grant from a ruler for military or administrative services by a client

**Iran** (ee-RAWN): Preferred name since 1935 for what was Persia

**Iran-Contra Affair:** Reagan administration's arms sales to Iran to secure release of American hostages in Lebanon and donation of the proceeds to aid Contra insurgents in Nicaragua (1986)

**Iran-Iraq War:** Ideological and territorial conflict between Iran and Iraq (1980–1988)

**Iraq** (ee-ROCK): Arabic name for Mesopotamia

**Irgun Tzvei Le'umi** (ear-GOON TSVAY le-oo-MEE): Right-wing Zionist guerrilla group, commanded by Begin and active up to 1948

**Isfahan** (iss-fa-HAWN): City in central Iran and Safavid capital (1597–1736)

**Ishmael** (ISH-mayl): Mythic ancestor of the Arabs

**Islam** (iss-LAM): The religion, now prevalent in the Middle East and many other parts of Asia and Africa, believing in one God revealed to a series of prophets, ending with Muhammad, to whom the Quran was entrusted

**Islamic Group:** Egyptian underground Islamist movement

**Islamic Republican party:** Revolutionary Iran's leading political movement (1979–1987)

**Islamist:** Pertaining to any person or group advocating government according to strict Muslim principles

**Isma'il** (iss-ma-EEL): Final legitimate imam, for Seven-Imam Shi'is

**Isma'il, Khedive:** Viceroy of Egypt (1863–1879)

**Isma'il Shah:** Founder (1501–1524) of the Safavid dynasty

**Isma'ili** (iss-ma-EE-lee): Pertaining to Seven-Imam Shi'ism

**Ismailia** (iss-ma-ee-LEE-ya): Suez Canal city

**Ismet** (iss-MET): Turkish general, Turkey's representative at the Lausanne Conference (1923), and president of the republic (1938–1950 and 1961–1965), surnamed Inonu

*isnad* (iss-NAD): Chain of witnesses verifying a hadith

**Israel** (IZ-real or iss-raw-EL): (1) The surname of Jacob and his descendants; (2) the ancient northern Jewish kingdom; (3) the modern Jewish state, located in what used to be Palestine

**Israelites:** Descendants of Jacob, or Jews

**Istanbul** (iss-tahm-BOOL): Modern name for Constantinople

**Izmir** (iz-MEER): West Anatolian city, formerly called *Smyrna*

**Jabotinsky, Vladimir** (zha-buh-TIN-skee): Founder of the Revisionist (right-wing Zionist) party (d. 1940)

**Jacobite:** Syrian Monophysite Christian

**Jaffa:** Port city in Palestine/Israel, now part of Tel Aviv

**janissary** (JAN-i-se-ree): Christian conscript foot soldier in the Ottoman army, converted to Islam and trained to use firearms

**Jarring, Gunnar** (YAR-ring, GUN-nar): UN mediator between Israel and the Arab states (1967–1971)

**Jawhar** (JOW-har): Arab general who conquered Egypt for the Fatimids in 969

**Jem:** Brother and rival to Ottoman Sultan Bayezid II (d. 1495)

**Jemal** (je-MAWL): Young Turk leader and Syria's governor (d. 1922)

**Jenghiz Khan** (JENG-giz KHAWN): Mongol warrior, conqueror, and ruler of most of Asia (d. 1227); also called *Genghis Khan*

**Jerusalem:** Judea's main city; major religious center for Jews, Christians, and Muslims; proclaimed by Israel as its capital

**Jewish Agency:** Organization set up under the Palestine mandate to work with Britain toward the Jewish national home; later charged with aiding Jewish immigration and absorption into Israel

**Jewish National Fund:** Zionist land-purchasing and development agency in Palestine/Israel, founded in 1901

**jihad** (jee-HAD): (1) Defense of Islam against attackers; (2) Muslim struggle against evil within oneself, one's associates, and the *ummah*; (3) name of several Islamist groups

**jinn:** In Muslim belief, invisible creatures living on earth, capable of doing good or harm

*jizyah* (JIZ-ya): Per capita tax paid by non-Muslim males living under Muslim rule up to the nineteenth century

**Johnston, Eric:** U.S. magnate sent by Eisenhower in 1953 to negotiate Jordan River development scheme for Israel and Jordan

**Jordan, Hashimite Kingdom of:** State formed from the Emirate of Transjordan and parts of Arab Palestine (commonly called the West Bank) annexed by Abdallah in 1948

**Jordan River:** River flowing through Syria, Jordan, and Israel

**Judea:** Mountainous area of eastern Palestine/Israel

**Jumayyil, Amin** (zhe-MYE-yel, ah-MEEN): President of Lebanon (1982–1988); also spelled *Gemayel*

**Jumayyil, Bashir** (ba-SHEER): Prominent Phalangist leader, elected Lebanon's president in 1982 but killed before he could take office

**Jumblat, Kamal** (zhum-BLOT, ke-MAL): Lebanese Druze leader (d. 1977)

**Junayd, Shaykh** (joo-NAYD): Turcoman Shi'i Sufi leader of the Safavids in Azerbaijan (d. 1460), grandfather of Shah Isma'il

**Jundishapur** (joon-dee-shah-POOR): Sasanid and Muslim center of learning

**Justice party:** Turkey's conservative party (1961–1980)

**Juvaini, Ata Malik** (jo-VAY-nee): Administrator in Mongol Persia (d. 1283)

**Ka'bah** (KAH-ba): Muslim shrine in Mecca housing the Black Stone, serving as the focal point for the hajj, and setting the direction for Muslim worship

**Kabul** (KAW-bul): Capital of Afghanistan

**Kalb** (KELB): Southern Arab tribe important in early Islam

**Kamil, Mustafa** (KA-mel, moos-TAH-fa): Egyptian nationalist (d. 1908)

**Kapu Kullar** (KAH-puh kul-LAWR): Slaves of the Gate; sultan's officers or officials, hence members of the Ottoman elite

**Kara-Khitay** (KAH-rah-khee-TIE): Thirteenth-century confederation of non-Muslim Mongol tribes in Central Asia

**Karamah** (ka-RAH-may): Jordanian village, site of 1968 Israeli attack against which Palestinian *fidaiyin* claimed victory

**Karbala** (KAR-ba-la): Iraqi city, site of Husayn's uprising and martyrdom (680); since then a Shi'i pilgrimage center

**Karlowitz:** 1699 treaty in which Ottomans ceded Hungary to Austria

**al-Kawakibi, Abd al-Rahman** (el-ka-WA-ke-bee, AB-dur-rah-MAN): Arab nationalist writer (d. 1902)

**Kayi** (KY-eh): Central Asian Turkish tribe, from which Ottomans claimed descent

**Kemal, Mustafa** (Ataturk) (ke-MAWL, MOOS-ta-fa [a-ta-TEWRK]): Turkish general, nationalist leader, and westernizing president (d. 1938)

**Kemalism:** Kemal's principles of Turkish nationalism and westernizing reform

**Khadijah** (kha-DEE-jah): Muhammad's first wife (d. 619)

**Khalid ibn al-Walid** (KHA-lid ib-nel-wa-LEED): Arab general; conqueror of Arabia, Syria, Iraq, and Persia

**Khamanei, Ayatollah Seyed Ali** (kha-ma-NAY-ee): Khomeini's successor as Iran's *faqih*

*kharaj* (kha-RODGE): Land tax paid by peasants on produce

**Kharijite** (KHA-re-jite): "Seceder" who opposed Ali after he accepted arbitration of the Battle of Siffin (657) and killed him (661); later an anarchist group believing that any sinless Muslim could be caliph

**Khartum** (khar-TOOM): (1) Capital of the Sudan; (2) site of 1967 Arab summit opposing peace negotiations with Israel

**Khatami, Mohammad** (KHAW-ta-mee): Iran's president (1997-)

**Khazar** (KHAH-zar): Turkic tribe north of the Caspian, which converted to Judaism in the eighth century

**khedive** (khe-DEEV): Title of Egypt's viceroy (1867–1914)

**Khomeini, Ayatollah Ruhollah** (kho-MAY-nee): Leader of Islamic revolution in Iran (1978–1979) and *faqih* (1979–1989)

**Khurasan** (kho-ra-SAWN): Persian province east of Caspian Sea; center of many dissident movements in early Islamic history

**Khuzistan** (khoo-ze-STAWN): Oil-rich province of southwestern Iran

**Khwarizm** (KHAW-rezm): Region south of the Aral Sea

**Khwarizm-Shah** (khaw-rezm-SHAH): Central Asian Turkic dynasty (1077–1231) defeated by Jenghiz Khan

**kibbutz** (pl. kibbutzim) (kee-BOOTS, kee-boo-TSEEM): Jewish settlement in Israel, initially agricultural, now mainly industrial, in which most property is collectively owned

**Kilometer 101:** Site of Egyptian-Israeli military talks following 1973 war

**Kinda** (KIN-da): Central Arabian tribe prominent in the sixth century

**al-Kindi** (el-KIN-dee): Muslim philosopher and scientist (d. 873)

**King-Crane Commission:** U.S. committee sent by 1919 Paris Peace Conference to ascertain Syrian and Palestinian aspirations, but its report, sympathetic to Arab nationalism, was not acted upon

**Kipchak** (kip-CHOCK): Central Asian Turkish tribe, source of many mamluks

**Kitchener, Lord** (KITCH-ner): Commander of Anglo-Egyptian army that retook the Sudan (1896–1898), who later became the British consul-general in Egypt (1911–1914)

*kizilbash* (KEE-zel-bosh): Shi'i Turks, especially Safavid horse soldiers

**Knesset:** Israel's unicameral legislature

**Konya:** Southern Anatolian city, capital of the Rum Seljuk state (1077–1300)

**Koprulu** (kuh-prew-LIEW): Family of Ottoman *vezirs*

**Koran:** *See* Quran

**Kosovo, Battle of** (KOH-so-vo): Site of 1389 Ottoman victory over Serbia

**Kufah** (KOO-fa): Iraqi garrison town founded by Umar; later an important commercial and intellectual center

*kufiyah* (kef-FEE-ya): White or colored headcloth worn by men in Arabia and parts of the Fertile Crescent

**Kunaitra** (koo-NAYT-ra): Main city in the Golan Heights, captured by Israel in 1967, fought over in October 1973, and returned to Syria in 1974

**Kurd:** Member of linguistic-cultural group concentrated in southeastern Turkey, northern Iraq, northwestern Iran, and parts of Syria

**Kurdistan:** Autonomous state projected by Treaty of Sèvres (1920) and still desired by many Kurdish nationalists

**Kuwait** (koo-WAYT): Oil-rich principality on the Gulf, occupied by Iraq from August 1990 to February 1991

**Labor Alignment:** Coalition of Israel's labor parties, ruling up to 1977, governing jointly with the Likud (1984–1990), and in power from 1992 to 1996 and 1999 to 2001

**Ladino** (la-DEE-no): Spanish dialect spoken by Sephardic Jews and written in Hebrew characters

**Lakhmid** (LAWKH-mid): Arab tribe near Iraq, prominent before Islam and usually allied with the Sasanids

**Lampson, Sir Miles:** British high commissioner and ambassador in Egypt (1934–1946)

**al-Lat** (el-LAT): Meccan goddess before Islam

**Lausanne** (loe-ZAHN): (1) 1923 conference and treaty between Turkey and the World War I Allies, replacing the Treaty of Sèvres; (2) abortive 1949 peace conference between Israel and the Arab states

**Lawrence, T. E.:** British intelligence officer who aided the Arab Revolt; gifted writer and advocate of Arab nationalism (d. 1935)

**Lazar** (lah-ZAHR): Serbian King defeated by Ottomans at Kosovo

**Lepanto, Battle of** (le-PAHN-toe): European naval victory over Ottomans (1571)

**Levantine:** Pertaining to the Levant or the eastern shores of the Mediterranean, or to its inhabitants, especially non-Muslims

**Likud** (lee-KOOD): Coalition of Israel's right-wing parties, in power from 1977 to 1984, in coalition with Labor (1984–1990) and with the religious parties (1990–1992 and 1996–1999)

**Lydda:** Israeli city, renamed Lod; site of civil airport

**Macedonia:** Much-disputed area of northern Greece and southern Yugoslavia

*madhhab* (MEDH-heb): Sunni legal rite or school

*madrasah* (MED-ra-sah): Muslim school, especially for law

*mahdi* (MEH-dee): Rightly guided one, precursor of the Judgment Day

**Mahdi of the Sudan:** Muhammad Ahmad (d. 1885), leader of successful Sudanese rebellion against Egyptian rule

**Mahmud II** (mah-MOOT): Ottoman sultan (1808–1839) and westernizing reformer

**Mahmud of Ghazna** (mah-MOOD): Ghaznavid ruler (998–1030)

**Majlis** (MODGE-liss): Iran's bicameral legislature

**Maliki** (MA-li-kee): Rite of Sunni Muslim jurisprudence, which originated in Medina and stresses use of hadiths as authoritative legal sources

**Malikshah** (ma-lik-SHAH): Seljuk sultan (1072–1092)

**mamluk** (mem-LOOK): (1) Turkish or Circassian slave soldier; (2) (cap.) member of a military oligarchy ruling Egypt (1250–1517) and Syria (1260–1516) and retaining power in some areas up to the nineteenth century

**Mamun** (ma-MOON): Abbasid caliph (813–833)

**al-Manat** (el-ma-NAT): Meccan goddess before Islam

**mandate:** (1) Commission given by the League of Nations to a Western power to prepare a former territory of Germany or the Ottoman Empire for eventual self-rule; (2) a country governed under this tutelary relationship

**Manichaeism** (ma-ni-KEE-izm): Dualistic religion formulated by Mani, a third-century Persian, calling for the liberation of the body from the soul by various ascetic spiritual exercises, strong formerly in Iraq, Persia, and some parts of Central and East Asia

**Mansur:** *See* Abu-Ja'far al-Mansur

**al-Mansurah** (el-man-SOOR-ah): Egyptian city besieged in the Seventh Crusade

**Manzikert, Battle of** (man-zi-KERT): Seljuk victory over the Byzantines (1071)

**Mapai** (ma-PIE): Israel's moderate labor party

**marches:** Frontier areas between two countries or cultures

**Maronite:** Pertaining to a Christian sect, mainly in northern Lebanon, whose distinguishing belief is that Christ contained two natures within one will and which has been in communion with the Roman Catholic church since the Crusades

**Marwa:** Hill in Mecca, important in hajj ritual

**Marwan I** (mar-WAHN): Umayyad caliph (684–685)

**Marxism:** System of socialist thought, founded by Karl Marx and others, which teaches that capitalism must be overthrown by a revolution leading to a workers' state, which will later give way to a classless and harmonious society; accepted by some Middle Eastern leaders at various times

*mawla* (pl. *mawali*) (MOW-la, ma-WA-lee): (1) Client member of Arab tribe, entitled to protection but not all membership privileges; (2) non-Arab convert to Islam during the early Arab conquests

**Mazandaran** (ma-zawn-da-RAWN): Province in northern Iran, home of Reza Khan

**McMahon, Henry:** British high commissioner in Egypt (1914–1916), who initiated the Husayn-McMahon Correspondence

**Mecca:** Birthplace of the Prophet Muhammad and chief commercial and pilgrimage center of western Arabia

**Medina** (ma-DEE-nah): Northwest Arabian farming oasis, formerly Yathrib, to which Muhammad and his followers went in 622

**Mehmet I** (meh-MET): Ottoman sultan (1413–1421)

**Mehmet II:** Ottoman sultan (1451–1481), conqueror of Constantinople

**Mehmet Ali:** Albanian adventurer who took control of Egypt and instituted many westernizing reforms (1805–1849), also called *Muhammad Ali*

**Meir, Golda** (may-EER): Israel's prime minister (1969–1974)

**Mersin** (mer-SEEN): Port city in southern Anatolia

**Merv:** City in Khurasan

**Mesopotamia:** Greek name for the land between the Tigris and Euphrates rivers, especially Iraq

**Messiah:** According to the Bible, the expected deliverer of the Jewish people and, according to Christians, Jesus Christ

**Middle East Supply Center:** Cairo-based British organization that coordinated manufacturing and distribution in Arab states and Iran during World War II

**Midhat** (mit-HOT): Ottoman liberal reformer (d. 1884)

*millet* (mil-LET): Ottoman political-social community based on religious membership and whose leaders were named by the sultan

**Milner, Lord:** British statesman who headed 1919 commission of inquiry to Egypt and later negotiated unsuccessfully with Sa'd Zaghlul

**minaret:** Turkish name for the mosque tower from which a muezzin calls Muslims to worship five times daily

**Mithraism:** Ancient Persian religion involving various mystery rites limited to men; popular among Roman soldiers and competing in the empire against Christianity in the third century

**Mitla Pass:** Strategic point in the western Sinai, captured by Israel in 1956 and 1967 and ceded to a UN buffer force in 1975

**Mixed Courts:** Egyptian tribunals for civil cases involving foreign nationals (1876–1949)

**Mohammad Reza Shah Pahlavi** (moe-HAHM-mad REH-za shah pah-luh-VEE): Iran's shah (1941–1979)

*mollah* (MUL-la): Persian Muslim teacher

**Mongol:** Nomadic horseman from northeastern Asia; member of a tribal coalition that under Jenghiz Khan and his descendants overran most of Asia in the thirteenth century

**Monophysite** (muh-NAW-fiz-ite): Pertaining to (mainly Middle Eastern) Christians who believe that Christ had only one nature, wholly divine; view condemned by the Council of Chalcedon in 451

**Monotheistic:** Pertaining to belief in one god, as in Judaism, Christianity, and Islam

**Morea** (mo-REE-a): The Peloponnesus, or southern Greece

**Mosaddiq, Mohammad** (mos-sa-DEGH): Iranian nationalist prime minister (1951–1953), who nationalized the Anglo-Iranian Oil Company and was later ousted in a coup engineered by the shah, the British, and the CIA (d. 1967)

**mosque:** Place of communal worship for Muslims

*mostaz'afan* (mos-TAZ-a-FAWN): People who have been dispossessed as a result of westernizing policies

**Mosul** (MOE-sel): City in northern Iraq

**Mu'awiyah** (moo-AWE-wee-ya): Umayyad caliph (661–680)

**Mubarak, Husni** (moo-BAH-rak, HOOS-nee): Egypt's president (1981-)

**Mudros:** Aegean island on which the Ottoman Empire formally surrendered to World War I Allies in October 1918

muezzin (moo-EZ-zin): Man who calls other Muslims to communal worship, usually from a mosque roof or minaret balcony

mufti (MOOF-tee): (1) Sunni Muslim legal consultant; (2) in modern times, leader of the ulama in a Sunni Muslim state

Mughal: *See* Timurid dynasty

Muhammad (moo-HOM-mad): Arab religious leader, born in Mecca and founder of the Islamic *ummah*, viewed by Muslims as God's messenger, whose revelations were recorded in the Quran

Muhammad: Khwarizm-Shah leader defeated by Jenghiz Khan

Muhammad al-Muntazar (el-moon-TAZ-er): Last of the twelve legitimate imams, who vanished around 874 but is expected, by Twelve-Imam Shi'is, to return someday

Muhammad ibn Abd al-Wahhab (ibn AB-dul-wah-HAB): Founder of the Wahhabi movement in the eighteenth century

*muhtasib* (MOOH-ta-sib): Muslim market inspector

Mu'izz (moo-IZZ): Fatimid caliph (953–975)

*mujtahid* (MOOJ-ta-hid): Learned Muslim who interprets the Shari'ah, especially in Shi'i jurisprudence

Mukhtar (mookh-TAHR): Leader of Kufah rebellion (685–687)

*multezim* (MOOL-te-zim): Ottoman tax collector allowed by the government to keep a share of what he collected

Murad I (moo-ROT): Ottoman sultan (1360–1389)

Murad II: Ottoman sultan (1421–1451)

Murad IV: Ottoman sultan (1623–1640)

*muruwwah* (mu-ROO-wa): Pre-Islamic code of Arab virtues

Muslim (MOOS-lim): (1) A person who submits to God's will; (2) anyone who believes that God revealed the Quran to Muhammad

Muslim Brothers, Society of the: Political group, strong in Egypt (1930–1952, 1978-) and in several other Arab countries, calling for an Islamic political and social system and opposing Western power and cultural influence

Mustafa II (MOOS-ta-fa): Ottoman sultan (1695–1703)

Mu'tasim (MUH-ta-sim): Abbasid caliph (833–842)

Mu'tazilah (muh-TA-zee-la): Rationalist formulation of Islamic theology, stressing that God created the Quran

Nader Afshar (NAW-der awf-SHAWR): Military leader who became shah of Persia (1736–1747), expelled Afghan invaders, and conquered part of India

Nagib, Muhammad (ne-GEEB): Titular leader of 1952 Egyptian revolution

al-Nahhas, Mustafa (en-nah-HASS, moos-TAH-fa): Leader of Egypt's Wafd party (1927-l952)

Najaf (NED-jef): Iraqi city where Ali was assassinated (661), hence a Shi'i pilgrimage center

Najran (nej-RAHN): Southern Arabian city, important in early commerce

Nasir, Gamal Abd al- (NAW-ser, ga-MAL AB-dun): Leader of the 1952 military coup that overthrew Egypt's monarchy; later prime minister, then president (1954–1970); also known as *Nasser*

**Nasirism:** Western term for Nasir's political philosophy and program, including nationalism, neutralism, and Arab socialism

**Nasiruddin Shah** (NAW-ser ud-DEEN): Qajar ruler (1848–1896)

**Nasiruddin Tusi** (TOO-see): Muslim astronomer (d. 1274)

**Nasser:** *See* Nasir, Gamal Abd al-

**National Charter:** 1962 Egyptian document describing the goals of Arab socialism

**National (Liberation) Front:** Aden's successful independence movement in 1967

**National Pact:** 1943 power-sharing agreement among Lebanon's religious and political groups

**National party:** Egyptian movement seeking independence from foreign control, led by Urabi in 1881–1882 and by Mustafa Kamil in 1895–1908

**National Religious party:** Party of observant Jews in Israel

**nationalism:** (1) Desire of a group of people to preserve or obtain common statehood; (2) ideology stressing loyalty to the nation-state or seeking independence of a national group

**Nationalist party:** Syria's main party after World War II

**Negev** (ne-GEV): Desert in southern Israel

**Neoplatonist:** Supporter of a philosophical system, founded in the third century, based on Plato's ideas and common in the Middle East up to the Arab conquests

**Nestorian:** Pertaining to Christians who believe in Christ's separate divine and human natures, condemned at the 430 Council of Ephesus

**Netanyahu, Benjamin** (ne-tan-YAH-hoo): Israel's prime minister (1996–1999)

**New Ottomans:** Turkish political movement in the 1870s demanding a constitution, parliamentary government, and other westernizing reforms

**Nicaea** (nye-SEE-ya): Northwest Anatolian city, site of the Christian church council in 325 that accepted the Trinitarian view of the nature of God: Father, Son, and Holy Spirit

**Nishapur** (nee-sha-POOR): City in Khurasan

*nizam-i-jedid* (ne-ZAWM-e-je-DEED): Military reform program promulgated by Selim III but crushed by the janissaries in 1807

**Noble Rescript of the Rose Chamber:** 1839 Ottoman promise of judicial and administrative reforms; sometimes called the *Hatt-i-Sherif* of Gulhane, ushering in the Tanzimat era

**Nur al-Din** (NOOR-ed-DEEN): Zengid sultan of Mosul and Damascus (1146–1174)

**Nuri al-Sa'id** (NOOR-ees-sa-EED): Pro-Western Iraqi leader, killed in 1958 revolution

**October War:** War started by Egypt and Syria in 1973 to regain lands occupied by Israel since 1967; also called the Yom Kippur War or Ramadan War

*olim* (oh-LEEM): Jewish immigrants to Israel

**Oljeitu** (uhl-JAY-tu): Il-Khanid ruler (1304–1317)

**Oman** (oh-MAN): Country in southeast Arabian Peninsula

**Organization of Petroleum Exporting Countries (OPEC):** A group formed in 1960 to maintain a minimum price for oil

**Orhan** (or-HAHN): Ottoman sultan (1326–1360)

**Oslo:** (1) Site of secret Israeli-PLO negotiations (1992–1993); (2) Term applied to 1993 Declaration of Principles; (3) Term applied to 1995 Israeli-PLO agreement

**Osman I** (oss-MAHN): First Ottoman sultan (ca. 1280–1326)

**Osman II:** Ottoman sultan (1618–1622)

**Osmanli** (oss-MAHN-lih): Pertaining to descendants of Osman I or to their soldiers and administrators, or to their language

**Ottoman Decentralization party:** Liberal political movement favored by moderate Arab nationalists before World War I

**Ottoman Empire:** Multinational Islamic state (1299–1922) that began in northwestern Anatolia and spread through the Balkans, most of southwest Asia, Egypt, and coastal North Africa

**Ottomanism:** Identification with the Ottoman Empire (as opposed to separatist nationalism), encouraged by early westernizers

**Oxus River:** Roman name for the Amu Darya, a Central Asian river flowing from the Pamir Mountains northwest to the Aral Sea

**Ozal, Turgut** (ew-ZAL, tewr-GEWT): Turkey's prime minister (1983–1989) and president (1989–1993)

**Pahlavi** (pah-luh-VEE): (1) Pre-Islamic Persian language; (2) ruling family of Iran (1925–1979)

**Palestine:** (1) Geographical term for southern Syria; (2) name of the British mandate from 1922 to 1948; (3) term preferred by many Arabs for some or all of the lands currently governed by the State of Israel

**Palestine (Self-Governing) Authority:** Political organization set up by Oslo I agreement to administer areas relinquished by Israel to the Palestinians; headed by Yasir Arafat

**Palestine Liberation Organization (PLO):** Group formed in 1964 by Arab heads of state, now the umbrella for most Palestinian military, political, economic, and social organizations

**Palestinian:** Inhabitant of Palestine; now the term used for Arabs who live in Palestine, came from there, or descend from emigrants from that land

**Palmyra:** Ancient Arab city in central Syria that challenged Roman power in the third century

**pan-Arabism:** Movement to unite all Arabs in one state

**pan-Islam:** Idea or movement calling for unity of all Muslims, promoted by some Ottoman sultans and some popular leaders

**pan-Slavism:** Movement to unite all Slavs, especially under Russian leadership

**pan-Turanism:** Movement to unite all peoples speaking Turkic languages

**Paris Peace Conference:** Meeting of the victorious Allies after World War I to establish peace in Europe and the Middle East

**Parthian:** Persian dynasty (248 B.C.E.–227 C.E.) preceding the Sasanids

**Partition Plan for Palestine:** Proposed division of the Palestine mandate into Jewish and Arab states, approved by the UN General Assembly in 1947

**Passfield White Paper:** British official report blaming both Jews and Arabs for the 1929 Wailing Wall riots in Palestine

**Peel Commission:** British committee that visited Palestine in 1937 and first recommended partition into Jewish and Arab states

**People's Democratic Republic of Yemen:** Name used (1969–1990) for what used to be called Aden and the Aden Protectorate, then South Arabian Federation, then South Yemen

**Peres, Shim'on** (PER-es, shim-OAN): Israel's prime minister (1984–1986), Labor Alignment leader (1977–1992), foreign minister (1992–1996), and acting prime minister (1995–1996)

**Permanent Mandates Commission:** League of Nations body supervising mandates' administration

**Persia:** Name used for Iran to 1935

**Persian:** Pertaining to the main language or culture of Persia/Iran

**Persian Gulf:** *See* Gulf

**Persian Gulf War:** *See* Gulf War

**Petra** (PET-ra): City in southern Jordan carved from stone by Nabatean Arabs in the first century

**petrodollars:** Dollars earned by oil-exporting countries

**Phalanges** (fa-LAHNJ): Paramilitary organization dedicated to preserving Maronite Christian dominance in Lebanon

**Pinsker, Leo:** Russian Zionist, author of *Auto-Emancipation* (1882)

**pogrom** (puh-GRAWM): Organized massacre of Jews

**Popular Front for the Liberation of Palestine:** Marxist Palestinian group, noted for its airplane hijackings and led by George Habash

**Port Said** (sa-EED): Egyptian city at which the Suez Canal meets the Mediterranean

**positive neutralism:** Nasir's policy of not siding with either the communist countries or the West but seeking to reconcile the two blocs

**predestination:** The belief that God has determined what will happen to every living person; the opposite of free will

**Prester John:** Mythic Christian ruler in East Asia or Ethiopia, thought by some medieval Western Christians to be a potential ally against the Muslims

**Punjab** (poon-JAWB): A region of northwestern India, now partly in Pakistan

**al-Qadhafi, Mu'ammar** (el-gad-DOF-fee, moo-AHM-mer): Libya's president (1969-)

*qadi* (KAW-dee): Muslim judge

**Qadisiyah** (kaw-de-SEE-ya): Central Iraqi region and site of 637 battle in which the Arabs defeated the Sasanid Persians

**Qajar dynasty** (GHAW-jar): Family of Turkic origin ruling Persia (1794–1925)

*qanat* (kah-NAWT in Arabic or ghaw-NAWT in Persian): Canal or channel carrying irrigation water underground

*qanun* (ka-NOON): A ruler's edict, as opposed to the rules or laws contained in the Shari'ah

**Qarmatian** (kar-MAH-te-an): Member of an Isma'ili Shi'i group that established a republic, allegedly practicing communism of property and spouses, in tenth-century Bahrain and Arabia

**Qasim, Abd al-Karim** (KAW-sem, AB-del-ka-REEM): Iraq's president (1958–1963) and Nasir's rival in Arab politics

*qawm* (KOWM): Arab clan

**Qayrawan** (KAY-ruh-wahn): City in northeastern Tunisia; also called *Kairouan*

**Qays** (KICE): Northern Arabian tribe, Kalb's rival in early Muslim times

**Qazvin** (ghaz-VEEN): City in northwestern Iran, briefly the Safavid capital

**Qom** (GHOM): Shi'i religious and educational center in Iran

**Qubilai Khan** (KOO-bi-lie): Mongol ruler in the late thirteenth century; sometimes called *Kubla Khan*

**Quran** (koor-AWN): The collection of revelations that Muslims believe God vouchsafed to Muhammad via Gabriel, and one of the main sources of Islamic law, literature, and culture; also known as the *Koran*

**Quraysh** (koo-RAYSH): Leading tribe of northwest Arabia, especially Mecca

**Rabat Summit** (ra-BAWT): 1974 meeting of Arab heads of state, recognizing the PLO as the sole Palestinian representative

**Rabin, Yitzhak** (ra-BEEN, yits-KHAHK): Israel's prime minister (1974–1977 and 1992–1995)

**Rafsanjani, Ali Akbar Hashimi** (raf-san-JAW-nee): Iran's president (1989–1997)

**Ragib, Mehmet** (raw-GHIP): Influential Ottoman *vezir* (d. 1763)

**Ramadan** (ra-ma-DAWN): Month of the Arabic calendar during which Muslims refrain from eating, drinking, and sexual intercourse from daybreak to sunset, commemorating first revelations of the Quran to Muhammad

**Ramleh:** Strategic town in central Palestine/Israel

**Rashid al-Din** (ra-SHEED ed-DEEN): Muslim historian and Il-Khanid *vezir* (d. 1318)

**Rashid dynasty:** Ruling family in northeastern Arabia and rival of the Saudis in the early twentieth century

**Rashidun caliphs** (ra-shee-DOON): For Sunni Muslims, Muhammad's successors as *ummah* leaders: Abu-Bakr, Umar, Uthman, and Ali

*re'aya* (re-AH-ya): Member(s) of the Ottoman subject class

**refugees, Palestinian:** Arabs who were forced or who chose to leave their homes in areas now part of Israel, during the 1948 or 1967 wars

**Reginald of Chatillon** (sha-tee-YAWH): French military leader in the Latin Kingdom of Jerusalem

**Republican People's party:** Liberal Turkish party founded by Kemal Ataturk in 1923

**Reshid, Mustafa** (re-SHEET, MOOS-ta-fa): Westernizing Ottoman reformer in the early Tanzimat era (d. 1858)

**Reuter, Baron de** (ROY-ter): British entrepreneur offered a lucrative concession in Persia by Nasiruddin Shah in 1873

**Revisionist party:** Right-wing Zionist movement founded by Jabotinsky

**Revolutionary Guards:** Iranian-organized Islamic guerrilla movement active in various Middle Eastern countries

**Reza Shah Pahlavi** (REH-za shah pah-luh-VEE): Iran's ruler (1925–1941)

**Rhodes:** Mediterranean island; site of the 1949 "proximity talks" between Arab states and Israel, mediated by Ralph Bunche

*riddah* (RID-da): Rebellion of the Arab tribes against rule from Medina after Muhammad's death, quelled under Caliph Abu-Bakr

**Riyadh** (ree-YODH): Saudi Arabia's capital; site of 1976 Arab summit meeting that tried to end Lebanon's civil war

**Rogers Peace Plan:** U.S. proposal in 1969–1970 to end the War of Attrition, calling on Israel to withdraw from lands occupied since 1967 and on Arabs to recognize Israel

**Rum** (ROOM): (1) Arabic, Persian, and Turkish word for Anatolia; (2) collective term for Greek Orthodox Christians

**Rumaylah:** Large oil field shared by Iraq and Kuwait

**Rushdi, Husayn** (ROOSH-dee): Egypt's prime minister (1914–1919)

**Russo-Turkish War:** Conflict (1877–1878) between Russia and the Ottoman Empire, in which the latter lost land in Anatolia and the Balkans

**Saba** (SAH-ba): Ancient Arabian kingdom in Yemen

**Sabah, Al-** (sa-BAH, AL): Ruling family of Kuwait

**Sabra** (SOB-ra): (1) Jewish native of Israel; (2) Beirut refugee camp, site of Palestinian massacre in 1982

**al-Sadat, Anwar** (es-sa-DAT, AN-war): Egypt's president (1970–1981)

**Saddam Husayn** (sad-DAM): Iraq's president (1979-), who began the Iran-Iraq War (1980–1988) and invaded Kuwait in 1990, leading to Operation Desert Storm

**Sa'di** (sah-DEE): Popular Persian poet (d. 1292)

**Safa** (SAH-fa): Hill in Mecca, important in the hajj ritual

**Safavid dynasty** (SAH-fa-vid): Azerbaijani Turkish family, Sufi at first, that ruled Persia (1501–1736) and upheld Twelve-Imam Shi'ism and promoted Persian culture

**Safed** (sa-FED): City in northern Israel

**Sa'id** (sa-EED): Egypt's viceroy (1854–1863)

**Salah al-Din** (sa-LAH ed-DEEN): Arabic name for a Kurdish military adventurer who took over Egypt from the Fatimids and Syria from the Zengids, defeated the Crusaders in 1187, and regained Jerusalem for Islam but failed to expel the Crusaders from Acre; also known as *Saladin* (r. 1171–1192)

*salam* (sa-LAM): Arabic word for "peace," sometimes having the sense of "truce"; also a Muslim greeting

*salat* (sa-LAWT): Ritual prayer, or worship, in Islam

**Samanid dynasty** (sa-MAWN-id): Persian family that took over Khurasan and Transoxiana in the late ninth century and later imported Turkic nomads, such as the Ghaznavids and the Seljuks, to serve as border guards

**Samaria:** Biblical name used by some Israelis for the northern part of the West Bank

**Samarqand** (sa-mar-KAWND): Major city in Transoxiana

**Samarra** (sa-MAR-ra): City in northern Iraq; Abbasid capital (836–889)

**al-Samu'** (es-sa-MOO-ah): Arab village subjected to harsh Israeli reprisal following Palestinian border raids in 1966

**Samuel, Sir Herbert:** British high commissioner in Palestine (1920–1925)

**San'a:** Yemen Arab Republic's capital

**San Remo** (san RAY-mo): 1920 conference in which Britain and France determined the mandate borders

**Sanskrit:** The classical language of India

**San Stefano** (san STEH-fuh-no): Village near Istanbul; site of abortive Russo-Turkish Treaty in February 1878 that would have strengthened Russia's position in the Balkans

**Saracen:** Medieval European word for "Arab" or "Muslim"

**Sarkis, Elias** (sar-KEESS, il-YASS): Lebanon's president (1976–1982)

**Sasanid dynasty** (sa-SAW-nid): Persian ruling family (227–651)

**Sa'ud ibn Abd al-Aziz** (sa-OOD): Saudi Arabia's king (1953–1964)

**Sa'ud dynasty:** Arab family of Najd supporting Wahhabi doctrines since the reign of Muhammad ibn Sa'ud (1746–1765); rulers of most of the Arabian Peninsula during the twentieth century

**Saudi Arabia** (SOW-dee): Kingdom in the Arabian Peninsula ruled by the Sa'ud dynasty

**SAVAK** (sah-VAWK): Iran's secret police under Mohammad Reza Shah Pahlavi

**al-Sayyid, Ahmad Lutfi** (es-SAY-yid, AH-mad LOOT-fee): Egyptian liberal nationalist and educator (d. 1963)

**Scopus, Mount:** Hill northeast of Jerusalem, site of first Hebrew University campus and Hadassah Hospital, surrounded by Jordanian-held land (1949–1967)

**Sebuktegin** (suh-BEWK-tuh-GEEN): Central Asian Turkish chieftain, Samanid vassal, and founder of the Ghaznavid dynasty (d. 997)

**Security Council Resolution 242:** November 1967 statement of principles for achieving peace between the Arabs and Israel, accepted by both sides but with differing interpretations

**Security Council Resolution 338:** Cease-fire resolution ending the October 1973 war, calling for direct Israeli-Arab talks

**Security Council Resolution 598:** Resolution calling for an end to the Iran-Iraq War, accepted by Iraq in 1987 and by Iran in 1988

**Selim I** (se-LEEM): Ottoman sultan (1512–1520) who conquered Syria, Egypt, and the Hijaz

**Selim II:** Ottoman sultan (1566–1574)

**Selim III:** Ottoman reforming sultan (1789–1807)

**Seljuk** (sel-JOOK): (1) Central Asian Turkic tribal leader who adopted Islam in 956; (2) ruling family descended from Seljuk

**Semitic:** Pertaining to a subgroup of Asian languages, including Arabic and Hebrew, having consonantal writing systems, inflected grammars, and structured morphologies, or to a speaker of one of these languages

**separation-of-forces agreement:** Kissinger's formula to secure Israel's withdrawal from some lands taken in the October War

**Sephardim** (se-FAR-dim or sfah-ra-DEEM): Jews whose ancestors came from Spain, Portugal, or the Muslim world

**Serbia:** Ancient Balkan kingdom, later part of Yugoslavia

**Seven-Imam Shi'i:** Any Muslim who believes that the true leadership of the *ummah* was passed from Ali through a line of heirs ending in Isma'il; also called *Isma'ilis* or *Seveners*

**Sèvres, Treaty of** (SEVR): Abortive treaty imposed by the World War I Allies on the Ottoman Empire in 1920; later replaced by the Treaty of Lausanne

**Shafi'i** (SHA-fi-ee): Rite of Sunni Muslim jurisprudence, originating in Cairo, making considerable use of analogy

*shahid* (SHA-hid): Professional witness in Muslim law

**Shajar al-Durr** (SHA-jar ed-DOR): Woman ruler of Egypt in 1250; sometimes called *Shajarat al-Durr*

**shaman** (sha-MAHN): Pre-Islamic Turkish wizard or soothsayer believed capable of communicating with the dead, healing the sick, and preserving tribal lore

**Shamir, Yitzhak** (sha-MEER, yits-KHAHK): Israel's prime minister (1983–1984 and 1986–1992), head of the Likud coalition and former Stern Gang leader

**Sham'un, Kamil** (sham-OON, ka-MEEL): Lebanon's President (1952–1958)

**Shari'ah** (sha-REE-a): The highly articulated code of approved Muslim behavior, based primarily on the Quran and sunnah and secondarily on analogy, consensus, and judicial opinion

**sharif** (sha-REEF): Descendant of Muhammad

**Sharm al-Shaykh** (sharm esh-SHAYKH): Fortified point in southern Sinai near the Straits of Tiran

**Sharon, Ariel** (sha-ROAN, ah-ree-EL): Israeli general, defense minister during Israel's 1982 invasion of Lebanon and alleged facilitator of Sabra and Shatila killings; prime minister (2001-)

**Shatila** (sha-TEE-lah): Beirut refugee camp, site of 1982 massacre of Palestinians

**Shatt al-Arab** (shot-el-AH-rab): Confluence of Tigris and Euphrates rivers, contested in Iran-Iraq War

*shaykh* (SHAYKH): (1) Arab tribal leader; (2) ruler; (3) learned Muslim

*shaykh al-Islam* (SHAY-khul-iss-LAHM): Chief Ottoman legal and religious officer, appointed by the sultan

**Shaytan** (shye-TAWN): Satan, or the devil, in Muslim belief

**Shihab, Fuad** (she-HAB, foo-ODD): Lebanon's president (1958–1964)

**Shi'i** (SHEE-ee): Muslim who believes that Muhammad's leadership of the *ummah* was bequeathed to Ali, to whom special legislative powers and spiritual knowledge were vouchsafed

**Shiraz** (she-RAHZ): City in southern Iran

**Shishakli, Adib** (she-SHEK-lee, a-DEEB): Syria's president (1949–1954)

**shofar** (SHOW-far): Ram's horn blown by Jews on religious occasions

**al-Shuqayri, Ahmad** (esh-shoo-KAY-ree): First PLO leader (1964–1968)

*shura* (SHOO-ra): Council chosen by Umar in 644 to elect his successor

**shuttle diplomacy:** Kissinger's method of mediating between the Arab countries and Israel in 1974–1975

**Shu'ubiyah** (shoo-oo-BEE-yah): Ninth-century literary movement in which Persians sought equal power and status with Arabs

**Sidon:** City in southern Lebanon

**Sidqi, Isma'il** (SID-kee, iss-ma-EEL): Egyptian politician (d. 1950)

**Siffin, Battle of** (sif-FEEN): Indecisive clash in 657 between partisans of Ali and those of Mu'awiyah, who wished to avenge Uthman's death

**Sind:** Lower Indus valley region, now part of Pakistan

*sipahi* (se-PAW-hee): Ottoman horse soldier supported by a *timar*

**Skanderbeg:** Fifteenth century Albanian military leader

**Smyrna:** *See* Izmir

**Sogut** (suh-EWT): Northwest Anatolian town where Ottoman Empire started

**Stern Gang:** Zionist group, also called *Lehi*, which broke with the *Irgun* and committed guerrilla acts in Palestine up to 1949

**Suez Affair:** 1956 British, French, and Israeli attack on Egypt, following Nasir's nationalization of the Suez Canal Company

**Suez Canal:** Human-made channel between the Mediterranean and Red seas

**Sufi** (SOO-fee): Pertaining to Muslim mystics or to their beliefs, practices, or organizations

**Sufism:** Organized Muslim mysticism

**Suleyman the Magnificent** (suh-lay-MAHN): Ottoman sultan (1520–1566)

*sulh* (SOOL-h): Comprehensive peace settlement

**sultan** (sool-TAWN): Title for ruler of various Muslim states, including the Seljuk and Ottoman empires

**Sultaniyah** (sool-taw-NEE-ya): Il-Khanid capital city in northern Persia

*sunnah* (SOON-na): The sayings and actions of Muhammad regarding correct Muslim belief or behavior; hence, next to the Quran, the most important source of Muslim law

**Sunni** (SOON-nee): (1) A Muslim who accepts the legitimacy of the caliphs who succeeded Muhammad and adheres to one of the legal rites developed in the early caliphal period; (2) careful adherent to Muhammad's *sunnah*

**Sykes-Picot** (pee-KOE): Secret pact (1916) among Britain, France, and Russia outlining their plan to partition the Ottoman Empire

**Syria:** (1) Region east of the Mediterranean, including parts of southern Turkey, the Republic of Syria, Lebanon, Israel, Jordan, and the northern Sinai, also called the Levant; (2) the Republic of Syria

**Syrian Protestant College:** American University of Beirut, up to 1920

**Tabaristan** (ta-BAHR-i-stahn): Persian region between the Elburz Mountains and the Caspian Sea

**Tabatabai:** *See* Ziya ud-Din Tabatabai, Sayyid

**Tabriz** (ta-BREEZ): City in Azerbaijan and early Safavid capital

**Tahirid dynasty** (TAW-her-id): Ruling family in eastern Persia (820–873)

**Taif** (TAH-if): Mountain city in western Arabia, near Mecca; site of 1989 conference that restructured Lebanese politics

**Talal** (ta-LAHL): Jordan's king (1951–1952)

**Talat** (ta-LAHT): Influential Young Turk leader (d. 1921)

**Talhah** (TULL-ha): Muhammad's associate who challenged Ali in the 656 Battle of the Camel, in which Talhah died

**Taliban** (taw-li-BAWN): Islamist group that has taken control of most of Afghanistan since 1996

**Talmud** (TAHL-mood): Collection of Jewish law and tradition

**Tanzimat** (tan-zee-MAHT): Program of intensive westernizing reforms by the Ottoman government, especially from 1839 to 1876

**Taurus** (TAW-rus): Mountain range in southern Anatolia

**Tawfiq** (tow-FEEK): Egypt's viceroy (1879–1892)

**Tehran** (teh-RAWN): Capital of Persia/Iran since 1794

**Tel Aviv:** Coastal city and commercial center in Israel

**Temple:** When capitalized, one of several edifices built in Jerusalem as the main centers of Jewish worship in biblical times

**Tengri** (TENG-gree): Turkic and Mongol god of the blue sky

**terrorism:** Any coercive act directed against noncombatants to attain political ends; often used as a propaganda term

**Thrace:** Area on the northern shore of the Aegean Sea

**Tigris:** The more eastern of Iraq's two rivers

*timar* (tee-MAHR): Land grant by Ottoman sultans for military service

**Timur Leng** (tee-MOOR): Central Asian Turkish conqueror of Khurasan, Persia, Iraq, and Syria (1369–1405); also known as *Tamerlane*

**Timurid dynasty:** Family descended from Timur, ruling Central Asia in the fifteenth century, and later India, where they were called *Mughals*

**Tiran** (tee-RAHN): Straits linking the Gulf of Aqaba to the Red Sea

**Tobacco Boycott:** Organized Persian refusal to buy tobacco in 1891–1892 after Nasiruddin Shah had sold to a British company the concession to process and market the product

**Trans-Iranian Railway:** Line linking the Caspian Sea and the Gulf, built under Reza Shah

**Transjordan:** Emirate or principality east of the Jordan River excised by the British from their Palestine mandate in 1921

**Transoxiana:** Land northeast of the Oxus River, conquered by the Arabs in the eighth century and later invaded successively by Turks and Mongols

**Transylvania:** Region between Romania and Hungary

**Trench, Battle of the:** Unsuccessful Meccan siege of the Medinan Muslims in 627

**tribe:** Group of people (often nomadic) sharing real or fictitious descent from a common ancestor, as well as common traditions, customs, and leaders

**Tripoli:** (1) City in northern Lebanon; (2) twelfth-century Crusader state; (3) Libya's capital city

**Truman Doctrine:** U.S. policy statement of 1947 promising aid to Greece and Turkey against communist aggression

**Tudeh** (too-DAY): Procommunist worker's party of Iran

**Tujueh** (TEW-jweh): Chinese name for the sixth-century Turkic empire

**Turk:** (1) Speaker of a Turkic language; (2) citizen of Turkey

**Turkish:** Pertaining to the language and culture of the Turks

**Twelve-Imam Shi'i:** Any Muslim who believes that the *ummah* should have been led by Ali and his descendants, of whom the twelfth is hidden but will someday return to restore righteousness; also known as *Imami, Ja'fari,* or *Twelver*

**Twitchell, Karl:** American oil prospector in Saudi Arabia during the 1930s

**Ubaydallah** (oo-bay-DUL-la): Founder (909–934) of the Fatimid dynasty, having his capital at Mahdiyah, near modern Tunis; called the Mahdi (rightly guided one) by his followers

**Uhud, Battle of** (OH-hood): Meccan defeat of Muslims in 625

**Uighur** (oo-ee-GOOR): Turkic people of northwestern China, who ruled a large kingdom in the eighth and ninth centuries

**Ukaz** (oo-KAHZ): Town near Mecca, site of pre-Islamic poets' fair

**ulama** (OO-le-ma): Muslim scholars and jurists

**Umar I** (OH-mar): Second of the Rashidun caliphs (634–644); leader of the early Arab conquests

**Umar II:** Umayyad caliph (717–720) who reduced discrimination against non-Arab converts to Islam

**Umayyad dynasty** (om-MYE-yad): Clan of the Quraysh tribe that ruled in Damascus (661–750) and in Cordoba (756–1030)

*ummah* (OOM-ma): The political, social, and spiritual community of Muslims

**Uniat Catholics:** Christians of various Middle Eastern rites who are in communion with the Roman Catholic church

**United Arab Emirates:** Federation of Gulf principalities

**United Arab Republic:** Union of Egypt and Syria (1958–1961)

**United Nations Disengagement Observer Force:** International army stationed between Syria and Israel (1974-)

**United Nations Emergency Force (UNEF):** International army between Egypt and Israel (1957–1967 and 1974–1979)

**United Nations Relief and Works Agency (UNRWA):** International organization providing aid and education to Palestinian refugees since 1949

**Urabi, Ahmad** (oo-RAH-bee): Egyptian army officer and nationalist who led a popular uprising against the Dual Control in 1881–1882

**Urban II:** Pope (1088–1099) who inspired the First Crusade

**Uthman** (oth-MAHN): Third of the Rashidun caliphs (644–656)

**Uzbeks:** Central Asian Turks, sixteenth-century rivals to the Safavids

**al-Uzza** (el-OZ-zah): Meccan goddess before Islam

**Varna:** Bulgarian port city, site of Crusader defeat by the Ottomans in 1444

**Venizelos, Eleutherios** (veh-neh-ZAY-los): Greek prime minister during invasion of Anatolia (1919–1922) and strong advocate of a greater Greece

*vezir* (ve-ZEER): Government minister in a Muslim state; *wazir* in Arabic

*wadi* (WAH-dee): Valley

**Wafd** (WAHFT): (1) Unofficial Egyptian delegation to the 1919 Paris Peace Conference; (2) Egypt's main nationalist party from 1923 to 1952, revived in 1978

**Wahhabi** (wah-HAH-bee): Puritanical Muslim sect founded by Muhammad ibn Abd al-Wahhab, now dominant in Saudi Arabia

**Wailing Wall Incident:** Fracas in Jerusalem (1929), leading to widespread Arab attacks against Jews in Palestine

**Wallachia** (wal-LAY-ke-ya): Balkan region now part of Romania

*waqf* (pl. *awqaf*)(WAHKF, ow-KAHF): Muslim endowment of land or other property, usually established for a beneficent or pious purpose

**Weizmann, Chaim** (VITES-man, KHIME): British Zionist leader who helped to obtain the Balfour Declaration; Israel's first president (1948–1952)

**Welfare party:** Islamist party that won a plurality of seats in Turkey's 1995 elections and led a coalition government until 1997

**West Bank:** Area of Arab Palestine annexed by Jordan in 1948 and captured by Israel in 1967, called "Judea and Samaria" by some Israelis; partly governed by the Palestine Authority since 1996

**Western Wall:** Remnant in Jerusalem of the last Temple, revered by Jews, sometimes incorrectly called the *Wailing Wall*

**White Paper:** 1939 British policy statement limiting Jewish immigration and land purchase rights within the Palestine mandate, assailed by Zionists

**White Revolution:** Broad reform program proclaimed by Iran's shah in 1963

**Wingate, Sir Reginald:** British high commissioner in Egypt (1916–1919)

**Yad Mordechai** (yod MOR-de-khye): Israeli kibbutz near the Gaza Strip

**Yamit** (ya-MEET): Israeli industrial town built in occupied Sinai and destroyed before its restoration to Egypt in 1982

**Yarmuk River** (yar-MOOK): Tributary of Jordan River, site of Arab victory in 636

**Yathrib** (YATH-rib): Original name of Medina

**Yazid I** (ye-ZEED): Umayyad caliph (680–683)

**Yemen** (YEH-men): (1) Mountainous region of southwestern Arabia; (2) common name for the Yemen Arab Republic or "North Yemen"; (3) the People's Democratic Republic of Yemen (PDRY) or "South Yemen"; (4) republic formed by the union in 1990 of the Yemen Arab Republic and the PDRY

**Yom Kippur War:** *See* October War

**Young Egypt:** Egyptian nationalist movement in the 1930s

**Young Turks:** Group of Turkish nationalists who took control of the Ottoman government in 1908, restored its constitution, and instituted westernizing reforms; their main organization was the Committee of Union and Progress

**Zaghlul, Sa'd** (zagh-LOOL, SOD): Egyptian nationalist leader (d. 1927)

**Zagros** (ZAH-gross): Mountain range in southwestern Iran

*zakat* (za-KAT): Fixed share of income or property that all Muslims must pay as tax or charity for the welfare of the needy

**Zayd:** Fifth Shi'i imam, leader of an abortive revolt in the early eighth century, and founder of the Zaydi branch of Shi'ism

**Zayd ibn Harithah** (ZAYD ibn-ha-REE-thah): Muhammad's adopted son

**Zaydi Shi'i** (ZAY-dee): Muslim who believes that Zayd bequeathed his *ummah* leadership to designated successors

**Zaynab** (ZAY-nub): Wife of Muhammad's adopted son, Zayd ibn Harithah, who divorced her so that Muhammad might marry her

**Zengi** (ZENG-kee): Turkish general who founded a state in Mosul (1127–1146)

*zindiq* (zin-DEEK): (1) Muslim heretic; (2) (cap.) Manichaean or supporter of any other pre-Islamic Persian religion

**Zionism:** (1) Nationalist ideology stressing solidarity of the Jewish people; (2) movement to create or maintain a Jewish state, especially in Palestine/Israel

**Zionist:** Believer in Jewish nationalism

**Ziya al-Din Tabatabai, Sayyid** (zee-yahd-DEEN ta-ba-ta-BAW-ee): Civilian leader of 1921 Persian nationalist revolt, which brought Reza to power

**Ziyad ibn Abihi** (zee-YAD ibn-a-BEE-hee): Arab governor of Iraq under Caliph Mu'awiyah

**Zoroastrianism:** Pre-Islamic Persian religion popularized in the sixth century B.C.E. by Zoroaster, preaching the existence of a supreme deity and of a cosmic struggle between Good and Evil

**Zubayr** (zoo-BAYR): Muhammad's associate who challenged Ali in the 656 Battle of the Camel, in which Zubayr died; father of Abdallah ibn al-Zubayr

# BIBLIOGRAPHIC ESSAY

As this work is intended to introduce the history of the Middle East to college students primarily and to the public secondarily, the books and other sources that I will recommend are chosen for readability and reliability. This essay is directed to students, not specialists, and to acknowledge my debt to many scholars whose works have influenced what I wrote. Professional historians, including instructors using this work as a textbook, should consult *The Study of the Middle East* (New York: Wiley, 1977), edited by Leonard Binder and sponsored by the Middle East Studies Association. For sample course syllabi, see Guity Nashat, *Middle Eastern History* (New York: Marcus Wiener Publishing, 1987).

For well-written syntheses of Islamic history, see Ira M. Lapidus, *History of Islamic Societies* (New York: Cambridge University Press, 1988), Albert Hourani, *History of the Arab Peoples* (Cambridge: Harvard University Press, 1991), and John Esposito, ed., *The Oxford History of Islam* (Oxford: Oxford University Press, 1999). Marshall G. S. Hodgson, *The Venture of Islam*, 3 vols. (Chicago: University of Chicago Press, 1975), is seminal but far too advanced for most undergraduates.

This introductory textbook might be read together with a collection of original sources in translation; I have several in mind: James Kritzeck, *An Anthology of Islamic Literature* (New York: Holt, Rinehart & Winston, 1964); Bernard Lewis, *Islam: From the Prophet Muhammad to the Capture of Constantinople*, 2 vols. (New York: Harper & Row, 1974); William H. McNeill and Marilyn Waldman, *The Islamic World* (Chicago: University of Chicago Press, 1983); and F. E. Peters, *A Reader on Classical Islam* (Princeton: Princeton University Press, 1994). Drs. Waldman and William A. Graham have edited a useful collection of readings entitled *Islamfiche*, published by the Islamic Teaching Materials Project and distributed by Inter Documentation of Zug (Switzerland).

## GENERAL RESEARCH AIDS

A good reference tool for students is Jere Bacharach's *Middle East Studies Handbook*, 2nd ed. (Seattle: University of Washington Press, 1986), which contains dynastic tables, lists of rulers, maps, chronology, abbreviations, and other aids. More specialized reference books include Richard Bulliet, et al. (eds.), *Encyclope-*

*dia of the Modern Middle East*, 4 vols. (New York: Macmillan, 1996); Peter Mansfield, ed., *The Middle East: A Political and Economic Survey*, 5th ed. (London and New York: Oxford University Press, 1980); and Trevor Mostyn and Albert Hourani, eds., *Cambridge Encyclopedia of the Middle East and North Africa* (Cambridge: Cambridge University Press, 1988).

As the modern period is naturally more changeable, a yearbook may serve both beginners and specialists better than a handbook. Two yearbooks that I use are *The Middle East and North Africa* (London: Europa Publications, 1950–), and *Middle East Contemporary Survey*, edited by Bruce Maddy-Weitzmann and others, of which Vol. 21: 1997 (Boulder, Colo.: Westview Press, 2000) is the latest one that I have seen. The most established U.S. periodical publication in this field is the *Middle East Journal* (Washington, D.C., 1947–), which includes a quarterly chronology of events and bibliography of new books and articles. Middle East historians use the *International Journal of Middle East Studies* (New York and London, 1970–) and *Middle Eastern Studies* (London, 1965–). A stimulating and unconventional source is the monthly *Middle East Report*, which should be balanced against *Middle East* (1974–) from London and *Middle East Quarterly* (1994–) from Philadelphia. For event data, a useful biweekly is *Middle East International* (1971–) from London. On a daily basis, read the *New York Times* or the *Christian Science Monitor*.

While writing this book, I relied often on *The Encyclopaedia of Islam* (Leiden: E. J. Brill, 1913–1938; 2nd ed., 1954–). Also useful are the *Encyclopedia Judaica*, 16 vols. (Jerusalem: Keter Publishing House, 1972), updated annually; and the *Oxford Encyclopedia of the Modern Muslim World*, 4 vols. (New York and London: Oxford University Press, 1995), edited by John Esposito.

Historical atlases include William Brice, ed., *An Historical Atlas of Islam* (Leiden: E. J. Brill, 1981); Ismail R. and Lois Lami' al-Faruqi, *Cultural Atlas of Islam* (New York: Macmillan, 1986); and Francis Robinson, *Atlas of the Islamic World Since 1500* (New York: Facts on File, 1982).

Librarians, students, and general readers have welcomed an annotated bibliography called *The Middle East in Conflict: A Historical Bibliography* (Santa Barbara, Calif.: ABC-Clio Information Services, 1985). I also recommend George N. Atiyah, *The Contemporary Middle East, 1948–1973* (Boston: G. K. Hall, 1975); Diana Grimwood-Jones, *The Middle East and Islam: A Bibliographical Introduction* (Zug: Inter Documentation, 1979); and Sanford R. Silverburg, *Middle East Bibliography* (Metuchen, N.J., and London: Scarecrow Press, 1992). Bibliographical control often breaks down when periodical articles are needed. We had two useful tools: *Middle East Abstracts and Index*, Vols. 1–4 (1976–1981), and *Mideast File*, Vols. 1–7 (1982–1988). Without them, readers should use the *Index Islamicus* (London: Mansell, 1955–), preferably in the CD-ROM version, available since 1998.

## CHAPTER 1

Several well-known writers on the Middle East have shared their views on history: Sir Hamilton Gibb, *Studies on the Civilization of Islam*, eds. Stanford J. Shaw and William R. Polk (Boston: Beacon Press, 1962); Albert Hourani, *Islam in European Thought* (Cambridge: Cambridge University Press, 1991); and Bernard Lewis, *History—Remembered, Recovered, Invented* (Princeton: Princeton University Press, 1975). Recent compendia of the views of Middle East historians include Nancy E. Gallagher, *Approaches to the History of the Middle East* (LPC Inbook, 1997), and Thomas Naff, ed., *Paths to the Middle East: Ten Scholars Look Back* (Albany: State University of New York Press, 1993).

The best introduction to the area's geography remains Stephen H. Longrigg and James Jankowski, *The Middle East: A Social Geography* (Chicago: Aldine, 1970). Students should then read Colbert C. Held, *Middle Eastern Patterns: Places, Peoples, and Politics*, 3rd ed. (Boulder, Colo.: Westview Press, 2000). The traditional societies and cultures of the Middle East are surveyed in Carleton Coon, *Caravan: The Story of the Middle East*, 2nd ed. (New York: Holt, Rinehart & Winston, 1959; reprinted 1976); and Dale Eickelmann, *The Middle East and Central Asia: An Anthropological Approach*, 3rd ed. (Upper Saddle River, N.J.: Prentice-Hall, 1998). For ethnographic data, beginners may refer to Joyce Moss and George Wilson, *Peoples of the World: The Middle East and North Africa* (Detroit: Gale Research, 1992).

## CHAPTER 2

The history of the Middle East before Muhammad is a field unto itself. The best introduction now available is William W. Hallo and William Kelly Simpson, *The Ancient Near East: A History* 2nd ed.(New York: Harcourt Brace Jovanovich, 1997). I like Milton Covensky's *The Ancient Near Eastern Tradition* (New York: Harper & Row, 1966); Jacquetta Hawkes, *The First Great Civilizations* (New York: Knopf, 1973); and two works by Henri Frankfort: *Before Philosophy* (Harmondsworth, Middlesex: Penguin Books, 1951) and *The Birth of Civilization in the Near East* (Bloomington: Indiana University Press, 1957). Byzantine history is covered in detail by George Ostrogorsky, *History of the Byzantine State*, trans. Joan Hussey (New Brunswick, N.J.: Rutgers University Press, 1986). Beginners may prefer John Julius Norwich, *Byzantium: The Early Centuries* (New York: Alfred A. Knopf, 1989) and later volumes, or Tamara Talbot Rice, *Everyday Life in Byzantium* (New York: Dorset Press, 1987). On the Eastern Christian churches, see Aziz S. Atiya, *A History of Eastern Christianity* (South Bend, Ind.: Notre Dame University Press, 1968); and on Zoroastrianism, see Mary Boyce, *The Zoroastrians: Their Religious Beliefs and Practices* (New York: Routledge, 1985), Peter Clark, *Zoroastrianism: An Introduction to an Ancient Faith* (Brighton, U.K.: Sussex Academic Press, 1998), or S. A. Nigosian, *The Zoroastrian Faith* (Montreal and Buffalo: Queens University Press, 1993). For quick reference, G. W. Bowersock, Peter Brown, and Oleg Grabar, eds., *Late Antiquity* (Cambridge, Mass.: Harvard University Press, 1999) has detailed articles and short entries.

General books on Iran (or Persia) require special attention. Probably the best for beginners are Elton Daniel, *History of Iran* (Westport, Conn.: Greenwood Press, 2000); Richard N. Frye, *Persia*, rev. ed. (New York: Schocken, 1969); or

Donald Wilber, *Iran: Past and Present*, 9th ed. (Princeton: Princeton University Press, 1981). Advanced students should use *The Cambridge History of Iran*, 8 vols. (Cambridge: Cambridge University Press, 1968–1991). I acknowledge the help I received from Taghi Nasr's *The Eternity of Iran* (Tehran: Iranian Ministry of Culture and Arts, 1974). Increasingly useful is the *Encyclopedia Iranica*, edited by Ehsan Yarshater (London: Routledge and Kegan Paul, 1982–1992; Costa Mesa, Calif.: Mazda Publishers, 1993–), which has now reached "Gavbazi" in vol. 10. It is also available online.

The Arabs before Islam are covered in M. J. Kister, *Studies in Jahiliyya and Early Islam* (London: Variorum Reprints, 1980), and D. T. Potts, *The Arabian Gulf in Antiquity*, 2 vols. (Oxford: Clarendon Press, 1990). The classic and oft-reprinted description of the Arabian desert is Charles Doughty, *Travels in Arabia Deserta* (Cambridge: Cambridge University Press, 1888). Richard Bulliet's *The Camel and the Wheel* (Cambridge, Mass.: Harvard University Press, 1975) is an engaging book on domesticating the camel. Translations of early Arabic poetry, traditionally called "pre-Islamic," include Arthur J. Arberry's *The Seven Odes* (New York: Macmillan, 1957). On the south Arabian kingdoms, read Wendell Phillips's *Qataban and Sheba* (New York: Harcourt Brace, 1955).

Surveys of early Arab history include Hugh Kennedy, *The Prophet and the Age of the Caliphates* (London and New York: Longman, 1986); Bernard Lewis, *The Arabs in History* (London: Hutchinson, 1950; 6th ed., 1993); Francis E. Peters, *Allah's Commonwealth* (New York: Simon & Schuster, 1973); John J. Saunders, *A History of Medieval Islam* (New York: Routledge, 1978); and W. Montgomery Watt, *The Majesty That Was Islam* (New York: Praeger Publishers, 1974). Start with Saunders. The chronicles of Tabari have been translated into English and published in forty volumes by the State University of New York Press, a real boon to students of early Islamic history.

## CHAPTER 3

A good life of the Prophet for beginners is W. Montgomery Watt's *Muhammad: Prophet and Statesman* (London: Oxford University Press, 1961), based on his two longer works, *Muhammad at Mecca* (Oxford: Clarendon Press, 1953) and *Muhammad at Medina* (same publisher, 1956), which stress the social and economic context. Another analytical biography is Maxime Rodinson's *Mohammed* (New York: Pantheon, 1974). Closer to the Muslim spirit are Martin Lings, *Muhammad: His Life Based on the Earliest Sources* (New York: Inner Tradition International, 1983); Karen Armstrong, *Muhammad: Biography of the Prophet* (San Francisco: HarperCollins, 1992); and Michael Cook, *Muhammad* (New York: Oxford University Press, 1983). Of the many biographies by Muslim writers, those easiest for non-Muslims to read are Muhammad Husayn Haykal, *The Life of Muhammad*, trans. Ismail R. al-Faruqi (American Trust Publications, 1976); Seyyed Hossein Nasr, *Muhammad: Man of Allah* (London: Muhammadi Trust, 1982); and Rafiq Zakaria, *Muhammad and the Quran* (1991).

Although the Quran cannot really be translated, English versions will help the reader who knows no Arabic. The most literary one is Arthur J. Arberry, *The Koran Interpreted*, 2 vols. (New York: Macmillan, 1955); the most technically accurate is Bell's *Introduction to the Qur'an*, revised by W. Montgomery Watt (Chicago: Aldine, 1970). These may be supplemented by Watt's *Companion to the Quran* (London: George Allen & Unwin; New York: Humanities Press, 1967); Hanna E. Kassis's *A Concordance of the Quran* (Berkeley: University of California Press, 1983); and Mustansir Mir's *Dictionary of Quranic Terms and Concepts* (New York: Garland Publishers, 1987). If you know or are learning Arabic, you should try reading the Quran in its original language with an English-annotated interpretation. King Fahd of Saudi Arabia ordered the printing and distribution of a well-prepared version, *The Holy Qur-an: English Translation of the Meanings and Commentary* (Medina: King Fahd Holy Qur-an Printing Complex, n.d.).

## CHAPTER 4

Books by Western writers about Islamic beliefs and practices often betray assumptions that offend Muslims, whereas those written by Muslims may confuse instruction about their faith with religious indoctrination. Exceptions in the former group include Frederick M. Denny, *Islam and the Muslim Community* (San Francisco: Harper & Row, 1987); John Esposito, *Islam: The Straight Path*, 3rd ed. (New York: Oxford University Press, 1998); Richard C. Martin, *Islamic Studies: A History of Religions Approach*, 2nd ed. (Upper Saddle River, N.J.: Prentice-Hall, 1996); and Ira G. Zepp Jr., *A Muslim Primer: Beginner's Guide to Islam*, 2nd ed. (Fayetteville: University of Arkansas Press, 2000). Among the latter, see Jamal Elias, *Islam* (Upper Saddle River, NJ: Prentice-Hall, 1999); Seyyed Hossein Nasr, *Ideals and Realities of Islam* (London: George Allen & Unwin, 1966; New York: Praeger, 1967); and Fazlur Rahman, *Islam*, 2nd ed. (Chicago: University of Chicago Press, 1979). Many books on Islam seem to slight Shi'ism, but Moojan Momen's *An Introduction to Shi'i Islam: The History and Doctrines of Twelver Shi'ism* (New Haven and London: Yale University Press, 1985) redresses the balance, together with Roy Mottahedeh's *The Mantle of the Prophet* (New York: Simon & Schuster, 1985). The pilgrimage rites are described in Ali Shari'ati, *Hajj*, 2nd ed., trans. Ali A. Behzadnia and Najla Denny (Houston: Free Islamic Literatures, 1978). Detailed works include David E. Long, *The Hajj Today: A Survey of the Contemporary Makkah Pilgrimage* (Albany: SUNY Press, 1979); Ian R. Netton, ed., *Golden Roads: Migration, Pilgrimage, and Travel in Mediaeval and Modern Islam* (Richmond, U.K.: Curzon Press, 1993); and F. E. Peters, *The Hajj: The Muslim Pilgrimage to Mecca and the Holy Places* (Princeton: Princeton University Press, 1994).

## CHAPTER 5

For the history of the caliphate as an institution, see Thomas W. Arnold, *The Caliphate* (Oxford: Clarendon Press, 1924). It was reprinted in 1965, with a concluding chapter by Sylvia Haim. On the early caliphs, see Wilferd Madelung, *The Succession to Muhammad* (New York: Cambridge University Press, 1997), then C. E. Bosworth, *The Arabs, Byzantium and Iran* (Aldershot, U.K.: Variorum Reprints, 1996) and Martin Hinds, *Studies in Early Islamic History* (Princeton: Darwin Press, 1996). Short and readable biographies of Umar and Mu'awiyah (and other early "greats") can be read in Philip Hitti, *Makers of Arab History* (New York: Harper & Row, 1968). On the early conquests, an introductory history in English is Sir John Bagot Glubb, *The Great Arab Conquests* (London: Hodder & Stoughton, 1963; Englewood Cliffs, N.J.: Prentice-Hall, 1964), which should be supplemented by Elias Shoufani's *Al-Riddah and the Muslim Conquest of Arabia* (Toronto: University of Toronto Press, 1973) and Fred Donner's *The Early Islamic Conquests* (Princeton: Princeton University Press, 1980). Any student contemplating writing a seminar paper or a thesis for a graduate degree in the history of this period, or of those covered in Chapters 6–7, should read carefully R. Stephen Humphreys, *Islamic History: A Framework for Inquiry* (Princeton: Princeton University Press, 1991), as it defines major historical issues and evaluates the work done so far by Muslim and non-Muslim scholars.

## CHAPTER 6

For the period of the High Caliphate, in addition to the general histories by Hodgson, Kennedy, and Saunders cited earlier, see Sir William Muir, *The Caliphate: Its Rise, Decline, and Fall*, 3rd ed. (London: Smith, Elder, 1898; reprinted 1963), and Julius Wellhausen, *The Arab Kingdom and Its Fall*, trans. Margaret Graham Weir (Calcutta: University of Calcutta, 1927; reprinted 1963). Controversial but well worth reading are two books by M. A. Shaban: *The Abbasid Revolution* (London and New York: Cambridge University Press, 1971) and Part 2 of *Islamic History: A New Interpretation* (London and New York: Cambridge University Press, 1976). The most readable histories are those of Sir John Bagot Glubb: *The Empire of the Arabs* (Englewood Cliffs, N.J.: Prentice-Hall, 1963), *The Course of Empire* (London: Hodder and Stoughton, 1965), and *Haroon er-Rasheed and the Great Abbasids* (London: Hodder and Stoughton, 1976). Recent scholarly works include C. E. Bosworth, *The History of the Saffarids of Sistan* (Costa Mesa, Calif.: Mazda Publishers, 1994); Richard W. Bulliet, *Conversion to Islam in the Medieval Period: An Essay in Quantitative History* (Cambridge, Mass.: Harvard University Press, 1979); Gerald R. Hawting, *The First Dynasty of Islam*, 2nd ed. (London: Routledge, 2000); Hugh Kennedy, *The Early Abbasid Caliphate* (London: Croom Helm; Totowa, N.J.: Barnes & Noble, 1981); Jacob Lassner, *The Shaping of Abbasid Rule* (Princeton: Princeton University Press, 1980); Michael Morony, *Iraq After the Muslim Conquest* (Princeton: Princeton University Press, 1984); Roy Mottahedeh, *Loyalty and Leadership in an Early Islamic Society* (Princeton: Princeton University Press, 1980); and Moshe Sharon, *Black Banners from the East: The Establishment of the Abbasid State* (Jerusalem:

Magnes Press, 1985). On Baghdad, see Jacob Lassner, *Topography of Baghdad in the Early Middle Ages* (Detroit: Wayne State University Press, 1970); and Gaston Wiet, *Baghdad: Metropolis of the Abbasid Caliphate*, trans. Seymour Feiler (Norman: University of Oklahoma Press, 1971). Important for history as well as art is Oleg Grabar, *The Formation of Islamic Art*, rev. ed. (New Haven: Yale University Press, 1987).

## CHAPTER 7

If you wish to read more about this challenging era, you may start with P. M. Holt, *The Age of the Crusades: The Near East from the Eleventh Century to 1517* (London and New York: Longman, 1986), or Sir John Bagot Glubb, *The Lost Centuries* (London: Hodder and Stoughton, 1967). A good introduction to Turkish history is Clement Dodd's update to Roderic Davison, *Turkey*, 3rd ed. (Huntingdon, U.K.: Eothen Press, 1998), to be supplemented for the early period by Claude Cahen's *Pre-Ottoman Turkey*, trans. J. Jones-Williams (London: Sidgwick & Jackson; New York: Taplinger, 1968), and two books by Clifford E. Bosworth: *The Ghaznavids* (Edinburgh: University of Edinburgh Press, 1963) and *The Later Ghaznavids* (New York: Columbia University Press, 1977).

The Crusades are amply treated from a Western point of view. Start with Hans Eberhard Mayer, *The Crusades*, trans. John Gillingham (New York and Oxford: Oxford University Press, 1972); then see Steven Runciman's very readable *History of the Crusades*, 3 vols. (Cambridge: Cambridge University Press, 1951–1954). On a more advanced level, turn to Kenneth Setton, ed., *A History of the Crusades*, 6 vols. (Madison: University of Wisconsin Press, 1955–1989). A Muslim perspective appears in Philip K. Hitti, ed. and trans., *An Arab-Syrian Gentleman and Warrior in the Period of the Crusades* (New York: Columbia University Press, 1929; reprinted 1964). Amin Maalouf, *The Crusades Through Arab Eyes*, trans. Jon Rothschild (New York: Schocken Books, 1985), is highly readable. Among the many books on Salah al-Din, see Andrew Ehrenkreuz, *Saladin* (Albany: SUNY Press, 1972); Sir Hamilton Gibb, *The Life of Saladin* (Oxford: Clarendon Press, 1973); Malcolm C. Lyons, *Saladin: The Politics of Holy War* (Cambridge: Cambridge University Press, 1982); and Geoffrey Regan, *Saladin and the Fall of Jerusalem* (London: Croom Helm, 1987).

You can pick up some background to the Mongols from René Grousset, *The Empire of the Steppes*, trans. Naomi Walford (New Brunswick, N.J.: Rutgers University Press, 1970), Leo de Hartog, *Genghis Khan: Conqueror of the World* (London: Tauris, 1989), and David Morgan, *The Mongols* (Oxford: Basil Blackwell, 1986). Some contemporary sources have been translated and edited in Bertold Spuler's *History of the Mongols*, trans. Helga Drummond and Stuart Drummond, reprint ed. (New York: Dorset Press, 1989). A recent series of lectures show how the Persians adapted and survived: Ann Lambton, *Continuity and Change in Medieval Persia* (London: Tauris, 1988).

CHAPTER 8

Many authors, both Muslim and Western, have written synoptic descriptions of Islamic civilization. Aside from the works cited earlier, these include Edward W. Lane, *Arabian Society in the Middle Ages* (London: Curzon Press, 1883; reprinted 1971); Seyyed Hossein Nasr, *Islamic Life and Thought* (Albany: SUNY Press, 1985); and Gustave Von Grunebaum, *Medieval Islam*, 2nd ed. (Chicago: University of Chicago Press, 1953; numerous reprints). Collaborative efforts include C. E. Bosworth and Joseph Schacht, eds., *The Legacy of Islam* (London and New York: Oxford University Press, 1974); John R. Hayes, ed., *The Genius of Arab Civilization: Source of the Renaissance*, 2nd ed. (Cambridge, Mass.: MIT Press, 1983); Bernard Lewis, ed., *Islam and the Arab World* (New York: Knopf, 1976); and Francis Robinson, ed., *The Cambridge Illustrated History of the Islamic World* (Cambridge: Cambridge University Press, 1996).

On the Shari'ah, see Joseph Schacht, *An Introduction to Islamic Law* (London: Oxford University Press, 1964), and Noel J. Coulson, *A History of Islamic Law* (Edinburgh: University of Edinburgh Press, 1965). Political thought is covered by Ann K. S. Lambton, *State and Government in Medieval Islam* (London: Oxford University Press, 1981). On theology, start with W. Montgomery Watt, *Islamic Philosophy and Theology* (Edinburgh: University of Edinburgh Press, 1962; reprint ed., 1985). Sympathetic treatment of Sufism can be found in Seyyed Hossein Nasr, *Sufi Essays* (Albany: SUNY Press, 1972); James Fadiman and Robert Frager, *Essential Sufism* (San Francisco: HarperSanFrancisco, 1997); and Annemarie Schimmel, *Mystical Dimensions of Islam* (Chapel Hill: University of North Carolina Press, 1975). Synthesizing recent scholarship on Sufi history is Julian Baldick's *Mystical Islam* (New York and London: NYU Press, 1989). A recent synoptic work on Islamic spirituality is John Renard's *Seven Doors to Islam* (Berkeley: University of California Press, 1996).

On the literature of the Muslim peoples, see Edward G. Browne, *A Literary History of Persia*, 4 vols. (Cambridge: Cambridge University Press, 1928); Sir Hamilton Gibb, *Arabic Literature: An Introduction*, 2nd ed. (Oxford: Clarendon Press, 1963); and Reynold A. Nicholson, *A Literary History of the Arabs* (New York: Scribner's, 1907; London: Unwin, 1914; many reprints). I have already suggested some anthologies of original literary works in English translation. Ibn Khaldun's *Muqaddimah* has been translated into English in three volumes by Franz Rosenthal (New York: Bollingen, 1958) and abridged by N. J. Dawood (Princeton: Princeton University Press, 1967). The most readable introduction to Islamic art, profusely illustrated, is Ernst Grube's *The World of Islam* (New York and Toronto: McGraw-Hill, 1966).

Some of the technical achievements of Muslims can be gleaned from Andrew M. Watson, *Agricultural Innovation in the Early Islamic World* (Cambridge: Cambridge University Press, 1983); Seyyed Hossein Nasr, *Islamic Science: An Illustrated Study* (London: World of Islam Festival Publishing Co., 1976); and Donald R. Hill, *Islamic Science and Engineering* (Edinburgh: Edinburgh University Press, 1993).

CHAPTER 9

I derived my views on the significance of gunpowder from Carlo M. Cipolla, *Guns, Sails, and Empire* (New York: Minerva Press, 1965), and from Hodgson, *The Venture of Islam*, cited earlier.

The Il-Khanid phase of Mongol history is covered by Bertold Spuler in *The Muslim World: A Historical Survey, Part 2: The Mongol Period*, trans. F.R.C. Bagley (Leiden: E. J. Brill, 1960). A readable introduction to the Mamluks is Sir John Bagot Glubb, *Soldiers of Fortune: The Story of the Mamlukes* (New York: Stein & Day, 1973). It should be followed by Daniel Pipes, *Slave Soldiers and Islam: The Genesis of a Military System* (New Haven: Yale University Press, 1981); David Ayalon, *The Mamluk Military* (London: Variorum Reprints, 1979); and Ira M. Lapidus, *Muslim Cities in the Later Middle Ages* (Cambridge, Mass.: Harvard University Press, 1967). On specific cities of this era, see A. J. Arberry, *Shiraz: Persian City of Saints and Poets* (Norman: University of Oklahoma Press, 1960); Gaston Wiet, *Cairo: City of Art and Commerce*, trans. Seymour Feiler (Norman: University of Oklahoma Press, 1964); and Nicola Ziadeh, *Damascus Under the Mamluks* (Norman: University of Oklahoma Press, 1964). A recent work, Beatrice Forbes Manz, *The Rise and Fall of Tamerlane* (Cambridge: Cambridge University Press, 1989) supersedes Harold Lamb, *Tamerlane: The Earth Shaker* (Garden City, N.Y.: Garden City Publishing Co., 1928), which may still be read for pleasure.

A comprehensive history of the Ottoman Empire, based heavily on Turkish sources, is Stanford J. Shaw (with Ezel Kural Shaw in Volume 2), *History of the Ottoman Empire and Modern Turkey*, 2 vols. (London, New York, and Melbourne: Cambridge University Press, 1976–1977). Because this work may seem formidable to beginners, I also suggest Jason Goodwin, *Lords of the Horizon: A History of the Ottoman Empire* (London: Chatto & Windus, 1998); Bernard Lewis, *Istanbul and the Civilization of the Ottoman Empire* (Norman: University of Oklahoma Press, 1963); Raphaela Lewis, *Everyday Life in Ottoman Turkey* (London: Batsford; New York: G. P. Putnam's Sons, 1971); Alan Palmer, *The Decline and Fall of the Ottoman Empire* (New York: M. Evans and Co., 1992); and Andrew Wheatcroft, *The Ottomans* (New York: Viking, 1993).

Regarding Ottoman institutions, Albert Howe Lybyer's *The Government of the Ottoman Empire in the Time of Suleiman the Magnificent* (Cambridge, Mass.: Harvard University Press, 1914) is well written and still often cited; but it has been superseded by later works, especially H.A.R. Gibb and Harold Bowen, *Islamic Society and the West*, vol. 1 (London: Oxford University Press, 1950–1957). A vivid account of the Ottoman conquest of Istanbul is Steven Runciman's *The Fall of Constantinople, 1453* (Cambridge: Cambridge University Press, 1965). On Mehmet II, see Franz Babinger, *Mehmed the Conqueror and His Time*, ed. William C. Hickman, trans. Ralph Manheim (Princeton: Princeton University Press, 1977). Another great sultan is studied in Andre Clot, *Suleiman the Magnificent* (New York: New Amsterdam, 1992); and, more lightly, in Harold Lamb, *Suleiman the Magnificent* (Garden City, N.Y.: Doubleday & Co., 1951; reprinted 1978). See also Paul Cole's *The Ottoman Impact on Europe* (London: Thames & Hudson, 1968); Halil Inalcik, *The Ottoman Empire: The Classical Age, 1300–1600*, 2nd ed. (New Rochelle, N.Y.: Caratzas Publishing, 1989); and L. S. Stavrianos, *The Balkans Since 1453* (New York: Rinehart & Co., 1958). Historians now analyze economic and social trends in the Ottoman Empire, notably in cities. See for example Edhem Elhem, Daniel Goffman, and Bruce Masters, *The Ottoman City between East and West* (New York: Cambridge University Press, 1999), drawing on their earlier monographs.

The standard work on the Safavids is Roger M. Savory, *Iran Under the Safavids* (Cambridge: Cambridge University Press, 1980). The same author's more specialized studies are available in *Studies on the History of Safavid Iran* (London: Variorum Reprints, 1987). On Isfahan's art and architecture, see Wilfrid Blunt, *Isfahan: Pearl of Persia* (New York: Stein & Day, 1966). On relations between the two states, see Adel Allouche, *The Origins and Development of the Ottoman-Safavid Conflict* (Berlin: Klaus Schwarz Verlag, 1983). J. J. Saunders, ed., *The Muslim World on the Eve of Europe's Expansion* (Englewood Cliffs, N.J.: Prentice-Hall, 1966), contains some original and often highly readable sources in translation.

## CHAPTER 10

The Eastern Question was a staple of the vanishing breed of European diplomatic historians. The most thorough, albeit arduous, treatment is M. S. Anderson, *The Eastern Question* (London: Macmillan; New York: St. Martin's Press, 1966). Easier for students is A. L. Macfie, *The Eastern Question*, rev. ed. (London: Longman, 1996). On British Middle East policy, see especially H. L. Hoskins, *British Routes to India* (London: Longman's Green, 1928; reprinted 1966); Marvin Swartz, *The Politics of British Foreign Policy in the Era of Disraeli and Gladstone* (New York: St. Martin's Press, 1985); Harold W. V. Temperley, *England and the Near East: The Crimea* (London and New York: Longman's Green, 1936; reprinted 1964); and Sir Charles Webster, *The Foreign Policy of Palmerston*, 2 vols. (London: G. Bell, 1951; reprinted 1969). A series of books by Edward Ingrams focuses on Persia: *Beginnings of the Great Game in Asia, 1828–1834* (Oxford: Clarendon, 1979), *Commitment to Empire* (same publisher, 1981), and *Britain's Persian Connection, 1798–1828* (same publisher, 1992). On the Middle Eastern rivalry between England and France, see John Marlowe [pseud.], *Perfidious Albion* (London: Elek, 1971). On the two countries' activities in Egypt, see David S. Landes, *Bankers and Pashas* (Cambridge, Mass.: Harvard University Press, 1958). Leon Carl Brown argues that the rules of the Eastern Question influence contemporary Middle East policies and politics in *International Politics and the Middle East: Old Rules, Dangerous Game* (Princeton: Princeton University Press, 1984).

The Russian warm-water port theory comes from Robert J. Kerner, *The Urge to the Sea* (Berkeley and Los Angeles: University of California Press, 1942), now corrected by Barbara Jelavich, *Russia's Balkan Entanglements, 1806–1914* (New York:

Cambridge University Press, 1991). On the Balkan crisis of 1875–1878, see William L. Langer, *European Alliances and Alignments, 1871–1890*, 2nd ed. (New York: Knopf, 1950); Richard Millman, *Britain and the Eastern Question* (New York: Oxford University Press, 1979); and B. H. Sumner, *Russia and the Balkans, 1870–1880* (Oxford: Oxford University Press, 1937; reprinted 1962).

On the Middle East during the eighteenth and nineteenth centuries, see (in addition to works already cited) P. M. Holt, ed., *Political and Social Change in Modern Egypt* (London: Oxford University Press, 1968), and his *Egypt and the Fertile Crescent, 1516–1922* (Ithaca, N.Y.: Cornell University Press, 1966); Thomas Naff and Roger Owen, eds., *Studies in Eighteenth-Century Islamic History* (Carbondale and Edwardsville: Southern Illinois University Press, 1977); William Polk and Richard Chambers, eds., *The Middle East in the Nineteenth Century* (Chicago: University of Chicago Press, 1967); Marion Kent, ed., *The Great Powers and the End of the Ottoman Empire* (London: George Allen & Unwin, 1984); and M. E. Yapp, *The Making of the Modern Middle East, 1792–1923* (New York and London: Longman, 1987). Amusing anecdotes about the later Ottoman Empire can be found in Noel Barber's *The Sultans* (New York: Simon & Schuster, 1973).

*The Modern Middle East* (Berkeley and Los Angeles: University of California Press, 1993), edited by Albert Hourani, Philip S. Khoury, and Mary C. Wilson, collects scholarly articles and book chapters dealing with aspects of Middle East history from the Eastern Question to the *Intifadah* in a form accessible to both teachers and students. Another recent work, Edmund Burke III, ed., *Struggle and Survival in the Modern Middle East* (Berkeley and Los Angeles: University of California Press, 1993), contains biographical sketches of Middle Eastern men and women, most of them "ordinary" but some quite famous, who have lived during the nineteenth or twentieth century.

Original sources in English translation include M. S. Anderson, ed., *The Great Powers and the Near East, 1774–1923* (London: Edward Arnold, 1970), and J. C. Hurewitz, ed., *The Middle East and North Africa in World Politics*, 2 vols. (New Haven: Yale University Press, 1975).

## CHAPTER 11

For a survey of modern Egyptian history, start with Arthur Goldschmidt, *Modern Egypt: The Formation of a Nation State* (Boulder, Colo.: Westview Press, 1988), and then read P. J. Vatikiotis, *History of Modern Egypt from Muhammad Ali to Mubarak*, 4th ed. (Baltimore and London: Johns Hopkins University Press, 1991). On intellectual changes, see Nadav Safran, *Egypt in Search of Political Community* (Cambridge, Mass.: Harvard University Press, 1961; reprinted 1981). Egypt's early westernization can be traced through Christopher Herold, *Bonaparte in Egypt* (New York: Harper & Row, 1962); Khalid Fahmy, *All the Pasha's Men: Mehmed Ali. His Army and the Making of Modern Egypt* (New York: Cambridge University Press, 1997); and Helen Rivlin, *The Agricultural Policy of Muhammad*

*Ali in Egypt* (Cambridge, Mass.: Harvard University Press, 1961). The era follow-ing Mehmet Ali is covered in Ehud R. Toledano, *State and Society in Mid-Nine-teenth-Century Egypt* (New York: Cambridge University Press, 1990).

Your study of Ottoman westernization should start with Bernard Lewis, *The Emergence of Modern Turkey*, 2nd ed. (London and New York: Oxford University Press, 1968), and Erik Jan Zurcher, *Turkey: A Modern History* (London: I. B. Tau-ris, 1993; New York: St. Martin's Press, 1994). On Selim III, read Stanford J. Shaw, *Between Old and New* (Cambridge, Mass.: Harvard University Press, 1971). On the Tanzimat era, see Roderic H. Davison, *Reform in the Ottoman Empire, 1856–1876* (Princeton: Princeton University Press, 1963; reprinted 1972); Carter V. Findley, *Bureaucratic Reform in the Ottoman Empire: The Sublime Porte, 1789–1922* (Princeton: Princeton University Press, 1980), and *Ottoman Civil Offi-cialdom: A Social History* (same publisher, 1989); and Serif A. Mardin, *The Gene-sis of Young Ottoman Thought* (Princeton: Princeton University Press, 1962). Also useful is Niyazi Berkes, *The Development of Secularism in Turkey* (Montreal: McGill University Press, 1964). Leila Fawaz, *An Occasion for War: Civil Conflict in Lebanon and Damascus in 1860* (Berkeley: University of California Press, 1994), tells of an instance where westernizing reforms led to dismal consequences.

On nineteenth-century Iran, read Hamid Algar, *Religion and State in Iran: The Role of the Ulama in the Qajar Period* (Berkeley and Los Angeles: University of California Press, 1980); Abbas Amanat, *Pivot of the Universe: Nasir al-Din Shah Qajar and the Iranian Monarchy* (Berkeley: University of California Press, 1997); Ann K. S. Lambton, *History of Qajar Persia* (London: Tauris, 1987); Guity Nashat, *The Origins of Modern Reform in Iran* (Urbana: University of Illinois Press, 1981); and A. Reza Sheikholeslami, *Structure of Central Authority in Qajar Iran, 1871–1896* (Atlanta: Scholars Press, 1997).

Two source collections useful for this and later chapters are Robert G. Landen, ed., *The Emergence of the Modern Middle East* (Cincinnati: Van Nostrand Rein-hold, 1970), and George Lenczowski, ed., *The Political Awakening of the Middle East* (Englewood Cliffs, N.J.: Prentice-Hall, 1970).

## CHAPTER 12

The rise of Egyptian nationalism during the heyday of British imperialism is cov-ered in Peter Mansfield, *The British in Egypt* (New York: Holt, Rinehart & Win-ston, 1972); John Marlowe, *Spoiling the Egyptians* (New York: St. Martin's Press, 1975), and *Cromer in Egypt* (London: Elek; New York: Praeger Publishers, 1970); Afaf Lutfi al-Sayyid [Marsot], *Egypt and Cromer: A Study in Anglo-Egyptian Rela-tions* (London: John Murray, 1968; New York: Praeger Publishers, 1969); Robert Tignor, *Modernization and British Colonial Rule in Egypt, 1882–1914* (Princeton: Princeton University Press, 1966); and Charles Wendell, *The Evolution of the Egyptian National Image* (Berkeley: University of California Press, 1972). The book on Urabi mentioned in the chapter is Alexander Schölch, *Egypt for the*

*Egyptians!* (London: Ithaca Press, 1981). A newer analysis is Juan R. Cole's *Colonialism and Revolution in the Middle East: Social and Cultural Origins of Egypt's Urabi Movement* (Princeton: Princeton University Press, 1993).

On nationalism in Turkey, see Kemal Karpat, *Inquiry into the Social Foundations of Nationalism in the Ottoman State* (Princeton: Center for International Studies, 1973); David Kushner, *The Rise of Turkish Nationalism, 1876–1908* (London: Frank Cass, 1977); and the works already cited by Niyazi Berkes, Bernard Lewis, and Stanford and Ezel Kural Shaw. A popular biography of Abdulhamid is Joan Haslip's *The Sultan* (New York: Holt, Rinehart & Winston, 1958). M. Sukru Hanioglu, *The Young Turks in Opposition* (New York: Oxford University Press, 1995) covers the CUP before it took power; for the later period, see Feroz Ahmad, *The Young Turks: The Committee of Union and Progress in Turkish Politics, 1908–1914* (Oxford: Clarendon Press, 1969); Ahmet Kansu, *The Revolution of 1908 in Turkey* (Leiden: E. J. Brill, 1997); and Erik Jan Zurcher, *The Unionist Factor: The Role of the Committee of Union and Progress in the Turkish National Movement, 1905–1926* (Leiden: E. J. Brill, 1984). Ziya Gokalp's *Turkish Nationalism and Western Civilization*, trans. Niyazi Berkes (New York: Columbia University Press, 1959), is supplemented by Robert Devereux's *The Principles of Turkism* (Leiden: E. J. Brill, 1968).

On both Egypt and Turkey, see also the essays edited by William Haddad and William Ochsenwald, *Nationalism in a Non-national State* (Columbus: Ohio State University Press, 1977; reprinted 1986). On Jamal al-Din al-Afghani, see Nikki Keddie, *Sayyid Jamal al-Din "al-Afghani"* (Berkeley and Los Angeles: University of California Press, 1972). Keddie has written many articles on early Persian or Iranian nationalism, but see also the writings of Algar and Cottam cited elsewhere. The Persian constitutionalist movement is covered by Janet Afari, *The Iranian Constitutional Revolution, 1906–1911* (New York: Columbia University Press, 1996); Mangal Bayat, *Iran's First Revolution: Shi'ism and the Constitutional Revolution of 1905–1909* (New York: Oxford University Press, 1991); and Vanessa Martin, *Islam and Modernism in the Iranian Revolution of 1906* (London: Tauris, 1989; Syracuse: Syracuse University Press, 1989). The rise of the Gulf principalities is treated in Frederick F. Anscombe, *The Ottoman Gulf: The Creation of Kuwait, Saudi Arabia, and Qatar* (New York: Columbia University Press, 1997), which refutes Iraq's territorial claims on Kuwait.

## CHAPTER 13

On the origins and rise of Arab nationalism, the classic account is George Antonius's *The Arab Awakening* (Philadelphia and New York: J. P. Lippincott, 1939; many reprints). It has been corrected in some details by Sylvia Haim's introduction to *Arab Nationalism: An Anthology* (Berkeley: University of California Press, 1962; reprinted 1976). See also David Dean Commins, *Islamic Reform: Politics and Social Change in Late Ottoman Syria* (New York: Oxford University Press,

1990); Albert Hourani, *Arabic Thought in the Liberal Age, 1798–1939* (London: Oxford University Press, 1962; many reprints); James Jankowski, ed., *Rethinking Nationalism in the Arab Middle East* (New York: Columbia University Press, 1997); Hasan Kayali, *Arabs and Young Turks: Ottomanism, Arabism, and Islamism in the Ottoman Empire, 1908–1918* (Berkeley: University of California Press, 1997); Rashid Khalidi et al., eds., *The Origins of Arab Nationalism* (New York: Columbia University Press, 1991); Philip S. Khoury, *Urban Notables and Arab Nationalism in the Politics of Damascus* (Cambridge: Cambridge University Press, 1984); Hisham Sharabi, *Arab Intellectuals and the West: The Formative Years, 1875–1914* (Baltimore: Johns Hopkins University Press, 1970); and Zeine N. Zeine, *Emergence of Arab Nationalism* (Beirut: Khayat's, 1966).

Anglo-Arab relations during World War I have been analyzed by Elie Kedourie in *England and the Middle East, 1914–1921* (London: Bowes and Bowes, 1956), *The Chatham House Version and Other Middle Eastern Studies* (London: Weidenfeld & Nicolson, 1970), and *In the Anglo-Arab Labyrinth* (London, New York, and Melbourne: Cambridge University Press, 1976). As a balance to Kedourie's antipathy toward Arab nationalism, read C. Ernest Dawn, *From Ottomanism to Arabism* (Urbana, Chicago, and London: University of Illinois Press, 1973); Rashid Khalidi, *British Policy toward Syria and Palestine* (London: Ithaca Press, 1980); and A. L. Tibawi, *Anglo-Arab Relations and the Question of Palestine* (London: Luzac, 1977). Closer to Kedourie's view is volume 1 of Isaiah Friedman's *Palestine: A Twice-Promised Land?* (New Brunswick, N.J.: Transaction Publishers, 2000).

Many books have been written about T. E. Lawrence, of which I recommend Lawrence James, *The Golden Warrior: The Life and Legend of Lawrence of Arabia* (New York: Paragon, 1993); Philip Knightley and Colin Simpson, *The Secret Lives of Lawrence of Arabia* (New York: McGraw-Hill, 1969); and Jeremy Wilson, *Lawrence of Arabia: The Authorized Biography of T. E. Lawrence* (New York: Atheneum, 1990). Lawrence's own account of the Arab revolt, a classic, is *The Seven Pillars of Wisdom* (Garden City, N.Y.: Doubleday, Doran & Co, 1935; numerous reprints).

On Middle East diplomacy during and after World War I, see Briton Cooper Busch, *Britain, India and the Arabs, 1914–1921* (Berkeley: University of California Press, 1971); David Fromkin, *A Peace to End All Peace: Creating the Modern Middle East* (New York: Henry Holt, 1989; reprint 2000); Elizabeth Monroe, *Britain's Moment in the Middle East, 1914–1971*, 2nd ed. (Baltimore: Johns Hopkins University Press, 1981); and Howard M. Sachar, *Emergence of the Middle East, 1914–1924* (New York: Knopf, 1969).

On Iraq under the British, see Reeva Simon, *Iraq Between the Two World Wars: The Creation and Implementation of a Nationalist Ideology* (New York: Columbia University Press, 1986); and Peter Sluglett, *Britain in Iraq, 1914–1932* (London: Ithaca Press, 1976). On Syria, see Philip S. Khoury, *Syria and the French Mandate: The Politics of Arab Nationalism, 1920–1945* (Princeton: Princeton University Press, 1986). To compare both countries, read Eliezer Tauber, *The Formation of Modern Syria and Iraq* (London: Frank Cass, 1995).

## CHAPTER 14

As this book moves into the modern period, let me recommend some general books on various aspects of the Middle East in the twentieth century. The most serviceable, though very detailed, political surveys are William Cleveland, *History of the Modern Middle East*, 2nd ed. (Boulder, Colo.: Westview Press, 2000), and Malcolm Yapp, *The Near East since the First World War* (New York: Longman, 1996).

No book better captures the life and character of the Middle East's most renowned twentieth-century westernizer than Lord Kinross's *Ataturk* (London: Weidenfeld & Nicolson, 1964; New York: William Morrow, 1965). Halide Edib [Adivar], *Turkey Faces West* (New Haven: Yale University Press, 1930; reprinted 1973); Irfan Orga, *Phoenix Ascendant: The Rise of Modern Turkey* (London: R. Hale, 1958); and Ahmed Amin Yalman, *Turkey in My Time* (Norman: University of Oklahoma Press, 1956), provide Turkish views of the Kemalist era. Psychohistory entered Turkish studies with Vamik D. Volkan and Norman Itzkowitz, *The Immortal Ataturk: A Psychobiography* (Chicago: University of Chicago Press, 1984). In addition to the histories of Turkey cited earlier, I recommend George S. Harris, *Turkey: Coping with Crisis* (Boulder, Colo.: Westview Press, 1985), and Mary Lee Settle, *Turkish Reflections: A Biography of a Place* (New York: Prentice-Hall, 1991).

Because the Pahlavi dynasty has been so controversial, unbiased histories of Reza Shah are rare. I used Donald N. Wilber, *Riza Shah Pahlavi: The Resurrection and Reconstruction of Iran, 1878–1944* (Hicksville, N.Y.: Exposition Press, 1975), supplemented by Hassan Arfa, *Under Five Shahs* (London: John Murray, 1964; New York: William Morrow, 1965), and Amin Banani, *The Modernization of Iran, 1921–1941* (Stanford, Calif.: Stanford University Press, 1961). On modern Iran generally, see Richard Cottam, *Nationalism in Iran*, 2nd ed. (Pittsburgh: University of Pittsburgh Press, 1979), and Nikki Keddie and Yann Richard, *Roots of Revolution: An Interpretive History of Modern Iran* (New Haven: Yale University Press, 1981). Homa Katouzian has written a comprehensive biography, *Musaddiq and the Struggle for Power in Iran* (London and New York: I. B. Tauris, 1990).

The best accounts of Ibn Sa'ud's life are David Howarth's *The Desert King* (New York: McGraw-Hill, 1964) and Leslie McLaughlin's *Ibn Saud: Founder of a Kingdom* (New York: St. Martin's Press, 1993). Introductions to the rise of Saudi Arabia include Joseph Kostiner's *The Making of Saudi Arabia, 1916–1936: From Chieftaincy to Monarchical State* (New York: Oxford University Press, 1993); H. St. John Philby's *Sa'udi Arabia* (London: Benn; New York: Praeger Publishers, 1955); Karl Twitchell's *Saudi Arabia, with an Account of the Development of Its Natural Resources*, 3rd ed. (Princeton: Princeton University Press, 1958); and D. Van der Meulen's *The Wells of Ibn Saud* (London: John Murray, 1957). Background studies include R. Bayly Winder, *Saudi Arabia in the Nineteenth Century* (New York: St. Martin's, 1965), and William Ochsenwald, *Religion, Society, and State in Arabia: The Hijaz Under Ottoman Control* (Columbus: Ohio State University Press, 1984). On Aramco's beginnings, see Wallace Stegner, *Discovery: The Search for Arabian Oil* (Beirut: Middle East Export Press, 1971), which also was serialized in *Aramco*

*World* in 1968–1969. More accessible are the relevant sections of Daniel Yergin's *The Prize: The Epic Quest for Oil, Money, and Power* (New York: Simon & Schuster, 1991). For Saudi Arabia's U.S. connection, read Rex J. Casillas, *Oil and Diplomacy: The Evolution of American Foreign Policy in Saudi Arabia, 1933–1945* (New York: Garland Publishers, 1987), and Nadav Safran, *Saudi Arabia: The Ceaseless Quest for Security* (Cambridge, Mass.: Belknap Press, 1985).

## CHAPTER 15

A new collaborative work on Egypt's history since the Arab conquest will benefit both scholars and students, the two-volume *Cambridge History of Egypt* (New York: Cambridge University Press, 1998), of which the first volume was edited by Carl Petry and the second by M. W. Daly.

Much of the best writing on twentieth-century Egypt has been done by French authors, such as Jacques Berque, *Egypt: Imperialism and Revolution*, trans. Jean Stewart (London: Faber; New York: Praeger Publishers, 1972); and Jean and Simonne Lacouture, *Egypt in Transition*, trans. F. Scarfe (New York: Criterion Books, 1958). Other good books on this period include Joel Beinin and Zachary Lockman, *Workers on the Nile: Nationalism, Communism, Islam and the Egyptian Working Class* (Princeton: Princeton University Press, 1987); Israel Gershoni and James Jankowski, *Egypt, Islam, and the Arabs: The Search for Egyptian Nationhood, 1900–1930* (New York: Oxford University Press, 1986); Afaf Lutfi al-Sayyid Marsot, *Egypt's Liberal Experiment, 1922–1936* (Berkeley: University of California Press, 1977); Richard Mitchell, *The Society of Muslim Brothers* (London and New York: Oxford University Press, 1969; reprinted 1993); Charles Smith, *Islam and the Search for Social Order in Modern Egypt: A Biography of Muhammad Husayn Haykal* (Albany: SUNY Press, 1983); William Stadiem, *Too Rich: The High Life and Tragic Death of King Farouk* (New York: Carroll and Graf, Publishers, 1991); and Robert L. Tignor, *State, Private Enterprise, and Economic Change in Egypt, 1918–1952* (Princeton: Princeton University Press, 1984).

On the overthrow of the monarchy, start with Joel S. Gordon, *Nasser's Blessed Movement: Egypt's Free Officers and the July Revolution* (New York: Columbia University Press, 1997), followed by some personal accounts: Khaled Mohi El Din, *Memories of a Revolution* (Cairo: AUC Press, 1995); Gamal Abdel Nasser, *Egypt's Liberation: The Philosophy of the Revolution* (Washington, D.C.: Public Affairs Press, 1955); Mohamed Neguib, *Egypt's Destiny: A Personal Statement* (London: Gollancz; Garden City, N.Y.: Doubleday, 1955); and Anwar El Sadat, *Revolt on the Nile* (London: Allan Wingate; New York: John Day, 1957).

## CHAPTER 16

Literature abounds on the contest for Palestine, but it is hard to separate scholarship from propaganda. Works closest to the former include Ian Bickerton and

Carla L. Klausner, *A Concise History of the Arab-Israeli Conflict*, 3rd ed. (Paramus, N.J.: Prentice-Hall, 1997); Benny Morris, *Righteous Victims: A History of Zionist-Arab Conflict, 1881–1999* (New York: Knopf, 1999); relevant portions of Howard M. Sachar's *Emergence of the Middle East* (cited earlier) and *Europe Leaves the Middle East, 1936–1954* (New York: Knopf, 1972); Charles D. Smith, *Palestine and the Arab-Israeli Conflict*, 4th ed. (New York: St. Martin's Press, 2000); Kenneth Stein, *The Land Question in Palestine, 1917–1939* (Chapel Hill: University of North Carolina Press, 1983); and Mark Tessler, *A History of the Israeli-Palestinian Conflict* (Bloomington: Indiana University Press, 1994). An accessible collection of documents is Walter Laqueur and Barry Rubin, eds., *Israel-Arab Reader*, 5th ed. (New York: Penguin, 1995).

Engaging biographies have been written about most of Israel's founders. See, for example, Amos Elon, *Herzl* (New York: Schocken Books, 1985); Jehuda Reinharz, *Chaim Weizmann: The Making of a Zionist Leader* (New York: Oxford University Press, 1985) and *Chaim Weizmann: The Making of a Statesman* (same publisher, 1993); Shabtai Teveth, *Ben Gurion: The Burning Ground* (Boston: Houghton Mifflin, 1987); and Joseph Schechtman's two-volume work, *The Life and Times of Vladimir Jabotinsky* (Washington: Bnai Brith, 1986).

Personal accounts of the early struggle for Palestine include Robert John and Sami Hadawi's *Palestine Diary*, 2 vols. (New York: New World Press, 1970) for the Arabs, Storrs's *Orientations* (already cited) for the British, and Chaim Weizmann's *Trial and Error* (New York: Harper, 1949) for the Zionists. On the British mandate, see Tom Segev, *One Palestine, Complete: Jews and Arabs under the British Mandate*, trans. Haim Watzman (New York: Henry Holt, 2000), Naomi Shepherd, *Ploughing Sand: British Rule in Palestine, 1917–1948* (New Brunswick, N.J.: Rutgers University Press, 2000) and Bernard Wasserstein, *The British in Palestine: The Mandatory Government and the Arab-Israeli Conflict, 1917–1929*, 2nd ed. (Oxford, U.K., and Cambridge, Mass.: Blackwell, 1991). Putting Britain's Palestine policy in broader perspective is William Roger Louis, *The British Empire in the Middle East, 1945–1951* (Oxford: Clarendon Press, 1984).

Among general histories of Israel, useful also for my later chapters, the best are Yossi Beilin, *Israel: A Concise Political History* (New York: St. Martin's Press, 1994); Martin Gilbert, *Israel: A History* (New York: William Morrow, 1998); Moshe Raviv, *Israel at Fifty* (London: Weidenfeld & Nicolson, 1998); and Nadav Safran, *Israel: The Embattled Ally* (Cambridge, Mass.: Belknap Press, 1978). Especially readable are Abba Eban, *My Country* (New York: Random House, 1972), and Amos Elon, *The Israelis: Founders and Sons*, rev. ed. (New York: Penguin Books, 1983). The history of Zionism is covered by Shlomo Avineri, *The Making of Modern Zionism* (New York: Basic Books, 1981); Simha Flapan, *Zionism and the Palestinians* (London: Croom Helm, 1979); Rafael Medoff, *Zionism and the Arabs: An American Jewish Dilemma, 1898–1948* (Westport: Praeger, 1997); and three histories by David Vital: *The Origins of Zionism* (New York: Oxford University Press, 1980), *Zionism: The Formative Years* (Oxford: Clarendon Press, 1982), and *Zionism: The Crucial Phase* (same publisher, 1987). Complementary readings appear in Arthur Hertzberg, ed., *The Zionist Idea* (Philadelphia: Jewish Publication Society, 1960).

The politicization of Palestine's Arabs can be traced in Yehoshua Porath's *The Emergence of the Palestinian National Movement, 1918–1929* (Jerusalem: Hebrew University Press, 1973) and *The Palestine Arab National Movement, 1929–1939. II: From Riots to Rebellion* (London: Frank Cass, 1978). See also Baruch Kimmerling and Joel Migdal, *The Palestinians: The Making of a People* (Cambridge, Mass.: Harvard University Press, 1994); Philip Mattar, *The Mufti of Jerusalem: Al-Hajj Amin al-Husayni and the Palestinian National Movement*, 2nd ed. (New York: Columbia University Press, 1992); and Muhammad Y. Muslih, *The Origins of Palestinian Nationalism* (same publisher, 1988). These may be supplemented by A. W. Kayyali, ed., *Zionism, Imperialism, and Racism* (London: Croom Helm, 1979), and Walid Khalidi, ed., *From Haven to Conquest* (Beirut: Institute for Palestine Studies, 1971). See also the works by Antonius, Khouri, and Tibawi, already cited, as well as Sami Hadawi, *Bitter Harvest: Palestine Between 1914 and 1967* (New York: New World Press, 1961), and Rashid Khalidi, *Palestinian Identity: The Construction of Modern National Consciousness* (New York: Columbia University Press, 1997). Favoring Palestine's Arabs is David Hirst, *The Gun and the Olive Branch: The Roots of Violence in the Middle East*, 2nd ed. (London and Boston: Faber & Faber, 1984).

The last days of British policy in Palestine are covered by Yehuda Bauer, *From Diplomacy to Resistance: A History of Jewish Palestine, 1939–1945* (New York: Atheneum, 1973); Michael J. Cohen, *Palestine and the Great Powers, 1945–48* (Princeton: Princeton University Press, 1982); Martin Jones, *Failure in Palestine: British and United States Policy After the Second World War* (London and New York: Mansell, 1986); William Roger Louis and Robert W. Stookey, *The End of the Palestine Mandate* (London: Tauris, 1986); Richie Ovendale, *Britain, the United States, and the End of the Palestine Mandate* (London: Royal Historical Society, 1989); and Ilan Pappé, *The Making of the Arab-Israeli Conflict, 1947–1951* (London: I. B. Tauris & Co., 1994). On U.S. support for Zionism, read Peter M. Grose, *Israel in the Mind of America* (New York: Knopf, 1983).

## CHAPTER 17

On the 1948 Palestine War, or Israel's war of independence, see Jon and David Kimche, *A Clash of Destinies* (New York: Praeger Publishers, 1960), also published as *Both Sides of the Hill* (London: Secker, 1960). In addition, see Dan Kurzman, *Genesis, 1948: The First Arab-Israeli War* (New York: World Publishing Co., 1970; reprinted 1992). Sir John Bagot Glubb eloquently defends his role in *The Story of the Arab Legion* (London: Hodder & Stoughton, 1948) and *A Soldier with the Arabs* (same publisher, 1957; New York: Harper Brothers, 1958). The *Journal of Palestine Studies* has published relevant memoirs by several Arab leaders, including Fawzi al-Qawuqji (in 1972) and Gamal Abd al-Nasir (in 1973). See also Larry Collins and Dominique Lapierre, *O Jerusalem!* (New York: Simon & Schuster, 1972). On the aftermath of the 1948 war, see George Kirk, *The Middle East, 1945–1950* (London and New York: Oxford University Press, 1954); Don Peretz, *Israel and the Palestine Arabs* (Washington, D.C.: Middle East Institute, 1956); and Nadav Safran, *From War to War* (New York: Pegasus, 1969). Benny Morris leads the Israeli revisionists with three books on Israel's relations with the Arabs: *The Birth of the Palestinian Refugee Problem* (New York and Cambridge: Cambridge University Press, 1987); *1948 and After: Israel and the Palestinians* (New York: Oxford University Press, 1990); and *Israel's Border Wars, 1949–1956: Arab Infiltration, Israeli Retaliation, and the Countdown to the Suez War* (same publisher, 1993). Paralleling the Arab exodus from Israel was an influx of Jews from the Arab countries, on which see Norman Stillman, *The Jews of Arab Lands in Modern Times* (Philadelphia: Jewish Publication Society, 1991).

On the new State of Israel, see David Ben Gurion, *Rebirth and Destiny of Israel*, trans. Mordekhai Nurock (New York: Philosophical Library, 1954), and on the Arab countries at this time, consult Barry Rubin, *The Arab States and the Palestine Conflict* (Syracuse: Syracuse University Press, 1981); Jon Kimche, *Seven Fallen Pillars* (New York: Praeger Publishers, 1953); Bruce Maddy-Weitzman, *The Crystalization of the Arab State System, 1945–1954* (Syracuse: Syracuse University Press, 1993); Phebe Marr, *The Modern History of Iraq* (Boulder, Colo.: Westview Press, 1985); Malek Mufti, *Sovereign Creations: Pan-Arabism and Politics* (Ithaca: Cornell, 1996); and Matthew Eliot, *"Independent Iraq": The Monarchy and British Influence, 1941–1958* (London: I. B. Tauris, 1996).

On the background to the 1956 Suez Affair, see Erskine Childers, *The Road to Suez: A Study in Western-Arab Relations* (London: Macgibbon & Kee, 1962); Sir Anthony Eden, *The Suez Crisis of 1956* (Boston: Beacon Press, 1968), reprinted from *Full Circle* (London: Times Publishing; Boston: Houghton-Mifflin, 1960); Mohamed H. Heikal, *Cutting the Lion's Tail* (New York: Arbor House, 1987); Keith Kyle, *Suez* (London: Weidenfeld & Nicholson, 1991); William Roger Louis and Roger Owen, eds., *Suez 1956: The Crisis and Its Consequences* (New York: Oxford University Press, 1989); and Hugh Thomas, *Suez* (New York: Harper & Row, 1966).

Gamal Abd al-Nasir and his policies are covered by Kirk Beattie, *Egypt During the Nasser Years* (Boulder, Colo.: Westview Press, 1994); R. Hrair Dekmejian, *Egypt Under Nasir: A Study in Political Dynamics* (Albany: SUNY Press, 1971); Jean Lacouture, *Nasser*, trans. Daniel Hofstadter (New York: Knopf, 1973); P. J. Vatikiotis, *Nasser and His Generation* (New York: St. Martin's Press, 1979); and Peter Woodward, *Nasser* (London: Longman's, 1992). Nasir's Arab policies are treated sympathetically in Charles D. Cremeans, *The Arabs and the World: Nasser's Nationalist Policy* (New York: Praeger Publishers, 1963). Mohamed Heikal, *The Cairo Documents* (Garden City, N.Y.: Doubleday, 1972), stresses Nasir's relations with foreign leaders. On his relations with Washington, compare

Miles Copeland [pseud.], *The Game of Nations* (New York: Simon & Schuster, 1969), with Wilbur Crane Eveland, *Ropes of Sand: America's Failure in the Middle East* (London and New York: W. W. Norton, 1980). On the dynamics of inter-Arab politics during this period, read sequentially Patrick Seale, *The Struggle for Syria: A Study of Postwar Arab Politics, 1945–1958*, rev. ed. (London: Tauris, 1987), and Malcolm H. Kerr, *The Arab Cold War: Gamal Abd al-Nasir and His Rivals, 1958–1970*, 3rd ed. (London: Oxford University Press, 1971).

Nasir's rival in Iraq is sympathetically treated by Uriel Dann, *Iraq Under Qassem: A Political History, 1958–1963* (London: Pall Mall; New York: Praeger Publishers, 1969). Dann also wrote *King Husayn and the Challenge of Arab Radicalism: Jordan, 1955–1967* (New York: Oxford University Press, 1989). Recent books on Jordan include Kamal Salibi, *The Modern History of Jordan* (London: I. B. Tauris, 1993), and Robert Satloff, *From Abdullah to Husayn: Jordan in Transition* (New York: Oxford University Press, 1994). The standard account of Lebanon's 1958 civil war is Fahim Qubain, *Crisis in Lebanon* (Washington, D.C.: Middle East Institute, 1961). A good survey of Syria is A. L. Tibawi, *A Modern History of Syria, Including Lebanon and Palestine* (London: Macmillan; New York: St. Martin's Press, 1969). Books on the Ba'th include Raymond A. Hinnebusch, *Authoritarian Power and State Formation in Ba'thist Syria* (Boulder, Colo.: Westview Press, 1990); Robert W. Olson, *The Ba'th and Syria, 1947 to 1982* (Princeton: Kingston Press, 1982); and Itamar Rabinovich, *Syria Under the Ba'th, 1963–1966* (Jerusalem: Israel Universities Press, 1972).

On the events leading up to the June 1967 war, see Theodore Draper, *Israel and World Politics* (New York: Viking Press, 1967); Walter Laqueur, *The Road to Jerusalem* (New York: Macmillan, 1968), also published as *The Road to War* (Harmondsworth, U.K.: Penguin, 1969); and Kennett Love, *Suez: The Twice-Fought War* (New York and Toronto: McGraw-Hill, 1969). U Thant's memoirs, published posthumously in 1978, try to shift some of the blame from himself to Nasir; but those of the UNEF commander, Major General Indar Jit Rickye, *The Sinai Blunder* (London: Frank Cass, 1980), serve as a corrective.

# CHAPTER 18

Because Israel made more facilities available to foreign journalists than Arab countries did, we have far more literature on Israel's version of the June 1967 war. Best for beginners is Randolph and Winston Churchill's *The Six Day War* (London: Heinemann; Boston: Houghton Mifflin, 1967), and then Eric M. Hammel's *Six Days in June: How Israel Won the 1967 Arab-Israeli War* (New York: Scribner's, 1992). Moshe Dayan's daughter, Yael Dayan, wrote her impressions of the front in *Israel Journal, June 1967* (New York: McGraw-Hill, 1967), also published as *A Soldier's Diary: Sinai 1967* (London: Weidenfeld & Nicolson, 1967). Jordan's role is described by two journalists who interviewed King Husayn (Vick Vance and Pierre Lauer), in *My "War" with Israel*, trans. J. P. Wilson and W. B. Michaels (New York:

Morrow; London: Own, 1969). A general sense of the Arabs' reaction to the war can be gleaned from Halim Barakat's novel *Days of Dust*, trans. Trevor Le Gassick (Wilmette, Ill.: Medina University Press International, 1974). See also Elias Sam'o, ed., *The June 1967 Arab-Israeli War: Miscalculation or Conspiracy?* (Wilmette, Ill.: Medina University Press International, 1971), and Fred J. Khouri, *The Arab Israeli Dilemma*, 3rd ed. (Syracuse, N.Y.: Syracuse University Press, 1985). A pro-Israel and anti-Soviet account of this period is Walter Z. Laqueur's *The Struggle for the Middle East*, rev. ed. (New York: Macmillan, 1972). Soviet policies are analyzed in Michael Confino and Shimon Shamir, eds., *The U.S.S.R. and the Middle East* (Jerusalem: Israel Universities Press, 1973). The pro-Israeli policy of the United States during and after the 1967 war is criticized in Maxime Rodinson, *Israel and the Arabs*, trans. Michael Perl (New York: Pantheon, 1968); Hisham Sharabi, *Palestine and Israel: The Lethal Dilemma* (New York: Pegasus Press, 1969); and David Waines, *The Unholy War: Israel and Palestine, 1897–1971* (Wilmette, Ill.: Medina University Press International, 1971). Personal accounts by Palestinians are Leila Khaled's *My People Shall Live: The Autobiography of a Revolutionary*, ed. George Hajjar (London: Hodder & Stoughton, 1973); and Fawaz Turki, *Soul in Exile: Lives of a Palestinian Revolutionary* (New York: Monthly Review Press, 1988). On Palestinian politics generally, read Yazid Sayigh, *Armed Struggle and the Search for State: The Palestine National Movement, 1949–1993* (Oxford: Clarendon Press, 1997).

There are numerous books about the October (or Yom Kippur) War of 1973. On the Arab background, see Mohamed Heikal, *The Road to Ramadan* (New York: Quadrangle, 1975); regarding Israel, see Michael Handel, *Perception, Misperception, and Surprise: The Case of the Yom Kippur War* (Jerusalem: Hebrew University Press, 1975). On the events of the war itself, I recommend Saad al-Shazly, *The Crossing of the Suez* (San Francisco: American Mideast Research, 1980), an Egyptian account hostile to Sadat; Chaim Herzog's two books, *The War of Atonement* (Boston: Little, Brown, 1975) and *The Arab-Israeli Wars* (New York: Random House, 1982); and *Insight on the Middle East War* (London: Deutsch, 1974), edited by the "Insight Team of the *Sunday Times*." On the political side, see Walter Z. Laqueur, *Confrontation: The Middle East War and World Politics* (London: Abacus; New York: Quadrangle, 1974), and the essays edited by Naseer Aruri called *Middle East Crucible: Studies on the Arab-Israeli War of 1973* (Wilmette, Ill.: Medina University Press International, 1975).

Kissinger's role in the postwar peace negotiations is praised in Edward Sheehan's *The Arabs, Israelis, and Kissinger* (New York: Reader's Digest Press, 1976) and attacked in Matti Golan's *Secret Conversations of Henry Kissinger* (New York: Quadrangle, 1976). On U.S. policies generally, compare Joseph Churba, *The Politics of Defeat: America's Decline in the Middle East* (New York: Cyrco Press, 1977), with William B. Quandt, *Peace Process: American Diplomacy and the Arab-Israeli Conflict since 1967* (Washington, D.C.: Brookings Institution, 1993).

Several major actors in the search for Middle East peace justify their roles: Henry Kissinger, in *Years of Upheaval* (Boston: Little, Brown, 1982); Golda Meir,

*My Life* (New York: Dell, 1976); and Boutros Boutros-Ghali in *Egypt's Road to Jerusalem* (New York: Random House, 1997).

OPEC and Middle Eastern oil attracted much attention after 1973. See Dankwart Rustow and John R. Mugno, *OPEC: Success and Prospects* (New York: New York University Press, 1976); George Lenczowski, *Middle East Oil in a Revolutionary Age* (Washington, D.C.: American Enterprise Institute, 1976); Abdul Amir Kubbah, *OPEC Past and Present* (Vienna: Petro-Economic Research Centre, 1974); Ragaei El Mallakh, ed., *OPEC: Twenty Years and Beyond* (Boulder, Colo.: Westview Press, 1982); and Benjamin Shwadran, *Middle Eastern Oil Crises Since 1973* (Boulder, Colo.: Westview Press, 1986). More attention is now being paid to oil-producing countries rarely mentioned in my book, such as the United Arab Emirates. See John Duke Anthony, *Arab States of the Lower Gulf: People, Politics, Petroleum* (Washington, D.C.: Middle East Institute, 1975); Alvin J. Cottrell, gen. ed., *The Persian Gulf States: A General Survey* (Baltimore and London: Johns Hopkins University Press, 1980); and F. Gregory Gause III, *Oil Monarchies: Domestic and Security Challenges in the Arab Gulf States* (New York: Council on Foreign Relations Press, 1994).

The 1978 peace talks are covered from various angles in Jimmy Carter, *Keeping Faith: Memoirs of a President* (New York: Bantam, 1982); Moshe Dayan, in *Breakthrough: A Personal Account of the Egypt-Israel Peace Negotiations* (New York: Knopf, 1982); Mohamed Ibrahim Kamel, *The Camp David Accords* (London and Boston: Routledge & Kegan Paul, 1986); William B. Quandt, *Camp David: Peacemaking and Politics* (Washington, D.C.: Brookings Institution, 1986); and Shibley Telhami, *Power and Leadership in International Bargaining: The Path to the Camp David Accords* (New York: Columbia University Press, 1990).

The best books I have seen so far on the Lebanese civil war are Latif Abul-Husn, *The Lebanese Conflict: Looking Inward* (Boulder, Colo.: Lynne Rienner Publishers, 1998); Robert Fisk, *Pity the Nation: The Abduction of Lebanon* (New York: Atheneum, 1990); Walid Khalidi, *Conflict and Violence in Lebanon* (Cambridge: Harvard University Press, 1979); and Itamar Rabinovich, *The War for Lebanon, 1970–1985*, rev. ed. (Ithaca: Cornell University Press, 1985). A moving personal account is Jean Said Makdisi, *Beirut Fragments: A War Memoir* (New York: Persea Books, 1990).

CHAPTER 19

Thanks to the late Ayatollah Khomeini, the cottage industry for Middle East specialists is the writing of books about Islam and its resurgence; but you can best start by reading the work of a nonspecialist, Edward Mortimer, *Faith and Power: The Politics of Islam* (New York: Random House, 1982). It may be followed by Nazih Ayubi's two books: *Political Islam: Religion and Politics in the Arab World* (London and New York: Routledge, 1991) and *Overstating the Arab State: Politics and Society in the Middle East* (London: Tauris, 1995); R. Hrair Dekmejian, *Islam in Revolution: Fundamentalism in the Arab World* (Syracuse: Syracuse University Press, 1985); John L. Esposito, *The Islamic Threat: Myth or Reality*, 3rd ed. (New York: Oxford University Press, 1999); Michael Gilsenan, *Recognizing Islam: Religion and Society in the Modern Arab World*, 2nd ed. (New York: Tauris, 2000); Malise Ruthven, *Islam in the World*, 2nd ed. (New York: Oxford University Press, 2000); and John Obert Voll, *Islam: Continuity and Change in the Modern World*, 2nd ed. (Syracuse: Syracuse University Press, 1994). Collections of Muslim writings include John J. Donohue and John L. Esposito, eds., *Islam in Transition: Muslim Perspectives* (New York and Oxford: Oxford University Press, 1982), and Yvonne Yazbeck Haddad, ed., *Contemporary Islam and the Challenge of History* (Chicago: Kazi Publications, 1996). Political terrorism is another favorite topic for writers; the book most relevant to the Middle East is Robin Wright, *Sacred Rage: The Wrath of Militant Islam*, rev. ed. (New York: Simon & Schuster, 1986). In addition, see Juan R. Cole and Nikki Keddie, eds., *Shi'ism and Social Protest* (New Haven: Yale University Press, 1986). Edward Said has written many books on the mistakes in Western thinking about the Middle East: *Orientalism* (New York: Pantheon Books, 1978) on scholars; *The Question of Palestine* (New York: Random House, 1979) on policymakers; and *Covering Islam* (New York: Pantheon Books, 1981) on journalists.

The Iranian revolution has been described from various angles. In particular, see Ervand Abrahamian's *Iran Between Two Revolutions* (Princeton: Princeton University Press, 1982), as well as his *Khomeinism: Essays on the Islamic Republic* (Berkeley: University of California Press, 1993); Said Amir Arjomand, *The Turban for the Crown: The Islamic Revolution in Iran* (New York: Oxford University Press, 1988); Shaul Bakhash, *The Reign of the Ayatollahs: Iran and the Islamic Revolution* (New York: Basic Books, 1984); Asaf Hussein, *Islamic Iran: Revolution and Counterrevolution* (New York: St. Martin's Press, 1985); Robin Wright, *In the Name of God: The Khomeini Decade* (New York: Simon & Schuster, 1989), and *The Last Great Revolution: Turmoil and Transformation* (New York: Knopf, 2000); and Dariush Zahedi, *Iranian Revolution Then and Now: Indicators of Regime Instability* (Boulder, Colo.: Westview Press, 2000). U.S. policy is discussed in James A. Bill, *The Eagle and the Lion* (New Haven: Yale University Press, 1988); Kuross Samii, *Involvement by Invitation: The American Experience in Iran* (University Park: Pennsylvania State University Press, 1987); and Gary Sick, *All Fall Down: America's Tragic Encounter with Iran* (New York: Random House, 1985). For background to the Iran-Iraq War, see Shahram Chubin, *Iran and Iraq at War* (Boulder, Colo.: Westview Press, 1988); Dilip Hiro, *The Longest War: The Iran-Iraq Military Conflict* (New York: Routledge, 1991); and Stephen C. Pelletiere, *The Iran-Iraq War: Chaos in a Vacuum* (New York: Praeger Publishers, 1992).

Recent developments in the Arab states are covered in Fouad Ajami, *The Arab Predicament: Arab Political Thought and Practice Since 1967*, 2nd ed. (New York: Cambridge University Press, 1992); Ali E. Hillal Dessouki, ed., *Islamic Resurgence in the Arab World* (New York: Praeger Publishers, 1982); Saad Eddin Ibrahim, *The*

*New Arab Social Order: A Study of the Impact of Oil* (Boulder, Colo.: Westview Press, 1982); Malcolm Kerr and Sayyid Yassin, *Rich and Poor States in the Middle East: Egypt and the New Social Order* (Boulder, Colo.: Westview Press, 1982); David Lamb, *The Arabs: Journeys Beyond the Mirage* (New York: Random House, 1987); Kenan Makiya, *Cruelty and Silence: War, Tyranny, Uprising, and the Arab World* (New York: W. W. Norton, 1993); and Alan R. Taylor, *The Arab Balance of Power* (Syracuse: Syracuse University Press, 1982).

A hostile but readable book on Egypt's late president is David Hirst and Irene Beeson, *Sadat* (London: Faber & Faber, 1981). More scholarly is Raymond Hinnebusch, Jr., *Egyptian Politics Under Sadat*, 2nd ed. (Boulder, Colo.: Lynne Rienner Publishers, 1988). On Sadat's Syrian rival, read Patrick Seale, *Asad: The Struggle for the Middle East* (Berkeley and Los Angeles: University of California Press, 1988), or Lisa Wedeen, *Ambiguities of Domination* (Chicago: University of Chicago Press, 1999). On Iraq's recent history, see Marion Farouk-Sluglett and Peter Sluglett, *Iraq Since 1958: From Revolution to Dictatorship*, rev. ed. (London: I. B. Tauris, 1991). A readable introduction to Saudi Arabia is Sandra Mackey's *The Saudis: Inside the Desert Kingdom* (New York: NAL/Dutton, 1990).

Recent books on Israel include Zeev Chafets, *Heroes and Hustlers, Hardhats and Holy Men: Inside the New Israel* (New York: Morrow, 1986); Thomas Friedman, *From Beirut to Jerusalem*, 2nd ed. (New York: Anchor Books, 1995); Amos Oz, *In the Land of Israel*, trans. Maurie Goldberg-Bartura (New York: Vintage Books, 1983); Don Peretz, *The Governments and Politics of Israel*, 3rd ed. (Boulder, Colo.: Westview Press, 1997); and David K. Shipler, *Arab and Jew: Wounded Spirits in a Promised Land* (New York: Times Books, 1986). In addition to works cited earlier by Gilmour and Rabinovich, books on Israel's invasion of Lebanon include George Ball, *Error and Betrayal in Lebanon: An Analysis of Israel's Invasion of Lebanon and the Implications for U.S.-Israeli Relations* (Washington, D.C.: Foundation for Middle East Peace, 1984); Ze'ev Schiff and Ehud Yaari, *Israel's Lebanon War*, trans. Ina Friedman (New York: Simon & Schuster, 1984); and Jonathan C. Randal, *Going All the Way: Christian Warlords, Israeli Adventurers, and the War in Lebanon* (New York: Viking, 1983). The political aftermath is extensively discussed in a volume edited by Robert O. Freedman, *The Middle East After the Israeli Invasion of Lebanon* (Syracuse: Syracuse University Press, 1985).

The raising of women's consciousness has added a major dimension to the study of the Middle East. A good book for students to read first is Geraldine Brooks's *Nine Parts of Desire: The Hidden World of Islamic Women* (New York: Anchor Books, 1995), to be followed by Leila Ahmed's scholarly work, *Women and Gender in Islam: Historical Roots of a Modern Debate* (New Haven: Yale University Press, 1992). Two anthologies are Lois Beck and Nikki Keddie, eds., *Women in the Muslim World* (Cambridge, Mass.: Harvard University Press, 1978), and Elizabeth Warnock Fernea and Basima Qattan Bezirgan, eds., *Middle Eastern Muslim Women Speak* (Austin: University of Texas Press, 1977). See also Elizabeth Warnock Fernea, ed., *Women and the Family in the Middle East* (Austin: University of Texas Press, 1985); Fatima Mernissi, *Islam and Democracy: Fear of the Modern World* (Reading: Addison-Wesley, 1992); and Wiebke Walther, *Women in Islam: From Medieval to Modern Times*, 2nd ed. (New York: Marcus Wiener, 1993).

## CHAPTER 20

Of the textbooks now available on Middle East politics, the best are James Bill and Robert Springborg, *Politics in the Middle East*, 5th ed. (New York: Addison-Wesley, 2000), and David E. Long and Bernard Reich, eds., *The Government and Politics of the Middle East and North Africa*, 4th ed. (Boulder, Colo.: Westview Press, 2002). On economics, see Alan Richards and John Waterbury, *A Political Economy of the Middle East: State, Class, and Economic Development*, 2nd ed. (Boulder, Colo.: Westview Press, 1996).

The basic book on prewar Iraqi politics is Samir al-Khalil [pseud.], *Republic of Fear: The Inside Story of Saddam's Iraq*, 3rd ed. (Berkeley: University of California Press, 1998). Of the many books that appeared on the Gulf War and its immediate aftermath, I suggest starting with Deborah Amos, *Lines in the Sand: Desert Storm and the Remaking of the Arab World* (New York: Simon & Schuster, 1992); Adel Darwish and Gregory Alexander, *Unholy Babylon: The Secret History of Saddam's War* (New York: St. Martin's Press, 1991); Elaine Sciolino, *The Outlaw State: Saddam Hussein's Quest for Power and the Gulf Crisis* (New York: Wiley, 1991); and *Triumph Without Victory: The Unreported History of the Persian Gulf War* (New York: Times Books, 1993). For a broader view of the context within which the crisis occurred, see Walid Khalidi, *The Gulf Crisis: Origins and Consequences* (Washington, D.C.: Institute for Palestine Studies, 1991). On Kuwait, see two books by Jill Crystal: *Kuwait* (Boulder, Colo.: Westview Press, 1991) and *Oil and Politics in the Gulf: Rulers and Merchants in Kuwait and Qatar* (Cambridge: Cambridge University Press, 1990).

Books on the Palestinian uprising are becoming steadily more numerous. Some of the best are Samih K. Farsoun, *Palestine and the Palestinians* (Boulder, Colo.: Westview Press, 1997); Robert Hunter, *The Palestinian Uprising: A War by Other Means* (Berkeley: University of California Press, 1991); Don Peretz, *Intifada: The Palestinian Uprising* (Boulder, Colo.: Westview Press, 1990); and Ze'ev Schiff and Ehud Yaari, *Intifada: The Palestinian Uprising; Israel's Third Front* (New York: Simon & Schuster, 1990). A broader perspective is provided by Glenn Frankel, *Beyond the Promised Land: Jews and Arabs on the Hard Road to a New Israel* (New York: Simon & Schuster, 1994). See also Geoffrey Kemp and Jeremy Pressman, *Point of No Return: The Deadly Struggle for Middle East Peace* (Washington, D.C.: Carnegie Endowment for International Peace, 1997). Israel's efforts to achieve peace are analyzed by its former ambassador to the U.S., Itamar Rabinovich, in *Waging Peace: Israel and the Arabs at the End of the Century* (New York: Farrar, Straus and Giroux, 1999).

On Syria, see Nikelaos van Dam, *The Struggle for Power in Syria* (London: I. B. Tauris, 1996). Today's Egypt is described in Mary Anne Weaver, *Portrait of Egypt* (New York: Farrar, Straus and Giroux, 1999); Geneive Abdo, *No God but God: Egypt and the Triumph of Islam* (Oxford: Oxford University Press, 2000); and Saad Eddin Ibrahim, *Egypt, Islam, and Democracy: Twelve Critical Essays* (Cairo: AUC Press, 1996). The Kurdish problem in Turkey is covered in Henri J. Barkey, *Turkey's Kurdish Question* (Lanham, Md.: Rowman and Littlefield, 1998) and Robert Olson (ed.), *The Kurdish National Movement in the 1990s* (Lexington: University of Kentucky Press, 1996). Turkey's oft-postponed admission to the European Union is analyzed in Mehmet Ugur, *The European Union and Turkey: An Anchor-Credibility Dilemma* (Aldershot, U.K.: Ashgate, 1999).

Three recent personal accounts of the Middle East by foreign travelers are Elizabeth Warnock Fernea and Robert A. Fernea, *The Arab World: Forty Years of Change* (New York: Anchor Books, 1997); Tony Horwitz's *Baghdad Without a Map* (New York: Dutton, 1991); and Tim Mackintosh-Smith, *Travels in Dictionary Land* (London: John Murray, 1997).

\* \* \*

Feel free to write either to Westview Press, 5500 Central Avenue, Boulder, CO 80301, or to me, c/o Department of History, Pennsylvania State University, University Park, PA 16802–5500 (Internet: axg2@psu.edu), to suggest future additions, corrections, or deletions for this bibliographic essay.

TABLE 1    Basic Statistics for Middle East Countries

| Name of country | Land Area (sq. mi./km²) | Population (mid–2000 estimate) | Languages Spoken | Religion Sn=Sunni Sh=Shi'i Ch=Chr'n |
|---|---|---|---|---|
| Bahrain | 240/620 | 634,137 | Arabic Persian | 56% Sh 37% Sn 7% Ch |
| Cyprus | 3,572/9,250 | 758,363 | Greek Turkish | 78% Ch 18% Sn |
| Egypt[1] | 386,900/1,001,450 | 68,359,979 | Arabic | 94% Sn 6% Ch |
| Iran | 636,293/1,648,000 | 65,219,636 | Persian Azeri Kurdish | 95% Sh 4% Sn 1% Ch |
| Iraq | 167,920/437,072 | 22,675,617 | Arabic Kurdish Turkish | 60% Sh 37% Sn 3% Ch |
| Israel[2] | 8,020/20,770 | 5,842,454 | Hebrew Arabic | 82% Jewish 14% Sn 2% Ch |
| Jordan[3] | 34,573/89,213 | 4,998,564 | Arabic | 92% Sn 6% Ch |
| Kuwait | 6,880/17,820 | 2,076,805 | Arabic | 50% Sn 30% Sh 6% Ch |
| Lebanon | 4,015/10,400 | 3,578,036 | Arabic French | 38% Ch 32% Sh 21% Sn 7% Druze |
| Libya | 679,536/1,759,540 | 5,115,450 | Arabic | 97% Sn |
| Oman | 82,030/212,460 | 2,533,389 | Arabic | 64% Ibadi 22% Sn 13% Hindu |
| Qatar | 4,468/11,439 | 744,483 | Arabic | 92% Sn 4% Ch 2% Hindu |
| Saudi Arabia | 865,000/1,960,582 | 22,023,506 | Arabic | 95% Sn 5% Sh |

*(Continues)*

*(Continued)*

| | | | | |
|---|---|---|---|---|
| Sudan | 967,491/2,505,810 | 35,079,814 | Arabic<br>various<br>languages | 70% Sn<br>20% Animist<br>5% Ch |
| Syria | 71,498/185,180 | 16,305,659 | Arabic | 70% Sn<br>15% Ch<br>12% Alawi<br>3% Druze |
| Turkey | 300,947/780,580 | 65,666,677 | Turkish<br>Kurdish | 99% Sn&Sh[4] |
| United Arab<br>Emirates | 32,375/82,880 | 2,369,153 | Arabic<br>Persian | 78% Sn<br>18% Sh<br>4% Ch |
| Yemen | 203,850/527,970 | 17,479,206 | Arabic | 99% Sn&Sh |

1. Area figures and population for Egypt exclude the Gaza Strip, whose estimated population in 2000 was 1,132,063 in a land area of 139 sq. mi./360 km2.

2. Area figures and populations for Israel and Syria are based on their boundaries as of 4 June 1967.

3. Area figures and population for Jordan exclude the West Bank, whose estimated population in 2000 was 2,020,298 in a land area of 2,263 sq. mi./5,860 km2.

4. Turkey and Yemen do not enumerate Sunni and Shi'i Muslims separately.

SOURCE: *2001 Time Almanac* (Boston: Information Please, 2000).

# INDEX